FOUNDATIONS OF HYPNOSIS

From Mesmer to Freud

FIGURE 1. Frontispiece from Father Kircher's book on *experimental physiology*, published in 1680.

FOUNDATIONS OF HYPNOSIS

From Mesmer to Freud

By

MAURICE M. TINTEROW, M.D., F.A.C.A., F.A.S.C.H.

Director of Anesthetic Services
Wesley Medical Center
Wichita, Kansas

CHARLES C THOMAS • PUBLISHER
Springfield • Illinois • U.S.A.

Published and Distributed Throughout the World by
CHARLES C THOMAS • PUBLISHER
BANNERSTONE HOUSE
301-317 East Lawrence Avenue, Springfield, Illinois, U.S.A.
NATCHEZ PLANTATION HOUSE
735 North Atlantic Boulevard, Fort Lauderdale, Florida, U.S.A.

With THOMAS BOOKS careful attention is given to all details of manufacturing and design. It is the Publisher's desire to present books that are satisfactory as to their physical qualities and artistic possibilities and appropriate for their particular use. THOMAS BOOKS will be true to those laws of quality that assure a good name and good will.

Printed in the United States of America
II-ii

Preface

The science of hypnotism has been evolved from such a labyrinth of idle superstition and wild speculation that even those keenly interested in the development of human knowledge have held aloof from a subject which apparently presents so entangled a maze of insoluble riddles. The publication of Faulconer and Keys of their historical masterpiece, *Foundations of Anesthesiology,* set the stage for me to think along these lines in the field of hypnosis and hypnotherapy. Today, it is easy to acquire modern thought on the subject through the textbooks and publications which have been published by scientific investigators and clinicians. However, it is easy to forget and not to recall the names of the early investigators and their work which laid the basic groundwork for our continued study of this important subject.

My interest in hypnosis led to the accumulation of a large library in excess of six hundred books and articles by such authors as Mesmer, de Puysegur, Esdaile, Elliotson, and Reichenbach; these publications gave me the total picture in the development of hypnosis. In particular, it was interesting to accumulate all of the publications of Mesmer and to read the works of James Braid, who was responsible for the word, hypnosis, and for a total investigation of the field of hypnosis. One can read in each textbook published today a chapter on the history of hypnosis, but one cannot satisfy his interest in any particular article or chapter of a book which is not available to him. A search of many major libraries revealed few books published in the latter part of the eighteenth and nineteenth centuries.

Most of the early works in mesmerism or animal magnetism were written in French, with a few in German, Italian, and Spanish. They arouse the curiosity of the historian, and it was felt that the translations would fill the gap in the field of study that has been overlooked by many because of the language barrier and the time involved in acquiring translations. In translating from one language to another, some of the original investigation may not be presented as written, but we have attempted to translate accurately, keeping in mind the changes in sentence structure and the ease of reading.

Many articles may not be of interest to some of the readers, but because of the necessity to build a subject from its inception, they have been included. Many of the works are complete; others are the most important chapters in the book; while others are separate paragraphs joined together to make the completed story. They are chronologically placed and separated into sections on mesmerism or animal magnetism, braidism or neurypnology, hypnosis in the late nineteenth century, and hypnosis prior to World War I—including the works of Sigmund Freud.

A.E. Waite, in his book *Braid on Hypnotism* (London, 1899), writes: "No copy of Braid's *Satanic Agency and Mesmerism Reviewed* is known to the present writer." This little booklet covers twelve pages, and in it Braid laid the foundation of medical hypnotism. W. Preyer, in the course of a sojourn in England for the purpose of tracing all of Braid's writings could locate no copy of this work. No copy can be traced in Great Britain or in the United States. This booklet, together with two other rare works, *The Physiology of Fascination and the Critics Criticised* and *The Power of the Mind over the Body*, will be reproduced as written by Braid. I was fortunate in being able to locate copies of the three rare books, and their inclusion in this book enables the historian to read and study what has otherwise not been available.

Much of the material published on animal magnetism will not be included other than by representative articles and selections from the published texts. A review of the literature of mesmerism is presented for those interested in pursuing other facets of the subject. The serious student of history and the historian may perceive that his favorite author and text of the past are not included in the many pages of this book. The inclusion of all related material would create a voluminous work that would have no value for the occasional student of the subject. Many published works repeat and verify the works of others so that the major works are representative of a given era.

I have included at the end of the present book a Selected Bibliography of all of the books in my collection with a short description of the work, so that those who are interested in completing their own collections of these rare books may compare the list with their own. The art of collecting these old and rare books is very enlightening and interesting. The friendships and associations I have made through my search for these books are lasting and invaluable. For those who are interested in a particular book, I will be more than happy to provide copies of portions of the books to further the interest in the history of hypnosis.

In writing this book, I am indebted to many helpful people. Particularly singled out is Mrs. J.J. Slay, who is associated with the French Department at Wichita State University, for her translations of the publications written in French. Appreciation is accorded to Mrs. Valerie Stallings, Mrs. Sandra York, Mrs. Pat Stewart, and Mrs. Joyce Warkentin for their excellent help in preparation of the manuscript, and to Jackie Speer for her interest in helping to read and prepare the manuscript prior to its final arrangement and organization.

M. M. TINTEROW

2322 E. Central
Wichita, Kansas 67214

Introduction

To those of us who would have a clear knowledge of what hypnotism is and what it is not, a study of the history is a necessity. In the long course of its history, hypnotism has been the frequent trade of the unscientific investigator, and indeed, almost all of the quacks at one time or another have endeavored to make some use of it. Its peculiar attraction for these men lay in the fact that the ordinary run of mankind knew nothing of the hypnotic state, and in the narrowness of their philosophy they were willing to attribute to the supernatural or to the unknown all that they, in their ignorance, could not appreciate or understand. However, many of these unscientific advocates were painfully in earnest, and the study of the subject was still making headway when the professional entertainer, the charlatan, the juggler, and the trickster laid their hands on the much-suffering science. No sooner had the showman's heart been gladdened by his latest "find" than he proceeded to add some "business" that his entertainment might still be more effective; in a space as short in time as it was in its effect, mesmerism became a byword for all that was low and contemptible.

It is unlikely that a definite condition of the human mind could for long be entirely unknown to all, and a study of the ancient writings shows that, however curious the ancient ideas may have been, the state of hypnotism itself had been observed in the earliest times. Thus, the history of hypnotism begins almost in fable. Methods were in use among the Egyptians, the Greeks, and the Romans, which present a striking similarity to the means adopted by modern hypnotists. In the British Museum there is a bas-relief taken from a tomb in Thebes; the subject, as he would be termed in modern phraseology, is sitting down while at a short distance from him a man is standing with his hand uplifted and evidently about to "pass" over his patient. The goddess Isis on the zodiac of her temple at Denderah is represented as making the same "passes." The earliest Greek physicians were in the habit of using processes having a strong resemblance to the "cutaneous irritations" of Heidenhain. The *Ebers Papyrus,* which gives us some account of the medical methods practiced in Egypt prior to 1552 B.C., mentions the laying of hands on the head of the patient as a part of treatment.[1]

Even the clairvoyant theories of the mesmerists seem to have a history since probably the early soothsayers and oracles relied largely upon the hypnotic state; and the acuteness which the faculties often gained in a deep state of hypnosis would enable the subject to speak with a foresight and wisdom calculated to excite the admiration and reverence of those who made use of their services.

Asclepiades was in the habit of putting frenzied persons to sleep by rubbing, and when these frictions were prolonged, the patient was plunged into a deep lethargy. One of the earliest, and at the same time most striking, references to the use of some form of nerve stimulation as a curative agent occurs in a book, *History of Philosophy* 1666, and gives the following translation:
> "The smallest hurt sometimes increase and rage more than
> all art of physic can assuage: sometime the fury of the
> worst disease the hand, by gentle stroking, will appease."

Tacitus and Suetonis testified to the cures performed by the Emperor Vespasian. Finally, St. Augustine told of a priest he knew who could reduce himself to a state not to be distinguished from death.

Everyone has heard of the cures due to the "royal touch." Numerous cures were effected in this manner by the early kings of France, and the "touch" was still in vogue in Queen Anne's time. It seems to have been first exercised by the Scandinavian princesses and princes, and particularly by St. Olaf, who was supposed to have reigned from 1020 to 1035. Thus, we notice in various times a number of phenomena which may, at first sight, strike the reader as but distantly connected with one another; the nature and extent of their connection can be more apparent as more history is understood.

How far the Egyptians, Persians, Greeks, and Romans knew of the scientific import of these phenomena, and how much they knew, seem impossible to decide. We have but the bare records of a number of isolated facts; there seems to be no evidence of any common method or principle. It is not improbable, since many of the phenomena are connected with the oracles, or with the most learned physicians, that the people either took no trouble to look for any explanation or attributed the result to a supernatural agency. The first traces of any system for these phenomena appeared toward the end of the Middle Ages, and this system grew out of the doctrines of astrology. Some of the famous men of the time were at work on the subject, and the student who peruses their writings will usually find them curiously interesting, though lengthy and ponderous. Prominent among the writers are Theophrastus Paracelsus, Petrus Pomponatius, Glocenius, Athanasius Kircher, van Helmont, Sir Kenelm Digby, Gul Maxwell, J.G. Burggrav, Sebastian Wirdig, and others, including Fludd and Helinotius.[2-5, 8, 9]

All these men, in various ways attempted to demonstrate the existence of a universal magnetic force by which the reciprocal action of bodies, in general, upon each other, and particularly the phenomena of the human body and mind were to be explained. The human will was capable of producing an effect upon the mind and organisms of other persons. Pomponatius and van Helmont were the two most systematic upholders of this view. Pomponatius, Professor of Philosophy at Padua, was born in Mantua in 1462 and died in 1525. He sought to prove that sickness and disease were curable by means of "magnetism" existing in each person. "When those who are endowed with this faculty operate by employing the force of the imagination and the will, this force effects their blood and their spirits, which produce the intended effects by means of an evaporation thrown outward."[7]

John Baptist van Helmont was born in Brussels in the year 1577. He was educated for the medical profession but spent his life in chemical researches. The discovery of laudanum, or the spirit of hartshorn, and of the volatile salts is due to him. He also discovered the existence of the aeriform fluids, to which he gave the name, *gas*, a name they still retain. He died in 1644. His book was intended partly as an answer to Glocenius and earlier writers, who had advocated the doctrine of magnetism, but not in a manner agreeable to van Helmont. It was also intended as a reply to

xi

Father Roberts, a Jesuit, who had contended that cures performed by means of this magnetism were diabolical agency spirits. "Magnetism," stated von Helmont, "is a universal agent; there is nothing new in it but the name; and it is a paradox only to those who are disposed to ridicule everything and who ascribe to the influence of Satan all those phenomena which they cannot explain." He defines magnetism as "that occult power which bodies exert over each other at a distance, whether by attraction or repulsion."[8]

The source of the spirits of magnetism gained force and precision with each successive writer. Paracelsus and Glocenius hint at rather than advocate the doctrine of magnetism; Wirdig takes up a much more decided position[9]; while Maxwell's "spiritus vitalis" indicates a great development and, in fact, was the legitimate precursor of Mesmer's doctrine of the "universal fluid."[5] In the spirit of this ecclesiastical age, they made no effort to prove their conclusions—the more impossible the theory, the more vehemently they advocated it, thus their works are full of fruitless discussions of untenable premises. Still it is not difficult to be wise after the event, and a study of the report of the Psychical Research Society and the works of Hack Tuke—together with the works of Kircher, van Helmont, and others—affords, in some respect, a demonstration of the relations of the latest psychology to its embryonic form.

In the middle of the eighteenth century, many men were attracted to the whole question of magnetism by witnessing the wonderful "cures" performed by Father Hehl, a Jesuit. These cures were supposed to be due to the subtle influence on body fluid by magnetism, which was imparted to the patients from steel plates and magnets especially prepared for the purpose. Maximillian Hehl, Professor of Astronomy at Vienna, was born at Chemnitz, in Hungary, in the year 1720. During the years 1745 and 1746 he assisted Father J. Francois, the head of the Jesuits' observatory at Vienna. He then went to Clausenberg in Transylvania to teach mathematics and was recalled some years later to Vienna, where he became the chief astronomer. From 1757 to 1786 he published the yearly *Ephemerides*. Upon the value of the mineral magnet in the cure of sickness and disease, numerous early authors had written dissertations. Its use seems to have been recommended by Galen and Descorides. The following titles are examples of publications showing the relationship between magnets and disease.

1. Ludwig: *Dissertation de Magnetismo in Corpore Humano.* Leipzig, 1772.
2. Unzer: *Beschreibung der mit dem Kuntslichen magnet augestellten Versuche.* Altona, 1775.
3. Heinsius: *Beytrage zu meinen Versuchen welche mit Kunstlichen Magneten in Verschiedenen Krankheiten angestellt worden.* Leipzig, 1776.
4. Heinsius: *Sammlung der neusten gedruckten und geschriebenen Nachrichten von Magnetcuren.* Leipzig, 1778.
5. Heinsius: *Historia Trismitonici quadraginta fere septimarum a Philiatro de Wocher curati.* Freiburg, 1778.

Friedrich Anton Mesmer came upon the scene with his theories of animal magnetism and published his first dissertation in the year 1766. The work of Mesmer and his disciples was the beginning of the development of hypnosis, and is the first chapter of the history of hypnosis.

REFERENCES

1. BURGGRAV, J.G.: *Cura Morborum Magnetica que Theophrasti Mumia Significatur.* 1611.
2. DIGBY, SIR KENELM: *Of the Cure of Wounds by the Power of Sympathy.* London, 1660.
3. KIRCHER, ATHANASIUS, S.J.; *Magnes Sive de Arte Magnetica.* Coloniae, 1643.
4. KIRCHER, ATHANASIUS, S.J.: *Natural Regnum.* Amsterdam, 1667.
5. MAXWELL, G.: *De Medicina Magnetica.* Frankfurt, 1679.
6. MOLL, ALBERT: *The Study of Hypnosis.* Julian, New York, 1958.
7. STANLEY: *History of Philosophy,* 1666.
8. VAN HELMONT, J.B.: *De Magneticum Vulneratum Curatione.* Paris, 1661.
9. WIRDIG, S.: *Nova Medicina Spiritium.* Hamburg, 1673.

Contents

FOUNDATIONS OF HYPNOSIS
From Mesmer to Freud

SECTION ONE

The Era of Animal Magnetism
(1780-1834)

A. P. Sinnett

Controversy still continued even in the late nineteenth century over the factual evidence of animal magnetism versus hypnosis. Many authors were still of the opinion that animal magnetism and hypnosis were one and the same. A controversial figure was A.P. Sinnett, President of the Theosophical Society of Simla, India. He was a practitioner of the occult sciences, and many of his books were published in England as well as in the United States. In the first chapter of his book, *The Rationale of Mesmerism*, he states: "It is necessary at the onset that I should explain why I am writing about mesmerism and not hypnotism. Names are, after all, but tickets put by conventional agreement upon things or branches of knowledge, and if, in the first instance, when the matter first began to attract attention in Europe a hundred years ago, the word, hypnotism, had been adopted to describe certain abnormal conditions of the human body and the human faculties, we need not, at this stage, have quarreled with the expression".

His chapter, "The Real Literature of Mesmerism," is one of the most complete reviews of the early history of hypnosis and is utilized at this point to give completeness to the subject at hand.

THE REAL LITERATURE OF MESMERISM*

Mesmer himself—Frederick Anthony Mesmer—according to Picard, was born at Weiler-on-the-Rhine, in the year 1734. He studied medicine in his youth and settled as a doctor in Vienna, where he ultimately married advantageously. In 1766 he wrote a dissertation on "The Influences of the Planets on the Human Body," which drew upon him much ridicule and professional opposition. The attempt to account for this influence led him to make the experiments which introduced him to the facts with which his name has since been indissolubly associated. At first he worked entirely with magnets, obtained some cures by this means, and wrote "A Letter To A Foreign Physician on the Magnetic Rem-

---

*From SINNETT, A.P.: *The Rationale of Mesmerism*. Boston, Houghton, 1897, pp. 36-84.

5

edy." But he was much persecuted for his audacity. For the further development of his inquiries he established a private hospital in his own house for the relief of destitute individuals. He soon came to the conclusion that the magnetic rods with which his first experiments were made, only served as conductors for a fluid emanating from his own person. To this he at once gave the name Animal Magnetism, and theorized boldly concerning its diffusion through nature. But he was accused of deceiving his public, and of having magnetic rods concealed about his person—an accusation which was very amusing, in view of the fact that, when he really used magnetic rods, he was ridiculed for expecting to obtain curative results by such means. His reputation was assailed and his fortune impaired. He sought some more favorable theater for the development of his experiments, and moved from Vienna to Paris in 1777. Two years later he published a short treatise, entitled "Mémoire sur la découverte du Magnétisme Animal." The theory put forward rested on Mesmer's conviction that "there exists a reciprocal influence between the heavenly bodies, the earth, and animated beings." The medium of this influence he conceived to be "a very subtle fluid pervading the whole universe, which from its nature is capable of receiving, propagating, and communicating every impulse of motion. The reciprocal action is subject to certain mechanical laws which have not yet been discovered . . . the animal body experiences the alternative effects of this agent, which, by insinuating itself into the substance of the nerves, affects them immediately." Mesmer's suggestions to this effect were treated by the men of science in Paris at the time with contempt. One, indeed, of the members of the Medical Faculty of Paris, Dr. D'Eslon, became a warm partisan of Mesmer's views. But, instead of inquiring into them, the Faculty suspended Dr. D'Elson for a year, in order that, at the expiration of this time, his name should be erased from the list of the Society, unless he recanted his declaration of belief. The public meanwhile became interested to some extent in the new ideas, as the fame of various magnetic cures had been spread about. Various persons testified to the fact that Mesmer had cured them, but the public journals ridiculed him, and the medical profession reviled him. In 1781 he published a work entitled "Précis Historique des Faits relatif au Magnétisme Animal." The opposition he encountered only stimulated his own enthusiasm, and led him to proclaim magnetism as a panacea. He declared "there is but one health, one disease, one remedy." An unfortunate private misunderstanding between himself and Dr. D'Eslon led him to move from Paris to Spa. Ultimately he returned to Paris, and then took a step which has led to much animadversion on his character. He established a secret society, under the name of "The Harmony," where he initiated pupils into the mystery of his process, taking from them fees of hundreds louis d'or each. By this means "he is said," according to Mr. J.C. Colquhoun, a relatively recent writer on Mesmerism, "to have realized a considerable fortune". M. Deleuze, a leading writer on the subject, justifies his action in this matter by pointing out that his whole professional prospects were merged in his magnetic discoveries, which had ruined him as an ordinary doctor. He took the fees from wealthy people, and is said to have remitted them when would-be pupils were less prosperous. Moreover, admits Mr. Colquhoun, it is very doubtful whether he really acquired the large sums he is alleged to have received.

In 1784 a Royal Commission of orthodox savants was appointed to inquire into the claims advanced in behalf of the theory of animal magnetism. The report was unfavorable, after an inquiry which the representatives of the new science declared to have been improperly conducted; though one eminent physician (de Jussieu) refused to subscribe to the report of his colleagues, and, after a great deal of attention paid to the subject, published an independent report of his own, entirely favorable to Mesmer. Even the general body of the commissioners admitted the effects produced by magnetic treatment, but repudiated Mesmer's theory of a fluid, and preferred hypotheses concerning "sensitive excitement, imagination, and imitation."

Mesmer eventually retired in disgust to Switzerland, and died at an advanced age in 1815, closing his career, as he had begun it, by practicing magnetic cures gratuitously for the benefit of the poor. Beyond a certain fancy for surrounding his mode of life in Paris with a flavor of mystery and theatrical affect, it is difficult to find any circumstances in Mesmer's life that afford the slightest color for the offensive terms for which he has constantly been spoken of, even by some students and adherents of his great subject.

During Mesmer's life the phenomena of animal magnetism, to which attention was chiefly called, were those connected with the cure of disease. Many societies were formed as branches of that first set on foot, and while on the one hand the orthodox medical scientists of today continue to treat with contempt the belief of those who declare that such and such results were accomplished, the volume of experience rolled on for those who paid attention to the work and progress. A very ludicrous aspect is thus put, for students of mesmeric literature, on the ignorant conceit of the dominant majority, who were all the while denying the possibility of that which was actually occurring. After the foolish bigotry of the doctors at large had thus been at war with the plain facts of the case for more than forty years, medical mesmerism at last received a grudging recognition from orthodox science in 1831. At this date a committee of the Medical Section of the French Royal Academy of Sciences was appointed to examine into the alleged phenomena of animal magnetism. The report made by this committee, after long and careful investigation, constitutes a remarkable record of experiments on the physical phenomena of the mesmeric state; it also goes in length into cases in which the patients of the medical mesmeric treatment were clairvoyant in their trances, and accurately prophetic concerning the subsequent course of their malady. The report, signed by nine members of the Academy, is apologetic in regard to its assurance that the alleged phenomena were true; the members say in effect, "How can we help ourselves?" We have taken every possible precaution to guard ourselves from mistakes, and we cannot resist complete conviction. An English translation on this report, by Mr. J.C. Colquhoun, was published in 1833.

From this date the reality of the phenomena of mesmerism, as far as those associated with its aspects as a curative agent, as a method of producing anesthesia, and as a means of producing abnormal mental states in which a mesmerized subject may foresee the future progress of his own disorder, must be regarded as finely established, although scientific and educated men up to our own day maintain an attitude of incredulity on the subject, which puts them, for better instructed persons, on the intellectual level of the African savage, who does not believe in ice. Since 1831 moreover, the experience which has accumulated on our hands concerning the higher and more purely psychic phenomena of the mesmeric state is such that the same remark really applies to everyone, however cultivated along some lines of mental activity, who remains in an attitude of incredulity concerning the typical phenomena of clairvoyance and mesmeric thought transfer.

As far back as 1808, Dr. Pététin published in Paris a book called "Electricité Animale," of which the well-known later writer on the same subject, Dr. Esdaile, says: "Dr. Pététin's cases alone are sufficient to establish the reality of natural clairvoyance." Plentiful testimony will be found in this book concerning the powers of mesmeric subjects of a certain kind to read the contents of closed letters and books, and to exercise many other faculties of perception quite independently of the ordinary sense.

Among the earliest of Mesmer's disciples, the Marquis Chastenet de Puységur has left voluminous writings on the subject of his own prolonged and varied practice as a curative mesmerist. The edition of his works before me is in four volumes, the last dates 1809, but this is a second edition, and I gather that the first must have appeared in 1807. This is entitled "Mémoires pour servir á l'histoire et á l'établissement du Magnétisme Animal." The second volume is a general continuation of the first, and the third is more especially devoted to "Recherches, Éxperiences, et Observations Physiologiques sur L'homme dans l'État de Somnambulisme Natural et dans le Somnambulisme Provoqué par L'acte Magnétique." The fourth volume, published in 1812, is entitled "Les Fous, Les Insensés, Les Maniaques et Les Frénétiques, ne seraient-ils que des Somnambules désordonnés." The whole collection of writings embodies an immense accumulation of experiences with persons clairvoyant during illness in respect to their own maladies. No recent writings on mesmerism in its medical aspects have an equal value with these, for de Puységur, working with straightforward and earnest faith in his own power of alleviating suffering with the help of Mesmer's glorious discovery, attained brilliant successes, and above all—for later students of the subject—has done unrivaled service in investigating the prophetic and clairvoyant faculties of mesmeric patients, not only in reference to their own but in respect also of other persons' ailments. On this development of their powers he says: "of all the facts of magnetism the most inexplicable, and above all the least conceivable, is, without doubt, that of the vision possessed by patients in a perfect state of somnambulism in reference to the sufferings of others and the knowledge which they show at the remedies and measures necessary for their cure. . . . Anyhow, although there is no known phenomena (in other branches of science) to which one can compare the faculty—the fact is nevertheless real, as certain as the other manifestations of somnambulism already recognized." De Puységur gives full details of the cases both of this and of the simpler kinds of clairvoyance—in reference to the patients' own illnesses—that he had the opportunity of dealing with, and they are both numerous and remarkable. It seems strange that he never apparently investigated the extent to which the clairvoyant perceptions he evoked could be directed to other subjects besides those having to do with physical illness, but in the beginning mesmerism was introduced to the world in reference almost exclusively to its medical aspects, and it was reserved for later inquirers to bring its psychological importance into view. De Puységur never seems to have expected the clairvoyance of his patients to be prolonged beyond the period of their recovery.

J.P.F. Deleuze was a voluminous, and one of the earliest, writers on mesmerism. He published several books on the subject, amongst others a critical history of animal magnetism. He himself was a Frenchman, born in 1763. He was attracted to the subject of mesmerism by reading accounts of magnetic cures in 1785 and subsequently accomplished many such cures himself. He was a naturalist attached to the Jardin des Plantes. In his "Histoire Critique du Magnétisme Animal" (Paris, 1813), he very effectually rebuts the accusation of imposture brought against Mesmer-This extraordinary man he says, gifted with an energetic character, was carried away by the wonderful successes he obtained into an exaggerated belief in the range of his discovery, but the attitude of incredulity, on the other hand, in regards to his achievements M. Deleuze shows to be altogether untenable. Not only were his numerous pupils convinced of the reality of his treatment, but the assurances and proofs furnished by persons who had been cured themselves, and who had taken part in establishing societies for the cure of others, were such that no opposition or ridicule could arrest the progress of so useful and well-established a discovery. M. Deleuze himself, since he had occupied himself with magnetism could attest that he had known more than three hundred persons who occupied with it like himself, and who had produced or experienced its vivid effects. M. Deleuze deplores that Mesmer had not the magnanimity to make public his discoveries for the good of mankind without deriving pecuniary benefit from them, but points out that after all he had spent money to acquire the right of practising as doctor, and by all ordinary considerations was entitled to take money for teaching pupils. M. Deleuze devotes himself chiefly to establishing the reality of the magnetic influence as a curative agent by records of cases and protracted arguments, and in his second volume gives an interesting summary of the books on the subject that had appeared up to the date at which he wrote. His "Practical Instructions on Animal Magnetism" were published in 1825, and have been translated into English. The book is described by the translator as a result of a consummate experience. In 1836 an early admirer of Deleuze's work had written: "A new era has commenced for magnetism. Authentically recognized by the Royal Academy of Medicine in 1831, and regarded by the commission as a very curious branch of Psychology and Natural History, it has taken rank among positive truths. The rising generation will be prompted to cultivate the new field laid open to them. What surer guide could they take than the man who, by the superiority of his intelligence, the sagacity of his conclusions, and the example of his own life, has so powerfully contributed to the triumph of his noble discovery?"

Deleuze says that his object is to give plain and simple instructions for people who wish to practice magnetism. "It is not the object of this work," he writes, "to convince men who, otherwise well-informed, still doubt the reality of magnetism." He employs the expression, "the magnetic fluid," he says, because he believes in the existence of such a fluid, though its nature is unknown. The directions which he gives go into great detail in regard to manipulation and passes, and most later handbooks of mesmerism seemed to have derived their inspiration very largely from this code of rules. The author also discusses the accessory means by which magnetic acts may be increased, namely, mesmerized water, woolen and cotton cloth, plates of glass, etc. The purpose in view is almost exclusively to instruct the reader in methods of mesmerism to be employed for the cure of disease, and the book is entirely concerned with such directions, or with criticisms on various modes of mesmerizing, the risks to be avoided, and the method that may be employed for "developing and fortifying one's self in magnetic power." A voluminous appendix added to an American edition of the work by the translator, Mr. Hartshorn, gives an immense quantity of testimony selected by him concerning curious and remarkable cases of mesmerism. J.J.A. Ricard, a Paris professor, is a thoroughly satisfactory exponent of mesmeric experience, who published in 1841 a volume entitled "Traité Théorique et Pratique du Magnétisme Animal." He must have been himself a mesmerist of most unusual force, and evidently combined with this attribute characteristics which, properly handled, would have made him himself a sensitive of great value, for he appears to have been a spontaneous somnambulist, capable on some occasions of writing long strings of verses in his sleep, in reference to the production of which he retained no recollection whatever in his waking state. However, this fact crops up merely incidentally; his book is devoted entirely to the record of his work, which chiefly has to do with curative mesmerism directed by the pathological clairvoyance of his patients, for with him it seemed as if almost everyone who approached could be thrown into a magnetic trance. There is something very puzzling to modern practical students in the immense advantage apparently enjoyed by the early mesmerists, as compared with ourselves, in reference to the prevalent condition of people around them. In the present day we may be able to get results which when obtained are fully as good in all respects as those described by the early French writers; but the persons with whom such results are procurable seem to be dotted here and there about the world, by ones and twos, whereas such mesmerists as M. Ricard seem always to have been puzzled if they did not succeed with a premier venu. Their records of distinct successes run into percentages like seventy-five or eighty of the total number of persons with whom they made experiments. Ricard treats with scorn the pretenses of some disputants to account for mesmeric phenomena by imagination, fascination, and other vague hypotheses in conflict with the simple and, to him, undeniably true theory of mesmeric fluid. The falsity of their judgment he thinks may easily be demonstrated, and he records a case in which in order to prove the reality of his own position he magnetizes one of his patients at a distance, and puts him to sleep without any expectation on his part that the experiment was going to be tried. For psychological students, however, Ricard's book has claims on their interests which far transcend its importance as, what it certainly is also, a very advanced and intelligent treatise on curative mesmerism. Ricard appears to me to have been the first experimentalist, or at all events the first writer, who gets entirely free of the belief that clairvoyance is merely a pathological condition, and to whom the dazedly interesting phenomenon of clairvoyance, having to do with other states of nature, presents itself in the light of its real importance. He gives a very full account of his first experience in this region of inquiry with a girl named Adèle Lefrey, who exhibited a new kind of lucidity at the conclusion of some curative treatment received at her mesmerist's hand. It may be worthwhile here to translate a short passage illustrative for all who have themselves been privileged to work with sensitives qualified to discern higher states of nature, of what may be called the inevitable routine of impression such people go through in the first instance. M. Ricard's Adèle said to him words conveying exactly the same ideas which I have heard uttered by sensitives under my own influence, young girls to whom the ABC's of mesmerism are wholly unknown. M. Ricard writes: "She was near the completion of her cure, when, in the midst of some new medical instructions which she was given, she said to me in a singular tone, 'You hear what he orders me?' 'Who,' I asked, 'is ordering you anything?' 'Why, Monsieur, do you not hear him?' 'No, I neither hear nor see anyone.' 'Ah, that is true,' she replied, 'you sleep while I am awake.' 'What do you mean? You dream, my dear child; you pretend that I sleep, when I have my eyes open and I can appreciate all that passes before me, while I know that I actually hold you in command by my magnetic influence, and that it only depends upon my will to bring you back to the state you were in recently. You believe yourself awake because you speak to me, and you have to a certain extent your free will, although you could not open your eyelids, and might be plunged in an instant into the most profound slumber. You do not reflect upon what you are saying.' 'You do not understand me, Monsieur, but that is nothing surprising.' 'You are asleep,' I replied. 'I am, on the contrary, as completely awake as we shall all be some day in the future. I will explain myself more clearly; all that you see at present is gross, material; you distinguish apparent forms; the real beauties escape you. How could it be otherwise? Your spirit is cramped, obscured, by the exterior impressions that your material senses give you. It can only reach out feebly, while my corporeal sensations are actually annihilated, while my soul is almost disintegrated from its ordinary fetters. I see what is invisible to your eyes, I hear what your ears cannot hear, I understand what for you is uncomprehensible. For example, you do not see what emanates from yourself and comes to me when you magnetize me; I, from the contrary, see it very clearly; at each pass you direct towards me I see a little column of fiery dust which comes from the end of your finger and seems to incorporate itself in me. Then when you isolate me I seem surrounded by an atmosphere of this fiery dust, which is often the reason why objects of which I seek to distinguish the forms take a ruddy tinge from me. I hear, when I desire, a sound that is made at a distance, sounds which may arise a hundred leagues from here. In a word, I am not obliged to wait till things come to me, I can go to them wherever they are, and appreciate them more correctly than anyone could who is not in a similar state to that which I find myself.' " This is a perfectly sound and correct exposition of the state in which the liberated ego of the sensitive finds itself. Phrases of precisely similar import have, as I say, been given to me more than once; and I venture to say that anyone in whom the facility of clairvoyance, in reference to other plains of nature, is possible will, on first entering into that state, if questioned, take the same view of the position.

Under the title "Archiv für den Thierischen Magnetismus," an immense collection of writings on mesmerism and all its branches, as then understood, was published in Germany in 1817. This work is in twelve volumes, edited by Dr. von Eschenmayer, Dr. Kiefer, and Dr. Nasse. It consists of narratives of experiments and magnetic cures, and careful critical essays, including speculation from the meaning of clairvoyance prevision, which show a more intelligent attitude of mind on the part of the German writers of that date than was common in England.

Baron du Potet, sometimes called de Sennevoy, after an ancestral domain, is to be ranked among the early French writers on mesmerism, though he lived to within a few years ago. He was born at Sennevoy, in the department of the Yonne, in 1796. He has given us a sketch of his own career at the beginning of one of his later books, and it appears that he was first attracted to the study of human magnetism in 1815. The whole subject burst upon him as a revelation "En sortant de ce premier entretien," he says, "j'étais magnétiseur." He at once obtained the mesmeric trance with the two persons on whom he first tried his hand. He became acquainted with Deleuze and de Puységur. He undertook the cure of some patients; dazzled with the results, he entered himself regularly for the study of medicine. As a mesmerist he rapidly distanced his teachers. He boldly confronted the ridicule and opposition of conventional science. He gave gratuitous courses of instructions in mesmerism from the year 1826, and at the same period began to write on the subject. He published a journal called the "Propagateur du Magnétisme;" also in 1838, in London, a volume entitled "An Introduction to the Study of Animal Magnetism." This is an admirable book. It shows us the author still unable to believe that the tenacity of ignorant prejudice could hold out against an overwhelming demonstration of the truth. "Hitherto" he says, "there has been a disinclination to entertain this investigation, but I trust the evidence now adduced will tend to dispel the prejudice that can only have arisen from the science not having been yet fairly represented." The book opens with a good review of the history of the subject. Speaking of Mesmer, the Baron says: "Surrounded as he was by enemies, both public and private, his unassuming manners, his manifest sincerity, his earnest yet silent enthusiasm, and, above all, his benevolent disposition, conciliated for him the esteem of persons of almost all ranks and pretensions." Later on the Baron goes into a full and detailed description of the physical and psychical phenomena of mesmerism as illustrated by his own experience. His records are of great instructive value and would alone be sufficient to establish the reality of clairvoyance as a fact in nature, even if they were not, as they are, merely one set of such experiences among a great number.

The only fault that can be found with du Potet's books is, that their style is a little inflated or bombastic. In this respect he is, however, the product of French and not English literary traditions, and throughout he is immensely impressed with the prodigious spiritual importance of the discoveries with which he is dealing. As he himself says, he felt a new philosophy forming itself in his mind around these germs; it was nebulous and undefined, but stupendous. He was filled with ideas that he felt to be too far advanced for his generation. He only ventured in 1845 to give them some expression in a work entitled "Essai sur l'enseignement philosophique du Magnétisme." But though this volume is relatively timid and reserved, the author was quickly outgrowing the limits of magnetic practice as familiar to his predecessors. He was becoming something more than a mesmerist—an occultist, and eventually became too theatrical and sensational. He printed an important quarto called "La Magie Dévoilée" which was never published, in the ordinary sense of the word, but delivered to a few persons under definite pledges taken from them in regard to the use they would make of it. The experiments described in this book, though startling and almost entirely of psychological interest, do not really outrun those related in the "Animal Magnetism" in scientific value for the student of mesmerism. The Baron seems to have been himself almost alarmed by the power he acquired over all kinds and conditions of people by causing them to look at signs and figures he drew with charcoal upon the floor. He got these signs from books on medieval magic, and was apparently inclined to attach too much objective importance to the diagrams themselves, thinking that other people would be able to obtain his results by following the same procedure, and that powers of a dangerous character might thus be acquired through his teachings by persons of evilly disposed nature if his instructions were carelessly disseminated. He did not realize how far the magic lay in his own magnetic force—how little of it had to do with the signs.

In 1840 Baron du Potet published another volume called "A Course of Magnetism in Seven Lessons," and in the course of his addresses to his pupils, in themselves a numerous body, to whom he dedicates this volume, he indulges in some very scornful language concerning the obstinate incredulity exhibited by the scientific world at large in regard to the accumulated facts of mesmeric experience.

M. Alexandre Bertrand seems to have been the first writer who quarreled with the straightforward theory of the magnetic fluid adopted by Mesmer, de Puységur and Deleuze. In 1826 he published a treatise entitled "Du Magéntisme Animal en France," in which he promulgated a theory of his own on what he calls "l'Extase"—the condition of those whom the earlier writers described as somnambules. This is not a work of any value in itself, and is chiefly remarkable as showing how very little originality there was in Mr. Braid's later claim to have put the whole subject on a new and scientific footing. M. Bertrand incidentally admits that his own somnambules bear testimony to the reality of the fluid. Many of these, he says, "declare in fact that they see the fluid by means of which I exert an effect upon them coming out from my fingers." The patients with whom he worked would also declare that they discerned a peculiar taste in water that he had magnetized, and experienced pronounced effects from objects he had magnetized, such as a handkerchief, a glove, or a piece of money. For all this, however, he found a sufficient explanation in the theory that they had been possessed by such ideas before going to sleep; and for him magnetism is "une pure chimère." That which he conceives to be a reality is "l'extase"—"a condition into which human creatures are capable of falling, altogether distinct from any state that had been previously recognized." The argument amounts to nothing in itself, explains nothing, and is only carried on by disregarding the larger part of the phenomena admitted as facts and requiring to be brought within the area of any genuine mesmeric theory.

M. Aubin Gautier is one of the early writers who must by no means be overlooked. He seems to have written, to begin with, in 1840 a volume entitled "Introduction au Magnétisme," a volume written in a very reverent spirit, and on the basis of much careful research in ancient history, aimed at showing the wide diffusion of magnetism in one shape or another as a psychological agent in Egypt, Greece, and Rome. M. Gautier seems to have been among those from the first who took the subject seriously and in the spirit of an occult student. Whoever expects to find these pages amusing, he says at the beginning, "deceives himself strangely. The study and practice of magnetism demand an unheard of patience, silence, and self control."

The book is more a review and a speculation rather than a narrative. It rests, of course, in complete reliance on the mesmeric fluid theory, and only fails in bringing out really scientific conceptions because the writer was not himself in possession of those sidelights on mesmerism which I propose to deal with directly, and without which the various phenomena themselves can never be coordinated.

In 1842 M. Gautier published his "Histoire du Somnambulisme," again sweeping the wide areas of ancient history for illustrations of his theme. This volume, including many narratives of more modern origin, gives a full account of M. Pigeaire's experience with the Académie de Médecine of Paris. Monsieur Pigeaire was a country doctor who discovered fine clairvoyant faculties in the youngest of his daughters, Léonide, age 10 years. No experimentalist in those days seemed to have realized the lengths a clairvoyant faculty could reach to when properly cultivated, so that the only experiments tried with the girl had to do with recognizing an object and reading from books when blindfolded. Her powers in this direction were brought to high perfection in a long series of private and domestic seances. When at last M. Pigeaire decided to claim on his daughter's behalf the prize which had been offered by a member of the Académie de Médecine, the family genius was brought out of her retirement and introduced in Paris to a great number of learned observers. The prize in question had been offered by Dr. Burdin to anyone who could read without the use of the eyes, of the sense of touch, or of light. The Académie de Medécine was to arbitrate on any claims that might be made. While the Pigeaire family were staying in Paris they seemed to have given a series of private entertainment at which Léonide's faculties were exhibited, and a large number of persons distinguished in science, literature, and social rank signed records of the successful experiments. When the time came, however, for M. Pigeaire to interview the committee appointed by the Académie de Médecine, he found them perfectly unprepared to investigate and adjudicate upon what actually took place and only willing to deal with Mlle. Léonide if she would conform precisely to their own arrangements and conditions, among which were that she would wear a peculiar kind of helmet mask which they had constructed, and let one of their number keep his hands on her eyelids all the time. In all its details the story is instructive to anyone interested in looking back on the thoroughly unscientific attitude of mind taken up by the representatives of physical science in those days in their dealings with mesmerism. But I can hardly give space here to all the ramifications of the story. M. Pigeaire tried to make his surly inquisitors understand that the whole psychic condition of his daughter required delicate and gentle treatment, that their own proposals were calculated to throw her into convulsions rather than into clairvoyant state, that the bandages he employed, using masses of cotton wool to cover the eyes completely, were of such a kind that any pretense of distructing their efficacy was ridiculous, but all to no purpose. The committee refused even to look at the bandages, and after he had left them in disgust sent in the report, the general drift of which was the proposed experiments had been declined except under conditions which the committee did not receive for evidence of bona fides.

In their zeal to discredit the subject the committee even ventured upon some statements that were positively false, wishing to lead the reader into the belief that they had interviewed the clairvoyant. But nowhere in 1848 was any scientific body prepared to observe the conditions of fair play or common honesty in dealing with the representatives of mesmerism.

In telling the story, however hastily, one should not omit to mention one concluding incident. A group of those persons, who had witnessed the earlier series of preliminary seances with Léonide, took M. Pigeaire's part very warmly. They raised a considerable guarantee fund and publicly offered a prize ten or twelve times larger than that originally offered by the Academy to any member of that body who should be able to read a single word of print when his eyes had been bandaged on the plan adopted with Mlle. Léonide by her father. It is needless to say nobody took up the challenge, and that the whole incident thus constitutes a very round and complete illustration of the gross dishonesty with which the high authorities in Paris conducted the war against the new discovery.

A year or two later, in 1845, M. Gautier published a third book called a "Traité Pratique du Magnétisme et du Somnambulisme." This is a well-arranged and well-indexed treatise on magnetism in all the branches then studied, and though very imperfectly divining the real potentialities of psychic mesmerism, is even to this day a solid book of careful record in earnest thinking, immeasurably better worth attention than any of the recent volumes that play up to the fashionable errors of the moment.

M.L.A. Cahagnet seems to have been one of the very few French writers of this period thoroughly alive to the psychic possisibilities of clairvoyance. He undertook a prolonged series of mesmeric seances with clairvoyants whose attention he directed to other planes of existence, and these are recorded in a book entitled "Arcanes de la Vie Future Dévoileé." The value of the statements made by his clairvoyants in reference to the future life will of course be variously estimated by different readers, but from the point of view of mesmeric sciences, the facts concerning the mental phenomena exhibited by the subjects under treatment are of the highest interest. An English translation of this book has been published in America.

Dr. Esdaile's "Mesmerism in India" is a record of the author's extraordinary success in the application of mesmerism to his surgical practice at the government hospital in Calcutta, of which he was in charge. The book was published about 1842. It includes not only minute surgical reports of frightful operations performed upon the mesmerized patients of the hospital without any suffering or consciousness of what was taking place on their part, but also corroborative testimony from a great many of the most distinguished people resident at Calcutta at the time, who were called in by Dr. Esdaile to be present at these wonderful performances.

A later work by the same author, "Natural and Mesmeric Clairvoyance," published in 1852, includes, besides a quantity of fresh testimony connected with the medical aspects of mesmerism, an epitome of evidence extracted from the "Zoist," and from other sources, on the subject of clairvoyance exhibited during the mesmeric state. In this book Dr. Esdaile also recounts the progress of his own struggle at Calcutta in the effort to press the importance of mesmerism upon the attention of the other doctors of the place, who would only plod along the beaten path. This narrative is, in some respects, the history of Mesmer's own career over again. Instead of being treated by his professional brethren as a benefactor of humanity, Esdaile was opposed and vilified by all the devices that prejudice and professional jealousy could suggest; and while it was notorious that he was daily performing painless operations on patients under mesmerism, the other doctors continued to torture their own unfortunate victims rather than confess that they had been in error in resisting the use of the new curative agent.

Dr. Esdaile's remarkable works are not the only records of capital operations performed without pain to the patient with the help of mesmerism. A paper read before the Royal Medical and

Chirurgical Society of London, in 1842, and published as an independent pamphlet, gives full details concerning a case in which Mr. Ward, a surgeon attached to St. Bartholomew's Hospital, had, about that time, amputated a man's leg above the knee while he, the patient, remained completely unconscious of the operation in a mesmeric sleep, put upon him by the influence of Mr. Topham, a barrister interested in the practice of mesmerism. The pages of the "Zoist," to which I will refer directly, are laden with reports of other similar cases.

Dr. Scoresby, the Arctic voyager and well-known writer on various branches of maritime science, was a careful experimenter in mesmerism, and a work of his called "Zoistic Magnetism" records a great deal of his work. He had only a limited experience of the higher phenomena, but a very extensive familiarity with the physical phenomena of the mesmeric state, including those on the border-land between the lower and higher, having to do with the transfer of sensation from the mesmerizer to the subject. His book was published in 1849, and is interesting for students of the science for its careful observation in regard to the polarity of different parts of the human body in respect to the emanations of its animal magnetism.

An interesting "Report upon the Phenomena of Clairvoyance or Lucid Somnambulism, From Personal Observation," was published in 1843 by Edwin Lee, Fellow of the Royal Medico-Chirurgical Society, and of many other societies abroad of a similar character. The cases here described have reference altogether to clairvoyance on the physical plane, that is to say, to the observation by the clairvoyants concerned, of distant places and houses, and also of objects in their own immediate neighborhood, which they had no means of cognizing through the usual senses. Mr. Lee also wrote about the same time a book on "Animal Magnetism," containing a comprehensive review of similar experiments by other observers.

Another work well worth notice is entitled "Facts in Mesmerism, with Reasons for a Dispassionate Inquiry Into It," by the Rev. Chauncy Hare Townsend, first published in 1839. This opens with a dedication to Dr. Elliotson, from whose experiments, the author says, the greater part of the English world have derived their ideas of mesmerism. He quotes Dr. Wilson, of the Middlesex Hospital, who having been present at a lecture in Dresden, when several fish in a large tub of water were stunned by an electric shock, tried the effect of mesmerizing the water. The fish revived. The incident suggested the proposal that great use might be made of mesmerized water in medicine. In a preface to his second edition Mr. Townsend says: "I now cast my mite into the treasury of evidence that is accumulating in favor of mesmerism with a deep regret that prejudice should yet stand in the way of so much alleviation of human suffering as it is calculated to afford." The book consists of a patient record of the author's own experiments, which were largely concerned with interesting phenomena of "sleep waking," as Dr. Elliotson called it, or mesmeric clairvoyance of the simpler kind. Mr. Townsend began with incredulity, but was drawn into serious inquiry in 1836. He worked at this for a long time and with a great number of subjects. His records include a great variety of facts in thought and sensation transference, and in connection with the development, by a mesmerized person, of perceptive faculties in nerve-centres not usually betraying these. He also throws out a good deal of intelligent speculation concerning the media through which mesmeric effects are wrought. Though priding himself on keeping his experiments and investigations on a relatively humble level, and testing the faculties of his subjects by applying them to the commonplace facts of life, Mr. Townsend treats with contempt "the imagination theory" as "really too absurd to merit a serious refutation. A thousand times I have seen mesmeric patients placed under circumstances where the action of imagination was plainly impossible." And later on he writes: "An elastic ether modified by the nerves, and the conduction of which depends on their condition; which can be thrown into vibration mediately by the mind of man and immediately by the nervous system, which manifests itself when thrown out of equilibrium, and produces mental effects through unusual stimulation of the brain and nerves, cannot but be allowed to be a cause which answers to all the conditions that we desire to unite, and which is sufficient to account for the phenomena that we have been considering."

The "Zoist" was a magazine, published, I believe, under the editorship of Dr. Elliotson, "to collect and diffuse information connected with two sciences—Cerebral Physiology and Mesmerism." "The science of mesmerism," says the inaugural article in the first number, brought out in April, 1843, "is a new physiological truth of incalculable value and importance; and though sneered at by the pseudo-philosophers of the day, there is not the less certainty that it presents the only avenue through which is discernible a ray of hope that the more intricate phenomena of the nervous system—of life—will ever be revealed to man. Already it has established its claim to be considered a most potent remedy in the cure of disease; already enabled the knife of the operator to traverse and divide the living fibre unfelt by the patient. If such are the results of its infancy, what may not its maturity bring forth?" The thirteen volumes of this magazine, for it was continued up to 1856, constitute a splendid reservoir of information on all branches of mesmeric science. In the farewell address, published with the last issue of the review, the conductors say their mission has been accomplished. Their object was neither gain nor worldly reputation, but the establishment of truth. For thirteen years they have amassed fresh facts in cerebral physiology and mesmerism, "and presented them in such numbers, and with such proofs, that to question them would be absurd." They speak of the "glorious doings of Dr. Esdaile in India," which the "Zoist" has chronicled, and though mainly dwelling on the achievements of medical mesmerism, they point to the examples of clairvoyance which abound in their volumes, and which render the phenomenon unquestionable, though of course gross imposition is practiced in regard to it by professional clairvoyants and private persons "influenced by vanity or wickedness."

Only less abundant than the proofs of the reality of mesmeric phenomena with which the pages of the "Zoist" teem, are the illustrations it gives of the senseless and bitter hostility which was opposed to it by the majority of the medical men of its time, and of what Dr. Elliotson, in one letter to the Review early in the proceedings, calls the "anti-mesmeric falsehoods of medical men." The favorite theory of the anti-mesmeric doctors in regard to celebrated surgical operations conducted painlessly under mesmerism, used to be that the sufferers had "feigned" insensibility. That anyone could soberly pretend to believe that patients undergoing the frightful torture of first-class surgical operations could subdue all outward signs of suffering in the interests of the new "imposture," shows us the depth of folly to which prejudice and bigotry may sink the understandings of people still capable of exhibiting a form of intelligence in connection with their own commonplace pursuits.

Dr. Elliotson says of his medical confreres at large that they were as brainlessly indifferent to mesmeric phenomena "as the cattle grazing in the meadows are to the wonders of the steam carriages passing by them on the railroads." With sorrow we must recognize that this contemptuous lament is hardly even as yet out of date.

"Isis Revelata, An Inquiry into the Origin, Progress, and Present State of Animal Magnetism," by J.C. Colquhoun, 1836, is a very comprehensive review of the subject, up to the period at which the author wrote. Its publication is justified, in the introduction, on the ground that the report of the French Academy of Sciences, of 1831, had completely superseded the earlier unfavorable report of 1784. It had been supposed, Mr. Colquhoun points out, that animal magnetism was a system of quackery and delusion. "This objection, which might perhaps have had some plausibility during the infancy of the discovery, has now become utterly ludicrous, and betrays either consummate ignorance of the subject or gross dishonesty." Mr. Colquhoun takes a highly favorable view of Mesmer's life and character, and quotes a dignified letter in which he refuses an offer of a pension of 30,000 francs a year, made to him by the King of France through the Minister Maurepas, on the ground that the offer relates to his pecuniary interest alone, and does not recognize the importance of his discovery as its principal motive. The question ought, Mesmer thinks, to have been approached in a totally opposite way. This, Colquhoun remarks, "is not the language of avarice."

"The Modern Bethesda, or The Gift of Healing Restored," is a narrative, or rather a compilation from letters, newspapers, and testimonials of all sorts, relating to the almost innumerable achievements in healing the sick, performed both in America and England by Dr. J.R. Newton. This wonderful mesmerist—a worker of miracles by wholesale—was born in Rhode Island in 1810. The earlier part of his life was spent in a prosperous mercantile career, and his peculiar gifts were not developed till 1858. Then he began to travel about in the United States, visiting thousands of patients, and performing "those marvelous and inexplicable cures which astonish the world and threaten to revolutionize all former laws and experience of medical science." He had discovered his own powers during a voyage in a crowded passenger steamer, where the yellow fever broke out among thirteen hundred passengers. In Ohio, where he began public ministrations, he treated about one hundred persons a day, performing in the course of time many thousands of wonderful cures.

My purpose in reviewing the books mentioned above has not been to compile anything resembling a complete bibliography of the subject, but simply to show my readers what a wide field the early literature of mesmerism offers for their exploration. But even this rapid survey of its resources would be incomplete without a reference to one which for many modern readers is the standard work on the subject, Dr. Gregory's "Animal Magnetism," first published, I believe, in 1851, and again in other editions at later dates. It is a very fine review of the whole subject in all its branches, and is a good first book for any new student of mesmerism to take up.

The "Mesmerist," a weekly journal of Vital Magnetism, was published in London in 1843. It was begun in May of that year, and continued till September, when its publication ceased. It abounds in interesting records of mesmeric experience in all branches and in good articles vainly combating the crass indifference and incredulity of the public.

In contrast to this mass of literature, which in reality renders any dispute as to the truth of mesmerism equivalent to a dispute as to whether Columbus was right in believing that a continent exists to the west of the Atlantic Ocean, we may usefully turn for a moment to the conventional, orthodox notices of the subject in those mirrors of popular ignorance concerning all psychic science—the encyclopaedias of the day.

The Oxford Encyclopaedia, published in 1828, describes Animal Magnetism as "an appellation given to a pretended science, which during the last century excited considerable attention in several parts of Europe." After giving a caricature account of Mesmer's operations, the writer goes on to declare that in the end it became evident the patients "were impostors, or in a most wretched state of debility both of mind and body." The article concludes by remarking, "It is needless to add that his doctrine is now almost entirely exploded."

Dr. Rees' "Cyclopaedia of Arts, Sciences, and Literature," 1819, disposes of the whole subject in a very charming paragraph. "Animal Magnetism," it says, "is an appellation given by some designing or self-deceived operators upon the credulity and purses of mankind, to certain practices by which, under the pretense of curing diseases, various effects were produced on the animal economy, such as faintings, partial and even general convulsions, etc.;" and referring to the "able investigation" of 1784, which demolished Mesmer's pretensions, the writer concludes by saying that an account of it will be found "under the article Imagination."

Chambers' Encyclopaedia, in the edition of 1884, after briefly glancing in a colorless tone at the earlier history of mesmerism, takes refuge in the investigations of Mr. James Braid as settling the character of mesmeric phenomena all round. "Unfortunately," it says, "the evil reputation which the subject had so naturally obtained prevented the due appreciation of Braid's discoveries,"— the discovery in question being really little more than an incomplete and misleading theory concerning a subdivision of mesmeric phenomena, unscientifically separated for the purposes of a preconceived hypothesis. The writer in the encyclopaedia follows Braid's plan, however, and confines his attention to incidents of mesmeric experience which seem to lend color to the hypnotic theory, lightly remarking of the rest, "No scientific observer has ever confirmed the statements of mesmerists as to clairvoyance, reading of sealed letters, influence on unconscious persons at a distance, or the like;" a statement which might be paralleled if we were to say, "No scientific observer has ever confirmed the statements of travelers and sailors concerning the existence of an

American continent with trees, population, lakes, rivers, and the like."

The eighth edition of the Encyclopaedia Britannica, in a brief account of Mesmer's life, represents him as a detected impostor, and without one word to indicate that there is even any considerable body of opinion opposed to that view, ignores the report of 1831, and refers to the report of the committee of 1784 in the following terms: "The proceedings of Deslon, the pupil of Mesmer, were scrutinized by a committee of inquiry, consisting of the physicians Majault, Sallin, d'Arcet, and Guillotin, and the academicians Franklin, Le Roy, Bailly, de Bory, and Lavoisier. The report drawn up by Bailly thoroughly exposed the falsehood and imposture of the mesmeric process. . . . The disciples of animal magnetism attempted to check the advance of their enemies by forming themselves into societies. Mesmer, more politic, escaped amid the general confusion, carrying with him a subscription of 340,000 francs, and at the same time the secret for which that sum had been given to him."

A somewhat different tone is taken up in the recent ninth edition. Mesmer is now spoken of cautiously as a man who made many converts, who was stigmatized as a charlatan, but who was undoubtedly a mystic, and who was honest in the belief that the phenomena produced were real. A timid reference to Reichenbach's discoveries in odylic force is then put forward. "The idea that some such force exists has been a favorite speculation of scientific men having a bias towards mysticism, and it makes its appearance not unfrequently." "The next great step in the investigation of these phenomena," the "Britannica" then proceeds, "was made by James Braid, a surgeon, in Manchester, in 1841,"—and it goes on to connect the whole remainder of a long article with the weak and insufficient hypothesis of this very shallow thinker.

To comment adequately on the attitude of mind of writers who, remaining thus entirely outside the area of knowledge concerning psychic science in any of its branches, have, nevertheless, the audacity to flirt their incredulity in the faces of wiser and better informed men, would claim the use of stronger language than I care to employ. No one, it is true, deserves blame for leaving any subject that does not attract him altogether unstudied. But in most cases people who are conscious of limited intellectual resources entertain a decent respect for others better furnished. A man may be nothing but a sportsman himself and yet refrain from asserting that chemists and electricians must be impostors, and a chemist may know nothing of Italian art, and yet may refrain from declaring that Raphael never existed. But all through the commonplace world, whether in its upper or lower strata, people who are ignorant of psychic science encourage one another in the brainless and absurd denial of facts exhibited in the encyclopaedias, and in an even more grotesque and impudent fashion by the newspapers of the day, whenever any of its phenomena come up for treatment. The average country grocer, the average newspaper reporter, the average student of physical science, are all steeped in the same dense incapacity to understand the propriety of respecting the knowledge of others, even if they do not share it themselves, whenever they brush up against any statement relating to the work of those who are engaged in any branch of psychic inquiry. From the occult point of view, indeed, one can understand why this should be so. The incredulity of unspiritual mankind is Nature's own protection against those unfit as yet to use her higher gifts. That is all in the legitimate order of things; but the most spiritualized minority need not play up, on their part, to that incredulity. It is their duty to war against it, and in the course of that strife, by slow degrees, the intelligence of the commonplace herd will be leavened, and their minds, growing within them in spite of their own complacent unconsciousness for the process, be qualified gradually for a more progressive evolution.

For the moment, of course, the mesmeric fluid theory is altogether out of fashion, and the most recent inquirers who have set to work within the last few years to rediscover the facts already included in books written from fifty to eighty years ago, have been conspicuous illustrations of one very common human frailty in reference to all advances of knowledge. There is something positively ludicrous to readers familiar with the earlier books in the great library of mesmeric literature, in the way the least intelligent of modern students always train themselves to treat the whole subject, if they handle it at all, as something which they, for the first time, at last have ascertained to be really worth inquiry, and in reference to which it is now important that mankind should begin, in company with them, to observe facts and lay a foundation for reasoning.

Franz Anton Mesmer
(1734-1815)

The subject of the following pamphlet created considerable excitement and conversation in France during the latter part of the eighteenth century. M. Mesmer was a German physician who was considered the inventor of animal magnetism. He first distinguished himself by publishing a thesis he had written while at the University of Vienna in 1766 entitled "Dissertation upon the Influence of the Stars on the Human Body." This thesis was publicly defended by Mesmer when it was critically attacked by his colleagues. In 1774, he became a convert to the work of Father Hehl, a German philosopher, who strongly recommended the use of the loadstone in the art of medicine.

Mesmer adopted a new set of principles which he conceived to be more general in their application and importance. He involved himself in a quarrel with Father Hehl and the celebrated Ingenhousze, by whom he had formerly been patronized. Since their credit in Vienna was extremely high, and their exertions against Mesmer untiring, his system fell immediately into general disrepute. Mesmer appealed in 1776 to the Academy of Sciences at Berlin. His principles were rejected as "destitute of foundation and unworthy of the smallest attention." He left Germany and traveled to Paris.

M. Mesmer was, from the first, desirous of submitting his system to the examination of the faculty of medicine at the University of Paris, but he would not submit it to a regular and authentic committee appointed for that purpose. This misunderstanding between him and the faculty resulted in no examination being made.

In France, the success of Mesmer was the reverse of what it had been in Germany. His number of patients increased rapidly, and his cures were numerous and exciting. He organized a number of pupils to administer animal magnetism under his supervision. He, therefore, published in 1779 a dissertation reflecting the "Discovery of Animal Magnetism," and promised to make a system on the subject which would revolutionize not only the thinking in medicine but also in philosophy. Struck with the clearness and accuracy of his reasonings, the extraordinary and unquestionable cures he performed, some of the greatest and most prominent physicians and philosophers of France became his converts.

DISSERTATIONS ON THE DISCOVERY
OF
ANIMAL MAGNETISM*

This discovery, which has so long been sought, of a principle acting on the nerves should be of interest to all. It has the two-fold aim of adding to their knowledge and of making them happier, by affording a means of curing the maladies which have hitherto been treated with but scant success. The advantages and the singular nature of this system were responsible, some years ago, for the eagerness of the public to grasp the first hopes which I held out; and it is by perverting them that envy, presumption and incredulity have in a very short space of time succeeded in relegating them to the status of illusions, causing them to fall into oblivion.

I have vainly endeavoured to resuscitate them by the enormous number of facts; nevertheless, prejudices won the day and truth has been sacrificed. But, it will be asked today, of what does this discovery consist? How have you come by it? What idea may be formed of its advantages, and why have you not enriched your fellow-citizens therewith? Such are the questions that have been put to me since my stay in Paris by persons who are highly qualified for taking up a new question.

It is with the object of giving a satisfactory reply and in order to provide a general idea of the system I propose, to free it from the errors with which it has been surrounded and to make known the vicissitudes which have formed an obstacle to its being made known, that I am publishing this Dissertation; which is merely the forerunner of a theory I shall impart as soon as circumstances

---

Mémoire sur la Découverte du Magnétisme Animal. Par M. Mesmer, Docteur en Médecine de la Faculté de Vienne. A geneve; et se trouve a Paris, Chez P. Fr. Didot le jeune Libraire—Imprimeur de Monsieur, quai des Augustins, 1779.

enable me to indicate the practical rules of the method I am announcing.

From this standpoint, therefore, I entreat the reader to consider this little work. I am well aware that it will raise many difficulties, but it must be borne in mind that they are of such a nature as not to be solved by any amount of reasoning without the assistance of experience.

Experience alone will scatter the clouds and shed light on this important truth: that NATURE AFFORDS A UNIVERSAL MEANS OF HEALING AND PRESERVING MEN.

Man is by nature an Observer. From his birth, his sole occupation is to observe in order to learn how to use his organs. The eye, for instance, would be useless to him if Nature did not cause him to pay attention to the slightest variations of which his observation is capable. It is by the alternating effect of enjoyment and deprivation that he learns of the existence of light and its different degrees but he would remain in ignorance of the distance, size and shape of objects if he did not learn, by comparing and combining the impressions of other organs, how to correct one by the other. Most sensations are therefore the result of his reflections on the impressions assembled in his organs.

Thus Man spends his early years in acquiring the prompt and correct use of his senses. His gift of observation, which he has from Nature, enables him to form himself, and the perfection of his faculties depends on its more or less constant application.

Among the infinite number of objects which come successively before him, his attention is chiefly attracted by those which interest him for more particular reasons.

Observation of the effects which Nature is universally and constantly producing on each individual is not the exclusive domain of Philosophers; universal interest makes an observer of almost every individual. These observations, multiplied in every age and every place, leave nothing to be desired as regards their reality.

The activity of the human mind, together with its ambition for knowledge, which is never satisfied, in seeking to perfect knowledge previously acquired, abandons observation, replacing it by vague and often frivolous speculation. It forms and accumulates systems which have only the merit of their mysterious abstraction. It departs imperceptibly from truth, to such an extent as to lose sight thereof, setting up ignorance and superstition in its stead. Human knowledge, thus perverted, ceases to possess any of the reality which it had to begin with.

Philosophy has occasionally made efforts to free itself of errors and prejudices, but by overturning those edifices with too much vigour it has covered the ruins with disdain, without fixing the attention on the precious things contained there.

We see among the different peoples the same opinions preserved in a form so disadvantageous and dishonourable for the human mind that it seems improbable that they could have been set up in that form.

Imposture and aberration of reason would have attempted in vain to win over nations and cause them generally to adopt such obviously absurd and ridiculous systems as we see today; truth alone and the general interest should have conferred their universal nature on these opinions.

It may therefore, nevertheless, be asserted that among the vulgar opinions of all ages, whose principles are not rooted in the human heart, there are but few which, however ridiculous and even extravagant they may appear, cannot be regarded as the remains of an originally recognized truth.

Such are my reflections on knowledge in general, and more particularly on the fate of the doctrine of the influence of celestial bodies on the planet we inhabit. These reflections have induced me to seek, among the ruins of that science, brought so low by ignorance, what it might have contained that was useful and true.

In accordance with my ideas on this subject, I published at Vienna in 1766 a thesis on the influence of planets on the human body. According to the familiar principles of universal attraction, ascertained by observations which teach us how the planets mutually affect one another in their orbits, how the sun and moon cause and control the ocean tides on our globe and in the atmosphere, I asserted that those spheres also exert a direct action on all the parts that go to make up animate bodies, in particular on the nervous system, by an all-penetrating fluid. I denoted this action by the INTENSIFICATION AND THE REMISSION of the properties of matter and organic bodies, such as gravity, cohesion, elasticity, irritability, and electricity.

I maintained that just as the alternate effects, in respect of gravity, produce in the sea the appreciable phenomenon which we term ebb and flow, so the INTENSIFICATION AND REMISSION of the said properties, being subject to the action of the same principle, cause in animate bodies alternate effects similar to those sustained by the sea. By these considerations I established that the animal body, being subjected to the same action, likewise underwent a kind of ebb and flow. I supported this theory with different examples of periodic revolutions. I named the property of the animal body that renders it liable to the action of heavenly bodies and of the earth ANIMAL MAGNETISM. I explained by this magnetism the periodical changes which we observe in sex, and in a general way those which physicians of all ages and in all countries have observed during illnesses.

My object then was only to arouse the interest of physicians; but, far from succeeding, I soon became aware that I was being taxed with eccentricity, that I was being treated like a man with a system and that my tendency to quit the normal path of Medicine was being construed as a crime.

I have never concealed my manner of thinking in this respect, being unable to convince myself that we have made the progress of which we boast in the art of healing.

Indeed, I have held that the further we advanced in our knowledge of the mechanism and the economy of the animal body, the more we were compelled to admit our insufficiency. The knowledge that we have gained today about the nature and action of the nerves, imperfect though it be, leaves us in no doubt in this respect. We know that they are the principal agents of sensation and movement, but we are unable to restore them to their natural order when this has been interfered with. We confess this to our shame. The ignorance of bygone centuries on this point has sheltered physicians. The superstitious confidence which they had and which they inspired in their specifics and formulae made them despotic and presumptuous.

I have too much respect for Nature to be able to convince myself that the individual preservation of Man has been left to the mere chance of discovery and to the vague observations that have been made in the course of a number of centuries, finally becoming the domain of the few.

Nature has provided everything for the existence of the individual. Propagation takes place without "system" and without trickery. Why should preservation be deprived of the same advantage? The preservation of animals affords proof that the contrary is the case.

A non-magnetized needle, when set in motion, will only take a determined direction by chance, whereas a magnetized needle, having been given the same impulse, after various oscillations proportional to the impulse and magnetism received, will regain its initial position and stay there. Thus the harmony of organic bodies, when once interfered with, goes through the uncertainties of my first hypothesis, unless it is brought back and determined by the GENERAL AGENT, whose existence I recognize; it alone can restore harmony in the natural state.

Thus we have seen, in all ages, maladies which become worse or are cured with and without the help of Medicine, in accordance with different systems and by the most conflicting methods. These considerations have removed all doubt from my mind that there exists in Nature a universally acting principle which, independently of ourselves, operates what we vaguely attribute to Art *and* Nature.

These reflections have caused me to stray imperceptibly from the beaten track. I have subjected my ideas to experience for over twelve years, which I have devoted to the most accurate observations of all types of disease, and I have had the satisfaction of seeing the maxims I had forecast being borne out time and time again.

It was chiefly in the years 1773 and 1774 that I undertook in my house the treatment of a young lady, aged twenty-nine, named Oesterline, who for several years had been subject to a convulsive malady, the most troublesome symptoms of which were that the blood rushed to her head and there set up the most cruel toothache and earache, followed by delirium, rage, vomiting, and swooning.

For me it was a highly favourable occasion for observing accurately that type of ebb and flow to which ANIMAL MAGNETISM subjects the human body. The patient often had beneficial crises, followed by a remarkable degree of alleviation; however, the enjoyment was always momentary and imperfect.

The desire to ascertain the cause of this imperfection and my own uninterrupted observations brought me time and time again to the point of recognizing Nature's handiwork and of penetrating it sufficiently to forecast and assert, without hesitation, the different stages of the illness. Encouraged by this first success, I no longer had any doubts as to the possibility of bringing it to perfection, if I were able to discover the existence, among the substances of which our globe is made, of an action that is also reciprocal and similar to that of the heavenly bodies, by means of which I could imitate artificially the periodic revolutions of the ebb and flow just referred to.

I possessed the usual knowledge about the magnet: its action on iron, the ability of our body fluids to receive that mineral. The various tests carried out in France, Germany, and Britain for stomach ache and toothache were known to me. These reasons, together with the analogy between the properties of this substance and the general system, induced me to regard it as being the most suitable for this type of test. To ensure the success of this test, in the interval of the attacks, I prepared the patient by the continuous use of chalybeates.

My social relations with Father Hehl, Jesuit and Professor of Astronomy at Vienna, then provided me with an opportunity of asking him to have made for me by his craftsmen a number of magnetized pieces, of convenient shape for application. He was kind enough to do this for me and let me have them.

On 28th July 1774, after the patient had had a renewal of her usual attacks, I applied three magnetized pieces to the stomach and both legs. Not long afterwards, this was followed by extraordinary sensations; she felt inside her some painful currents of a subtle material which, after different attempts at taking a direction, made their way towards the lower part and caused all the symptoms of the attack to cease for six hours. Next day, as the patient's condition made it necessary for me to carry out the same test again, I obtained the same success with it.

My observation of these effects, coupled with my ideas on the general system, provided me with fresh information. While confirming my previous ideas about the influence of the GENERAL AGENT, it taught me that another principle was causing the magnet to act, the magnet itself being incapable of such action on the nerves, and I saw that I only had a short way to go in order to arrive at the IMITATIVE THEORY, which formed the subject of my research.

A few days afterwards, having met Father Hehl, I mentioned to him in the course of conversation that the patient was in a better state of health, also the good effects of my process and the hopes that I had, on the strength of this operation, of soon finding a means of curing nerve sufferers.

I found out not long afterwards, from the public and from the newspapers, that this man of religion, abusing his fame in astronomy and wishing to appropriate for himself a discovery of whose nature and benefits he was entirely ignorant, had taken upon himself to publish the fact that by means of some magnetized pieces, to which he attributed a specific virtue depending on their shape, he had obtained the means of curing the gravest nerve disorders. To lend support to this opinion, he had sent to a number of Academies some sets consisting of magnetized pieces of all shapes, mentioning according to their outline their analogy with the various maladies.

This is how he expressed himself: "I have discovered in these shapes, which agree with the magnetic vortex, a perfection on which depends their specific virtue in cases of illness; it is owing to the lack of this perfection that the tests carried out in England and France have met with no success." And by affecting to confuse the manufacture of the magnetized shapes with the discovery I had mentioned to him, he finished by saying "that he had communicated everything to the physicians, and particularly to myself, and would continue to avail himself of them for his tests."

The repeated writings of Father Hehl on this subject inspired the public, which is always eager for a specific against nervous disorders, with the illfounded opinion that the discovery in question consisted in the mere use of the magnet. I in my turn wrote to refute this error, by publishing the existence of ANIMAL MAGNETISM, essentially distinct from the Magnet; however, as the public had received its information from a man of high repute, it remained in its error.

I continued my experiments with different disorders so as to generalize my knowledge and perfect the application thereof.

I knew particularly well Baron de Stoerck, President of the Faculty of Medicine at Vienna and Chief Physician to Her Majesty. It was moreover seemly for him to be acquainted with the nature of my discovery and its purpose. I consequently placed be-

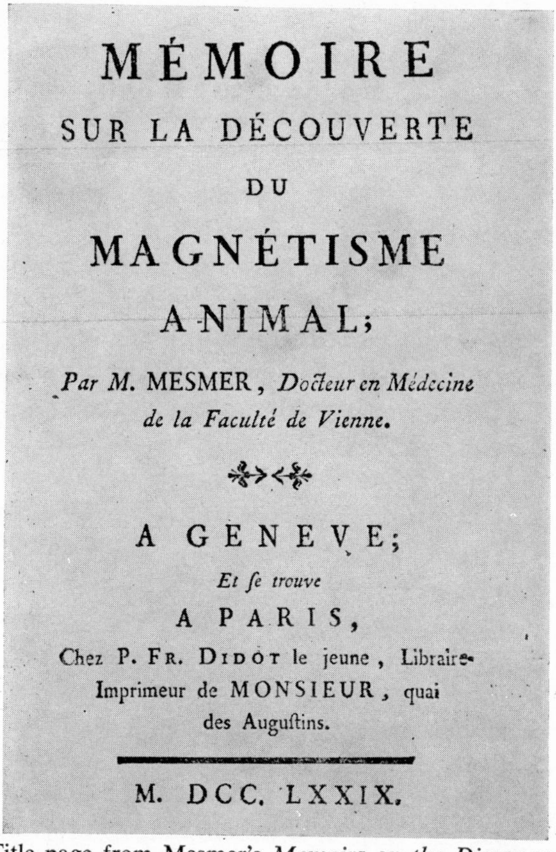

MÉMOIRE
SUR LA DÉCOUVERTE
DU
MAGNÉTISME
ANIMAL;

Par M. MESMER, *Docteur en Médecine de la Faculté de Vienne.*

A GENEVE;
Et se trouve
A PARIS,
Chez P. FR. DIDOT le jeune, Libraire-Imprimeur de MONSIEUR, quai des Augustins.

M. DCC. LXXIX.

FIGURE 2. Title page from Mesmer's *Memoirs on the Discovery of Animal Magnetism,* published in 1779.

fore him the circumstantial details of my operations, particularly as regards the communication and currents of animal magnetic matter, and I invited him to verify them for himself, stating that it was my intention to report to him in the future all progress that I might make in this new science. To give him certain proof of my good faith, I made known my methods to him without reserve. The natural timidity of this physician, no doubt based on motives which it is not my intention to penetrate, induced him to reply that he wished to have nothing to do with what I was telling him about, and he begged me not to compromise the Faculty by giving publicity to an innovation of this kind.

Public prejudice and uncertainty as to the nature of my methods decided me to publish, on 5th January 1775, a Letter to a Foreign Physician, in which I gave an exact idea of my theory, the success I had hitherto obtained and the success I had reason to hope for. I set fourth the nature and action of ANIMAL MAGNETISM and the analogy between its properties and those of the magnet and electricity. I added "that all bodies were, like the magnet, capable of communicating this magnetic principle; that this fluid penetrated everything and could be stored up and concentrated, like the electric fluid; that it acted at a distance; that animate bodies were divided into two classes, one being susceptible to this magnetism and the other to an opposite quality that suppresses its action." Finally, I accounted for the various sensations and based these assertions on experiments which enabled me to put them forward.

A few days prior to the publication of this Letter, I heard that Mr. Ingenhousze, member of the Royal Academy of London and Inoculator at Vienna, by entertaining the nobility and distinguished personages with experiments in electricity, and by the skill with which he varied the effects of the magnet, had acquired the reputation of being a physician. I heard, as I said, that when this gentleman learned of my operations, he treated them as vain imaginings, going so far as to say that only the English genius was capable of such a discovery, if it could be done. He came to see me, not to gain information, but with the sole intention of persuading me that I was laying myself open to error and should suppress all publicity with a view to avoiding inevitable ridicule.

I replied that he was not sufficiently talented himself to give me this advice, and that I should moreover have pleasure in convincing him at the first opportunity. This presented itself two days afterwards.

Miss Oesterline took fright and contracted a chill, causing a sudden stoppage, and she relapsed into her former convulsions. I invited Mr. Ingenhousze to call. He came, accompanied by a young physician. The patient was then in a fainting fit with convulsions. I told him that it was the most favourable opportunity for convincing himself of the existence of the principle I announced, and the property which it has to communicate. I told him to approach the patient, while I withdrew from her, instructing him to touch her. She made no movement. I recalled him to me, and communicated ANIMAL MAGNETISM to him by taking him by the hands; I then bade him approach the patient once more, while I kept at a distance, telling him to touch her a second time. This resulted in convulsive movements. I made him repeat this touching process several times, which he did with the top of his finger, changing the direction each time. Always, to his great astonishment, he brought about a convulsive effect in the part touched.

When this operation was over, he told me he was convinced, and I suggested a second visit. We withdrew from the patient, so as not to be perceived even had she been conscious. I offered Mr. Ingenhousze six china cups and asked him to tell me to which one he wished me to communicate the magnetic quality. I touched the one of his choice and then applied the six cups to the patient's hand in succession; on reaching the cup that I had touched, the hand made a movement and gave signs of pain. Mr. Ingenhousze obtained the same result when he applied the six cups.

I then had these cups taken back to the place whence they had come, and after a certain interval, holding him by one hand, I asked him to touch with the other any cup he wished; he did so, the cups were brought to the patient, as before, with the same result.

The communicability of the principle was now well-established in Mr. Ingenhousze's eyes, and I suggested a third experiment to show its action at a distance and its penetrating quality. I pointed my finger at the patient at a distance of eight paces; the next instant, her body was in convulsion to the point of raising her on her bed with every appearance of pain. I continued, in the same position, to point my finger at the patient, placing Mr. Ingenhousze between herself and me. She underwent the same sensations.

Having repeated these tests to Mr. Ingenhousze's satisfaction, I asked him if he was convinced of the marvellous properties about which I had told him, offering to repeat our proceedings if he were not. His reply was to the effect that he wished for nothing further and was convinced; but owing to his friendship with me, he entreated me not to make any public statement on this subject, so as not to lay myself open to public incredulity. We parted, and I went back to the patient to continue the treatment, which was most successful. That same day I managed to restore the normal course of nature, thereby putting an end to all the trouble brought about by stoppage.

Two days later I was astonished to hear that Mr. Ingenhousze was making statements in public that were quite the reverse of his utterances in my house, and was denying the success of the different experiments he had witnessed. He effected to confuse ANIMAL MAGNETISM with the magnet and was endeavouring to damage my reputation by spreading the report that with the aid of a number of magnetized pieces which he had brought with him, he had succeeded in unmasking me, proving that it was nothing but a ridiculous prearranged fraud.

I must confess that such words at first seemed to me to be unbelievable, and I had some difficulty in bringing myself to regard Mr. Ingenhousze as their author. However, his association with the Jesuit Hehl, and the latter's irresponsible writings in support of such odious insinuations, aimed at ruining the effect of my Letter of 5th January 1775, removed all doubt from my mind that Mr. Ingenhousze was the guilty party. I refuted Father Hehl and was about to draw up an indictment when Miss Oesterline, who had been informed of Mr. Ingenhousze's procedure, was so affronted at finding herself thus compromised that she relapsed into her former state, which was aggravated by a nervous fever.

Miss Oesterline's condition claimed the whole of my attention for a fortnight. In these circumstances, by continuing my research, I was fortunate in overcoming the difficulties which stood in the way of my progress and of giving my theory the desired perfection. The cure of this young lady represented the first fruits of my success, and I had the satisfaction of seeing her henceforth in excellent health. She married and had some children.

It was during this fortnight that, being determined to justify my conduct and to give the public a correct idea of my abilities by unmasking Mr. Ingenhousze's behaviour, I informed Mr. de Stoerck, requesting him to obtain orders from the Court for a Commission of the Faculty to be acquainted with the facts, so that it might verify and make them known to the public. This step appeared to be agreeable to the senior physician; he seemed to share my viewpoint and promised to act accordingly, remarking, however, that he could not be on the Commission.

I suggested several times that he should come and see Miss Oesterline and satisfy himself as to the success of my treatment. His replies in this matter were always vague and uncertain. I explained to him how it would benefit humanity to have my method adopted by the hospitals, and asked him to demonstrate its utility forthwith at the Spanish Hospital. He agreed to this and gave the necessary instructions to Mr. Reinlein, physician at that hospital.

The latter was witness of the effects and usefulness of my visits over a period of eight days. On several occasions he expressed surprise and reported to Mr. de Stoerck. However, I soon became aware that different impressions had been given to this leading physician. I met him almost every day and insisted on my request for a Commission, reminding him of the interesting matters about which I had told him, but saw nothing but indifference, coldness, and reserve in his attitude whenever the topic was broached.

Being unable to obtain any satisfaction, and as Mr. Reinlein had ceased reporting to me (I moreover found out that this change of front was the result of steps taken by Mr. Ingenhousze), I realized my inability to stem the course of the intrigue and sought consolation in silence.

Emboldened by the success of his plans, Mr. Ingenhousze acquired fresh vigour; he vaunted his incredulity and it was not long before he succeeded in having those who suspended judgment or who did not share his opinion classed as feebleminded. It will readily be understood that all this was quite enough to alienate the masses and have me looked upon at least as a visionary, especially as the indifference of the Faculty appeared to support that opinion.

What I felt to be the most strange was that the same opinion should be shared the following year by Mr. Klinkosch, Professor of Medicine at Prague, who, without knowing me and without the slightest idea of the true state of the matter, was sufficiently foolish (to use no stronger term), as to publish in the public journals the curious details of the impostures attributed to me by Mr. Ingenhousze.*

Whatever public opinion might be, I felt that truth could not find better support than in facts. I undertook the treatment of various disorders, including a hemiplegia, the result of apoplexy; stoppages, spitting of blood, frequent colics and convulsive sleep from childhood, with spitting of blood and normal ophthalmia. Mr. Bauer, Professor of Mathematics at Vienna and a man of outstanding merit, was attacked by this latter malady. My work was crowned with the best possible success, and Mr. Bauer himself was honest enough to make public a detailed report on his cure. However, prejudice had the upper hand. Nevertheless, I had the satisfaction of being quite well known to a great Minister, a Privy Councillor and an Aulic Councillor, friends of humanity, who had often recognized truth for themselves, seeing that they upheld and protected it. They even made several attempts to lighten the shadows in which it was being wrapped. They met with little success, however, it being objected that only the opinion of physicians was capable of deciding, and their good will was thus confined to their offers to give my writings the necessary publicity in foreign lands.

It was through this channel that my explanatory Letter of 5th

---

*Letter on Animal Magnetism and the Electrophorus, addressed to Count de Kinszky. It was included in the *Proceedings of the Scientists of Bohemia,* Vol. II, 1776. It was also printed separately and published at Vienna in the following year.—F. A. M.

January 1775 was transmitted to the majority of the scientific institutions, and to a few scientists. Only the Berlin Academy, on the 24th March that year, made a written reply in which by confusing the properties of ANIMAL MAGNETISM which I had expounded with those of the magnet, which I only spoke of as a conductor, it incurred a number of errors and its opinion was that I was the victim of illusion.

This Academy was not the only one to make the mistake of confusing ANIMAL MAGNETISM with mineral magnetism, although I have always stressed in my writings that the use of the magnet, however convenient, was always imperfect without the assistance of the theory of ANIMAL MAGNETISM. The physicians and doctors with whom I have been in correspondence, or who have endeavoured to find out my methods in order to usurp this discovery, have taken upon themselves to spread about either that the magnet was the only means I employed, or else that I used electricity as well, because it was well known that I had availed myself of both. Most of them have been undeceived by their own experience, but instead of realizing the truth I was expounding, they have concluded from the fact that they obtained no success from the use of these two agents that the cures announced by myself were imaginary and that my theory was nothing but an illusion.

The desire to refute such errors once and for all, and to do justice to truth, determined me to make no further use of electricity or of the magnet from 1776 onwards.

The poor reception given to my discovery and the slight hopes it held out to me for the future made me resolve to undertake nothing of a public nature at Vienna, but instead to travel to Swabia and Switzerland and add to my experience, thus arriving at the truth through facts. Indeed, I had the satisfaction of making some striking cures in Swabia, and of operating in the hospitals, before the eyes of doctors from Berne and Zurich. They were left in no doubt as to the existence of ANIMAL MAGNETISM and the usefulness of my theory, which corrected the error into which they had been led by my opponents.

Between the years 1774 and 1775 an ecclesiastic, a man of good faith but of excessive zeal, was operating in the diocese of Ratisbon on various disorders of a nervous nature, using means that appeared to be supernatural to the less well informed in that district. His reputation extended to Vienna, where society was divided into two halves; one regarded his methods as imposture and fraud, while the other looked upon them as miracles performed by Divine Power. Both, however, were wrong, and my experience at once told me that the man in question was nothing but a tool of Nature. This was because his profession, assisted by fate, had furnished him with certain natural talents enabling him to find out the periodical symptoms of maladies without knowing their cause. The end of such paroxysms was held to be a complete cure, and time alone could undeceive the public.

On returning to Vienna towards the end of 1775, I passed through Munich, where his Highness, the Elector of Bavaria, was kind enough to consult me on this subject, asking me whether I could account for these pretended miracles. I carried out before his eyes some experiments that removed any prejudices he may have had and left him in no doubt as to the truth I announced. Shortly afterwards, the Scientific Institution of that city paid me the honour of admitting me as a member.

In 1776 I again visited Bavaria and secured similar success there in illnesses of different kinds. In particular, I effected the cure of an imperfect amaurosis, accompanied by paralysis of the limbs, which was afflicting Mr. d'Osterwald (factually Oesterwald, G.F.), director of the Scientific Institution of Munich; he was kind enough to make public mention of this and of the other results he had witnessed.*

After returning to Vienna, I persisted until the end of that year in undertaking no further work; neither would I have altered my mind if my friends had not been unanimous in opposing my decision. Their insistences, together with my desire to see the truth prevail, aroused in me the hope of accomplishing this by means of fresh successes, particularly through some striking cure. With

*There was published at the beginning of 1778 a Collection of Cures effected by Magnetism, printed at Leipzig. This bulky Collection, whose authority is unknown to me, has the sole merit of assembling faithfully, without partiality, the reports and writings for and against my system.—F. A. M.

this end in view, among other patients I undertook the treatment of Miss Paradis, aged eighteen, whose parents were well known; she herself was known to Her Majesty the Queen-Empress, through whose bounty she received a pension, being quite blind since the age of four. It was a perfect amaurosis, with convulsions in the eyes. She was moreover a prey to melancholia, accompanied by stoppages in the spleen and liver, which often brought on accesses of delirium and rage so that she was convinced she was out of her mind.

I also undertook the treatment of one Zwelferine, a girl, nineteen years of age, who had been blind since the age of two owing to amaurosis accompanied by a very thick, wrinkled albugo with atrophy of the ball; she was also afflicted with periodic spitting of blood. I found this girl in the Vienna orphanage and her blindness was attested by the Governors.

At the same time I also treated Miss Ossine, aged eighteen, who was in receipt of a pension from Her Majesty, as being the daughter of an officer in her armies. Her malady consisted of purulent phthisis and irritable melancholia, accompanied by fits, rage, vomiting, spitting of blood and fainting. These three patients and others besides were accommodated in my house so that I might continue my treatment without interruption. I was fortunate in being able to cure all three.

The father and mother of Miss Paradis, who witnessed her cure and the progress she was making in the use of her eyesight, hastened to make this occurrence known and how pleased they were. Crowds flocked to my house to make sure for themselves, and each one, after putting the patient to some kind of test, withdrew greatly astonished, with the most flattering remarks to myself.

The two Presidents of the Faculty, at the head of a deputation of their corps, came to see me at the repeated instances of Mr. Paradis; and, after examining the young lady, added their tribute to that of the public. Mr. de Stoerck, one of these gentlemen who knew this young person particularly well, having treated her for ten years without the slightest success, expressed to me his satisfaction at so interesting a cure and his regret at having so far deferred his acknowledgment of the importance of my discovery. A number of physicians, each for himself, followed the example set by our leaders and paid the same tribute to truth.

After such authentic recognition, Mr. Paradis was kind enough to express his gratitude in his writings, which went all over Europe. It was he who afterwards published the interesting details of his daughter's recovery in the newspapers.

Among the physicians who came to see me to satisfy their curiosity was Mr. Barth, professor of anatomy of diseases of the eye, and cataract specialist; he had even admitted on two occasions that Miss Paradis was able to use her eyes. Nevertheless, this man's envy caused him to state publicly that the young lady could not see, and that he had satisfied himself that she could not. He founded this assertion on the fact that she did not know or confused the names of objects shown to her. He was answered from all quarters that he was therein confusing the necessary inability of those blind from birth or at a very tender age with the knowledge acquired by blind persons operated on for cataract. How, he was asked, is it that a man of your profession can be guilty of so obvious an error? His impudence, however, found an answer to everything by asserting the contrary. It was in vain that the public told him again and again that a thousand witnesses had given evidence of the cure; he alone held the opposite view, in which he was joined by Mr. Ingenhousze, the Inoculator of whom I have spoken.

These two individuals, who were at first regarded as fanatics by sensible, honest folk, succeeded in weaving a plot to withdraw Miss Paradis from my care, her eyes still being in an imperfect state, and made it impossible for her to be presented to Her Majesty, as was to have been the case. This inevitably lent credence to their assertion of imposture. To this effect they worked on Mr. Paradis, who began to be afraid that his daughter's pension and several other advantages held out to him might be stopped. He consequently asked for his daughter back.

The latter, supported by her mother, showed her unwillingness and fear lest the cure might be imperfect. The father insisted, and this dispute brought on her fits again and led to an unfortunate relapse. However, this had no effect on her eyes, and she continued to improve the use of them. When her father saw she was better, being still egged on by the conspirators, he returned to the charge. He demanded his daughter with some heat and compelled his wife to do likewise.

The girl resisted for the same reasons as before. Her mother, who had hitherto supported her, and had apologized for the lengths to which her husband had gone, came to tell me on 29th April 1777 that she intended to remove her daughter instantly. I replied that she was free to do so, but if fresh accidents were the result, she could not count on my help.

These words were overheard by the girl, who was so overcome that she went into a fit. She was assisted by Count de Pellegrini, one of my patients. Her mother, who heard her cries, left me abruptly and seized her daughter angrily from the hands of the person who was assisting her, saying: "Wretched girl, you too are hand in glove with the people of this house!" as she flung her in a fury head-first against the wall.

Immediately all the troubles of that unfortunate girl recommenced. I hastened towards her to give her assistance, but her mother, still livid with rage, hurled herself upon me to prevent me from doing so, while she heaped insults on me. I had the mother removed by certain members of my household and went up to the girl to assist her. While I was so engaged, I heard more angry shouts and repeated attempts to open and shut the door of the room where I was.

It was Mr. Paradis who, having been warned by one of his wife's servants, now invaded my house sword in hand with the intention of entering the room where I was, while my servant was trying to remove him by guarding the door. The madman was at last disarmed, and he left my house breathing imprecations on myself and my household.

Meanwhile, his wife had swooned away. I had her given the necessary attention, and she left some hours afterwards, but the unhappy girl was suffering from attacks of vomiting, fits and rages, which the slightest noise, especially the sound of bells, accentuated. She had even relapsed into her previous blind state through the violence of the blow given her by her mother, and I had some fears for the state of her brain.

Such were, for my patient and for me, the sinister effects of that painful scene. It would have been easy for me to take the matter to court, on the evidence of Count de Pellegrini and eight persons who were with me, to say nothing of other neighbours who could have acted as witnesses too, but, as I was solely concerned with saving Miss Paradis, if possible, I refrained from availing myself of legal redress. My friends remonstrated in vain, pointing out the ingratitude exhibited by her family and the wasted expenditure of my labours. I adhered to my first decision and would have been content to overcome the enemies of truth and of my peace of mind by good deeds.

Next day I heard that Mr. Paradis, in an endeavour to cover up his excesses, was spreading about the most wicked insinuations regarding myself, always with a view of removing his daughter and proving, by her condition, the dangerous nature of my methods. I did indeed receive through Mr. Ost, Court physician, a written order from Mr. de Stoerck, in his capacity as head physician, dated Schoenbrunn, 2nd May 1777, who called upon me "to put an end to the imposture" (his own expression) "and restore Miss Paradis to her family, if I thought this could be done without risk."

Who would have believed that Mr. de Stoerck, being so well informed by the same physician of all that had taken place in my house and, after his first visit, having come twice to convince himself of the patient's progress and the success of my methods, could have taken upon himself to use such offensive and contemptuous language to me? I had indeed reason to expect the contrary, because being well placed for recognizing a truth of this kind, he should have been its defender. I would even go so far as to say that as the repository of Her Majesty's confidence, one of his first duties under these circumstances should have been to protect a member of the Faculty whom he knew to be blameless, and to whom he had time and time again given assurances of his affection and esteem. I made answer to this irresponsible order that the patient was not in a position to be moved without running the risk of death.

Miss Paradis's critical condition no doubt made an impression on her father, and caused him to reflect. Through the intermediary of two reputable persons, he begged me to continue attending his daughter. I told him that I would do so on condition that neither he nor his wife ever again appeared in my house. My treatment indeed exceeded my hopes, and nine days sufficed to calm down the fits entirely and put an end to the disorders. But her blindness remained.

Fifteen days' treatment cured the blindness and restored the eye to its condition prior to the incident. To this period I added a further fortnight's attention to improve and restore her health. The public then came to obtain proof of her recovery, and everybody gave me, even in writing, fresh evidence of satisfaction. Mr. Paradis, being assured of the good health enjoyed by his daughter through Mr. Ost, who, at his request and by my permission, followed the progress of the treatment, wrote a letter to my wife in which he thanked her for her motherly care.

He also wrote thanking me and apologizing for the past; he finished by asking me to send back his daughter so that she might enjoy the benefit of country air. He said that he would send her back to me whenever I might think necessary, so as to continue the treatment, and he hoped that I would attend her. I believed him in all good faith, and returned his daughter to him on the 8th of June.

Next day I heard that her family asserted that she was still blind and subject to fits. They showed her thus and compelled her to imitate fits and blindness. This news evoked some contradictions by persons who were convinced of the contrary, but it was upheld and accredited by the obscure intriguers who used Mr. Paradis as their tool, and I was unable to check its spread by the highest testimony, such as that of Mr. de Spielmann, Aulic Councillor of Their Majesties and Director of the State Chancellery; Their Majesties' Councillors, Messrs. de Molitor and de Umlauer, physician to Their Majesties; de Boulanger, de Heufeld and Baron de Colnbach and Mr. de Weber, who, independently of several other persons, had almost every day followed for themselves my processes and results.

Thus in spite of my perseverance and my work, I have little by little been relegated to the position of a conjecture, or at least of something uncertain, a truth that has been authentically proven.

It is easy to imagine how I might have been affected by the relentlessness of my enemies to do me harm and by the ingratitude of a family on which I had showered kindnesses. Nevertheless, during the last half of 1777 I continued with the cure of Miss Ossine and the aforementioned Zwelferine, whose eyes, it will be remembered, were in an even more serious condition than Miss Paradis's. I also persevered successfully with the treatment of my remaining patients, in particular Miss Wipior, aged nine, who had in one eye a growth on the cornea, known by the name of staphyloma; this cartilaginous excrescence, of three to four lines, prevented her from seeing with that eye.

I succeeded in removing the excrescence to the extent that she was able to read sideways. There only remained a slight albugo in the centre of the cornea, and I have no doubt that I would have caused it to disappear entirely had circumstances permitted me to continue the treatment. However, being wearied by my labours extending over twelve consecutive years and still more so by the continued animosity of my adversaries, without having reaped from my research and efforts any satisfaction other than that of which adversity could not deprive me, I felt that I had done my duty by my fellow-citizens.

With the conviction that justice would one day be done me, I decided to travel for the sole purpose of securing the relaxation I so much needed. However, to guard against prejudice and insinuations as far as possible, I arranged matters so as to leave at home in my absence Miss Ossine and the girl Zwelferine. I next took the precaution of telling the public of the reason for this arrangement, stating that these persons were in my home so that their condition could be ascertained at any moment and thereby lend support to truth. They remained there eight months after my departure from Vienna and only left on orders from a higher authority.

On arriving at Paris in February 1778,* I began to enjoy the delights of repose there, in the interesting company of the scientists and physicians of that capital. However, acceding to their requests and to repay the kindness shown to me, I decided to satisfy their curiosity by speaking of my system. They were astonished at its nature and results and asked me for an explanation. I gave them my concise assertions in nineteen articles.* They seemed to them to bear no relation to established knowledge. I felt indeed how difficult it was, by reason alone, to prove the existence of a principle of which people had not the slightest conception. With this in mind, I therefore yielded to the request made to me to show the reality and the usefulness of my theory by the treatment of a few serious maladies.

A number of patients placed their trust in me. Most were in so desperate a plight that it required all my desire to be of use to make me decide on attending them. Nevertheless, I cured a vaporous melancholia with spasmodic vomiting, a number of longstanding stoppages in the spleen, liver and mesentery, an imperfect amaurosis, to the extent of preventing the patient from moving about alone, and a general paralysis with trembling which gave the patient (aged forty) every appearance of old age and drunkenness. This malady was the result of frost-bite; it had been aggravated by the effects of a putrid and malignant fever which the patient had contracted six years before in America.

I also obtained the same success in a case of total paralysis of the legs, with atrophy; one of chronic vomiting, which reduced the patient to a state of progressive emaciation; one of general scrofulous debility, and finally in a case of general decay of the organs of perspiration.

These patients, whose condition was known and verified by the

---

*My adversaries, who were ever on the watch to harm me, lost no time in spreading warnings about me on my arrival in France. They went to the length of compromising the Faculty of London by causing an Anonymous Letter to be inserted in the *Journal Encyclopedique for March 1778, page 506;* Mr. Hell, bailiff of Hirsingen and Lundzer, did not scruple to lend his name to this libellous document. Nevertheless I was not known to him, and I only saw him afterwards, at Paris, to receive his apologies. The untrustworthiness, inconsistency and maliciousness of this Letter are merely deserving of contempt, as will be found on perusing it.—F. A. M.

*These same Assertions had been forwarded in 1776 to the Royal Society of London by Mr. Elliott, English Envoy to the Diet of Ratisbon; I communicated them to that Minister at his own request, after carrying out before him various experiments at Munich and Ratisbon. — F. A. M.

physicians of the Paris Faculty, were all subject to considerable crises and evacuation, on a par with the nature of their maladies, without making use of any medicaments. After completing their treatment, they gave me detailed declarations.

That should have been more than enough to prove beyond all doubt the advantages of my method. I had reason to flatter myself that recognition would follow. However, the persons who had induced me to undertake the foregoing treatments were not enabled to see their effects, owing to considerations and reasons which it would be out of place to enumerate in this dissertation.

The result is that the cures which, contrary to my expectation, were not communicated to bodies whose duty it might have been to call the attention of the public to them, only imperfectly fulfilled the task I had set myself, and for which I had been praised.

This induces me to make a fresh effort today in the cause of truth, by giving more scope and the publicity which they have hitherto lacked to my original Assertions.

PROPOSITIONS ASSERTED

1. There exists a mutual influence between the Heavenly Bodies, the Earth and Animate Bodies.

2. A universally distributed and continuous fluid, which is quite without vacuum and of an incomparably rarefied nature, and which by its nature is capable of receiving, propagating and communicating all the impressions of movement, is the means of this influence.

3. This reciprocal action is subordinated to mechanical laws that are hitherto unknown.

4. This action results in alternate effects which may be regarded as an Ebb and Flow.

5. This ebb and flow is more or less general, more or less particular, more or less composite according to the nature of the causes determining it.

6. It is by this operation (the most universal of those presented by Nature) that the activity ratios are set up between the heavenly

bodies, the earth and its component parts.

7. The properties of Matter and the Organic Body depend on this operation.

8. The animal body sustains the alternate effects of this agent, which by insinuating itself into the substance of the nerves, affects them at once.

9. It is particularly manifest in the human body that the agent has properties similar to those of the magnet; different and opposite poles may likewise be distinguished, which can be changed, communicated, destroyed and strengthened; even the phenomenon of dipping is observed.

10. This property of the animal body which brings it under the influence of the heavenly bodies and the reciprocal action of those surrounding it, as shown by its analogy with the Magnet, induced me to term it ANIMAL MAGNETISM.

11. The action and properties of Animal Magnetism, thus defined, may be communicated to other animate and inanimate bodies. Both are more or less susceptible to it.

12. This action and properties may be strengthened and propagated by the same bodies.

13. Experiments show the passage of a substance whose rarefied nature enables it to penetrate all bodies without appreciable loss of activity.

14. Its action is exerted at a distance, without the aid of an intermediate body.

15. It is intensified and reflected by mirrors, just like light.

16. It is communicated, propagated and intensified by sound.

17. This magnetic property may be stored up, concentrated and transported.

18. I have said that all animate bodies are not equally susceptible; there are some, although very few, whose properties are so opposed that their very presence destroys all the effects of magnestism in other bodies.

19. This opposing property also penetrates all bodies; it may likewise be communicated, propagated, stored, concentrated and transported, reflected by mirrors and propagated by sound; this constitutes not merely the absence of magnetism, but a positive opposing property.

20. The Magnet, both natural and artificial, together with other substances, is susceptible to Animal Magnetism, and even to the opposing property, without its effect on iron and the needle undergoing any alteration in either case; this proves that the principle of Animal Magnetism differs essentially from that of mineral magnetism.

21. This system will furnish fresh explanations as to the nature of Fire and Light, as well as the theory of attraction, ebb and flow, the magnet and electricity.

22. It will make known that the magnet and artificial electricity only have, as regards illnesses, properties which they share with several other agents provided by Nature, and that if useful effects have been derived from the use of the latter, they are due to ANIMAL MAGNETISM.

23. It will be seen from the facts, in accordance with the practical rules I shall draw up, that this principle can cure nervous disorders directly and other disorders indirectly.

24. With its help, the physician is guided in the use of medicaments; he perfects their action, brings about and controls the beneficial crises in such a way as to master them.

25. By making known my method, I shall show by a new theory of illnesses the universal utility of the principle I bring to bear on them.

26. With this knowledge, the physician will determine reliably the origin, nature and progress of illnesses, even the most complicated; he will prevent them from gaining ground and will succeed in curing them without ever exposing the patient to dangerous effects or unfortunate consequences, whatever his age, temperament and sex. Women, even in pregnancy and childbirth, will enjoy the same advantage.

27. In conclusion, this doctrine will enable the physician to determine the state of each individual's health and safeguard him from the maladies to which he might otherwise be subject. The art of healing will thus reach its final stage of perfection.

Although there is not one of these Assertions regarding which my constant observation over a period of twelve years leaves me in any uncertainty, I quite realize that compared with old-established principles and knowledge my system may appear to contain as much illusion as truth. I must, however, ask the enlightened to discard their prejudices and at least suspend judgment, until circumstances enable me to furnish the necessary evidence of my principles. Consideration for those languishing in pain and unhappiness through the very inadequacy of known methods is well calculated to inspire the desire for and even the hope of more useful methods. Physicians, being the repositories of public trust for everything connected with the preservation and happiness of mankind, are alone enabled, by the knowledge on which their profession is founded, to judge of the importance of the discovery I have just announced and realize its implications. In a word, they alone are qualified to put it into practice.

As I have the privilege of sharing the dignity of their profession, I am in no doubt whatever that they will hasten to adopt and spread principles intended to alleviate the sufferings of humanity, as soon as they realize the importance of this Dissertation, written essentially for them, on the true conception of ANIMAL MAGNETISM.

Le Comte Maxime de Chastenet de Puysegur
(1751-1825)

After the report of the Commissioners appointed by King Louis XVI was completed, animal magnetism lost some of its popularity. Later on, a pupil of Mesmer, the Comte de Puysegur attracted all the scientific world to Buzancy, near Soissons, where he obtained most remarkable results. Puysegur may be said to have resuscitated magnetism. Public opinion became infatuated once more about this new agent that was to be the gratuitous means of curing mankind. Puysegur's "tree," impregnated with the fluid, was touched by hundreds of persons who came from all parts of the country, and the effects were most beneficial.

Puysegur offered a striking contrast to Mesmer, and avoided all public exhibitions and everything that could affect the imagination, never choosing special subjects but experimenting on peasants, male and female, afflicted with stubborn and matter-of-fact diseases. He admitted the marvelous, and believed in somnambulistic lucidity.

In his report of cures at Bayonne, he reports how he was induced to magnetize in public during his regiment's drill session and also on a small dog wounded by a fall. This shows that magnetization of animals at that time was already established.

Puysegur soon had more patients than he could handle. The results of his cures are verified and established in official form before a commission of officers, physicians, and civil servants.

REPORT OF CURES BY ANIMAL MAGNETISM
OCCURRING AT BAYONNE WITH VERIFICATIONS*

Of the cures that have been used in Bayonne, since the 19th of August, 1784, until the following first of October. By the procedures utilizing animal magnetism; M. the Comte Maxime De

---

*Chastenet De Puyseguér, le Comte Maxime de: *Rapport des Cures Opérées a Bayonne par le Magnétisme Animal*. Adresse a M. l' Abbé de Poulouzat, Conseiller-Clerc au Parlement de Bordeaux. Avec des Notes de M. Duval d'Esprémenil, Conseiller au Parlement de Paris. Bayonne et Paris, 1784.

Puysegur, second in command of the Regiment of Languedoc, addressed to M. the Abbot de Poulouzat, counsellor-clerk at the Parliament of Bordeaux, with the notes of M. d'Espremenil, counsellor at the Parliament of Paris. (Italics added.)

* * *

At Bayonne, the 20th of September, 1784

You know, my dear Abbot, that my intention was not to occupy myself with animal magnetism in Bayonne: I had told you so when I passed through Bordeaux. As a matter of fact, coming to command a corps to whom I did not have the honor to be known, it was not as a doctor that I had to introduce myself. I even pretended a few times to be absolutely indifferent to everything that could have a connection with animal magnetism; but soon an unforeseen accident forced me to leave the "incognito". Rainy weather obliged me to exercise my officers in the cloister of the Jacobins; they were under arms, formed in a column, when one of them surprised at the word "march" had an apoplectic fit, and instead of going forward, fell like a plank that one would have knocked down, lying face down on the pavement, lying there without any feeling; then, I interrupted the exercise, his comrades picked him up, and each one was willing to give him the help that they thought he needed. I waited a few minutes, wanting sincerely to see him recover without my help. But finally impatient of the poor results of their effort, I approached him; I asked all the bystanders to form a chain, trying very hard the resort that can suggest to me the doctrine of M. Mesmer, and soon my efforts are crowned with success; I have the satisfaction of feeling him coming back alive in my arms, and making him recover enough that he can go back home.

The contusion of the head was very serious. The lower lip was split inside and out. There was also a wound on the chin and at the exterior angle of the right eye. The face was all bloody. After having him washed, I prevented any one from applying any kind of remedy. The wounds were dressed with dry coth, the patient was cured, and until perfect recovery he had no other treatment except magnetism.

This scene happened so publicly, you see, my dear Abbot, that it was impossible for me to hide any longer: in a few hours, all my Regiment and the whole town, knew that I was a disciple of M. Mesmer. Everyone was questioning me, and talking to me about magnetism. But that is not all; this same day the events seemed to succeed one another to make me known. The same afternoon, the weather became nice again, and allowed our young men to perform a foot race in the presence of the ladies of the town. The runners would overcome any obstacle to distinguish themselves. One of them meeting a little dog in his path, who was stubbornly tormenting him, and in order to get rid of the dog, he grabbed him by the tail, and with a strong arm, threw him a considerable distance. The dog, shocked by the fall, lay without movement and without any sign of life. The race continued; but soon someone came to complain to me. The master of the dog was seeking justice for the murder that had been committed. Here I am, obliged to punish, and to change gaiety to sorrow, if I can not stop the complaint. Then, without making any noise, and imposing silence to the complainer, I approached the maltreated dog, I found him without motion, vomiting blood from his mouth and from his nose. But examining him with care, I noticed that the artery was still beating. Then, using on him the magnetic proceeding, I brought him back to life. Soon he moved his eyes. My hand being close to his mouth, the first movement he made was to lick me in a sign of thankfulness. Little by little his strength increased. I put him back on his four feet, and I made him take a standing posture in which he stood with a remarkable patience. Doing this, I wanted to be sure that he had nothing broken. Then leaving this little animal to himself, he began to walk as if he had a pain in the kidney. Because of this the master was still not satisfied. I called the dog back, and in one minute, I restored him in perfect recovery. Seven or eight minutes at the most were employed in this treatment, and since I did not want any witnesses, but the crowd was still all around me, I was, to my regret, the subject of their surprise and of their curiosity.

Nevertheless, they continued the race until night came. Coming into town somebody came to notify me that a young officer, whom

I did not have the honor to know yet, dared not to call me to relieve him of strong pain that was caused by a sprain that he had received at the race. I ran to him immediately and in less than two minutes, he found himself able to walk without pain, and to follow me to the house of my first patient of that same morning that I was going back to see. It is here that another scene, much more remarkable, was waiting for me to surprise all the spectators. Many officers went to see the patient, many of them because of the interest that they were attaching to his health, and also a little bit by curiosity, to be a witness of his treatment. Each one was talking in his own way on animal magnetism. Some were for it, and others against it. The majority were laughing, jesting, and had very much doubt of the reality of its effects, as it is practiced among those who have never seen it.

In such cases, you know that I do not like the unoccupied; so, wanting to use all the members of the audience, I invited them to form a chain. Some of them had left the same morning, feeling bad, and thinking that it was because of the shock of the accident. One of them, suffering of a delicate health, and having a disturbed stomach, was present then. He had joked and was still joking very pleasantly. Soon because the effect of the chain was not indifferent to him, he began to feel the same impressions of the morning, and he wanted to leave. But realizing the cause, I insisted that he stay, and soon he was obliged to confess the anguish that he felt and to give himself an irrevocable evidence of the effects of magnetism. A nausea attack hit him at the same time. Finally the speed of the effects gave him no time to leave his place, and he was forced to reveal to the spectators signs of his relief.

After so much proof, on the effects of animal magnetism, you would think that many people came to consult me. I refused, but every day the number of patients grew. They were coming to my door. Finally I could not resist any longer to the soft satisfaction of helping so many unfortunate, and I opened a public treatment for the poor.

Considering that there exists in all regiments a class of man designated by the name of "patient in the bedroom" which makes a burden for the hospitals, and for their comrades in doing nothing

RAPPORT

DES CURES

OPÉRÉES A BAYONNE

PAR LE MAGNÉTISME ANIMAL,

ADRESSÉ

A M. L'ABBÉ DE POULOUZAT,

Confeiller-Clerc au Parlement de Bordeaux,

Par M. LE COMTE MAXIME DE PUYSÉGUR,

Avec des Notes de M. DUVAL D'ESPRÉMENIL,

Confeiller au Parlement de Paris.

A BAYONNE,

Et fe trouve à PARIS,

CHEZ PRAULT, IMPRIMEUR DU ROI,

quai des Auguftins, à l'Immortalité.

1784.

FIGURE 3. Title page from de Puysegur's *Report of Cures Performed at Bayonne by the Use of Animal Magnetism*, published in 1784.

for their company, I decided to reduce the number of those, beginning to cure many; and I had the pleasure of succeeding. Soon, the place that I had taken to assemble my patients became too small. It was time to choose a new location. The season, promising some beautiful days, I established my hospital on the Bastion Saint-Etienne. There are some trees, strong, that nourish themselves in a fertile ground. Their leaves and the grass that grow at their feet, make the most agreeable green, and testify that nature deploys in this place all its power. I chose three of those trees, and then, taking all I could find, I gathered in a few days under their shade, more than 300 patients.

It is here, my dear Abbot, that I would have liked to have seen you! Your sensible soul would have given you a very pleasant feeling. In spite of all I had seen of the effects of animal magnetism, I was always surprised at the success that was crowning my cares. Each day, each minute, was showing new help, and marked by some action of grace. In the midst of those good people, I was seized by a sincere attachment for each one of them. None of their sensations were indifferent to me. At the extremity of France, I thought I had a new family, and I do not say too much, when I say that they were all looking to me as their father. It is so, that in perpetual happiness, I have passed all my free time since the 19th of last month. But the coming review, left me very little time. It was impossible for me to take care of what I had started, if the zeal and the charity of many people had not come to my aid. Two of the officers of the regiment, the surgeon, one of the first citizens of the town, and three people of the art, hastened to second my efforts, and I instructed them in the art of magnetism as M. Mesmer taught me.

It is to them, as much as to me, that a large number of patients, in less than a month's time, had some real help and perfect recovery. One will bring you a list of sixty recoveries verified in an incontestable way. I do not send you this list in this letter, because I want them to verify the facts that it contains. It is one more precaution that I do not want to neglect, and to be sure that I do not dupe myself. I will let them give you a second copy at the same time, containing the state of the patients who are still actually under treatment, but who have experienced great relief, and of an unusual nature. I could cite you many more without trickery that happened, and which I had just realized. After a few days, seeing my three trees full, I was forced to reject all those who were pretending, and the crowd grew every day. I had given some cards to my patients, so that a sentinel could recognize them and let them pass. But those, having parents or friends who wanted to be admitted, and being afraid to be refused, were leaving without saying a word when they were cured, and were giving their cards to others, so an important part of the treatment has been renewed many times, without payment. Nevertheless, the number of the recoveries that will be recognized must be sufficient to give much thought to the men of good will. Of course, if it is here that the effects of the imagination are of value, the academie will be forced to agree that the imagination is the most important doctor on earth. Almost all the ailments that I had to treat had previously undergone the yoke of ordinary medicine, but without any success. Those are the dangers of this antique and religious chimera that the beneficial influence of animal magnetism came to recover.

I was under my trees, and I had in front of my eyes this affecting spectacle of humanity relieved! I render thanks to our good master, Mesmer, of the happiness that he had helped me bring, when one brings me to read the certificate of the report of M.M. Commissionaire. Like the guest who at the end of a good meal laughs about the frost that threatens the vineyard, the same for me. Drunk of the pure joy that brings the beneficence and the truth, I first only laughed about it, feeling sorry for man to be so often duped of their self-styled knowledge. But considering then how much our good Mesmer is tormented for having wanted to do some good, a movement of indignation took me from my indifference. I was telling myself, the ingratitude—is it then the necessary price of charity? Some men that he has helped have betrayed and persecuted him. The arrogant philosophy condemns all which does not feed its vanity, and does not blush to use the means that are most unjust for striking at the foundation of the system of beneficence that his genius has conceived! And the good Mesmer was doubting the sincerity of man! Ah! It added the last straw!

Those thoughts distress me and put me imperceptibly into a painful reverie. It was even more painful that it contrasted very much with the precedent situation of my soul. But fortunately the concern of the necessary cares to all who were around me, soon changed the way of my thoughts, and reminded me of my first feeling. I was being useful; my sorrow disappeared. I felt at that moment more than ever, this important truth proved physically by Mesmer. "How powerful is the influence exerted from one man to another, and the mutual need that we have for one another?" I remembered the patience of Mesmer, and I thought of imitating him! Anyway, why feel sorry for him? The beneficence compensates for everything, and the pleasure of being tender and useful to the pains of others, must elevate one above the caprice of the chance and of the inconstancy of the events.

Yes, if it is possible that I am mistaken, the doctrine of Mesmer could prove to me that the physical utility of man is null. I assure you that I would enjoy to publish it. It is nothing, for one who has done it right once, to make it better, more attached to his duties, more fair, more humane, more sensible, and in consequence very happy.

I respect the society which was formed a long time ago to conserve the deposit of science. I have great regard, and I love many of their members; but truly my dear Abbot, in any weight I price their opinion, I find it very light, when I weigh it on the scales with what I do myself every day. I would like that each one of these gentlemen would do it also, one hour, in my place, and that he could feel nature obey his simplest move. Then we could see them blush because their judgment has precipitated, and rises above the shame to welcome with ecstasy a simple, consoling, truth, which would make them more just, more useful, and more happy!

Finally, I do not dream it is really true that I am in Bayonne, and that it has only been a month in which I am using my moment of freedom to relieve the patients. It is not possible to think that I have seen so many sick people, and that I now see them cured. It has opened by eyes, and their obstinacy in not believing that I have helped them has sustained me.

Anyway, after all the precautions that I have prescribed to take for verifying the facts in my absence, it would seem necessary, that they put many, many people in conspiracy. Eh! This quantity of certificates that must be signed by so many people, would then design that destiny has put together to prove that I am only stupid? The illusions of vanity, my dear Abbot, are the source of our biggest illness. The abuse of the "knowledge" has produced the incredulity on the existence of the master of worlds. It is not surprising to see him today rejecting the proof of the wordly wisdom.

Yet, how is it possible that the people of wit, erudite, nice people, as are most of M.M. the Commissionaires, named by the king, to judge a discovery announced as useful on more than one aspect, established like axiom that the facts do not prove any thing? For me, I always believed that the reasoning had become absurd when they contradicted the facts. And what! At the present time, when it is about the life or death of a man, the health and illness, let's make an exception of the rule. I must believe that the facts do not prove any thing! But why should I care about what cured me, as long as I am cured? Why should I care about the theory of my doctor, as long as he brings back my strength and re-establishes my health?

The use that M. Mesmer makes of the magnetic action in the treatment of the illnesses, is it useful? Does it cure? Does it cure better than the ordinary routine of medicine? There is really, my dear Abbot, the essential point that was necessary to be made clear, and on which all humanity had the right to expect from them a sane judgment, moderate, and even more determinant that it would have been supported on facts, and facts that are comparative, repeated even many times, if it would have been necessary.

For me, from those that I have applied myself to establish, I believe I have the right to have an opinion. I insist then, and I pretend that the method of M. Mesmer is preferable to the one of the faculty, which circumstances have also forced me to learn, in order to be more able to judge.

These gentlemen, the Commissionaries, say that in principle the facts do not prove any thing. They say that one has often seen the illnesses most rebellious to the art, abandoned to the resources of the simple nature, cured better and faster than by the usage of the ordinary means of medicine. And those are doctors who are saying it! Don't they realize that this is the argument that people are opposed to since there are doctors in the world? What sort of confession does the truth extort from them, even when they are trying to suffocate it?

But gentlemen, if you recognize so well the power of this good nature, try then to conceive better the principle of the doctrine that you want to destroy. This nature is the base of it, and the theory is dictated by an intimate feeling which dwells in all humans: there is at least one that M. Mesmer made me aware of. The discovery of any truth is a flash of light that strikes the human intelligence. The first development of each science begins with a sudden inner glimpse, of an intimate feeling in man.

It is a radio impulse of the genius that proves the exactness, in going straight to the objective. Meanwhile the thought is always looking for proof in the reasoning, invents nothing, perfection rarely, and often misleads us.

The medicine of our day has undergone the strength of other human knowledge; and going away in time from the source that produced it, the principles on which this art is founded have disappeared.

The only thing left has been a shapeless structure that the spirit of men has tried in vain to support.

Finally, the faculty is not more sure to cure today, than it was in the beginning, even though there are a tremendous quantity of volumes, which their respectable members have written. It is not, that there is a small number of books that contain some truths felt of the first order, and I feel myself very much in line with them.

But if the doctors would recognize the empire and the resources of nature, they would have to listen for a moment, with a delicate sense of touch, a discernment marked by a true feeling. They make a rigorous sorting that burns them mercilessly, a confused mass of uselessness. Soon we will all agree, and if the words shock them, we will change them: we do not mind.

Nature taking back its rights will make them know that there exists an energy capable of preserving the human from the disorders which menace without losing their existence. When those disorders exist, we still can work to destroy them in using some simple means to reinforce its action.

We will see a simple and sublime theory establish itself, and replace a maze of incoherent opinions accumulated by time. They are related to each other only by the titles which look alike, and by the same mark that brings them into close proximity. In subsisting the obscure and gloomy method of our faculty of medicine, with a method easy to conceive and easy to practice in the treatment of the illnesses, each individual will become able, more or less, to appreciate and know it.

Man learning to know his own forces will feel how much he can be useful to his fellow-men. We will see him revive the zeal of a charity educated to work with fervour to relieve their pains.

A medicine of specific "hazard", will succeed a medicine of "educated" cares. It is true, simple, but more sure. By this, it is even more at the reach of every one. Finally, a medicine like nature itself, gives to every one it carries in its bosom.

What will become of the doctors? . . . That is what abuses them! And it is again an incontestable proof that they conceive nothing of the method that we are proposing. The faculty of speaking which each man makes use of, and often abuses, does it prevent in case of an important discussion, to take an advocate? This advocate is your advisor. Not only does he talk for you, but he dictates your answers when you must speak. Henceforth such will be the role of the doctors.

But then later on, there will be less patients? . . . I do not see any answer to that. . . . What to do? . . . I would sincerely want that we agree! . . .

I only see one means, by dear Abbot. Let's work together to procure for those gentlemen an honorable state which can compensate for them the fee that their frankness could perhaps make them lose. Soon, we will see them, the most zealous defenders of the doctrine of M. Mesmer.

Their particular knowledge of the organs of man will illuminate them with a precious light, to understand everything which can have a connection with that. The medical material which I must have studied, the art of knowing the productions of nature, will put them more than anyone else, able to second the efforts of a nature full of life, diminishing on purpose by some strange means the resistance of some obstacles which it seems to forget. Their habits in physiology will make them feel and verify immediately some simple and sublime axiom, ascending rapidly from a multitude of symptoms diversely varied and combined to some simple causes, and almost always unified. Finally, in the debris of the gigantic edifice which crumbles under their feet, they will find some useful material to build with Mesmer, a temple for the truth. It is on its frontispiece that will be engraved: *"Nature offers a universal means to cure, and to preserve man!"*

Such are, my dear Abbot, the reflections which came to me at this moment. I only wanted to relate to you what I am doing in Bayonne, but the facts have necessarily brought me to the consequences. And imperceptibly I have expatiated myself without realizing it. If you think that what I am saying can be useful for something, make of it what you judge to be the best.

Many others, more capable, are in the process of extending and of verifying this little number of ideas that this material has suggested to me, and I would like very much for some one to apply his thoughts on it very seriously.

As for me, I will always be content myself, by simply saying what I feel, what I think, and I will never have the fear of seeing it published.

The interest that I am taking to the success of the discovery of M. Mesmer is dictated by the gratitude of the good that it has made me do, and by my sincere friendship for the person. Even more happy, if in working like this for my own satisfaction, humanity may one day benefit the fruit of my labor.

It is in this state of mind that, not only happy of the good that I could have done, I wanted to leave after my departure, a continued treatment in this town, and I have informed some pupils. It is with a true pleasure that I see them devote themselves with fervour to the relief of the unfortunate. Their light and the straightforwardness of their intentions are for me a sure guarantee of the success which will crown their cares.

These gentlemen are going to continue the free treatment for the poor. The approaching season will find the patients leaving the trees of the Bastion Saint-Etienne, to get together in one of the rooms of the Convent of the Augustins, that the Reverend Fathers had the charity to offer me, and also the dependable help, in gratitude of one of their Monks.

I have the honor to be, etc.

Comte Maxime de Puysegur

RESULT OF THE MAGNETIC TREATMENT OF BAYONNE SINCE THE 19th OF AUGUST 1784, EPOCH OF HIS ESTAB-LISHMENT, UNTIL THE FIRST OCTOBER, EXCLUSIVELY.

* * * *

AVIS

M. Le Comte Maxime de Puysegur, desirous to be sure of the reality of the facts, has taken all the possible precautions to verify the existence of it. In consequence, in the principle, he has asked all the People of the Art, as many doctors and Surgeons who, at first attracted by the simple curiosity, were willing to come, to be willing to come, to be willing to verify, without his participation, the condition of the patients who would come for the treatment.

When he was ready to leave, he collected the certificates of each patient in particular, and confronted them with the People of the Art with their daily condition.

Those patients are divided into three classifications—first: the soldiers of the Regiment of Languedoc; second: the residents of the country; third: the residents of the town of Bayonne.

Afterwards, when ready to leave, he gave the order to hand over the certificates of the first class to M. De Raigneau, Lieutenant Colonel, then commanding the Regiment; who had agreed to verify them and have them signed by the Sergeant-Major, and by the Commander of each Company.

Those of the second and third class who are gathered together, have been placed in the hands of M. De La Laune, Mayor of the town of Bayonne, with the request of M. de Puysegur, that he be willing to verify the validity of it.

M. De La Laune, with a zeal and an impartiality that renders honor to his love for the truth, has put his utmost care in the verifications. The patients have been invited to go in the Town Hall. Reading has been made of the certificates they gave, and they have certified again the reality of the facts that are contained in it.

We regret that the business of many patients did not permit them to fulfil this formality. But there is not one that M. Mayor has not been able to verify, that we can not have confidence in, from their certificates, and by consequence to address ourself directly to them, to be assured of the truth.

This formality accomplished, all the certificates or originals, also the attestations of the Gentlemen, the Mayors and Echevins, and of the People of the Art, have been deposited in the office of M. Duhalde, Notary Royal at Bayonne, to whom he has delivered a copy.

It is the same copy that is printed, and that contains wholly sixty cures.

Subsequently of those cures, we will find again an exact state of the situation of sixteen patients in the process of recovery, and who have been feeling some marked relief.

NOTE

M. de Puysegur . . . learned that the Society of Harmony, established in Guyenne, offered to make public the Letter to M. l'Abbe de Poulouzat, and the verified copies of the certificates of recovery which he had made at Bayonne, since the originals were placed in the offices of M. Duhalde, a Notary. For this, a sum of six hundred pounds was deposited, having been remitted at first in part, and finally as payment in full, to defray the expenses of verification and stamping with the seal of the Notary. It is of value to verify the truthfulness of these reports, and to have many copies of the letter and the testimonials reproduced so that there now exists the condition that evidence is proof against refutation. This is a mere formality which endows the authenticity in the establishment of facts and the desire to remain as always truthful and above reproach.

If there is a disbeliever among you who would desire to be known, and who would want to refute the published facts, let him take action at the office of the Notary before the first day of January, 1785.

Signed—
M. Le Comte Maxime De Puysegur

The Societies of Harmony

Mesmer established his reputation in Paris with everyone except his medical colleagues who were intent on disclaiming his mesmerism or animal magnetism as a cure for many diseases.

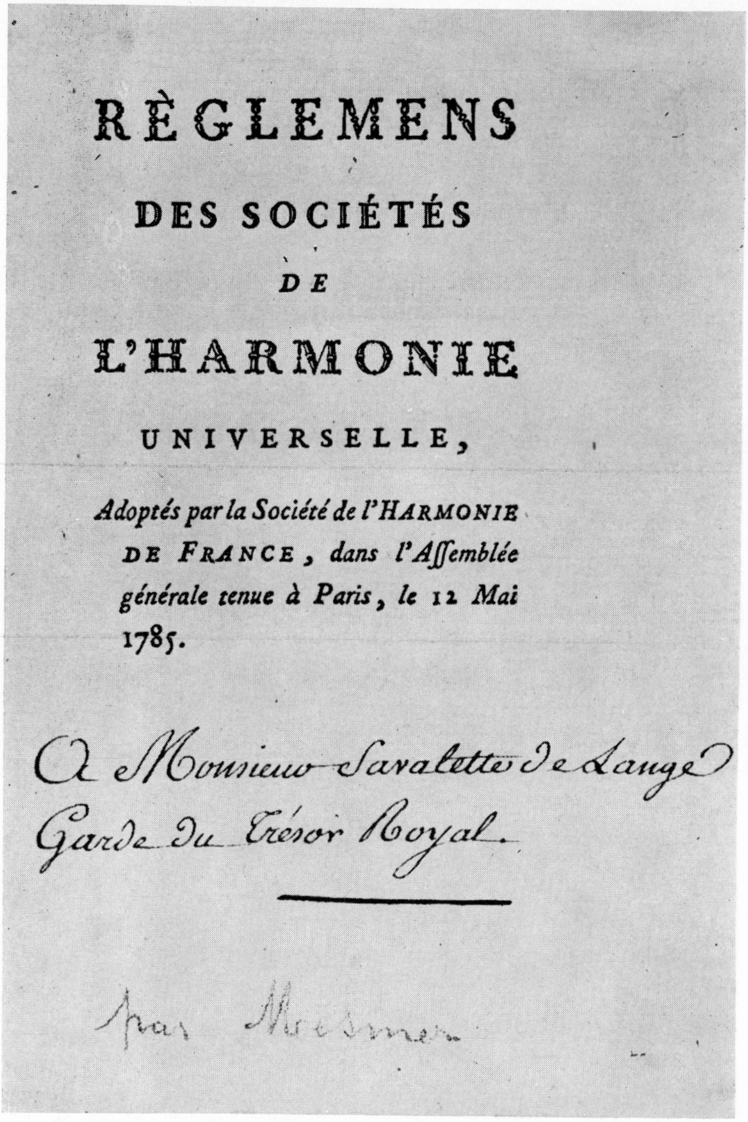

FIGURE 4. Title page from Mesmer's *Rules of the Societies of Universal Harmony*, published in 1785.

Mesmer proclaimed animal magnetism as a panacea, and when he had a misunderstanding with d'Eslon, one of his closest friends, he left Paris for a little while.

On his return, he took a step for which he was criticized. He established a secret society under the name of The Societies of Universal Harmony, where he initiated pupils into the mystery of his process, taking from them fees which he converted to his own use. The constitution of the society is printed in its entirety and is interesting in its organization and function.

CONSTITUTION OF THE SOCIETIES OF UNIVERSAL HARMONY OF FRANCE*

Chapter I

On the Formation and the Organization of the Societies of Harmony

Article I

A certain number of pupils, instructed by M. Mesmer, in the different towns of the kingdom, today formed, through their meeting and through their adherence to the present regulations, the different societies of harmony.

Article II

Each of the Societies carry the name of the town in which they were formed, except here in Paris, where the only title to be used is *The Society of Harmony of France.*

Article III

Each student of M. Mesmer, before being free to accept, refuse, or to renounce his membership in the Society, and it being essential, however, that each Society know the state of its membership, it will be necessary that those who adhere to the present regulations,

---

*Mesmer, F.A.: *Réglemens des Sociétés de l'Harmonie Universelle.* Adoptés par la Société de l'Harmonie de France, dans l 'Assemblée générale tenue a Paris, le 12 Mai, 1785.

sign in the space for their signature, date the day of their accept-ance, in particular those who make up the majority in the assembly convened for that purpose. Those who find themselves absent from the place of the Assembly, will try to send their consent in the interval of two months.

Article IV

Those students who do not carry out this formality, will be censured by renouncing the title of member of *The Society of Harmon*y; he will not participate as a result of this in any of the advantages, or in any of the instructions which will be attached; they will not be counted in the number of *Correspondents*.

Article V

The members who are absent from their towns are not obligated to carry out the prescribed formality in the preceding article until two months after their arrival in France.

Article VI

Those students of Paris, who have permission from their customary residence will be *preference members* in one of the Societies of a Province, being selected according to the prescribed details of Article III of the *Present Regulations*.

Article VII

The members of each Society shall fix their membership at *fifty (50)*, except *The Society of France* which shall have at least *one hundred (100)*.

Article VIII

If any of the Societies find themselves in excess of the prescribed membership for the present, they shall not admit any new members, only up to that number fixed by the preceding article.

Article IX

The new students will receive, after they finish their instruction, the title of *Correspondent of the Society* and their number will be fixed for deliberation by each Society.

Article X

M. Mesmer will have the title of *Founder and Perpetual President* of all *The Societies of Harmony,* and at all times will place this title on all of the actions, diplomas, and actions which come from this administration.

Article XI

The title of *Perpetual President* has been deferred to M. Mesmer as Founder of the *Doctrine of Magnetism;* it will never be given to others after him who are members of *The Societies of Harmony.*

Article XII

It will be necessary to inform M. Mesmer the moment a vacancy exists, and this shall come from the Secretary of each Society, each of the changes, abstracts, of the history of the Society and important deliberations which occur during the year.

Article XIII

M. Mesmer will name a Representative having the title of General Vice-President upon the presentation of three (3) names, which will have been given by the Society of France from the Assembly, scheduled to convene next January, and in the future, through the General Assembly, the Vice-President will be renominated every *Five Years,* the term he will serve.

Article XIV

The Society of Cap, the first created in the French Colonies, have bestowed on Count Chastenet-Puysegur, their founder, the title of *Perpetual Vice-President* of the Societies which were established in the French Colonies in America; this title will be bestowed on this individual alone, and will not be replaced in the future.

Article XV

Each Society will proceed immediately with the election of four Syndics (trustees), a Treasurer, and two Secretaries, whose election will take place in the Assembly during the month of January of each year, and will conform exactly with the forms which are prescribed for the elections.

Article XVI

The Secretaries will serve in their office for a period of *three years* because of the importance of their functions, and the preliminary instructions which the office demands.

Article XVII

The four Trustees, the Treasurer and the two Secretaries shall form permanently the *Permanent Committee,* in order that in the interval between the *Assembly,* the Committee shall act in its place on all urgent business which may interest the *Society;* but this shall be only temporary, and they shall reserve the right to make a report to the main Assembly which in all of these transactions shall pronounce definite action.

Article XVIII

Each of the four Trustees shall have three months indoctrination and experience, during which time they shall travel to the outlying Societies after their election, so that they may be known to the members of those Societies and their visit shall be announced by the Secretary.

Article XIX

The Trustee, who is serving as President, will be particularly charged with calling the extraordinary assembly, according to the circumstances, to determine the *Subjects* which will be discussed, and to maintain order and decency; and to execute on all occasions the dispositions of the present Society. The Treasurer and Secretaries shall realize the consequences of their administration, and they shall conform to the actions of the Assembly.

Article XX

The functions of the *Treasurer* shall be to receive from each member of the Society their personal contribution, which shall have been set at the first *Assembly;* to make inquiries and the choice of a convenient meeting place for the *Assembly of the Society*, to provide the finances for the expenses of the *Secretaries of the Society*, and all other objects of expense which have been approved by the Society, and to account for these expenses to each Assembly. A state Society shall have a signed summary for receipts and expenses with papers to support them, shall present them at the end of each year, showing the condition of their administration, and shall so deposit it with the *Secretary of the Society*.

Article XXI

The functions of the *Secretaries* shall be to receive the letters, reports and observations of the Societies and their *Correspondents*, to investigate, and to collect the various works which shall create interest in the *Doctrine of Animal Magnetism*, its effect and its progress, and to make a report to the Assembly, of the correspondence and the results of the deliberations of the Society, and to record their deliberations. They shall always write in the name of the *Society* of which they are Secretaries, and they shall affix their title to their *signatures* with care. He shall check each month with the state *Societies* for the expenses of their correspondence, salaries of their clerks, who do their work in the Society, and sign for one of them and remit the report to the Treasurer, who is charged with disposing of them.

Article XXII

The *Ordinary Assemblies* of the *Harmony Society of France* shall have a meeting take place at least once a month from the *First of November* until the *First of June*. They shall suspend the meeting for the next five months of the year. This article permits the *Societies of the Provinces* to fix the seven months most suitable for their *Assemblies*.

Article XXIII

The *Day* and the *Hour* of the Assemblies shall be set at the first assembly of each year, and the Journal shall always be posted by the Secretary, so that each member may not be ignorant of the fact; the Assembly should in consequence have a good reputation.

Article XXIV

The day of the reopening of each Society shall be stated at the last meeting of the Assembly of each year for the next year. The Committee shall serve for the entire year, depending on the vacation itself, but they should not take upon themselves any definitive actions or deliberations in the name of the *Society*.

Article XXV

The *Trustee* in *Authority* shall be authorized during the seven months of the *Assembly,* only to call the *Assembly* as many times as he feels necessary, by giving notice of the meeting five days in advance, through general and regular invitations, in which shall be made known the object of the meeting.

Article XXVI

All *Elections, Deliberations* and *Admissions,* shall be a result of passage by *balloting,* in order to always preserve the liberty and equality of each of the members of the Society; they will for that purpose cast a ballot with the Secretary of each Society, and one of the Secretaries shall be in charge of receiving and counting the ballots.

Article XXVII

In order to proceed with the election of *Officers of The Society,* which shall be in the month of *January* of each year, each of the members will have the right to bring his nomination in writing; they will make those nominations in succession, and be received in the *Assembly* by one of the *Secretaries;* he will count the votes, and name the one who receives the greatest number, and burn immediately in the Assembly the other votes which have been counted for other candidates.

Article XXVIII

The choice of members of the Society should always be made among the Corresponding members once a year, in the Assembly during the month of *January*.

Article XXIX

The persons who desire to be admitted to the number of disciples, will be proposed to each Society by their Trustee in Charge, who will assure himself of their good morals, of the purity of their views, and who have reached *twenty-five* years.

Article XXX

The choice and the admission will be made in the Society during the same Assembly in the month of January, from among the proposed subjects, without any expense or retribution.

Article XXXI

The persons who are admitted from the number of *Disciples* shall be informed separately on the elementary topics, conforming to that which is prescribed in Article IV of the second chapter of the present regulations, by the professors who will have special charge of the Society, after they have first subscribed to the obligations conforming to the joint model of the Present Regulations.

Article XXXII

The Certificate of the Correspondent will not be sent to the disciple on *Admission,* but the Certificate will be given to them by the Professor, who will attest to the fact that he has been instructed perfectly in the basis of the *Doctrine of Animal Magnetism.*

Article XXXIII

As it is essential for each Society to know at all times the exact state of their members, before proceeding with the elections, however if one of the members should be absent from more than *three* ordinary and consecutive meetings, without having been warned, then one of the *Secretaries* shall write to him asking his definite plans and his intentions of remaining a member of the Society.

Report on Animal Magnetism by Benjamin Franklin *et al.*

This is the famous report which dealt the death blow to mesmerism or animal magnetism in Paris. By order of King Louis XVI, a commission was appointed from the Faculte de Medecine and the Academie Royale des Sciences to investigate the practices of Mesmer, or rather his disciple, d'Eslon. The president of the commission was Benjamin Franklin, and this report usually goes under his name. Also included on the commission were the scientist Lavoisier and M. de Guillotin.

After carefully conducted experiments, the members concluded that animal magnetism, as claimed by Mesmer, does not exist, and that its apparent successes were to be explained by suggestion and imagination. Franklin, at that time at the height of his career as the representative of the United States at the court of Louis XVI, had attained some reputation as an authority on mesmerism. He had known Mesmer some years earlier and was familiar with his practices. Franklin was president of the commission but was ill with gout in his home at Passy. The other members of the commission actually conducted the necessary experiments.

One of the leading commissioners was the great chemist and academician, Lavoisier, and the published report seems to be written in his style. Afraid of the results of this commission, Mesmer left Paris and went to Switzerland where he later died.

REPORT OF THE COMMISSIONERS CHARGED BY THE KING TO EXAMINE ANIMAL MAGNETISM*

The King named on the twelfth of March, 1784, four physicians of the faculty of Paris, Messieurs Borie, Sallin, d'Arcet, and Guillotin, to enter into the examination, and to lay before him an account of the Animal Magnetism as practised by M. d'Eslon.

---

*Franklin, Benjamin, *et al.*: *Report of Dr. Benjamin Franklin and the other Commissioners, Charged by the King of France, with the Examination of the Animal Magnetism, as now practised at Paris.* Translated from the French, with a Historical Introduction (by Wm. Godwin). London, 1785.

Upon the petition of these physicians, His Majesty joined with items for the purpose of this inquisition, five members of the Royal Academy of Sciences, Messieurs Franklin, le Roy, Bailly, de Borie, Lavoisier, M. Borie having died at the beginning of the investigation, His Majesty appointed M. Majault, doctor of the faculty, to replace him.

M. Mesmer has described the agent he professes to have discovered, and to which he has given the name of Animal Magnetism, in the following manner: "It is a fluid universally diffused, the vehicle of a mutual influence between the celestial bodies, the earth, and the bodies of animated beings; it is so continued as to admit no vacuum; its subtlety does not admit of illustration; it is capable of receiving, propagating, and communicating all the covered, and to which he has given the name of Animal Magnetism, and reflux. The animal body is subject to the effects of this agent; and these effects are immediately produced by the agent insinuating itself into the substance of the nerves. We particularly discover in the human body qualities analogous to those of the loadstone; we distinguish in it poles, different and opposite. The action and the virtue of Animal Magnetism are capable of being communicated from one body to another, animated or inanimate; they exert themselves to considerable distances, and without the least assistance from any intermediate bodies: this action is increased and reflected by the mirrors; it is communicated, concentrated and transferred. Though the fluid be universal, all animal bodies are not equally susceptible of it; there even are some, though very few, of so opposite a nature, as by their mere presence to supersede its effects upon any other contiguous bodies."

The Animal Magnetism is capable of curing immediately diseases of the nerves and immediately other distempers; it improves the action of medicines; it forwards and directs the salutary crises so as to subject them totally to the government of the judgement; by means of it the physician becomes acquainted with the state of health of each individual, and decides with certainty upon the causes, the nature and the progress of the most complicated distempers; it prevents their increase, and effects their extirpation, without at any time exposing the patient, whatever be his age, sex, or constitution to alarming incidents, or impleasing consequences.

In the influence of the magnetism, nature holds out to us a sovereign instrument for securing the health and lengthening the existence of mankind.

Such is the agent, with the examination of which the commissioners have been charged, and whose properties have been avowed by M. d'Eslon, who admits all the principles of M. Mesmer. This theory forms the basis of a memoir, which was read at the home of M. the lieutenant general of the police, and the commissioners. It is asserted in this memoir, that there is but one nature, one distemper and one remedy; and this remedy is Animal Magnetism. This physician, at the same time that he acquainted the commissioners with the doctrine and the process of the magnetism, instructed them in its practise by discovering in them the poles, showing them the manner of touching the diseased, and directing, in regard to them, the magnetic fluid.

M. d'Eslon undertook to inform the commissioners, in the first place, and to convince them of the existence of Animal Magnetism; secondly, to communicate to them his knowledge respecting this discovery; and thirdly, to prove the utility of this discovery and of the Animal Magnetism in the cure of diseases.

After having thus made themselves acquainted with the theory and practise of Animal Magnetism, it was necessary to observe the effects. For this purpose the commissioners adjourned and each of them witnessed the public method of M. d'Eslon. They saw in the center of a large apartment a circular box, made of oak, and about a foot or a foot and a half deep, which is called the baquet; the lid of this box is pierced with a number of holes, in which are inserted branches of iron, elbowed and moveable. The patients are arranged in ranks about this baquet, and each has his branch of iron which by means of the elbow may be applied immediately to the part affected; a cord passed around their bodies connects them one with the other; sometimes a second means of communication is introduced by the insertion of the thumb of each patient between the forefinger and thumb of the patient next to him; the thumb thus inserted is pressed by the

RAPPORT

Du 11. Août 1784.

DES COMMISSAIRES

CHARGÉS PAR LE ROI,

DE L'EXAMEN

DU

MAGNÉTISME ANIMAL.

Imprimé par ordre du Roi.

A PARIS,

DE L'IMPRIMERIE ROYALE.

M. DCCLXXXIV.

FIGURE 5. Title page from the *Report of the Commissioners*. Findings of the commission, headed by Benjamin Franklin, were published in 1784.

person holding it; the impression received by the left hand of the patient, communicated through his right and thus passes through the whole circle.

A piano is placed in one corner of the apartment, and different airs are played with various degrees of rapidity; vocal music is sometimes added to the instrumental.

The persons who supervise the process, have an iron rod in their hand, from ten to twelve inches in length.

M. d'Eslon made to the commissioners the following declarations: (1) that this rod is a conductor of the magnetism, has the
power of concentrating it at its points, and of rendering its emanations more powerful; (2) that found, conformably to the theory of
M. Mesmer, is also a conductor of the magnetism, and that to
communicate the fluid to the piano, nothing more is necessary
than to approach it with the iron rod; that the person who plays
upon the instrument furnishes also a portion of the fluid, and
that the magnetism is transmitted by the sounds to the surrounding
patients; (3) that the cord which is passed round the bodies is
destined, as well as the union of their fingers, to the effects by
communication; (4) that the interior part of the baquet is so
constructed as to concentrate the magnetism, and is a grand
reservoir, from which the fluid is diffused through the branches
of iron that are inserted in its lid.

The commissioners in the progress of their examination discovered, by means of an electrometer and a needle of iron not
touched by the loadstone, that the bucket contained no substance
either electric or magnetic; and from the detail that M. d'Eslon
made to them respecting the interior construction of the baquet,
they cannot infer any physical agent, capable of contributing to
the imputed effects of the magnetism.

The patients then, arranged in large numbers and in successive
ranks round the baquet, derive the magnetic virtue at once
from all these conveyances: from the branches of iron, which
transmit to them that of the baquet, from the cord which is
passed round their bodies, and the union of their fingers, which
communicate to them that of their neighbors; and from the sound
of the piano, or of a musical voice, which diffuses it through the
air. The patients are besides magnetized directly, by means of a
finger or a bar of iron, guided before the face, above or behind
the head, and over the surface of the parts affected, the distinction
of the poles are still observed; they are also acted upon by a look,
and by having their attention excited. But especially they are magnetized by the application of the hands, and by the pressure of
the fingers upon the hypochonders and the regions of the lower

abdomen; an application frequently continued for a long time, sometimes for several hours.

In this situation the patients offer a spectacle extremely varied in proportion to their different habits of body. Some of them are calm, tranquil, and unconscious to any sensation; others cough, spit, are affected with a slight degree of pain, a partial or an universal burning, and perspirations; a third class (of patients) are agitated and tormented with convulsions. The convulsions are rendered extraordinary by their frequency, their violence, and their duration. As soon as one person is convulsed, others presently are affected by that symptom. The commissioners saw examples of this kind, which lasted upward of three hours; they were accompanied by the violence of their efforts. Sometimes these expectorations were accompanied with small quantities of blood, and there is among others a lad, a patient, who has brought up blood in considerable abundance. These convulsions are characterized by precipitate and involuntary motions of all of the limbs or of the whole body, by a contraction of the throat, by sudden affections of the hyperchonders and the epigastrium, by a distraction and wildness in the eyes, by shrieks, tears, hiccuppings, and immoderate laughter. They are either preceded or followed by a state of languor and reverie, by a species of dejection, and even drowsiness. The least unforeseen noise occasions starting; and it has been observed, that the changing of the key and the time in the airs played upon the piano, had an effect upon the patients; so that a quickened motion agitates them more, and renews the vivacity of their convulsions.

There is an apartment lined with quilting, which was originally destined for the patients in whom the magnetism produced convlusions, and is designated as the apartment of crises; but M. d'Eslon has not tried to make any use of it; and all the patients, whatever be the accidents of their situation, are placed together in the apartment of public exhibitions.

Nothing can be more astonishing than the sight of these convulsions; he that has not had it, can have no idea of it: and in beholding it, a man is not less struck with the profound repose of one class of patients, than with the violence which agitates

another; he observes with admiration the various accidents that
are repeated, and the sympathies that are developed. He sees some
patients seek each other with eagerness; and in approaching, smile,
converse with all the demonstrations of attachment, and soothe
their mutual crises. They are entirely under the government of the
person who distributes the magnetic virtue; in vain they may appear
to be in a state of the extreme drowsiness, his voice, a look, a sign
from him rouses them. It is impossible not to recognize in these
regular effects an extraordinary influence, acting upon the patients,
making itself matter of them, and which he who superintends the
process, appears to be the depository.

These convulsive seizures are improperly called crises in the
theory of animal magnetism; according to this doctrine indeed they
are regarded as a salutary crisis, of the same kind as those which
nature produces, or of a skillful physician who has the art to
facilitate the cure of diseases. The commissioners will adopt this
expression in the following report; and wherever they employ the
word crisis, they will always understand it as the convulsive,
drowsy, or lethargic symptoms, produced by the means of animal
magnetism.

The commissioners observed, that in the number of patients in
the state of crises, there were always many women and few men;
that it was one or two hours before these crises took place; and
that when one had taken place, all the others commenced successively, and without any considerable interval. But after having
made these general remarks, the commissioners were speedily of
the opinion, that the public exhibition could not be made the
scene of their experiments. The multiplicity of the effects is one
obstacle; too many things are seen at once for any of them to be
seen well. Beside, the patients of rank on account of their health,
might be displeased with the investigation of the commissioners;
the very act of watching them might appear a nuisance; and the
recollection of this might be burdensome, and impede the commissioners in their turn. They therefore resolved, that their frequent attendance at the public exhibitions was unnecessary, it
would be sufficient for a few of them to go from time to time to
observe the former general observations, to make new ones in

case an opportunity should occur for that purpose, and to report them to the commission assembled.

After having observed these effects at the public exhibition, it behoved them, in the next place, to endeavour to discover their causes, and inquire into the possibility of the existence and utility of the magnetism. The question of its existence is first in order; that of its utility was not to be examined until the other shall have been fully resolved. The animal magnetism may indeed exist without being useful, but it cannot be useful if it does not exist.

Of consequence the first object of attention with the commissioners and the direct tendency of their first experiments ought to be to ascertain this existence. Again, this was itself an object of considerable comprehension, and had need of being simplified. The animal magnetism embraces the whole compass of nature; it is the vehicle we are told, of the influence exerted upon us by the celestial bodies; the commissioners were of the opinion, that they ought, in the first place, to have this more extensive influence out of the question, and to consider only that part of the fluid which is diffused over the earth, without troubling themselves from whence it comes; in a word, to determine the action it exercises upon us, around us, and within the sphere of our inspection, before they undertook to examine its relation to the universe.

The most certain method of determining the existence of the animal magnetic fluid, would have been to have rendered its presence capable of being perceived by the senses; but it did not take long to convince the commissioners that this fluid was too subtle to be subjected to their observation. It is not, like the electrical fluid, luminous and visible; its action is not, like the attraction of the loadstone, the object of one sight; it has neither taste nor smell, its process is silent, and it surrounds you or penetrates your frame, without your being informed of its presence by the sense of touch. If therefore it exists in us and around us, it is after all perfectly insensible. There are persons among those who profess the magnetism, who pretend that it may sometimes be seen passive from the extremity of the fingers, which serve it as conductors, or who believe, that they feel its passage when you guide your finger before their face, or along their hand. In the first of these cases, the emanation perceived is merely that of transpiration, which becomes completely visible when viewed through a solar microscope; in the second, the impression of cold or freshness, which is felt are impressions which are more perceptible the warmer one is. It results from the motion of the air which follows the finger, and the temperature is always below that of animal heat. When on the other hand, the finger approaches the surface on the face, which is colder than the finger, and it is held at rest, the consequence is a sensation of heat, which is none other than the transference of the animal heat.

It is also assumed that this fluid has a smell, and that it is perceived when either the finger or an iron conductor is brought into contiguity with the nostrils; it is even said, that the sensation is different, depending on whether the finger or the rod of iron is directed parallel with, or opposite to the poles. M. d'Eslon performed the experiment upon several of the commissioners, and the commissioners themselves have repeated it upon different subjects. Not one has experienced this difference of sensation; and if by giving it close attention, any scent has been perceived, it has been that of iron, when the rod has been presented, rubbed and heated. It might have been the emanation of the transpiration, when the finger has been presented; a scent frequently combined with that of iron with which the finger itself has been impressed. These effects have been erroneously attributed to the magnetism, but they may be traced in reality to natural and definite causes.

Indeed M. d'Eslon has never insisted upon these transient impressions. He did not think that they were to be offered in evidence; on the contrary, he expressly assured the commissioners, that he could not demonstrate to them the existence of the magnetism, otherwise than by the action of this fluid, producing certain changes in the animated bodies. This existence is so much the more difficult to be demonstrated by effects, which shall be incontrovertible, and the whole causes shall be unequivocal by authentic facts. In cases where moral circumstances cannot exert their influence; in a word, by proofs calculated to convince and compel the understanding, the only ones which can yield any solid satisfaction are persons really proficient in the study of nature.

The action of magnetism upon animated bodies may be observed in two different ways; either as it conflicts in that action continued for a long time and in its solitary effects in the treatment of different diseases, or in its momentary effects upon the animal economy and the perceptible changes there produced. M. d'Eslon insisted that the former of these methods should be employed principally, and nearly exclusively. The commissioners have been of a different opinion, and their reasons are as follow:

The majority of diseases have their seat in the interior part of one frame. The collective experience of a great number of centuries has made us acquainted with the symptoms, which indicate and discriminate them. The same experience has taught the method in which they are to be treated. What is the object of the efforts of the physician in this method? It is not to oppose and to subdue nature. It is to assist her in her operations. Nature, says the father of the medical science, cures the diseased; but sometimes she encounters obstacles, which constrain her in her course and uselessly consume her strength. The physician is a minister of nature; an attentive observer. He studies the method in which she proceeds. If that method be firm, strong, regular, and well directed, the physician looks on in silence, and bewares of disturbing it by remedies which would at least be useless. If the method be embarrassed, he facilitates it. If it be too slow or too rapid, he accelerates or retards it sometimes to accomplish his object. He confuses himself to the reputation of the diet; sometimes he employs medicines. The action of a medicine, introduced into the human body, is a new force, combined with the principal force by which one's life is maintained. If the remedy follows the same route, which the force has already opened for the expulsion of diseases, it is useful, and it is salutary. If it tend to open different routes, and to turn aside this interior action, it is pernicious. In the meantime it must be confessed that this salutary or pernicious influence, real as it is, may frequently escape common observation. The natural history of man presents as in this respect with very singular phenomena. It may seem that opposing regimens have not prevented the attainment of an advanced old age. We may see men, attacked according to all appearance with the same disease, recover in the pursuit of opposite regimens. In the use of remedies totally different from each other; nature is, in these instances, sufficiently powerful to maintain the vital principles in spite of the improper regimens and to triumph at once over the distemper and the remedy. If it has this power of resisting the action of medicine, by a still stronger reason, it must have the power of operating without medicine. The experience of the efficacy of remedies is always therefore attended with some uncertainty. In the case of the magnetism, the uncertainty has thus in addition, the uncertainty of its existence. How then can we decide upon the action of an agent, whose existence is contested from the treatment of diseases, when the effect of medicine is doubtful, and whose existence is not at all problematical?

The cure which is principally cited in favor of the magnetism is that of M. le baron de . . . and all classes are acquainted with its history. We shall not at this time enter into a discussion of the facts. We shall not inquire whether the remedies precedingly employed might have contributed to this cure. On the one hand, the very critical condition of the patient is admitted, and on the other the inefficacy of all the ordinary views of medical science is likewise admitted. The magnetism has been employed and M. le baron de . . . has completely recovered. But might not a natural crisis have singly caused this recovery? A woman of low rank and extremely poor, who lived at the Groscaillou, was attacked in 1779 with a malignant fever and all its symptoms. She resolutely refused every assistance, and she only desired that a vessel which she had near her should be kept constantly replenished with water. She remained quiet upon the straw which served her for a bed, drinking water continually and doing nothing more. The disease developed itself, passed successively through its different stages and terminated in a complete cure. Madam E. . . . who lived at the lesser royal mews, had two indurations found in her right breast, which gave her great pain. A surgeon recommended to her the use of the Eau du Peintre as an excellent dissolvent, at the same time informing her that if this remedy did not succeed in a month, it would be necessary to remove them by incision. The lady, terrified at this sentence, consulted M. Sallin, who gave as his opinion, that the indurations were susceptible of resolution. M. Bonvart, who was also consulted, confirmed the opinion of M. Sallin. Before proceeding upon any course of remedy, they prescribed dissipation. Fifteen days after, she was seized at the opera with a violent cough, and a profuse expectoration, she was carried home, and spit in the space of four hours about three pints of a viscid lymph. One hour after this, M. Sallin examined the breast and discovered no trace of induration. M. Bonvart, called in the next day, proved on his part the happy effect of this natural crisis. If Madam E . . . had taken Eau du Peintre, the honor of her cure would have been attributed to this medicine.

The uninterrupted observation of ages proves, and the professors of physic acknowledge that nature alone and without our interference cures a great number of persons. If the magnetism were absolutely inactive, the patients who undergo this method of cure, might be considered as abandoned to nature. It would be absurd to choose a method of deciding upon the existence of this agent, which, by attributing to it all the cures performed by nature, would tend to prove that it had an action useful and curative, when in reality, it might have no action at all.

Upon this reasoning, the commissioners had to agree with M. Mesmer. He rejected the cure of diseases, when this method of proving the magnetism was proposed to him by a member of the Academy of Sciences. "It is a mistake," he replied, "to imagine that this kind of proof is unanswerable. It cannot be demonstrated that either the physician or the medicine causes the recovery of the patient."

The treatment of diseases can do nothing more than furnish a result, but a result is always uncertain, often deceitful. Nor can this uncertainty be dissipated, and all the causes of illusion compensated, but by an infinity of cures, perhaps by the experience of successive centuries. The object and importance of the commission demand means of a speedier description. It was the duty of the commissioners to confine themselves to arguments purely physical, that is, to the instantaneous effects of the fluid upon the animal frame excluding from these effects all the illusions which might mix with them. They must assure themselves that they could proceed to make experiments upon single subjects, who might be willing to submit to the various experiments which they should invent; and who, some of them by their simplicity, and others by their intelligence, should be capable of giving an exact and faithful account of their sensations. These experiments we shall not confine ourselves to relate in the order of time, but shall follow the order of the facts they were intended to elucidate.

The commissioners in the first place resolved to make their first experiments upon themselves, and personally to experience the action of the magnetism. They were extremely curious to become acquainted by their own sensations with the effects ascribed to this agent. They, therefore, submitted themselves to these effects, and in such a way, that they would not have been sorry to have undergone some accidents, and a partial derangement of health, which being evidently produced by the operation of the magnetism, should have enabled them to decide this important question on the spot, and with their own testimony. But in submitting themselves to the magnetism in this manner, the commissioners have employed one necessary precaution. There is not an individual, in a state of good health, who, if he be sensible to an infinity of interior notions and variations, either of a slight pain, or of heat in different parts of his body, will not recognize these variations which exist at all times as being independent of the magnetism. To turn and fix in this manner one's attention upon oneself, is not perhaps itself entirely without its effects. There is so intimate a connection between the volitions of the soul and the motions of the body, that it is not easy to prescribe limits to the influence of attention, which appears to be nothing more than a train of volitions directed, constantly and without interruption, to the same object. When we recollect that the arm is moved by the will as it pleases, how can we be certain that the attention, being fixed upon some interior part of our frame, may not excite some slight emotion in it, direct the heat towards it, and so modify its actual situation as to produce in it new sensations? The first thing, therefore, to which the commissioners were bound to attend, was not to observe so minutely what passed within them. If the magnetism were a real and operative cause, there was no need that it should be made an object of thought, in order to perceive its action and manifest itself. It ought, so to express ourselves, to compel and arrest this attention, and to render itself perceptible to a mind that should even be distracted from it by design.

But in deciding to make experiments upon themselves, the commissioners unanimously resolved to make those experiments private, without admitting any strangers except M. d'Eslon, by whom the operation was to be performed, or such persons as they should choose. In like manner, they engaged not to submit to the magnetism at the public exhibition, in order that they might discuss freely their observations, and be in all events the sole, or at least the first judges of the symptoms observed.

In order to pursue these determinations, a particular apartment and a separate baquet were designated to be used in the house of M. d'Eslon, and the commissioners met there once every week. The operation was continued in each experiment for two and a half hours, and the rod of iron was in contact with the subject, surrounded by a cord of communication, and forming from time to time the chain of fingers and thumbs. They were magnetized either by M. d'Eslon, or in his absence, by one of his pupils, some of them for a longer period of time and more frequently than others; there were those with whom this was the case, and who appeared to the commissioners from constitution and habit the most susceptible.

The operation was performed sometimes with the fingers, and the rod of iron was presented and guided along the different parts of the body. Sometimes it was performed by the application of the hands and the pressure of the fingers, either upon the lower part of the body or upon the pit of the stomach.

Not one of the commissioners felt any sensation, or at least none which ought to be ascribed to the action of the magnetism. Some of the commissioners are of a robust constitution. Others have more delicate habits, and are subject to interruptions of their health; one of these last was sensitive of a slight pain in the pit of the stomach, due to considerable pressure that was employed upon that part. This pain continued all that day and the next day, and was accompanied with a sensation of fatigue and dejection. Another felt, in the afternoon of one of the days in which the experiments were performed, a slight irritation of the nerves, to which he is very subject. A third, endowed with an extreme restlessness of the nerves, was subject to a higher degree of pain and a more perceptible irritation. These lesser accidents are the results of perpetual and ordinary variations in the state of their health, and are as a result foreign to the operation they had undergone, or proceed only from the pressure employed upon the region of the stomach. The commissioners do not speak of these slight details, but from a scrupulous fidelity. They relate them, because they have imposed upon themselves in every particular to say the truth.

The commissioners could not avoid being struck with the difference of the private experiments made upon themselves from the public experiments. All was calm and silence in the one, all restlessness and agitation in the other. Then multiplied symptoms, violent cries, and the ordinary state both of body and mind were interrupted and overthrown, and nature was wrought up the highest pitch. Here the body, free from pain, and the mind from anxiety, pressures nature in her ordinary course and her equilibrium. In a word, the absolute privation of every kind of effect, the stupendous influence, which creates such an astonishment in the public experiment appears no longer. The magnetism, stripped of its energy, seems perfectly supine and inactive.

The commissioners, having at first submitted to the experiment only once a week, were anxious to ascertain whether a continuity of experiments would produce any effect. They submitted to it three days in succession, but their insensibility was the same, and the magnetism appeared to be perfectly impotent. This experiment, made once upon eight different subjects, several of whom were subject to habitual derangement of health, authorizes the conclusion that the magnetism has little or no action in a state of health, or even in a state of lesser infirmity. We then resolved to make experiments upon persons really diseased, and we chose them out of the lower class.

Seven of these were assembled at Passy, at the house of M. Franklin. The experiment was performed upon them by M. d'Eslon in the presence of all the commissioners.

The widow Saint-Amand, asthmatic, having swollen belly, legs, and thighs; and dame Anseaume, who had a swelling upon her thigh felt no sensation. The little Claude Renand, a child of six years of age, scrophulous, almost consumptive, having swollen knees, legs bent inward, and the articulation of the knees nearly deprived of motion, a very interesting child, and possessing a greater degree of understanding than is usual at his age, was likewise conscious to no sensation. Anymore than Genevieve Leroux, nine years of age, subject to convulsions, and to a disorder greatly resembling that which is called St. Vitus's Dance. Francois Grenet experienced some effects. He had a distemper in his eyes, particularly in the right, in which he had scarcely any sight, and in which there was a very large tumor. When the operation was directed towards the left eye, by approaching and moving the thumb backward and forward for a considerable time, he was very sensitive to a pain in the ball of the eye, and the eye watered. When the operation was directed to the right eye, which was the most disordered, he felt no sensation in it. He felt the same pain in the left eye, and nothing in any other part of the body.

Dame Charpentier, who had been thrown against a log of wood by a cow two years before, had experienced the most unfortunate consequences from this accident. She lost her sight, recovered it afterwards in part, but remained in a state of habitual illnesses. She stated that she had two ruptures, and the belly so sensitive that she could not stand the pressure of the strings of her petticoats. This sensibility belongs to the case of nervous irritation. The slightest pressure upon the region of the belly is capable of determining this irritation, and producing, through the correspondence of the nerves, effects in every part of the body.

The operation was performed upon this woman as upon the rest by the application and the pressure of the fingers. The pressure was extremely painful to her, and afterwards, in directing the finger towards the rupture, she complained of a pain in her head. When the finger was placed before her face, she said she could not draw her breath. Upon the repeated motion of the finger upwards and downwards, she had sudden starts of the head and shoulders, like those which are commonly occasioned by surprise mixed with terror; for instance, that of a person who has some drops of cold water suddenly thrown in his face. She appeared to have the same startings when her eyes were closed. As the fingers were held under her nose, while her eyes were shut, she complained of a sensation of faintness as long as they remained there. The seventh subject, Joseph Enningi, experienced sensations of a similar nature, but much less severe.

Of these seven patients, four felt no sensation at all, and three experienced some effects from the experiments. These effects engaged the attention of the commissioners, and demanded an accurate examination.

The commissioners, to obtain further light, and to define their ideas upon this part of the subject, resolved to make the experiment upon patients, placed in other circumstances. They selected from the polite world those who could not be suspected of sinister views, and whose understanding made them capable of inquiring into and giving a faithful account of their sensations. Mesdames B . . . and de V..., Messieurs M... and R... were admitted to the private baquet together with the commissioners. They were asked to describe their sensations, without fixing upon them too regular an attention. M. M... and Madame de V... were the only persons who experienced any sensation. M. M... had an indolent swelling over the whole articulation of the knee, and a constant pain in the patella. He declared, during the experiment, that he felt nothing in any part of his body, except at the moment the finger was passed over the diseased knee. He then thought that he felt a slight degree of heat in the place, in which he habitually had sensation of pain. Madame de V..., attacked with a nervous disorder was several times at the point of falling asleep during the operation. The experiment having continued for an hour and nineteen minutes without interruption, and for the greater part by the application of the hands, she was sensible to nothing but a sensation of irritation and dejection. These two subjects underwent the experiment only once. M. R... whose distemper was the remainder of an obstruction in the liver, the consequence of a very violent disorder of that kind, underwent the experiment three times and felt nothing. Madame de B...

severely attacked with obstructions, underwent the experiment constantly at the same time with the commissioners, and felt nothing. It is necessary to observe, that she submitted to the magnetism with an extreme tranquility which originated in the highest degree of incredulity.

Experiments were made at other times upon different subjects, but without the assistance of the baquet. One of the commissioners in a violent headache, had the experiment performed upon him by M. d'Eslon, brought his foot near that of the patients. The foot did not get warmer, and the headache lasted its ordinary period of time. The patient, having placed himself near a fire, obtained from it the curative effects which heat has constantly given him, without experiencing, either that day or night following, any effect from the magnetism.

Dr. Franklin, though the weakness of his health hindered him from coming to Paris and assisting at the experiments which were performed there, was magnetized by M. d'Eslon at his own house at Passy. The assembly was large; every person who was present underwent the experiment. Some sick persons, who had come with M. d'Eslon, were subjected to the effects of the magnetism, in the same manner as at the public demonstration, all but Madame de de B.... Dr. Franklin, his two relations, his secretary, and an American officer felt no sensation, though one of Dr. Franklin's relations was convalescent, and the American officer had at that time a regular fever.

The experiments we have related, furnish a number of facts, calculated to illustrate to the commissioners who were at liberty to deduce certain inferences. Of fourteen sick persons, five only appeared to feel any effect from the experiment, and nine felt no effect at all. The commissioner who had the headache and coldness in the feet, derived no benefit from the magnetism, nor did his feet recover their natural heat. This agent does not have the property which has attributed to it of communicating heat to the feet. The magnetism has also been said to have the property of discovering the species, by the pain, which the action of this fluid infallibly reacts in that part. Such an advantage would be of great consequence, and the fluid which was the instrument of it would be a valuable means in the hands of the physician. It is often deceived by equivocal symptoms; but Francis Grenet felt no sensation and no pain in the eye least affected. If the redness and tumor of the other eye had not furnished external symptoms, in judging from the effect of the magnetism we should have concluded that it was understood. M. R... and Madame de B... were conscious of no sensation or the seat of their diseases. And yet obstructions are among the disorders, which are said to be particularly subject to the action of the magnetism, since according to the new theory, the free and rapid circulation of this fluid through the nerves, is a means of opening the channels and destroying the obstacles, that is, the obstructions, which it encounters in its passage. It is at the same time said that the magnetism is the touch stone of health. If therefore, M. R... and Madame de B... had not experienced the derangements and sufferings inseparable from obstructions, they would have had a right to believe that they enjoyed the best health in the world. The same thing may be said of the American officer; the magnetism therefore announced as the discoverer of diseases completely failed of its effects.

The heat that M. M... felt in the patella, is an effect too slight to come to any conclusions. It may already attract too great an attention to observe what passes within us. The same attention would discover similar sensations at any other time, when the magnetism was not employed. The drowsiness experienced by Madame de V... was attributed to the regularity and fatigue of preserving the same situation. If she was sensible to any vaporous emotion, it must be remembered that it is a known property of nervous illnesses, to have much dependency upon the attention that is paid them. To renew them, it is only necessary to hear them spoken of or to think of them. It is easy to judge what ought to be expected from a woman, whose nerves are extremely irritable, and who, being magnetized for an hour and a half, had, during that time, no other thought than that of the disorders which are chronic to her. She might have had a nervous crisis greater than we have described, without our having a right to be surprised at it.

There remains then only the effects produced upon Dame Charpentier, Francois Grenet and Joseph Ennuye, which can be thought to be derived from the experiments of magnetism. In comparing these three particular facts to the rest, the commissioners were astonished that three subjects of the lower class should be the only ones who felt anything from the experiments while those of a more elevated rank, of more enlightened understandings, and better qualified to describe their sensations, have felt nothing. Without doubt, Francois Grenet experienced a pain and a watering in the eye when the thumb approached very near to it. Dame Charpentier complained that in touching her stomach the pressure corresponded to her rupture; and the pressure might have been in part the cause of what she felt. But the commissioners suspected that these sensations were augmented by moral causes.

Let us imagine the situation of a person of the lower class, and of considerable ignorance, attacked with a distemper and desirous of a cure. He is introduced with some degree of ceremony to a large company, partly composed of physicians, and where an experiment is performed upon him which is new to him and from which he persuades himself beforehand that he is about to experience prodigious effects. Let us add to this that he is paid for his cooperation and that he thinks he shall contribute more to our satisfaction by professing to experience sensations of some kind. We shall have definite causes to which to attribute these effects, and we shall at least have just reason to doubt whether their true cause be the magnetism.

Besides it may be asked why the magnetism produced these effects upon persons, who knew what was done to them and might imagine they had an interest in saying what they said. However it took no sort of hold upon the little Claude Renard, an organization endowed with all the delicacy of infancy, so irritable and so susceptible. The sound understanding and ingenious temper of this child provides us with the veracity of his relation. Why, too, has this agent produced no effect upon Genevieve Leroux, who was in a perpetual state of convulsion? Her nerves were certainly sufficiently irritable. Why is it that the magnetism did not display its power, either in augmenting or diminishing her convulsions?

Her indifference and impossibility induced the belief, that the reason she felt nothing, was the idiotism which did not permit her to judge whether she ought to have felt anything.

From these facts, the commissioners are at liberty to observe, that the magnetism has seemed to have no existence for those subjects, who have submitted to it with any degree of incredulity. The commissioners, even those who have had their nerves most irritable, having expressly turned their attention to other objects, and having armed themselves with that philosophic doubt which ought always to accompany inquiry, have felt none of those sensations, which were experienced by the three patients of the lower class. They have a right to suspect that these sensations, supposing their reality, were the fruits of anticipated persuasion, and might be operated by the mere force of imagination. Of this suspicion another class of experiments has been the result. Their subsequent researches were directed towards a new object. It was necessary to destroy or confirm the suspicion they had formed and to determine to what degree the power of the imagination can influence our sensations. It must be demonstrated whether it can be cause, in whole or in part, of the effects attributed to the magnetism.

At this time the commissioners heard of the experiments, which were made at the house of M., the dean of the faculty, by M. Jumelin in a body at the house of M. Majault, one of the commissioners. M. Jumelin declared that he was neither a disciple of M. Mesmer, nor of M. d'Eslon. He had learned nothing about animal magnetism from them, but he had formed his principles and learned his process from what he had heard about the subject during conversation. His principles consisted in regarding the animal magnetic fluid, as a fluid which circulates in the human body, and which flows from it, but which is the same principle as body heat. Like all other fluids it remained in equilibrium, and therefore passes from the body which has the least amount. His method does not differ from that of Messieurs Mesmer and d'Eslon in spite of his principles. Like them, he performs the operation with the finger, the rod of iron is the conductor, and the application of the hands is without any reference to poles.

Eight men and two women submitted to the operation in the

first experiment, and felt nothing. Finally a woman, who wanted, in the hall of M. Alphouse le Roy, doctor of physic, to be magnetized in the forehead, but not by being touched, said that she felt the sensation of heat. M. Jumelin, guiding his hand, and presenting the five fingers of his hand over her face, produced a sensation of heat which she claimed passed like a flame from place to place. When magnetized in the stomach, she stated that she felt the heat; magnetized upon the back, she made the same declaration and said that she also felt hot in every part of her body, and that her head also ached.

The commissioners observed that of the eleven persons who underwent the experience of the experiment, only one was sensitive to the magnetism of M. Jumelin; and they were of the opinion that this person had experienced certain sensations, only because she probably had an imagination that was more easily excited than the rest. It was the right time to clear up the point. Since this woman was very sensitive, it was necessary to protect her from the illusions of the imagination, or at least to keep anything from directing the operation of her imagination. The commissioners proposed to blindfold her, in order to observe what her sensations would be when she could no longer realize the conduct of the experiment. She was then blindfolded and magnetized but she could not perceive the places on her body where the magnetism was directed. When she was magnetized successively on her stomach and in the back, she felt only heat in her head, a pain in both eyes and in the left ear.

The bandages were removed from her eyes, and M. Jumelin applied his hands upon her stomach and she said she felt the heat; after a few minutes she said that she was ready to faint, and she promptly fainted. When she recovered somewhat, the experiment was resumed. She was again blindfolded, M. Jumelin left the room, and the woman was told that the experiment was being performed. The effects were the same, though no operation, either distant or near was being performed. She felt the same heat, the same pain in her eyes and in her ears. She felt heat in her back and loins.

After a quarter of an hour, a sign was made to M. Jumelin to magnetize her in her stomach, but she felt no sensation; in the back the same thing. The sensations diminished instead of augmenting themselves. The pains in her head continued, the heat in her back and loins ceased.

We see in this instance certain effects produced, and these are similar to those which were experienced by the three subjects whose experiments have already been detailed. But the former and the latter were obtained in different methods, but this is of no consequence. The process utilized by M. Mesmer and M. d'Eslon, and an opposite process have produced the same phenomena. It may be observed that while the woman was permitted to see the procedure, she placed her sensations precisely in the part towards which it was directed. On the other hand, when she did not see the operation, she placed them haphazardly in parts very distant from those which were the object of the magnetism. It was natural to conclude therefore that these sensations, real or pretended, were determined by the imagination. We were really convinced when we saw the patient at rest, having recovered from her previous sensations, still blindfolded, still experiencing the same effects although no operation was performed. After the demonstration was complete, her imagination cooled down, and when the operation was renewed for augmentation, the sensations actually diminished.

If she was seized with a faintness, it could have probably been caused, as is sometimes true with women, by her garments being tight and otherwise burdensome. The weather was extremely hot, and the woman unquestionably felt some emotional disturbance at the beginning of the experiment, but she had made an effort to submit to a new and unknown operation. It was possible that this added effort, continued over a long period of time, could cause the patient to faint.

This fainting could be said to have a known and natural cause, but the sensations, which she experienced when no procedure was performed, could only be the result of imagination. In similar experiments which M. Jumelin made the next day at the same place, while the commissioners were present, the result was precisely the same, when performed upon a man who was blindfolded and a woman who was not blindfolded. It was evident that their answers were determined by the questions that were put to them, that is, the question pointed out where the sensation ought to be. In the room where the experiments were performed, all that was done was to direct and stimulate their imagination. A child, five years of age, was magnetized but felt nothing but the heat which he had just contacted while playing extremely hard.

These experiments appeared sufficiently important to the commissioners, for them to desire a repetition of them in order to obtain further light into the subject, and M. Jumelin had the complaisance to comply with their request. It would have no purpose to object to the fact that the method of M. Jumelin was a bad method, for at the moment it was not proposed to prove the magnetism, but the imagination.

The commissioners agreed to blindfold subjects who had already undergone the magnetical operation; for the most part not to magnetize them at all, but to put to them questions so framed as to point out their answers to them. This means of calculating was not to deceive them; it only misled their imagination. In reality, when no operation was performed upon them, their sole answer ought to have been, that they felt no sensation at all, and when the experiment was performed, the impression they felt, not the manner in which they were questioned, ought to have dictated their replies.

The commissioners adjourned to the house of M. Jumelin, and began an experiment upon his servant. They fixed a bandage over his eyes, prepared for the purpose, and which they employed in all the succeeding experiments. The bandage was made of two calottes of elasticgum, whose concavity was filled with edredon, the whole enclosed and sewn up in two pieces of a circular four. These pieces were then fastened to each other, and to two strings which were tied in a knot at the back part of the head. Placed over the eyes, they left room for the nose, and the entire freedom of respiration, without the person blindfolded being permitted to receive even the smallest particle of light, either through, or above, or below the bandage. These precautions, having been observed, and with the comfort of the subject in mind, and with the certainty of result, the servant of M. Jumelin was persuaded that there was an experiment being performed upon him. With this, he felt an almost universal sensation of heat and certain emotions in the region of the belly, together with an extreme heaviness. By degrees he grew very drowsy, and appeared to the point of falling asleep. This experiment proved what we had already said, that the symptoms of heaviness and drowsiness is (*sic*) the effect of situation and weariness, not of the magnetism.

The same person was magnetized afterwards with his eyes uncovered, and a rod of iron placed in front of his forehead. He experienced a sensation of pricking. The bandage was then replaced and the experiment repeated, and he was conscious of no sensation. The rod of iron was then removed and the patient was questioned if he felt anything in his forehead. He stated he felt something move backwards and forwards from one side to the other.

M. B . . ., a man of learning, and particularly acquainted with the science of medicine, was then blindfolded, and he presented the same situation, feeling certain sensations when he was not acted upon, and often feeling nothing when the experiment was performed. These sensations went to such length that, previously to being magnetized in any manner, but believing that the experiment had been performed for at least ten minutes, he suddenly felt heat in his loins which he compared to that of a stove. It is evident that M. B... had a very strong sensation, since in order to convey an idea of it, he thought it necessary to have recognized such a comparison. This sensation he owed solely to his imagination, which was the only agent concerned in the affair.

The commissioners, particularly those of the faculty of medicine, made an infinite number of experiments upon different subjects whom they either magnetized themselves, or persuaded to have the procedure. They performed the procedure indifferently, either opposite to, or in the direction of the poles, or at right angles with them, and in each case, obtained the same results. They were therefore convinced that the imagination alone is capable of producing various sensations, and causing the patient to experience both pain and heat, and even a very considerable degree of heat, in all parts of the body. They concluded that it of course entered for a considerable share into the effects attributed to animal magnetism. It must at the same time be admitted, that the process of magnetism produces in the animated body changes more distinguished, and derangements more considerable than those we have just reported. None of those subjects, whom we have described as the imaginary objects of the magnetical operation, were so far impressed as to produce convulsions. It was therefore a new subject for the experiments of the commissioners to inquire whether by the mere energies of the imagination it were possible to produce crises, similar to those which we have stated in the public exhibition.

Many experiments were thought of for the decision of this question, when a tree has been touched according to the principles and method of the magnetism, every person who stops under it, ought to experience in a greater or lesser degree the effects of this agent. There have been some in this situation who have swooned, or experienced convulsions. We discussed our ideas upon this subject with M. d'Eslon, who replied that the experiment ought to succeed, provided the subject was extremely susceptible, and it was agreed that it should be made in Passy in the presence of M. le Dr. Franklin. The necessity that the subject should be susceptible, led the commissioners to believe, that to render the experiment decisive and unanswerable, it should be read on a person with whom M. d'Eslon had contact and of whose suscepti- bility he was already convinced. M. d'Eslon therefore brought with him a twelve year old boy. An apricot tree was fixed upon in the orchard of Dr. Franklin's garden, considerable distance from any other tree, and calculated for the preservation of the magnetical power which might be impressed upon it. M. d'Eslon was asked to perform the procedure, the boy in the mean time remaining in the house with another person. We could have presented the subse- quent part of the experiment, but he declared that he could not answer for its success if he did not direct his cane and his countenance towards the tree, in order to augment the action of the magnetism. It was therefore resolved, that M. d'Eslon should be placed at the greatest possible distance, and that some of the commissioners should stand between them, shielding the boy from him, in order to ascertain the impracticality of any signals being made by M. d'Eslon, or any intelligence being maintained between them. These precautions in an experiment the essence of which must be authenticity, are indispensable, without giving the person with respect to whom they are employed a right to think himself offended.

The boy was then brought into the orchard, his eyes covered with a bandage, and successively taken to trees upon which the procedure had not been performed, and he embraced them for the space of two minutes, the method of communication which had been prescribed by M. d'Eslon.

At the first tree, the boy, being questioned at the end of a minute, declared that he had perspired in large drops, he coughed, spit, and complained of a slight pain in his head; the distance of the tree which had been magnetized was about twenty-seven feet.

At the second tree he felt the sensations of stupefaction and pain in his head; the distance was thirty-six feet.

At the third tree, the stupefaction and headache increased considerably, and he said that he believed he was approaching the tree which had been magnetized. The distance was then about thirty-eight feet.

In line with the fourth tree, one which had not been rendered the object of the procedure, and at a distance of about twenty-four feet from the tree which had, the boy fell into a crisis, he fainted, his limbs stiffened, and he was carried on to a plot of grass, where M. d'Eslon hurried to his side and revived him.

The result of this experiment is entirely contrary to the theory of animal magnetism. M. d'Eslon accounted for it by observing that all the trees, by their very nature, participated in the magnetism, and that their magnetism was reinforced by his presence. But in that case, a person, sensitive to the power of magnetism, could not hazard a walk in the garden without the risk of convulsions, an assertion which is contradicted by the experience of every day. The presence of M. d'Eslon had no greater influence here than in the coach, in which the boy came along with him. He was placed opposite the coach and he felt nothing. If he had experienced no sensation even under the tree which was magnetized, it might have been said that at least on that day he had not been sufficiently susceptible. However, the boy fell into a crisis under a tree which was not magnetized. The crisis was therefore the effect of no physical or exterior cause, but is to be attributed solely to the influence of imagination. The experiment is therefore entirely conclusive. The boy knew that he was about to be led to a tree upon which the magnetical operation had been performed, his imagination was struck, it was increased by the successive steps of the experiment, and at the fourth tree it was raised to the height necessary to produce the crisis.

Other experiments were made, calculated to support this, and the result was the same. One day, when the commissioners were all together at the house of M. le Dr. Franklin, including M. d'Eslon, they asked him to bring some of his patients, selecting those of the lower class who were the most susceptible to the magnetism. M. d'Eslon brought two women, and while they were witnessing the performing of the procedure upon Dr. Franklin and several persons in another apartment, the two women were separated, and placed in different rooms.

One of them, Dame P. . . , had films over her eyes, but as she could always see a little, the bandage already described was used. She was told that M. d'Eslon had been brought into the room to perform the magnetical operation. Silence was suggested; three commissioners were present, one to interrogate, another to take minutes of the transaction, and one to impersonate M. d'Eslon. The conversation was pretended to be addressed to M. d'Eslon, and he was told to begin the experiment. The three commissioners in the mean time remained perfectly quiet, and were occupied with observing the symptoms of the patient. At the end of three minutes, the patient began to feel a nervous shuddering, she then successively complained of a pain in her head, her arms, a creeping in her hands, and she grew stiff. She struck her hands violently together, rose from her feet, stamped her feet on the floor and the crisis had all of the symptoms. Two other commissioners, who were in the adjoining room with the door shut, heard the stamping of the feet and without seeing anything were witnesses to this noisy experiment.

The two commissioners we have mentioned were with the other patient, Mademoiselle B..., who was subject to nervous distempers. No bandage was employed, and her eyes were not bandaged. She was seated with her eyes towards the door which was shut, and was told that M. d'Eslon was on the other side, performing the magnetical operation upon her. This had scarcely taken place for a minute before she began to feel the symptoms of shuddering; in another minute she had chattering of her teeth and a universal heat; at the end of the third minute she fell into a regular crisis. Her respirations were rapid, she stretched out both her arms behind her neck twisting them in extreme fashion. Bending the whole body forward, she began to tremble all over. The chattering of her teeth became so loud that it could have been heard on the outside. She bit her hand with such force that the marks of the teeth remained perfectly visible.

It is proper to observe that neither of these subjects were touched in any manner, their pulse was not even felt, that it might not be possible to say that the magnetic fluid was communicated, the crises, however, were complete. The commissioners, who wanted to know the effect of the influence of the imagination and to appreciate the part it plays in the magnetical crises, had now obtained all that they desired. It is impossible to see this influence displayed in a clearer or more incontrovertible manner than in these two experiments. If the subjects have declared that their crises were stronger in the public experiment, it must be attributed to the power of communication possessed by the numerous emotions, and that in general, every individual symptom has been increased by the anticipation of similar symptoms.

We had occasion to try a second experiment upon Dame P..., and to experience how much she was under the dominion of her imagination. The experiment of the magnetic basin was proposed. This experiment consists of discovering among a number of basins one that has been magnetized. They are successively presented to a patient susceptible to magnetism. He ought to fall into a crisis or at least to experience sensible effects, when the magnetic basin is presented to him. He ought to be perfectly indifferent to all the rest. All that was necessary according to the recommendation of M. d'Eslon, was to present them to him in the direction of the poles in order that he who presents the basins may not himself magnetize the patient, and that there may be no other effect than that of the magnetism of the basin itself.

Dame P... was sent to the house of M. d'Eslon who was staying with M. Lavoisier. She began falling into a crisis in the anti-chamber, before she had seen either the commissioners or M. d'Eslon, and merely from the knowledge she had that she was about to see him, a distinguished effect of the influence of imagination.

When she had sufficiently recovered, she was led into the room that was scheduled for the experiment. Several china basins were presented to her which had not been magnetized. At the second basin, she began to feel the usual symptoms, and at the fourth, fell into a complete crisis. It may be stated that her actual state was a state of crisis, that it had begun in the anti-chamber, and was renewed by its own single energy. A circumstance which was decisive, was, that having asked for something to drink, the basin, which had been magnetized by M. d'Eslon himself was presented to her. She drank with perfect calmness and said that she felt much better. The basin and the magnetism had therefore failed of their effect, since the crisis was tranquilized in the room.

Some time after, while M. Majault examined the films she had over her eyes, the magnetic basin was placed at the back of her head, and was held there for twelve minutes. She was not conscious of the operation, and felt no effect from it. She was very quiet in her actions because her imagination had been diverted, and fixed upon the examination which was being performed on her eyes.

The commissioners were informed that while this woman had been left alone in the anti-chamber, different people not acquainted with the animal magnetism had approached her, and the convulsive emotions commenced again. She was observed and it was noticed that the magnetical operation was not performed on her, but her imagination was such, that she replied, "If you did nothing to me, I should not be in the condition in which I am."

She knew that she had been sent for in order that she be the subject of the experiments; and the approach of any person toward her, or the slightest noise, attracted her attention, excited the idea of magnetism, and renewed her convulsions.

The imagination in order to act with considerable strength, has often the need to touch several cords at a time. It has a correspondence with each of the senses, and its reaction may be expected to be in proportion, both to the number of senses applied to, and of the sensations received. The commissioners were led to this observation by the following experiment.

M. Jumelin had spoken to them of a young lady, twenty years of age, whom he had deprived of the faculty of speech by the influence of the magnetism. The commissioners repeated the experiment at his house, the young lady consenting to submit to it and to be blindfolded.

The first object of the experiment was to endeavor to obtain the same effect without performing the procedure but though in this situation she felt or believed she felt the effects of the magnetism, we were not able to strike her imagination with the force that was necessary for the success of the operation. The procedure was then really performed, the bandage was not removed and the success was the same. The bandage was then taken away, her imagination was not stirred through the different channels of sight and hearing, and the effects were a little more marked. Though she complained of a heaviness in her head, an obstruction in the superior part of her nostrils, and a number of symptoms which she had felt under the operation of M. Jumelin, she did not lose the faculty of speech. She observed herself, that the hand by which she was magnetized in the forehead, ought to descend to the level of her nose, recollecting that there was the situation at the time in which she had felt the loss of her voice. What she demanded was performed, and in three-quarters of a minute she was dumb. Nothing was now to be heard from her but low and inarticulate sounds, though the exertion of the muscles of the throat for the formation of sound, and that of the tongue and lips in order to articulate were visible. The state lasted only a minute. It is obvious to observe that, finding herself precisely in the same circumstances, the seduction of the understanding, and the effect of that seduction upon the organs of speech were the same. But it was not enough that she should be informed that she was magnetized, it was also necessary that a sense of feeling should yield her the testimony, stronger and capable of greater effects. It was necessary to have a gesture with which she was already acquainted to re-excite her former ideas. It should therefore seem that this experiment is calculated to display the manner in which the imagination acts, the degrees by which it is exalted, and the different exterior stimuli it requires in order to display itself in its greatest energy.

The power which the sense of sight exercises over the imagination, explains the effects attributed by the doctrine of the magnetism to the eyes. The eyes possess in an eminent degree the power of magnetizing. Signs and gestures, as the commissioners were informed, have commonly no effect except upon a subject who had been previously mastered by the employment of the eyes. The reason for this is very simple. It is that the eyes convey the most energetic expressions of passions. It is this expression that develops all that the human character has of the commanding or the attractive. It is therefore natural that the eyes should be the source of a very high degree of power. This power consists merely in the aptitude they possess of moving the imagination, and that they are more or less strong in proportion to the activity of the imagination. It is for this reason, that the whole process of the magnetism commences from the eyes of the operator, and their influence is so powerful and leaves traces so strong and lively, that a woman, who just came to the house of M. d'Eslon, having encountered a look of one of his pupils, who had performed the procedure upon her, just as she was recovering from a crisis had her eyes set in her head for three-quarters of an hour. For a long time she was haunted with the remembrance of this look. She always saw before her this very eye; fixed to regard her, and she carried it uninterruptedly in her imagination, sleeping as well as waking for three days. We see from this instance what an imagination is capable of doing. It can preserve one impression for so long a time, that is, can renew, of itself, and by its single power, the same sensation regularly and without interruption, for three days.

The experiments which we reported, are uniform in their nature, and contribute alike to the same decision. They authorize us to conclude that the imagination is the true cause of the effects attributed to the magnetism. But the partisans of this new agent will perhaps reply that the identity of the effects does not always prove an identity of causes. This will grant that the imagination is capable of exciting these impressions without the magnetism, but they will maintain that the magnetism is also capable of exciting them without the imagination. The commissioners might easily destroy this assertion by applying the principles of all reasoning and the laws of natural philosophy, of which the first is to admit no new causes without an absolute necessity. When the effects observed are capable of having been produced by a known cause, and a cause whose existence, other phenomena have already established, sound philosophy teaches that the effects ought to be ascribed to that cause, and when on the other hand, we are acquainted with the discovery of a cause hitherto unknown, sound philosophy requires that its existence be made out by effects which do not belong to a known cause, and which cannot be explained but by the new cause. It therefore belongs to the partisans of the magnetism, to bring forward other proofs, and to discover effects which shall be entirely stripped of the illusions of the imagination. But the facts are more demonstrative than reasoning, and as their evidence is more universally striking, the commissioners have been desirous of establishing by experiment, what the magnetism can do in cases where the imagination is concerned.

For this experiment they made the choice of two rooms, contiguous to each other, and united by a door of communication. The door was taken away, and a frame of wood substituted in its place, with transverse bars, and covered with a double texture of paper. In one of these rooms was a commissioner, who undertook to take minutes of the transaction, and a lady who had just arrived from the county and to have a suit of linen which she wanted to have made up. Mademoiselle B . . ., a seamstress by profession, who had already been employed in the experiments at Passy, and whose sensibility to the magnetism was well known, was sent for. Everything was all set up for her arrival in such a manner that there was but one seat upon which she could place herself and that seat stood within the frame of the door of communication.

The commissioners were in the other apartment, and one of them, a physician, who had upon former occasions performed the magnetical operation with success, had undertaken to magnetize Mademoiselle B . . . through the paper partition. It is a principle in the theory of the magnetism that this agent passes through doors, walls, etc. A partition of paper could therefore be no obstacle; beside M. d'Eslon had positively declared that the magnetism passes through paper.

Mademoiselle B . . . was accordingly magnetized during the next half hour, at the distance of a foot and a half, and in a direction opposite to that of the poles, in conformity to the rules taught by M. d'Eslon, and which the commissioners had seen practised at his house. During the operation she conversed with much gaiety, and in answer to an inquiry concerning her health, she readily replied that she was perfectly well. At Passy she had fallen into a crisis in the course of three minutes; in the present instance she underwent the operation of the magnetism without any effect for thirty minutes. The only reason for this difference must be that here she was ignorant of the operation, and that at Passy, she thought it had been performed. The inevitable conclusion is that the imagination singly produces all the effects attributed to the magnetism, and that where the imagination ceases to be called forth, it has no longer the smallest efficacy.

Only one objection can be suggested for this experiment; and that is that Mademoiselle B . . . might not be prepared to receive the magnetic fluid, and might be less susceptible to its operation than usual. The commissioners foresaw this objection, and for this reason made the following experiment. as soon as they had ceased to magnetize the patient through the paper partition, the same commissioner passed into the other apartment. He found no difficulty in engaging Mademoiselle B . . . to submit to the magnetical operation. It was accordingly repeated in precisely the same manner as in the former instance, at the distance of a foot and a half, and by the intervention of gestures only, together with the employment of the right finger and the rod of iron. If he had applied the hands, and touched the body, it might have been objected that any difference of effect, was to be ascribed to the application having been more immediate in the latter instance. But the only difference between the two experiments was, that in the former Mademoiselle B... was magnetized in a direction opposite to that of the poles, and conformable to the rules of the magnetical theory; and in the second she was magnetized in the direction of the poles, or in the transverse line. On this account according to the principles of the magnetism, no effect ought to have been produced.

In three minutes, however, she felt a sensation of dejection and suffocation, an interrupted hiccup, a chattering of teeth, a contraction of the throat, and extreme pain in her head. She was restless in her chair; she complained of a pain in the loins. Now and then she struck her foot with extreme quickness on the floor; afterwards she stretched her arms behind her, twisting them extremely as at Passy. In a word, the convulsive crisis was complete and accompanied with all the regular symptoms. All these accidents appeared in consequence of a process of twelve minutes, though the same process, employed for thirty minutes a little before had been ineffectual. The only ground of difference that remains is the play that was afforded in the latter influence to the imagination. To this therefore the difference of the effects is to be ascribed.

If the crisis originated in the influence of the imagination, it was the imagination also that put a stop to it. The commissioner who magnetized her observed that it was time to have this done, at the same time presenting to her his two forefingers in the form of a cross. It is proper to observe that in so doing he magnetized her in the direction of the poles, in the same manner as he had done through the whole experiment. No actual alteration had therefore been made, and the process being continued, the impression ought also to have continued. But the declared intention of the operator was sufficient to dissipate the crisis. Her heat and the pain in her head were immediately alleviated. The disorder of her frame was in this manner followed from place to place, announcing at the same time that it was going to disappear. In this manner in obedience to the voice to which the imagination was subjected, the contraction of the throat ceased, then the accidents of the breast, lately those of the stomach and the arms. The whole required only three minutes; after which Mademoiselle B . . . declared that she no longer felt any sensation, but was perfectly restored to her normal state.

These last experiments as well as several of those that were made at the house of M. Jumelin, have the double advantage of demonstrating at once the efficacy of the imagination, and the importance of the magnetism in regard to the symptoms which were operated.

If the symptoms are more considerable and the crisis more violent at the public exhibition, it is because various causes are combined with the imagination, to operate, to multiply and to enlarge its effects. They begin with subduing the minds of the patients by the employment of the eyes. This is followed by the touch, the application of the hands, and it is proper to develop in this place the physical effects of this method of procedure.

The symptoms are more or less numerous. The less numerous are hiccupping, qualms of the stomach and purging. The greater are the convulsions to which they have given the name of the "crises." The parts upon which the touch is employed are the chest, the pit of the stomach and sometimes the ovaries, if the patient is a female. The hands are pressed with a greater or lesser stress, as are the fingers, upon these different regions.

The colon, one of the larger intestines, runs through both the regions of the upper abdomen and the region of the epigastrium which separates them. It is placed immediately under the integuments. It is therefore upon this intestine that the pressure falls, an intestine full of sensibility and irritability. A repeated voluntary effort, without assistance from any other cause, excites the muscular action of this intestine, and sometimes results in evacuations. Nature, as it were by instinct, indicates this maneuver to persons hypochondriacally affected. The process of the magnetism is nothing more than this very maneuver. The evacuations are calculated to be produced by the magnetical process, by the frequent and almost habitual use of a real laxative, the cream of tartar in their drink.

But while the motion which is produced excites principally the irritability of the colon, this intestine offers other phenomena. It swells in a greater or lesser degree, and sometimes distends itself to a considerable volume. At such times it relays to the diaphragm such an irritation, that this organ becomes more or less convulsed. It is this convulsion to which they have given the name of crisis in animal magnetism. One of the commissioners had occasion to see a woman, subject to a kind of spasmodic vomitings, with which she was seized several times every day. Her efforts produced nothing but a turbid and viscous water, similar to that which is brought up by the patients in the crisis of the magnetical operation. The convulsion had its seat in the diaphragm, and the region of the colon was so sensitive, that the slightest touch upon that part, a strong commotion of the air, the surprise caused by a sudden noise sufficed to excite the convulsion. The woman had therefore regular crises without the assistance of the magnetism, by a single irritability of the colon and diaphragm; and the women who are magnetized, obtained their crises from the same cause and through the same irritability.

The application of the hands upon the stomach has physical effects that are no less remarkable. The application is made directly upon that organ. Sometimes a strong continuous compression is utilized, sometimes a number of slight and successive compressions, sometimes a discomposure of the stomach by a rotary motion of the rod of iron in contact with the part, or by the successive and rapid passage of the thumbs over it one after the other. These methods convey almost immediately to the stomach an irritation, more or less strong and durable, in proportion to the susceptibility of the subject. The part is also previously conditioned to the reception of this irritation by being first compressed. This compression prepares it to act upon the diaphragm and to relay to it the impressions it receives. It is irritated, the diaphragm is also irritated, and from thence result in the same manner as by the action of the colon, the nervous accidents which had been already stated. In women who are peculiarly susceptible, the mere compression of the upper abdomen, without their being acted in any other manner, occasions a contraction of the stomach and fits of swooning. This happened in the case of the woman magnetized by M. Jumelin, and it often happens from no other cause than an improper degree of tightness in their dress. These cases are not followed by the crisis, because the stomach is compressed without being irritated, and the diaphragm remains in its natural state. The same methods employed upon the ovaries of the female sex, beside their particular effects, produce with great force the above accidents. The empire and extensive influence of the uterus over the animal economy is well known.

The intimate connection of the colon, the stomach and the uterus with the diaphragm is one of the causes of the effects ascribed to the magnetism. The regions of the lower belly, which are the subject of these operations, answer to the different plexuses which constitute a regular nervous center in this part, by means of which, leaving every particular system out of the question, there most certainly exists a sympathy, communication, or correspondence between all parts of the body, such in this center affects the other parts of the body, and reciprocally a sensation experienced in any part affects and calls into play the nervous center, which often transmits the impression back again to all the parts of the body.

The truth thus stated not only explains the effects of the magnetic touch, but also the physical effects of the imagination. It has been constantly remarked that the affections of the soul make their first corporeal impression upon the nervous center, which commonly leads their subject to describe himself as having a weight upon his stomach, or a sensation of suffocation. The diaphragm enters into this business from where the sighs, the tears, and the expressions of mirth originate. The viscera of the lower belly then experience a reaction. It is by this automatous process that we are able to account for the physical disorders produced by the imagination. Surprise occasions the colic, terror causes a diarrhea, melancholy is the origin of icterical distempers. The history of medicine presents to us an infinity of examples of the power of imagination and the mental affections. The terror occasioned by a fire, a violent degree of desire, a strong and undoubting hope, a fit of choler have restored the use of his limbs to one who has been crippled with the gout or to a paralytic person. A strong and unlooked for degree of joy has dissipated a quartan ague of two months' standing. Close attention is a remedy for the hiccup; and persons, who by some accident have been deprived of the faculty of speech, have recovered it in consequence of some of the vehement emotions of the soul. This last assertion is supported by the testimony of history and the commissioners have themselves witnessed a suspension of this faculty, occasioned singly by the imagination. The action and reaction of the physical upon the moral system, and of the moral upon the physical, have been acknowledged ever since the phenomena of the medical science have been remarked, that is, ever since the origin of science.

Tears, laughter, coughs, hiccups, and in general all the effects which are observed in what have been styled crises in animal magnetism, do therefore originate either in the interruption of the functions of the diaphragm by a physical vehicle, such as the touch and the pressure, or from the power with which the imagination is endowed of acting upon this organ and interrupting its functions.

If it is objectionable that touch is not always necessary to these effects, it may be stated that the imagination may be sufficiently fertile in resources to produce them all by its sole instrumentality. Especially is this true of the imagination exerted in a public exhibition, called into play at once by methods in which it is itself addressed, and also by the effects observed in those who surround it. It has already been seen what were its effects in the experiments made by the commissioners upon isolated subjects. It may easily be conceived in what degree those effects must be multiplied in the case of a number of patients collected together in a public meeting. These patients are assembled in a narrow space, if the space be compared with the number of patients. The air of the apartment is heated although care is used to renew it, and it is always more or less impregnated with mephitic gas, which has the property of acting immediately upon the head and the nervous system. When the introduction of music is added, it affords another means of acting upon and exciting the nerves.

In the public gathering, several women are magnetized at the same time, and they experience at first no effects, but such as are similar to those obtained by the commissioners in various experiments. It is even acknowledged that for the most part the crises do not begin sooner than two hours. Little by little, the impressions are communicated from one to the other, and reinforced, in the same manner as the impressions which are made by theatrical representation, where the impressions are greater in proportion to the number of spectators, and the liberty they enjoy of expressing their sensations. The applause, by which the emotions of individuals are announced, arouses a general emotion, which everyone partakes in the degree in which he is susceptible. The same observation has been made in armies upon a day of battle, where the enthusiasm of courage, as well as the impressions of terror, are propagated with so amazing rapidity. The drum, the sound of military musical instruments, the noise of the cannon, the musketry, the shouts of the army, and the general disorder impress the organs, have a uniform effect upon the understanding, and exalt the imagination in the same degree. In this equilibrium of inebriation, the external manifestation of a single sensation immediately becomes universal. It hurries the soldiery to the charge or it causes them to flee. The same cause is seen in rebellions; the multitude are governed by the imaginations. The individuals in a large assembly are more subjected to their senses, and less capable of submitting to the dictates of reason, and where fanaticism is the presiding quality, its fruits are the tremblers of the Cevennes. It has been usual to forbid larger assemblies in seditious towns as a means of stopping a contagion so easily spread. Everywhere example acts upon the moral part of our frame, mechanical imitation upon the physical part. The minds of individuals are calmed by dispersing them. The same method puts a stop to their spasmodic affections, always contagious in their nature. We have had a recent example of this in the young ladies of Saint Roch, who were in this manner cured of the convulsions with which they were affected when together.

The magnetisms then, or rather the operations of the imagination are equally discoverable at the theatre, in the camp, and in all larger assemblies, as at the baquet, acting indeed by indifferent means, but producing similar effects. The baquet is surrounded by a crowd of patients. The sensations are continually communicated and recommunicated. It should be expected that the nerves should be worn out with this exercise, and they are irritated accordingly, and the woman who is the most sensitive in the company gives the signal. Immediately the cords, stretched to the same degree and in perfect unison from all directions, respond to each other. The crises are multiplied. They mutually reinforce each other and are rendered violent. In the meantime, the men who are witnesses to these emotions, take part in them in proportion to their nervous sensibility, and those in whom the sensibility is greatest and most easily excited, become themselves the subject of a crisis.

This propensity to irritation, partly natural and partly acquired, becomes in each sex habitual. The sensations, having been felt once or more often, nothing is now necessary but to recall the memory of them, and to exalt the imagination to the same degree in order to operate the same effects. This will never be difficult when the subject is placed in the same circumstances. The public exhibition is no longer necessary, you have only to touch the upper abdomen and to place the finger and the rod of iron in front of the face, the signs are well known. Even these are not necessary. It is sufficient that the patients be blindfolded, made to believe that these signs are repeated upon them, and that they are magnetized. The ideas are again made excitable. The sensations are reproduced, the imagination, employing its accustomed instruments and resuming its former routes, gives birth to the same phenomena. These cases happen exactly to the patients of M. d'Eslon, who fall into a crisis, without the baquet and without being excited with the spectacle of the public exhibition.

Compression, imagination, imitation are therefore the true causes of the effects attributed to this new agent known by the name of animal magnetism. This fluid is said to circulate through the human body and to be communicated from individual to individual. Such is the result of the experiments of the commissioners, and the observations they made upon the means employed and the effects produced. This agent, this fluid, has no existence. Chemically, however, as it is, the idea is by no means novel. Some authors, particularly physicians of the last age, have expressly treated it in various performances. The curious and interesting inquiries of M. Thouret have convinced the public, that the theory, the operations and the effects of animal magnetism proposed in the last few years, were nearly the same as those revived in the present. The magnetism is no more than an old falsehood. The theory is now presented with a greater degree of pomp and ceremony, but it is not less erroneous. Human nature is prone to seize, to quit and to resume the mistake which is flattering to its wishes. There are errors which will be eternally dear to the sublunary state. How often has the pretended science of astrology vanished and reappeared? The magnetism is calculated to lead us back to it. Its professors have been desirous of connecting it with the celestial influences, that it might have a stronger seduction, and attract mankind by the hopes that are nearest to their heart, that of looking into the future, and that of prolonging their existence.

There is room to believe that the imagination is the principle of the three causes which we have assigned to the magnetism. It appears by the experiments we have related that imagination alone produces the crisis. The pressure and the touch seem to serve as preparatives. It is by touch that the nerves begin to be excited, imitation communicates and extends the impressions. But the imagination is that active and terrible power, by which we are accomplishing the astonishing effects that have excited so much attention to the public process. The effects strike all the world, the cause is enveloped in the shades of obscurity. When we consider that these effects seduced in former times men, venerable for their merit, their illumination and even their genius, Paracelsus, Van Helmont, and Kircher, we cease to be astonished that persons of the present day, learned and well-informed, that even a great number of physicians have been dupes of this system. Had the commissioners been admitted only to the public presentations, where there is neither time nor opportunity for making decisive experiments, they might well themselves have been led into error. It was necessary to have liberty to insulate the effects in order to distinguish the causes. It was necessary to see as they have done the imagination act, if we may be allowed the expression, partially, and produce its effects one by one in detail, to have an idea to what the accumulation of those effects might amount to. It was necessary to conceive the extent of its power and to account for all its prodigies. Such an examination demanded a sacrifice of time, and a number of systematical researches, which we have not always the leisure to undertake for our private instruction or private curiosity, nor even the power properly to pursue without being like the commissioners charged with the mandates of the sovereign, and honored with the confidence of the public.

M. d'Eslon is not much averse to the admission of these principles. He declared in our session held at the house of Dr. Franklin the 19th of June, that he thought he might lay it down as a fact that the imagination had the greatest share in the effects of animal magnetism. He said that this new agent might be no other than the imagination itself, whose power is as extensive as it is little known. He affirmed that he always acknowledged the concern of this faculty in the treatment of his patients, and he affirmed with equal confidence that many persons have been either entirely cured or infinitely amended in the state of their health under his direction. He remarked to the commissioners that the imagination thus directed to the relief of suffering humanity would be a most valuable means in the hands of the medical profession. Persuaded by the reality of the power of the imagination, he invited the commissioners to embrace the opportunity which his practice afforded to study its procedure and its effects. If therefore M. d'Eslon is still attached to his first idea, that these effects are to be ascribed to the agency of a fluid, which is communicated from individual to individual by the touch or under the guidance of a conductor, he cannot however avoid conceding to the commissioners that only one cause is requisite to one effect. Since the imagination is a sufficient cause, the supposition of the magnetic fluid is useless. It cannot be denied that we are surrounded with a fluid which peculiarly belongs to us. The insensible perspiration forms around us an atmosphere of insensible vapors, but this fluid has no agency such as is common to other atmospheres. It cannot be communicated by the touch but in infinitely small quantities. It is not capable of being directed either by conductors, or by the eyes, or by the will. It is neither propagated by sound, nor reflected by mirrors, and is in no case susceptible to the effects ascribed to it.

It remains for us to inquire, whether the crises or convulsions, excited by the methods of pretended magnetism in the assemblies around the baquet, is capable of any utility, or is calculated to cure or relieve the patients. The imagination of sick people has unquestionably a very frequent and large share in the cure of their diseases. With its effect, we are otherwise not acquainted except through general experience. Though it has not been traced in positive experiments, it should seem reasonable not to admit doubt. It is a well-known adage, that in psychic as well as religion, men are saved by faith. This faith is the product of the imagination. In these cases the imagination acts on a gentle means, and it acts by diffusing tranquility over the senses, by restoring the harmony of the functions, by recalling into play, every principle of the frame under the genial influence of hope. Hope is an essential constituent of human life; the man that yields us one contributes to restore to us the other. But when the imagination produces convulsions, the means it employs are violent, and such means are almost always destructive. There are indeed a few rare cases in which they may be useful. There are desperate diseases in which it is necessary to overturn everything for the introduction of an order totally new. These critical shocks are to be employed in the medical art in the same manner as poisons. It is obvious that necessity should demand and economy employ them. The need of them is momentary. The shock ought to be single. Very far from repeating it, the intelligent physician exerts himself to invent the means of repairing the indispensable evil which has thus been produced, but in the public process of the magnetism, the crises are repeated every day and they are long and they are violent. Now, since the state produced by these crises is pernicious, the habit cannot be other than fatal. How indeed can it be conceived, that a woman, for instance, attacked with pulmonary distemper, can undergo with impunity, a crisis, some of whose symptoms are a convulsive cough, and compulsory expectorations? She can safely fatigue, perhaps shatter the lungs by repeated and violent efforts. How can we imagine that a man, be his disorder what it will, finds that, in order for him to recover, needs the intervention of the crisis? During this time, his sight appears to be lost, he strikes his breast with precipitous and involuntary motions. These crises are terminated by an abundant spitting of viscous humour and even blood. The blood that is spit up is neither vitiated nor corrupted. It flows from vessels which were torn by the violence of effort and contrary to the intention of nature, these effects are therefore to be treated as a real and not a salutary evil.

Nor is this the only danger that is present. Man is incessantly enslaved by custom, and nature is modified by habit only in a progressive manner. Yet she is so often completely modified, as to suffer an entire metamorphosis, and is scarcely capable of being known for the same. Who will assure us, that this state of crises, at first voluntarily induced, shall not become habitual?

The commissioners, having convinced themselves that the animal magnetic fluid is capable of being perceived by none of our senses, and had no action either upon themselves or upon the subjects of their many experiments. They are assured that the touches and compressions employed in its action rarely had favorable charges in the animal economy. The impressions thus made are always dangerous to the imagination. Therefore, having demonstrated by decisive experiments that the imagination without the magnetism produces convulsions, and that the magnetism without the imagination produces nothing, they have concluded with a unanimous voice, respecting the existence and the utility of the magnetism, that the existence of the fluid is absolutely destitute of proof, and that the fluid, having no existence, can consequently have no use. The violent symptoms observed in the public exhibition are to be ascribed to the compression, to the imagination called into action, and to that propensity to mechanical imitation which leads us in spite of ourselves to the repetition of what strikes our senses.

And at the same time they think themselves obliged to add as an important observation, that the compressions and the repeated action of the imagination employed in producing the crises may be harmful. The sight of these crises is not less dangerous on account of that imitation which nature seems to have imposed upon us as a law. Consequently, every public exhibition, in which the means of animal magnetism shall be employed, cannot fail in the end of producing the most pernicious effects.

Paris, the 11th day of August, 1784.

(Signed)

B. Franklin,

Majault,

Le Roy,

Sallin,

Bailly,

D'Arcet,

De Borie,

Guillotin,

Lavoisier.

The principles of M. d'Eslon are the very same as those included in the twenty-seven propositions disseminated from the press by M. Mesmer in 1779. If M. Mesmer now announces a more extensive theory, it is not necessary for the commissioners to be acquainted with the theory to decide upon the existence and the utilization of the magnetism, it was sufficient to estimate the effects. It is by the effects that the existence of a cause is determined. It is also by effects that its utilization must be demonstrated. The phenomena are learned from observation long before we can arrive at the theory which connects and explains them. The theory of the loadstone does not yet exist, and its phenomena are ascertained by the experience of successive axes. The theory of M. Mesmer is in this case, indifferent and superfluous. The methods employed, the effects produced, was what was necessary to be examined. Now it is easy to prove that the essential practice of the magnetism is known to M. d'Eslon.

M. d'Eslon was for many years the pupil of M. Mesmer. Constantly he saw the method of animal magnetism and the means employed in exciting and directing it. M. d'Eslon, himself, administered the magnetism in the presence of M. Mesmer, and separated from him, he achieved the same effects. After their reconciliation, they united their patients, and without distinguishing the patients, undertook the management of them and consequently the methods were the same. The method which is followed to this day by M. d'Eslon can be no other than the method of M. Mesmer.

The effects are not less dissimilar. There are crises which occur equal in frequency, and accompanied by similar symptoms, at the house of M. d'Eslon and at the house of M. Mesmer, proved that the effects do not belong to an individual, but to the practice of magnetism in general. The experiments of the commissioners demonstrate that the effects obtained by M. d'Eslon were due to compression, to imagination and to imitation. These are therefore the causes of the magnetism in general. The observations of the commissioners have convinced them that these convulsive crises and these violent means cannot be as useful in medicine as are poisons, and they have judged independent of all theories, that wherever it shall be the object to excite convulsions, they may become habitual and pernicious. They may be epidemically diffused and even extend to future generations.

The commissioners were obliged to conclude that not only the measures in a particular mode of proceeding, but the measures of the magnetism in general might in the end produce the most pernicious effects.

Artificial Somnambulism

In 1784, the Marquis de Puysegur, while magnetizing a young peasant whom a diseased chest kept bedridden, produced without effort the magnetic sleep, fascination, lucidity, second sight—in fact, somnambulism. Mesmer, who understood at once what the discovery would entail, was not pleased with it. Theoretically Puysegur's discovery resulted in the elimination of the universal fluid theory, to be replaced by the animal or nervous fluid, which had become the magnetic agent.

At this time, many attempts were made to explain the resulting states of animal magnetism. Artificial magnetism represented a magnetic state during which the subject, even though he is under the physiological influence of the operator, is in possession of his intellectual autonomy to such a degree that, owing to the isolation in which he is placed, he obtains results which would be absolutely unattainable by anyone while awake. It was also assumed that the ease in which certain subjects fall into the state of artificial somnambulism was the result of bad health, or at any rate a result of organic weakness accompanied by a certain degree of nervous irritation. It is interesting to note that recall of conversation or thoughts during sleep is one of the essential characteristics of somnambulism.

Memory is exercised in a most indubitable way whenever the subject, while asleep, receives orders which he is bound to carry out when awaken. Recall is still absent in all cases since the subject is totally unaware that he had received an order and can in no way account for the action he is performing.

The following reprint is a translation of a book stating the facts of somnambulism. The author is only identified by initials, but the book was a recognized work at the time when magnetism was being questioned by the philosophers and the scientists.

ESSAY ON THE PROBABILITIES OF
MAGNETIC SOMNAMBULISM*

Of all the new things that the practice of Animal Magnetism offers to public curiosity, the most interesting is, without contradiction, Magnetic Somnambulism.

By these terms is designated an intermediate state between sleep and wakefulness, which has characteristics of both, and produces also a great number of phenomena which belong to neither.

The patient reduced to somnambulism hears nothing of what is happening beside him; immobile in the midst of great movement, he seems separated from all nature, preserving communication for only him who has put him into that state.

The latter has acquired (by the single fact of magnetization) an intimate rapport with the patient; with the help of a kind of invisible lever, he makes him move as he pleases. Such is the strength of his power, that not only does he make himself understood by talking to the patient, and through signs, but also by thought alone. What is even stranger, is that Magnetism can communicate its property to other persons, by simple contact; and from this moment communication is carried on between the somnambulist and his new director.

The patient being put into a state of Somnambulism, a disorganization occurs within him which interrupts the equilibrium of his senses; so that certain ones experience an extreme lessening, while certain others acquire a prodigious degree of subtlety.

Thus, the hearing of certain persons is lost or weakened, while sight becomes prodigiously penetrating; others, loss of sight and of hearing is compensated by an unbelievable sensitivity of touch or of taste.

In others, a sixth sense seems to appear, through an extreme extension of the intellectual faculty, which surpasses the extent of ordinary human wit.

In short, the phenomena which the state of Somnambulism presents, offer daily new subjects for astonishment for the very

---

*Essai sur Les Probabilités du Somnambulisme Magnétique, Pour Servir a l'Histoire du Magnétisme Animal. Par M. F. . . . A Amsterdam; et se trouve a Paris, Chez les Marchands de Nouveautés, 1785.

same persons which ought to be the most familiar with them.

It remains to be known if all these alleged wonders are as real as one might wish it to be believed, and if on the contrary, these are not illusions undertaken by the bad faith of certain persons, and by the credulity of others.

For it is known that the human mind, naturally borne to the wonderful, quickly seizes all that is to its taste; and exalted wits which then use their ardor and their talents to realize their fancies are not lacking.

Among the persons who have been witnesses to the singularities of Magnetic Somnambulism, there is a party who, struck with astonishment and admiration, ended up by giving it his full credence, and regarded it as an irresistible proof of Animal Magnetism.

Others, after having been convinced of the reality of these phenomena, have nevertheless conserved their incredulity about the cause to which they (the phenomena) were attributed. They (the witnesses) preferred to suppose that there was some secret mainspring in this affair which produced illusion adroitly. Although they did not manage to understand these means of intelligence, they nonetheless supposed their existence, quoting, for example, these feats with those by which a subtle Physician astounded Paris for several years.

As for Scholars, Doctors, and Physicians, they have, for the most part, disdained being witnesses to the effects of Magnetic Somnambulism. Upon the pretext that it was enough for them that this phenomenon offended the ideas received in Physics, in Physiology, they regarded these alleged wonders as so many fancies unworthy of serious examination.

A scholarly Body was even seen to forbid its members all uncertainty upon this point, and to exclude from its body those of its members who had given themselves to the study of this novelty.

However, from another point of view, Magnetic Somnambulism acquires from day to day more confidence. A multitude of persons distinguished by their reason, their probity, the excellence of their judgment, and their sagacity, attest to the reality of Magnetic Somnambulism. This disagreement of respectable authorities

E S S A I

SUR LES PROBABILITÉS

D U

SOMNAMBULISME

MAGNÉTIQUE,

Pour fervir à l'Hiftoire du Magnétisme
Animal.

Par M. F***. *ouvrel, avocat.*

A AMSTERDAM;

Et fe trouve à PARIS

Chez les Marchands de Nouveautés.

1785.

FIGURE 6. Title page from the *Essay on the Probabilities of Magnetic Somnambulism*, published in 1785.

on the one side and the other, leaves in suspense the part of the public which is waiting, to make up its mind, for this matter to be put into its proper light.

The following reflections can serve to prepare the opinion of impartial persons, about what one is to think of Magnetic Somnambulism.

In order to more successfully achieve this objective, I believe it is necessary to divide this discussion into three parts.

The first point to examine is that of effectively knowing whether the Public has been witness to phenomena of some importance, worthy of exciting its curiosity, and which might merit that its cause be researched.

Supposing that the effects which are in question be worthy of being delved into, it will be necessary to see if they might not reasonably be suspected to be frauds.

Finally, admitting that fraud is not discovered, it will remain for us to examine whether it is true that they are in contradiction with common notions.

Are the Phenomena of Magnetic Somnambulism of a Nature to Merit the Curiosity of the Public and of Scholars?

It is easy, I believe, to understand the object of this question; I mean, that before we take the trouble of examining whether Magnetic Somnambulism is an illusion, or a truth, it is necessary to establish that there exist (at least in appearance) singularities of such a nature, that they interest the public and the progress of the Sciences.

There are many persons who would be within their rights to doubt it, because they have had no occasion to witness it. They are authorized to ask, before passing on to the two other propositions, that they be assured of the fact, "that there exist, be it in Paris, or be it in the Provinces, or be it anywhere else, persons struck by a state of sleep, during which they offer the phenomena which are under examination."

For if it wasn't quite certain that this sight might take place anywhere, it would be a waste of time to examine the principle behind it.

It is thus a preliminary obligation above the others (obligations), to clearly establish the existence of Magnetic Somnambulism, real or false.

This point has been the subject of general incredulity for a long time. That there were such individuals anywhere was flatly denied, and the account which a few people have made upon this head was regarded, as pure fable intended to be amusing.

The first piece of writing which discussed Somnambulists, if I am not mistaken, was a Letter from M. Cloquet, *Payeur des Rentes* at Soissons, who, telling what he had seen at the treatment of Buzanci, allowed several traits which characterized Magnetic Somnambulism to escape.

Since this Letter, a man of quality, whose candor it is impossible to question, consigned in a writing, interesting in all respects, phenomena which he had observed at the treatment of Buzanci, much more astonishing than those which M. Cloquet had outlined.

The reading of this Work having inspired in persons of the highest consideration the desire to witness such a Somnambulism, the Author of the Work in question had the chance to procure from them this satisfaction in the course of the winter of 1785.

More than five hundred persons have been at hand to attend these phenomena, real or false, about which the national papers, even the foreign papers have not failed to talk. These somnambulists were submitted to multiple proofs, which had more or less success.

Independently of those about which I am talking, several others have been formed, in Paris, and in the Provinces. The example of this Somnambulism having engaged the Magnetizers in attaching themselves to this part of Magnetism, they added to it all the more zeal. This state appeared to be leading to cure; thus, the interest of Magnetism and that of the patient were united to prefer this proceeding. It became the object of the efforts of all the Magnetists, and there was no treatment where people did not take pride in showing it more or less perfected.

Finally, the report of MM., the commissioners named by the King to examine Animal Magnetism, makes mention of this

Somnambulism, as of the most constant and the most extraordinary thing.

It cannot be then, as to the present, doubted for a moment that there exist individuals struck by an apparent Somnambulism. If I have begun by establishing this question, it was to proceed methodically, following the constant and noteworthy facts, which can lead me to infallible consequences.

Then let us hold for certain, as incontestable, that there exist, as much in Paris as in the Provinces, in the public treatments, and in private houses, claimed Somnambulists, who offer to the eyes of spectators marvellous phenomena.

At the present it is a question of knowing what must be thought of these Somnambulists; as to whether this isn't a simulated state, through which they are trying to seduce the credulity of those around them.

What Degree of Belief Can Be Added to Magnetic Somnambulists?

Among the somnambulists with whom I concern myself here, I do not understand at all this multitude of men or of women of the people (common) that are found in the treatments, and who can reasonably be suspected of pretending somnambulism, through imitation, or to appear more interesting, or for some other motive.

Never being conserved in the pure state is a misfortune attached to good things, and never being able to escape the mixture which malice or cupidity do not fail to introduce.

Those who, through prepossession or through self-interest, seek to discredit the discovery, take care to examine it on its side which most resembles charlatanism. They do not fail to offer it to the public in this light.

But those who desire to enlighten themselves in good faith, give this consideration only a very moderate value, and leaving aside charlatanism and the exaggerations of the people, delve into the principle. It is thus that a Botanist who wants to have the pit of a fruit to discover its quality, is not turned aside by the decay of the flesh which accompanies it. Casting aside the disgusting superfluities, he goes straight to the kernel which is to serve his study.

This is also the way all judicious men must operate who seek the truth with frankness, without interest and no design to evade it.

Let us then brush aside, without consideration, this suspect cohort claimed (unreal) somnambulists, to give our time to those who, through their civil existence, their character, their surroundings, silence the suspicious, and in which moreover Somnambulism is found accompanied by the last degree of perfection.

I say that through preference those patients with the purest cases of Somnambulism ought to be chosen, and I think that this precaution is essential.

Actually, the more imperfect the Somnambulist, the easier it is for him to impose on you. If he responds badly to your signs, if he follows your movements with awkwardness and clumsiness, and he gets along badly stating that he hasn't yet reached a state of full Somnambulism, the observer, who conceives that actually such a state must have degrees, is completely put off the track, not knowing if he is to attribute his poor success that he has experienced, to the maladresse of the Somnambulist, or to the imperfection of his state.

But when I settle myself upon a Somnambulist given to me as perfect, it is evident that his task becomes painful. In this case, no more excuses, no more pretexts; the observer is at his ease, and Somnambulism is found to be submitted to a test which must create its shame or its triumph.

This winter, this kind of perfect somnambulists have not been lacking, and among those who have been submitted to my experiments, there is *one* with whom I stayed half an hour and who executed before me, and at my will, the movements which I prescribed to him.

Given over to my disposition, without witnesses, without contradictors, there is no human means which I did not use to find fraud, if there was any. The rapidity of the evolutions, the precision of his movements, a multitude of facts which is too great to mention here, turned aside all my efforts.

Several others experiments having succeeded regarding other equally perfect Somnambulists, all gave me the same results.

There are in Paris and in the Provinces more than six thousand persons who are in the same case.

Now, to destroy the consequence which results from similar experiments, there is no other resource than persevering in supposing that there was a fraud on the part of the Somnambulists.

But this supposition brings out the greatest difficulties, and offers improbabilities more outrageous than Somnambulism itself.

To admit that the phenomena in question are the result of fraud, the assembly of two conditions are necessary.

First, that the Somnambulists intend to deceive;

Secondly, that they have the skill for it.

But first, it is necessary to state that among the persons who have been struck by Somnambulism, and who have it daily, there are some (people) who are above all suspicion. These are mothers of respectable families, serious men of known probity, simple people, children, in whom design and not the interest of stimulating such a situation cannot be reasonably supposed.

Could it be party spirit and the intention of giving some apparent reality to Animal Magnetism? But most of these persons are not at all concerned with the fortune of Animal Magnetism. Several of them had no idea of it at the time when they were put into magnetic sleep.

Could it be said that it is possible that some of these individuals are secretly encouraged by the partisans of Animal Magnetism, and that they are even only an instrument in the hands of these latter, for the advancement of the system?

But for what reasons would the partisans of Animal Magnetism have taken recourse in such a queer stratagem? The supposition would be, at the very most, admissible if Somnambulism had originally been revealed as a necessary result of Magnetism; so that it was necessary to renounce Animal Magnetism, if the resource of Somnambulism failed: but the situation is not thus.

Animal Magnetism was revealed, from the outset, without being accompanied by Somnambulism. This singularity is a posterior discovery, which has resulted from the habitual practice of Magnetism.

Even at the present, there are several Magnetizers who are very talented, who do not regard Somnambulism as being an essential part of Animal Magnetism, but only as an accessory which can be joined with the use of Magnetism, or separated from it, indifferently.

M. Mesmer himself has always seemed to me to be of this last opinion.

From which it results, that if the partisans of Animal Magnetism needed a resource which imposed it on the Public, assuredly they would have been very maladroit to have entangled themselves (without need) in a maneuver so strange, which bore a prodigious complication of results, and insurmountable difficulties of execution.

Observe that through this even if there had been artifice, there would have been no hope of bringing in any honest person.

It would thus have been necessary to stick to depraved people, taken from the vilest class, admit them into this confidence, at the risk of seeing them betray and publish the next day. This isn't all, it would have been necessary to find in these individuals an unheard of talent to play such a difficult role, and to deceive the tests of an enlightened and suspicious public, before which it is necessary to appear.

If things had gone thus, Somnambulism would have been of short duration, and far from gaining confidence through time, it would soon have revealed its illusion and fraud, through the difficulty of finding actors able to perpetuate this imposture.

But the contrary happened; each day Somnambulism acquires partisans; and the credit that it obtains opposes all idea of fraud.

Daily patients are seen put into this state, in the bosom of their family, under the eyes of their relatives who are nearest (to them) and the most concerned about verifying their situation.

Can it be thought that these patients, surrounded by the horrors of death and struck with sufferings, are thinking about playing a Comedy, in the interest of Magnetism? Their relatives, fathers, husbands, wives, children, are they in the midst of the plot?

Could it be said they are feigning illness? This is an equally inadmissible supposition; for beyond the fact that it isn't so easy to feign a feverish illness, a pneumonia, hydropsy, and other illnesses of this type, there are some that are so established, that it would be madness to call them into question.

Let us add here a consideration, that is while admitting that a healthy man might be able to resolve to play patient for a long time, or that a sick man might resolve to play Somnambulist, and that hidden persons behind a curtain presided at this tomfoolery, I say that the thing would be impossible in execution, and that, whatever talent might be supposed on the one side or the other, fraud must reveal itself by the end of a few hours. I defy the finest buffoon, the most adroit, the best broken away from the actions of the body, to play Somnambulist before enlightened persons, and also to execute anything which has been observed in the Somnambulists in question. I defy him to remain with his eyes closed for eight or ten hours, the eyelids glued shut, without (during this interval) one eyelid separating from the other.

Such perseverance seems beyond human skill and patience to me. What man can stay in an immobile position for five or six hours, without showing any sensation of what is passing around him, inaccessible to all emotions, and to the sudden and unforeseen outbursts which it pleases those around him to give to surprise his attention? What Historian is subtle enough to ever be able, with his eyes shut, to follow the signs presented to him, and to describe the lines which will be traced for him with such exactness and such rapidity, that there is no interval between the command and the obedience? Only a few experiments of this kind would be necessary to demonstrate the most consummate Showman, and to make him give up his undertaking at the end of two hours.

Now, when one sees all these effects constantly repeated, without any effort, by a multitude of people of all sexes, of all ages, and of all rank, one is necessarily drawn to recognizing that they are acting through a natural impulse, where *art* has no use, for one knows that what is impossible in art is nothing to nature.

Thus, physical probabilities are united with moral probabilities, to establish the reality of Magnetic Somnambulism. We cannot reject Somnambulism, without supposing a fraud just as difficult to conceive, and however you go about it, there will always be a moral or physical phenomenon. I vow that the last costs much more of the mind than the other. I make fewer efforts to conceive a natural phenomenon, which, after all, is susceptible to explanation, than to conceive a fraudulent plot devoid of interests, complicated by resources, and impracticable in its execution.

But there are some persons for whom such considerations are not victorious. Whatever difficulties there might be in making these stratagems work, they suppose that this skill takes place, because they say, in the things which wound reason, the authority of witnesses is nil.

This evident impossibility serves to fortify the public's part, since it has not seen the phenomena in question, and inspire mistrust in those who have seen them.

If it was a question only of an ordinary fact, which might be in accord with the march of nature, it is generally agreed that there would be more proof than would be necessary to believe it on its word, and without having seen it. But for a phenomenon so little natural, which is neither explainable nor conceivable, which reverses all received notions, one is authorized, not only to challenge the witness of others, but even that of his own senses; it is from this that it has been heard about several Scholars, "that when they saw it they would not believe it."

It is thus presently a question of seeing if it is true that Magnetic Somnambulism and the phenomena with which it is accompanied, are as inconceivable as these gentlemen (MM.) want it to be understood.

Are the Phenomena of Magnetic Somnambulism Against the Order of Nature?

The Physicians and Doctors, in affecting the greatest incredulity about Magnetic Somnambulism, under the pretext that this phenomenon is inconceivable, give no satisfactory reason for their incredulity, because the difficulties which they argue, cannot enter into concurrence with the imposing evidences which are raised in favor of Magnetic Somnambulism.

The difficulties of conceiving a phenomenon do not destroy its reality. We are surrounded with natural wonders which no one doubts, while they cannot be understood; for it is well known that the power of nature has inaccessible limitations for the conception of man.

But, perhaps it will be said, "it thus will follow from this reasoning, that one will be held to add faith to all the ineptitudes that will be related, and to submit (his) credulity to the most bizarre things in the world. Those who demand this belief will be free to invoke the great power of nature and the extent of her resources."

"With this way of reasoning, the Arts will soon lose their rules, principles will be banished from Science, to make way for bold assertions, and our knowledge, instead of becoming surer and more widespread, will fall back into chaos and confusion."

But this objection doesn't seem applicable to me, since it is not here a question of admitting a phenomenon, on the sole consideration that all is possible in nature. On the contrary it is a question of submitting to the test of opposition, of experimentation, and of reasoning, a fact attested to by the crowd of persons who have been visual witnesses of it.

Thus, up to this time, presumption remains in favor of Somnambulism, since it is based on the strongest considerations. These considerations are neither destroyed nor weakened by the disbelief claimed by those who oppose it.

But how would it be if it came to be discovered that Magnetic Somnambulism, instead of offering inconceivable phenomena, incompatible with the admitted notions of Physics and Physiology, to scholars, is on the contrary a consequence of these same received principles, an accessory of common notions, with which it mixes and it reconciles itself in a quite natural manner?

This is what I propose to make clear. To proceed with the method, I am going to successively examine the two articles on Magnetic Somnambulism which have excited the protest of Doctors and Physicians; to know, firstly, the ease of putting a patient into Somnambulism; secondly, the phenomena which accompany this state.

Article One: *The Communication of Somnambulism is in the Order of Accepted Notions of Physiology*

It is rather singular to see Doctors deny, with heat, that it is possible to put, by any art whatsoever, a patient into Somnambulism, when it is considered that it is one of their maxims that art can manage to imitate, in the human body, all the natural changes. It is upon this principle that the partisans of inoculation support their stand to defend its practice and the success of this proceeding.

All Doctors agree that the art of inoculation consists of forewarning in an individual, through the artificial indisposition, that which nature would sooner or later have occasioned.

It is from this very maxim that Doctors have thought of inoculating several types of illnesses, either for preventing them, or for serving as a counter-balance against other illnesses. Presently it is regarded in Medicine as the height of skill, to be able to cure one illness through another.

This mentioned, and from the time that it is recognized that nature can be imitated, by introducing some illness into the human body, is it strange, is it inconceivable that Somnambulism also is transmissible through artificial means?

Somnambulism is placed among illnesses by Physiologists. It is thus, through this quality, in the class of changes which art can introduce, that there is, for this condition, only one other step to take in the career of inoculation of illnesses. But this extension, from contradicting the principles of Physiology, only serves to confirm them.

However, it is certainly expected that Doctors will seek to combat this parity, by establishing differences and distinctions. They will even go so far as to want to withdraw Somnambulism from the class of illnesses, disavowing on this point their *nosologistes*.

In order to remove all pretext for subterfuge, it is necessary to lay aside illnesses, to stick to sleep.

Up to the present, there is no Doctor, nor Physician, nor Philosopher who has been able to explain the cause of sleep, nor how it occurs.

Everything said on this subject offers only conjectures, and work of the imagination. Only one thing is certain, that is, that sleep happens any time the body is in any disposition, proper to produce it, and that it is possible to put the body into this disposition through art. Such is the well-known effect of narcotic plants, such as opium, cockle (darnel), etc.

Now, if there exists any art which can put the body into a disposition for sleep, there is thus nothing astonishing about the fact that magnetic proceedings can also produce it.

It will be said that there is a lack of similarity, in that the magnetic processes do not use any decoctions or infusions to produce sleep. I answer that there is a lot lacking if drinks or drugs are necessary, for the state of wakefulness to be changed into the state of sleep. There are a multitude of other means which produce the same effect, and it is even one of the singularities which belong to sleep. It is produced by an infinite variety of causes; and causes which are completely opposed to one another; for example, if great warmth gives birth to sleep, it is equally produced by extreme cold. Soldiers have been seen to fall asleep upon the snow, and to perish from cold in this state of drowsiness.

If light and gentle massages bring sleep, atrocious pain produces it also; which is proved by the example of several unfortunate men who, being tortured, fell asleep in the middle of this supplice. Others have been cited who, stretched on the wheel, gave in to sleep.

Gemelli Carreri says, being in China, he was on the road with a Tartar who, every night, was obliged to fall asleep, to have himself struck with a rod upon the belly, like a drum.

Hunger and an excess of food, fatigue and rest, cooling drinks and warm drinks equally produce sleep. It results from the diminution of blood which is borne to the brain, as it results from its augmentation; it comes after baths and from bleeding. Fever, which causes insomnia, also causes drowsiness. A small difference in the dose of wine, wakens or induces sleep. There would be no end if one assembled the diverse causes which bring a man to this state, whether these causes engender as many different combinations, equally capable of producing sleep, whether, despite their apparent difference, they achieve the same result.

But in either case, one is obliged to admit that the means of sleep are of great number, and that we are not able to determine their nature or their quantity.

This consideration suffices doubtless to cast aside the quality of disbelief about sleep, which results from a magnetic touch.

This means, which appears at first glance so strange, loses much of its wonder when it is compared to others which are even stranger, whose certitude cannot be denied, such as those about which I have just spoken.

The efficacy of touching to produce sleep, seems moreover a necessary consequence of a general law of nature, which meant for the five senses to watch over the introduction of sleep. If touching did not produce it, this would be the only sense which fails to have this property.

In effect, if we take a look at hearing, smell, sight, and taste, we see therein many conductors of sleep. No one will deny that the ear is a very useful path for sleep. The noise of a windmill, the murmur of a stream, the spurting of water, a dragging conversation, the monotony of the voice, a slow and sad music, more or less promptly organizes the body in a proper way for sleep.

The smell of aromatic plants and narcotics puts (the body) into drowsiness, and Chemists have given in their works the recipes for soporific essences, which misusers have often abused.

Taste too is an introducer of sleep, and Medicine uses this means in the administration of narcotics, to bring it back to those who naturally lack it, or to make patients insensible to painful operations.

It is to be noticed that most drugs which produce this effect, develop their virtue before they have decomposed in the stomach, even before they have gotten that far down, and only through the contact with the palate or the tongue alone; which proves that this state belongs to the (sense of) taste.

Finally, sight is no less powerful for production of sleep. Too bright a light, obliging the eyelids to close, brings sleep unconsciously.

It is also known how reading is fitted to provoking it. There are many people who do not resist this impression, and who even make a resource of it when needed.

And it must not be said that sleep is then the effect of boredom, since most of the time sleep is involuntary, and that it happens in the middle of interesting reading without feeling any inclination to sleep.

Thus it truly is that sight then serves as a vehicle of sleep.

From which it follows that it is well established that sleep comes through four of our senses. This observation leads us almost necessarily to believing that touch is given the same virtue, because the uniformity which is noticed in nature, does not allow it to be supposed that it makes a particular exception for this sense.

But there is more; a little reflection shows us that the property in question must belong to touch more especially than to all the other senses. It is agreed, to speak exactly, there is only one sense, which is the sense of touch, and that the four others are only a modification of touch.

Sight, hearing, taste and smell, produce sensations in us, only through means of contact. Light, sound, tastes, odors do not act upon us except by shaking the nerve clusters of our organs, and they achieve this effect (shaking up), only after having touched them: this truth is incontestable.

Touch properly speaking does not differ then from the other senses except through a greater energy, and by its extension. The other senses occupy only a very circumscribed place, and are susceptible only to a local impression. Touch, through excellence, is spread over all the body's surface: and that suffices alone to make clear that touch must play a superior role in the property of opening a pathway to sleep. Being the main sense, thus to speak, the principal sense, from which the others are only a derivation, how could one conceive it deprived of a faculty which is found in its subordinates?

Finally, it is so true that sleep is introduced through touch, that Doctors themselves order opium taken as a local remedy and applied to the skin; which effectively produces sleep. The touch of an organized body can thus, without any marvel to it, occasion sleep. This is the point I wanted to reach to answer the reproach of disbelief.

But, it will be said, supposing the Magnetists have the power of producing sleep, there is not the same reason for believing that they procure Somnambulism.

The answer is simple.

Somnambulism is itself only a modification of sleep; there is no Somnambulism without sleep.

It could even be added that there is no sleep without Somnambulism, and that all men are born somnambulists.

This proposition, which seems to be a paradox, is no less incontestable, provided that there is no haste to give too much extension to the term Somnambulist.

Perfect sleep is a time of rest during which the sensations are reduced to a state of concentration which allows no sign of life other than breathing and the movement of the pulse to appear externally.

Imperfect sleep is that where this concentration is not complete, so that it leaves still some means for the external play of the organs. It is rare that the first kind of sleep is enjoyed.

In the deepest and happiest sleep, the sleeping person retains some portion of wakefulness more or less active, by means of which he executes diverse movements. Isn't it known that during sleep the body moves, arranges itself to choose a more advantageous position, the hand goes toward the parts which suffer some incommodity, it arranges the covers, crushes insects, all things which incontestably belong to the state of wakefulness, and which constitute consequently a kind of Somnambulism. For it must be understood under this name the exercise of movements, however operated, during sleep.

Ordinary men push Somnambulism even further, since there is an infinity of people who talk while sleeping, make gestures, hold long discourses, speak to those whom they think surround them, leave their bed and get back into it, etc.

These singularities are so ordinary, that there is hardly a house where one doesn't find a few examples of it.

When Somnambulism acquires a few more nuances, it produces astonishing things.

It is then that one sees the sleeper write, work, open doors, light fires, climb upon roofs, swim streams, curry horses, etc.

But observe that Somnambulism carried to this last degree, is not a new state, nor contrary to the nature of sleep; it is simply a reinforced modification of a natural state of man, and an adherent of sleep.

Which brings us to this proposition, that every sleeper is a budding Somnambulist, that whosoever gives himself to sleep is in a state near Somnambulism, which is to develop in a more or less striking manner, according to the physical constitution of the sleeper, the nature of his illness, and above all according to the different causes which produce, precede, or accompany his sleep.

From there, it is easy to conceive that a patient already borne, either through temperament or through the nature of his illness, to a somewhat pronounced Somnambulism, is susceptible to receiving, with magnetic sleep, a greater determination toward Somnambulism.

Is a similar state useful to the cure of the illness? It is not a question of examining this at this time. Whether the Somnambulism is beneficial or not, it is still true that it is one of the dependencies of sleep, that it is introduced with it, and that it must consequently develop more or less, and it is that which I want to establish.

There are persons in whom magnetic drowsiness is accompanied by no striking signs of Somnambulism, who are only dulled and struck by a continual somnolence, meaning moreover quite well everything that is happening around them.

Others get drowsy from time to time, wake up at certain intervals, then fall back asleep. The differences are multiplied to infinity, beginning with the sleepers, who offer nothing except the appearance of sleep, to those who execute wondrous things which everyone talks about.

If these wonders which are left for me to render conceivable: for having proved that magnetic proceedings, that is to say, progressive contact combined according to the principles, can produce sleep, and, as a result, Somnambulism; at least it will be necessary to reduce Somnambulism to that which is already known. But the adversaries of Animal Magnetism will not fail to throw themselves upon the fact that Magnetic Somnambulism goes much further, offering the spectacle of a Somnambulism about which there is no idea, and which is accompanied by phenomena that had never been noticed in natural Somnambulism.

Such is the last allegation which serves as a refuge for the incredulity of those who have not seen Somnambulists, and the mistrust of those who have seen them. But one will be very surprised, in a moment, to see that Magnetic Somnambulism has nothing superior to Natural Somnambulism; that on the contrary it is found in a way exactly like that of this latter state, of which it is only the development. This consideration will appear to many people one of the most victorious arguments for the reality of Magnetic Somnambulism.

Francois Foveau de Courmelles

The first recorded experiments in hypnotism were performed on animals and were described by Athanasius Kircher, S.J., a Jesuit priest. A very concise historical survey of all the methods of magnetism and hypnotism was written by Francois Foveau de Courmelles, a French physician, who became interested in the utilization of hypnotism in his medical practice. In his book, special

PHYSIOLOGIA
KIRCHERIANA
EXPERIMENTALIS,

QUA

SUMMA ARGUMENTORUM
MULTITUDINE & VARIETATE

Naturalium rerum scientia per experimenta
Physica, Mathematica, Medica, Chymica, Musica, Magnetica, Mechanica comprobatur atque stabilitur.

QUAM

EX VASTIS OPERIBUS
Adm.Revdi. P. ATHANASII KIRCHERI

extraxit , & in hunc ordinem per classes redegit Romæ,
Anno M. DC. LXXV.

JOANNES STEPHANUS KESTLERUS Alsata,
Authoris discipulus, & in re litterariâ assecla, & coadjutor.

Levinus de Spiritu, Monasteriensis,

AMSTELODAMI,
Ex Officinâ JANSSONIO-WAESBERGIANA.
Anno cIↃ IↃc Lxxx.

FIGURE 7. Title page from Father Kircher's book on *experimental physiology,* published in 1680.

149

chapters are devoted to the schools of the Salpetriere at Nancy (Liebault) and the Charite of Paris (Charcot), and another to the anesthetizing effects of hypnotism and the dangers of hypnosis.

The work of Father Kircher covers an enormous field of endeavor in the scientific world. Of interest is the title page from one of his works:

ATHANASII KIRCHERI E., Soci Jesu: *Magneticum Naturae Regnum sive Disceptatio Physiologica de Triplica in Natura Rerum Magnetica.* Luxta Triplicem Eiusdem Naturae Gradum Digesto—Inanimato, Animato, Sensitivo, qua Occultae Prodigiosarum Qurundam Motionum Vires et Proprietates, Quae in Triplici Naturae Decononia Non-Nullis in Corporibus Noviter Delectis Observantur, in Apertam Lucim Eruuntur et Luculentis Argumentis, Experientia Duci, Demonstrantur, 1667.

This work is divided into four sections:

Sectio I. "De Viribus Naturae in Genere."
Sectio II. "De Magnetibus Animalis."
Sectio III. "De Magnetibus in Vegetabili Natura Existentibus —Sive de Solisequis et Lunesequis Magnetibus."
Sectio IV. "De Sensitivae Naturae Magnete."

SLEEP INDUCED IN ANIMALS*

Man is not the only being in creation in whom sleep can be artificially produced. I have shown this in a recent work on the mental faculties of animals, from which I shall quote largely. As early as the year 1636, Daniel Schwenter hypnotized cocks and hens, and invented an amusement which soon became popular in many countries. It was, however, only in 1646 that this mode of investigation was followed up—at least authentically—by Father Kircher, the ingenious inventor of the Eolian harp, and of magic lanterns. He put hens to sleep by tying their legs together and placing them before a chalk line drawn on the ground. This recalls the magic circle of the famous magnetizer, Baron du Potet,

*From De Courmelles, Foveau: *Hypnotism*. New York, George Routledge and Sons, Limited, 1819, pp. 257-275.

who with a bit of charcoal or chalk would trace on the ground some geometrical figure which his subjects were unable to cross; for when Father Kircher released the bird it remained motionless.

Binet and Féré mention a curious practice of the farmers' wives in Normandy. In order to induce a hen to sit on her eggs, they place her head under her wing and gently rock her to and fro. The bird falls asleep, and when she awakes will remain upon the nest she has been placed on. This method is used either to force the hen to sit, or to transfer her from one nest to another, without her manifesting any wish to return to the old one.

Colonel Albert de Rochas quotes several curious cases of hypnotism applied to animals. We will now give a detailed account of several of these experiments.

At Boston, in 1881, Bérard produced a cataleptic state in animals by means of fear, or a bright light, or music, magnetic passes, or a fixed gaze.

The magnetiser Lafontaine had already held public exhibitions in Paris, in which he reduced cats, dogs, squirrels, and lions to such complete insensibility that they felt neither pricks nor blows. He could throw lizards into a sleep that would last several days.

The Harvys or Psylles of Egypt impart to the ringed snake the appearance of a stick, by pressure on the head which induces a species of tetanus.

Monsieur Jacolliot tells us that the fakirs produce a cataleptic stiffness in snakes by soft and monotonous music, followed up by a fixed gaze and magnetic passes.

And as we have quoted the ex-judge at Chandernagor, we will now borrow from his book "Voyage au pays des perles", a few more remarks concerning the Aissaouas, or serpent charmers, of the province of Sous (Morocco), who publicly performed at the Paris Exhibition of 1889. He states that the fakirs perform similar feats. We have mentioned the insensibility of the Aissaouas themselves, and will now treat of their action on serpents.

Their instruments are long reeds shaped like flutes, and pierced at each end. By blowing into one of the holes they produce a melancholy sound, which they prolong harmoniously.

". . . The principal charmer began by whirling with astonishing rapidity in a kind of frenzied dance around the wicker-basket that contained the serpents, which were covered by a goat skin. Suddenly he stopped, plunged his naked arm into the basket, and drew out a cobra-de-capello, or else a haje, a fearful reptile which is able to swell its head by spreading out the scales that cover it, and which is thought to be Cleopatra's asp, the serpent of Egypt. In Morocco it is known as the buska. The charmer folded and unfolded the greenish-black viper, as if it were a piece of muslin; he rolled it like a turban round his head, and continued his dance while the serpent maintained its position, and seemed to follow every movement and wish of the dancer.

"The buska was then placed on the ground, and raising itself straight on end, in the attitude it assumes on desert roads to attack travellers, began to sway from right to left, following the rhythm of the music. The Aissaoua, whirling more and more rapidly in constantly narrowing circles, plunged his hand once more into the basket, and pulled out two of the most venomous reptiles of the deserts of Sous; serpents thicker than a man's arm, two or three feet long, whose shining scales are spotted black and yellow, and whose bite sends, as it were, a burning fire through the veins. This reptile is probably the torrida dipsas of antiquity. Europeans now call it the leffah.

"The two leffahs, more vigorous and less docile than the buska, lay half-curled up, their heads on one side ready to dart forward, and followed with glittering eyes the movements of the dancer . . . Hindoo charmers are still more wonderful; they juggle with a dozen different species of reptiles at a time, making them come and go, leap, dance, and lie down at the sound of the charmer's whistle, like the gentlest of tame animals. These serpents have never been known to bite their charmers."

Having considered the power of fascination which the charmer possesses over reptiles, we may mention the same power that the serpent itself possesses, which enables it to fascinate its prey with the fixed gaze of its glittering eye. After a certain time the exhausted victim yields to the reptile.

We have often heard it said by country folk—though we have had no opportunity of verifying the fact ourselves—that the common snake can fascinate in this way small birds, toads, and mice, with the result that the wretched little animals throw themselves into their enemy's jaws. The fear or ophidiophobia that produces this sensation is common to men and animals alike; it even attains in certain lower species a peculiar state of passive torpor. In such cases the brain is in a state of inhibition, or complete suspense; the motor muscles are paralysed, and cataleptic rigidity ensues.

The mere noise of the rattlesnake's tail has been known to render a man motionless and unable to escape. Travellers state that they have felt themselves forcibly impelled towards boa-constrictors.

In a letter to Sir E. Tennent—which he has published—Reyne relates that a charmer, whom he ascertained to have no tamed serpent about him, had on one occasion taken him to an ant-hill which he (Mr. Reyne) knew to be inhabited by an enormous cobra (Naja). At the sound of a fife the serpent appeared and danced, after having, however, bitten the knee of the charmer, who cured himself immediately by applying to the wound a serpent-stone.

Major Skinner was acquainted with a family at Negomba who used cobras as watch-dogs; the serpents were allowed to enter the apartments freely, and never hurt any one belonging to the house.

Houzeau denies the possibility of charming snakes. He holds that the charmers extract the venomous fangs of the reptiles which, notwithstanding the steadiness of the look fixed upon them, often rebel. In 1862 he saw at Matamoras, a half-breed charm a rattlesnake which turned out to be a harmless serpent, to which the fellow had attached the rattle of a real crotalus. Broderip mentions that he has observed movements of self-defence in reptiles.

Houzeau relates that though it is impossible to catch a pigeon by going straight up to the bird, it can be done by turning round and round it. The pigeon turns upon itself, so as not to lose sight of the person who is trying to catch it, and, as it seems to lose the notion of space, can soon be seized.

Romanes, Pennant, Thompson, and Le Vaillant believe in the

power of fascination, or rather in that of fear exercised by serpents on small animals. They have witnessed cases of death in squirrels, mice, and shrikes resulting from such fascination. Sir Joseph Fayrer maintains that fascination is only a synonym of fear. Dr. Barton of Philadelphia is very positive on the subject. He says that it is only the danger threatening their nests that causes fear in birds, and that fascination does not exist. Dr. Liebeault once saw a small bird fall to the ground in terror of a hawk. Montaigne mentions a bird which let itself fall, half-dead with fright, into the claws of a cat. A partridge will remain motionless before the eyes of a pointer. It has been found, in London, that a rabbit placed in front of a boa, becomes completely paralysed.

Fascination—linked probably with a sentiment of curiosity—may also be produced by fire or a light. A moth will flutter round a lamp and dash itself against it. The Paraguay horse and the African donkey are attracted by camp fires. Dolphins are attracted by the fires lit by fishermen. Migrating birds will deviate in their nocturnal flight, to hover in serried masses over the lights of a large city, of a lighthouse, or of a conflagration. The nature of this kind of fascination may become purely emotional, when, for instance, a flock of sheep, mad with terror, will rush into a blazing shed.

This hypnotic fascination has often been made use of by man.

Thus Balassa in 1828 stated that the most vicious horse can be shod if a person looks at it steadily in the eyes during the opeartion. Rarey mastered restive horses by magnetic passes over the neck and muzzle, and the incessant repetition of words uttered in a caressing tone. Czermack in 1873 induced catalepsy in birds, salamanders, crayfish and rabbits by simply fixing an object (either the finger or a match) before their eyes, and holding them motionless for a few minutes. Dr. Liebeault has on two occasions used the method proposed by Monsieur Morin for Martin's Menagerie, to appease snarling and ill-tempered dogs. He gives the following account: "I fixed my gaze steadily on a hound, that showed me his teeth whenever I entered his master's house, at the same time pointing two of my fingers at him like a fork. He barked for a long time, then drew back and cowered between the legs of one of the persons present. Then I called him; he came to me, allowed me to pat him and lay down near me. I tried a similar experiment on another dog of the same species said to be dangerous. But this time it was in the street and he was loose; he barked a great deal, but did not dare to approach me."

Hypnotism was, however, in full force, even before the word existed, in wild beast shows. A wild beast never attacks a man in front. The tamer's art is nothing else than suggestion in the waking state, such as it is practised on man; and does not consist in implanting a will foreign to his own, as suggestion is generally defined, but calling into action the subject's own disturbed imagination. Only in this case it is always the same idea that is suggested to the animal by fear—that of a power superior to its own.

The suggestion made by the more or less powerful or glittering gaze of the tamer, is assisted by mechanical means of correction or intimidation, and—magnetisers add—by the magnetic fluid. The animals are weakened either by being deprived of sleep and food, or by an abundant supply of purposely chosen debilitating food. But the tamer must above all be possessed of presence of mind, a steady eye, and calm and imperative audacity. Surrounding circumstances also aid him; the eyes of the spectators riveted on the performance intimidate the lion, and excite the man; a sudden, vivid light dazes the animal, and a diabolical, mad strain of music, ever the same, cows the beast. The man then appears; everything is at once hushed, as at the approach of a master; and the trembling, uneasy animal gives way before the man, who now advances with a firm step, strikes a violent blow on the bars with the loaded whip he holds in his hand, and goes in and out of the cage, without taking his eyes off the beast for one moment.

These performances go on for some time; then one fine day, we learn that the obedient animal has devoured his tamer; or, as was seen during a recent trial, that a young hypnotised girl who had been placed in a wild beasts' cage, has been torn to pieces.

The animal has taken its revenge, as was to be expected. Wild beast shows must be suppressed if we wish to avoid the repetition of similar accidents.

All the different degrees of sleep are to be met with in animals; lethargy, with complete inertia; catalepsy, with corpse-like rigidity; and somnambulism with the dreams and hallucinations of natural sleep, or the suggestions produced by provoked sleep. Dr. Tissie mentions that he had a goldfinch which he taught to whistle by hearing him during its sleep.

Simulated death is frequently seen in animals, and is generally due to catalepsy. In this case it is involuntary and the result of paralysis of the motor power, occasioned by fear.

"In a dark library cupboard," Couch relates, "there were certain articles of food which the mice evidently considered more worthy of their attention than the books. One day, on suddenly opening the cupboard, a mouse was seen on one of the shelves. The little creature was so transfixed by fear, that it looked dead, and did not stir even when taken up in the hand. Another day, on opening the drawing room door, a mouse was seen fixed and motionless in the middle of the room. On going up, it was found that it presented all the appearance of a dead animal, except that it had not turned over on its side. On various other occasions, several mice were seen together, completely deprived of motion. None of the little creatures made the slightest effort to escape; and they could be leisurely picked up. They were in no way injured, for in a short time they entirely recovered.

"It is by no means easy, as we know, to catch a weasel asleep, or at least off its guard; it would therefore seem still more unlikely that a weasel would allow itself to be rolled over, mawled about, and trampled on with impunity by a cat. This did however happen, for one day that pussy was lying quietly stretched out, seemingly regardless of all around her, a weasel most unexpectedly passed near her, and was in a second caught up and carried off to the house near at hand. The door, however, being shut, pussy deceived by the apparent death of her victim, laid it down on the doorstep and mewed according to her custom, for it to be opened. But, at this moment, the sharp little creature recovered its senses, and stuck its teeth in its enemy's nose. It is probable that beside the surprise of its sudden capture, the way in which the cat had held the weasel by the middle of the body, had till then prevented it from offering any resistance. By taking hold of these little quadrupeds in this manner, one can avoid being bitten; for it is difficult to believe that the weasel had the intention of deceiving the cat, all the time it was held in her mouth."

Professor Preyer has made some studies on hypnotism in animals, and declares that fear is a powerful predisposing cause of catalepsy (or mesmeric sleep) in animals. He even attributes the appearance presented by insects that simulate death, exclusively to a cataleptic state. This influence producing an analogous condition in the neuro-muscular system of a higher order of animals, even with the crayfish, which can be made, in an hypnotic condition, to stand on its head, it seems reasonable to attribute simulated death in insects to the same cause. Death and simulated death are easily distinguishable in every species of animal.

Insects, spiders, centipedes or death-watch, and crayfish fall into a state of complete insensibility (catalepsy) the moment they are alarmed, "but they recover," Romanes tells us, "directly after the exciting cause of alarm is removed."

Duncan, after having remarked that spiders, which simulate death, will allow pins to be stuck in them, and even be cut up, without betraying the slightest sign of terror, adds, that if the cause of this phenomenon were, as is often supposed, "a kind of stupor induced by terror," the insect would not recover immediately after the cause of its terror had disappeared. This is, however, really the case, for the cataleptic state continues even after the exciting cause has been removed. An owl, placed on its back, becomes insensible and remains so, even after it has been replaced in a natural position.

When the tail of a newt or the leg of a frog are suddenly pinched, the creature will remain for some time petrified, sometimes, indeed, for several minutes, and cannot move a limb.

To induce hypnosis in animals, it is necessary to make use of either gentle and prolonged, or strong, short, cutaneous excitations. If the nostrils of a guinea-pig are gently squeezed with a pair of pincers, it will be found, after a certain lapse of time, that its stupor is so great that it can be made to assume the most whimsical attitudes, without being awakened.

Heubel made experiments on frogs. If a frog is gently held between the fingers with the thumb on its abdomen, and the four fingers on its back, at the end of two or three minutes the creature will become perfectly motionless. It can then be stretched out on its back, or be put in the most fantastic positions, without its attempting to resist or escape. A similar paralytic state may be induced by gently scratching the frog on its back.

Catalepsy, caused either by disease or in provoked sleep, produces such rigidity in a human being, that it seems as though he would break like glass if any attempt were made to bend him. And is it not an analogous phenomenon that makes the little reptile called the slow-worm, with its rudimentary limbs hidden under its skin, break when caught hold of, just like a glass stick?

Darwin, in treating of simulated death in animals, has compared it with real death; and has ascertained that there is a vast difference between the attitudes of real and the simulated death.

Wrangel says that geese migrate in the direction of Tuddras at the moulting season, and that they are then incapable of escaping. They simulate death so completely—in cases of danger—that "their legs and necks are stretched out stiff and stark," and he himself has believed the geese to be dead, on seeing them in this position. The natives, the wolves, and the foxes, are, however, not deceived by this.

Darwin relates that, in Patagonia, a frightened lizard simulated death by "stretching itself out on the sand, which was the same colour as itself, and closing its eyes; if again disturbed, it would rapidly burrow in the sand."

Lethargy—sleep with inertia—exists also during hibernation. It seems as though the condition of those animals, such as dormice, marmots and bats, that sleep long days and months, should come under the definition of phenomena attributable to induced sleep. It is almost an exaggeration to call the hibernal condition cataleptic sleep, as Dr. Liebeault has done in his book on sleep. No special rigidity, proper to this phase of hypnotism, has ever been noticed in animals thus asleep, neither can it be attributed to suggestion—as Dr. Forel of Zurich seems to think.

"The accumulation of fat in the tissues predisposes man to sleep, and may well be the organic cause of hypnotic suggestion in the dormouse, as has been already supposed. A gradual emaciation would therefore finally induce the suggestion to awake. The theory of suggestive action is corroborated by the fact that in this state, sleep is succeeded by waking in a relatively abrupt manner, and vice versa, besides certain intermittences of sleep observed before the final and definitive awakening."

The same experimentalist has observed certain reflex movements in the sleeping dormouse; he has, for instance, seen one hang from a branch in this condition, and instinctively climb down without awaking.

J. C. Colquhoun

About the time that animal magnetism created controversy in England, J.C. Colquhoun translated the report of a committee of the medical section of the French Royal Academy of Sciences which appeared in 1831. Colquhoun noted that this report completely superseded the earlier unfavorable report of 1784. "The earlier report," so Colquhoun states, "supposed that animal magnetism was a system of quackery and delusion." This objection was thought to have had some plausibility during the infancy of the discovery of animal magnetism but now is a matter of ignorance, dishonesty, and selfishness. He felt that jealousy was at the seat of disclaiming the actual methods of animal magnetism.

Mr. Colquhoun takes a highly favorable view of Mesmer's life and character and quotes a dignified letter in which Mesmer refused a pension of 30,000 francs a year, made to him by the King of France through the Minister Maurepas, on the ground that the offer relates to his pecuniary interest alone and does not recognize the importance of his discovery as its principal motive.

Colquhoun also published in 1836 a very comprehensive review of the subject up to the period at which he wrote. The title was quite elaborate and mystic in its phraseology. "Isis Revelata, An Inquiry into the Origin, Progress, and Present State of Animal Magnetism."

REPORT ON THE MAGNETIC EXPERIMENTS MADE BY A COMMITTEE OF THE ROYAL ACADEMY OF MEDICINE*

Gentlemen,

More than five years have elapsed since a young physician, M. Foissac, whose zeal and talent for observation we have had frequent opportunities of remarking, thought it his duty to draw

---

*Report of the Experiments on Animal Magnetism, Made by a Committee of the Medical Section of the French Royal Academy of Sciences. Read at the meetings of the 21st and 28th of June, 1831; translated, and now for the first time published with historical and explanatory introduction by J.C. Colquhoun, Esq. Edinburgh, Printed for Robert Cadell, Edinburgh and Whittaker & Co., London, 1833.

160

the attention of the medical section to the phenomena of Animal Magnetism. With regard to the Report made by the Royal Society of Medicine in 1784, he recalled to our recollection, that, amongst the commissioners charged with conducting the experiments, there was one conscientious and enlightened man, who had published a Report in contradiction to that of his colleagues; that since the period in question, magnetism had been the object of new experiments and of new investigations; and, with the consent of the section, he proposed to submit to their examination a somnambulist who appeared to him to be capable of throwing light upon a question, which several of the most intelligent men in France and Germany considered as far from being resolved, although, in 1784, the Academy of Sciences and the Royal Society of Medicine had pronounced an unfavourable judgment.

A committee, composed of MM. Adelon, Burdin the elder, Marc, Pariset, and myself (M. Husson,) were appointed by you to report upon the proposition of M. Foissac.

The Report, which was presented to the Section of Medicine at its meeting of the 13th December 1825, concluded that magnetism ought to be subjected to a new investigation. This conclusion gave rise to an animated discussion, which was prolonged during three meetings—the 10th and 24th of January, and the 14th of February, 1826. At this last meeting, the committee replied to all the objections which had been made to their Report; and at the same meeting, after mature deliberation, after adopting the mode hitherto unusual in matters of science, of an individual scrutiny, the Section decided that a special committee should be appointed, in order to investigate anew the phenomena of animal magnetism.

This new committee, consisting of MM. Bourdois, Double, Itard, Gueneau, de Hussy, Guersent, Fouquier, Laennec, Leroux, Magendie, Marc, and Thillaye, was appointed at the meeting of the 28th of February 1826. Some time afterwards, M. Laennec, having been obliged to leave Paris on account of his health, I was named to replace him; and the committee, thus constituted, proceeded to discharge the duty with which it had been entrusted.

Their first care, previous to the retirement of M. Laennec, was to examine the somnambulist who had been offered to them by M. Foissac.

Various experiments were made upon her within the premises of the Academy; but we must confess that our inexperience, our impatience, our distrust, perhaps too strongly manifested, permitted us only to observe certain physiological phenomena sufficiently curious, which we shall communicate to you in the sequel of our Report, but in which we did not recognize any peculiar phenomena of somnambulism. This somnambulist, fatigued, no doubt, with our importunities, ceased, at this time, to be placed at our disposal; and we were obliged to search the hospitals for the means of prosecuting our experiments.

M. Pariset, physician to the Salpetriere, was more capable, than any other, of assisting us in our search. He set about the task with an ardour, which, unfortunately, led to no result. The committee, who founded a great part of their hopes upon the resources which this hospital might be capable of furnishing, whether in regard to the individuals who might be subjected to experiment, or to the presence of M. Magendie, who had requested to accompany them as one of the committee; the committee, we say, seeing itself deprived of those means of instruction which it had expected to find, had recourse to the zeal of each of its individual members.

M. Guersent promised us his assistance in the hospital des Enfans, M. Fouquier in the hospital de la Charite, MM. Gueneau and the Reporter in the Hotel-Dieu, M. Itard in the Institution for the Deaf and Dumb; and thenceforward, each prepared to make experiments, which were subsequently to be witnessed by the other members of the committee. Other and more powerful obstacles soon arrested our labours; the causes from which these obstacles proceeded are unknown to us; but, in virtue of a decree of the general council of the hospitals, of date the 19th of October 1825, which prohibited the use of every new remedy which had not previously been approved of by a committee appointed by the council, the magnetic experiments could not be continued at the hospital de la Charite.

Reduced to their own resources, to those which the particular relations of each of its individual members might present, the committee made an appeal to all the physicians who were known to make animal magnetism the object of their researches. We requested them to allow us to witness their experiments, to accompany them during their progress, and to confirm the results. We are bound to declare that we have been most effectually assisted in our investigations by several of our brethren, and especially by the gentleman who first suggested the enquiry, M. Foissac. We do not hesitate to declare that it is to his constant and persevering intervention, and to the active zeal of M. Dupotet, that we are indebted for the greater part of the materials embodied in the Report which we now present to you. Nevertheless, gentlemen, do not believe that your committee, in any circumstances intrusted to others than its own members the task of directing the experiments which we witnessed, that any others than the Reporter held the pen, at any instant, for the purpose of compiling the minutes of procedure, and of commemorating the succession of the phenomena which presented themselves, and exactly as they presented themselves. The committee proceeded to fulfill their duties with the most scrupulous exactness; and if we render justice to those who assisted us with their kind co-operation, we must, at the same time, destroy even the slightest suspicion which might arise in your minds with regard to the share, greater or less, which others than ourselves may be supposed to have had in the investigation of this question. Your committee always suggested the different modes of experimenting, traced the plan of inquiry, directed the course to be perused, followed and described its progress. Finally, in availing ourselves of the services of auxiliaries more or less zealous and enlightened, we have always been present, and always impressed our own direction upon everything that has been done.

Thus you will see that we admit no experiment made without the presence of the committee, even by members of the academy. Whatever confidence the spirit of confraternity, and the reciprocal esteem with which we are all animated, ought to establish amongst us, we felt that in the investigation of a question of which the solution is so delicate, we should trust none but ourselves, and that you could trust only to our guarantee. From this rigorous exclusion, however, we have thought proper to except a very curious phenomenon observed by M. Cloquet, which we have admitted, because it was already, in a manner, the property of the academy, the section of surgery having been occupied in its investigation at two of its meetings.

This reserve, gentlemen, which the committee imposed upon itself, in regard to the use of various facts relative to the question which we studied with so much care and impartiality, would give us the right to demand a return of confidence, if any persons who had not witnessed our experiments should be inclined to raise discussions in regard to their authenticity. For the same reason that we only demand your confidence in respect of what we ourselves have seen and done, we cannot admit that those who, at the same time as ourselves and along with us, had neither seen nor done, can attack or call in question that which we allege to have observed. And, moreover, as we always entertained the greatest distrust of the announcements which were made to us of wonders to come, and this feeling constantly predominated during all our researches, we think we have some right to require that, although you may suspend your belief, you will, at least, raise no doubt in regard to the moral and physical dispositions with which we always proceeded to the observation of the various phenomena of which we were witnesses.

Thus, gentlemen, this Report, which we are far from presenting to you with the view of fixing your opinion upon the question of magnetism, cannot and ought not to be considered in any other light, than as the combination and classification of the facts which we have hitherto observed: We offer it to you as a proof that we have endeavoured to justify your confidence; and while we regret that it is not founded upon a greater number of experiments, we trust that you will receive it with indulgence, and that you will hear it read with some interest. At the same time, we think ourselves bound to make you aware, that what we have seen in the course of our experiments bears no sort of resemblance to what the report of 1784 relates with regard to the magnetizers of that period. We neither admit nor reject the existence of a fluid, because we have not verified the fact; we do not speak of the baquet,—of the baguette,—of the chain established by the medium of a communication of the hands of all the magnetized patients,—of the application of means prolonged, sometimes during several hours, to the hypochondriac region and the stomach, —of the vocal and instrumental music which accompanied the magnetic operations,—nor of the assemblage of a great number of people together, who were magnetized in the presence of a crowd of witnesses; because all our experiments were made in the most complex stillness, in the most absolute silence, without any accessory means, never by immediate contact, and always upon a single person at a time.

We do not speak of that which, in the time of Mesmer, was so improperly called the crisis, and which consisted of convulsions, of laughter, sometimes irrepressible, of immoderate weeping, or of piercing cries, because we have never met with these different phenomena.

In all these respects, we do not hesitate to declare, that there exists a very great difference between the facts observed and decided upon in 1784, and those which we have collected in the work which we have the honour to present to you; that this difference establishes a most glaring line of demarcation between the one and the other; and that, if reason has done justice in regard to a great proportion of the former, the spirit of observation and research should endeavour to multiply and appreciate the latter.

It is with magnetism, gentlemen, as with many of the other operations of nature, that is to say, a certain combination of conditions is required in order to the production of such and such effects. This is an incontrovertible principle, which, if it required any proof, might be confirmed by that which takes place in diverse physical phenomena. Thus, I am sure that you have all likewise heard of a case, which, at the time, attracted the attention of the surgical section, and which was communicated to it at the meetings of the 16th of April, 1829, by M. Jules Clocquet. Your committee have thought it their duty to notice it here, as affording one of the most unequivocal proofs of the power of the magnetic sleep. The case is that of a lady, P . . . aged 64 years, residing in the street of St Denis, No. 151, who consulted M. Clocquet, upon the 8th of April, 1829, on account of an ulcerated cancer on the right breast, of several years standing, which was combined with a considerable swelling (engorgement) of the corresponding axillary ganglions. M. Chapelain, the ordinary physician attending this lady, who had magnetized for her some months, with the intention, as he said, of dissolving the swelling (engorgement) of the breast, had obtained no other result than that of producing a most profound sleep, during which all sensibility appeared to be annihilated, while the ideas retained all their clearness. He proposed to M. Clocquet to operate upon her while she plunged in this magnetic sleep. The latter having deemed the operation indispensable, consented. The two previous evenings, this lady was magnetized several times by M. Chapelain, who, in her somnambulism, disposed her to submit to the operation,—who had even led her to converse about it with calmness, although, when awake, she rejected the idea with horror.

Upon the day fixed on for the operation, M. Clocquet arriving at half-past ten in the morning, found the patient dressed and seated on an elbow-chair, in the attitude of a person enjoying a quiet natural sleep. She had returned about an hour before from mass, which she attended regularly at the same hour. Since her return, M. Chapelain had placed her in a state of magnetic sleep, and she talked with great calmness of the operation to which she was about to submit. Every thing having been arranged for the operation, she undressed herself, and sat down upon a chair.

M. Chapelain supported the right arm, the left was permitted to hang down at the side of the body. M. Pailloux, house pupil of the hospital of St. Louis, was employed to present the instruments, and to make the ligatures. A first incision commencing at the arm pit was continued beyond the tumour as far as the internal surface of the breast. The second, commenced at the same point, separated the tumour from beneath, and was continued until it met the first: The swelled ganglions (ganglions engorges) were dissected with precaution on account of their vicinity to the axillary artery, and the tumour was extirpated. The operation lasted from ten to twelve minutes.

During all this time, the patient continued to converse quietly with the operator, and did not exhibit the slightest sign of sensibility. There was no motion of the limbs or of the features, no change in the respiration nor in the voice, no emotion even in the pulse. The patient continued in the same state of automatic indifference and impassibility, in which she was some minutes before the operation. There was no occasion to hold, but only to support her. A ligature was applied to the lateral thoracic artery, which was open during the extraction of the ganglions: The wound was united by means of adhesive plaster, and dressed. The patient was put to bed while still in a state of somnambulism, in which she was left for forty-eight hours. An hour after the operation, there appeared a slight hemorrhage, which was attended with no consequence. The first dressing was taken off on the following Tuesday, the 14th,—the wound was cleaned and dressed anew— the patient exhibited no sensibility nor pain—the pulse preserved its usual rate.

After this dressing, M. Chapelain awakened the patient, whose somnambulistic sleep had continued from an hour previous to the operation, that is to say, for two days. This lady did not appear to have any idea, any feeling of what had passed in the interval; but upon being informed of the operation and seeing her children around her, she experienced a very lively emotion, which the magnetizer checked by immediately setting her asleep.

To all these facts which we have so laboriously collected, which we have observed with so much distrust and attention, which we have endeavoured to classify in such a manner as might best enable you to follow the development of the phenomena which we witnessed, which we have, above all, exerted ourselves to present to you disengaged from all those accessory circumstances which might have embarrassed or perplexed the narrative; we might add those which ancient, and even modern history have recorded on the subject of previsions which frequently have been realized, on the cures effectuated by the imposition of the hands, on ecstasies, on the convulsionaries, on oracles, on hallucinations; in short, on all that, remote from those physical phenomena which may be explained upon the principle of the action of one body upon another, enters into the domain of physiology, and may be considered as an effect depending upon a moral influence not appreciable by the senses. But the committee was appointed for the purpose of investigating somnambulism, for the purpose of making experiments relative to this phenomenon, which had not been studied by the commissioners of 1784, and of reporting to you. We should, then, have exceeded the limits prescribed to our inquiries, if, in attempting to support that which we ourselves had seen by the authority of others who had observed analogous phenomena, we had swelled out our report with facts which were foreign to it. We have related with impartiality what we have seen with distrust; we have exposed in order what we have observed in different circumstances,—what we have prosecuted with the most anxious, minute and unremitted attention. We are conscious that the report which we present to you is the faithful exposition of all we have observed. The obstacles which we have encountered in our progress are known to you. They are, in some measure, the cause of the delay which has taken place in presenting our report, although the materials have been for a long time in our hands. Nevertheless, we are far from wishing to excuse ourselves or to complain of this delay, since it confers upon our observations a character of maturity and of reserve, which ought to secure your confidence in the facts which we relate, divested of that prejudice and enthusiasm with which you might have reproached us, had we collected them in haste. We may add, that we are far from thinking that we have seen all; we do not, therefore, pretend to desire you to admit as an axiom, that there is nothing positive in magnetism beyond what we have noticed in our report. Far from setting limits to this part of physiological science, we hope on the contrary, that a new field has been opened up to it; and warranting the authenticity of our own observations, presenting them with confidence to those who, after us, may wish to engage in the investigation of magnetism, we shall only deduce from them the following.

CONCLUSIONS

The conclusions of the report are the result of the observations of which it is composed.

1. The contact of the thumbs or of the hands; frictions, or certain gestures which are made at a small distance from the body, and called passes, are the means employed to place ourselves in magnetic connection, or, in other words, to transmit the magnetic influence to the patient.

2. The means which are external and visible are not always necessary, since, on many occasions, the will, the fixed look, have been found sufficient to produce the magnetic phenomena, even without the knowledge of the patient.

3. Magnetism has taken effect upon persons of different sexes and ages.

4. The time required for transmitting the magnetic influence with effect, has varied from half an hour to a minute.

5. In general, magnetism does not act upon persons in a sound state of health.

6. Neither does it act upon all sick persons.

7. Sometimes, during the process of magnetizing, there are manifested insignificant and evanescent effects, which cannot be attributed to magnetism alone; such as a slight degree of oppression, of heat or of cold and some other nervous phenomena, which can be explained without the intervention of a particular agent—upon the principle of hope or of fear, prejudice and the novelty of the treatment, the ennui produced by the monotony of the gestures, the silence and repose in which the experiments are made; finally, by the imagination, which has so much influence on some minds and on certain organizations.

8. A certain number of the effects observed appeared to us to depend upon magnetism alone, and were never produced without its application. These are well established physiological and therapeutic phenomena.

9. The real effects produced by magnetism are very various. It agitates some, and soothes others. Most commonly, it occasions a momentary acceleration of the respiration and of the circulation

fugitive fibrillary convulsive motions resembling electric shocks a numbness in a greater or less degree, heaviness, somnolency and in a small number of cases, that which the magnetizers call somnambulism.

10. The existence of an uniform character, to enable us to recognize, in every case, the reality of the state of somnambulism has not been established.

11. However, we may conclude with certainty that this state exists, when it gives rise to the development of new faculties, which have been designated by the names of clairvoyance; intuition; internal prevision; or when it produces great changes in the physical economy, such as insensibility; a sudden and considerable increase of strength; and when these effects cannot be referred to any other cause.

12. As among the effects attributed to somnambulism there are some which may be feigned, somnambulism itself may be feigned, and furnish to quackery the means of deception.

Thus, in the observation of those phenomena which do not present themselves again but as insulated facts, it is only by means of the most attentive scrutiny, the most rigid precautions, and numerous and varied experiments, that we can escape illusion.

13. Sleep produced with more or less promptitude, is a real but not a constant effect of magnetism.

14. We hold it as demonstrated that it has been produced in circumstances, in which the persons magnetized could not see or were ignorant of the means employed to occasion it.

15. When a person has once been made to fall into a magnetic sleep, it is not always necessary to have recourse to contact, in order to magnetize him anew. The look of the magnetizer, his volition alone, possess the same influence. We can not only act upon the magnetized person, but even place him in a complete state of somnambulism, and bring him out of it without his knowledge, out of his sight, at a certain distance, and with doors intervening.

16. In general, changes, more or less remarkable, are produced upon the perception and other mental faculties of those individuals who fall into somnambulism, in consequence of magnetism.

A. Some persons amidst the noise of a confused conversation hear only the voice of their magnetizer; several answer precisely the questions he puts to them, or which are addressed to them by those individuals with whom they have been placed in magnetic connection; others carry on conversation with all persons around them.

Nevertheless, it is seldom that they hear what is passing around them. During the greater part of the time, they are completely strangers to the external and unexpected noise which is made close to their ears, such as the sound of copper vessels struck briskly near them, the fall of a piece of furniture, etc.

B. The eyes are closed, the eyelids yield with difficulty to the efforts which are made to open them; this operation, which is not without pain, shows the ball of the eye convulsed, and carried upwards, and sometimes towards the lower part of the orbit.

C. Sometimes the power of smelling appears to be annihilated. They (the subjects) may be made to inhale muriatic acid, or ammonia without feeling any inconvenience, nay, without perceiving it. The contrary takes place in certain cases, and they retain the sense of smelling.

D. The greater number of the somnambulists whom we have seen were completely insensible. We might tickle their feet, their nostrils and the angle of the eyes with a feather, we might pinch their skin so as to leave a mark, prick them with pins under the nails, &c. without producing any pain, without even their perceiving it. Finally, we saw one who was insensible to one of the most painful operations in surgery, and who did not manifest the slightest emotion in her countenance, her pulse, or her respiration.

17. Magnetism is as intense, and as speedily felt, at a distance of six feet, as of six inches; and the phenomena developed are the same in both cases.

18. The action at a distance does not appear capable of being exerted with success, excepting upon individuals who have been already magnetized.

19. We only saw one person who fell into somnambulism upon being magnetized for the first time. Sometimes, somnambulism was not manifested until the 8th or 10th sitting.

20. We have invariably seen the ordinary sleep, which is the repose of the organs of sense, of the intellectual faculties, and the voluntary motions, precede and terminate the state of somnambulism.

21. While in the state of somnambulism, the patients, whom we have observed, retain the use of the faculties which they possessed when awake. Even their memory appeared to be more faithful and more extensive, because they remembered every thing that passed at the time, and every time they were placed in the state of somnambulism.

22. Upon awaking, they said they had totally forgotten the circumstances which took place during the somnambulism, and never recollected them. For this fact we can have no other authority than their own declarations.

23. The muscular powers of somnambulists are sometimes benumbed and paralyzed. At other times, their motions are constrained, and the somnambulists walk or totter about like drunken men, sometimes avoiding, and sometimes not avoiding the obstacles which may happen to be in their way. There are some somnambulists who preserve entirely the power of motion; there are even some who display more strength and agility than in their waking state.

24. We have seen two somnambulists who distinguished, with their eyes closed, the objects which were placed before them; they mentioned the color and the value of cards, without touching them they read words traced with the hand, as also some lines of books opened at random. This phenomenon took place even when the eyelids were kept exactly closed with the fingers.

25. In two somnambulists we found the faculty of foreseeing the acts of the organism more or less remote, more or less complicated. One of them announced repeatedly, several months previously, the day, the hour, and the minute of the access and of the return of epileptic fits. The other announced the period of his cure. Their previsions were realized with remarkable exactness. They appeared to us to apply only to acts or injuries of their organism.

26. We found only a single somnambulist who pointed out the

symptoms of the diseases of three persons with whom she was placed in magnetic connection. We had, however, made experiments upon a considerable number.

27. In order to establish with any degree of exactness the connection between magnetism and therapeutics, it would be necessary to have observed its effects upon a great number of individuals, and to have made experiments every day, for a long time, upon the same patients. As this did not take place with us, your committee could only mention what they perceived in too small a number of cases to enable them to pronounce any judgment.

28. Some of the magnetized patients felt no benefit from the treatment. Others experienced a more or less decided relief: viz. one, the suspension of habitual pains; another, the return of his strength; a third, the retardation for several months of his epileptic fits; and a fourth the complete cure of a serious paralysis of long standing.

29. Considered as a cause of certain physiological phenomena, or as a therapeutic remedy, magnetism ought to be allowed a place within the circle of the medical sciences; and, consequently, physicians only should practise it, or superintend its use, as is the case in the northern countries.

30. Your committee have not been able to verify, because they had no opportunity of doing so, other faculties which the magnetizers had announced as existing in somnambulists. But they have communicated in their report facts of sufficient importance to entitle them to think, that the Academy ought to encourage the investigations into the subject of animal magnetism, as a very curious branch of psychology and natural history.

Arrived at the termination of our labours, before closing this Report, your committee have asked themselves, whether, in the precautions which we have multiplied around us, in order to avoid all surprise; whether in the feeling of continual distrust, in which all our proceedings were conducted; whether in the examination of the phenomena observed, we have scrupulously fulfilled our commission. What other course could we have followed? What means more certain could we have adopted? With what distrust more decided and more discreet could we have been actuated? Our conscience, gentlemen, proudly answers, that you could expect nothing from us but what we have done. In short, have we been honest, exact and faithful observers? It is for you who have long been acquainted with us, for you who see us continually near you, whether in the intercourse of the world, or at our frequent meeting,—it is for you to answer this question. Your answer, gentlemen, we expect from the long friendship of some of you, and from the esteem of all.

Indeed, we dare not flatter ourselves with the hope of making you participate entirely in our conviction of the reality of the phenomena which we have observed, and which you have neither seen, nor followed, nor studied along with us. We do not, therefore, demand of you a blind belief of all that we have reported. We conceive that a great proportion of these facts are of a nature so extraordinary, that you cannot accord them such a credence. Perhaps we ourselves might have dared to manifest a similar incredulity, if, in changing characters, you came to announce them here to us, who, like you, at present, had neither seen, nor observed, nor studied, nor followed any thing of the kind.

We only request that you would judge us, as we should judge you,—that is to say, that you be completely convinced, that neither the love of the marvellous, nor the desire of celebrity, nor any views of interest whatever, influenced us during our labours. We were animated by higher motives and more worthy of you— by the love of science, and by an anxiety to justify the expectations you had formed of our zeal, and of our devotion.

Signed by Bourdois de la Motte, President; Fouquier, Gueneau, de Hussy, Guersent, Husson, Itard, J.J. Leroux, Marc, Thillaye.

Note: MM. Double and Magendie did not consider themselves entitled to sign the Report, as they had not assisted in making the experiments.

Baron Du Potet de Sennevoy

Baron Du Potet was one of the early French writers on mesmerism; he lived at the same time as did de Puysegur and Deleuze. He was very successful in his therapy and did not mind the criticism and ridicule he received from his colleagues. He published many books on mesmerism and was the product of French and not English literary tradition.

He quickly outgrew the limits of magnetic practice which was familiar to his predecessors. He became more than a mesmerist and occultist, and became attached to the use of medieval magic. He found these signs in books and was inclined to attach too much objective importance to the diagrams. He did not realize how far the magic lay in his own magnetic force and how little of it had to do with the signs.

Baron Du Potet invented the magic mirror which convulsed so many people. In all this, he fancied he saw magic; but hypnotism obtained by physical means brings about the same results.

In his book, *A Course in Animal Magnetism,* he indulges in some very scornful language concerning the lack of acceptance of mesmerism exhibited by the scientific world at large in regard to the accumulated facts of mesmeric experience.

A COURSE IN ANIMAL MAGNETISM*

Sirs,

Convinced of a real truth, I hesitated for a long time to say it. I thought that if I was to confess it a little at a time, I would not frighten the people who are going to suffer because of it. My speeches did not touch them. My cries found them deaf, and the phenomena that should have enlightened them did not get through to them. Should I have said nothing and kept for me the germ I believe to be prolific? Should I have imitated our scholars? Just let the generation who push us try to develop and to make known a truth which will enlighten all the sciences? No, I push away

---

*Du Potet de Sennevoy, M. le Comte: *Cours de Magnétisme Animal par Du Potet de Sennevoy.* A l' Athénée Central, Passage du Saumon, Galarie du Salon, Paris, 1834.

175

the cold hearts,—hearts which the pains of humanity do not move, more sensible to their own interest of science.

I realized but too late, that my sincere speeches would not find any echo among them; and regretting the time vainly lost, I took the resolution to spread to the world what the scholars would have usually been the first to know. So let them accuse themselves. Let them suffer the scorn that people have the right to address to them. And if some irreparable mistake has happened, the ones who have to be blamed are the scholars. They were the ones who should have showed the way, and they did not.

We are going to unfold in front of you all the intricacies of a famous process. This process will interest all humanity, because it is about a new art of curing the pains from which we suffer, and it must replace the sciences, morals and physics in this examination. We are going to overcome our weakness. We will talk to you without hate and without passion. Our language will be sincere and our confession perhaps stronger than prudence would require. Our language will leave you no doubt on the sincerity of my intentions. Let us start, therefore, the examination of this important question.

Let us plant deeply into your spirit the conviction that dominates us, and seeing that you are here you will become one of my judges. It is your duty to listen to me attentively.

Sirs, from everywhere honorable men with the same judgment are calling to the world an old discovery which has always been contested. They say man has wonderful powers which equal him almost to God. Man can act on his likeness and on all of nature. Man can be put in a condition or state where his greater destiny on earth is revealed to him. Man can also, as he wishes, modify what seems to escape his senses. This moral and physical action can be recognized, studied, proven, because all men are able to feel and communicate it. There is only the ignorance or the insincerity that can put it in doubt.

To those positive assertions, what is the answer to the people in possession of the science and at the head of opinion? They say all the marvels you are telling us are lies. The oldest antiquity believed in the power of men over men, at the revelations, the previsions, and every time people have been found who were pretending to have a supernatural power. But there have also been found some scholars like us, who were earning the true light and who justified all those dreams. Stop pursuing us with your propositions of examinations, since science does not have anything to learn from you. You are crazy or imbeciles. We only pity you!

Happy scholars, we kneel in front of your lights, your genius, and the nation must build your altars!

Vulgarity bends and lowers the head! She quotes with pride the names of those illustrious scholars whose judgments she adopts for articles of faith. This does not surprise me at all. Men seem to be made for lying, without that it would have been difficult to exploit him. Ah! Sirs, I cannot predict for you the feeling that I experience. It is not anger. It is not scorn. It is a deep affection, especially the view of the obstacles which have always opposed the reign of the truth on earth. So it is really *"that God has delivered the world to the plight of man."* It is true that every thing will always be doubt and uncertainty, and that the nations like the individual will disappear from the earth without leaving any thing else for proof of their passage, only vain opinions.

Man in the middle of this chaos will come to say to the world: "Stop your running, the truth you are after is deep within you. It has followed you everywhere, although you have not recognized it. When you thought that you had caught it you were only holding its shadows!" This man will obtain as a reward for his virtue and his happy genius, only exile and the gallows. Dismiss far from us this sad truth. Let us forget, if it is possible, the history of the old times; but brand with a red hot iron the scholars of our time, who less cruel than their predecessors, have not been more concerned for their honor or for more friends of the truth.

Let the torch of truth shine in your eyes; that her bright clarity penetrate you, that her rays show you the untrue knowledge covered by the coat of the truth. It will not be possible to abuse you and to make you believe in a superiority that only comes from a default of examination and habit. You have let the others have the responsibility of ruling your destiny. What will happen to our great doctors, if we prove to you that each individual has in himself a natural, superior, principal intelligence? What will they do with their knowledge amassed with so much care, if their fallacy is soon recognized in their virgin brain? Is it possible to find material which would confuse them?

And you philosophical dreamers, who believe that you know man and his destiny. Tear your system, because when you wrote it, each one of you had less sense.

Ah! I feel how important and beautiful my mission is, but I do not have any illusions. I know in advance the dangers that are strewn on my road, but I do not mind. I am proud of my courage, it won't leave me. My only fear is that the weaknesses of my means do not offer you, Sirs, a defender as good and as important as truth requires.

So, I am calling all generous men and I am telling them: "The magnetism is a powerful lever that can lift the moral world and the physical world. Help me to make it move; but why this doubt and this hesitation?"

Let me convince you, and if your good faith attracts ironic comments in you, then throw off the yoke of indifference and selfishness. They do not have ears and no entrails. Nothing can move them.

Nevertheless my speeches did not find any echo among you. Ah! I will not be angry with you. I know too well the power of all the presumption, and the vain systems that reign today. But then, it was the scholars of our academy, who under the veil of prudence kept a cowardly silence. The light that they are running from will spread in spite of them. They will soon hear people who are strangers to all science say to them, "Those men have backed up in front of everything that could enlighten them. They thought that lies could serve their interest. They have fought honesty and virtue; and when under their eyes some facts of indignation will happen—facts that they won't be called to judge, because they will have lost the sight of it—let each one realize the confusion of their soul and remember that truth for one who denied it is a worm that gnaws at the heart, and an iron that burns, and he cannot escape from the remorse of his bad actions."

And when the doctors come to complain that magnetism invades medicine, and that without their knowledge one can cure their patients, here is what will be said to them, "When Mesmer came among you, you thought that you deserved to know his doctrine. He pleased you, begged you to examine the results. He wanted you, and you alone for judges of his system. You have said and published without even wanting to hear him. You have said that he was a charlatan, a visionary. Then, after having heard him, you added your sickening epithet that the magnetic doctrine was dangerous and treacherous. You have even encouraged the government to forbid it."

Later, some men recognizing the falsity of your judgments, men like Puysegur, Deleuze and hundreds of others called you in good faith. You did not want to hear them. Your ears were deaf to the truths that their works revealed. You did not want to hear the accusations that were thrown against them. The people used to defend only the abused. When some generous men came as far as your sanctuary to try to convince you in curing a few of your patients; the laughs and the sarcasm were the first welcome that you gave them. But forced to give themselves up to the evident proofs that were furnished you by the magnetizers, you have kept silent. You had to justify to yourselves the denial of justice for which you were being accused. You have again, in some insignificant reports confessed half of the facts. You have not published what you recognized to be the real truth.

Although the truth in spite of your shackle came out of the circle you had drawn around it, the magnetism that you had thought dead is rising after many centuries. It is now triumphant, and spreading its wings over the world.

Powerful genius who embraces the universe! Ah, if a bad destiny wanted you to stay unknown for a long time, and if you had supported those fights, your triumph would be all the more glorious!

The public has read your reports, Sirs. They have even printed and delivered them in spite of you to the judgment of men who love to be clever. One has penetrated the causes of your reticence, guessed your cause of hate; and, learning that you needed six years to produce so little work, one has said to himself that never in our days would the truth be welcome by you. The magnetism, even if it could not bury anyone, would still be too important by all the news that it would bring.

You wanted to hide the truth; but it happened at a time where lies crumble by themselves. Misfortune has resisted the truth too long because their defeat is more than ignominious.

The truth goes directly to the objective. It works in the open. It does not cheat; but each time it strikes, it strikes right.

We will make the one who has accused our intentions tremble. And one day all together, we will invert the altar where one adores the false gods, the temples where they sacrifice only human victims, and, taking off the mask of the lying priests who receive the offering, we will show them covered with the blood of their brothers. We will take back the power that they have usurped, power of life and death. Society, taking back its rights, will not be a herd of sheep that power shears whenever it wants to, and that a body known as the "Faculty of Medicine" decimates as it wishes without having to justify it even in front of its accomplices.

Raise now the statue of Aesculapides, place it under your porch, but remember that it was in the temples of this god that people were going to sleep for the recovery of their health, and that they only go in yours to die.

It is time to pull off the mask of the impostor. We will go together and we will see all its deformities. A thousand times more hideous, it is put on the side of the truth as pretty as it is. We will show this power of man that makes us so happy. We will despise the feeling of the perverse.

It is to the man of good that we will talk, and instead of following the device of our antagonist who is: "our self for our self, and the other for us," we will say: "our self for the others, our self for humanity!"

Magnetism! Power that come from the soul! Power that is born with man, and dies with him. Power that covers the distance with the rapidity of the thoughts, and that strikes the object to whom it has attached itself. Unnatural power that we cannot express with words is power which comes from the divinity and makes man big, noble, and equal to God. This power can crush man like lightning, and, although invisible it is stronger and more powerful than all the physical forces that man has put together.

But it is necessary to experience that man has an absolute empire on all his thoughts. It is necessary for him to be sane of any impure thoughts, so no remorse will come to take possession of him in all his vigour. O, you who wanted to magnetize, think that this force is divine and that it cannot unite itself with vice.

Begin to purify your soul, hunt all bad thoughts, and do not touch Holy things with profane hands. Let only the desire of doing good to humanity be your only valour, and you will have enough of it.

You will crush the head of the ugly monster of imposture, and the enjoyment in doing good will make you taste in advance the happiness of pure joy that the wise expect for the end of their life. But do not mistake all those joys and pleasure. Do not come without penalty and without words. Keep your self out of the nonchalance, tell yourself it is necessary, I want it! And let a continued action emit from your heart this principle of life more precious than all your riches. As soon as the lazy man stops wishing, his arms will stop obeying him. Do not complain of your weakness, we always have enough physical forces when the soul and the heart agree.

The wise who are really wise have always the forces of the soul that they received from nature. Only death can take it away from him. Well, imitate him, be like him, do not let the trouble go into your soul. Armed with a strong will, and full of confidence in the truth, you will find some men who will tell you that you are an impostor, an enthusiastic, a dreamer, and perhaps they will call you roguish, even killer. So that your heart does not get discouraged, keep on doing good to man by relieving his pain and spreading a doctrine, simple and consoling. It is the only true one, because it relies entirely on nature and on its immutable laws. By this approach you will even gain your enemies. Do not flee from them. Go straight to them, ask them what is the cause of their incredulity. Try to make them come to see the facts. Show them that nature obeys your desires when they are founded on good.

If they still do not believe, submit them to your action. Penetrate into their organs the facts of life which you can dispose of. Do it without hate and without anger. You will have much more power. The smallest facts that you will produce will be more convincing for them than all those they have seen you produce on others. Teach them the mechanism of your action. Tell them that the will to act is the first step. Put them then in the most favorable circumstances.

Do so, and let them try their new born power on children or on sleeping men. And when they see those people sensibly woven from far away by some simple movements of the hand, you will have attained your objective. You will have convinced the incredulous, you will have then only to moderate your zeal.

He called you enthusiastic. He will be enthusiastic himself. He will be even more enthusiastic than you! Because you know how you act, this will be your reason. Illuminate by experience and by truth, but he will not yet know it. You will see him provoke the effect that he will be able to control. You will have to help him with your advice, to correct his mistakes, and perhaps to repair the accidents for which he would have been responsible. He will soon learn to read in the book of nature. He will then feel all that is great and sublime in magnetism. He will cherish you who have taken the lead. Even though his eyes were covered, and his soul grateful, he will find a way to pay for the services that you have rendered to him. Some expressions will touch your heart, because it exists as a moral in the deep of magnetism, a moral pure as the Divine essence, Ah! If only those who feel it could talk. They would express to you what the mouth can say. The Divine things are not made to be explained by man in this state of nature because, "It is only flesh that is talking." Corrupt man, filthy man! How do you want your creation to be sublime? You deny what the great genius has done because you cannot tolerate their work. Blind, you deny light because you need an organ to be able to see it.

Let us stop to draw so sad a picture. The man who does not care about any body, does he need us to care about him? It is to you, man of good heart, that we are directing our doctrines. It is you that we are willing to convince. When you will be convinced, the ignorance and the stupidity will back up with fear, or perhaps they will come by themselves to bring you the tribute of their defeat. "Listen," I will say to the good and sensible man who wants to be interested in magnetism, "Do you want to know the enjoyment that will be the fruit of your studies? I cannot express them to you; it is nature itself that will give them to you."

When relieving a patient at the expense of your life, you will see him fall into a good sleep. Interrogate him and he will answer you. You will learn from him the cause of his illness, the necessary remedy, and then, you will become a doctor, a prophet, and a philosopher. He will teach you everything by his lessons, everything that nature has hidden from our weak eyes. Your eyes are spread by the entrancing pictures that will draw his genius, will charm your spirit. You will then stop to be in the common crowd. You will begin to become a real man. The presumption is that education and time had amassed your intelligence. It will disappear by degree, like the night at the approach of the sun which illuminates us.

Never abuse my secrets! The one who plays with magnetism is crazy, because it is a divine emanation, and to use it to satisfy a vain curiosity, it is like committing a sacrilegeous action!

"Sleep, magnetic! Sleep of happiness, where the soul is free of the body, where the soul hovers and seems to fly"! Nature is its domain. It tastes the felicity and the body is not its prison any more. Happiness, inexpressible, that no word can make you feel! Words, echo without life, you can only give sounds without value. The soul has other organs than you, but to hear it, it is not ears that you need, it is a conscience, and then its language is even more expressive because the flesh is more asleep!

How could they be erudite, those who wrote on the doors of their temples: "Man, know yourself." They knew without any doubt what exists under our opaque and rough body. Nature taught it to them, and if their secret has not come on to us, it is only the arrogance of man and his vanity who has to be accused, because he thinks he knows every thing, but he knows nothing.

He does not want to recognize sobriety, even the one who thinks he is a genius! Why then, unveil the mystery to him; if his heart does not feel the kindness and is grateful for it.

It is not enough to be persistent in work, it is necessary to recognize what leads to the truth.

So, man has looked everywhere to find some means of conservation, which he thought he had found in the "inorganic body" that relieves the pains he suffers from. So, the electricity, the galvanization, the mineral magnetism has been praised like some sovereign remedy for certain illnesses.

But a dead body lying beside a live body would not reheat him! So, the dead fluid instead of giving life like it pretends, only carries in his organ a spirit of perturbation, and an excitement that is always dangerous, because those fluids are strangers to the vitality. Man has always looked for life in places where it was not. His nature was carrying it, but he was looking for it some where else! He only has to accuse his madness and in spite of all the effort he did to know the truth, the mistake has always been in the depth of the crucible.

It has been necessary at all times to have a curse for humanity; the ignorance and the barbarity have always weighed on it.

Ah! Keep yourself confounding the truth which we are defending, with the vile charlantanism of those who walk next to it! You will distinguish them by their great work.

The truth is simple. It walks straight and openly, the other is suspicious, and it stumbles at every step and always asks for gold.

Unfortunate condition of men soothed by lies, big children that we are, we are dying without having learned during our life anything else than words without value.

What is left of so much trouble and care? The doubt and the boredom, nothing else. But you who want to know the truth, take possession of the magnetism. It is the door of the sciences. Knock! Knock! Armed with a strong will, they will open to you. It is necessary that your desires be sincere and that the thought to do good accompany you all the time. It is easy by speeches to excite some uncivilized peoples to revolt, but to express true things, sublime things, and to make them understand, is not the work of only one day, it is the work of many centuries. So, since antiquity, the most ancient men to whom nature has talked, cried to you. You have a natural medicine, a superior medicine. It is very much greater than the one that art teaches and practices. This one makes victims, the other does not. It would not hurt. The medicine of art is all conjectures and it has for support only vain systems, all fallible, like man. The other is sure like nature, because it relies on one of his laws. This is the one that we would make you understand, and make you recognize the superiority.

Ah! Believe our intentions. They are sincere, and no desires to fool you will enter our minds. It is the tribute of twenty years of work and observation that we bring to you. It is your cause we are pleading, because it is your pain that touches us. It is for that reason that the truth which we feel is protested by our voices against one of the biggest mistakes of the human spirit. This mistake is medicine, because if we were obligated to quote the names of the victims it has made, there would not be a library big enough to contain all the volumes.

Ah! If this art is true, why then this fear when they have treatments in your hospitals? Why this repugnance that pain would not always know how to vanquish? It is because like the fox next to the cavern of the lion, they see some enter, but they see very few coming out. The unfortunate know all the experiences they are destined to undergo!

Your philanthropy is great, sirs. Your cares are generous! If I would dare to say here the truth on all those things, if I would dare to say the attempts made daily, attempts in which you have praised yourself and your newspapers repeated occasionally. For example, the potion of Bicetre, when eight unfortunate people died on the same day. The earth, we say, covers your mistakes! Ah! If a supreme justice exist, one day we shall be accountable for our work. Ah! Sirs, how sorry we will feel for the pain that is reserved for you!

Who will dare to say what is going on in the amphitheater, and the profanations that are happening therein? Ah! I feel a deep horror of it. What have they done to nurture those unfortunate people who are dying in your hospitals, to be first mutilated and then sold? If at least their contaminated remains would receive the burial that is due to them! But it is necessary to have been a witness of what you are doing to them. To believe in all the miseries of man. "Humane justice, you have only one name!"

Let's draw the curtains on all those scenes where man learns to degrade his soul, in receiving in his organ the poison that must in the next day demolish the harmony of it.

Let's keep the silence of the tomb, and if we see something that would revolt the uncivilized peoples, let's remember that in our country we killed their soul by indifference. Their medicine wanted to cure your illness, but it killed your body with the remedy.

I do not exaggerate, Sirs, and if you still have a doubt of the veracity of this picture, tell me then what has served the science of medicine during an attack of cholera? Have we ever shown more ignorance of the medicine that cures? They were reduced to counting the victims of this terrible plague, and then, the doctors seemed to believe in fatality, like the orientals did a long time ago! Stricken they were, letting themselves die, knowing that their art was only futile. The heart failed in thinking all those things! The mind is shocked to see so much and so poor merit, and the memory that retains the souvenir of so much and so recent disaster, reminds you constantly of their weakness and of their carelessness.

This was your medicine, Sirs: now there is ours.

We have talked of dispensaries, which we do not have, of machinery, which we have never known. We have talked of many instruments, but we decline however, to give the doctors the justice that they deserve. Their knowledge of science—this is incontestable! But one more time, it is not the science that cures.

On the contrary, the more a doctor is erudite, "if he is erudite," the more patients he will lose, and the examples that we can quote exist at each step. They have disserted on all the diseases with a very great knowledge. If you want to consider their works, their efforts; they have devastated the vegetable, cut the throat of the animals, dissected hundreds of cadavers, discerned the most subtle and the most hidden parts, and then they have flattered themselves by saying that they enjoy inflicting misery, and then stop at their will, the pain. This is the objective of their art, of their science, of the works of their days and dreams of their nights! They have made a character where they have seen the sovereign happiness, a medicine in which they thought they had found a perfect health!

Insensate! They must consider what comes back to them of their chimera. Their false morals wanted to cure their passion, but they have the use of them. It is in our power and in our organs that we are going to derive the whole principle of our medicine.

We do not have, like you, a Body, and a Faculty. Our knowledge is easy, and can be made without the dissection of a corpse. Our science is not a science of words, but a science of real facts, and we do not need a language to thoroughly study it. All our secrets rest on nature, and, it is nature itself that teaches them to us. This is where we have derived our secrets, and we are only the depositary of it. So, it is not only a sacred trust that authorizes us to diffuse the beneficial kindness, kindness that we must give to all and not only to a few. The rich do not have more rights to hope for them than the poor, because the two are submissive equally to its laws.

Ah, this precious gift that we call "the life" and that passes away with us!

There are our potions, there are our draughts. We do not admit any others. It is not the carrying in some one else's body the principle that maintains life in us, that we are going to replace in the others the same principle that is gone!

There are all our secrets, there are all our mysteries; mysteries which reveal all the power of man, mysteries which reverse all the systems that the centuries have amassed until us, and which will establish, I hope, the empire of truth on earth.

Yes, we have already said it, we do not want any potions. Any draught that is pointed out by men of the art, we do not admit any treatment from them, "except the one that will have been prescribed by the mouth of the patient himself," or by the one who "mingled with him," feels at the same time the same pains and the same sufferance. We go even further, we only admit for being able to cure, those who can cure themselves! But, Sirs, this medicine, so simple and however so marvellous that the ancients knew and that they transmitted only to some men they had selected, has fallen into the public property. Everywhere they speak of the marvellous things that it breeds, and some men, strangers to all sciences, produce some phenomena which surpass in importance all that the physical sciences have offered of the most admirable.

The magnetism that we are talking about has been destined at all times to galvanize the dying corpse of a depraved Society; and why at our age is he (man) retarding his action? It is up to you man who hear me to help my efforts and to find out exactly who you are; here you can settle down. An enormous truth that nature will teach you is that the desires of man can stop running from one thing to another and that his doubts can be resolved. But we repeat it: man can not know without work. It is necessary that he plunge his soul in the mysteries of infinity, because all that is around him is mystery, and his life is the biggest of all. If he penetrates those doctrines, his soul will fraternize with the divine essence, because the soul looks for what is most hidden, even to our senses.

Ah! How much this career is great and beautiful! Happy the one who can penetrate the secrets of it! They offer some pure enjoyment that we do not find elsewhere. Penetrate yourself with it, Sirs! Come, follow us in our march, and we will lead you like a sincere guide on this road that you did not know.

I will take care of removing all that could rebuff you. I will teach you to look for the pitfalls of hypocrisy. I will affirm your tottering steps until you become capable enough yourselves. You can drive yourselves alone, and like me at your turn propagate a truth that will never have enough defenders. The call that I am making here, Sirs, can not escape notice. If by a guilty abuse of the word I have looked to spread among you the error and to divert a blame not merited on a numerous class of men of science, my name will stay attached to the stake of the infamy. But if I have said the truth, the negligence that you would bring to defend it would then be inexcusable. You would have no right to complain when your turn arrives to be victim of the false science that I have pointed out to you.

Du Potet de Sennevoy

SECTION TWO

The Era of Cerebral Physiology and Mesmerism
(1843-1851)

John Elliotson

Under the editorship of Dr. John Elliotson, a magazine, *The Zoist*, was published to collect and diffuse information connected with two sciences, cerebral physiology and mesmerism. The first number was brought out in April, 1842, to report "a new physiological truth of incalculable value and importance." Mesmerism was thought by Elliotson to be a potent remedy in the cure of disease and "already enabled the knife of the operator to divide and traverse the living fiber unfelt by the patient." The thirteen volumes of this magazine, continued up until 1856, constituted a reservoir of information on all branches of mesmeric sciences.

In the farewell address, published with the last issue of the review, the editors stated that their mission had been accomplished. Their object was neither gain nor worldly reputation, but the establishment of truth.

There is documentation of the efforts of Esdaile in India and Chenevix on the Continent, as well as illustrations of the senseless and bitter hostility shown toward mesmerism by the majority of medical men at that time. The favorite theory of anti-mesmeric doctors, in regard to the celebrated surgical operations conducted painlessly under mesmerism, used to be that the sufferers had "feigned" insensibility.

The following three articles are taken from *The Zoist* as illustrations of the sincerity of the mesmerists in furthering their cause. The article entitled "Mesmerism" demonstrates the work of Chenevix after his visit to England. The second article is a rebuttal by Elliotson after the Hospital Committee of the University College Hospital passed a resolution to prevent the practise of mesmerism or of animal magnetism in the hospital. The third article is a review of Elliotson's book on numerous cases of surgical operations without pain by means of mesmerism.

These representative articles are included because they are from a period in the history of mesmerism which forms a bridge between the old and the new advocates of hypnotism. Elliotson's name appears at a time when, again, medical opinion formulated the route which the practice of hypnosis was to take in the annals of medical practice.

MESMERISM*

Mesmerism is established. Mesmerism has always been true. Dimly known for thousands of years in barbarous and semi-barbarous countries, it was known by its high results in many of the great nations of antiquity, though the knowledge was confined to the chosen. It is only now beginning to be seen in its various aspects and ramifications, and to assume the character of a science. It is a science of the deepest interest and importance, inasmuch as the phenomena of life transcend those of all inanimate matter. The faculties of the brain—the mind—are the highest objects in the universe that man can study; and inasmuch as its power over the faculties of the body at large, and especially over the brain and whole nervous system, is immense, it is therefore capable of application to prevent and remove suffering, and to cure disease, far beyond the means hitherto possessed by the arts of medicine.

"Animal Magnetism is true,"—was the opening sentence of a series of five papers published by Mr. Chenevix on the subject in 1829, in the *London Medical* and *Physical Journal*.

The second sentence was the following: "In the whole domain of human acquirements, no art or science rests upon experiments more numerous, more positive, or more easily ascertained."

If this was the case then, how much more is it not the case now? Within these very few years, thousands of persons have made successful experiments upon the subject; and, although as far as mesmerism has for ages been proved, it has been in one sense established. It is established as a TRUTH, the multitude of positive facts, and the multitude of persons cognizant of these facts, are at this moment such, that it is beyond all shadow of doubt established as a POSSESSION by mankind, which can never be demolished, never be neglected, or lost.

Accident determines the knowledge, the opinions, and the pur-

---

*Elliotson, John, M.D.; Mesmerism. *The Zoist*, A Journal of Cerebral Physiology and Mesmerism and their Application to Human Welfare, *1*: 58-94, April 1843.

suits, both of most individuals and of most nations. Where any cerebral organ, or group of organs, preponderates over the others, it will impel the individual, with little reference to the influence of surrounding circumstances, or even in spite of them. The generality of men are without such preponderance, and take the kind of knowledge which is offered them, imbibe the opinions of those around them, and fall into the habits and pursuits of their countrymen. The knowledge, the opinions, and pursuits of a nation, must necessarily depend much upon natural cerebral development, but very greatly also upon accident. It is dependent upon the physical circumstances which surround them, rendering one mode of life and action absolutely inevitable, or at least more suitable than another. It is dependent upon accidental impediments to one or another kind of knowledge, opinion, or pursuit. It also is dependent upon the accidental impartment to them, by individuals of remarkable cerebral organization among themselves or by other nations, of one or another kind of knowledge, or upon a similar accidental influence upon their opinions and pursuits. When a subject does not require a peculiar organization for excellence, as music or colouring does, it is but merely a good development of the group of superior intellectual faculties. Chance chiefly directs whether it shall be known and cultivated by a nation. Consequently nations, at an equal point of civilization and most different in their intellectual organization, differ greatly in their knowledge and opinions. Mr. Priault, in his learned *Questiones Mosaice,* asks, "Who can assert a priori the particular direction which civilization shall take? The Greeks were long without any true knowledge of the year, and yet Mexico at its discovery had a year of three hundred and sixty monthly, and five intercalary days. The Otaheitans too, built curiously carved canoes, and wove cloth and mats, and were, nevertheless, ignorant that water could be made to boil. And the Peruvians, similarly, had constructed roads throughout their dominions, and had established posts of communication between the several parts of their country and their capital; they had learned also to card and weave wool, and could work silver into vessels and tools, and would even, occasionally, mould it into images, which prettily imitated nature; and yet the iron that was at their

THE ZOIST:

A JOURNAL

OF

CEREBRAL PHYSIOLOGY & MESMERISM,

AND

THEIR APPLICATIONS TO HUMAN WELFARE.

" This is TRUTH, though opposed to the Philosophy of Ages."—*Gall.*

VOL. I.

MARCH, 1843, TO JANUARY, 1844.

LONDON:

HIPPOLYTE BAILLIÈRE, PUBLISHER,
219, REGENT STREET;

PARIS: J. B. BAILLIÈRE, RUE DE L'ECOLE DE MEDÈCINE;

LEIPSIZ: T. O. WEIGEL.

M DCCC XLIV.

FIGURE 8. Title page from *The Zoist,* a journal published by John Elliotson in 1844.

feet they had never observed and knew not how to turn to account. When, therefore, we compare that which the early nations are said, at any given time, to have known with what they remained in ignorance of, we may often be surprised as well at the subtlety and ingenuity of their discoveries, as at the stupidity of their ignorance: but we cannot from this ground argue against their inventions. Neither can we, on the other hand, infer the untruth of alleged science or the inefficiency of art, because in a country of much science and art it is unknown and disregarded, or even despised."

The greatest events in history have been determined very much by accident. There is, indeed, a general working, or influence of general causes, which renders an accidental circumstance availing or unavailing, so that what appears accidental may not be so altogether, nay, perhaps in but small part. But, nevertheless, fortuitous circumstances, that is to say circumstances not in a natural sequence of occurrence, and arising from other and independent causes, do most materially influence events, both for their production and their prevention.

Thus it has been with mesmerism. One would suppose that a thing so easily practised by every one would long ago have been known universally in Europe. But the subtle Greeks had no sure knowledge of the year, the carving and weaving Otaheitan never boiled water, nor did the sagacious Peruvian use the iron he possessed. The time and trouble demanded for its practice, the disinclination of persons to permit such powerful effects to be produced over the whole frame of their friends without immediate evident good, and the brutally ignorant prejudices of the superstitious, who unquestionably form the mass of mankind in every country, in referring the natural phenomena of mesmerism to imaginary beings and agencies, have probably been sufficient to deter men from its investigation. But the longer time rolls on, the greater and more numerous the opportunities for favourable chances to turn up and exert their influences; and thus, at last, is caught hold of and fixed what might have been in our possession ages back, had attention been directed towards it, and impediments manfully opposed; and its constant cultivation for the future is secure. Mesmerism has at length had its happy chances, and as certainly as civilization itself is now secure, through the art of printing and some other modern inventions, so certainly may mesmerism henceforth defy oblivion or neglect.

Till the present moment mesmerism never attracted more than a very partial and temporary notice in this country. Maxwell wrote respecting it in 1679, laying down all the very propositions afterwards advanced by Mesmer, just as before him in the beginning of the seventeenth century Van Helmont, a Belgian physician, had written of it in the language which a disciple of Mesmer would have employed. In the middle of the seventeenth century an Irish Protestant gentleman named Greatrakes, of spotless character, receiving no recompense, writing in the purest spirit of piety and benevolence, and not pretending to explain how he did it, "stroked" thousands of the sick with his own hands, and, though he did not pretend to cure all, is said to have cured large numbers, and two celebrated men, Boyle and Cudworth, put themselves under his care, which we presume they would not have done, if the great doctors of the day had not failed to cure them. The Lord Bishop of Derry declared that he himself had seen "dimness cleared and deafness cured," pain "drawn out at some distant part," "grievious sores of many months date, in a few days healed, obstructions disappear, and stoppages removed, and cancerous knots in the breast dissolved," by his manipulations. The Royal Society published some of his cures, and accounted for them "by a sanative contagion in Mr. Greatrakes' body, which had an antipathy to some particular diseases, and not to others." A gardener, named Leveret, did the same, and used to say that so much virtue went out of him that he was more exhausted by touching thirty or forty people than by digging eight rods of ground.

Dr. Elliotson mentions in the chapter on mesmerism in his *Human Physiology*, p. 563, that a lady named Prescot, who died at an advanced age a few years back, in Bloomsbury Square, practised mesmerism there during the greater part of her life; and that he recollects that, now about thirty years ago, a woman mesmerized for a time at Kennington.

The establishment of mesmerism in England sprung from the

visit of an Irish gentleman, named Chenevix, who had fixed his residence for several years in Paris, to London in 1828. His visit was short, but during it he solicited and prevailed upon several persons to see him make trials of mesmerism: and afterwards prevailed upon the editors of the *London Medical and Physical Journal* to publish the report of all that took place.

Notwithstanding the sentence of the Royal Commission appointed in France to pronounce upon the truth of animal magnetism in 1784, when Mesmer had drawn it from oblivion and discredit, and proved its truth and power, the facts had taken firm root in France and some other parts of the continent, and several clever and estimable persons had always practised and cultivated it. Indeed it could not be otherwise, for the Commission, like all the adversaries of mesmerism in every country and at every period, whether a body of men or private individuals, behaved most unfairly. Whenever a person resolves to oppose mesmerism he seems to forget himself entirely, to part with common sense, common morality, and common propriety. This Commission would not examine it with Mesmer, but with one of his pupils, named d'Eslon; Mesmer himself being not only more capable of demonstrating it, but one of the most powerful mesmerizers that ever existed. Mesmer protested in vain to Franklin, and to the Baron de Breteuil, who did not even condescend to reply to his letter. Their examination was immediately shown to be most incomplete and superficial, by a host of writers. The members were careless in their attendance and did not all regularly assemble, but went casually, and as each or two or three felt inclined. They asked no questions of the patients, took no trouble to observe. They took up the subject prejudiced against it; and in their experiments omitted the conditions which they were expressly told were indispensable.—"Point de questions aux personnes soumises aux epreuves,—pas le soin d'observer,—pas assidus aux seances—allant de temps en temps. Nous les voyons dans une disposition peu bienveillante; nous les voyons malgre toutes les representations qui leur sont faites, faire des essais, tenter des experiences dans lesquelles ils omittent les conditions morales exigees et announcess comme indispensables aux succes." These are the words of Drs. Adelon, Pariset, Marc,

Burdin, sen. and Husson, appointed by the Royal Academy of Medicine of Paris, in 1825, to report upon the propriety of examining the subject again.

Franklin gave himself very little trouble about the matter. One, however, a truly celebrated man, the illustrious botanist Jussieu, paid the utmost attention; and what was the result? Why, that he refused to put his signature to the report of the rest, notwithstanding the pressing solicitation of his colleagues and the menaces of the minister—Baron de Breteuil; but drew up a report of his own, in which he declared that the facts which he had witnessed depended upon an external agent independent of the imagination.

Mesmer found a large number of pupils who resolutely took up the subject among them. The Marquis de Puysegur, a truly virtuous man and a soldier, produced somnambulism by the process, though unprepared for it by Mesmer, who however was conversant with the fact; and he published at the end of 1784 and in 1785. He had not been converted by a course of lectures by Mesmer, though he attended diligently; but subsequently by mesmerizing in the way of joke the daughter of his steward, and the next day the wife of his game-keeper. The shortest mode of ascertaining the truth of the matter, is thus to make experiments for one's self. His third patient was a peasant, who fell into a quiet sleep, and into somnambulism, in a quarter of an hour. In this state she talked aloud of her affairs. He awoke her, and left her in an hour. She slept the whole of the night; and a severe cold, for which he had mesmerized her, was sensibly better the next morning.

He was the first who accurately described this state, and pointed out the intuitive knowledge possessed in it by some patients with reference to their own complaints and those of others. Puysegur relinquished the road to certain power and fortune in order to devote himself both on his estate and in Paris to cultivate and establish mesmerism. "All those who had the honor of knowing," says Foissac, "knew that the love of benefitting others was his religion, and that he undeviatingly pursued, to the last day of his existence, the course which Providence had pointed out to him." Like his ancestors, M. de Puysegur, placed on the high road to honours and fortune, might have attained the highest dignities;

but he sacrificed all to the more tranquil and true happiness of comforting, assisting, and enlightening his fellow-men. Indeed he often said that his mission on earth was to place mesmerism in the hands of physicians. This mission he fulfilled with incomparable zeal and complete success: for soon after his death, in 1824, the Royal Academy of Medicine appointed a committee, which admitted all the phenomena of mesmerism and somnambulism.

M. Deleuze, originally destined like Puysegur for the army, but afterwards devoted to literature and science, and established in an appointment in the Jardin des Plantes, heard in 1785, when thirty-two years of age, and, at his native place Sisteron, of the cures effected by Puysegur on his estate, and thought the whole must be nonsense. A physician, however, at Aix, converted him, and he wrote admirably and extensively upon mesmerism till 1825, and cultivated it assiduously in Paris. He avoided all speculation, all mystery, and showed that the phenomena of mesmerism were in harmony with the laws of nature. He showed that the adversaries of mesmerism, precisely like the adversaries at the present day, "are ignorant of mesmerism and imagine absurdities to be held by its partisans which they do not hold,—pass over in silence the most convincing proofs,—refute statements that nobody makes,— and when obliged to confess incontestable facts, ascribe them to insufficient causes." In 1828, he was appointed librarian of the Museum of Natural History. He has been spoken of in the most respectful and honorable terms. "His rare qualities," says M. Foissac, "his kind and instructive intercourse, gained for him many friends among the most celebrated learned men—Levaillant, Duperron, Cuvier, de Humboldt, etc.; the unanimous opinion of his contemporaries concedes to him and M. le Marquis de Puysegur, the honour of having preserved, defended, and propagated one of the most beautiful discoveries of modern times."

Many other men of less prominence in mesmerism, kept up the subject both in France and Germany, and even Russia, and it found its way temporarily into some German universities and hospitals. In 1818, the Academy of Sciences at Berlin offered a prize of 3340 francs for the best treatise on mesmerism; it was practised in Russia, in 1815, when a committee, appointed by the emperor, declared it to be a most important agent; in Denmark, in 1816; in Prussia, in 1817, where the practice of mesmerism was by law ordered to be confined to physicians. But its head was held above the surface of the waters with difficulty.

At the insistence of Dr. Foissac, in 1825, a committee was appointed by the Royal Academy of Medicine of Paris, to determine whether a commission should be appointed to investigate mesmerism. The committee reported in the affirmative. A long discussion took place, in which as much nonsense was talked by the opponents as could be desired by its most malicious supporter;— and to this the Committee drew up a powerful and in every respect admirable answer, which settled the matter; and a commission was appointed in 1826. One difficulty however after another occurred. The conduct of Dr. Magendie, one of the commission, was shuffling and contemptible in the extreme. He wrote to Dr. Foissac, that the secretary of the committee took careful notes and drew them up, when it had been resolved that none should be drawn up. He made an appointment at his own house with Dr. Foissac for the latter to be present at a meeting for experiment, kept Dr. Foissac waiting from four till six,—never saw him,—and had him let out by a back door. When one of the committee— Dr. Husson—wrote a very polite letter to inform him that permission was obtained for epileptic patients at his hospital to be mesmerized for experiment, and begged him, as a physician of the hospital and one of the committee of the enquiry, to be present,— he, in apish imitation of the Baron de Breteuil forty years before, did not condescend to notice the invitation! "M. Magendie ne repondit pas." All this may be seen in Dr. Foissac's book. The business languished, and no report was heard of for five years,— until 1831, when indeed a most favourable report was given, acknowledging the truth of mesmerism, and its most wonderful facts; and displaying earnestness, labour, candour, and a truly philosophical spirit. But in the mean time (and indeed afterwards, for this report was not allowed to be printed or lithographed, but was put in a box and thought no more of by the academy) mesmerism had little prospect, for miserable obstacles were thrown in the way, and particularly by Dr. Magendie who, it is said, not only violated truth and acted as he knows so well how, with vulgar impoliteness, but ceased as well as Dr. Double (who with Magendie had no singleness of purpose) to attend the experiments, and consequently could not sign the report.

The learned and important, and those in authority, would not condescend to notice mesmerism; the superficial herd of time-serving practitioners, vulgar medical journalists, and all kinds of ephemeral medical writers, railed at it and all who upheld it, so that it was a poor outcast, neither legitimate nor respectable. Still, being the offspring of an eternal and vigorous parent—TRUTH, it was sturdy, and lived on, without being indebted for food, lodging, clothes, or countenance to the flourishing and respectable members of learned or fashionable society.

"In France," says Mr. Chenevix, and his article in the *Edinburg Review,* 1819, on France and England, shows that his long residence in Paris had made him perfectly acquainted with the French character and habits, "where words and jargon are more valuable than facts, it has been treated as a matter of opinion, not of experiment." "It has been believed, and reviled, and believed again, and has followed all the vicissitudes of fashions." "Through all the phenomena have been produced over and over again, yet, as these phenomena are not phrases, the academy of medicine thinks it can argue down somnambulism, and talk lucidity out of existence."

The influence of the opinions of those around him had their full weight upon Mr. Chenevix:—

"Whenever animal magnetism was mentioned, I joined," he says, "the general tribe of scoffers, and so much was I convinced(!) of its absurdity, that, being at Rotterdam in 1797, I laughed to scorn a proposal made to me by an English resident there to witness some experiments in which he was then engaged." "The respectability and general understanding of this person left no mode of accounting for so extraordinary an illusion, but to suppose him labouring under a monomania."

In 1803 and 1804, while traveling in Germany, he continues—

"I heard many very enlightened men of the universities talk of animal magnetism, nearly with the same certainty as mineral magnetism; but their credulity I set down to the account of German mysticism." "I remained an unbeliever."

At length, after nineteen years, Mr. Chenevix condescended to witness mesmerism in the person of a young lady in Paris. "I went to laugh," says he; "I came away convinced."

"To suspect any thing like a trick in the parties concerned was impossible. They were of the highest respectability and distinction, and some of them I had known for many years. The magnetizer was, indeed, in the frivolous French metropolis, called a charlatan, which made me suppose he was not so; and the event proved that I was right. He was, indeed, poor; he exercised his art for money; he gave public lectures at three francs a ticket. Many young physicians have as fair a claim to the title as he had. But from the hour above alluded to till the period of his death, I remained acquainted with the Abbe Faria, and never knew a man to whom the epithet impostor was less applicable.

"No sooner had the Abbe Faria begun to operate than the countenance of the lady changed, and in two seconds she was fast asleep, having manifested symptoms which could not be counterfeited. The sitting lasted about two hours, and produced results which, though I still remained a sceptic upon some of the most wonderful phenomena, entirely convinced me of the existence of a mesmeric influence, and of an extraordinary agency which one person can, by his will, exercise upon another. The Abbe Faria offered every means to dispel my remaining doubts, and gave me all necessary instructions to obtain total conviction from experiments of my own. I most zealously attended his labours, public and private, and derived complete satisfaction upon every point relating to mesmerism; even upon those which appeared supernatural. Many of the experiments I repeated, not only upon persons whom I met at his house, but upon others totally unacquainted with him or with his studies, and was ultimately compelled to adopt the absolute and unqualified conclusion announced above: —Mesmerism is true."

And what then was his conduct? Did he content himself with saying, "It's very wonderful, certainly," "I don't understand it," and then think no more about it, turn to something by which he was making money, or which was pretty or popular? Did he content himself with saying, "I should like to know the use of it?" as though the sight of any of nature's wonders were not in itself useful,—a high, and invigorating, a noble, intellectual, and truly delicious and improving occupation, far beyond the occupation, however necessary, of procuring food and raiment and property, the administration of which to the more humble wants of our nature constitute the only view possessed by many of utility,—as though every fact of nature were not a part of the mighty, the universal whole;—as though a knowledge of any fact in nature could fail directly or indirectly, sooner or later, to give power to good. Did he content himself with saying, "It cannot be doubted; but it is a dangerous power and may be turned to mischievous purposes!"—as though whatever is a power is not a power to evil as well as to good, and greater power to evil in the very same degree in which it is a greater to good; as though heat, without which we die, without high degrees of which the arts administering most to our advantage and comfort and prosperity of all kinds cannot be practiced, is not converted to the most destructive purposes by the ill disposed and a source also of incalculable unintentional accidental mischief;—as though the steel instruments always on our eating tables, and in our hands, and in all parts of our dwellings, might not in one moment be made implements of injury and death;—as though half our medicines in hourly use may not be made instruments of death? Did he content himself saying, "Well, I am sure the medical profession will see its truth and importance, and I shall leave it to them . . ." as though any revolution in science or institutions had ever come from those in whose hands the subject was placed; and had not always been forced upon them, and forced upon them with toil and anguish and persecution to those who effected it? He had read that Christ, for his efforts to substitute, in the room of long public prayers and sanctimonious scrupulousness about indifferent things, and the pomp and ceremony and mechanism of worship, and nicety of doctrines, and priestly assumption,—to substitute humility, disinterestedness, and universal benevolence, saying, "It was said of old time; but I say unto you," was vilified by all the Jewish establishment and the so-called respectable Jews, and then nailed on high in the open air to two crossed pieces of wood. He (Faria) knew that the discoveries of Newton were long excluded from the University of which he was a member, and were introduced through stratagem by Dr. Samuel Clarke who explained them in notes, without any appearance of argument or controversy to the book of Deacartes which was used as a text book by all the tutors. Though, like these notable fellows, now forgotten and in the dust, unseen and unremembered, the exploded and unfounded system of Descartes kept its ground for more than thirty years after the publication of Newton's discoveries. He knew that the medical profession laughed Harvey to scorn and made the public think him too great a fool and visionary to be fit to physic them, when he taught the circulation of the blood, and were so perversely obstinate that not one doctor who had arrived at years of discretion—had attained his fortieth year—when the discovery was announced, ever relented, or admitted the truth of the circulation, or allowed himself to the day of his death to be the wiser for Harvey's discovery, but lived on perversely and piggishly boasting of error; though probably many noisy professors of unbelief did, like a host of noisy living doctors who declare their unbelief at this moment in mesmerism and, like gentlemen of a dark hue in the basement story, "believe and tremble." Mr. Chenevix knew that beneficial changes in bodies of men, united as an institution or corporation, or even in a profession or occupation, and standing up for their vested rights or ignorance, unimprovability, and undisturbed motionlessness, required always heavy blows and pressure from without before these bodies bestir themselves and think of moving onwards. Did he think a truth less important because neglected and despised? No, Mr. Chenevix.

"Surprised at the pusillanimity of the French Academy, which could not deny and yet had not the manliness to avow the facts which one half of its members declared they had witnessed, resolved, with all due humility, yet without shrinking from the task, to devote some time to the collection of facts, and to offer the result to a much more enlightened public than that to which the art is compelled to appeal in France."

We really think the last remark, however national, to be well founded, when we compare the slight hold that mesmerism has taken of the Parisians, who are more struck with its marvels than its scientific bearings and practical applications, who derive a sensation from it rather than an enlightenment, with the deep root it has now taken all over England and the intense earnestness with which so many of both sexes study and cultivate it, now that they have recovered from the stupor into which the ignorant misrepresentations and misconceptions and the bold falsehoods of journalists, medical and literary, and the clamor of the medical profession, the lucky, leading practitioners all vociferating and the little ones in due imitation snarling and making the best little noises they could, had thrown them.

In 1837 a Frenchman named Dupotet, and styled Baron Dupotet, who had long practised mesmerism, came over to London to propagate it and gain money. He had an introduction to the Middlesex Hospital and was allowed to make experiments upon several patients. He produced decided effects; but Mr. Mayo, and all those to whom he was introduced, disregarded them more and more, and at last left him to make the experiments by himself; and the poor man was in despair, when Dr. Wilson advised him to go to Dr. Elliotson, who, he added, would look into the subject and soon see if there was anything in it. M. Dupotet followed this advice, was well received by Dr. Elliotson, who said he was glad of the opportunity of investigating a subject, of the truth of which Mr. Chenevix had convinced him eight years before, and which he had ever since hoped one day to enquire into for the purpose of ascertaining the amount of its truth. He daily mesmerized several patients and produced marked results, that is, mesmeric coma and involuntary movements. Among the rest was Elizabeth Okey, in the hospital for epilepsy and whose sister had been also in the hospital for the same disease. After several trials she was sent to sleep, but roused again almost as soon as she lost herself; and the appearance she thought so ridiculous that she was always unwilling to undergo the process. Gradually the sleep lengthened, and at last ecstatic delirium occurred, and, after he had ceased to visit the hospital, all those wonderful phenomena which so many witnessed, of which all the world has heard, and of which Dr. Elliotson has engaged to furnish this work with a full account, as well as an ample answer to the ignorant persecutors and slanderers of her and her sister. In the autumn Dr. Elliotson left London for his annual tour, which he found always absolutely necessary for his health, and left M. Dupotet to mesmerize three or four patients, whose treatment he had begun. That person, however, with great weakness and want of propriety, gave out that all people who wished to be mesmerized might apply to him at the hospital and would be attended to by him there. The committee were obliged to put a stop to this, and Dr. Elliotson on his return highly approved of the step and disapproved of the liberty taken by M. Dupotet. Dr. Elliotson, having returned, now took the care of his mesmeric patients into his own hands, and M. Dupotet commenced daily demonstrations of mesmerism at half-a-crown a head at a house which he hired in Orchard-street, Portman-square. His rooms were always crowded, and he exhibited several genuine and remarkable cases; and he made very many converts, who still talk of the wonders they beheld. At last, notwithstanding his ample receipts, he got into difficulties, though we believe through no fault of his own, but the mismanagement of some and the bad conduct of others; and after vain attempts to borrow money, left London, and is now at Paris. Having been afforded every facility at the hospital by Dr. Elliotson to whom entirely he owed his success, for before he saw that gentleman he was about to leave England in despair; having been shown every kindness by him, except that of lending money, which he ought not to have required and which could have been of use but for a moment, he employed himself as soon as he returned home again in writing a very shallow book, containing no information, but silly abuse of Dr. Elliotson for having been so grand as to make his annual tour for fresh air and health, while M. Dupotet was showing mesmeric facts, although by so doing Dr. E. placed M. Dupotet in a situation for which he could not have hoped,—that of treating a certain number of patients in one of our public hospitals. On the cause of his anger,— the refusal of pecuniary loans,—he is silent. In truth, he was an innocent sort of man, very weak and of little information, and he knew no more, and would have been detrimental had he stayed. All things serve a prupose for a certain time only, and are then destined to waste away as useless.

Dr. Elliotson and his clinical clerk, Mr. Wood, regularly mesmerized certain patients. Some excellent cures were effected, and such striking phenomena produced that the students regularly attended; then students from other schools; then they all requested to bring their friends, so that for convenience he was obliged to mesmerize no longer in the wards but in the theatre, just as the surgeons perform their operations not in the wards but in the theatre. Requests were poured in upon him from all classes of medical men and from others to be permitted to witness the cases; the highest nobility and even royalty attended. This of course excited the jealousy of his colleagues. The school, which was at a low ebb when he condescended to join it on account of the wise and liberal plan of the institution, (and no other man of his station would have joined it,) had thriven more and more every year, and his classes continued to thrive during that time. But his colleagues determined he should not occupy, what he never once thought of, a more conspicuous place in the public view than themselves; the truth and benefits of mesmerism they cared not one straw for. They would not witness his facts,—they boasted of this, began every sort of petty, disgraceful annoyance, and at last, without any previous communication or hint, while effecting easy and satisfactory cures, he received an abrupt order from the council that his patients were not medical nor at all conversant with literature or any science, except two or three of their number. The very moment he received this insult, worthy of the most ignorant, miserable, bigotted, and despotic only, he sent his resignation, and has never since entered either college or hospital.

We extract the following account from Dr. Elliotson's farewell Letter to his class:—

"My enquiries were soon attended with such results that a large number of medical men, most distinguished noblemen, nay royalty itself, members of the House of Commons, some of the first men of science in the country, Professors of Oxford, Cambridge, King's College, and Edinburgh, the Presidents of the Royal and Linnaean Societies, and teachers of the various hospitals, flocked to witness my facts. Some of these gentlemen made handsome donations to the hospital in consequence, and others expressed their intention to do the same, but have declined in consequence of my resignation. This soon excited envy, and this excited a commotion; and the late Dean advised me to desist. He urged that, whether the wonderful facts were true or not, and whether great benefit in the treatment of diseases would result or not, we ought to consider the interests of the school;—not of science and humanity, observe —but of the school: that, if the public did not regard the matter as true and the benefits as real, we ought not to persevere and risk the loss of public favour to the school, that I was rich, and could afford to lose my practice for what I believed the truth, but that others were not:—in short, his argument was "rem—rem;" and "virtus post nummos." I replied that the institution was established for the dissemination and discovery of truth; that all other considerations were secondary to this; that, if the public were ignorant, we should enlighten them; that we should lead the public, and not the public us; and that the sole question was, whether the matter were a truth or not. I laughed at the idea of injury to the pecuniary interests of the school.

"The commotion increased. My demonstrations were debated upon at meetings of the faculty, and discussions went on between members of the holders of office. At one meeting of the medical faculty, a professor boasted that he had seen none of my experiments and should have considered himself disgraced if he had; that animal magnetism had been proved about forty years ago to be a perfect humbug and imposture; and that it was now in as bad repute with the public as Christianity had been at its first promulgation.

"Another professor boasted that he had seen none of the facts, and, though invited by my clinical clerk to observe them while visiting his own patients in the ward, that he had declined the invitation. One professor declared that he never could procure a vacant bed because I detained my patients so long in order to mesmerize them: and another reported that patients would not apply for admission, lest they should be mesmerized, and that others left the hospital to avoid mesmeric treatment. But, when I enquired of the officer whom I understood to have furnished these absurdities, he assured me that he was blameless, and made the general scape-goat of the place; and he entreated me to accept his denial without an enquiry which would emboil him with the professors. Not conceiving that any thing but reputation could accrue to the hospital from the demonstration of physiological and pathological facts to crowds of the first men in the country, among whom were characters totally opposed in politics to the place and who otherwise never would have entered it,—I persevered. The president of the college—Lord Brougham and five other members of the council did not refuse to attend the demonstrations; nor did the professors of the faculty of arts; nor Dr. Grant, Dr. Lindley, nor M. Graham. But, with the exception of these three last gentlemen, whose conduct throughout has commanded my respect, I never saw any of the medical faculty: if any ever were present, it could have been only to reconnoitre unobserved by me. The Irish, the Welsh, and four of the six Scotch medical professors, held meeting after meeting of the faculty or of the hospital committee, which my disgust prevented me from attending. At these meetings I know that the most bitter feelings against me were manifested, and matters discussed which were perfectly irrelevant, but the introduction of which showed the hostility of certain parties. I have always acted in the most honourable and correct manner; and dare any examination of my conduct.

"Dr. Lindley and Mr. Cooper confessed to me that they could not imagine that my demonstrations would hurt the hospital; and Dr. Lindley, in his own noble and honest manner, declared that he thought the facts which he had witnessed were very curious and deserved investigation. The feeling, however, for what reason they could not tell, was so strong, that they conceived my best course was to give up the demonstrations. Mr. Cooper suggested, as indeed Dr. Davis had done, that I should show the patients in my own house, or some house in the neighbourhood. One professor recommended a public-house. But I declined to exhibit hospital patients to a number of persons anywhere but in the hospital. For the sake of peace, therefore, I consented never to show the phenomena again in the theatre of the hospital, unless my colleagues approved of the list of those to whom I wished to demonstrate them: and both gentlemen agreed that this ought to content the party. It, however, did not content them. They still refused to come and examine into the phenomena; and, when I sent to the medical committee a list of many of the highest names in and out of the profession, who had applied for permission to witness my facts, they absolutely refused to read it.

"Entreated on all sides to exhibit the phenomena, I requested of the council permission to demonstrate them in one of those theatres of the college, when this was not in use. But I was refused. One of the council, whose goodness and liberality render him an ornament to the Jewish nation and to England, moved the reconsideration of the refusal or made a motion for permission, but in vain. I hear that he entreated the council to witness the phenomena and judge for themselves as he had done, but in vain. Yes, the majority of the council, perfectly ignorant of the subject, refused to go to learn anything of it before they passed judgment upon it; and among these were legislators, barristers, and one physician. Yet this same council gave permission for the exhibition of a calculating boy to the public, at so much a head, and tickets were purchased by any one, as for a concert." Yet these experiments on a subject of which he is as ignorant as of Latin, French, or Mathematics; and from his effrontery at once frightened the medical profession, and those, who firmly believed, but now imitated Peter and denied their convictions. Nothing daunted, however, from the time of his resignation to the present, Dr. Elliotson has shown the phenomena at his own house very frequently to those who requested the favour, and has made many hundreds of converts, who in their turn have converted others.

Another Frenchman named La Fontaine, came over two years ago, like Dupotet, on a pecuniary speculation. He also showed some genuine and striking cases. He lectured in the provinces, and the sister countries; but at last found the affair unsuccessful. He appeared a less educated man than Dupotet, and his knowledge of mesmerism was as limited. He did great good, however; and more ostensible good than Dupotet, because he came at a period when the conviction of the truth had become much more diffused, and persons were more disposed to attend to the subject.

The converts have gone on steadily increasing; the converted experimenting for themselves and converting others, till, during the last twelvemonth, the conviction has spread far and wide, and people need no more be afraid of being laughed at for expressing their belief. Numbers of persons originally converted at University College Hospital and in Dr. Elliotson's house, but afraid to express their mind, have now taken courage, and talk of the convincing wonders they long ago saw, and speak of the absurdity of doubting the truth of the cases of the Okeys. Those who were terrified by Mr. Wakley's firing and ran away, have now stopped to take breath, looked back, and found that he had no shot, produced merely noise and smoke, and that the giant himself was an unwieldy, feeble, short-breathed, puffing mortal, only able to throw his arms about menacingly and make ugly noises, so that little boys need not be at all afraid of him and may laugh at him. It will soon be considered ridiculous for a man to declare he believes mesmerism to be nonsense. The honest among the most noisy opponents will become Sauls of Tarsus and be the most strenuous proselytes; each of this class will confess his sorrow, as Mr. Chenevix did, that this—

"Presumptuous ignorance had shut in his own face the door of a science more directly interesting to man than all that chemistry and astronomy can teach." "Nine-tenths," he continues, "who may read will laugh at this as I did, in 1797, at my friend in Rotterdam. Let them do so; but while they laugh, let them learn, and not, thirty years afterwards, have to lament that so short a remnant of life is left to them to enjoy this new and valuable secret of nature."

The uncandid will be silent, and then at last begin to allow there is something in it, and pretend that they always allowed as much, but did not think it right to be precipitate, and only objected to the nonsense of the matter.

So at last it will be spoken and written of as a matter of course, lectured upon as a matter of course, and employed as a matter of course; and all the folly, ignorance, injustice and vulgarity that have been exhibited must be most charitably forgotten; only that copies of the *Lancet,* its heavy offspring the *Provincial Medical Journal,* the *Dublin Medical Journal, Dr. Johnson's Journal,* and *Dr. Forbes's,* will still be accessible on the shelves of public medical libraries, and we "before we forget them," must from time to time present our readers with a tid-bit of an extract, sometimes from one of them and sometimes from another, to show the world how wild and vulgar doctors can be among themselves, and how closely their conduct resembles that of one of the most uneducated, who wonder at what they never saw before, and refuse to believe their senses because they wonder, forgetting that what they do believe is all equally wonderful, but not thought so because they are accustomed to it.

"Wonderful," says Mr. Chenevix, "indeed, it may appear; but what makes anything wonderful to us, if not our ignorance. In my recollection, they have wondered at hydrogen and oxygen; at a dead frog jumping between two slips of metal; at gas lights and steam boats; and now they wonder at all who wonder at these familiar things. They would pity the wretch who would not instantly believe that a stone falls, and a balloon rises, by the same impulse; or that the taste which his tongue receives when placed between a piece of silver and a piece of zinc, has the same origin as the thunder which strikes his soul with awe. Everything in creation is wonderful, or nothing is so, but the last known truth always appears the most miraculous to unreflecting minds." "Since the world began, men have been wondering at every thing till habit tamed their minds upon it."

We ask not the aid of those medical journalists. On the contrary we entreat them to continue in their present course of absurdity, for their "fantastic tricks," like those of "angry apes before high heaven, will amuse us in our leisure moments, and enable us to amuse our readers as well as ourselves, by playing with them, and teasing them, and showing the world what comical creatures they are when well worried". The facts of mesmerism which we possess are now profusely abundant and extensively scattered without the assistance of professors, examiners, colleges, halls, medical journalists, or fashionable practitioners. It must go on conquering and to conquer—for MESMERISM IS ESTABLISHED.

John Elliotson

CASES OF CURES BY MESMERISM*

"Mr. Wakley says he is resolved that Mesmerism shall no longer be employed in this or any other hospital."—Speech of Mr. Wakley's Clerk to Dr. Elliotson in the ward of University College Hospital, where he was allowed as a favour to see Elizabeth Okey, November, 1838.

Resolved—"That the Hospital Committee be instructed to take such steps as they shall deem most advisable, to prevent the practice of Mesmerism or Animal Magnetism in the future within the Hospital."—Resolution of the Council of University College, December 27, 1838.

To the Editor of the Zoist:

June, 1843

Sir,

For six years I have carefully and constantly investigated the powers of mesmerism over different diseases, and, to increase the extent of my observation, a gentleman who was my pupil, and mesmerized extensively for me in University College Hospital up to the day on which I shook the dust of my feet upon it, has, at my request, mesmerized patients for me during the whole of this period.

I have found it one of the most important remedies, and accumulated a great amount of decisive evidence of its marvellous powers, even when all other means have failed in the hands of the most noted practitioners. This evidence I shall gradually send to your publication. It would probably not be received by medical journals, and I should indeed be unwilling to transmit it to any medical journal or society, since the conduct of the medical profession has been so disgraceful, both intellectually and morally. My statements will, I know, be relied upon. They are not only true to the letter, but are the result of the most patient and careful labour, gone through with no view to emolument or reputation,

*Elliotson, John: Cases of Cures By Mesmerism. *The Zoist,* A Journal of Cerebral Physiology and Mesmerism and Their Application to Human Welfare, *1*:161-208, June 1843.

but for the love of acquiring and disseminating knowledge. I have never received a fee, and never will, for practising mesmerism, from the humblest or the highest; and, unless the case of a person above the humble class of society occurs among my particular friends, or is likely to prove interesting, I send it to some medical man who practises mesmerism professionally, as he would other medical means. Reputation is out of the question. The medical profession, being totally ignorant of the subject, have thought proper to stigmatize me as a fool, a visionary, a madman, aye, and a quack, for understanding something of it.—Their ignorance and conceited obstinacy have been my disgrace. From being thought "a careful and conscientious observer," "a most skillful physician in ascertaining the real nature of a disease, and in employing remedies;" "a great contributor to the improvement of the medical art;" and "worthy to have the largest and most leading practice"; "destined to divide the town with Dr. Chambers who was to be the Halford and I the Baillie of the day," "possessing the highest claim to be physician in ordinary to the monarch;" styled "the first physician of the age," in letters brought by patients without end, the only effect of which was to make me work the harder that I might one day really deserve such commendation; I was all at once considered destitute of all my previous knowledge and skill, incapable of observation and investigation, and unworthy of any practice, which, by their good care and cooperation with one whom they previously abused, has been reduced to one third of what it was; though during the whole of this time I have prosecuted inquiries into diseases and remedies far more assiduously than before, and certainly have far more knowledge, far more skill in treating diseases than I ever possessed. I am some ten thousand pounds less rich than I should have been. But I have been amply rewarded in reflecting that I was making a proper use of my intellect and time, and that I was right; and in feeling myself superior to those whose delight is to disparage me, as they have successively and successfully done at my advocacy of every new thing, though now established and employed by them when they could hold out no longer, and who are at this moment in what they regard as prosperity, and are silent upon the opposition they once made to what they now admit. They have their reward and I have mine; and, though I shall probably be another ten thousand pounds or so the less rich before the day of ignorance and sin is past, I shall not deviate from the course which I have ever pursued since I began practice,—of working and trying to deserve success, and leaving all worldly wisdom, sycophancy, religious hypocrisy, authoritativeness, utterance of truisms and of opinions which are known to be those of the persons spoken to, and trading industry, to others who can stoop to these things and feel happy without self-respect.

The first cases I present to you are instances of INSANITY.

Mr. D., aged 18, had an attack of rheumatism on the 6th day of January, 1837. It was severe, and at first confined to his knees; but, on the 8th it suddenly seized his scalp also, causing the most excruciating pain. His pulse was 120, his skin hot, his tongue white. He was bled to twelve ounces by his medical attendant, Mr. Chandler of Rotherhithe; took colchicum, opium, calomel, and salines. On the 9th he was better in the morning, but the symptoms returned with increased violence in the afternoon, and he suddenly became delirious in the evening. He was occasionally violent, but easily restrained. His pulse was now 132, and very hard: his bowels were torpid, and he chewed some pills of compound extract of colocynth which were given him: the removal of twelve ounces of blood from his arm reduced the pulse and appeared to calm him a little. Calomel and saline aperients were given. On the 10th he passed a quiet though sleepless night, and seemed much as he had been the preceding evening,—still perfectly delirious. His head was shaved and wetted with an evaporating lotion. He immediately began to improve, and in half an hour was perfectly rational, though he had been delirious for sixteen hours. The rheumatism left the scalp and, no doubt, the membranes within the skull which also it had seized; but it continued in the knees, which were constantly half bent, especially the right, so that his right heel was constantly drawn up. On the 11th the delirium returned at seven in the evening, and lasted two hours, but without violence. The lotion was applied again to the scalp, and sinapisms were put upon the feet, with decided benefit: and the calomel and saline aperients were continued.

An attack of this delirium without violence, in which he stared a great deal and pointed at imaginary objects, now returned every evening, at the same time within an hour, and usually lasted an hour or two, followed by a sleepless night, though he was tolerably well in the day-time. As the disease had become periodical, two grains of sulphate of quinine were given every four hours, and six grains an hour before the attack was expected. Under this treatment the attack came later every evening, and lasted a shorter time; and it ceased at the end of twelve days from its first assumption of a periodical character, though on the fifth night a cause of excitement produced an attack. Curiously enough, in this attack, his right heel, which previously had applied itself flatly on the ground, was again drawn up more than an inch, and remained so for about twenty-four hours.

On the 6th of December he had another attack of rheumatism, followed, as in the preceding January, by periodical attacks of delirium, though far more violent. Sulphate of quinine was tried, in much larger doses than before, but in vain. Dr. James Blundell was called in, and prescribed first musk, and afterwards arsenic with it, and the disease ceased about the 23rd. During the severe weather of January, 1838, he experienced upon the 22nd a third attack of rheumatism, followed as before by periodical delirium, occurring about seven o'clock, sometimes a little earlier, sometimes a little later, every evening. It began with severe pain of the head, wildness of look, and slight catchings of the limbs. In about a quarter of an hour the eyes became fixed, and the full force of the fit burst forth, of the approach of which he was perfectly conscious. There was now such violence that three strong men were required to hold him in his bed, besides sheets confined across his body in several directions.

He raised his head, opened his eyes, and stared violently, and frightfully; snapped at every person who went near him, maliciously and slyly watching for opportunities; he bit the pillows and sheets, looked ferocious and menacing and grinned horridly; made the most terrific howlings and vociferations so as to disturb the neighbourhood, and after a while he invariably began whistling, at first imperfectly, but at length he got into a perfect tune, and this was a sure sign that the attack was near its end. He would next sink into a deep sleep for only a few minutes, and then wake completely exhausted. He next suffered violent headache for half an hour, then intense itching of the scalp for two hours, and then went to sleep. Cold applications to the head made him more violent. Sixteen grains of musk were given daily, as well as arsenic, sulphate of quinine, creosote, and carbonate of iron, all in large quantities, but in vain. Five drops of Scheele's prussic acid, and the second night eight, quieted him a little.

He always lay upon his back during the whole of the paroxysm, and turned upon his right side the instant that it went off. The length of the attack was from one hour to two and a half. He had not the least recollection of what had occurred, but always said he had been very ill.

Before mesmerism was practised, he not only turned on his back as the attack began, but always pulled off his nightcap. In an analogous manner, I see patients have peculiar ways as they first go into the mesmeric coma, unless the sleep comes on instantaneously. One lady always flings her head and chest violently over the right side of the bed, and, if precautions were not taken, would injure herself severely, as a small table with various articles stands close to the bedside. A youth flings himself to the right side of a sofa on which I mesmerize him. Sometimes the head balances backwards and forwards before it drops.

In this state of things, I was requested by his medical attendant, my former pupil, Mr. Chandler of Rotherhithe, to visit the patient in the evening during an attack.

On the 8th of February, the seventeenth night of the present attacks, I found him in bed confined by ropes across it, and further restrained by three men. He was howling, shouting, vociferating, barking, menacing, grinning, spitting, snapping, etc. I mesmerized him with passes for three quarters of an hour, he moving his head in every direction, sometimes to avoid me, sometimes to bite me. No effect was apparent. I advised Mr. Chandler to mesmerize him the next evening before the attack was expected,

because during the violence of any disease the system is less impressionable to all agencies, whether drugs or other medical
means. Mr. Chandler was totally unacquainted with mesmerism,
but trusted to my carefulness of observation and to my integrity
when I assured him of its powers; and, on my giving him a little
instruction, he cheerfully and amiably promised to comply with
my advice. Although the medicines taken at the time had hitherto
proved useless, I thought it right to give the patient the chance
of benefit from their continuance. The doses of prussic acid and
of creosote before the attack were respectively eight and twelve
drops: the daily amount of the sesquioxide of iron was two ounces,
and of the sulphate of quinine sixteen grains: and I advised the
augmentation of the latter quantities to four ounces and to twenty
grains. The length of the attack had gradually extended, and this
evening reached three hours.

The patient held mesmerism—"mere pawing before his eyes,"
as some wiseheads consider it—in perfect contempt; but he submitted at eight o'clock on the evening of the 9th. He was mesmerized for two hours and a quarter. The attack commenced
at nine but lasted only an hour and a quarter. It was distinctly
seen, he made no noise; he was so tranquil that no restraint was
required, his eyes instead of being always wide open and staring,
he evidently seeing, were closed, except when he raised his head
and half-opened them from time to time, apparently without dis-
cerning objects as before; and he sometimes seemed asleep for a
few moments. The attack terminated suddenly in a burst of
laughter, after several attempts at this in vain. He then said,
"That will do," and was very cheerful.

The mighty power of mesmerism over him was most decided.
His own words were, "There is something in it." The doses of
creosote and prussic acid had been the same as on the preceding
evenings.

February 10. Mesmerism was begun at a quarter past eight and
continued for an hour and a half. The attack commenced at a
quarter before nine and lasted only an hour. He raised his head
higher and stared more intently, but the snatches of sleep were
longer than on the preceding evening. On coming to himself, he

allowed that he was conscious now of having been influenced by mesmerism, and that it saved him great suffering, though he had denied this the day before with reference to Mr. Chandler's first attempt, and had treated this "marvellous remedy," as Mr. Chandler justly termed it in a letter to me, even with contempt. He slept both this night and the night before three hours, on recovering from the attack,—far longer than on any former nights.

The following is Mr. Chandler's letter, giving an abstract to the effect:—

"Rotherhithe, April 11, 1838."

"I am happy to inform you that our patient is much better. I tried the mesmerism, and it has succeeded to a miracle.

"I came home after leaving you on Thursday evening, and tried the operation upon Mrs. Chandler, who laughed very much at the idea. After five minutes she laughed still: but in ten minutes more, making fifteen, she was sound asleep, and no ordinary means could wake her.

"This converted me completely; and I went to work the next evening on Mr. . . ., and continued the operation two hours and a quarter.

"'The effect was to keep him perfectly quiet. Though he had the fit, the influence was very decided, and all the family were astonished.

"Last evening I practised it again, and with the same effect. He even acknowledged the influence himself, which he would not yesterday. It has produced quite a sensation in the parish."

"T. C."

11th. Mesmerism was begun at ten minutes past eight, and continued for an hour and a quarter. The attack commenced at five and twenty minutes before nine and lasted but fifty minutes. He raised his head still higher and stared still more intently, but his sleeps were longer; and, when from his horrible looks and his gestures he made Mr. Chandler almost afraid he would spring out of bed, his head would suddenly fall back upon the pillow like a lump of lead. The attack did not go off quite so pleasantly and he did not sleep so long as on the two previous nights. Still be it remembered that the attack lasted ten minutes less than the night before, and he required no restraint.—Here I must make an important remark. The aggravation of the symptoms tonight was nothing more than I continually observe in cases which advance steadily to a cure under mesmeric treatment. Mesmerizers should never be discouraged by such occurrences, but persevere if any good or even any sensible effect whatever has at any time been produced. The improvement generally returns. It is for want of perseverance with even the ordinary modes of treatment of diseases, that many chronic diseases are not cured.

12th. Mesmerism begun at eight and continued for an hour. The attack commenced at a quarter past eight and lasted but five and forty minutes. Only two drops of prussic acid had been given him.

13th. Neither creosote nor prussic acid was given him, for it was evident that the amelioration could not be ascribed to them. 1) A powerful and unquestionable impression was made upon the disease the first night that he was mesmerized before the attack. 2) The prussic acid had been reduced on the night of the 13th to two drops. 3) The patient, in spite of his prejudices, confessed the influence of the mesmeric process upon him from the diminished indisposition felt by him when the attack was over, and that it spared him much suffering; and he was always very anxious that Mr. Chandler should come in time to control the fit. 4) Whenever he raised his head upon the pillow, and was advancing it, a single pass of the hand now caused it instantly to drop back in sound sleep, though it would rise again in a minute; pointing at him with one finger had the same effect, and all this at the distance of ten feet and in the dark. 5) The mesmeric process brought on the attack. This had always begun at nine; but on the second mesmerization by Mr. Chandler it began a quarter before nine, on the third at five and twenty minutes to nine, and on the fourth at a quarter past eight. It is common for intermittent diseases, ague for example, or rheumatic pain of nerves, when they grow more and more severe, or longer and longer, to attack earlier and earlier; and as they grow more and more mild, or shorter and shorter, to attack later and later: it is unusual for them to attack earlier and grow milder and shorter, though sometimes they attack later and grow more severe. When this patient's attacks in January, 1837, lasted a shorter and shorter time, I mentioned that they commenced later and later. Now, when the attacks became milder, and regularly shorter and shorter, they commenced earlier and earlier. Any remedy but mesmerism, while it rendered the attacks milder and shorter, would have postponed them later and later. 6) The mesmeric effect of attachment to the mesmerizer, so common when striking effects are produced, was manifested; for the patient now always turned towards him, whether the room was in darkness or not, whereas previously to mesmerism being employed he aimed violence at Mr. Chandler and at everybody else.

Mr. Chandler, though unacquainted with mesmerism, saw clearly that the attack was under the control of the process, and justly conceived that he could bring it on at pleasure. He therefore mesmerized the patient at half-past seven. The attack began in five minutes; and the power of the process was more clearly demonstrated than ever, for the youth remained during the whole period as if in a mesmeric sleep, raising his head from time to time but not opening his eyes, as he invariably had done on raising his head before. The attack lasted five and twenty minutes only. Mr. Chandler awakened him suddenly, as it were magically, by passing his hand transversely three or four times, without contact, before the youth's face. On every former occasion he had been allowed to wake spontaneously, and this was always slowly. He passed a very quiet night, slept three or four hours, and was much better in the morning.

14th. Mesmerism was begun at eight o'clock. The attack took place in eight minutes and lasted five and twenty, in about the same degree as on the preceding evening. But the sleep was very profound in the intervals of his raising his head. Here it is worthy of remark, that little progress was made today. The attack lasted the same time—five and twenty minutes, and the degree of the symptoms was the same as on the preceding evening; the only manifestation of greater power in the process was the increased depth of the sleep in the intervals, and as a set off to this the production of the fit three minutes later. The explanation probably is that Mr. Chandler, from his engagements did not begin so early by half an hour as on the last evening. All remedies, given to obviate a periodical disease, act more efficiently if given at periods when the disease is completely absent or more nearly absent. Quinine, for instance, has comparatively little or no effect over ague if given in the fit: it should be given in the intermission:— when I mesmerized this patient in his fit, on first seeing him, I made not the least impression. During the intermission the effect of quinine is the greatest as soon as the fit is over,—that is, when the system may be regarded as well cleared of the disease. Its effect lessens as the period of the fit approaches: and thus, though efficient when given just before a fit, it controls the disease less than when given just after a fit; and the best practice is to give repeated doses during all the intermission, but as large a dose as can be borne at once just after the attack, and as many doses as possible in the early part of the intermission, though some of course up to the recommencement of the attack. As the period of the fit approaches, we cannot but consider that, although no change is discernible, the system is gradually working up into the condition of the fit; and therefore less and less impressionable by all agencies. The commencement of the mesmerization therefore tonight half an hour nearer the bursting forth of the attack rendered it less operative. I have no doubt that if it had been begun an hour earlier, the attack would have been brought on at once, and been far milder and shorter than ever. The power of the mesmerism was so manifest, and the amelioration so clearly owing to it, that Mr. Chandler now very properly at once discontinued the sesquioxide of iron which was taken in the quantity of four ounces and a half, and the sulphate of quinine which was taken in the quantity of thirty-six grains, in the day. Yet he passed a good night, and was in every respect much better in the morning.

15th. His right heel, which had been constantly drawn up day and night, just as in the previous rheumatic illnesses, was today flat upon the ground, though the knee remained weak. Mesmerism was not begun till a quarter before nine. In four minutes he fell asleep, and the attack began; and it lasted four and twenty minutes. The sleep was very profound between the movements of

his head, and it continued after these had entirely ceased, till
Mr. Chandler suddenly awakened him by a few transverse passes,
without contact, before his face. He awoke completely in his
senses. Mr. Chandler always knew when the fit was over and that
he might be awakened, from his turning on his right side, as already mentioned.

16th. He passed a good night. Mesmerism was begun at ten
minutes before nine. The attack began in three minutes, and lasted
twenty-two minutes, ending as usual in profound sleep. Mesmerization was continued during the sleep last night and tonight, but
with no evidence of increased effect.

17th. His condition even during the day regularly improves.
Mesmerism was begun at ten minutes after seven. The fit began in
three minutes and lasted but twelve minutes.

No prejudiced person will now venture even to suggest that the
fit could not be brought on at pleasure by mesmerism and rendered mild. The effect of mesmerism now was first to send him to
sleep. Then the fit would begin in a few minutes, as shown by his
turning on his back, raising his head occasionally, and sometimes
throwing his arms about. He lay with his face to the side of the
bed where Mr. Chandler sat, while being mesmerized, and when
asleep till the attack began; and then, as before he was ever mesmerized, he instantly turned on his back. Mr. Chandler thought it
worth while to ascertain whether the attack could be cut short
by mesmerism after it had begun. Therefore, before it was over,
while it was decidedly still present, he made transverse passes.
The patient instantly awoke, perfectly himself, and seemed better
than he usually was after an attack: he dressed himself again
and remained up for two hours, ate a hearty supper, passed a good
night and felt perfectly well the next morning.

18th. His nose having bled for two nights, some leeches were
put upon his temples; and, as he strongly objected to them, and
was compelled by his father to have them on, he was frightfully
irritable the whole day. On account of this, he was mesmerized
at a quarter past four. Though he was at the time in high excitement, he fell into a sound sleep in five minutes, and the little
features of the attack presented themselves as usual. Mr. Chandler

thought it more prudent to allow him to sleep rather than to awake him as early as had been done the night before, and therefore allowed the state to continue for seventeen minutes, when he was instantly awakened by a few transverse passes, and appeared perfectly well, having lost his excitement.

19th. Much better. Mesmerized at a quarter before one in the afternoon. He was sound asleep in two minutes, and very faint marks of an attack were visible. Mr. Chandler awoke him by transverse passes at the end of seven minutes, and he was quite well and so remained all day.

From this day he was not mesmerized and had no attack. For some time he was more unwell than usual and slept badly. But this would have been obviated had the mesmerism been repeated daily for a week or two, and then left off gradually.

Those who witnessed the exquisite phenomena of the two Okeys will be struck with the similarity of the present case; and will appreciate my feelings at receiving Mr. Chandler's accounts, proving an identity of condition, an identity of influence, though neither the youth nor the operator had even seen the Okeys, nor had any conception whatever of mesmerism—proving the reality of a peculiar state of body and of a peculiar influence.

ST. VITUS'S DANCE is a very common disease from six or seven to sixteen or seventeen years of age, and chiefly in females. I ascertained many years ago that iron is almost a specific remedy for it. The least disturbing form of iron is the sesquioxide, and I have never once failed to cure the disease with this remedy, when the disease was general throughout the body, and had not lasted some years. Purgatives, blisters, and all debilitating and irritating measures for the most part retard the cure. Arsenic, copper, and zinc, have great power over it; but iron cures the most cases, and the most rapidly, even when there is headache and a full habit. I have often seen the good of iron sadly interfered with by the practitioner being too busy with purgatives, and fiddle-faddling with other remedies, and not allowing the iron fair play by exhibiting it steadily and undisturbedly. A regular state of bowels is all that is required. Still, taking medicine is always disagreeable; and I resolved, when I first saw the power of mesmerism, to ascertain what it could do in this disease; and my success has been astonishing. It has been most beneficial even in a case of many years standing, such as in which I have found iron useless; and in which case itself, iron actually proved useless.

I recollect about twelve years ago smiling incredulously when a German physician, now no more, Dr. Kind, assured me in St. Thomas's Hospital that "animal magnetism was a good remedy for St. Vitus's dance." He had learned this in his own country, but Germany has very little availed itself of its knowledge; and it has been reserved to Britain to establish the universal acknowledgment and application of Gall's mighty discoveries and of the truths for which Mesmer laboured.

I. It is five years since I first treated St. Vitus's dance with mesmerism. Henrietta Power, aged 17, servant of all work, was admitted under my care in University College Hospital, April 28th, 1838, for St. Vitus's dance. About a fortnight previously, while taking in the tea things, she suddenly dropped them, and the disease at the same moment declared itself, but without any other disturbance of a single function. She was in constant motion, flexion, extension, rotation, twitching and catching; dragged one leg along the ground; rolled the face and chin on the neck and shoulders; grimaced; rubbed her eyes; could not continue to sit in the same situation. The least excitement rendered all the movements more violent. Her mother had been obliged to make her a bed upon the floor, and, sit up all night to prevent her injuring herself; and she had slept but little during the fortnight. The left arm and right leg were more affected than the others. She could swallow well, but had extreme difficulty in speaking. When asked to give me her hand, it went into all sorts of movements. Though she was ruddy and of a full habit, her pulse was quiet and weak. I ordered her no medicine, but mesmerism for half an hour every day, morning or afternoon. She was mesmerized in the afternoon for half an hour with no sensible effect. It was necessary to confine her in bed by straps to prevent her falling out; she slept only two hours altogether in the night, but during her sleep was quiet.

29th. More quiet than yesterday. She was mesmerized for half an hour. Slept six hours at night, and did not require to be confined in her bed.

30th. Movements rather increased, but she had a good night.

May 5th. Has improved daily since the last report; walks easily the length of the ward. During the mesmerism she moves much less, and is rather heavy.

8th. Has steadily improved; assists the nurse, and can carry a saucepan of water from an adjoining room to the fire place in the ward.

13th. Still better; can extend her arms and hands firmly and hold a book well enough to read it. Very heavy during the mesmerization.

24th. So much better that she does needle-work with ease.

29th. Several persons joined hands, and one held a hand of the mesmerizer; and under his manipulations she went to sleep.

June 3rd. Only drowsiness induced since the 29th.

4th. Not rendered even drowsy.

From this time she was rendered drowsy, but nothing more; and,

July 5th, was all but perfectly well, and I kept her till the 24th of July to see her cure established. She took no medicine all the time, and ate meat several times a week.

Here was another admirable cure without any expense for drugs. But it was beneath the notice of the doctors, and above all of the distinguished Dr. A. T. Thomson who had patients in the same ward: and such simple, inexpensive, and perfect cures were forbidden by the Committee of the College.

II. Mary Ann Vergo, aged 13. Ill three months with St. Vitus's dance. In the humble walk of life. Sent to me by Mr. Baker, surgeon, at Staines, August 4th, 1840. She had experienced the same disease in the spring, four times at intervals of two years; and it has always lasted six or seven months. I mesmerized her for half an hour daily myself, till the 8th of September, and gave her no medicine. She was always much quieter during the process, and for the first fortnight sleepy, but not afterwards. The improvement was very gradual; and she was well enough actually to make a straw bonnet before the middle of September, that is in about six weeks from the commencement of the treatment; and perfectly well before the end of that month.

I have just heard from Mr. Baker that she has remained well till this summer (1843), the interval of the attack now having been three years instead of two; and the present attack is much milder than ever it was before, and is yielding to iron and the cold shower bath. There can be no doubt that mesmerism without either would cure her more rapidly than before.

III. The following case was treated by Mr. Wood, and I give it in his words. "Elizabeth Alexander, 26 years old. When 13 years of age it was first observed that any sort of excitement produced catchings and twitchings of her hands, arms, and other parts, and any sudden fright produced the same symptoms, and caused the bowels to be very much relaxed. This state continued getting gradually worse until she was 19, when she was taken to Bath, used the waters, took cold shower baths, hot baths, etc."

Remained at Bath five months, and returned home quite well for five years.

January, 1841. About twelve months ago the same symptoms returned and have been gradually getting worse up to January, 1842. She has almost constant involuntary movements and catchings in the head and face, and also in the hands and feet, particularly the former. She was mesmerized by Mr. Wood during half an hour without any visible effect.

Mesmerism was continued by Mr. Wood daily for nearly two months. The involuntary movements gradually subsided, and at the end of that time she went home quite well.

IV. A friend of mine who has the largest provincial practice among physicians in England, and has had the virtue and manliness always to avow his conviction of the truth of mesmerism—Dr. Simpson of York, related to me, when in town three years ago, that he had cured a case of this disease at one sitting; and has just now sent me the following account of it.

"York, June 9th, 1843.

My Dear Sir,

I regret not having had an opportunity of writing to you.

A little girl, aged thirteen, had an attack of chorea, in the early part of the year, for three successive years. The indisposition was perfectly suspended by the carbon. ferri. in the course of six weeks, on two occasions; on the third attack two surgeons and myself determined to try the effects of mesmerism, without the use of any medicine taken internally; she was mesmerized for forty minutes. Very little apparent effect was produced at the time, but the disease was entirely suspended, and although the process was never repeated, she has had no relapse.

My dear sir, yours most faithfully,
T. Simpson."

V. Master Linnell, of Mercer Row, Northampton, nine years of age, a clever and healthy boy and always in action, was reading on Friday, November 4th, 1842, near the fireplace, when he was frightened by flames suddenly descending from the chimney, the communicating chimney of the kitchen below having caught fire. He screamed and ran out of the room; but took no further notice in particular of the circumstance. However, at night, after he had been in bed two hours, he "flew screaming down stairs, as white as a sheet," saying that he smelled fire, and that the fire had broken out again. His mother warmed him, gave him some wine, and took him to bed again. In another hour, he ran down screaming again with fright. His mother then kept him up till she went to bed herself. On Saturday he was "poorly, fretting, and low."

On Sunday, at church, he disturbed his mother by his fidgetiness during the whole of the service, on which account she punished him, and was so displeased that she would not allow him to go again in the evening.

On Monday and Tuesday he was observed to be in great motion; and his mouth frothed, which he said he could not help, for "his tongue was grown so large." He spoke so badly that his mother thought he was mimicking, and scolded him; when he cried and said he could not speak properly, she saw that he was ill, and supposed the fright had been the cause. A druggist told her that "the fright had caused too much blood to flow to the brain, and that he might have worms, but that by giving a little medicine and plenty of nourishment he would soon get better," and sent him three powders. "I gave him," writes his mother in a statement which she drew up, "two, and, after the action on the bowels, he was immediately worse; but finding him getting worse, sent him to Dr. Robertson, who said that it was the St. Vitus's dance, caused by fright, and ordered him a blister on the back of the neck and strengthening medicine.

"The next day I was obliged to send for Dr. Robertson, as the motions had increased so much that we could not hold him, and he had quite lost his speech.

"Dr. Robertson and Mr. Terry (surgeon) attended him daily for some time, and he had scarcely any sleep for ten nights, and took a great deal of medicine and a shower bath every morning. Not seeing him get much better, I asked the doctor if change might not be of use. He said certainly. I brought him to London. And, having read a book of the Rev. W. W. Mosely" (father of the Rev. Professor Mosely of King's College), "took my child to him. But after a week's trial found him getting worse, and was obliged to hire a carriage to draw him in and out of the house. I then went to Surgeon Cholmondley of Nottingham Place, who said he seldom saw a case of that kind cured in boys." She was advised by Mr. Dyer of Upper Marylebone Street to bring him to me. On January 4, 1843, he was brought in a coach to me and obliged to be carried into the house. Supported by his mother, he walked with great difficulty from my dining-room into my library.

His debility was such that he could not stand a moment unsupported; his head hung on one side; his tongue out of his mouth, which constantly slobbered; his look was quite fatuitous; he could not articulate, making only inarticulate noises, and these with extreme difficulty. Even yes and no were said in the strangest manner so as hardly to be understood. He often fell into a passion at not being able to articulate. He ground his teeth, and sighed greatly; continually blew bubbles of saliva from his mouth, and moved his tongue. The movements of the disease had lessened, so as not to be in proportion to his extreme muscular debility. He could use neither hand for any purpose, and scarcely ever raised the right. He was low-spirited and fretful, and often cried almost without cause.

His tongue was clear and moist; his appetite good, and his bowels in the most healthy condition. His pulse 74.

He cried sadly at being brought to me, thinking that I should give him loads of physic to swallow and blister him, as others had done.

I mesmerized him by vertical passes before his face for half an hour. He sat well supported in an easy chair, his head on his breast; but he sat so quietly in comparison with his usual state that his mother noticed it. He was mesmerized daily for the same time in the same way.

5th and 6th. Spoke less inarticulately after mesmerization today than before. Indeed, can walk and stand alone a little.

7th. Walks with less support: his countenance is clearer and its expression more intelligent. Perfectly still while mesmerized.

8th. Walks better; after being mesmerized walked twice round the room alone, without stopping, though unsteadily, and he stood well alone.

9th. Walked alone four times round the room after being mesmerized. Is always much stronger after it than before.

10th and 11th. Walked five times round the room alone and without stopping, faster and more upright.

12th and 13th. Walked much better and speaks better—said, "pudding." He blows no bubbles with his saliva while mesmerized; and has gaped, as if sleepy, for several days during the process.

14th and 15th. Walks still better; and speaks decidedly better.

17th. Stands about the room well, and has walked out of doors alone twice: articulates a great many words. He has sat less and less drooping and supported while being mesmerized; has sighed, slobbered, and blown bubbles less and less.

In a few days he read aloud freely in a book opened by me at random, and took a walk every day; and in three weeks from the first day of mesmerism he fed himself with his left hand, and walked from his lodgings, Park Street, Dorset Square, to my house.

On the 30th he walked five miles, and could talk well. He continued to improve rapidly; could use his right hand well on the 2nd of February; and by the 10th was perfectly cured: and is well at this moment—June 26.

I mesmerized him on the 15th of February for the last time, having omitted but once (February 6th). He says that for some time past he has been very sick of sitting still to be mesmerized, feeling so strong and active: whereas formerly he was glad to sit still, and sorry when I had finished.

Nothing could be more decisive of the power of mesmerism than this case. The disease was getting worse and worse at the time I began. An effect was visible in a few days; the benefit steadily increased; and, from being a slobbering idiot-looking child, his head hanging on one side, unable to speak or stand unsupported, in three weeks he could stand easily and walk five miles. Not a particle of medicine was given after the first day.

The true gratitude of the boy and his mother was delightful. But my medical reward was, that the surgeon who attended him, and whose very name I had never before heard of, gave way to such bad feeling as publicly to attack me, by reiterating a silly and ignorant string of sentences from a very dull and feeble medical periodical, called the *Provincial Journal*, but took care to omit all mention of the case which led to his hostility.

The following cases and remarks have been kindly sent me by Mr. Prideaux of Southampton.

VI. "In November, 1841, Eliza Beale, then about sixteen years of age, and residing with her parents in the village of Itchen, became a patient of the Southampton Dispensary for a severe attack of St. Vitus's dance. After being under treatment two months without benefit, the surgeon whose care she was under, Mr. G.B. List, with a freedom from prejudice which contrasts advantageously with the bigotry of too many of his professional brethren, offered me an opportunity of attempting her cure by mesmerism, which I willingly embraced. At the time I first saw the patient the convulsive movements were violent and incessant, whilst her countenance presented a pitiable expression of fatuity which it was painful to behold, and which indicated that her intellect had become much impaired. The state of her digestive functions was such that Mr. List proposed that he should administer a little aperient medicine at the same time that I was treating her by mesmerism. To this however I decidedly objected, not from any doubt as to the propriety of the treatment, but because I was aware from experience that the sittings would render such a course unnecessary, and was moreover desirous that the result of the case might be as conclusive as possible, that no loop-hole for doubt as to the means of cure might be opened, but that the single and unassisted power of mesmerism might be rendered clearly apparent.

"At the first sitting I mesmerized her energetically for three quarters of an hour, neither willing to entrance her nor the reverse, but with the desire that my influence might be exerted in just that way which would prove most beneficial to her. The only perceptible effects produced beyond a very slight manifestation of attraction and increase of attraction and increase of the convulsive moments, were, that the patient became intensely cold and experienced a pricking sensation running along the course of the spine. The first sitting took place on a Monday morning at 10 o'clock, and her mother was requested to bring her again at the same hour on Wednesday.

"On Wednesday morning she accordingly presented herself; the moment she entered the room it was apparent at a glance that the convulsive movements were very much lessened both in violence and frequency, but my feelings of pleasurable surprise at an amendment so rapid were speedily drowned in the astonishment which seized me, when, as she approached and I perceived the expression of her countenance, I saw a change so great that nothing but the evidence of my own senses could have made me credit it, and concerning which it is no exaggeration to say that she was transformed from a creature apparently verging on idiocy into a rational being. Could I present my readers with a daguerreotyped portrait of my patient taken on each occasion, I might then succeed in convincing them of the amount of change which took place. But without such a testimony I feel that any language I may employ will fail in effecting this object, since, had I myself, prior to witnessing so incredible a transformation, read any such account, I should certainly have concluded it to be exaggerated and made large deductions for the imagination of the writer.

"The second sitting, like the first, lasted three quarters of an hour, and the effects produced were the same except that the aggravation of the convulsive movements by the operation was more marked. The weather being stormy, to save the patient from exposure to the wet in crossing the ferry to Southampton, I promised her mother to visit her at her own house on Friday morning. I accordingly went, and to my surprise found my patient entirely cured of her chorea. Not a trace of convulsive movement was to be perceived, and upon asking her mother when they ceased, she replied, 'I have not seen her twitch once, Sir, since she left your house.'

"The patient's appetite remaining bad I again mesmerized her for three quarters of an hour, and on this occasion she manifested a disposition to sleep without however quite going off. I left the house with a promise to visit her again if it should prove necessary, and desired her mother to take an early opportunity of letting me know how she was. In the ensuing week the mother called to return her thanks and stated that her daughter's appetite was quite restored, and that she was more active, sprightly and better, in every respect, than she had been for years before, and from a visit I paid her a few days ago I find that she has remained quite well ever since.

"A case more conclusive than the foregoing of the power of mesmerism as a remedial agent in the cure of disease it would be difficult to conceive. It presents to us a case of severe chorea under medical treatment for two months without benefit, three-fourths cured by the first sitting; we see the disease in its subdued form continue up to and during the second sitting, which has the effect of aggravating its symptoms, but, behold, at its termination the patient walks out of the house cured, and in the language of her mother 'has never been seen to twitch since;' the occurrence of the crisis in her malady and the application of mesmerism, bearing such a relation to each other in point of time as irresistibly to impress all sane individuals with the conviction that the relation of cause and effect subsisted between them, and to entitle us to exclaim, that never was the cure of any disease more clearly attributable to the operation of any remedy.

"For my own part so intense has been the gratification which I have derived from having been the instrument of conferring such a benefit on a fellow-creature, so great the delight I have experienced in contemplating this new revelation of nature and musing on the happy consequences to man which its cultivation promises, that I can truly say that the pleasurable emotions which the successful result of this single case has afforded me, have more than compensated for all the obloquy, abuse, and ridicule, which have been heaped upon me for choosing to believe in the evidence of my senses and unhesitatingly on all occasions avowing my convictions."

VII. "The second case of St. Vitus's dance treated by me is that of a young woman of Ryde, twenty-six years of age, named Snudden, and was brought under my notice by a lady whose ever active benevolence is always on the watch to do good, and who had previously been witness of a most extraordinary cure I had effected by the agency of mesmerism, and assisted me not a little in its completion.

"The patient, Jane Snudden, about ten years prior to the commencement of her treatment by me in June, 1842, had begun to perceive a winking of the eyes and slight movements of the muscles of the face, which continually increased, till at length, four years after the accession of her disorder, she was affected with violent twitchings and contortions over her whole frame to such an extent as seriously to interfere with her occupation as a seamstress, the jerking of her arms being often so great as to break the thread she was sewing with: in other respects her health remained good and her appetite was not impaired. She continued in this state rather getting worse than better up to the time when I first saw her; at this period her figure was robust, her colour fresh, and her general appearance quite the reverse of an invalid.

"I mesmerized her on the first occasion for half an hour; this sitting lessened the severity of the disease fully one half, and I entertained the most sanguine hopes of a speedy cure. Elated with her amendment, at the interval of a week she walked seven miles under a hot sun to procure a sitting, and little if any benefit appeared to be derived on this occasion. I mesmerized her subsequently three or four times at intervals of a fortnight, but the cure, though progressing, not proceeding so rapidly as I desired, and attributing the slow progress to the length of time which intervened between the sittings, I relinquished the treatment of the case to a gentleman resident in the town, by whom she was mesmerized three times a week for three months, at the close of which time she considered herself cured; the only trace of her complaint remaining being a very slight and almost imperceptible twitching of the muscles of the face when she became excited.

"The only perceptible effect produced on this patient by the sittings I gave her was slight drowsiness, but subsequently, after she had been mesmerized regularly three times a week for a considerable period, she used to go to sleep on each occasion, was very difficult to be awakened, and manifested community of taste. A few days since, I called to see her, and regret to state that within the last month the disease has shown a disposition to return, and she proposes again to recur to mesmerism in the event of its increasing."

VIII. "Matilda Esther, aged eleven years, residing with her parents at No. 1, York Square, Southampton, became in the autumn of 1842 gradually affected with chorea and paralysis of the right side of the body. After being under treatment in the dispensary for six weeks with some improvement in her general health, but with little amendment of the chorea, and none of the paralysis, on the 13th of February her mother brought her to me by the advice of her medical attendant.

"At this period the convulsive movements though not severe were incessant, her arm hung powerless by her side, and her mother stated that her leg often suddenly gave way, so as to cause her nearly to fall to the ground. I commenced mesmerizing her for half an hour every morning. The twitchings diminished perceptibly from day to day, and at the end of the fifth sitting not a trace of them remained; about this period the patient also commenced endeavouring to use her right hand, and was able to feed herself at the end of the tenth sitting, which she had not done for upwards of three months. I now lessened the frequency of the sittings to every alternate day, and six more sufficed to complete the cure, and to restore the arm to its normal state of strength. The only visible effect of the sittings was a great increase of the convulsive movements; this was always very marked, and continued to the end; and though after the fifth sitting no traces of chorea appeared in the child in her ordinary state, the twitchings invariably began about two minutes after commencement of the sitting, continued to its termination, and could always be aggravated in any part by especially directing the operation to it.

"What will the medical scoffers at mesmerism say to these and similar cases? Will they have the assurance to vote them beneath their consideration, and affirm that their present mode of curing such diseases is so satisfactory, so mild in its nature, and so happy in its results, as to leave nothing to be desired? Or will they resort to their old tactics of making abortive attempts to explain away facts, and raise once more the hackneyed cry of imagination? Verily if imagination—pure imagination—work such wonders, she should be placed at the head of the materia medica, and the credit of many of the faculty would be more than a little improved by calling in her assistance.

"With what a choice tableau of the philosophers of the nineteenth century, will the scene recently enacted in the Royal Medical and Chirurgical Society furnish posterity? We see a set of men who are unable to specify one single cause why the phenomena of mesmerism should be impossible, beyond the mere circumstance of these being contrary to their previous experience, and who must know full well that this can be no test of truth, and who yet without examination suffer themselves so to be carried away by their passions and prejudices, that, with a violence proportionate to their lack of facts and arguments, each struggles to bawl the loudest against discoveries which the unanimous voice of future generations will confirm. How lamentable that man should so prostitute the noble heritage of reason, as to cast it from him when he forms his opinions, and only recur to its aid to search for plausibilities to defend the creed, which, slave as he is, has been dictated by his passions.

"Were the well-attested facts of mesmerism only one-tenth part so numerous as they are, still their production is so completely within the reach of all, that no language could be too strong to characterize the irrationality, the folly, and the blindness of those, who in hot haste rush forward and risk their reputation by affirming the impossibility of them, without having made one single attempt to elicit them. All who make such essays become of necessity converts, and all should make them except they are prepared to lay it down as an axiom, that whatever is incomprehensible is false; a doctrine, the innate silliness of which is only paralleled by its arrogance and presumption. We are diverted at the incredulity with which the eastern potentate received the tale, that water occasionally became solid as crystal in the native country of his guest, but after having all his life long as inseparably associated the idea of fluidity with water, as that of heat with fire, great allowance is to be made for his refusing to believe in a transformation he had no means of verifying, and we must not place him so low in the scale of rationality, as those who, surrounded with opportunities for observation, adhere to some bigoted prepossession against mesmerism without once availing themselves of their aid.

"As the ignorant become conversant from childhood with the various phenomena around them, till their frequent repetition has to their unthinking brains divested them of wonder, and they regard none as requiring explanation, so in phenomena, not one whit more wonderful or inexplicable, when presented for the first time, they behold an impossibility. The philosopher however sees that the more circumstance of his being conversant with one class of phenomena and not with another, can exert no influence on their intrinsic quality of wonderfulness, and smiles to see men whose minds are too permanently contracted to expand to the reception of a new truth, and who ludicrously mistake their own narrowness of view for profundity, and the inveteracy of their prejudices for superior penetration, complacently characterizing as visionaries, those whose more enlarged conceptions emancipate them from thinking by habit.

"The question is,—is truth to be determined by facts or by the priori reasonings,—the conjectures,—the fancies of individuals? If the latter, let the maxim—'Homo nature minister et interpres, tantum facit et intelligit quantum de nature ordine re vel mente observaverit; nec amplius scit, aut potest'—be at once exploded, and let us seek at the hands of these new luminaries of science a fresh edition of that Aristotelian philosophy which substitutes speculation for induction, and, when opposed by facts, coolly proclaims that if they do not agree with its theories so much the worse for them."

These are all the Cases of insanity and St. Vitus's dance that have been treated with mesmerism by myself or, to my knowledge, by my friends. I have therefore no failures to relate or I would relate them.

I request you to postpone the publication of Master Salmon's Case, as it was partly one of palsy and I propose to send you a group of Cases of palsy, cured by mesmerism, for your next number.

> I am, Sir,
> Yours, &c., &c.,
> JOHN ELLIOTSON.

June, 1843

John Elliotson

NUMEROUS CASES OF SURGICAL OPERATIONS
WITHOUT PAIN IN THE MESMERIC STATE;

With Remarks upon the Opposition of Many
Members of the Royal Medical and Chirurgical
Society and Others to the Reception of the
Inestimable Blessings of Mesmerism.
By John Elliotson, M.D., Cantab., F.R.S.
London, 1843*

This is a remarkable book, called forth by a most remarkable cause, and at a most extraordinary period. It not only exposes the ignorance and malevolence of certain members of the medical profession, but it places before us an instructive lesson—the fact of a strictly moral and intellectual physician promulgating a great truth—fighting with the prejudices of his compeers, and presenting to them against their desire, *as he has frequently done before,* a new engine with which to alleviate the miseries of suffering humanity. If we recall the proceedings of the last four years, how distressing the retrospect! On every side we behold injustice and persecution. From all quarters the most rabid animalism has been manifested, and too frequently by those whose situation should compel them to investigate every new physiological subject, and who, if they were conscientious in the discharge of their duty, would not prostitute the professional chair to the basest of all purposes—the retardation of a great truth, and the denunciation of scientific investigators.

We remember the disgraceful course pursued by the Professors of University College in 1838 and 1839; and we find in 1842 the same disreputable conduct characterizing the proceedings at the meetings of the Royal Medical and Chirurgical Society. However, notwithstanding all this odious bad feeling and unphilosophical opposition, we find Dr. Elliotson steadfastly adhering to the great fundamental principle upon which he erected his fame—a determination to search after truth, and moral courage to avow the same when he discovered it. How exalted and dignified such a

*Book review: *The Zoist,* A Journal of Cerebral Physiology and Mesmerism and Their Application to Human Welfare, *1*:211-217, June 1843.

course! How paltry, mean, and detestable, the contract—the conduct of those who filled chairs in the same University! "I think," said the Professor of Physiology, "that there is something in mesmerism, but if I avow my belief I shall lecture to empty benches."

Here at least, we have the truth. Here is a most substantial reason for neglecting investigation. Mammon is their god. Mammon they worship day after day. If their benches are full, they luxuriate in the sight and count their rent roll.* They confine themselves to the dry detail of their own particular department—they move on in the same jogtrot manner year after year, and if aught occurs to interfere with their preconceived ideas or premature theories, they either boldly pronounce an anathema on the enunciator of the new facts, or, they fig-leaf truth, flutter through their little day, and die enveloped in their ignorance. Can it be possible that such a course was, and is, pursued in the liberal University of the first city of the most liberal nation? Can it be possible that man undertaking the duty of public instructors should so forget the great cause to which they devoted (?), as to peril the immediate reception of a truth by a dastardly subserviency to the popular breath? Oh, how they mistake their calling! Oh, how they require that vitality which true philosophy alone can infuse! When scientific men shall be advanced so far in the practice of morality as to

---

*We do not think we can better demonstrate the high, liberal, and philosophic principles, which have always guided Dr. Elliotson through his career, than by contrasting his conduct at the period when he resigned his chair in University College, with the low, sordid, and grovelling motives influencing the conduct of the authorities. We quote from Dr. E.'s admirable farewell address to the students. The Dean urged, "that whether the wonderful facts were true or not, and whether great benefit in the treatment of diseases would result or not, we ought to consider the interests of the school;—not of science and humanity, observe—but of the school; that if the public did not regard the matter as true and the benefits as real, we ought not to presevere and risk the loss of public favour to the school; that I was rich, and could afford to lose my practice for what I believed the truth, but that others were not;—in short his argument was 'rem—rem' and 'virtus post nummos.' I replied that the Institution was established for the dissemination and discovery of truth; that all other considerations were secondary to this; that if the public were ignorant, we should enlighten them; that we should lead the public, and not the public us; and that the sole question was whether the matter were a truth or not. I laughed at the idea of injury to the pecuniary interests of the school."

abhor the moral turpitude, the result of even an attempt to suppress a truth—when they shall become sincere in the advocacy of their opinions and discard the "chirping of the sparrows" which flutter around them—when they shall boldly unite for the purpose of disenthralling first themselves, and then the world—how different will be the lessons taught in our colleges, and how pure and invigorating the philosophy which will flourish under such favourable culture. Men will then unite and mutually assist in the investigation of a scientific subject, and they will be all influenced by that ardour without which no progress, individually or collectively, can ever be made. Who can think of the machinery of such a cooperative system without being convinced of the important results which must accrue? Can low, selfish and individual interest, compete with exalted, liberal, and cooperative efforts? Can the pigmy wrestle with the giant, or scientific truths be promulgated faster by the efforts of one or a thousand advocates? Much as our enthusiasm may lead us to contemplate the consummation of our wishes at no distant period—we are compelled to confess that reflection and every day's experience convinces us, that *now* the majority of men are influenced by selfish motives, and the prospects of individual aggrandizement. We need no better proof than the recent proceedings at the Medico-Chirurgical Society, when the case of amputation, *without pain,* during the mesmeric trance, was brought forward by Mr. Topham and Mr. Ward. Not one manly form stood forth to assist the few struggling advocates for the freedom of scientific investigation—not one of the "world's great men" lifted up his voice to plead the cause of science, but all—

"Trammell'd and bound in custom's changeless school,
Absurd by system, frivolous by rule."

assisted to denounce as nonsense a natural fact, and to designate as visionaries and impostors, the only men who proved by their conduct that they were really sincere in their advocacy of a new and startling truth. The discovery of a new truth is but the recognition of one, or of a series, of previously unobserved facts. Why then did those who had not observed the facts, question the sincerity and intellectual acumen of those who had? Here is the answer. Science and ignorance—the world's wisdom and the world's folly—have both their boundaries marked by the same sign-posts—prejudice and obstinacy. How clearly was the truth of this opinion proved on the occasion referred to!

The absurdities and vulgarities which were indulged in, have been exposed in the most complete manner by Dr. Elliotson, and we would recommend every one to obtain a copy of this pamphlet for the purpose of being armed with the means to enable them to crush similar opposition. We will, however, assist those gentlemen—

"Who dare to trample where they scarce should tread."
in acquiring the notoriety they were so desirous for, by enrolling their names in our pages. Behold, a motley group! Mr. Coulson, Dr. Moore, Mr. Blake, Mr. Alcock, Dr. James Johnson, Dr. M. Hall, Dr. G. Burrows, Sir B. Brodie, Mr. Liston, Dr. Copland, and Mr. B. Cooper. These were the principal speakers on this memorable occasion, and to the uninitiated such an array of names, some of which they are accustomed to consider "great," might make them doubt the facts these gentlemen opposed. But can we not present a list composed of men far more intellectual, and who are as far superior, and differ as widely in scientific reputation from them, as, for the sake of example, Hippocrates or Celsus do from Dr. Moore of Saville Row, or Mr. Coulson of the city?* "It would not," says Mr. Chenevix, "disgrace the greatest man whom England ever has produced to attempt an experiment or two upon a doctrine which Hufeland, Jussieu, Cuvier, Ampere, and La Place believed. Nay, *would it not disgrace him more to condemn, without knowing anything about it, what they knew and credited? Is supercilious ignorance the weapon with which Bacon would have repelled a new branch of knowledge, however extraordinary*

---

*Dr. Moore has the distinction of being the first person who in a scientific society of gentlemen required that the detail of philosophical experiments should be supported by affidavits made before the lord mayor.

"Mr. Coulson, while the paper was reading, exclaimed, "What d——d stuff this is!' Mr. C. has also confessed to me since the discussion, that he has never seen a mesmeric fact and is quite ignorant of mesmerism."—Pamphlet, page 12.

it might have appeared to him? Surely what *great men* believe, *ordinary men* may try."

Dr. M. Hall receives a complete and well-merited castigation. His speech contained the most arrant nonsense, and most satisfactorily has it been dissected and answered.

"Man ever vaunts his worth beyond its due,
On his own wisdom pompously dilates,
And shines in precepts: but his actions view,
You'll find him tripping, even whilst he prates."

He took upon himself to explain to an assembly of his brethren, what kind of phenomena the nervous system *ought* to manifest when in a state, regarding which *he knew nothing at all*! But Dr. M. Hall shall speak for himself:

"Dr. MARSHALL HALL, some years ago, when my Demonstrations went on at University College Hospital, called mesmerism 'trumpery' that 'polluted the temple of science;' and now, being *like all the other opponent speakers, totally ignorant of the subject*, and glorying in his ignorance, very consistently considered the present case to be one of imposition, because the poor man's sound leg did not start or contract while the diseased leg was amputated! The case, he says, *'proved too much, or rather flatly contradicted itself,'* because the sound leg did not contract when the diseased one was cut. He asserted that, 'in cases of insensibility in brutes, from intercourse of any portion with the brain being stopped by division of the spinal cord, or from absolute decapitation, or from stunning by a blow upon the head, such an injury of an insensible *leg* as pricking it with anything, lacerating, or cutting, —such an injury for instance as plunging a sharp instrument into the muscles,' (I sat next to Dr. M. Hall and those were his very words,) 'invariably causes both legs to contract; and, unless man differs from all other animals, the same must take place in the human being; and, as this man did not move his *other* leg—did not enact the *reflex motions,* he was no physiologist.' Had he been such a physiologist as Dr. Marshall Hall and read about the reflex motions, 'he would have known better, and would have moved the other leg,—and enacted the reflex motions.' The ignorant man! Dr. Marshall Hall's right leg would have moved most physiologically, if a surgeon had plunged a knife into his left. It was very silly of the man not to allow his sound leg to start, nor his diseased leg, nor any part of his frame. But a horse has been just as silly, just 'as bad a physiologist,' and has just as 'flatly contradicted itself,' by not 'enacting the reflex motions.' 'A horse was struck with the pole-axe over the anterior lobes of the brain. It fell instantly, as if struck with a thunder-bolt; it was convulsed, and then remained motionless. It shortly began to breathe, and continued to breathe freely by the diaphragm. When lacerated or pricked with a sharp pointed instrument, as a *pin* or *nail,* on any part of the face or surface of the body, it was totally motionless, manifesting no evidence of sensation or volition.' In another account it is said, 'deep lacerations' of these parts produced no movement of any kind, nor any infliction on the skin by 'a pin or other pointed instrument.' Now this I quote against Dr. Marshall Hall on authority considered by Dr. Marshall at least equal to any in the world — equal to his own. But whose can this be? Can there be an authority equal to Dr. Marshall Hall's? It is Dr. Marshall Hall himself! Dr. Marshall Hall in print, against Dr. Marshall Hall in debate! Dr. Marshall Hall in print proving too much, or rather flatly contradicting Dr. Marshall Hall in debate! But Dr. Marshall Hall in print is quite right.

"The other extremity may move, but it may not. I cut off the heads of some frogs, and, in the presence of Professor Wheatstone of King's College, Mr. Atkinson, Mr. Symes, and Mr. Wood, pinched the toes of one leg with the forceps; the leg contracted but the other leg was still. I repeated the experiment twenty times, and, in almost every instance, the same leg only contracted; once or twice the other leg contracted, but it was when general contractions of the whole mass of the frog took place. I repeatedly pinched the muscles of the thigh, and they alone contracted, the other extremity being invariably unaffected. Provoking frogs! Why did you not contract your other leg? Impostors! You little thought you 'proved too much'—for Dr. Marshall Hall; and yet you were but like some other unphysiological frogs. For Dr. Marshall Hall says that, if, when he divides the spinal cord in frogs just below the occiput, so that the creatures remain motionless, he then pricks or pinches the toes, 'there is no movement at first, but soon distinct movements, take place, and generally retractions of the limb!'—not limbs."

Is it possible to point out in clearer language the ridiculous position in which Dr. M. Hall has placed himself? Really we feel for him most deeply.

"The *frog* a wooing in his op'ra hat—
The puss in Wellingtons—presumptuous cat!—
Cock-robin's rook in clericals and band—
A hog in armour, or a fish on land—
All move our laughter: but oh!"

Really his position instead of producing laughter, excites our pity. Fancy Dr. M. Hall dictating to dame Nature! Fancy the presumption of the man, asserting that the report of a certain natural phenomenon is untrue, "because I, Dr. M. Hall, have proved by means of certain experiments, such as the decapitation of frogs and tortoises, and the pithing of donkeys, that such a phenomenon is impossible." Dr. M. Hall who did not see the man's leg amputated, presumes to question the honesty of those who did! Sage physiologist! to suppose that the phenomena observed during the insensibility of the mesmeric trance, *must* of necessity be identical with those *sometimes* observed in your guillotined frogs and tortoises! And yet, this was advanced, aye, and was believed, in an assembly of men, said to be composed of the elite of the medical profession. *Proh pudor!* We have blushed more than once when non-medical readers have asked us how scientific men could be so easily deceived. Dr. M. Hall in 1837 said that mesmerism was "trumpery," and that Dr. Elliotson's experiments "polluted the temple of science." Query: what is the amount of disgrace to be attached to the man who could talk such nonsense, and to those who remained quiet and listened to such manifest absurdities?

We have been very much pleased with Dr. Elliotson's pamphlet, and this lengthened notice of it will convince our readers that we consider the subject most important. All mesmerizers should possess themselves of a copy. We cannot refrain from making one other quotation.

"The happiness of a scientific, liberal, and humane course they would find great beyond all expectations. They would feel raised as men, and be enabled not to view their poor coterie, or college, or profession, as their world, fashioning their opinions, and habits, and whole nature by its cramping influence; but, regarding themselves as a part of universal nature, would find themselves always moving freely in it, would keep their regards constantly upon its truths only, and, walking happily onwards, bestow no more attention upon the sayings and doings of the coteries and prosperous men of the moment, than upon the noisy sparrows which flutter and chirp outside their window today and will not be heard of tomorrow.

"If I have expressed myself strongly in this pamphlet, it is what I intended. The adversaries of mesmerism and of mesmerists have had their full sway hitherto, and they must be thankful for a change. Our turn is now come. Their conduct has shown that patience, sincerity, disinterestedness, and mild persuasion are lost upon them. Our objects are of incalculable importance,—the establishment of means to cure diseases at present more or less troublesome, difficult, or impossible to cure,—the prevention of pain in surgical operations,—and possibly other advances on which I will not venture at present to say anything. This must require a great effort, for it will form an era in the history of man; and those who are willing to assist must be in earnest. I feel no hostility to our opponents. They merely act the part of puppets;—not knowing why they so act, and blindly obeying the general laws by which a supply of opponents to every truth and improvement is always provided. The statistics of opposition to good things would show that their course obeys fixed laws; and they are to be pitied for being destined to the parts which they so eagerly perform."

This is sound philosophy, and we trust Dr. E.'s opponents will profit by his advice—*nous verrons*.

James Esdaile
(1808-1859)

James Esdaile performed a variety of surgical operations on Hindus in India and appears to have successfully induced hypnotism (mesmerism) and hypnotic anesthesia (mesmeric anesthesia) as the sole agent for surgery.

The book he wrote on this subject describes many major and minor surgical procedures in detail. His work was not accepted by the Royal Academy of Medicine in England, and he seemed to lose his enthusiasm in this field.

At this time, ether was discovered, and it was much easier to induce anesthesia by chemical means rather than by the time-consuming method of hypnotic techniques.

MESMERISM IN INDIA AND ITS PRACTICAL APPLICATION IN SURGERY AND MEDICINE*

If this production should be fortunate enough to attract attention at home, I hope that criticism will be chiefly expended upon a careful examination of the alleged facts, and their practical application to the improvement of Surgery and Medicine.

What I now offer to the public is the result of only eight months' mesmeric practice, in a country charity hospital; but it has been sufficient to demonstrate the singular and most beneficial influence that Mesmerism exerts over the constitution of the people of Bengal, and that painless surgical operations and other medical advantages are their natural birthright; of which I hope they will be no longer deprived.

Duty calls me to another and more extensive field (the Civil Surgeons being ordered to join the army of the Sutly;) where I hope to work out this curious and interesting subject in all its practical bearings, and to live to communicate my experience to the public.

Hooghly, February 1st, 1846.

---

*Esdaile, James: *Mesmerism in India and Its Practical Application in Surgery and Medicine.* Hartford, Silue Andrus and Son, 1851, pp. XVII-XXII.

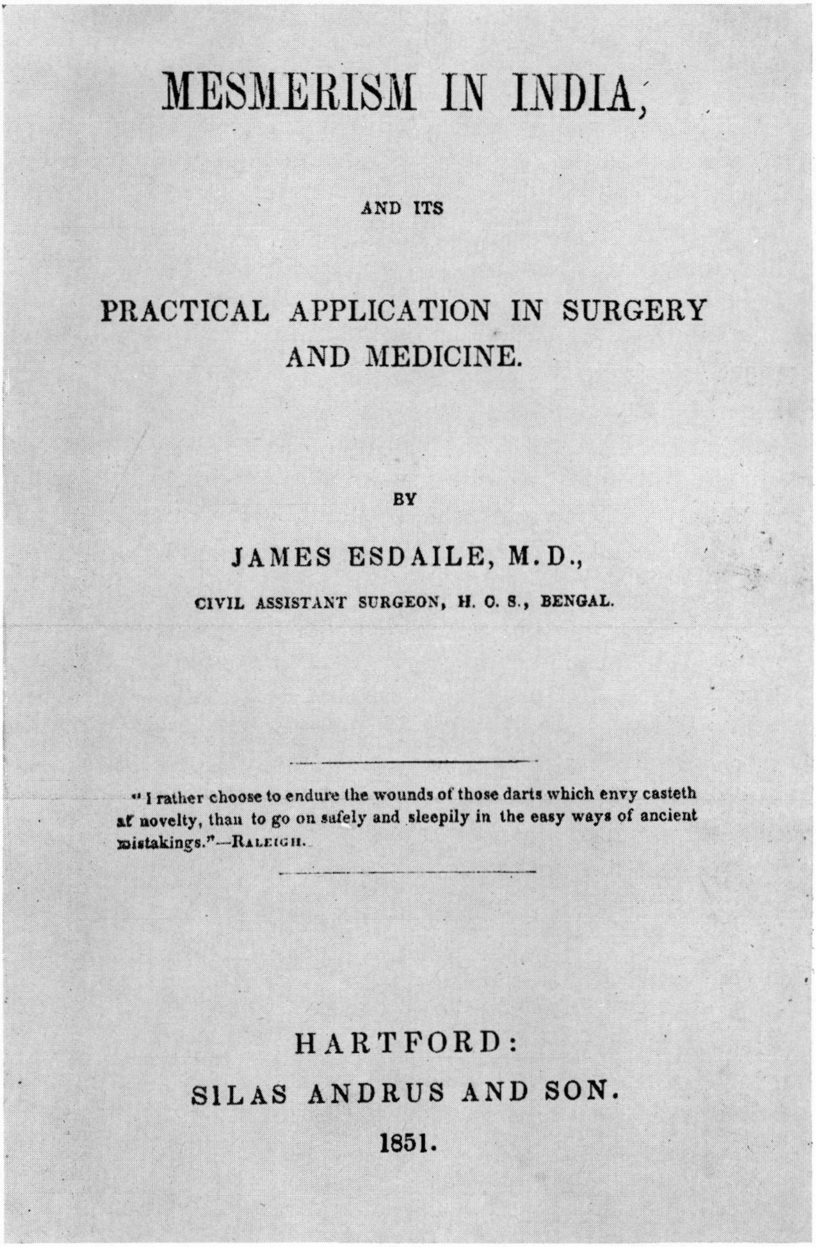

MESMERISM IN INDIA,

AND ITS

PRACTICAL APPLICATION IN SURGERY AND MEDICINE.

BY

JAMES ESDAILE, M.D.,

CIVIL ASSISTANT SURGEON, H. O. S., BENGAL.

" I rather choose to endure the wounds of those darts which envy casteth at novelty, than to go on safely and sleepily in the easy ways of ancient mistakings."—RALEIGH.

HARTFORD:

SILAS ANDRUS AND SON.

1851.

FIGURE 9. Title page from James Esdaile's *Mesmerism in India,* published in 1851.

Mesmeric Facts
Reported by James Esdaile, M.D.
To the Editor of *The Englishman*

Sir:—Before proceeding to join the Army, I have the pleasure to send you a "resume" of my mesmeric practice during the last eight months.

My experience has demonstrated the singular and beneficial influence exerted by Mesmerism over the constitution of the Natives of Bengal, and that painless surgical operations, with other advantages, are their natural birthright, of which they will no longer be deprived, I hope.

Duty calls me to another and more extensive field, where I hope to work out this curious and interesting subject in all its practical details, and to ascertain to what extent other varieties of mankind are capable of being benefitted by this natural curative power.

I am your obedient servant,
James Esdaile, M.D.

Hooghly, 22nd Jan., 1846.

* * *

A return showing the Number of painless Surgical Operations performed at Hooghly, during the last eight months.

Arm amputated	1
Breast ditto	1
Tumour extracted from upper jaw	1
Scirrhus testium extirpated	2
Penis amputated	2
Contracted knees straightened	3
Ditto arms	3
Operations for cataracts	3
Large tumour in the groin cut off	1
Operations for hydrocele	7
Ditto dropsy	2
Actual cautery applied to a sore	1
Muriatic acid ditto	2
Unhealthy sores pared down	7
Abcesses opened	5

Sinus, six inches long, laid open	1
Heel flayed	1
End of a thumb cut off	1
Teeth extracted	3
Gum cut away	1
Prepuce cut off	3
Piles ditto	1
Great toe nails cut out by the roots	5
Seton introduced from ankle to knee	1
Large tumour on leg removed	1
Scrotal tumours, weighing from 8 to 80 pounds, removed 17, painless	14
Operations	73

A Return of medical cases cured by Mesmerism, during the last eight months.

Nervous headache	3	Cured by one trance
Tic-douloureaux	1	Ditto
Nervousness and lameness from rheumatism of 2½ years standing	1	By chronic treatment*
Spasmodic colic	1	By one trance
Acute inflamation of the eye	1	By repeated trances in 24 hours
Chronic ditto	1	By chronic treatment
Acute inflamation of the testes	1	By repeated trances in 36 hours
Convulsions	1	By one trance
Lameness from rheumatism	2	By general and local mesmerizing for a week
Sciatica	1	Ditto

*By chronic treatment is meant daily mesmerizing without the intention of entrancing the patient, which is not necessary.

Pain in crural nerve	1	Ditto
Palsy of one arm	1	Ditto for a month
Ditto of half of the body	1	Ditto for six weeks
Feeling of insects crawling over the body	1	By one trance

It will be perceived that the above cases are chiefly diseases of the nervous system. But as sleep and the absence of pain are the best condition of the body for promoting the resolution of inflammation by the powers of nature, I have extinguished local inflammations by keeping the patients entranced till this was effected.

I beg to state, for the satisfaction of those who have not yet a practical knowledge of the subject, that I have seen no bad consequences whatever arise from persons being operated on when in the mesmeric trance. Cases have occurred in which no pain has been felt subsequent to the operation even; the wounds healing in a few days by the first intention; and in the rest, I have seen no indications of any injury being done to the constitution. On the contrary, it appears to me to have been saved, and that less constitutional disturbance has followed than under ordinary circumstances.

There has not been a death among the cases operated on. In my early operations, I have availed myself of the first fit of insensibility, not knowing whether I could command it back again at pleasure.

But if the trance is not profound the first time, the surgeon may safely calculate on its being deeper the next, and when operating in public, it will be prudent to take the security of one or two preliminary trances. Flexibility of the limbs till moved, and their remaining rigid in any position we put them in, are characteristic of the trance: but there are exceptions, and these are equally diagnostic, and to be depended upon. It sometimes happens, that the limbs become rigid as they lie, and on bending them, they have always a disposition to return to a state of spasmodic extension. At other times, there is a complete relaxation of the whole muscular system, and the limbs can be tossed about like those of a person just dead.

The eyes are usually closed, but the eyelids are sometimes seen a little separated, or half open and tremulous, and the eye is ocasionally wide open, fixed and insensible to light. On one occasion, having ordered the man to be entranced, I returned after two hours, and was told by my assistant that the man was not affected. I went to see, and found him with half-open eyes, quivering eyelids, and trembling hands. I immediately said that he was ready and, without further testing his condition, performed a most severe operation upon him, without his knowing anything about it.

I also wish to remark that I have seen no symptom of congestion of blood on the brain; the circulation in the trance being usually quite natural, like that of a sleeping person. My patients appear to escape the stimulating stage of the mesenteric influence altogether, and to pass at once from life to temporary death. This I am disposed to attribute to the concentrated uninterrupted manner in which the power is applied. As soon as it is felt, there is no time given to the system to rally from the first impression and it succumbs without a struggle to the constraining power.

Some patients, when suddenly awakened, say that their vision is hazy, and their heads light; but I take this to arise from the imperfectly recovered sensibility of the brain and the organs of sense, which are not at once roused up into the full possession of their waking powers, just as is seen in persons aroused from profound natural sleep.

That the mesmeric torpor of the brain and nerves does not arise from sanguine congestion, is often beautifully seen in the first actions of persons awaking from the trance.

They open their eyes, and at the same moment recover all their faculties; but it is seen that the pupil is insensible to light; this they also become aware of; they know that their eyes are open, and they ought to see, but do not. The thought fills them with horror, and with a fearful cry they bury their faces in their hands, like persons struck blind by lightning; but this soon passes off, and the retina recovers its sensibility by a little rubbing of the eye. The dreadful shock given to the mind under such circumstances, or when a somnambulist awakes and finds himself standing in some strange attitude naked, in the midst of strangers (an experiment I have often made), is a trial of nerves which it would be very imprudent and even dangerous to make with any but such singularly impassive subjects as my patients.

This, and the inconveniences of inducing the mesmeric disease (spontaneous mesmerism action in the system) by doing more than is necessary for the cure of the disease, appear to me to be the real dangers to be avoided in the use of mesmerism as a remedy.

I am now able to say from experience, that debility of the nervous system predisposes to the easy reception of the mesmeric influence, and I augur well of a patient's powers of submission, when I recognize in him the listless dejected air, "l'air abattu", that usually accomanies functional debility of the nerves.

Baron Charles Von Reichenbach

Baron Von Reichenbach devoted himself entirely to the branch of mesmeric inquiry having to do with the power of many "sensitives" to see visible emanations from human fingers as well as from physical magnetic apparatus. Von Reichenbach's experiments tried to constitute a complete demonstration of the theory of mesmerism, advanced by Mesmer, and adopted as entirely in harmony with their own extensive observations and practice by his immediate followers, de Puysegur and Deleuze.

Before the Baron's time, the whole subject had been discredited by the fierce opposition it encountered at the hands of the orthodox scientific world at the beginning of the nineteenth century.

Dr. John Ashburner translated the complete work of Baron Von Reichenbach in 1850. I have included the Preface from Ashburner's book in which he explains his reasons for translating the work and his opinion on the experiments performed by the Baron.

PREFACE*

The present edition of a translation of these Researches owes its existence perhaps to one, perhaps to a series of misapprehensions, with which the public may have little concern. Certain it is that at no time have I had the slightest intention to be guilty of a want of courtesy towards the gentleman who had, by the publication of a very skillful abstract of his labors in the year 1846, the merit of introducing the Baron von Reichenbach to the British public, as an investigator of the Philosophy of Mesmerism. Various efforts have been made to convince me that I did not act as I ought to have done, in omitting to place myself in communication with Professor Gregory when I was applied to by the Publisher, through a well-known literary physician, to furnish some notes to a complete edition of these Researches; but I confess my obtuseness shuts out from my mind the light of all the reasoning that has been brought to bear on this matter. All that I can allow is, that

---

*From Reichenbach, Baron Charles von: *Physico-Physiological Researches on the Dynamics of Magnetism, Electricity, Heat, Light, Crystallization and Chemism in their Relation to Vital Force*, translated by John Ashburner. New York, J.S. Redfield, 1851, pp. 4-10.

257

although I have no personal acquaintance with the Professor, I am very sorry in any way to have injured his feelings, and I am grieved to find myself in such a relative position with a man for whom I am bound to entertain a deep respect; for, besides his high scientific reputation, he is known to have courage to avow his belief in Phrenology and in Mesmerism, "even in the spirit of truth, whom the world cannot receive, because it seeth him not, neither knoweth him; but," to all like the Professor, it may be said, "ye know him, for he dwelleth with you, and shall be in you!" To me, feeling quite innocent of all wrong intention, in the perfect freedom of action, which, under the circumstances, I claim for myself, it is sad to be at opposite poles with one who is of the salt of this earth. To those who cannot know of the dire consequences resulting from the aggregation of the petty and repulsive mental forces concentrating and directing in society the baneful powers of their various influences upon characters who dare to think for themselves, — who are hardly aware that new truths are met so frequently by sneers, taunts, ridicule, or that unworthy social persecution, at once the proof of a want of capacity to be noble and just, and the disgrace of an advanced civilization,— the exalted courage of such persons must be lost. To those who know how to respect scientific ardor, and a pure love of truth, the fortitude of a faithful and sincere man is for high admiration, and for deep respect.

Such observations are perhaps equally applicable to the Professor, and to his friend the Baron, and I may be regarded as bold in remarking, as freely as I have done, on some of the philosophy in the following pages. No one can entertain a deeper veneration for large cerebral organizations than I do. I am clear, from the work before us, that so much patience, so much ingenuity, so much caution, so much concentration, so much ideal resource, so much just and honest desire to be true, could not characterize any individual, who had not a rare combination of organs in his magnificent head. Regarding any person in this point of view, one is immediately at liberty to look out for all those inconsistencies that belong to humanity; deeply respecting the excellencies, and always, with due humility doubting one's own power of detecting the weakness that may belong to any logical edifice he may construct.

There are not wanting persons who doubt entirely of the Baron's power of accurate and severe observation. They doubt some of his most striking facts. They deny the accuracy of his results with the magnet and photographic plate. Some, and among them are persons of no means note as scientific characters, affect to hold him in very secondary estimation—pitying him for wild ideas, and denying that his researches deserve any rank as philosophy.

But the Baron is not the builder up of a tall house of loose cards to be toppled down by a breath. I have not tried all his experiments. I have tried, comparatively, only a few. Where I have found the suitable cases, the results have been, with few exceptions, identical.

Then, because I have been disappointed in the results of many other experiments, I have no right to conclude that the Baron is at fault, but rather that I have not yet been fortunate enough to meet with exactly the same description of case he terms the "sick sensitive,"—a vague expression of an idea with which, surely, it is not criminal to disagree. Long before I had read Professor Gregory's abstract, I had arrived at conclusions on differences, as well as analogies, between electric, magnetic, and mesmeric agencies, and operating differently, have witnessed many confirmations of the facts established by the Baron. Dr. Elliotson has noted many remarkable analogies in many pages of the *Zoist*. But then, the greater number of our cases have been in mesmerized persons. How the Baron would have fared, as to his conclusions, if he had not taken up the study of his subject, in its most elemental form is another question. Seeing, as I do, the conditions of his patients, in a different point of view, from that in which he regards them, I cannot concede to him that, professing to condemn the mesmeric state, as one unfit for his purpose, he has not been operating with persons, who, though not at all asleep, have actually been in a state constituting the very condition which distinguishes some of the phenomena of somnambulism. One mistake has been, to suppose that the truthfulness of an individual depends upon a certain normal state of the general fibres of the brain, instead of the tendencies derived from a particular relative size, and combination of certain organs of that viscus. A patient, who is a sleep-walker, may, from a certain configuration of organs, be a most just and honorable character, and have that fine disposition considerably exalted by the state of somnambulism; while a wide-awake person may be a most cunning and habitual deceiver. Another mistake is, to suppose that the "sensitive," and "sick sensitive," form a category, independent of all phrenological, and all mesmeric considerations. They are, in fact, those most easily affected by mesmeric and crystallic agencies—those most easily stimulated to clairvoyance, in the state of wide vigilance. Certain I am, that with the advantages offered by the power of his head, the Baron would have advanced both further and faster, if, to all his other knowledge, he had combined a more extensive view of physiological pathology, with a study of phrenology and mesmerism. They may oppose the truth in Germany, as they do here. The Author exhibits some of their doings, but the Baron has courage flowing from a sense of justice. He worships the spirit of truth, which must eventually prevail. I marvel at many of the objectors to his philosophy, for in regarding these researches with the eeye of criticism, ready to seize a weak point, I feel that one is at a loss which most to admire—the plain, straightforward, philosophical acumen which guides each consecutive inquiry, or the combination of ingenuity and common sense with which questions of great delicacy are made subservient to the progress of severe inquiry. Time and opportunity only are required to corroborate rather than to correct the facts he advanced. Those who venture to risk their own reputations in throwing doubts on the Baron's results, should remember that the conditions under which the experiments were originally made, must, in justice, be strictly repeated. The discoverer of creosote, paraffin, eupion, and many other new compounds, for the knowledge of which the world is indebted to his laborious researches, is not a common-place authority; and he has now taken up a subject, the truth of which will roll with tremendous force over all obstacles.

Those who regard the science of Physics, in the isolated form in which it is generally presented in most of the Elements of Natural Philosophy, must necessarily have a very limited view of the importance of the researches now presented to the public. Indeed, it would be, at present, almost impossible to indicate all the points in cosmogony, to which the Baron von Reichenbach's commencement, in strict logical deduction, on imponderable agencies, may not, at a future period, have a positive reference. It may be remarked, that the evolution of each new fact is a step in that progress, which may be ultimately connected with the forces, agencies, fluids, or powers that pervade space in universal nature.

Undoubtedly, the attempt to place Mesmerism within the domain of physicis was a bold conception. It is an attempt to bring the whole of physiology into the strict limits of chemical philosophy. The establishment of the existence of the odic force is that which was wanting to reply to most of the questions respecting life. No doubt much is yet to be desired in order to clear the obscurities enveloping the innumerable modifications of this force; but enlightenment reaches us from the enlightened, and the Baron pursues his continued researches with a zeal which promises to unfold to us many a new principle, as well as many a new fact connected with this subject; and, considering the very curious investigations which will be published in the second part of this work, it is hardly too much to anticipate that we may, ere long, be favored with some insight into the philosophy of a subject evidently connected with the matter of light, or in some way allied with that of the development of either latent light, or of some combination of a share of this principle with certain organic re-agents. The researches into odic light by the Baron do not appear yet to belong immediately to clairvoyance, and yet the links which connect the inquiries are not far off. Numerous questions suggest themselves in an examination of the philosophy of this subject:—why the condition of brain favorable to the development of clairvoyance should belong to certain individuals, and not to others? Why it should belong to some nervous susceptible temperaments, and not to others? Why some insane persons should be in the category, and not others? Why in some brains these peculiar developments of mental lucidity should take place, quickly and easily, by peculiar stimulants, while others should require a long period for the attainment of the object? Why, in some, the phenomena are not produced without a long course of mesmeric sleep, while in others, the presence of certain individuals, or of certain crystals, or of clear bottles of clean mesmerized water, in the same room, suffice to excite the brain to the requisite condition? In one and the same person, one mesmerizer will establish it, at the first seance. I have no doubt of these facts: I have often witnessed them. I have produced the condition of clairvoyance; but the kind and the degree of the phenomena differed, very remarkably, from those produced by Major Buckley, in the same patients. Repeatedly I have tired, in vain, to make clairvoyant somnambules read printed words which were enclosed in a pill-box. Major Buckley, ignorant of the same words, has had them quickly read in the innermost of a nest of five, four of them tightly-fitting silver boxes. The stimulus afforded by the odic lights issuing from my brain, must then be very different from that of those emitted by his. I have elsewhere said, (*Zoist,* Vol. IV, p. 125) before the abstract of the work of Reichenbach appeared here, that "striking facts may be adduced which may tend to the conclusion that the exercise of the faculties of the human mind, and particularly that of the will, is attended by the emanation of a fluid from the brain, from the fingers, seats of the functional extremities of the nerves, or from some part of the person who may be exercising the mental faculties. I propose to show that the same series of events may be produced in individuals of a certain nervous diathesis, by the impingement of a fluid evolved by the will of another; or by manipulations attended by the emanation of the same fluid, or by certain emanations from magnets, or from some metallic wires, through which currents of electricity are passed; or from the direct application of certain metals. I do not attempt to establish the identity of these fluids, for the facts daily developing themselves tend to show that the distinctive properties of these fluids are as various as the substances from which they emanate; and it may be that the great power, antecedent to all consequence, may ordain the simplicity and unity of one electric, and gravitating with centrical force, evolving an infinite complication and variety of magnetic cohesive and repulsive agencies; the entire system emerging from the volonté directing *La Grande Formule.*" All these considerations are for inquiry. They must meet with scrutiny, and new truths will be elicited, multiplying the facts, prolonging the interest and the fame attached to the genius of the discoverer of the odic force. We are but at the commencement of the wonders of clairvoyance, and can certainly be in no position to estimate the great fund of new truths, that by means of its cultivated agency, are in store for us. We are so often met with objections as to the possibility of the phenomena of clairvoyance, that after the Baron von Reichenbach's arguments on the varying powers of various individuals to perceive the odic flames, one is tempted to adduce the fact discovered by Sir Isaac Newton, that the densest and heaviest metal, gold, has more pores in it than solid metallic particles, and consequently that light may be transmitted through it; and if so, it is quite possible to conceive of its being diaphanous to certain individuals possessed of a highly sensitive nervous system. But what are the marvellous things of clairvoyance, compared to those contained in a supplementary note to the relation between Holy Scripture and some parts of geological science, by Dr. Pye Smith? Here our object is not to display wonders, but while in passing we reply to objectors, we must continue to illustrate the leading purpose of these researches, really and truly the philosophy of mesmerism. Strange would it be if the wonders of clairvoyance; those of the phenomena detected by the telescope; the events accruing from the nature of living organisms, in all their infinite varieties, should finally be dependent on the same force, which Newton contemplated, in his acute conjecture that water was a compound body, and which gave rise to the wild but important speculations of Mesmer, on the existence of an universal fluid, when he led the way to the facts of a new science, which, after a struggle of eighty years has emerged in the hand of von Reichenbach into principles applicable to all nature.

A remarkable fact connected with the emergence of mesmerism into its present importance is the serious neglect of its merits

which has marked the conduct of those who were bound to encourage them, by study and inquiry. Really, practically, mesmerism
has deserved very different treatment. It has merited high civic
honors. It has, under the patient philosophic guidance of Dr.
Elliotson, conquered malignant cancer. It has removed enormous
growths known as polypus, as I can testify. I know that it has
chased away large ovarian tumors, and dropsies that have defied
all medical skill. It has cured malignant fevers in their advanced
stages. It has removed tubercles, and healed abscesses. To enumerate all the good that has been done by this agent, combined
with the essence of human kindness—for without that the practice
of mersmerism is useless—would take many volumes. Thousands
of cases are now extant of the benefits derived from this holy power.
The *Zoist* is the grand English work of testimony of this subject,
and it is full of useful information, as well as of noble essays to
advance the cause of humanity. The defenders of mesmerism have,
in that work, labored hard for the truth, which they have advocated
with the boldness belonging to sincerity. How much soever
they have been opposed by the sordid and the mean, by those
systematically opposed to the progress of expansion—with whatever success falsehood has retarded the march of useful knowledge—it is consoling to the writers in the *Zoist* to know that the
great cause is advancing. Small-minded men, not capable, from
unfortunate organization of brain, of believing truths at
variance with the idols they have been accustomed to worship, set
themselves up as oracles of wisdom. Too many implicitly give
up their convictions to such incompetent leaders! Fight, however,
as they will against the truth, it is always too strong for its opponents. Time, which settles all differences, by changing old things
and by bringing forward new, sweeps away the fallacies of the
obstinately proud and ignorant. Would it were possible for small
minds to reflect, that all their efforts to establish falsehood will
not alter the laws of nature, and no folly of striving to prove
that falsehood is truth can change these established laws! For
nearly eighty years has the professional world of science opposed
itself to the discovery of Mesmer, yet still the facts exist. Turn to
the truths placed before mankind by the stupendous powers of

observation and catenation of that rare genius, Gall! It is sickening to note the causes which have hiterto deprived society of the advantages, destined to accrue to our race, at a later period, by the cultivation of phrenology. How curiously and strikingly has mesmeric science verified all the discoveries of Gall! Still the flood of opposition pours on, and the pretenders to religion, real enemies of the spirit of truth, with awful pride and cunning, endeavor by sly arts to crush its rising lights.

It is remarkable that three great philosophers, each in succession, in some measure condemning the labors of his predecessor, should have arisen in the same spot; that each should have put forth a discovery of signal importance to the philosophy of mind; that Vienna should be the well-spring, whence these lights should radiate; that the sparkling, crystalline, luminous knowledge emanating from that fountain, placed in the central capital of European civilization, should have reflected a glory round the names of three philosophers, which will emblazon their researches as amongst the most important that can occupy the attention of mankind; that Mesmer, Gall, and Reichenbach, first announced their grand ideas from the capital of the Austrian empire.

The Baron von Reichenbach may not believe himself complimented by this allocation. He may have some scientific pride, notwithstanding the size and quality of the majority of the organs of his brain; nevertheless, the reflection must be made, that all knowledge is relative, as every atom of matter is relative. Nothing is fixed and absolute; but in the vast range of human acquirement, it would be difficult to exhibit three sets of facts, announced at separate intervals of time, having so intimate a relation to each other, and which are so interwoven in their dependencies, as those Viennese discoveries; having, moreover, such numerous alliances to all the circumstances to which man can, by turns, transfer his attentions.

Where will all this philosophy lead us? Can any sincere person entertain a doubt? It is the spirit of truth which is about to be victorious. It is not a question as to the appreciation, at the present moment, of the best knowledge, of the soundest philosophy. Educated in selfishness, we live in a world of hallucinations. It has been well said that we form one large lunatic establishment. We are surrounded by influences that are always tending to impress upon us a desire to succumb to the tyranny of falsehood. The conventional habits of our lives make us, more or less, hypocrites; and according to the energy, originality, or some other individual peculiarity of our character, we swerve from the leaning of our fellow-men. In the proposition to be offered to his innate desire for justice, it is not that man does not essentially love truth, but that the progress of his organization, through ages, has not yet ripened sufficiently to allow that expanded development which, as science advances, must have place in a more perfect arrangement of society. Man cannot yet worship truth as the best knowledge. He has not yet passed the age of idols. The knavery of the selfish and interested is always ready to excite his lower feelings against that which is really holy and reverential, the sacred will of the Most Just. But the good time approaches—for science advances with immensely rapid strides. Those who are now young have to witness many improvements, all tending, like the researches of the Baron von Reichenbach, to expand the intellects and morals of man, and to lead him finally to the realms of light.

JOHN ASHBURNER.

65, Grosvenor Street,
April 25, 1850.

SECTION THREE
The Age of Braidism (1843-1860)

James Braid
(1795-1860)

James Braid inaugurated modern hypnotism, the word itself being introduced by him. His theories were adopted by Broca, Charcot, Liebault, and Bernheim; thus he founded the French school.

Neurypnology; or, the Rationale of Nervous Sleep was the first book actually published with hypnosis as the subject. Braid carried on the work of Mesmer in England, although he recognized that the art of mesmerism was actually the result of suggestion and was not what was previously believed. Braid's work is monumental as a contribution to modern hypnotism.

Modern theories still trace their beginning to the work which Braid accomplished with his practice of hypnosis.

NEURYPNOLOGY, OR THE RATIONALE
OF NERVOUS SLEEP*

It was my intention to have published my "Practical Essay on the Curative Agency of Neuro-Hypnotism," exactly as delivered at the Conversazione given to the members of the British Association in Manchester, on the 29th June 1842. By so doing, and by appending footnotes, comprising the data on which my views were grounded, it would have conveyed a pretty clear knowledge of the subject, and of the manner in which it had been treated. It has since been suggested, however, that it might readily be incorporated with the short Elementary Treatise on Neuro-Hypnology, which I originally intended to publish, and which I am earnestly solicited to do, by letters from professional gentlemen from all quarters. I now, therefore, submit my views to the public in the following condensed form. I shall aim at brevity and perspicuity; and my great object will be to teach others all I know of the modes of inducing the phenomena, and their application in the cure of diseases, and to invite my professional

---

*Braid, James: *Neurypnology; or the Rationale of Nervous Sleep.* London, 1843, pp. 1-74.

brethren to labour in the same field of inquiry, feeling assured, that the cause of science and humanity must thereby be promoted.

It was with this conviction I offered my "Practical Essay on the Curative Agency of Neuro-Hypnotism," to the medical section of the British Association.

In November 1841, I was led to investigate the pretensions of animal magnetism, or mesmerism, as a complete sceptic, from an anxiety to discover the source of fallacy in certain phenomena I had heard were exhibited at M. Lafontaine's conversazioni. The result was that I made some discoveries which appeared to elucidate certain of the phenomena, and rendered them interesting, both in a speculative and practical point of view. I considered it a most favourable opportunity for having additional light thrown upon this subject, to offer a paper to the medical section of the British Association, which was about to meet in Manchester. Gentlemen of scientific attainments might thus have had an opportunity of investigating it, and eliciting the truth, unbiassed by local or personal prejudice. I hope to learn something from others, on certain points which were extremely mysterious to me, as to the *cause* of some remarkable phenomena. I accordingly intimated my intention to the secretaries, by letter, on 18th May, and on the morning of Wednesday, the 22nd June 1842, sent the paper I proposed reading for the consideration of the committee, intimating also, by letter, my intention to produce before them as many of the patients as possible, whose cases were referred to in proof of the curative agency of Neuro-Hypnotism, so that they might have an opportunity of ascertaining, for themselves, the real facts of the cases, uninfluenced by any bias or partiality that I might exhibit as the discoverer and adapter of this new mode of treatment. The committee of the medical section, however, were pleased to decline entertaining the subject.

Many of the most eminent and influential members of the Association, however, had already witnessed and investigated my experiments in private, and expressed themselves highly gratified and interested with them. In compliance with the repeated desire of these gentlemen, and many other eminent members of the Association to whom I could not possibly afford time to exhibit my experiments in private, and who were anxious to have an opportunity afforded them of seeing, hearing, and judging of the phenomena for themselves, I gave a gratuitous conversazione, when I read the "Rejected Essay," and exhibited the experiments in a public room, to which all the members of the Association had been respectfully invited. The interest with which the subject was viewed by the members of the Association generally, was sufficiently testified by the number and high respectability of those who attended on that occasion; in reference to which the chairman requested the reporters to put on record, "that he had been in the habit for many years of attending public meetings, and he had never in his life seen a more unmixed, a more entirely respectable assembly in Manchester." It was also manifested by their passing a vote of thanks at the conclusion of the conversazione, for my having afforded an opportunity to the members of the British Association of witnessing my experiments, to which they had previously borne testimony as having been "highly successful."

On that occasion I stated, there were certain phenomena, which I could readily induce by particular manipulations, whilst I candidly confessed myself unable to explain the *modus operandi* by which they were induced. I referred particularly to the extraordinary rapidity with which dormant functions, and a state of catalepti-form rigidity, may be changed to the extreme opposite condition, by a simple waft of wind, either from the lips, a pair of bellows, or by any other mechanical means. I solicited information on these points, both privately and publicly, from all the eminently scientific gentlemen who honoured me with their company during the meetings of the British Association in this town; but no one ventured to express a decided opinion as to the causes of these remarkable phenomena. I now beg to assure every reader of this treatise, that I shall esteem it a great favour to be enlightened on points which I confess are, at present, still above my compre-hension.

It will be observed, for reasons adduced, I have now entirely separated Hypnotism from Animal Magnetism. I considered it to be merely a simple, speedy, and certain mode of throwing the nervous system into a new condition, which may be rendered eminently available in the cure of certain disorders. I trust, therefore, it may be investigated quite independently of any bias, either for or against the subject, as connected with mesmerism; and only by the facts which can be adduced. I feel quite confident we have acquired in this process a valuable addition to our curative means; but I repudiate the idea of holding it up as a universal remedy; nor do I even pretend to understand, as yet, the *whole range of diseases* in which it may be useful. Time and experience alone can determine this question, as is the case with all other new remedies.

When we consider that in this process we have acquired the power of raising sensibility to the most extraordinary degree, and also of depressing it far below the torpor of natural sleep; and that from the latter condition, any or all of the senses may be raised to the exalted state of sensibility referred to, almost *with the rapidity of thought,* by so simple an agency as a puff of air directed against the respective parts; and that we can also raise and depress the force and frequency of the circulation, locally or generally, in a most extraordinary degree, it must be evident we have thus an important power to act with. Whether these extraordinary physical effects are produced through the imagination chiefly, or by other means, it appears to me quite certain, that the imagination has never been so much under our control, or capable of being made to act in the same beneficial and uniform manner, by any other mode of management hitherto known.

That we really have acquired in this process a valuable addition to our curative means, which enables us speedily to put an end to many diseases which resisted ordinary treatment, I think will be satisfactorily manifested by the cases which I have recorded. Many of these cases have been seen by other medical men, and are so remarkable, so self-evident to every candid and intelligent mind, that it is impossible, with any show of propriety, to deny them. Most unwarrantable and novel attempts have been made, not only to extinguish the farther prosecution of Hypnotism, but also to misrepresent all I had either said or done on the subject, and thus damage me, as well as Hypnotism, in public estimation. I am in possession of a mass of documentary evidence in proof of this, to an extent which could scarcely be credited. But I shall not trouble (sic) my readers with details of all that has been done in order to prejudice my patients against me.

As regards general principles, it has ever been attempted, by garbled statements, to set forth such gross misrepresentations as could only be credited by parties totally ignorant of the subject. Thus it was alleged, that my mode of hypnotizing was no novelty; on the contrary, that it was an unacknowledged plagiarism, and that it was the opinion and practice of Bertrand and the Abbe Faria. Now, so far as I have been able to comprehend the meaning of Bertrand, which Colquhoun observes, "it is rather difficult to comprehend," he adheres "to the theory of imagination, and imagination alone," (Colquhoun's *Introduction,* p. 94). At p. 34, Vol. IV of the "Encyclopaedia of Practical Medicine," Dr. Prichard says of Bertrand, that he "comes at last to the conclusion, that all the results of these operations are brought about through the influence of the mind;" that is, through the influence of the imagination of the patients acting on themselves. Bertrand also supports this opinion by the manner in which the Abbe Faria performed magnetization. His plan was this: "He placed the patient in an arm-chair, and after telling him to shut his eyes, and collect himself, suddenly pronounced, in a strong voice and imperative tone, the word 'dormez,' which generally produced on the individual an impression sufficiently strong to give a slight shock, and occasion warmth, transpiration, and *sometimes* somnambulism." Had his success by this method been as general as mine, would he have used the word *"sometimes"* on this occasion? It is farther added, "if the first attempt failed, he tried the experiment a second, third, and even a fourth time, after which he declared the individual incapable of entering into the state of lucid sleep." Whilst it is doubted that his success was equal to what he represented it, still Bertrand states in reference to the Abbe Faria, that it was incontestable, "that he very often succeeded." Now, is this not sufficient proof, that his success was by no means so general as mine? And who does not see, on persuing my directions for hypnotizing, that methods are very different?

It is farther added, "The complete identity of the phenomena thus produced by a method which operated confessedly through the imagination, with those which display themselves under the ordinary treatment of the magnetizers, affords a strong reason for concluding that the results in other instances depend upon a similar principle." It is still farther added, that M. Bertrand denies the necessity of strong intense volitions of the operator being necessary to produce the result. He declared, "that in trials made by himself, precisely the same results followed, whether he *WILLED* to produce them or not, provided that the patient was *inwardly persuaded that the whole ritual was duly observed."* Can any farther remarks be required to prove that Bertrand referred the result entirely to the effect of imagination? And can any one who has attended to what I have given as my opinion, say that this either *was,* or *is* my opinion? Certainly quite the contrary. The parties referred to, therefore, have only proved their belief of how easy it is, by garbled statements, to misrepresent the truth, when submitting such remarks to those ignorant of the subject, or who are blinded by prejudice.

The following remarks by Mr. H. Brookes, a celebrated lecturer on animal magnetism, will illustrate this point rather better than the individuals referred to. On hearing that I had changed my original opinion about *identity,* he writes thus: "I am very glad you have at length found reason to change your original opinion as to the identity of your phenomena with those of mesmerism. From the very first I freely admitted the value and importance of your discovery, but I could not admit that identity, and I blamed you for insisting upon it so hastily, and using such hard words against the animal magnetists, because they could not agree with you. I thought, and still think, you did wrong in that, and that you certainly did yourself injustice, for in fact you are the original discoverer of *a new agency,* and not of a mere modification of an old one."

But when so much had been said of Bertrand, with the hope of making it appear that I had either been ignorant of, or copied his views without due acknowledgment, which is evidently erroneous, why not have quoted him also to prove I was wrong in attributing curative effects as resulting from these operations? Let us hear what M. Bertrand says on this point. He declares, "it is difficult to imagine with what facility the practisers of the art succeed in relieving the most severe affections of the nervous system. Attacks of epilepsy, in particular, are rendered considerably less frequent and severe by their method skillfully employed; which displays in so remarkable a manner the influence of moral impressions on the physical state of the constitution." After such declarations in favour of the *curative power* of mesmerism, had M. Bertrand's method of inducing the condition been as generally and speedily successful as mine, will any one believe that it would not have been brought more generally into practice ere now? Mr. Mayo, one of our best authorities, in a letter to me on this subject, states distinctly that the great reason for its not being more generally introduced into practice, was the tediousness of the processes for inducing the condition, and the uncertainty, after all the time and trouble devoted to the manipulation, of producing any result whatever. He concludes his observations on this subject, by the remark, *"It took up too much time."* And Dr. Prichard, author of the article referred to in the Encyclopaedia of Practical Medicine, adds, "On the whole, when we consider the degree of suffering occasioned by disorders of the class over which magnetism exerts an influence, through the medium of the imagination, and the little efficacy which ordinary remedies possess, of alleviating or counteracting them, it is much to be wished that this art, notwithstanding the problematical nature of the theories connected with it, were better known to us in actual practice.

I am aware great prejudice has been raised against mesmerism, from the idea that it might be turned to immoral purposes. In respect to the Neuro-Hypnotic state, induced by the method explained in this treatise, I am quite certain that *it* deserves no such censure. I have proved by experiments, both in public and in private, that during the state of excitement, the judgment is sufficiently active to make the patients, if possible, even *more* fastidious as regards propriety of conduct, than in the waking condition; and from the state of rigidity and insensibility, either by being rudely handled, or even by a breath of air. Nor is it requisite this should be done by the person who put them into the Hypnotic state. It will follow equally from the manipulations of any one else, or a current of air impinging against the body, from any mechanical contrivance whatever. And, finally, the state cannot be induced, in any stage, unless with the knowledge and consent of the party operated on. This is more than can be said respecting a great number of our most valuable medicines, for there are many which we are in the daily habit of using, with the best advantages in the relief and cure of disease, which may be, and have been rendered most potent for the furtherance of the ends of the vicious and cruel; and which can be administered *without the knowledge of the intended victim.* It ought never to be lost sight of, that there is the *use* and *abuse of* every thing in nature. It is the *use,* and only the *judicious use* of Hypnotism, which I advocate.

It is well known that I have never made any secret of my modes of operating, as they have not only been exhibited and explained publicly, but also privately, to any professional gentleman, who wished for further information on the subject. Encouraged by the confidence which flows from a consciousness of the honesty and integrity of my purpose, and thorough conviction of the reality and value of this as means of cure, I have persevered, in defiance of much, and, as I think, unwarrantable and capricious opposition.

In now unfolding to the medical profession generally—to whose notice, and kind consideration, this treatise is more pratically presented—my views on what I conceive to be a very important, powerful, and extraordinary agent in the healing art; I beg at once distinctly to be understood, as repudiating the idea of its being, or ever becoming, a universal remedy. On the contrary, I feel quite assured it will require all the acumen and experience of medical men, to decide in what cases it would be safe and proper to have recourse to such a means; and I have always deprecated, in the strongest terms, any attempts at its use amongst unprofessional persons, for the sake of curiosity, or even for a nobler and more benevolent object—the relief of the infirm; because I am satisfied it ought to be left in the hands of professional men, and of them only. I have myself met with some cases in which I considered it unsafe to apply it at all; and with other cases in which it would have been most hazardous to have carried the operation so far as the patients urged me to do.*

In now submitting my opinions and practice to the profession in the following treatise, I consider myself as having discharged an imperative duty to them, and to the cause of humanity. In future, I intend to go on quietly and patiently, prosecuting the subject in the course of my practice, and shall leave others to adopt or reject it, as they shall find consistent with their own convictions.

As it is of the utmost importance, in discussing any subject, to have a correct knowledge of the meaning attached to peculiar terms made use of, I shall now give a few definitions, and explain my reasons for adopting the terms selected.

Neurypnology is derived from the Greek words for nerve; sleep; a discourse which Braid used and means the *rationale,* or *doctrine* of *nervous* sleep, which I define to be, "a peculiar condition of the nervous system, into which it can be thrown by artificial contrivance;" or thus, "a peculiar condition of the nervous system, induced by a fixed and abstracted attention of the mental and visual eye, on one object, not of an exciting nature."

By the term "Neuro-Hypnotism," then, is to be understood "nervous sleep;" and, for the sake of brevity, suppressing the prefix "neuro," by the terms—

HYPNOTIC,		The state or condition of *nervous* sleep.
HYPNOTIZE,		To induce *nervous* sleep.
HYPNOTIZED,		One who has been put into the state of *nervous* sleep.
HYPNOTISM,	will be understood,	*Nervous* sleep.
DEHYPNOTIZE,		To restore from the state or condition of *nervous* sleep.
DEHYPNOTIZED, and		Restored from the state or condition of *nervous* sleep.
HYPNOTIST,		One who practices Neuro-Hypnotism.

---

*The circumstances which render my operations dangerous, the symptoms which indicate danger, and the mode of acting when they occur, to remove them, are pointed out.

NEURYPNOLOGY;

OR, THE

RATIONALE OF NERVOUS SLEEP,

CONSIDERED IN RELATION WITH

ANIMAL MAGNETISM.

ILLUSTRATED BY

NUMEROUS CASES OF ITS SUCCESSFUL APPLICATION IN THE RELIEF AND CURE OF DISEASE.

BY

JAMES BRAID, M.R.C.S.E., C.M.W.S. &c.

" UNLIMITED SCEPTICISM IS EQUALLY THE CHILD OF IMBECILITY AS IMPLICIT CREDULITY."

Dugald Stewart.

LONDON:

JOHN CHURCHILL, PRINCE'S STREET, SOHO.
ADAM & CHARLES BLACK, EDINBURGH.

1843.

FIGURE 10. Title page from James Braid's *Neurypnology,* published in 1843.

Whenever, therefore, any of these terms are used in the following pages, I beg to be understood as alluding to the discovery I have made of certain peculiar phenomena derived and elicited by my mode of operating; and of which, to prevent misconception, and intermingling with other theories and practices on the nervous system, I have thought it best to give the foregoing designation.

I regret, as many of my readers may do, the inconvenient length of the name; but, as most of our professional terms, and nearly all those of a *doctrinal* meaning, have a Greek origin, I considered it most in accordance with good taste, not to deviate from an established usage. To obviate this in some degree, I have struck out two letters from the original orthography, which was Neuro-Hypnology.

Having, in the introduction, presented a cursory view of certain points, and given a few explanatory remarks, I shall now proceed to a more particular and detailed consideration of the subject. I shall explain the course I have pursued in prosecuting my investigation; the phenomena which I discovered to result from the manipulations had recourse to; the inferences I was consequently led to deduce from them; the method I now recommend for inducing the hypnotic condition, for applying it in the cure of various disorders, and the result of my experience, as to the efficacy of hypnotism as a curative agent.

By the impression which hypnotism induces on the nervous system, we acquire a power of rapidly curing many functional disorders, most intractable, or altogether incurable, by ordinary remedies, and also many of those distressing affections which, as in most cases they evince no pathological change of structure, have been presumed to depend on some peculiar condition of the nervous system, and have therefore, by universal consent, been denominated *"nervous complaints;"* and as I felt satisfied it was not dependent on any special agency or emanation, passing from the body of the operator to that of the patient, as the animal magnetizers allege is the case by their process, I considered it desirable, for the sake of preventing misconception, to adopt new terms, as explained in the introduction.

I was led to discover the mode I now adopt with so much

success for inducing this artificial condition of the nervous system, by a course of experiments instituted with the view to determine the cause of mersmeric phenomena. From all I had read and heard of mesmerism (such as, the phenomena being capable of being excited in so few, and these few individuals in a state of disease, or naturally of a delicate constitution, or peculiarly susceptible temperament, and from the phenomena, when induced, being said to be so exaggerated, or of such an extraordinary nature,) I was fully inclined to join with those who considered the whole to be a system of collusion or delusion, or of excited imagination, sympathy, or imitation.

The first exhibition of the kind I ever had an opportunity of attending, was one of M. Lafontaine's conversazioni, on the 13th November 1841. That night I saw nothing to diminish, but rather to confirm, my previous prejudices. At the next conversazione, six nights afterwards, *one* fact, the inability of a patient to *open his eyelids,* arrested my attention. I considered that to be a *real phenomenon,* and was anxious to discover the physiological cause of it. Next night, I watched this case when again operated on, with intense interest, and before the termination of the experiment, felt assured I had discovered its cause, but considered it prudent not to announce my opinion publicly, until I had an opportunity of testing its accuracy, by experiments and observation in private.

In two days afterwards, I developed my views to my friend Captain Brown, as I had also previously done to four other friends; and in his presence, and that of my family, and another friend, the same evening, I instituted a series of experiments to prove the correctness of my theory, namely, that the continued fixed stare, by paralyzing nervous centres in the eyes and their appendages,* and destroying the equilibrium of the nervous system, thus produced the phenomenon referred to. The experiments were varied so as to convince all present, that they fully bore out the correctness of my theoretical views.

My first object was to prove, that the inability of the patient to

---

*By this expression I mean the state of exhaustion which follows too long continued, or too intense action, of any organ or function.

open his eyes was caused by paralyzing the levator muscles of the eyelids, through their continued action during the protracted fixed stare, and thus rendering it *physically* impossible for him to open them.* With the view of proving this, I requested Mr. Walker, a young gentleman present, to sit down, and maintain a fixed stare at the top of a wine bottle, placed so much above him as to produce a considerable strain on the eyes and eyelids, to enable him to maintain a steady view of the object. In three minutes his eyelids closed, a gush of tears ran down his cheeks, his head drooped, his face was slightly convulsed, he gave a groan, and instantly fell into profound sleep, the respiration becoming slow, deep and sibilant, the right hand and arm being agitated by slight convulsive movements. At the end of four minutes I considered it necessary, for his safety, to put an end to the experiment.

This experiment not only proved what I expected, but also, by calling my attention to the spasmodic state of the muscles of the face and arm, the peculiar state of the respiration, and the condition of the mind, as evinced on rousing the patient, tended to prove to my mind I had got the key to the solution of mesmerism. The agitation and alarm of this gentleman, on being roused, very much astonished Mrs. Braid. She expressed herself greatly surprised at his being so much alarmed about nothing, as she had watched the whole time, and never saw me near him, or touching him in any whatever. I proposed that she should be the next subject operated on, to which she readily consented, assuring all present that she would not be so easily alarmed as the gentleman referred to. I requested her to sit down, and gaze on the ornament of a china sugar basin, placed at the same angle to the eyes as the bottle in the former experiment. In two minutes the expression of the face was very much changed; at the end of two minutes and a

---

*Attempts have been made to prove, that I got this idea from a person who publicly maintained that the patient referred to *could* have opened his eyes *if he liked*; to this the patient having replied, "I have tried all I could and cannot;" the individual referred to, in support of his opinion, alleged, that the inability *was only imaginary*; that he "could easily believe that a man may stand with his back to a wall, and may really believe that he has no power to move from the wall." It is therefore clear this individual attributed the phenomenon to a *mental*, whilst I attributed it to a *physical* cause.

half the eyelids closed convulsively; the mouth was distorted; she gave a deep sigh, the bosom heaved, she fell back, and was evidently passing into an hysteric paroxysm, to prevent which I instantly roused her. On counting the pulse I found it had mounted up to 180 strokes a minute.

In order to prove my position still more clearly, I called up one of my men-servants, who knew nothing of mesmerism, and gave him such directions as were calculated to impress his mind with the idea, that his fixed attention was merely for the purpose of watching a chemical experiment in the preparation of some medicine, and being familiar with such he could feel no alarm. In two minutes and a half his eyelids closed slowly with a vibrating motion, his chin fell on his breast, he gave a deep sigh, and instantly was in a profound sleep, breathing loudly. All the persons present burst into a fit of laughter, but still he was not interrupted by us. In about one minute after his profound sleep I roused him, and pretended to chide him for being so careless, said he ought to be ashamed of himself for not being able to attend to my instructions for three minutes without falling asleep, and ordered him down stairs. In a short time I recalled this young man, and desired him to sit down once more, but to be careful not to go to sleep again, as on the former occasion. He sat down with this intention, but at the expiration of two minutes and a half his eyelids closed, and exactly the same phenomena as in the former experiment ensued.

I again tried the experiment by causing Mr. Walker to gaze on a different object from that used in the *first* experiments, but still, as I anticipated, the phenomena were the same. I also tried him *a la Fontaine,* with the thumbs and eyes, and likewise by gazing on my eyes without contact, and still the effects were the same, as I fully expected.

I now stated that I considered the experiments fully proved my theory; and expressed my entire conviction that the phenomena of mesmerism were to be accounted for on the principle of a derangement of the state of the cerebro-spinal centres, and of the circulatory, and respiratory, and muscular systems, induced, as I have explained, by a fixed stare, absolute repose of body, fixed attention, and suppressed respiration, concomitant with that fixity of attention. That the whole depended on the physical and psychical condition of the patient, arising from the causes referred to, and not at all on the volition, or passes of the operator, throwing out a magnetic fluid, or exciting into activity some mystical universal fluid or medium. I farther added, that having thus produced the *primary* phenomena, I had no doubt but the others would follow as a matter of course, time being allowed for their gradual and successive development.*

For a considerable time I was of the opinion that the phenomena induced by my mode of operating and that of the mesmerizers, were identical; and, so far as I have yet personally seen, I still consider the condition of the nervous system induced by both

---

*It has been asserted, for the mere purpose of proving the contrary, that I had claimed being the first to discover that *contact* was *not* necessary, and that a magnetic fluid was not required to produce the phenomena of mesmerism. I never made any such claim, but illustrated these facts by the most simple and conclusive experiments probably which were ever adduced for that purpose. In one of my lectures, I gave a history of mesmerism, including Mesmer's attempt to mesmerize trees in Dr. Franklin's garden, to prove to the Commission of 1784, that the patients would become affected when they went under the mesmerized trees, from the magnetic fluid passing from the trees to the patients. This was proof sufficient, that even *Mesmer* did not hold that *contact* was necessary. I farther stated the fact, that the experiment was a failure, as the patient became affected, *not* under the *mes*merized, but under the *un*mesmerized trees, which led the Commission to infer, that the phenomena resulted from imagination, and not from the influence of a magnetic fluid. Here, then, we had two theories, neither of which considered contact necessary. Surely no one could suppose that I wished to lay claim to these facts as discoveries of my own, seeing I gave the dates when the occurrence took place, which was many years before I was born.

Moreover, I explained, at the same lecture, the different modes of mesmerizing, by passes *at a distance,* and by pointing the fingers at the eyes and forehead, adopted by others, long before I made any experiments on the subject; and at subsequent lectures, from observing the graceful attitudes some patients assumed during the hypnotic state, and the ease with which they could maintain any given position, by becoming cataleptiformly fixed in it, I hazarded the opinion, that it may have been to hypnotism the Grecians were indebted for their fine statuary; and the Fakirs for their power of performing their remarkable feats. I also expressed my belief, that the rapt state of religious enthusiasts, such as that of the Monks of Mount Athos, arose from the same cause, although none of the parties might have understood the true principle by which they were produced.

modes to be at least analogous. It appeared to me that the fixation of the mind and eyes was attained occasionally during the monotonous movements of the mesmerizers, and thus they succeeded sometimes, and as it were, by chance; whereas, by my insisting on the eyes being fixed in the most favourable position, and the mind thus riveted to one idea, as the *primary and imperative conditions,* my success was consequently general and the effects intense, while theirs was feeble and uncertain. However, from what the mesmerizers state as to effects which they can produce in certain cases, there seem to be differences sufficient to warrant the conclusion that they ought to be considered as distinct agencies; and for the following reasons. The mesmerizers positively assert that they can produce certain effects, which I have never been able to produce by my mode, although I have tried to do so.* Now, I do not consider it fair or proper to impugn the statements of others in this matter, who are known to be men of talent and observation, and of undoubted credit in *other* matters, merely because *I* have not *personally* witnessed the phenomena, or been able to produce them myself, either by my own mode or theirs. With my present means of knowledge I am willing to admit that certain phenomena to which I refer *have* been induced by others, but still I think most of them may be explained in a different and more natural way than that of the mesmerizers. When I shall have personally had evidence of the special influence and its effects to which they lay claim, I shall not be backward in bearing testimony to the fact.

However, the greatest and most important difference is this, that they can succeed so seldom, and I so generally, in inducing the phenomena which we both profess thus to effect. Granting, therefore, to the mesmerizers the full credit of being able to produce certain wonderful phenomena which I have not been able to produce by my plan, still it follows, that mine is superior to

---

*The effects I allude to are such as, telling the time on a watch held behind the head, or placed on the pit of the stomach; reading closed letters, or a shut book; perceiving what is doing miles off; having the power of perceiving the nature and cure of the diseases of others, although uneducated in medical science; mesmerizing patients at miles' distance, without the knowledge or belief in the patient that any such operation is intended.

theirs in as far as *general applicability and practical utility* are concerned. Mine has also this advantage, that I am quite certain no one can be affected by it, in any stage of the process, unless by the free will and consent of the patient, which is at once sufficient to exonerate the practice from the imputations of being capable of being converted to immoral purposes, which has been so much insisted on to the prejudice of animal magnetism. This has arisen from the mesmerizers asserting that they have the power of over-mastering patients irresistibly, even whilst at a distance, by mere volitions and secret passes.

I am fully borne out by the opinion of that eminent physiologist, Mr. Herbert Mayo, in my view of the subject, that my plan is "the best, the shortest, and surest for getting the sleep," and throwing the nervous system, by artificial contrivance, into a new condition, which may be rendered available in the healing art. At a private conversazione, which I gave to the profession in London on the 1st of March, 1842, he examined and tested my patients most carefully, submitted himself to be operated on by me both publicly and privately, and was so searching and inquisitive in his investigations as to call forth the animadversions of a medical gentleman present, who thought he was not giving me fair play; but which he has assured me proceeded from an anxious desire to know the truth, not being biassed by having any peculiar views of his own to bring forward; and because he considered the subject most important, both in a speculative and practical point of view.

Whatever I advance, therefore, in the following remarks, I wish to be distinctly understood as strictly in reference to my own mode of operating, and distinct from that of all others. The latter I shall merely refer to in as far as is necessary to point out certain sources of fallacy by which the phenomena of the one may be confounded with those of the other.

In proof of the general success of my mode of operating, I need only name, that at one of my public lectures in Manchester, fourteen male adults, in good health, all strangers to me, stood up at once, and ten of them became decidedly hypnotized. At Rochdale I conducted the experiments for a friend, and hypnotized twenty strangers in one night. At a private conversazione to the profession in London, on the 1st of March, 1842, eighteen adults, most of them entire strangers to me, sat down at once, and in ten minutes sixteen of them were decidedly hypnotized. Mr. Herbert Mayo tested some of these patients, and satisfied himself of the reality of the phenomena. On another ocassion I took thirty-two children into a room, none of whom had either seen or heard of hypnotism or mesmerism: I made them stand up three times, and in ten or twelve minutes had the whole thirty-two hypnotized, maintaining their arms extended while in the hypnotic condition, and this at mid-day. In making this statement, I do not mean to say they were in the *ulterior* stage, or state of *torpor*; but that they were in the *primary* stage, or that of *excitement,* from which experience has taught me confidently to rely that the torpid and rigid state will certainly follow, by merely affording time for the phenomena to develop themselves. At the conversazione given on the 29th of June, 1842, to the members of the British Association, two men and two youths were brought off the street. One man and both youths were operated on; all the three were hypnotized, and one of the youths reduced to the rigid state. In the *Stockport Chronicle* of 4th February 1842, there is a report of a lecture delivered in that town a few days before. A dozen male patients were made to stand up at once, and treated according to my method, six of them became hypnotized, and two of them so deeply, as to cause the lecturer very considerable trouble to rouse them. With one named "Charlie," all the usual means, including buffetings and frictions before a fire, did not succeed in restoring speech until he had been made to swallow nearly half a tumbler glass of *neat gin*. I consider this important as being the testimony of *an enemy*. It can take place also in the dark, as well as by day or by gas light; when the eyes are bandaged, as when they are uncovered, by merely keeping the eyes fixed, the body in a state of absolute rest, and the mind abstracted from all other considerations. In cases of children, and those of weak intellect, or of restless and excitable minds, whom I could not manage so as to make them comply with these simple rules, I have always been foiled, although most anxious to succeed.

This I consider a strong proof of the correctness of my views. By arresting the attention, and fixing the eyes, it is also successful with brute animals.

This general success of my plan, both with man and brute animals, I consider sufficient to prove it proceeds from a law in the animal economy. The exceptions to success are so few as to lead to the conclusion that they arise from a non-compliance with the conditions. It is, however, unquestionable, that there exists great difference in the susceptibility of different individuals, some becoming rapidly and intensely affected, others slowly and feebly so.

I am aware that some say they have tried my mode, and failed to produce the phenomena. The reason, I presume, is simply this. They will not believe the necessity of complying with the WHOLE of the conditions I have distinctly insisted on. But, in all fairness, if they do not comply with the WHOLE conditions, they have no right to expect the promised results, nor to be disappointed because they fail. If the patient and operator comply in *all* respects as I direct, success is almost certain; but, on the contrary, he is almost equally certain to fail if *all* the conditions are not *strictly* complied with.

When we consider the great difficulty to some persons of abstracting their minds, and the greater difficulty of ensuring that patients operated on in a public room shall be able to abstract their minds entirely from the circumstances with which they are surrounded, and from other considerations concentrate their ideas entirely on the subject in hand, and the equally great difficulty of securing absolute quiet where a large number of people are assembled, and the extreme quickness of hearing when patients are passing into the hypnotic state, which makes them liable to be roused by the slightest noise, it must be evident, that a public lectureroom is by no means a favourable place for operating on patients for the first time.

Prosecuting the investigation, as I have been doing, by experiments and observations, I have, as might be expected, had occasion to modify and alter some of my views and manipulations; but still the principle remains the same.

I now proceed to detail the mode which I practise for inducing the phenomena. Take any bright object (I generally use my lancet case) between the thumb and fore and middle fingers of the left hand; hold it from about eight to fifteen inches from the eyes, at such position above the forehead as may be necessary to produce the greatest strain upon the eyes and eyelids, and enable the patient to maintain a steady fixed stare at the object.* The patient must be made to understand that he is to keep the eyes steadily fixed on the object, and the mind riveted on the idea of that one object. It will be observed, that owing to the consensual adjustment of the eyes, the pupils will be at first contracted: they will shortly begin to dilate, and after they have done so to a considerable extent, and have assumed a wavy motion, if the fore and middle fingers of the right hand, extended and a little separated, are carried from the object towards the eyes, most probably the eyelids will close involuntarily, with a vibratory motion. If this is not the case, or the patient allows the *eyeballs to move,* desire him to begin anew, giving him to understand that he is to allow the eyelids to close when the fingers are again carried towards the eyes, but that the *eyeballs must be kept fixed in the same position, and the mind riveted to the one idea of the object held above the eyes.* It will generally be found, that the eyelids close with a *vibratory* motion, or become spasmodically closed. After ten or fifteen seconds have elapsed by gently elevating the arms and legs, it will be found that the patient has a disposition to retain them in the situation in which they have been placed, if *he is intensely affected.* If this is not the case, in a soft tone of voice desire him to retain the limbs in the extended position, and thus the pulse will speedily become greatly

---

*At an early period of my investigations, I caused the patients to look at a cork bound on the forehead. This was a very efficient plan with those who had the power of converging the eyes so as to keep them *both steadily* directed on the object. I very soon found, however, that there were many who could not keep *both* eyes steadily fixed on *so near* an object, and that the result was, that such patients did not become hypnotized. To obviate this, I caused them to look at a more distant point, which, although scarcely so rapid and intense in its effects, succeeds more generally than the other, and is therefore what I now adopt and recommend.

accelerated, and the limbs, in process of time, will become quite rigid and involuntarily fixed. It will also be found, that all the organs of special sense, excepting sight, including heat and cold, and muscular motion, or resistance, and certain mental faculties are at *first* prodigiously *exalted,* such as happens with regard to the primary effects of opium, wine, and spirits. After a certain point, however, this exaltation of function is followed by a state of depression, far greater than the torpor of *natural* sleep.* From the state of the most profound torpor of the organs of special sense, and tonic rigidity of the muscles, they may, at this stage, *instantly* be restored to the *opposite* condition of extreme mobility and exalted sensibility, by directing a current of air against the organ or organs we wish to excite to action, or the muscles we wish to render limber, and which had been in the cataleptiform state. By mere repose the senses will speedily merge into the original condition again. The *modus operandi* of the current of air producing such extraordinary effects, I acknowledge myself quite unable to explain, but I have no difficulty in producing and reproducing the effects by the same means, whether performed by myself or others, and whether the current of air is from the lips, from a pair of bellows, or by the motion of the hand, or any inaminate object. The extent and abruptness of these transitions are so extraordinary, that they must be seen before the possibility is believed.

An abrupt blow, or pressure over the rigid muscle, will de-hypnotize a rigid part; but, I have found pressing the nose will

---

*I wish to direct especial attention to this circumstance, as from overlooking the fact of the *first* stage of this artificial hypnotism being one of *excitement,* with the possession of *consciousness* and *docility,* many imagine they are *not* affected, whilst the acceleration of pulse, peculiar expression of countenance, and other characteristic symptoms, prove the existence of the condition beyond the possibility of a doubt, *to all who understand the subject.* I consider it very imprudent to carry it to the ulterior stage, or that of torpor, at a *first* trial. Moreover, there is great difference in the susceptibility to the neuro-hypnotic impression, some arriving at the state of rigidity and insensibility in a few minutes, whilst others may readily pass into the *primary* stage, but can scarcely be brought into the ulterior, or rigid and torpid state. It is also most important to note, that many instances of remarkable and permanent cures have occurred, where it has never been carried beyond the state of consciousness.

not restore smell, unless very gentle and continued, nor will pressing a handkerchief against the ear restore hearing when the ear has become torpid, nor will *gentle* friction over the skin restore sensibility to the dormant skin, or mobility to the rigid muscles underneath (unless so gentle as to be titillation, properly so called), and yet a slight puff of wind will *instantly* rouse the whole to abnormal sensibility and mobility; a fact which has perplexed and puzzled me exceedingly.

At first I required the patients to look at an object until the eyelids closed of themselves, involuntarily. I found, however, that in many cases this was followed by pain in the globes of the eyes, and slight inflammation of the conjunctival membrane. In order to avoid this, I now close the eyelids, when the impression on the pupil already referred to has taken place, because I find that the *beneficial* phenomena follow this method, provided the eyeballs are kept fixed, and thus, too, the unpleasant feelings in the globes of the eyes will be prevented. Were the object to produce astonishment in the person operated on, by finding himself unable to open his eyes, the former method is the better; as the eyes once closed it is generally impossible for him to open them; whereas they may be opened for a considerable time after being closed in the other mode I now recommend. However, for curative purposes, I prefer the plan which leaves no pain in the globes of the eyes.

In time, from a careful analysis of the whole of my experiments, which have been very numerous, I have been led to the following conclusion:—that it is a law in the animal economy, that by a continued fixation of the mental and visual eye, on any object which is not of itself of an exciting nature, with absolute repose of body, and general quietude, they become wearied; and, provided the patients rather favour than resist the feeling of stupor of which they will soon experience the tendency to creep upon them, during such experiments, a state of somnolency is induced, accompanied with that condition of the brain and nervous system generally, which renders the patient liable to be affected, according to the mode of manipulating, so as to exhibit the hypnotic phenomena. As the experiment succeeds with the blind, I consider it not so much the optic, as the sentient, motor, and sympathetic nerves, and the mind through which the impression is made. I feel so thoroughly convinced that it is a law of the animal economy that such effects should follow such condition of mind and body, that I hesitated not to give it as my deliberate opinion, that this is a *fact* which cannot be controverted. As to the *modus operandi* we may never be able to account for that in a manner so as to satisfy all objections; but neither can we tell why the law of gravitation should act as experience has taught us it *does* act. Still, as our ignorance of the cause of gravitation acting as it is known to do, does not prevent us profiting by an accumulation of the facts known as to its results, so ought not our ignorance of the *whole* laws of the hypnotic state to prevent our studying it practically, and applying it beneficially, when we have the power of doing so.

I feel confident that the phenomena are induced solely by an impression made on the nervous centres, by the physical and psychical condition of the patient, irrespective of any agency proceeding from, or excited into action by another—as any one can hypnotize himself by attending strictly to the simple rules I lay down; and the following is a striking example of the fact, which was communicated to me and two other gentlemen, by a most respectable teacher. He found that a number of his pupils had been in the habit of hypnotizing themselves, and he had ordered them to discontinue the practice. However, one day he ascertained a girl had hypnotized herself by looking at the wall, and that her companions had put a pen in her hand, with which she had written the word "Manchester;" and she held the pen very firmly—in fact, the fingers were cataleptiformly rigid. He spoke to her in a gentle tone of voice, and called her. She arose and advanced towards him, and when awoke, was not aware he had called her, or of what had passed.

I have also had the state of the patient tested before, during, and after being hypnotized, to ascertain if there was any alteration in the magnetic or electric condition, but although tested by excellent instruments, and with great care, no appreciable difference could be detected. Patients have been hypnotized whilst positively, and also whilst negatively, electrified, without any appreciable difference in the phenomena; so that they appear to be excited independently of electric or magnetic change. I have also repeatedly made two patients hypnotize each other, at the same time, by personal contact. How could this be reconciled with the theory of a special influence transmitted being the cause of the phenomena, *plus* and *minus* being equally efficient?

It is also well known, that occasionally the phenomena arise spontaneously in the course of disease.

It is now admitted even by the editor of the *Lancet,* one of the greatest opponents of mesmerism, in the leading article of 4th February, 1843, that the phenomena "are wonderful only to those who are unacquainted with the aspects of disease;" and "that we continually see patients labouring under hysteria, and analogous forms of nervous disease, falling suddenly into various states of stupor, trance, and convulsion, without *any* assignable cause." When it is acknowledged that such effects as those named, may spring from such slight influences as to be said to arise *"without any assignable cause,"* can it be wondered at that important changes may be induced by acting on the nervous system in the way I have adopted, of which Mr. Herbert Mayo (whose competence to give an opinion on *any* physiological subject no one will question, and who himself publicly submitted to be operated on by me) observed, in the course of our correspondence, that it induces "a feeling of stupor, which any one may observe has a disposition to creep upon him, when he tries your experiment of looking fixedly at an object as you direct."

I thought it desirable, therefore, to adopt the name I did, for the reasons explained in the introduction.

A patient may be hypnotized by keeping the eyes fixed in any direction. It occurs most *slowly* and *feebly* when the eyes are directed straight forward, and most *rapidly* and *intensely* when they can be maintained in the position of a double internal and upward squint.*

It is now pretty generally known, that during the effort to look at a very near object, there is produced, according to the direction of the object, a double internal squint, or double internal and downward or upward squint, or double internal and downward or upward squint, and the pupils are thereby powerfully contracted. I am not aware, however, that it has been recorded, that by directing the eyes loosely, upwards or downwards, to the right or to the left, as if looking at a very distant object, the pupils become very much *dilated,* irrespective of the quantity of light passing to the retina; so that in this manner we can contract or dilate the pupil at will. To those who consider the movement of the iris as the mere effect of irritability, I may observe, in that view, the former position increases, the latter diminishes, the

---

*It is not a little amusing to find any one try to distort so greatly, by garbled statements, the plain meaning of an author, as to make it appear that a writer of some articles on Animal Magnetism, in the *Medical Gazette* in 1838, was well acquainted with my mode of operating. He observes, "On the majority of persons no influence whatever is exhibited." How does this coincide with the general success of my mode as stated? "On those least affected a number of anomalous slight symptoms are produced." He then describes those "feelings of heat and cold, and those of creeping and trembling," which, he adds, "are only the usual imaginary feelings which most persons have if their attention be strongly directed to any particular part of the body, more especially if (as is generally the case with magnetic patients) something is expected to occur." Such are the symptoms attributed by this writer to "attention," but are these the symptoms or phenomena induced by Hypnotism? Or is there the slightest similarity in the cause? In this author's view it is the result of "attention strongly directed to *different parts of the body*," whereas mine is by attention riveted to something *without* the body. The best mode of gathering the opinion of an author appears to me to be that of his summing up at the conclusion of his subject. Now, the subject is concluded by the following observations:—"This, then, is our case. Every credible effect of magnetism has occurred, and every incredible is *said* to have occurred in cases where no magnetic influence has been exerted, but in all which excited imagination, irritation, or some powerful mental impression, has operated: where the mind has been alone acted on, magnetic effects have been produced without magnetic manipulations: where magnetic manipulations have been employed, unknown, and therefore without the assistance of the mind, no result has ever been produced." Now, can any thing more be required than this, to prove that this writer, as well as Bertrand, adheres to the theory of imagination? Such was the impression left on my mind by reading these papers when they were published; and, together with Wakley's experiments, determined me to consider the whole as a system of collusion or illusion, or of excited imagination, sympathy, or imitation. I therefore abandoned the subject as unworthy of farther investigation, until I attended the conversazione of Lafontaine, where I saw one fact, the inability of a patient to open his eyelids, which arrested my attention; I felt convinced it was not to be attributed to any of the causes referred to, and I therefore instituted experiments to determine the question; and exhibited the results to the public in a few days after.

irritability. I may farther remark, if the eyes are *much strained* in ANY direction, I think the pupils will be found to contract as a consequence.

It is important to remark, that the oftener patients are hypnotized, from assocation of ideas and habit, the more susceptible they become; and in this way they are liable to be affected *entirely through the imagination.* Thus, if they consider or imagine there is something doing, although they do not see it, from which they are to be affected, they *will become affected;* but, on the contrary, the most expert hypnotist in the world may exert all his endeavours in vain, if the party does not expect it, and mentally and bodily comply, and thus yield to it.

It is this very circumstance, coupled with the extreme docility and mobility of the patients, and extended range and extreme quickness of action, at a certain stage, of the ordinary functions of the organs of sense, including heat and cold, and muscular motion, the tendency of the patients in this state to approach to, or recede from, impressions, according as their intensity or quality is agreeable or the contrary, which I consider has misled so many, and induced the animal magnetizers to imagine they could produce their effects on patients at a distance, through mere volition and secret passes.*

---

*In the *Medical Times* of 26th March, 1842, I published a letter on this subject, from which I make the following extracts:—

"The supposed power of seeing with other parts of the body than the eyes, I consider it a misnomer, so far as I have yet personally witnessed. It is quite certain, however, that some patients can tell the shape of what is held at an inch and a half from the skin, on the back of the neck, crown of the head, arm, or hand, or other parts of the body, but it is from *feeling* they do so; the extremely exalted sensibility of the skin enabling them to discern the shape of the object so presented, from its tendency to emit or absorb caloric. This, however, is not *sight,* but *feeling.*

"In like manner I have satisfied myself and others, that patients are drawn, or induced to obey the motions of the operator, not from any peculiar inherent magnetic power in him, but from their exalted state of feeling enabling them to discern the currents of air, which they advance to, or retire from, according to their direction. This I clearly proved to be the case to-day, and that a patient could feel and obey the motion of a glass funnel passed through the air at a distance of *fifteen feet.*

"To remove all sources of fallacy as to the extent of influence exercised by the patient herself, independently of any personal or mental influence on my part, whilst I was otherwise engaged, my daughter, requested the patient to go into a room by herself, and when alone, try whether she could hypnotize herself. In a short time I was told the patient was found fast asleep in my drawing-room. I went to her, bandaged her eyes, and then, with the glass funnel (which I used to avoid the chance of electric or magnetic influence being passed from my person to that of the patient), elevated, or drew up her arms, and then her whole body. I now retired fifteen feet from her, and found every time I drew the funnel *towards* me, she approached nearer, but when it was forced sharply *from me,* she invariably retired; and if it was moved laterally, she moved to the right or left accordingly. I now continued drawing the funnel so as to keep up the currents towards the door, and in this way, her arms being extended, and eyes bandaged, she followed me down stairs and up again, a flight of twenty-two steps, with the peculiar characteristic caution of the somnambulist. After arriving at the top of the stair, I allowed her to stand a little, and again began the drawing motion. She evidently felt the motion, and attempted to come, but could not. I now endeavoured to lead her by the hand, but found that *the legs had become cataleptiform, so that she could not move.* I now carried her into the drawing-room, and, after she was seated on a chair, awoke her. She was quite unconscious of what had happened, and could not be made to believe she had been down stairs—said she was quite sure she could have done no such thing without falling—and to this moment believes we were only hoaxing her by saying she had had such a ramble.

"I had repeatedly performed this experiment with this patient and others before, with the same result in all respects but walking up and down stairs; and proved their readiness to be drawn by others equally as myself when in that state; so that I consider it quite evident to any unprejudiced person, that a patient can hypnotize himself independently of any personal influence of another; and that it is by extreme sensibility of the skin, and docility of the patients, that they are drawn after an operator, rather than by magnetic attraction; and that the power of discriminating objects held near the skin in different parts of the body, is the result of *feeling*, and *not of sight*.

"The moment I witnessed the attempts of a celebrated professor *to draw a patient,* I formed my opinion of the *cause;*—that it arose from currents of air produced by his hand, together with the extreme sensibility of the skin, and docility of the patients when in that state; and my experiments have clearly proved this, *some patients acknowledging the fact.*

"It may be interesting to remark, that whilst passing up and down stairs the door bell rang, which produced such a tremor through the whole frame as nearly caused the patient's fall—a fact quite in accordance with the effect of any abrupt noise on NATURAL *somnambulists.*"

It is owing to this extreme sensibility of the skin during hypnotism, that patients may walk through a room blindfolded, without running against the furniture—the difference of temperature, or rather degree of conducting power of objects, and the resistance of the air directing them.

I have frequently illustrated this with very sensitive patients in the most beautiful and satisfactory manner, thus: by throwing any fragrant and agreeable scent on a bare table the patients will approach, anxious to smell it, but are repelled before they come quite close to the cold table. Place a handkerchief on the table, on which place the scent, and now the patient will approach close to it, and revel in its fragrance. Remove the handkerchief, and the attractive and repulsive movements will again ensue.

This was beautifully illustrated at a private conversazione at my house lately, in the presence of several medical and other eminently scientific gentlemen. Two patients were hypnotized, when one became so enamoured of the scent of a gentleman's snuff-box as to follow him around the room. He then laid the box about eighteen inches from the edge of an uncovered table, when she advanced, her arms being extended, anxious to reach the box, but when about ten or twelve inches from it, she started back, from perceiving the impression of the cold table at that distance. She now made another attempt to approach the box, being attracted by the fragrance of its contents, but was as speedily repelled by the cold table before she approached it, and now kept bobbing over the box, much in the same manner as I have witnessed in the attempts of a hungry dog to partake of very hot food. The other patient, in passing round the table, also caught the smell of the box, and advanced from another point, and thus both kept bobbing over it much to the amusement of all present. I now covered the table with a handkerchief, and placed the box on it, when they instantly approached close to it, and seemed to feast on its fragrance; on removing the handkerchief they withdrew, and commenced bobbing over it as at first. The former patient had never seen such experiments, or been tested in this way before.

It would be difficult to adduce a more striking example than the following of the fact, that the phenomena are produced by the fixation of the mind and eyes, and general repose of the patient, and not from imagination, or the look or will of another. After my lecture at the Hanover Square Rooms, London, on the 1st of March, 1842, a gentleman told Mr. Walker, who was along with me, that he was most anxious to see me, that I might try whether I could hypnotize him. He said both himself and friends were anxious he should be affected, but that neither Lafontaine nor others who had tried him, could succeed. Mr. Walker said, if that is what you want, as Mr. Braid is engaged otherwise, sit down, and I will hypnotize you myself in a minute. When I went into the room I observed what was going on, the gentleman sitting staring at Mr. Walker's finger, who was standing a little to the right of the patient, with his eyes fixed steadily on those of the latter. I passed on, and attended to something else, and when I returned a little after, found Mr. Walker standing in the same position *fast asleep, his arm and finger in a state of cataleptiform rigidity,* and the patient wide awake, and staring at the finger all the while. After I had roused Mr. Walker, the gentleman observed, "This is really very strange, that no one can mesmerize *me;* I must have extraordinary powers of resistance." I requested him to stay a little, and I would try what I could do for him when all was quiet. In three mintues I had him asleep, and in a little more quite rigid. The following reasons may be assigned for my success after Mr. Walker had so signally failed. He tried it whilst there were several people in the room, who were moving about and talking; I took care not to commence till all was quiet—Mr. Walker had not taken the precaution to make the patient direct his eyes in the best possible manner, but I was careful that he should do so. Moreover, although Mr. Walker had not succeeded in putting him into the somnolent condition, he had, no doubt, partially affected him, and the influence had not entirely passed off when I began my operation. Two days after, Mr. Walker accompanied me when I called on one of the most celebrated mesmerizers in Europe, who, during our conversation, stated, that a glance of the eye was quite enough, in many cases, to produce the effects. During our conversation, I presume, he had determined to surprise both Mr. Walker and myself, by keeping his large intellectual eyes fixed on Mr. Walker. The latter, however, suspecting what was intended, and knowing my opinion as to the mode of *resisting* the influence of *such fascination,* kept his eyes moving, and his mind roaming, and thus frustrated the volition of one of the most energetic minds, and the glances and fascination of one of the finest pair of eyes imaginable for such a purpose. I must remark, that Mr. Walker was once magnetized by M. Lafontaine, after having been several times operated on by me, a circumstance which of course would render him more susceptible to the influence of the animal magnetizers' modes of operating, according to their own theory. Had Mr. Walker believed in the power, I know he would have become affected, even supposing the gentleman referred to had no such intention,—and I am not prepared to say he had. Mr. Walker, however, firmly believed he was trying to mesmerize him by the fascination referred to; but, relying on my opinion, and acting accordingly, he escaped. In order to show the efficacy of my simple plan, in a short time after, in the presence of the same gentleman, I requested Mr. Walker to hypnotize himself. By simply fixing his eyes and mind this was accomplished in about a minute.

I *consider* is unnecessary, in this treatise, to enter into a *detailed* account of the ordinary phenomena of sleep, dreaming and somnambulism, as contrasted with the walking state. Suffice it to say, the waking condition is that of mental and bodily activity, during which we are enabled to hold communion with the external world, by perceiving the ordinary impressions of appropriate stimuli through the organs of special sense, and of exercising the power of voluntary motion, and the mental functions generally. The state of *profound* sleep is exactly the *reverse* of this—a state of absolute unconsciousness of all that is going on around, and suspension of voluntary motion, and intellectual activity. In as far as regards the organs of special sense, and voluntary motion, and a temporary suspension of the mental energies, it is the emblem of death.

Between these extreme points there are *gradual* transitions, so that there are all possible varieties of condition imaginable, from the highest state of mental and bodily activity, to absolute torpor of both. There are two conditions, however, to which I may *briefly* advert,—that of dreaming and of somnambulism. In the former there are some of the mental and bodily functions in a state of partial activity, but, from the sensations arising from external stimuli being perceived very imperfectly, erroneous impressions are conveyed to the mind; and, as happens in some cases of insanity, the power of controlling the current of thought being absent, one idea excites another, until the most incongruous combinations are produced in many instances. Somnambulism, properly so called, is a state still more nearly allied to the waking condition than dreaming. The mental functions are more awake, a more just estimate of external impressions can be formed, and there is the power of voluntary motion present in a remarkable degree. Persons in this state are thus capable of being directed by those around, into certain trains of thought and action. The principal difference between the natural somnambulists, and those who become so through hypnotizing in the manner pointed out in this treatise, is the greater tendency of the latter to lapse into a state of *profound* sleep, unless prevented by being roused and directed by those present. Natural somnambulists seem to be impelled to certain trains of action by *internal* impulses; but, so far as I have seen, the artificial somnambulists have an inclination to remain at absolute rest, unless excited to action by some impression from without. In compliance with such excitement, however, they evince great acuteness and docility. There is also another remarkable difference. It is stated, that although natural somnambulists cannot remember, when awake, what they were engaged in when asleep, they have a vivid recollection of it when in that state again; but I have found no parallel to *this* in the somnambulism induced by hypnotism.

By this I mean that they cannot explain what happened during the former somnambulic state, but they may approximate to the words and actions which had formerly manifested themselves, provided they are placed under exactly similar circumstances. For the extent to which peculiar manifestations may be brought out by manipulating the head and face, at a certain stage of hypnotism, where examples are given of memory as regarded events which happened during the *waking* condition, whilst they seemed to have no recollection of what happened during a former state of hypnotism.

As to the causes of common sleep, I may remark, that, by the exercise of the mental operations, and the impressions conveyed through the organs of special sense, muscular effort, and the discharge of other animal functions, the brain become exhausted, and ceases to be affected by ordinary stimuli, and lapses into that dormant state we call sleep. During this condition it becomes recruited, and fitted for again receiving its wonted impressions through the organs of sense, and of holding intercourse with external nature, and exercising those powers of voluntary motion and mental function peculiar to the waking condition.

It will be generally admitted, that the most refreshing, and therefore the *most natural* sleep, accompanies that condition or languor which follows the *moderate* exercise or fatigue of *all* the bodily and mental functions, rather than an undue exercise of *one* or *more* to the neglect of the others. It is long since it was observed that inordinate attention to one subject caused *dreaming* instead of *sound sleep*. It will also be found that the absolute length of time during which any function may be exercised, depends very much on the *continuity* of its exertion, or its alternation with that of other functions; thus the mind may become confused and bewildered by continuing one particular study for a length of time, but may be able to return to it with energy and advantage, and prosecute the subject longer on the whole, by varying it with study of a different nature; moreover, bodily disease, and even insanity, frequently arises from allowing the mind to be occupied inordinately by one particular object or pursuit, whether that may be religion, politics, avarice, schemes of ambition, or any other passion, emotion, or object of unvaried contemplation.

In like manner, continued and over-intense muscular effort very soon exhausts the power of the muscles so exercised or over-exerted; and by keeping the eyes steadily and constantly exercised by gazing on a coloured spot, they soon cease to be able to discern the boundaries of the respective colours,* and ultimately seem scarcely to be capable of distinguishing the spot at all. The same might be proved of the other senses. It fine, *alternate action and repose is the law of animated nature.*†

---

*Muller.

†This subject is beautifully illustrated by Muller, at page 1410, Vol. II Baly's translation), which I now quote. "The excitement of the organic processes in the brain which attends an active state of the mind, gradually renders that organ incapable of maintaining the mental action, and thus induces sleep, which is to the brain what bodily fatigue is to other parts of the nervous system. The cessation or remission of mental activity during sleep, in its turn, however, affords an opportunity for the restoration of integrity to the organic conditions of the cerebrum, by which they regain their excitability. The brain, whose action is essential to the manifestation of mind, obeys, in fact, the general law which prevails over all organic phenomena,—that the phenomena of life being particular states induced in the organic structures, are attended with changes in the constituent matter of these structures. Hence, the longer the action of the mind is continued, the more incapable

does the brain become of supporting that action, and the more imperfectly are the mental processes performed, until at length sensations cease to be perceived, notwithstanding the impressions of external stimuli continue. This is entirely analogous to what frequently occurs during the waking state, in the case of individual sensations."

I must beg leave to take one exception to the correctness of these remarks, and that is, *moderate* exercise, I consider, instead of *exhausting,* seems rather to act *as a salutary stimulus,* and thus *strengthens* both *organ and function.* He (Muller) then goes on to state, most lucidly and fairly, "Nor merely the action of the mind, but the long continued exertion of other functions of animal life, such as the senses of muscular actions, induces the same exhaustion of the organic states of the brain, and thereby want of sleep and sleep itself; for these different systems of the body participate in the change which the organic condition of any one of them may undergo. Lastly, impairment of the normal organic state of the brain, by the circulation through it of blood charged with imperfectly assimilated nutriment, as after full meals in which spirituous drinks have been taken, also induces sleep. The narcotic medicaments act still more strongly by the change they produce in the organic composition of the sensorium. Even the increased pressure of the blood upon the brain, produced by the horizontal posture, may become the cause of sleep."

Here then is the opinion of this author in a few words. The exercise of function is attended with a change, deterioration, or wasting of the organic structure at a more rapid rate than can be repaired by the slow, but regular and persistent organic renovation continually going on in the whole system. A cessation of sentient, and mental, and muscular functions, therefore, as happens in sleep, becomes necessary to afford time for the renovation of the deteriorated organic structures of the respective organs, and of the brain in particular, which, in so eminent a degree, sympathizes and participates in the organic changes which have been induced in other organs.

Liebig's views seem confirmatory of this, where he points out the fact, that the chemical principles of those substances which act most energetically on the brain and nerves have a composition analogous to that of the substance of the brain and nerves, as in the case of the vegetable alkaloids. He believes that all the active principles which produce powerfully poisonous or medicinal effects, in minute doses, are compounds of nitrogen; and that those compounds, being resolved into their elements, take a share in the formation, or transformation, of brain and nervous matter.

It is this very principle, of over-exerting the attention, by *keeping it riveted to one subject or idea which is not of itself of an exciting nature,* and over-exercising one set of muscles, and the state of the strained eyes, with the suppressed respiration, and general repose, which attend such experiments, which excites in the brain and whole nervous system that peculiar state which I call Hypnotism, or nervous sleep. The most striking proofs that it is different from common sleep, are the extraordinary effects produced by it. In deep abstraction of mind, it is well known, the individual becomes unconscious of surrounding objects, and in some cases, even of severe bodily inflictions. During hypnotism, or nervous sleep, the functions in action seem to be so *intensely* active, as must in a great measure rob the others of that degree of nervous energy necessary for exciting their sensibility. This alone may account for much of the dulness of common feeling during the abnormal quickness and extended range of action of certain other functions.*

---

*It was certainly presuming very much on the ignorance of others for any one to attempt so to pervert the meaning of an author, as to twist what M'Nish has written on the article "Reverie," and represent it as the basis of my theory. How does M'Nish define it? "Reveries," he says, "proceeds from an unusual quiescence of the brain, and inability of the mind to direct itself strongly to any one point; it is often the prelude of sleep. There is a *defect* in the *attention*, which, instead of being fixed on *one* subject, *wanders over a thousand,* and even on these is feebly and ineffectively directed." Now this, as every one must own, is the very *reverse* of what is induced by *my plan,* because I *rivet* the *attention* to *one idea,* and the eyes to *one point,* as the *primary* and *imperative conditions.* Then, as to another passage, "That kind of reverie in which the mind is nearly divested of all ideas, and approximates nearly to the state of sleep, I have sometimes experienced while gazing long and intently upon a river. The thoughts seem to guide away, one by one, upon the surface of the stream, till the mind is emptied of them altogether. In this state we see the glassy volume of the water moving past us, and hear its murmur, but lose all power of fixing our attention definitively upon any subject; and either fall asleep, or are aroused by some spontaneous reaction of the mind, or by some appeal to the senses sufficiently strong to startle us from our reverie." Now, I should have read this passage a thousand times without discovering any analogy between it and my theoretical views. They appear to me to be "wide as the poles asunder." Instead of ridding the mind of ideas "one by one, till the mind is *emptied* of them *altogether,*" I endeavour to rid the mind at *once* of all ideas *but one,* and to fix *that* one in the mind *even after passing into the hypnotic state.* This is very different from what happens in the reverie referred to, in which M'Nish confesses the difficulty "of fixing our attention definitively upon *any* subject." Again, so far from a reaction of the mind being sufficient to rouse patients from the hypnotic state, as in the reverie referred to, I can only state, that I have never seen patients deeply affected come out of it without assistance; and I heard Lafontaine say, he had been unable to restore the Frenchman who was with him for twelve hours on one occasion, when a surgeon operated on him; and I have read the report of another, who operated on a patient at Stockport, "Charlie," according to my method, and, from having allowed him to go too far, experienced no small difficulty in rousing him, nor could he be restored to speech after much manipulation, and buffeting, and friction, till he had swallowed nearly *half a* *tumbler glass of neat gin.* To prevent misrepresentation, I shall quote the case as reported in the Stockport Chronicle of 4th February, 1842, — "To the final instance the lecturer now drew particular attention. It was that of a young man, recognized by many in the room by the familiar name of 'Charlie.' He was just entering upon the state of somnolence, and the attention of the audience was directed to the fact, that is was indicated, by the different members becoming rigid. Presently his eyelids closed, and he became as though apparently under the influence of catalepsy. It was tried to make him sit down, but his whole frame was perfectly rigid, and that object could not therefore be accomplished. He was then laid on the floor, and the usual means, with cold water added, were employed in order to bring him to a state of consciousness. After a time these partially succeeded, his limbs became once more supple, and he was set in a chair, apparently conscious, though his eyelids were not yet open. He was several times requested to open them, and as often made the most vigorous efforts to do so, but was unable; at last they were opened, and it was discovered that the operation had so far influenced the entire functions of his body, that he had for a time lost the power of utterance, the muscles of the throat and tongue still remaining in a state of the most perfect rigidity. In this state, and being affected by a tremor which seized every part of his person, while the operator continued to rub the parts, in order to excite them to renewed action, and to restore animation. All this, however, had not the desired effect for some time, during which the patient evinced feelings of considerable surprise at his condition; but nevertheless was exceedingly lively, and made several efforts to speak, but could not. At last half a tumbler glass of neat gin was brought, the greater portion of which he drank off, and this partially restored the power of utterance, for he was afterwards able to articulate a little, and asked, though only in a whisper, for his hat; and also requested that some water might be mixed with the remaining portion of the gin. He complained also of a sense of excessive fulness of the stomach; and said, in answer to inquiries, that although not feeling cold, he was yet unable to resist the tremor which had seized him."

Was not this a beautiful illustration of the facility with which patients might be roused from this condition *"by a reaction of the mind?"* Nor was this the only case that evening, in which great difficulty had been experienced in rousing patients from the hypnotic state.

The untoward result (of difficulty in rousing patients from the hypnotic state) . . ., I have no doubt, was the effect of permitting the experiment to be carried too far. No such consequence has ever followed in any of my operations, and for this reason, that I have always watched each case with close attention, and aroused the patient the moment I saw the slightest symptom of danger. I shall, therefore, now point out the symptoms of danger, with the mode of arousing patients, and thus preventing mischief which might ensue from want of due caution in the operator.

Whenever I observe the breathing very much oppressed, the

face greatly flushed, the rigidity excessive, or the action of the heart very quick and tumultuous, I instantly arouse the patient, which I have always readily and speedily succeeded in doing by a clap of the hands, an abrupt shock on the arm or leg by striking them sharply with the flat hand, pressure and friction over the eyelids, and by a current of air wafted against the face. I have never failed by these means to restore my patients very speedily.

I feel convinced hypnotism is not only a valuable, but also a perfectly safe remedy for many complaints, if judiciously used; still it ought not to be trifled with by ignorant persons for the mere sake of gratifying idle curiosity. In all cases of apoplectic tendency, or where there is aneurism, or serious organic disease of the heart, it ought not to be resorted to, excepting with the precaution, that it may be in the mode calculated to *depress* the force and frequency of the heart's action.

In passing into common sleep objects are perceived more and more faintly, the eyelids close, and remain quiescent, and all the other organs of special sense become gradually blunted, and cease to convey their usual impressions to the brain, the limbs become flaccid from cessation of muscular tone and action, the pulse and respiration become slower, the pupils are turned upwards, and inwards, and are *contracted*. (Muller.)

In the hypnotic state, induced with the view of exhibiting what I call the hypnotic phenomena, vision becomes more and more imperfect, the eyelids are closed, but have, for a considerable time *a vibratory motion* (in some few they are forcibly closed, as by spasm of the orbiculares); the organs of special sense, particularly of smell, touch, and hearing, heat and cold, and resistance, are greatly *exalted*, and afterwards become blunted, in a degree far beyond the torpor of natural sleep; the pupils are turned upwards and inwards, but, contrary to what happens in *natural* sleep, they are greatly *dilated*, and highly insensible to light; after a length of time the pupils become contracted, whilst the eyes are still insensible to light. The pulse and respiration are, at first, slower than is natural, but immediately on calling muscles into action, a tendency to cataleptiform rigidity is assumed, with rapid pulse, and oppressed and quick breathing. The limbs are thus maintained in a state of tonic *rigidity* for any length of time I have yet thought it prudent to try, instead of that state of flaccidity induced by common sleep; and the most remarkable circumstance is this, that there seems to be no corresponding state of muscular exhaustion from such action.*

In passing into natural sleep, any thing held in the hand is soon allowed to drop from our grasp, but, in the artificial sleep now referred to, it will be held more firmly than before falling alseep. This is *a very remarkable difference.*

The power of balancing themselves is so great that I have never seen one of these hypnotic somnambulists fall. The same is noted of natural somnambulists. This is a remarkable fact, and would appear to occur in this way, that they acquire the centre of gravity, as if by instinct, in the *most natural, and therefore, in the most graceful manner,* and if allowed to remain in this position, they speedily become cataleptiformly and immovably fixed. From observing these two facts and the general tendency and taste for dancing displayed by most patients on hearing lively music during hypnotism, the peculiarly graceful and appropriate movement of many when thus excited, and the varied and elegant postures they may be made to assume by slight currents of air, and the faculty of retaining any position with so much ease, I have hazarded the opinion, that the Greeks may have been indebted to hypnotism for the perfection of their sculpture, and the Fakirs for their wonderful feats of suspending their bodies by a leg or an arm.

It thus clearly appears that it differs from common sleep in many respects, that there is first a state of excitement as with opium, and wine, and spirits, and afterwards a state of corresponding deep depression or torpor.

In the case of two patients, symptoms very much the same as

---

*The average of a great number of experiments gives me the following results: The rise in the pulse from mere muscular effort, to enable patients to keep their legs and arms extended for five minutes, is about 20 per cent. When in the state of hypnotism it is upwards of 100 per cent. By arousing all the senses, and the head and neck, it will speedily fall to 40 per cent, (that is, twice what it was when so tested in the natural condition), and by rendering the whole muscles limber, whilst the patient is in the state of hypnotism the pulse very speedily falls to, or even below, the condition it was before the experiment.

those produced in them by the laughing gas, were produced twice on each patient, and the only time I know of their having been hypnotized. One lost the power of speech for two hours, as happened also after the gas. Both these patients had hypnotized themselves. There is a remarkable difference between the hypnotic condition, and that induced by the nitrous oxide. In the latter there is a great, almost irresistible inclination to *general muscular effort*, as well as laughter; in the former there seems to be no inclination to *any* bodily effort, unless excited by *impressions from without*. When the latter are used, there is a remarkable difference again in the power of locomotion and accurate balancing of themselves, when contrasted with the condition of intoxication from wine or spirits, where the limbs become partially paralyzed, whilst the judgment remains pretty clear and acute. The state of muscular quiescence, with acute hearing, and dreamy glowing imagination, approximates it somewhat to the condition induced by conium.

During the course of last spring some lectures were delivered in this town to prove that the *mesmeric phenomena* might be induced by an "undue continuance or repetition of the same sensible impression" on *any* of the senses. Immediately after the first lecture I instituted experiments according to this plan, but very soon ascertained, that the sleep induced by this mode of

---

*It has been suggested to me, that it can scarcely be doubted that the Bacchanalians, who had no feeling of wounds ("non sentit vulnera Moenas,"— *Ovid*), and whose condition was a stupor different from common sleep ("Exsomnis stupet Evias," —*Horace*), were in the hypnotic condition of nervous sleep, and therein excited to dance by music; and that, as uneducated maidservants, when under the full influence of that state of nerve, move with the grace and peculiar action of the most accomplished dancers of pantomimic ballet, there is reason to believe, not merely that the perfect grace exhibited in the attitudes represented in ancient sculpture and painting, was derived from studying the Bacchanalian and other mystic dancers, but that the movements used by stagedancers, in our days, have been transmitted to us by continued imitation, through Italy, from the dancers in the Greek mysteries. No person can see girls of humble education, under the influence of music while in the nervous sleep, without perceiving, that those individuals, if awake, could not move with the elegance they exhibit under that influence. The reason of such grace probably is, that it arises from the simple and pure efforts of nature to balance the body perfectly in all its complicated movements while the power of sight is suspended.

operation, *unless through the eye,* was nothing more than NATURAL or common sleep, *excepting in patients who had had the impressibility stamped on them, by having been previously mesmerized or hypnotized.* The lecturer concluded his course by stating his opinion, that he knew no sleep but natural or common sleep; and by representing that he considered the effects produced by the different modes to be the same.* I believe most, if not all the patients this gentleman exhibited at his lectures, had been previously mesmerized or hypnotized, which, if I am correct in this supposition, form the circumstances already referred to, would completely nullify the importance of his *apparent* results. However, I have never heard of his having *operated successfully, and exhibited the phenomena on numbers of patients taken indiscriminately from a mixed audience, who had never been operated on before;* or produced curative results such as I have so repeatedly done. I therefore consider it a fair inference, that until the same phenomena are produced by his method in cases of persons which have *never* been hypnotized or mesmerized, nothing is proved beyond the fact *which I have so often urged,* namely, the power of imagination, sympathy, and habit, in producing the expected effects ON THOSE PREVIOUSLY IMPRESSED.*

From overlooking another important fact which I have repeatedly explained, that all the phenomena are consecutive, that is, first increased sensibility, mobility, and docility, and afterwards a subsidence into insensibility and cataleptiform rigidity, this gentleman,

---

*This being his belief, there could be no novelty in his views. The following was the language of Cullen, long before he (M'Nish) was born, "If the mind is attached to a single sensation, it is brought very nearly to the state of the total absence of impressions; or, in other words, to the state most closely bordering upon sleep; remove those stimuli which keep it employed, and sleep ensures at any time."

M'Nish also writes, "Attention to a single sensation has the same effect (of inducing slumber). This has been exemplified in the case of all kinds of monotony, where there is a want of variety to stimulate the ideas, and keep them on the alert."

And again M'Nish writes, "I have often coaxed myself to sleep by internally repeating half a dozen times any well-known rhyme. Whilst doing so the ideas must be strictly directed to this particular theme, and prevented from wandering." He then adds, that the great secret is to compel the mind to depart from its favourite train of thought, into which it has a tendency to run, "and address itself solely to the *verbal* repetition of what is substituted in its place;" and farther adds, "the more the mind is brought to turn upon a *single impression,* the more closely it is made to approach to the state of sleep, which is the total absence of all impressions." Willich also, some forty years ago, wrote thus, "Sleep is promoted by tranquillity of mind, . . . by *gently and uniformly affecting one of the senses;* for instance, by music or reading; and lastly, a gentle external motion of the whole body, as by rocking or sailing." Counting and repeating a few words have been also long and generally known and resorted to for the purpose of procuring sleep.

Let any one read attentively the following extract from the *Medical Gazette* of February 24, 1838, on the power of weak monotonous impressions on the senses having the power of inducing sleep, and many phenomena usually attributed to mesmerism, and say what merit could be due to a person acquainted with the article referred to, for *recording a note to the same effects some six or eight months thereafter,* and that without having instituted a single experiment to prove the correctness of the hypothesis? "For the other slight symptoms" (others enumerated having been attributed to imagination or emotion of mind) "of vapours, drowsiness, and at last natural sleep, no other cause need be sought than the tediousness and ennui of passing the hands for more or less than an hour over the most sensitive parts of the body. This is only an instance of the well-known effect of weak monotonous impressions on the senses inducing sleep; analogous examples are found in the soothing influence of a body seen slowly vibrating, or of a distant calm scene, or the motions of the waves, or of quivering leaves; or in impressions on the sense of hearing by the sound of a waterfall, the rippling of billows, the humming of insects, the low howling of the winds, the voice of a dull reader; or on the nerves of common sensation by *gentle friction of the temple or eye-brow, or any sensitive part of the body;* the rocking of a cradle; any slow and regular motion of the limbs or trunk; all these instances show that the effect of monotonous impressions on the senses is to produce, in most persons, tranquillity, or drowsiness, and ultimately sleep."

Where, then, is the great merit of any one having recorded a note six or eight months after this was published, that these phenomena were induced by "the undue continuance and repetition of the same sensible impression?"

*A very decided proof of this was exhibited at one of my lectures, where, as may be seen from the report of it, twenty-two who had been operated on before, laid hold of different parts of each other's persons or dresses, and by concentrating their attention to that act, and anticipating the effect, they all became hypnotized in about a minute. After another lecture, in the ante-room, sixteen who had been hypnotized formerly, stood up in the same manner, and also *one* who *had never been hypnotized.* In about a minute all were affected *excepting the latter.* I then operated on him alone in my usual way, and in two or three minutes he was very decidedly affected. Suffice it to say, I have varied my experiments in every possible form, and clearly proved the power of imagination *over those previously impressed,* as the patients have become hypnotized or not by the same appliance, accordingly to the result which they previously expected. This readily accounts for the result of Mr. Wakley's experiments with the Okeys.

by mistaking and exhibiting the *primary* phenomena for the *secondary,* seems to have managed to deceive both himself and some others who are satisfied to look at such matters loosely. *This, however, is confounding things which are in themselves essentially different.* I beg especial attention to the note below.*

---

*In illustration of this, I may here state the following remarkable facts, which have been frequently repeated before many most competent witnesses, and of which, therefore, I consider there can be no doubt.

The first symptoms after the induction of the hypnotic state, and extending limbs, are those of extreme excitement of all the organs of sense, sight excepted. I have ascertained by accurate measurement, that the hearing is about twelve times more acute than in the natural condition. Thus a patient who could not hear the tick of a watch beyond 3 feet when awake, could do so when hypnotized at the distance of 35 feet, and walk to it in a direct line, without difficulty or hesitation. Smell is in like manner wonderfully exalted; one patient has been able to trace a rose through the air when held 46 feet from her. May this not account for the fact of Dr. Elliotson's patient Okey, discovering the peculiar odour of patients in *articulo mortis?* when she said on passing them, "There is Jack." The tactual sensibility is so great that the slightest touch is felt, and will call into action corresponding muscles, which will also be found to exert a most inordinate power. The sense of heat, cold, and resistance, are also exalted to that degree, as to enable the patient to feel any thing *without actual contact,* in some cases at a considerable distance (18 or 20 inches), if the temperature is very different from that of the body; and some will feel a breath of air from the lips, or the blast of a pair of bellows, at the distance of 50, or even 90 feet, and bend from it, and, by making a back current, as by waving the hand or a fan, will move in the opposite direction. The patient has a tendency to *approach to, or recede from impressions, according as they are agreeable or disagreeable, either in quality or intensity.* Thus, they will approach to soft sounds, but they will recede from loud sounds, however harmonious. A discord, such as two semi-tones sounded at the same time, *however soft,* will cause a sensitive patient to shudder and recede when hypnotized, although ignorant of music, and not at all disagreeably affected by such discord when awake. By allowing a little time to elapse, and the patient to be in a state of quietude, he will lapse into the opposite extreme, of rigidity and torpor of *all* the senses, so that he will not hear the loudest noise, nor smell the most fragrant or pungent odour; nor feel what is either hot or cold, although not only approximated to, but brought into actual contact with, the skin. He may now be picked, or pinched, or maimed, without evincing the slightest symptom of pain or sensibility, and the limbs will remain rigidly fixed. At this stage a puff of wind directed against any organ *instantaneously* arouses it to inordinate sensibility, and the rigid muscles to a state of mobility. Thus, the patient may be unconscious of the loudest noise, but by simply causing a current of air to come against the ear, a very moderate noise will *instantly* be heard so *intensely* as to make the patient start and shiver violently, although the whole body had immediately before been rigidly cataleptiform. A rose, valerian, or asafoetida, or strongest *liquor ammoniae,* may have been held close under the nostrils without being perceived, but a puff of wind directed against the nostrils will instantly rouse the sense so much, that supposing the rose had been carried 46 feet distant, the patient has instantly set off in pursuit of it; and even whilst the eyes were bandaged, reached it as certainly as a dog traces out game; but, as respects valerian or asafoetida, will rush *from* the unpleasant smell, with the greatest haste. The same with the sense of touch.

The remarkable fact that the whole senses may have been in the state of profound torpor, and the body in a state of rigidity, and yet by very gentle pressure over the eye-balls, the patient shall be instantly roused to the waking condition, as regards all the senses, and mobility of the head and neck, in short to all parts supplied by nerves originating above the origin of the fifth pair, and those inosculating with them, and will not be affected by simple mechanical appliance to other organs of sense, is a striking proof that there exists some remarkable connection between the state of the eyes, and the condition of the brain and spinal cord during the hypnotic state.

This is also a remarkably good illustration of the propriety of Mr. Mayo's designation of the origin of the fifth pair of nerves, which he styles "the dynamic centre of the nervous system." [1]

[1]"The Nervous System, and its Functions," p. 27.

Another remarkable proof to the same effect is this; supposing the same state of torpor of all the senses, and rigidity of the body and limbs to exist, a puff or air, or gentle pressure against ONE eye will restore sight to *that eye,* and sense and mobility to *one half of the body*—the same side as the eye operated on—but will leave the other eye insensible, and the other half of the body rigid and torpid as before. Neither hearing nor smell, however, are restored in this case to either side. Thus, by one mode of acting through the eye, we reduce the patient to a state of hemiplegia, by the other to that of paraplegia, as regards both sense and motion. In many cases, when the patient has been hypnotized by looking sideways, this gives a tendency to the body to turn round in that direction when asleep.

It seemed puzzling, that by acting on one eye, both sense and motion could be communicated to the *same* side of the body, seeing the motor influence is communicated from the *opposite hemisphere of the brain.* It has occurred to me that the partial decussation of the optic nerves may account for this, and that this partial decussation may be for the express purpose of perfecting the union of sensation and motion through the eyes, "on which we lean as on crutches;" thus enabling us to balance ourselves so much more perfectly than we could otherwise have done.

There is another most remarkable circumstance, that whilst the patient is in the state of torpor and rigidity, we may pass powerful shocks of the galvanic battery through the arms, so as to cause violent contortions of them, without his evincing the slightest symptom of perceiving the shocks, either by movement of the head or neck, or expression of the countenance. On partially arousing the head and neck, as by gentle pressure on the eyes, or passing a current of air against the face, the same shocks *will* be felt, as evinced by the movements of the head and neck, the contortions of the face, and the whine, moan, or scream of the patient. All this may happen, as I have witnessed innumerable times, and the patient be altogether unconscious of it when roused from the hypnotic condition.

Moreover, whilst the patient is in the condition to be unconscious of the shock passed through the arms whilst a rod is placed in each hand, if one of the rods is applied to any part of the head, or neck, or face, in short, to any part which is set at liberty by acting on *both eyes,* as formerly referred to, he will instantly manifest symptoms of feeling a shock, though it be much less powerful than that which had failed to produce any sensation or consciousness when passed through both arms. This might readily be accounted for on the principle of the circuit being shortened, and also by one of the rods being nearer the centre of the sensorium; but that it depends on something else is apparent from the following fact: without moving the rod placed on the neck, head, or face, carry the other rod *from the hand,* to any other part of the head, neck, or face, and all evidence of feeling will disappear, *unless the power of the galvanic current is increased.*

Analogous to this is another most puzzling phenomenon: the brain being in a state of torpor, the limbs rigid, and the skin insensible to pricking, pinching, heat or cold, by gently pressing the point of one or two fingers against the back of the hand, or any other part of the extremity, the rigidity will very speedily give place to mobility, and quivering of the arm, hand, and fingers, and which is greatly increased by pressing another finger against the neck, head, or face. Indeed, in the latter case, the commotion of the whole body is as violent in some patients as from shocks of the galvanic battery. By placing BOTH fingers on any part of the head, face, or neck, the commotion almost, or entirely ceases. By inching the skin or the hand or arm with one finger and thumb, and the skin of the neck or face with the other, no effect is produced. Pressure, made with insulating rods, glass, or sealing wax, is followed by the same phenomena as when done by the points of the fingers. The flat hand applied has very little effect. The pressure being made against both hands, the arms are contorted, and if the head is partially dehypnotized the patient will complain of pins running into the fingers, especially if one point of contact is the hand, and the other the face or head. These phenomena do not occur whilst the skin remains sensible to pricking or pinching.

Moreover, during the state of cataleptiform rigidity, the circulation becomes greatly accelerated, in many cases it has more than double the natural velocity; and may be brought down to the natural standard, in most cases in less than a minute, by reducing the cataleptiform condition. It is also found, that it may be kept at any intermediate condition between these two extremes, according to the manipulations used; and that the blood is circulated with less *force* (the pulse being always contracted) in the *rigid limbs,* and sent in correspondingly greater quantity and force into those parts which are not directly subjected to the pressure of rigid muscles. It is also important to note, that by acting on both eyes in the manner required to induce the state of paraplegia, as already explained, the force and frequency of the heart's action may be as speedily and perceptibly diminished, as the action of a steam engine by turning off the steam. By again fixing the eyes, its former force and velocity will be almost as speedily restored, as can be satisfactorily proved to any one who keeps his ear applied to the chest during these experiments. The amount of change in the pulse, by acting on the two eyes, and thus liberating the organs of special sense, and the head and neck, is about 60 per cent of the actual rise of the pulse when at the maximum above the ordinary velocity of the circulation. We might therefore, I think, *a priori,* infer, that in this new condition of the nervous system we have acquired an important power to act with.

N. B. — It is to be observed, that owing to the extreme acuteness of hearing during the first stage of hypnotism, it is extremely apt to mislead the operator, or those who do not understand this fact, during operations on the acuteness of the other senses, such as smell, currents of air, and heat and cold. To avoid such mistakes, therefore, it is best to allow the hearing to disappear, by which time all the other senses will have gone to rest, with the exception of the susceptibility to be affected by a current of air. I allow all the senses to become dormant, and then rouse only the one I wish to exhibit in the state of exalted function, when operating carefully.

Of all the circumstances connected with the artificial sleep which I induce, nothing so strongly marks the difference between it and *natural* sleep as the wonderful power the former evinces in curing many diseases of long standing, and which had resisted *natural* sleep, and every known agency, for years, e.g. patients who have been born deaf and dumb, of various ages, up to 32 years, had continued without the power of hearing sound until the time they were operated on by me, and yet they were enabled to do so by being kept in the hypnotic state for eight, ten, or twelve minutes, and have had their hearing still farther improved by a repetition of similar operations. Now, supposing these patients to have spent six hours out of twenty-four in sleep, many of them had had four, five, six, or eight years of *continuous* sleep, but still awoke as they lay down, incapable of hearing sound, and yet they had some degree of it communicated to them by a few *minutes of Hypnotism.* Can any stronger proof be wanted, or adduced, than this, that it is very different from *common* sleep? A lady, 54 years of age, had been suffering for 16 years from incipient amaurosis. According to the same ratio, she must have had four years of sleep, but instead of improving she was every month getting worse, and when she called on me, could with difficulty read two words of the largest heading of a newspaper. After *eight minutes* hypnotic sleep, however, she could read the other words, and in three minutes more, the whole of the smaller heading, soon after a smaller sized type, and the same afternoon, with the aid of her glasses, read the 118th Psalm, 29 verses, in the small diamond Polyglot Bible, which for years had been a sealed book to her. There has also been a most remarkable improvement in this lady's general health since she was hypnotized. Is there any individual who can fail to see, in this case, something different from common sleep? Another lady, 44 years of age, had required glasses 22 years, to enable her to see to sew, read, or write. She had thus five years and a half sleep, but the sight was still getting worse, so that, before being hypnotized, she could not distinguish the capitals in the advertising columns of a newspaper. After being hypnotized, however, she could, in a few minutes, see to read the large and second heading of the newspaper, and the next day, to make herself a blond cap, threading her needle WITHOUT the aid of glasses. This lady's daughter, who had been compelled to use glasses for two years, was enabled to dispense with them, after being *once* hypnotized. It is also important to note, that all these three, as well as many others, were agreeably surprised by improvement of *memory* after being hypnotized. The memory of one was so bad that she was often forced to go up stairs several times before she could remember what she went for, and could scarcely carry on a conversation; but all this remnant of a slight paralytic affection is gone, by the same operations which roused the optic nerves, and restored the sight. Now, with such cases as these, who can doubt that there is a real difference in the state of the brain and nervous system generally, during the hypnotic sleep, from that which occurs in common sleep? The same might be urged from various other diseases cured or relieved by this process, but I shall only briefly refer to a few.

In the second part of this treatise, where the cases are recorded, will be found many examples of the curative power of hypnotism, equally remarkable with those to which I have just referred: such as Tic Douloureux; Nervous headache; Spinal irritation; Neuralgia of the heart: Palpitation and intermittent action of the heart; Epilepsy; Rheumatism; Paralysis; Distortions and tonic spasm, etc.

I shall here give a few particulars of a case which shows in a most remarkable degree the difference of this and common sleep, or that induced by opium and the whole range of medicines of that class. Miss Collins, of Newark, Nottinghamshire, had a spasmodic seizure during the night, by which her head was bound firmly to her left shoulder. The most energetic and well directed means, under a most talented physician, and aided by the opinion of Sir Benjamin Brodie, had been tried, as far as known remedies could be carried (amongst other means, narcotics, in as large doses as were compatible with the safety of the patient); and although she was carefully watched by night and by day, there had never been the slightest relaxation of the spasm, which had continued nearly six months. When I first examined her, no force I was capable of exerting could succeed in separating the head and shoulder in the slightest degree. Experience led me to hope, however, that I might be able to do so after she was hypnotized. Having requested all present, excepting the patient, her father, and her physician, to retire, I hypnotized her, and in three minutes from commencing the operation, with the most perfect ease to myself, and without the slightest pain to the patient, her head was inclined in the opposite direction, and in two minutes more she was roused, and was quite straight. I visited this patient only three times, after which she returned home. Shortly afterwards, she had a nervous twitching of the head, and on one occasion it was again drawn down to her shoulder. Dr. Chawner, however, hypnotized her as he had seen me do, and put it right immediately; and she is now (about twelve months after she was hypnotized) in perfect health, ("her head quite straight, and she has perfect control over the muscles of the neck.")

Miss E. Atkinson had been unable to speak above a whisper for four years and a half, notwithstanding every known remedy had been perseveringly adopted, under able practitioners. After the ninth hypnotic operation she could speak aloud without effort, and has continued quite well ever since—now about nine months.

The extraordinary effects of a few minutes hypnotism, manifested in such cases (so very different from what we realize by the application of ordinary means) may appear startling to those unacquainted with the remarkable powers of this process. I have been recommended, on this account, to conceal the fact of the rapidity and extent of the changes induced, as many may consider the thing *impossible,* and thus be led to reject the *less* startling, although *not more* true, reports of its beneficial action in other cases. In recording the cases, however, I have considered it my duty to record *facts as I found them,* and to make no compromise for the sake of accommodating them to the preconceived notions or prejudices of others.

It may be proper to add, however, that I have afforded opportunities to many eminent professional and scientific gentlemen to see the patients, and investigate for themselves the real state of these respective cases; and to them I can confidently appeal as to the accuracy and fidelity of the reports of most of the cases recorded in this treatise.

After such evidence as this, no one can reasonably doubt that there is a remarkable difference between hypnotism and natural sleep, and that it is a valuable addition to our therapeutic means.

How these extraordinary effects are produced, it may be impossible absolutely to decide. One thing, however, I am certain of, that, in this condition, besides the peculiar impression directly made on the nervous centres, by which the mind is for the time "thrown out of gear," and which enables us, in a remarkable manner, to localize or concentrate the nervous energy, or sensorial power, to any particular point or function, instead of the more equal distribution which exists in the ordinary condition, we have also an extraordinary power of acting on the capillaries, and of increasing and diminishing the force and frequency of the circulation, locally and generally.* This can be done in a most remarkable

---

*By this I mean that any one examining the pulse by the radial artery, whilst the patient has his arms in the cataleptiform condition, and held at right angles with his body, (and when, of course, the circulation can only be influenced by the state of rigidity or flaccidity of the muscles), it will be found feeble or contracted, but the moment the rigidity of the muscles is reduced, by blowing on or fanning them, the pulse will become much more developed. This, of course, which may be done without the patient being conscious of the experiment, is totally different from what may be displayed as a trick, by a person voluntarily compressing the axillary and brachial arteries, by drawing his arm firmly against his side. The former is independent of volition, the latter is entirely voluntary, and a mere trick.

degree, both as regards the extent and rapidity of these changes.†
And, moreover, changes from absolute insensibility to the most
exalted sensibility, may be effected at a certain stage, almost with
the rapidity of thought. On the whole, I consider it is of great
importance to have acquired a knowledge of how these effects can
be produced and generally applied, and turned to advantage in
the cure of disease, although we should never ascertain the real
proximate cause, or principle through which we produce our
effects. Who can tell how, or why, quinine and arsenic cure
intermittent fever? They are, nevertheless, well known to do so,
and are prescribed accordingly.

Whilst I feel assured from personal experience, and the testimony
of professional friends, on whose judgment and candour I can
implicitly rely, that in this we have acquired an important curative
agency for a *certain class* of diseases, I desire it to be distinctly
understood, as already stated, that I by no means wish to hold it
up as a universal remedy. I believe it is capable of doing great work,
if judiciously applied. Diseases evince totally different pathological
conditions, and the treatment ought to be varied accordingly. We
have, therefore, no right to expect to find a universal remedy in
this, or *any other*, method of treatment.

---

†The first time I ever had an opportunity of examining a patient minutely
or of feeling the pulse of one, under the mesmeric influence, was on the 19th
November, 1841. I was much struck with the state of the pulse at the wrist—so
small and rapid as, combined with the state of tremor, or slight subsultus in
the arm, rendered it impossible to count it accurately at the wrist. This circumstance induced me to reckon the velocity of the pulse by the carotid artery, as
will be found recorded in the *Manchester Guardian* of the 24th of that month.
I adduced this as the cause of the discrepancy between the numeration of the
pulse by others and myself, that I had counted it by the *carotid artery,* and
considered it impossible for anyone to reckon it correctly by the radial artery
in such a case. The injected state of the conjunctival membrane of the eye,
and the whole capillary system in the neck, head, and face, was so apparent,
as Dr. Radford very correctly stated, that no one near the patient could fail to
observe it: this, together with the cold hands and contracted pulse at the
wrist, led me to infer, that the rigid state of the cataleptiform muscles, opposed
the free transmission of the blood through the extremities, and would thus
cause increased action of the heart and determination to the brain and spinal
cord, as resulted from the ingenious experiments of my late friend Dr. Kellie,
for speedily terminating the cold stage of ague, by putting a tourniquet round
one of the extremities.

James Braid

The following chapter is a complete reprint of James Braid's little-known *Satanic Agency and Mesmerism Reviewed* which is said to be the starting point of active, complex psychotherapy and of scientific hypnotherapy. This little booklet is twelve pages in length and in it Braid laid the foundation for medical hypnotism. The book, which is a part of my library, is believed to be the only existing copy. A.E. Waite and W. Preyer, who have made an intensive search for all of Braid's contributions to the field of hypnotism, claim that no other copy of this booklet has been located in the United States or England.

The age of mesmerism or animal magnetism was brought to a close by James Braid who practiced medicine in Manchester, England. He was a sober, keen-witted, and experimental physician. Braid demonstrated that the various phenomena attributed to animal magnetism could be obtained by simple suggestion.

In his first work on mesmerism, *Satanic Agency and Mesmerism Reviewed,* Braid coined the word *hypnotism* to replace *mesmerism* —and his first use of the term occurs in this work, and not, as is generally believed, in his later work, *Neurypnology.*

Satanic Agency, written in answer to an attack by Reverend H. Mc. Neile, of Manchester, was a response to only one of the many attacks made on Braid from several directions. Mc. Neile had charged Braid with refusing to state the laws of nature by the uniform action of which hypnotic phenomena were performed. To this, Braid replied that he had always explained the phenomena on physiological and psychological principles but that Mc. Neile had refused to attend his lectures or to read any account of them. In fact, Braid frequently referred to the almost incredible opposition he had to combat, both at the hands of the orthodox medical practitioners and of the mesmerists.

In Braid's own words: ". . . Like the originators of all new views, however, hypnotism has subjected me to much contention; for the sceptics, from not perceiving the difference between my method and that of the mesmerists, and the limited extent of my

own pretensions, were equally hostile to hypnotism as they had
been to mesmerists, thinking their craft was in danger—that their
mystical idol was threatened to be shorn of some of its glory by
the advent of a new idol—buckled on their armor and soon
proved that the *odium mesmericum* was an inevitable as the
odium theologicum."

SATANIC AGENCY AND MESMERISM REVIEWED, IN A LETTER TO THE REV. H. Mc. NEILE, A.M., OF LIVERPOOL*

Reverend Sir,

I have read in the newspapers a report of a Sermon on the
subject of Mesmerism which you are alleged to have delivered in
St. Jude's Church, Liverpool, on the evening of Sunday, the 10th
of April last. In that Sermon you are pleased to ascribe the
various phenomena exhibited in certain lectures then recently delivered, or in course of delivery, in Liverpool, on the subject of
Animal Magnetism and Mesmerism, to Satanic agency, and to
brand the lecturers as necromancers, and with other terms characterized neither by the gentle spirit of the Master whose precepts
your profess to inculcate, nor even by the ordinary dictates of
gentlemanly courtesy. You are pleased further, in that Sermon, to
refer to myself in the following terms: — "Or the other who is
in the town at this time, of whom I have read something, but
whose name I forget at this moment:" and to include me in the
charge of dishonesty which you have preferred against those who
"refuse to come forward and state the laws of nature by the uniform
action of which this thing (Mesmerism) is done;" and also as
being one of those who "confine themselves to experiments in a
corner, upon their own servants, or upon females hired for the
purpose."

Had you been content with the oral delivery of the Sermon
which contained these attacks upon myself, I should have been
satisfied with my own reply as given in the lecture delivered by
me in Liverpool on the 21st of April; but as you have thought

---

*Braid, James: *Satanic Agency and Mesmerism Reviewed.* Manchester, 1842.

proper to publish that Sermon, without, as it appears to me, the slightest modification of your strictures, notwithstanding the subsequent opportunity which I afforded you of ascertaining their utter foundlessness; — I consider that I have no course left for the proper vindication of my professional character, other than that of adopting the same medium for giving publicity to my statements which you have yourself adopted.

Without pausing to inquire into the motives which could have induced you, in this instance, to abandon the sacerdotal office for the discussion of simple physiological questions in your pulpit, (in which discussion, I may venture to remark, you have displayed a degree of ignorance of mental as well as medical philosophy which can hardly be credited of any man of education,) I proceed at once to the main subject of this letter.

On persuing the report referred to, I was inclined to exercise towards your proceeding that charity "which thinketh no evil." I was inclined on that occasion, as I am in all cases, to adopt the most charitable view which could be taken as to the motives of action which swayed you; and I thereupon addressed to you a letter, accompanied by a copy of the Macclesfield Courier, containing an ample report of a lecture which I had delivered a few days before, in which I explained the nature and causes of the phenomena on physiological and psychological principles, proving, from the *uniform* success of my mode of operating, that the whole arose from a law of the animal economy which had not hitherto heen found out. I referred to what had been done in this respect in the case of strangers, who had presented themselves to be operated upon, at my lectures; some from mere curiosity, — others to test the accuracy of my statements, and many others with the view of benefiting from the application of this new agency to cure diseases from which they had suffered much and long, in defiance of all other remedies which had been tried. I also appealed to the value of this agency from its success in curing such cases; and concluded by respectfully inviting you to attend my next lecture, for which I enclosed a free admission ticket, at which lecture you were to have an opportunity of testing the accuracy of what I had stated. What has been your conduct in this respect? First, you never had the courtesy to acknowledge the receipt of my letter either by note or verbally; nor to acknowledge it by attending the lecture; and, finally, in the face of all the evidence I had thus adduced, you publish, or suffer to be published, with your sanction, the said Sermon, which contains a number of statements which are utterly untrue, and most offensive and injurious to me as a professional man. There might have been some shadow of excuse for this when you could plead ignorance; but, after the documentary evidence with which I had *personally* furnished you, it is altogether without excuse. I shall give an extract or two from the report referred to in proof of this:

> "The various theories at present entertained regarding the phenomena of mesmerism may be arranged thus:—First, those who believe them to be owing entirely to a system of collusion and delusion; and a great majority of society may be ranked under this head. Second, those who believe them to be real phenomena, but produced solely by imagination, sympathy, and imitation. Third, the animal magnetists, or those who believe in some magnetic medium set in motion as the exciting cause of the mesmeric phenomena. Fourth, those who have adopted my views, that the phenomena are solely attributable to a peculiar physiological state of the brain and the spinal cord."

* * *

> "In answer to the first, or those who believe, the whole to be a system of collusion and delusion—or, in plain terms, a piece of deception—the UNIFORM and general success of the results by my method must be sufficient to prove that the mesmeric phenomena are not "humbug," but real phenomena. In answer to the second, I have to state, that I by no means deny that imagination, sympathy, or imitation, are capable of producing the phenomena; that I believe they do so in many cases, especially in cases where the impressibility has been determined by operating as I direct; and may heighten their effects in others; but my experiments clearly prove that they may be induced, and are generally induced in the first instance, independently of any such agency. In answer to the third, I have to state that I consider the theory of the animal magnetists as a gratuitous assumption, unsupported by fact; and that it is far more reasonable to suppose, that an exaltation of function in natural organs of sense is the cause of certain remarkable phenomena, and a depression of

them the cause of others, than that they arise from a transposition of the senses, or are induced by a silent act of the will of another. We know the exercise of the will is not adequate to remove sensibility to pain and hearing, etc., in our own bodies; and would it not be passing strange if it could exercise a greater effect on the bodies of others, whilst inoperative in our own?"

* * *

"I shall merely add, that my experiments go to prove that it is a law in the animal economy that, by the continued fixation of the mental and visual eye on any object in itself not of an exciting nature, with absolute repose of body and general quietude, they become wearied; and, provided the patients rather favour than resist the feeling of stupor which they feel creeping over them during such experiment, a state of somnolency is induced, and that peculiar state of brain, and mobility of the nervous system, which render the patient liable to be directed so as to manifest the mesmeric phenomena. I consider it not so much the optic, as the motor and sympathetic nerves, and the mind, through which the impression is made. Such is the position I assume; and I feel so thoroughly convinced that it is a law of the animal economy, that such effects should follow such condition of mind and body, that I fear not to state, as my deliberate opinion, that this is a fact which cannot be controverted."

* * *

"I have already explained my theory to a certain extent, namely, that the continued effort of the will, to rivet the attention to one idea, exhausts the mind: that the continuance of the same impression on the retina exhausts the optic nerve: and that the constant effort of the muscles of the eyes and eyelids, to maintain the fixed stare, quickly exhausts their irritability and tone; that the general quiet of body and suppressed respiration which take place during such operation, tend to diminish the force and frequency of the heart's action; and that the result of the whole is a rapid exhaustion of the sensorium and nervous system, which is reflected on the heart and lungs; and a feeling of giddiness, with slight tendency to syncopy, and a feeling of somnolency, ensue; and thus and then the mind slips out of gear."

* * *

"I must beg, however, that it be particularly understood, that I by no means hold up this agency as a universal remedy. Whoever talks of a universal remedy, I consider must either be a fool or a knave; for, as diseases arise from totally opposite pathological conditions, all rational treatment ought to be varied accordingly. I must also warn the ignorant against tampering with such a powerful agency. It is powerful either for good or for evil, according as it is managed and judiciously applied. It is capable of rapidly curing many diseases for which, hitherto, we know no remedy; but none but professional man, well versed in anatomy, physiology, and pathology, is competent to apply it with general advantage to the patient, or credit to himself, or the agency he employs. My experiments, moreover, open up to us a field of inquiry equally interesting, as regards the government of the mind as of matter."

Now, Sir, in the face of all this evidence to the contrary, with what propriety could you publish the following remarks (?): — "It belongs to philosophers *who are honest men*, and who make any discovery of this kind, to state the uniform action. But *this is not done at present; we hear of experiments, but we hear nothing of a scientific statement of the laws* on which they proceed."

In this paragraph you would brand me as being dishonest for not stating the nature or uniformity of its action, although I had most unequivocally stated that my mode of operating, from its uniform action, proved it to be a law of the animal economy

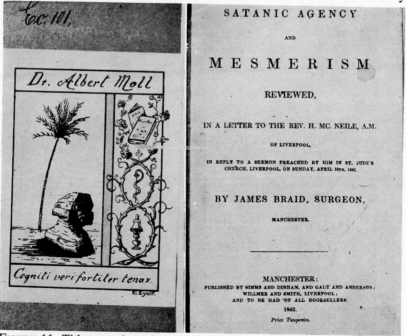

FIGURE 11. Title page from James Braid's *Satanic Agency and Mesmerism Reviewed,* published in 1842, with library plate of Dr. Albert Moll.

that certain effects shall follow certain compliances, mentally and bodily. And, moreover, in the fact of the elaborate details into which I had entered as to the scientific explanation of the laws on which they proceed — you publish your discourse flatly denying I had done any such thing. Is there any proof here that you were actuated by a sense of honesty, truth, or justice, in making such an attack upon me, a person who had never done you wrong? I, therefore, beg leave to ask, does not your conduct, in this instance, savour strongly of being influenced by *"Satanic agency?"*

But I must not omit another important point. You have quoted from Chambers' Journal; now, it is rather curious, if you wished to act honestly in this matter, that you should have quoted from that work what would answer your purpose in respect to Lafontaine, but should have overlooked the fact that, in the same work, they had referred to my having attended his Conversazioni, and discovered the cause of the phenomena, and had given lectures and successful courses of experiments, to prove its true nature to be neither in the operator nor in the Devil, but solely in the individuals operated on keeping their mind and eyes rivetted to one idea, and in one fixed position. I may reasonably ask, were you ignorant of this when you penned your notable sermon? — or had you taken pains to be correctly informed on the subject? — or was it "Satanic agency" which blinded your bodily eyes that you could not see it, or your mental eye that it might be wilfully dismissed?

The talented editors of that work introduce the article from which you quote, with the following pertinent remarks:

"There appears to us to be too great an inclination in the public to regard these phenomena as something out of the common course of nature. Ordinary sleep-walking, catalepsy, and some of the diseases of extreme nervousness, are not less wonderful—yet they occur every day. Why, then, may not mesmerism be only an artificial means of bringing on, in susceptible natures, conditions of a like remarkable kind? This we say, without wishing it to be understood that we are either believers or disbelievers in animal magnetism, and the subject is not yet ripe for either full belief or full rejection. It only appears to us that, in this art, (so to call it,) laying out of view some of the more extraordinary effects attributed to it, there is nothing, judging before hand, more wonderful, than in some conditions of the nervous system with which medical men are familiar. The vulgar disposition to look upon such things as supernatural, is one of the causes why sound thinkers and philosophical inquirers are deterred from them. THE MORE REAL KNOWLEDGE THAT ANY ONE POSSESSES OF THE NERVOUS SYSTEM, THE LESS, WE BELIEVE, WILL HE BE DISPOSED TO BE STARTLED BY THE ALLEGED WONDERS OF MESMERISM, AS OUT OF THE ORDINARY COURSE OF NATURE."

As these judicious remarks immediately precede the paragraph you quoted, it cannot be supposed you were ignorant of it. Now, if you wished mesmerism to be fairly tried, why not have given the above quotation? — And if you wished to do justice either to me or the subject, why deny that the laws by which it acted attempted to be explained? Is it not distinctly stated in the number of the same work for the 19th February last, that I had done so, where they say — "It is proper, however, to state Mr. Braid's own notions as the the physiological causes of both his own and Mesmer's phenomena. It is, briefly, that by an individual keeping up a steady gaze, or fixed stare at an object," etc., after which follows a condensed view of my theory. Now, Sir, was it fair or honest conduct to have promulgated such statements as you have done, in *direct opposition to evidence published in the very work from which you quoted*; or to have done so at all without taking pains to be correctly informed?

Besides the numerous cases referred to in my letter as having been operated on successfully at Liverpool and elsewhere, on individuals whom I had never seen before, that presented themselves on the platform in the public lecture-room, and which were reported in your own papers, you had an opportunity of observing, in the report of my lecture at Macclesfield, that five deaf and dumb patients and one paralytic, all adults, and who were strangers to me, were operated on successfully as regarded bringing them under the Hypnotic influence, and that four of the deaf and dumb patients acquired the power of hearing in consequence of the operation; and the patient who had been paralytic of the right leg and arm was enabled to walk much better, and acquired the power of picking up a pin with that hand, which she could not do at any time for fifteen years previously. These facts were seen and borne testimony to by the talented editor of the paper, a stranger to me until I met him that evening in the lecture-room; and by individuals who *might* be known to him, but who were utter strangers to me. It was also particularly remarked that my attention was chiefly devoted to the investigation with the view of rendering it comprehensible and available as a curative agency, and that I explained how any intelligent medical man might apply the agency to the amelioration of suffering humanity. Moreover, various maladies, in which it had been eminently useful where other means had failed, were enumerated, in order to induce other professional men to engage in this important investigation.

Now, Sir, with all these facts plainly laid before you, with what propriety could you implicate me in the charge of "refusing to come forward and state the laws of nature by the uniform action of which this thing is done;" or that I was one of those who "confine themselves to experiments in a corner upon their own servants, or upon females hired for the purpose"? Had I not, moreover, stated the fact, that impressed with the importance of the subject, I had, at great personal inconvenience as well as pecuniary sacrifice, gone to London, that my views might be subjected "to a rigid examination" of the most learned men in our profession, to propound to them the laws by which I consider it to act, and, above all, to prove to them "the uniformity of its action," and its practical applicability and value as a curative agency, by my mode of operating? I would therefore ask upon what principle, either of honour or candour, were you warranted in implicating me in such charges?

But even supposing the statements which were put forth could not explain the whole of the phenomena in a manner to satisfy all objections, and that various theories were adduced — as has happened on many scientific questions — surely, when beneficial application could be made of the extent of knowledge we had acquired, we ought to be at liberty to do so without being stigmatised from the pulpit as necromancers, or producing our effects by "Satanic agency," etc. Supposing a hundred passengers start in one of your packets, and twenty or thirty of them become seasick, and the others escape, would it be fair to implicate the captain in the charge of acting by Satanic agency because the whole were not sick, and because, according to Mr. Mc. Neile, "if it be in nature, it will operate uniformly" and not capriciously? If it operate capriciously, then there is "some mischievous agent at work; and 'we are not ignorant of the devices' of the Devil" Would any man but Mr. Mc. Neile say, that, because the captain gave the signal to heave anchor, to spread the sails, and other "talismanic tokens" for steering the vessel, and because only part of the passengers became sick, he was consequently affecting them through Satanic agency; — or that it would alter the matter one whit because medical men could not assign the true cause of this, or why any one should be so affected? Is it not lamentable that the sacred and important duties of the Sabbath ministration of the pulpit should be so degraded, and perverted to such unworthy purposes?

I also vindicated Neurohypnotism against the erroneous prejudices excited against it as having an immoral tendency. I prove by experiments, both in public and in private, that during the somnambulistic state, whilst consciousness lasts, the patients are more sensitive and fastidious in their feelings of strict propriety than in the natural condition. I did not, and do not, claim for it the power of implanting a principle. I do not say it will make a vicious person virtuous; but I am most confident it will not make a virtuous person vicious. On the contrary, I feel assured that a person of habitually correct feelings will, during the somnambulistic condition, whilst consciousness lasts, manifest fully as much delicacy and circumspection of conduct as in the waking state. And again, even supposing the contrary were the case, I have clearly proved that the animal magnetisers are in error, in supposing they had the power of *irresistibly* overpowering any one by mere volition and secret passes. In proof of this, I have challenged the whole of them to exert their combined influence to prevent me, by such secret means from delivering my lectures, in which I was exposing the fallacy of their assumptions; but hitherto I have felt no lethargic influence brought into operation to retard my proceedings. Moreover, I have proved that no one can be affected at all *unless by voluntary compliance,* and consequently it has no right to be held as an agency which could be converted to immoral purposes, as many have supposed. If any one would say it may have this tendency because in the state of torpor, insensibility, and cataleptiform rigidity, the party is unconscious, immovable, and incapable of self-defense, I beg to remind such individuals that the same argument might be urged against the proper use of wine, spirits, or opium, because excess in the use of either might be followed by like results. Had the mesmerisers' notions been true, that any individual could obtain such irresistible power over others by mere volition and secret passes of the operator, most assuredly it would have been a dangerous agency, and might be used for most improper purposes. And, did I believe any such dangerous power could thus be obtained by one individual over others. I would be as ready to denounce it, as I am now desirous of defending a valuable agency against what I know to be unmerited obloquy. Of the truth of these statements I shall furnish ample proofs in a small work on the subject which I intend to publish shortly.

I also defended Neurohypnotism against the charge of having a tendency to sap the foundation of the Christian creed, by making the Gospel miracles appear as wrought by this agency. I explained that were the animal magnetisers views correct, there were a few of the Gospel miracles the importance of which might be invalidated; but, as I distinctly deny the existence of a magnetic fluid or medium, according to my views the Gospel miracles are rendered more invulnerable than ever. I explained also that the phenomena of insensibility at one time, and exalted sensibility at another, were *real* phenomena, arising from the peculiar condition of the brain and spinal cord at different times. Now, I would ask any rational man, was there anything in all this like a wish to conceal, or savouring of Satanic agency? As to your remarks about the Estatica and Adolorata, I fully explained, and exhibited experiments to prove, that their exhibitions resulted entirely from the individuals hypnotizing themselves by their fixed gaze and deep contemplation. This I did at one of my early lectures, and it has since been done in the *Achill Herald* by some one else; so that your remarks on this subject are *not* only *not* original, but bear strong marks of being an *unacknowledged plagiarism*.

As you appeal to Scripture, I have no objection to do so too, and I consider the best plan is to take the Scripture rule, "By their works ye shall know them". Now, I shall adduce a few cases in illustration of what I *have* done and *can* do, and *can teach any intelligent medical man to do,* without being a "necromancer," or having any more to do with the devil than yourself, when, in the exercise of your vocation, you are composing and delivering your sermons.

By the aid of this agency I have extracted teeth from most sensitive patients without pain; I have performed many other important operations with present ease and future advantage; in a few minutes have removed rheumatic pains which had resisted every other remedy, and tortured the patients for months or years—in one case for thirteen years; have completely overcome the pain of a violent tic douloureux in a few minutes, which had tortured the patient for eight weeks before I saw him, in spite of the most approved remedies—and other cases in like manner; have restored strength and feeling to paralytic limbs in a few minutes—in one case of a patient twenty-four years of age, and who had been so from birth, in defiance of every other remedy; have restored hearing to the deaf, sight to the blind, smell to those who had been deprived of it; restored the crooked to proper form; calmed the irritable, and roused the desponding; restored the mind from imbecility to intelligence, and the memory from the listlessness and torpor to activity. Thus, those who could not for years read their Bible, or remember, or profit by what others have read, have been enabled, after a few minutes' hypnotic sleep, to do both. Now, I would ask any rational person, was it likely the Devil would have assisted me in doing any such thing? Is it not far more like Satanic agency for him to inspire any one to become the active agent in preventing the dissemination of what, when properly understood and applied, is calculated to prove such a vast blessing to mankind?

At page 149 you make a strange charge against the medical

profession. You there say, "It is a very unsuitable profession for the examination of such a matter as this. If there be anything connected with the spiritual world in it, it is wholly out of the cognizance of those gentlemen, whose whole professional study is connected with matter." In answer to the sweeping charge and insulting remarks contained in the above extract and what follows, I must tell you they are sufficient to prove that you know very little of medical men, or of their habits and pursuits. I must take leave to tell you that the medical man who has not studied the laws of *mind* as well as *matter,* and how they act and react on each other, is very unfit for practising his profession, either with credit to himself or advantage to his patient. Let such individual only attend to these studies, and the advantages will soon become apparent, both to himself and others. But I will go farther, and claim for the honour of the medical profession some of the brightest characters who have appeared to illuminate the dark domain of metaphysical science. Need I do more to prove this than name the fact, that Locke, Thomas Brown, and Abercrombie, etc., were medical men?

I by no means wish to laud Neurohypnology as an universal remedy. But that it is a means, when properly applied, of rapidly curing many diseases which resisted all other known remedies, there can be no doubt; and being a law of the animal economy— and, as such, no doubt implanted for some wise purpose—it is certain to prevail in defiance of all opposition.

I consider the uniformity of its action, as I apply it, is sufficient to *prove* it to be a law of the animal economy; and after the explanations I have given of it in the public lecture-room, to which I invited you that you might investigate the subject for yourself, where I stated my object was *"not to mystify, but to dispel all mystery,"* it has no right to be stigmatised as an *"occult* science," or the device of the Devil. I have always understood the Devil to be actively engaged in inflicting disease, blindness, and ignorance on mankind. But here we have works the very contrary—the cure of diseases which have resisted all other known remedies; the restoration of sight, hearing, and intelligence to the benumbed mind.

In reference to *your* profession, I may, with great propriety, quote the words you apply to mine—"For which no man has a higher respect in its proper place, and for its proper work, than I have;" but, unless by those who can bring to bear on it more extensive knowledge of the subject, or more candour than you have displayed on this occasion, I must be excused for saying that *yours* is not a profession which peculiarly fits its disciples for "the examination of such a matter as this." I would, therefore, recommend you to consider Gamaliel's advice, and should you wish to preach another sermon on the subject, that you should adopt it for your text—"Take heed what ye do, for if this work or this counsel be of men, it will come to nought; but if it be of God ye cannot overthrow it, lest haply ye be found even to fight against God."

James Braid

The first serious English critic of the researches of Reichenbach was James Braid, whose opposition to Reichenbach's opinions gave occasion to his pamphlet, *The Power of the Mind over the Body*: An Experimental Inquiry into the Nature and Cause of the Phenomena Attributed by Baron Reichenbach and Others to a "New Imponderable". In it Braid writes: "My experiments and researches are opposed to the theoretical notions of Baron Reinchenbach and the mesmerists . . . ." This work is one of the most interesting of Braid's publications, and it contains some of his most sagacious experiments and is in all respects entitled to the extended notice which has been given it in this place.

THE POWER OF THE MIND OVER THE BODY*

Few publications have lately issued from the press so well calculated to excite general interest and inquiry, as Baron Von Reichenbach's "Researches on Magnetism." The high reputation of the author, as well as that of his learned translator and annotator, Professor Gregory, who has furnished a condensed view of the subject in an English dress, were all calculated to produce an effect—the greater, because the subject discussed was represented as bringing under our notice "a new imponderable," through which we should realize a clear and satisfactory solution of many problems in the mental and physical constitution of man, which had puzzled and perplexed alike the savage and the sage from the earliest ages.

The vast interest which the above-named brochure has created, is evinced by the extent to which it has been quoted, referred to, and reviewed in our numerous periodicals. Nor is it devoid of interest to observe the various awards of these different authorities. Thus, one quotes at great length, and not only with seriousness sets down the whole as fully established, but, moreover, with much self-complacency exults in the proof thereby adduced of

---

*Braid, James: *The Power of the Mind over the Body*. London, John Churchill, 1846.

the correctness of all the most extreme views he and other Mesmerists may have promulgated on certain points of this keenly
debated science; whilst another writes a clever burlesque article
holding up the whole speculation as worthy only of unsparing
ridicule. Between these two extremes, again, we have every grade
of approval or scepticism.

On the first announcement of Dr. Gregory's abstract of Baron
Reichenbach's "Researches on Magnetism," I lost no time in
procuring a copy, which I perused with intense interest. I had not
proceeded far, however, when my experience with hypnotic
patients enabled me to perceive a source of fallacy, of which the
Baron must either have been ignorant, or which he had entirely
overlooked. From whatever cause this oversight had arisen, I felt
confident that, however carefully and perseveringly he had
prosecuted his experiments, and how ever well-calculated they had
been for determining mere physical facts, still no reliance could
be placed upon the accuracy of conclusions drawn from premises
assumed as true, where especial care had not been taken to guard
against the source of fallacy to which I refer—viz, the important
influence of the mental part of the process, which is in active
operation with patients during such experiments.* I resolved to
repeat his experiments, paying the strictest attention to this point;
and, as I had anticipated, the results were quite opposed to the
Baron Reichenbach. It is with considerable diffidence that I
venture to publish an opinion opposed to such high authority;
but I shall briefly state the grounds of my own opinion, and leave
it to others to repeat the experiments, and determine which opinion
is nearer the truth. The observations which I have to submit may,
moreover, prove suggestive to others, and enable them not only
to avoid sources of fallacy with which I am familiar, but may also
lead to the detection of many which may have escaped my own
observation.

The great aim of Baron Reichenbach's researches in this department of science has been to establish the existence of a new
imponderable, and to determine its qualities and powers in reference to matter and other forces, vital and inanimate. It unfor-

tunately happens, however, that the only test of this alleged new force (with one solitary exception, and that as I thought by no means a satisfactory one) is the human nerve; and not only so,

---

*Let it not be supposed that I intend by these observations to impute to Baron Reichenbach any want of ordinary caution, or even the strictest desire to guard against sources of fallacy of every sort. From what is recorded at pp. 13, 50, and 81, of the "Abstract," it is obvious that he had taken great precautions, and such, indeed, as would have been quite adequate to effect such purpose under ordinary circumstances. Moreover, I most cordially admit that a better devised series of experiments, or a more laborious and painstaking effort, for determining the question on strictly inductive principles, I have never met with in any department of science. Nor is small praise due to Professor Gregory, for the masterly manner in which he has performed his part of the task; still, when the extraordinary acuteness of the organs of special sense are taken into account, to which reference is made at p. 2 of the "Abstract," where it is admitted that "smell and taste become astonishingly delicate and acute;" vision so irritable that patients "are able, in very dark rooms, to distinguish not only the outlines, but also the colours of objects, where healthy people cannot distinguish anything at all;" and that "patients hear and understand what is spoken three or four rooms off;" I say, when these facts are taken into consideration, coupled with excitable state of their minds, it will readily be admitted that with all the precautions resorted to by Baron Reichenbach, various ideas may have been conveyed to his secluded patients, through the ordinary channels, of which he had no suspicion. For example, slight sounds in conducting the experiments, may have been overheard by the patients, and indicated to them changes in the arrangements, of which the operator had no notion; tones of voice, in proposing questions, may have had an equally certain and unintended influence; and it is an undoubted fact that, with such subjects, the slightest change in the concomitants always suggests a change in the fundamental or previously existing ideas. Such being the case, I can imagine no satisfactory mode of determining the subject with such patients as the Baron experimented with in the stair-case, but having them placed beyond the range of hearing, even to their quickened ears. The conducting wires should be securely fixed by thumb-screws near their distal ends, so as to prevent any vibration taking place beyond, when changing arrangements; which should be performed with the least possible noise; and a single sound of a bell should be the only signal for an answer, unless the patient should wish voluntarily to express some intelligence as to impressions, which he ought to be at liberty to do at any time. I would also suggest that there ought to be no regular order in the experiments; and that changes should be made without sounding the bell; and occasionally, that the bell should be sounded repeatedly without any change having been made. On no account should the experiments be conducted where the patients can have ocular observation of the features, or gestures of the investigators, even in apartments apparently dark. Such are the rigorous conditions I should consider requisite in the investigation of this subject, so as to guard against all obvious sources of fallacy.

but it is further admitted that its existence can only be demonstrated by certain impressions imparted to, or experienced by, *a comparatively small number of highly sensitive and nervous subjects.* But it is an undoubted fact that with many individuals, and especially of the highly nervous, and imaginative, and abstractive classes, a strong direction of inward consciousness to any part of the body, especially if attended with the expectation or belief of something being about to happen, is quite sufficient to change *the physical action of the part, and to produce such impressions from this cause alone, as Baron Reichenbach attributes to his new force.* Thus every variety of feeling may be excited from an internal or mental cause—such as heat or cold, pricking, creeping, tingling, spasmodic twitching of muscles, catalepsy, a feeling of attraction or repulsion, sights of every form or hue, odours, tastes, and sounds, in endless variety, and so on, according as accident or intention may have suggested. Moreover, the oftener such impressions have been excited, the more readily may they be reproduced, under similar circumstances, through the laws of association and habit. Such being the fact, it must consequently be obvious to every intelligent and unprejudiced person, that no implicit reliance can be placed on the human nerve, as a test of this new power in producing effects from *external* impressions or influences, when precisely the same phenomena may arise from an *internal* or *mental* influence, when no external agency whatever is in operation.

In order to guard against this source of fallacy, therefore, I considered it would be the best mode to throw patients into the *nervous sleep, and then operate on such of them as I knew had* no use of their eyes during the sleep (for some patients have), and to take accurate notice of the results when a magnet capable of lifting fourteen pounds was drawn over the hand and other parts of the body *without contact*, after the manner described as performed by Baron Reichenbach in his experiments.

I experimented accordingly, and the results were, that in no instance was there the slightest effect manifested, unless when the magnet was brought so near as to enable the patient to feel the abstraction of heat, (producing a sensation of cold), when a feeling of discomfort was manifested, with a disposition to move the hand, or head, or face, as the case might be, *from* the offending cause. This indication was precisely the same when the armature was attached, as when the magnet was open; and in both cases, if I suffered the magnet to *touch* the patient, instantly the part was hurriedly withdrawn, as I have always seen manifested during the primary stage of hypnotism, when the patients were touched with any *cold* object. Now, inasmuch as patients in this condition, generally, if not always, manifest their perceptions of external impressions by the most natural movements, unless the natural law has been subverted by some preconceived notion or suggested idea to the contrary, and as I have operated with similar results upon a considerable number of patients, we have thus satisfactory proof that there was no real attractive power of a magnetic or other nature, tending to draw the patient, or any of his members, so as to cause an adhesion between his body and the magnet, as between the latter and iron, as Baron Reichenbach had alleged. I conclude, therefore, that the phenomena of apparent attraction manifested in his cases were due entirely to a *mental* influence; and I shall presently prove that this is quite adequate to the production of such effects.

But I must now give an extract, so as to state Baron Reichenbach's views, as expressed in Professor Gregory's abstract. "Magnets of 10 lbs. supporting power, when drawn along the body, without contact, produced certain sensations in a certain proportion of human beings. Occasionally, out of twenty, three, or four sensitive individuals are found; and in one case, out of twenty-two females examined by the author, eighteen were found sensitive.

"The sensation is rather unpleasant than agreeable, and is like an *aura*: in some cases warm, in others cool; or it may be a pricking or the sensation of the creeping of insects on the skin; sometimes headache comes on rapidly. These effects occur when the patient does not see the magnet, nor know what is doing; they occur both in males and females, though more frequently in females; they are sometimes seen in strong, healthy people, but oftener in those whose health, though good, is not so vigorous, and in what are called nervous persons. Children are frequently found to be sensitive. Persons affected with spasmodic diseases, those who suffer from epilepsy, catalepsy, chorea, paralysis, and hysteria, are particularly sensitive. Lunatics and somnambulists are uniformly sensitive. The magnet is consequently an agent capable of affecting the living body. The object of the author is to solve some of the disputed questions, and to bring a number of phenomena under fixed physical laws.

"Healthy sensitive subjects observe nothing father than the sensations above noticed, and experience no inconvenience from the approach of magnets; but the diseased sensitive subjects experience different sensations, often disagreeable, and occasionally giving rise to fainting, to attacks of catalepsy, and to spasms so violent that they might possibly endanger life. In such cases, which generally include somnambulists, there occurs an extraordinary acuteness of the senses; smell and taste, for example, become astonishingly delicate and acute; many kinds of food become intolerable, and the perfumes most agreeable at other times become offensive. The patients hear and understand what is spoken three or four rooms off, and their vision is often so irritable, that, on the one hand, they cannot endure the sun's light, or that of a fire; while, on the other, they are able, in very dark rooms, to distinguish, not only the outlines, but also the colours of objects, where healthy people cannot distinguish anything at all. Up to this point, however strange the phenomena, there is nothing which may not be easily conceived, since animals and men differ very much in the acuteness of the senses, as is daily experienced."

Having met with a patient, Mdlle. Nowotny, who was subject to catalepsy, who possessed such a high degree of acuteness of the senses, that "she could not endure the daylight, and in a dark night perceived her room as well lighted as it appeared to others in the twilight, so that she could quite well distinguish colours;" from a consideration of this circumstance, and remembering that the aurora borealis appears to be a phenomenon connected with terrestrial magnetism, or electro-magnetism, it occurred to the Baron "that possibly a patient of such acuteness of vision might

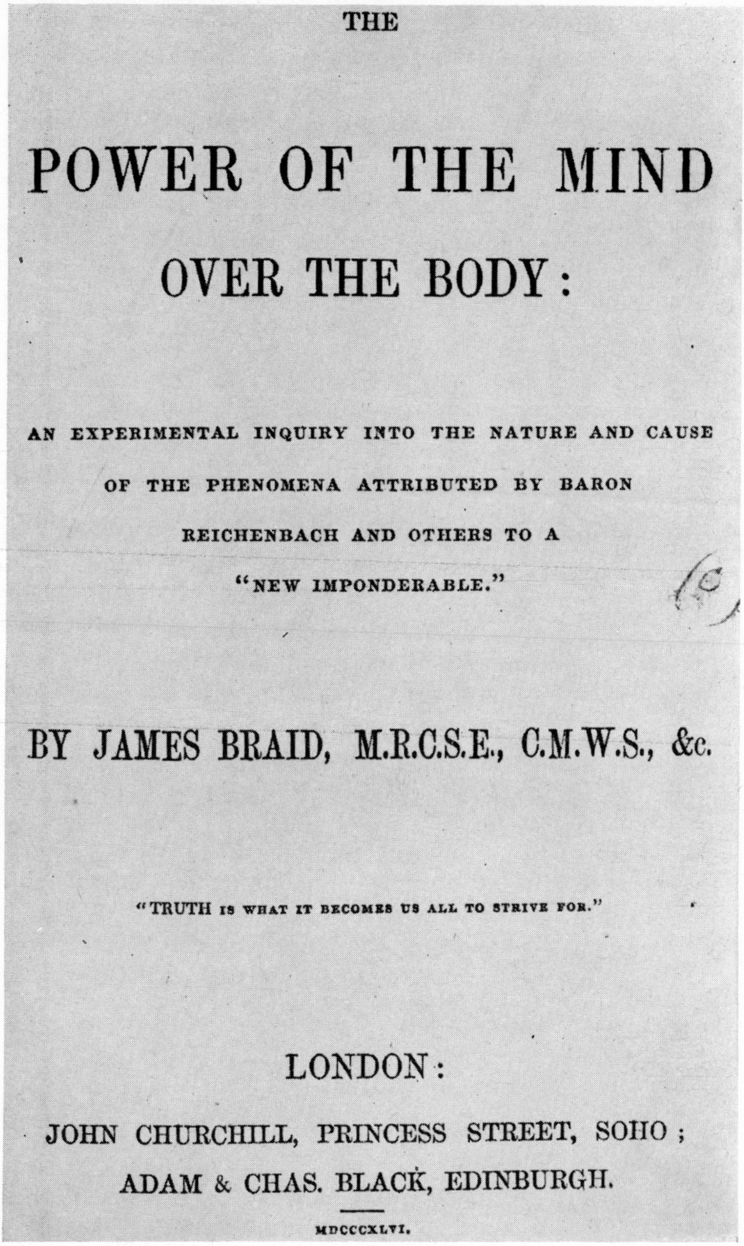

THE

POWER OF THE MIND

OVER THE BODY:

AN EXPERIMENTAL INQUIRY INTO THE NATURE AND CAUSE

OF THE PHENOMENA ATTRIBUTED BY BARON

REICHENBACH AND OTHERS TO A

"NEW IMPONDERABLE."

BY JAMES BRAID, M.R.C.S.E., C.M.W.S., &c.

"TRUTH IS WHAT IT BECOMES US ALL TO STRIVE FOR."

LONDON:

JOHN CHURCHILL, PRINCESS STREET, SOHO;

ADAM & CHAS. BLACK, EDINBURGH.

MDCCCXLVI.

FIGURE 12. Title page from James Braid's *The Power of the Mind Over the Body*, published in 1846.

see some luminous phenomenon about the magnet."

"The first experiment was performed by the patient's father;' no doubt by the suggestion of the Baron, and with the idea conveyed to him that some luminous appearance was likely to be discovered by the patient. It would be interesting to know whether the patient had not also been led, by some means, to understand the object of the inquiry, such as expectation, (which) according to my own experience with such subjects, was quite adequate to the production of the expected phenomenon; and, moreover, once realized, *it would be liable to recur ever after, under the same combination of circumstances.*

"In profound darkness, a horse-shoe magnet of nine elements, capable of carrying 80 lbs., was presented to the patient, the armature being removed; and she saw a distinct and continued luminous appearance, which uniformly disappeared, when the armature was applied.

"The second experiment was made on her recovery from a cataleptic attack, when the excitability of her senses was greatest. She saw two luminious objects, one at each pole, (the magnet was open,) which disappeared on joining the poles, and reappeared on removing the armature. At the moment of breaking contact, the light was somewhat stronger. The appearance was the same at both poles, without any apparent tendency to unite. Next to the metal, she described a luminous vapour, surrounded by rays, which rays were in constant shooting motion, lengthening and shortening themselves incessantly, and presenting, as she said, a singularly beautiful appearance. There was no resemblance to an ordinary fire; the colour of the light was pure white, sometimes mixed with iridescent colours."

The next patient "was far more sensitive to the magnet than the former. She declared that, at the moment the armature was withdrawn, she had seen fire rise from the magnet, the height of a small hand, white, *but mixed with* red and blue."

Mdlle. Maix.—"As often as the armature was removed from a large magnet, in the dark, she instantly saw the luminous appearance above the poles, about a hand-breadth in height. But when affected with spasms, she was more sensitive, and the phenomenon increased in her eyes amazingly. She not only now saw the magnetic light at the poles much larger than before, but she also perceived currents of light proceeding from the whole external surface of the magnet, weaker than at the poles, but leaving in her eyes a dazzling impression which did not for a long time disappear."

"Mdlle. Barbara Reichel saw the magnetic light not only in the dark, but also in such a twilight as permitted the author to distinguish objects, and to arrange and alter the experiments. The more intense the darkness, the brighter and larger she saw the flaming emanations; the more sharp and defined their outline, and the more distinct the play of colours." In the dark she saw the magnet giving out light, when shut, as well as when open, with this difference, that in the former case there were no points where the light appeared concentrated; but all the edges, joinings, and corners of the magnet gave out short flame-like lights, uniform in size, and in a constant undulatory motion. From the large magnet these were about as long as the thickness of a little finger; when the armature was removed, however, the light was concentrated at the two poles, from which the flames arose to about the height of eight inches and a half, rather broader than the bar. "At each depression, where two plates of the magnet were laid together, there appeared smaller flames ending in point-like sparks on the edges and corners. These small flames appeared blue, the chief light was white below, yellow higher up, then red and green at top. It was not motionless, but flickered and undulated, or contracted by starts continually, with an appearance as of rays shooting forth. There was no appearance of mutual attraction, or mutual tendency towards each other of the flames, or from one pole to the other; and as in the case of Mdlle. Nowotny, both poles presented the same appearance."

Mdlle. Reichel was tested with a straight magnet. "At the pole pointing to the north, or negative end of the magnet, the flame was larger than at the opposite end; it was sometimes undulating, sometimes starting, and shot out rays as in the horse-shoe magnet; it was red below, blue in the middle, green at top."

In order to enable the reader to form a correct estimate of what is represented in these several narratives, I have quoted the more important parts verbatim; and by comparing the results recorded by the different patients, no one can fail to be struck with the remarkable discrepancy in their description of what has been alleged as a physical fact. All expected, as I presume, to see light, and they saw light or flames accordingly; but let us remark another result: Mdlle. Nowotny, in her most sensitive state, saw luminous vapour surrounded by rays which were in a constant shooting motion. "The *colour* of the light was nearly *pure white, sometimes* mixed with iridescent colours." The appearance was the same at *both* poles; the length of the flames, about one-half or three-fourths of an inch. Mddle. Maix, in her ordinary state, saw flames (from the same magnet I presume,) a hand breadth in height, and when in the more sensitive state they were much larger; and she now saw currents of flame proceeding from the whole external surface of the magnet, but weaker than at the poles.

Mdlle. B. Reichel saw the magnet giving out light, not only when open, but also when closed. When open, the flames from the poles were about eight inches high, those at the joining of the plate of the magnet about a finger's breadth in length. "These *small flames* appeared blue, the *chief light* was white *below, yellow higher up, then red and green at top.*" As with the others, both poles seemed to have given out *similar* appearances of light and flame. This same patient being experimented on with the above straight bar magnet, about a foot and a half long, we are told that, *"at the pole pointing to north,* or negative end of the magnet, the flame was *larger* than at the *opposite* end;" and we are further told that, "it was *red below, blue in the middle,* and green at the top." When we advance to the flames seen to be given out by crystals, from the human hand, and other forms of matter, we have equally discordant descriptions as to *colour* and *size* of the flames as seen by different sensitive subjects. Now, to my mind, these discordant statements, as to the *colour* of the flames, are quite fatal to the notion of such representations proving a physical fact; and in an especial manner is that remark applicable to the statement of Mddle. Reichel, who not only saw the *colour* different which was emanating from a *straight* bar magnet from that of the horse-shoe variety, but also described the *size* of the flame as *larger* from the *north* pole of the straight bar magnet than from the other end, whereas it was always seen by her, as well as by others, to be the same size at *both* poles of a *horse-shoe magnet*. If there be a physical reality in these alleged flames and colours, there ought to be no discrepancies of this sort; and the fact of such discordant statements having been made will tend to prepare the mind of the reader for the solution of the problem which I have now to submit.

In prosecuting the inquiry, Baron Reichenbach considered he had not only proved the existence of this new force, which produced all the physical effects enumerated, with streams of light from the poles, and the power of attracting the human body, and adhering to it, as steel to the magnet—I say he alleged that he had established such a force, not only as residing in the magnet, in addition to the ordinary magnetic force, but moreover, that it was found equally active in crystals, where it existed quite pure and distinct from ordinary magnetism. He also now ascertained that his subjects could discover "that from the finger points of healthy men, fiery bundles of light streamed forth, exactly as from the poles of magnets and of crystals visible to the sensitive." He alleges, moreover, that he had proved that where it was passive, it could be excited into activity by the sun's rays, by the moon's rays, by starlight, by heat, by chemical or mechanical action, and finally, that this luminous or phosphorescent appearance, and certain other peculiar properties, might be discovered by the highly sensitive in almost every place, and from nearly every object or form of matter, solid or fluid, animate or inanimate. Also, that it could be conducted through all other matter, and that all substances, not naturally actively charged with it, could be so temporarily, by proximity and contact of those which were actively charged.

I have already stated the wonderful power of the human mind, when inward consciousness is strongly directed to any part of a sensitive person, in changing physical action, and leading the subject to attribute to an external cause what may have arisen entirely from an internal or mental cause. It has also been stated that, when I resorted to a mode of operating which ren-

Foundations of Hypnosis

dered the subjects more highly sensitive to external influences, and at the same time was calculated to obviate any source of fallacy, as to mental emotion or expectation being directed to the part from their seeing what was being done, the results were in direct opposition to what was represented as having been realized by the Baron. I have particularly adverted to this in respect to the alleged attraction of the magnet for the human frame; I have proved it to be equally so in respect to the human hand, and crystals, etc., *where all sources of fallacy are guarded against.* In my experience, moreover, with such cases, no light or flames have been perceived by patients either from the poles of a magnet, crystals, the points of the fingers, or other substance, unless the patients have been previously penetrated with some idea of the sort, or have been plied with such questions as were calculated to excite notions, when various answers were given accordingly, and when in the sleep, there appeared an equal aptitude to see something *when neither magnet nor fingers were in the direction indicated, as when they were*—a clear proof that the impressions were entirely imaginary, or mental in their origin.

I shall now proceed to detail the results of experiments with patients when wide awake, and when they had an opportunity of seeing what was being done, and expected something to happen; and also when the same patients saw nothing of what was doing, but supposed I was operating, and consequently expected something to occur.

With nearly all the patients I have tried, many of whom had never been hypnotized or mesmerized, when drawing the magnet or other object slowly from the wrist to the points of the fingers, various effects were realized, such as a change of temperature, tingling, creeping, pricking, spasmodic twitching, catalepsy of the fingers, or arm, or both; and reversing the motion was generally followed by a change of symptoms, from the altered current of ideas thereby suggested. Moreover, if any idea of what might be expected existed in the mind previously, or was suggested orally, during the process, it was generally very speedily realized. The above patients being now requested to look aside, or a screen having been interposed, so as to prevent their seeing what was being done, and they were requested to describe their sensations during the repetition of the processes, similar phenomena were stated to be realized, even when there was nothing whatever done, beyond watching them, and noting their responses. They believed the processes were being repeated, and had their minds directed to the part, and thus the physical action was excited, so as actually to lead them to believe and describe their feelings as arising from *external* impressions.

The above fact was most remarkably evinced in a young gentleman, twenty-one years of age. I first operated in this manner on his right hand, by drawing a powerful horse-shoe magnet over the hand, without contact, whilst the armature was attached. He immediately observed a sensation of cold follow the course of the magnet. I reversed the passes, and he felt it less cold, but he felt no attraction between his hand and the magnet. I then removed the cross-bar, and tried the effect with both poles alternately, but still there was no change in the effect, and decidedly no proof of attraction between his hand and the magnet. In the afternoon of the same day I desired him to look aside and hold his hat between his eyes and his hand, and observe the effects when I operated on him, whilst he could not see my proceedings. He very soon described a recurrence of the same sort of sensations as those he felt in the morning, but they speedily became more intense and extended up the arm, producing rigidity of the member. In the course of two minutes this feeling attacked the other arm, and to some extent the whole body, and he was, moreover, seized with a fit of involuntary laughter, like that of hysteria, which continued for several minutes—in fact, until I put an end to the experiment. His first remark, was, "Now this experiment clearly proves that there must be some intimate connection between mineral magnetism and Mesmerism, for I was most strangely affected, and could not possibly resist laughing during the extraordinary sensations with which my whole body was seized, as you drew the magnet over my hand and arm." I replied that I drew a very different conclusion from the experiments, as *I had never used the magnet at all,* nor held it, nor anything else, near to him; and that the whole proved the truth of my position as to the extraordinary power of the mind over the body, and how mental impressions could change physical action.

I operated on two other gentlemen the same day, who were much older, and with decidedly marked effects in both, though less so than in the last case. The experiment being tried with a lady of fifty-six years of age, by drawing a gold pencil-case slowly from the wrist to the finger ends, a creeping, twitching, sensation was felt, which increased until it became very unpleasant, and excited a drawing, crampy feeling in the fingers of that hand. On causing her to look aside, watch, and describe her feelings during my subsequent operations, the results were similar, and that whilst I had done nothing; and the whole, therefore, was attributable to the power of the mind in changing the physical action.

Another interesting case of a married lady, I experimented with in presence of her husband, as follows. I requested her to place her hand on the table, with the palm upwards, so situated as to enable her to observe the process I was about to resort to. I had previously remarked, that my drawing something slowly over the hand, without contact, whilst the patient concentrated her attention on the process, that she would experience some peculiar sensations in consequence. I took a pair of her scissors, and drew the bowl of the handle, slowly from the wrist downwards. I had only done so a few times, when she felt a creeping, chilly sensation, which was immediately followed by a spasmodic twitching of the muscles, so as to toss the hand from the table, as the members of a prepared frog are agitated when galvanized. I next desired her to place her *other* hand on the table, in like manner, but placed so, that by turning her head in the opposite direction, she might not see what was being done, and to watch her sensations in that hand, and tell us the result. In about the same length of time, similar pnenomena were manifested, as with the other hand, although in this instance I had done nothing whatever, and was not near her hand. I now desired her to watch what happened to her hand, when I predicted that she would feel it become *cold,* and the result was as predicted and vice versa, predicting that she would feel it become intensely hot, such was realized. When I desired her to think of the tip of her nose, the predicted result either of heat or cold, was speedily realized in that part.

Another lady, twenty-eight years of age, being operated on in the same manner, whilst looking at my proceedings, in the course of half a minute, described the sensation as that of the blood rushing into the fingers; and when the motion of my pencil-case was from below, upwards, the sensation was that of the current of blood being reversed, but less rapid in its motion. On resuming the downward direction, the original feeling recurred, still more powerfully than at first. This lady being requested now to look aside, whilst I operated, realized similar sensations, and that whilst I was doing nothing.

The husband of this lady, twenty-eight and a half years of age, came into the room, shortly after the above experiment was finished. She was very desirous of my trying the effect upon him, as he was in perfect health. I requested him to extend his right arm laterally, and let it rest on a chair with the palm upwards, to turn his head in the opposite direction, so that the might not see what I was doing, and to concentrate his attention on the feelings which might arise, during my process. In about half a minute he felt an *aura* like a breath of air passing along the hand; in a little after, a slight pricking, and presently a feeling passed along the arm, as far as the elbow, which he described as similar to that of being slightly electrified. *All this, while I had been doing nothing,* beyond watching what might be realized. I then desired him to tell me what he felt now,—speaking in such a tone of voice, as was calculated to lead him to believe I was operating in some different manner. The result was that the former sensations ceased; but, when I requested him once more, to tell me what he felt *now,* the former sensations recurred. I then whispered to his wife, but in a tone sufficiently loud to be overheard by him, observe now, and you will find his fingers begin to draw, and his hand will become clenched,—see how the little finger begins to move, and such was the case; see the next one also going in like manner, and such effects followed; and finally, the entire hand closed firmly, with a very unpleasant drawing motion of the whole flexor-muscles of the forearm. I did nothing whatever to this patient until the fingers were nearly closed, when I touched the palm of his hand with the point of my finger, which caused it to close more rapidly and firmly. After it had remained so for a short time, I blew upon the hand, which dissipated the previously existing mental impression, and instantly the hand became relaxed. The high respectability and intelligence of this gentleman rendered his testimony very valuable; and especially so, when he was not only wide awake, but had never been either mesmerized, hypnotized, or so tested before.

Another gentleman, twenty-one years of age, was tried by drawing a gold pencil-case along the palm of the hand, without contact. At the fourth traction, looking at the part and my process, he described a cold *aura* following the course of the pencil, then a pricking, and after a few more courses, he described it as rather a warm pricking sensation such as that experienced by the sun's rays concentrated on the skin by a lens. By reversing the passes, from the points of the fingers towards the wrist, the *aura* was changed, and he described the sensation as that of forcing back the blood in the veins, when they are much distended. I then proposed to experiment on his other hand whilst his head was held aside. When similar sensations were realized, although on this occasion I had done nothing,—the whole results arose from his own concentration of inward consciousness, changing the physical action of the part, and recalling his former association of ideas in reference to the other hand. I thereupon explained to him the law, (for he was a very acute young gentleman), which caused the production of such phenomena, and told him to satisfy himself of the fact, by concentrating his attention on the upper part of his foot and watching the result. Here, also, he experienced similar sensations to arise, even whilst he was aware that I was doing nothing; but the effects took place less rapidly than was the case in the former experiments with his hands. It is also worthy of remark, that this gentleman experienced a very severe headache from these experiments, which, however, I was able to remove by another process.

A lady, thirty years of age, was requested to hold out her

right hand over the arm of an easy chair, whilst she turned her head to the left, which prevented her from seeing what I was doing, and to watch and describe to me the feelings she experienced in the hand during my process which was to be performed without contact. She soon felt a pricking in the point of the third finger, which increased in intensity, and at length extended up the arm. I then asked her how her thumb felt, and presently the same feeling was transferred to it; and when asked to attend to the middle of the forearm, in the manner the feeling was presently perceived there. All the time I had been doing *nothing;* the whole was the result of her own mind acting on her hand and arm. I now took the large magnet, and allowed her to watch me drawing it slowly over the hand. When the feeling was much as before, she felt the cold from the steel when brought very near to the skin. It was precisely the same when closed as when opened, and the *same* sensations occurred when the north pole alone was appromixated, or the south alone, or both together. She experienced no sense of attraction between her hand and the magnet from either pole, nor from both combined. I now requested this lady to keep a steady gaze upon the poles of the large horse-shoe magnet, and tell me if she saw anything, (the room was not darkened nor was the light strong) but nothing was visible. I then told her to look steadily, and she would see flame or fire come out of the poles. After this announcement she calmly started, and said, "Now I see it, it is red; how strange my eyes feel," and instantly she passed into the hypnotic state. This lady had been repeatedly hypnotized. I now took the opportunity of testing her as to the alleged power of the magnet to attract her hand when asleep, but, as in the other cases, the results were quite the contrary—the cold of the magnet (and of either pole alike) caused her to withdraw her hand the moment it touched her. I now requested her to tell me what she *saw* (she being still in the sleep). She said she still saw the red light. I told her to put her finger to the place where she saw it. This she declined to do, being afraid that it would burn her. I thereupon assured her that it would not burn her, upon which she pointed *to the same place where the magnet was held before she went into the sleep,* instead of to where it was now held, which was near her face, but towards the *opposite* side of the chair. This lady does not see from under her closed eyelids when hypnotized, as some patients do; and the evidence her testimony affords in support of my opinion upon this subject is very conclusive, as she is a lady of very superior mental attainments, and one whose testimony merits unlimited confidence.

I beg to call particular attention to the fact, that in this latter case, as with the fifth of the vigilant cases narrated, the *first* experiments were tried without any magnet or other object being pointed at or drawn over them, and still the mental influence was quite sufficient to change the physical action, and produce decided and characteristic effects, where there could be no influence from without, of the nature alleged by Baron Reichenbach and the mesmerists.

A lady, upwards of fifty-six years of age, in perfect health, and wide awake, having been taken into a dark closet, and desired to look at the poles of the powerful horse-shoe magnet of nine elements, and describe what she saw, declared, after looking a considerable time, that she saw nothing. However, after I told her to look attentively, and she would see fire come out of it, she speedily saw sparks, and presently it seemed to her to burst forth, as she had witnessed an artificial representation of the volcano of Mount Vesuvius at some public gardens. Without her knowledge, I closed down the lid of the trunk which contained the magnet, *but still the same appearances were described as visible.* By putting leading questions, and asking her to describe what she saw from another part of the closet, (where there was nothing but bare walls) she went on describing various shades of most brilliant coruscations and flame, according to the leading questions I had put for the purpose of changing the fundamental ideas. On repeating the experiments, similar results were repeatedly realized by this patient. On taking this lady into the said closet after the magnet had been removed to another part of the house, she still perceived the same visible appearances of light and flame when there was nothing but the bare walls to produce them; and, two weeks after the magnet was removed, when she went into the closet by herself, the mere association of ideas was sufficient to cause her to realize a visible representation of the same light and flames. Indeed such had been the case with her on entering the closet ever since the first few times she saw the light and flames. In like manner, when she was made to touch the poles of the magnet when wide awake, no manifestations of attraction took place between her hand and the magnet, but the moment the idea was suggested that she would be held fast by its powerful attraction, so that she would be utterly unable to separate her hands from it, such result was realized; and, on separating it, by the suggestion of a new idea, and causing her to touch the *other* pole in like manner, predicating that *it* would *exert no attractive power* for the fingers or hand, such negative effects were at once manifested. I know this lady was incapable of trying to deceive myself, or others present; but she was self-deceived and spell-bound by the predominance of a preconceived idea, and was not less surprised at the varying powers of the instrument than others who witnessed the results.

In like manner several other patients whom I took into the dark closet could see nothing, until told to look steadily at a certain point and they would see flame and light of varying colours, proceeding from it, which predications were speedily realized, whilst they were wide awake, and with nothing but bare walls toward which to direct their eyes. Not only so, but I have moreover ascertained, that, even in broad daylight, a strong mental impression is adequate to produce such delusions with certain individuals of a highly imaginative and concentrative turn of mind. This fact was beautifully illustrated in the case of a gentleman, twenty-four years of age, who had suffered severely from epilepsy for eleven years, (notwithstanding the persevering use of medicine of various sorts prescribed by many of the most able members of the profession, but who is recovering very satisfactorily under the hypnotic treatment,) was taken into the above closet and tested as the latter. He likewise saw nothing till I suggested that he would see flame and light, after which prediction he very speedily saw it accordingly, not merely where the magnet was, but also from other parts of the apartment. Now, this patient, and the last two referred to, when taken into the closet *after* the magnet had been a long time removed to a distant part of the house, still saw the flames, and changing colours as before—a clear proof that the whole was a mental delusion arising from an excited imagination, on the point under consideration, changing physical action. The same gentleman being made to look at the point of a piece of brass wire, could be made to imagine that he saw any sort of flame or colour indicated issuing from it, *even in broad daylight*; and when made to touch it with a finger, and then told he would find it impossible to draw it away, the mere idea was sufficient to paralyze his volition, the whole muscles became rigid, and he looked with astonishment at his condition; but the moment I said *now the attraction* is gone, and his hand will separate, such results followed. Moreover, now that his finger was a little withdrawn, by simply saying confidently that it would *now* be found that he could not touch the wire, as it would repel him, the idea once more paralyzed his volition, and he again manifested his incapacity, and in spite of his anxious, but misdirected efforts, there he remained fixed as a statue. On hitting that *now* the influence was suspended, the hand and arm became limber; when I told another person watching the experiment that now he would find the hand irresistibly drawn to the wire, and such result was presently manifested. No one had touched this wire for hours; it was merely a piece of bent brass wire which was lying loosely and projecting from the chimney-piece. This power seems to have been understood by Virgil, when he said—

"Possunt, quia posse videntur."

In like manner having intimated to a friend the remarkable vividness of this patient's imagination, implicit belief, and credulity, which rendered him liable to believe that he had an ocular perception of an external change, according to whatever idea might be suggested to him by others, I requested this friend, when we went into the room, to look at the end of the above wire at the same time with the patient, and that the former should pretend to me, when asked what coloured flame she saw emanating from it, to give a new idea at each inquiry. By this mode the patient caught the ideas suggested, having no notion that he was deluded in the way indicated. He left with the full conviction of the physical reality of all he had seen and described; and he has manifested like phenomena as frequently as he has been so tested.

I have detailed the above case so much at length, because it is a very good type of a class of patients to be met with, who readily became the dupes of suggestions, in the manner presently to be explained, without the least desire to deceive others, or the most distant idea that they are themselves decieved. I have proved all I have advanced by so many concurrent examples, with individuals of the utmost probity and competency to describe their feelings, that there can be no doubt of the facts.

But not only may patients, in the waking state, be made to believe that they see various forms, and colours, and perceive variable sensible impressions and irresistible powers, drawing, repelling, or paralyzing them, from a strong mental impression changing the physical action of the organ or part usually engaged in the normal manifestation of such function; but I have, moreover, ascertained that the same influence may be realized in respect to sound, smell, taste, heat, and cold,—so that suggested ideas, and concentration of inward consciousness are competent, with some individuals, to excite ideas, not merely of hearing vague sounds, but particular tunes, the smell of particular odours, and to discriminate particular tastes, and feel heat or cold. All this I have proved may be realized with some excitable subjects when they were wide awake; and when there was neither actual sound, nor odour, nor taste, in the situations and substances to which they were referred; and by merely asking what tune, what colour, what animal, or what substance, they perceived now, I clearly proved that ideas may be thus excited in the minds of subjects totally different from those existing in my own, at the time. The subjects with whom I made these experiments were worthy of implicit credit as to their integrity in describing their feelings, and belief; and the results, therefore, are attributable to the remarkable reciprocal actions of the mind and body on

each other, to which I have so often referred.* Indeed, one of the
most beautiful examples I have had of these "vigilant phenomena,"
in respect to all the senses, occurred in the case of a gentleman
of high classical and mathematical attainments, as well as in general science. He had seen no experiments of the sort before I
tested himself. On finishing my round of experiments with him,
he begged of me to expain the *rationale* of what had occurred. I
requested him to read what I had written on the subject, which
he perused with great attention; after which he expressed himself
perfectly satisfied that I had hit upon the true solution of the
problem. Indded, he was so kind as to authorize me to refer any
one to him for a confirmation of the *rationale* I had given of the
phenomena, as experienced by him in his own person when wide
awake, and in the bright light of day.

It is stated by Baron Reichenbach that the sensitive can uniformly detect water which has had the magnetic current passed
through it, by having an open magnet brought over and in contact with the opposite sides of the glass in which the water is
contained. I have tried this experiment in such a manner as was
calculated to guard against various sources of fallacy which I
knew were likely to mislead the unwary; such as the varied tone
of voice or look of the experimentalist, when investigating the
subject and trying to elicit from the patient his candid opinion
as to the qualities of each glass of water. The results were, that
none of the patients tried could detect either by smell, taste, or
any other sensible effect, any difference between the magnetized

---

*For remarkable examples of the extent to which mental impression is
capable of changing physical action, I beg to refer to my papers in the Medical
Times for December, 1844, and January and February, 1845. It is particularly
gratifying to be able to refer in confirmation of most of the views I advocate,
to Dr. Holland's "Medical Notes and Reflections"—one of the most masterly
works I ever read, which I had the pleasure of perusing for the first time in
June, 1845.

Farazi, the Persian necromancer's answer to Firuz Shah, is also quite corroborative of my views. When asked how it was possible for him to bring a person
immediately to that spot, who was known to be at the time 800 or 900 miles
distant, he replied that "HE COULD NOT BRING HER IN PERSON, BUT COULD PRODUCE
SUCH A LIKENESS OF HER THAT HE COULD SWEAR TO HER BEING HIS OWN WIFE."—
Late Right Hon. Sir Gore Ouseley's "Biographical Notices of Persian Poets."

and the unmagnetized water. At each trial I made use of our similar glasses, filled to the same height, two of which, by the contact to the glass of a power magnet for a minute or two, were magnetized, the other two not magnetized. The patients were all first tested in this way when awake, and then when asleep. Magnetizing by passes, or breathing on the water, I should not consider a fair experment, and for this reason, that the *halitus* of the breath, or from the skin, might very readily be detected by a highly sensitive patient, by *smell,* and *probably also by taste.* I have met with a patient who could very readily detect water so treated from that which had not, and I ascertained that she did so by *smell.*

The extreme acuteness of the organs of special sense, under certain circumstances, is well illustrated in certain states of disease, and by what is realized in the feats of some savage tribes. They appear quite as exalted as anything I have met with, in the hypnotic or mesmeric state; and which has been sufficient to enable me to account, on *natural* principles, for what others have attributed to some new faculty or sense developed by their processes, and distinct from the ordinary organs of sense.

However, I have never met with any case of accurate thought-reading, where the patients could generally and accurately interpret my unexpressed thoughts and desires regarding him, without some sensible sign to indicate my ideas to him; but, as already stated, I feel confident that there are many, who, from their excited and concentrated state of mind, and quickened senses, will catch ideas far more quickly than in the ordinary condition, who may be thus imposed upon, and excited to act by means of impressions received through the senses, which would entirely escape them in the ordinary condition.

In consequence of the statement made in the third section, of the tranquilizing effect of causing highly sensitive patients to lie with the head towards the north, and the extreme discomfort of other directions of the body, in reference to the magnetic meridian, I had a patient who had been long an extreme sufferer, and in whose welfare I felt the deepest interest, to submit to the trouble of such a change in the position of her bed, but,

I am sorry to say, it was followed by no beneficial effect.

I am perfectly aware that the results of a single case are not competent to refute what has been alleged, as proved by a number of others. However, I have stated my fact on the point; and, whilst I readily admit my firm conviction that, with sensitive patients, who, from whatever cause they may have imbibed notions that certain directions of the body, either when asleep or awake, might be followed by feelings of physical as well as mental discomfort, the mere idea would be adequate to the production of such effects; still, I do not believe there is any adequate *physical* cause for such results, merely as regards the polarity of the earth and human frame. The following are the grounds for this opinion. The constitutent parts of the human frame are *diamagnetic,* that is, under the magnetic influence, they have a tendency to assume the *equatorial axis,* instead of the *polar* direction; and it therefore appears to me extremely improbable that a combination of dia-magnetics should, merely in consequence of their combination become invested with the *very opposite qualities of the constitutent parts.* To say the least of it, this would be at variance with all which has yet been ascertained of such powers in the inanimate, physical, and chemical world. It therefore appears to me, that the peculiarities referred to by Baron Reichenbach, under this head, are more likely to have arisen from a *mental* than a *physical* cause.

A few days after the above paragraph was written, I read it to a most intelligent friend, who told me, that she had just received a letter from her brother, who had been attending some lectures by Professor Faraday, and kindly offered to send me an extract from his letter, corroborative of what I had read to her. The following is the extract which I received the following morning, and is particularly gratifying, coming as it does from the very highest authority we have on this subject. "I have been greatly interested lately, with a course of lectures by Faraday on Electricity and Magnetism, which I am sorry to say, is just concluded. You will no doubt be gratified to learn that, in common with the whole human race, you are a magnet! With this peculiarity only, that if you were suspended by the middle, you would point East and West, instead of North and South—with which interesting fact, I leave you to your meditations."

That some of Baron Reichenbach's patients should have manifested the power of seeing luminous emanations in the dark, over the graves of the dead, more especially of those recently buried, I think admits of a more probable explanation than that propounded by the Baron. We know that during certain stages of decay of vegetable and animal matter, a phosphorescent appearance is manifested in the dark to ordinary vision, and, of course, it must be still more so to the highly sensitive. But there is another result of such organic decay still more powerfully felt by all, namely, its disagreeable odour. Few can escape the recognition of this, even in the bright light of day. Again: we are so much in the habit of associating visible or tangible forms with impressions which are conveyed to our minds through any of the organs of sense, that the blind are in the habit of expressing themselves as *seeing* such and such persons, whom they recognize approaching, merely by the sound of their voices, or tread of their steps, and so on.

In like manner a smell of any sort suggests corresponding ideas; and I have found hypnotic patients who recognized individuals of their acquaintance quite readily by *smell*, who always said, when asked how they knew who was present, "I see him or her," and, when the nostrils were stopped, thought the party had gone away. The sympathy which exists between the eyes and the nose is well proved by a strong light producing sneezing; and the converse of this is very natural, that a strong impression on the olfactory nerves might excite in the mind of a highly sensitive and imaginative person the idea of some visible appearance. This will account for the ghost-story quite as readily as the theory of the Baron, and will be found more generally available, as few people are so constituted as to be able to pass through such places without being painfully reminded, through their olfactory organs, that they are treading on the mortal remains of friends departed.

But I may be met with the objection to my arguments by an appeal which has been made to the Daguerreotype, which could not be influenced by mind,—for an experiment has been recorded by Baron Reichenbach, where, by the mere exposure of a sensitive plate in a box with a magnet, all light being excluded, an impression had been made, as if it had been exposed to the full influence of light, which did not happen, when another plate was so confined *without* the magnet. It appeared to me that such an important deduction ought not to have been arrived at, from one or two experiments of such a ticklish nature; and more especially so, when the iodized plates were so long kept before being exposed to the mercurial vapour; for it was natural to expect some chemical change might take place with them irrespective of light. I have repeated these experiments with nine plates, prepared at different times with the greatest care by Mr. Akers, the patentee of the Manchester photographic gallery, (one of the most correct professors of his art,) and the experiments varied so as to guard against error, by mutual correction. The experiments have been tried by close and free exposure of three plates to the poles of a powerful horse-shoe magnet, (originally of 80 lbs. lifting power, but somewhat reduced from use,) and of other three similarly situated, only with two sheets of black paper interposed so as to intercept the rays of light, if any were emitted from the magnetic poles, and another was enclosed in a box at a distance from the magnet, and all kept from 66 to 74 hours; but in no instance was there any appearance of them having been acted on by light,—the only change being such chemical changes as generally arise from keeping prepared plates for some time before being exposed to mercury. The latter process was also performed by Mr. Akers for the purpose of insuring greater accuracy from his daily practice of the art. Two other plates were enclosed in a camera and exposed at such a distance as must have given a picture of the poles of the magnet, and flames issuing from them—for the camera was adjusted to 4½ times the distance of ordinary light, and on left 66, the other, 35½ hours—but no such indications manifested themselves. I think, therefore, that I am warranted to conclude that no light, capable of affecting an iodized plate, is given out at the poles of magnets, as alleged from the experiments referred to by Baron Reichenbach.*

Having thus far investigated Baron Reichenbach's speculations, and proved the *major* propositions to be erroneous, as respects proving the phenomena he refers to as resulting from a new imponderable, I consider it unnuecessary to prosecute the subject in the minor details. I may, however, remark that I can readily imagine, from the exalted sensibility of particular individuals, and their highly concentrative state of mind, that they may be competent to detect electric, calorific, and physical qualities of objects, which would escape the observations of themselves and others, when in the ordinary and less sensitive condition. And again: whilst I deny that we have any satisfactory proof of this new imponderable, passing from the operator to the patient, as alleged, during the processes of the mesmerists, still I readily admit that the operator, for the reasons already assigned, of mental impression changing physical action, is very likely to feel an *aura* in his finger ends, the position, action, and mental direction, all tending to excite in them turgescence and increased sensibility. I can also easily conceive that the passes, through their physical, electrical, and other effects, tending to draw the patient's attention *to* particular parts, thus exciting their functions, and withdrawing it *from* others, thereby depressing their functions, and especially if the patient expects such results to ensue from such processes, are very likely to be followed by such results, irrespective of any special influence being transmitted from the operator to the patient, of the nature alleged by Baron Reichenbach and others.

The mesmerists, who have entertained the notion that the sleep and other phenomena occurring during their processes arose from a magnetic fluid, or some special influence issuing from their persons, and passing into that of the patient, of course hail these speculations of Baron Reichenbach as demonstrative proof of the correctness of their theory of mesmerism. Some of their patients having declared that they saw blue or variegated sparks passing from the fingers of the operator, when making passes in mesmerizing a patient, water, or other inanimate object, or

---

*Mr. Dancer, the optician, kindly lent me apparatus, and saw and approved of my arrangements, as well adapted for the purpose.

that they saw a blue fluid, or one of still brighter hue, issuing from the eyes of the operator and darting towards them, when gazing fixedly for the purpose of mesmerizing; or that they perceived a luminous halo surrounding the head of a person engaged in deep thought, must have felt gratified by the announcement, considering it well calculated to confirm in their minds, the notion of the physical entity of the agent. But, when those patients have further described that when the operator has been engaged in silently willing, for example, that a patient should be made to come towards him, there is seen by the patient, a stream of something passing from the head of the operator to that of the patient, like a rope, and that he not only sees this, but feels its influence as a rope, or innumerable threads drawing him irresistibly towards the operator, the entity must now appear fully confirmed. But again, when some of these subjects become, at length, so accomplished and susceptible as to be able to perceive these visible appearances *in the wide waking state,* it cannot be wondered at that those whose long cherished opinions lay in that direction, should jump to the conclusion that now the point is fully and satisfactorily settled. Under such a combination of circumstances, individuals may be excused for overlooking what to others is a very obvious source of fallacy—viz., the tendency of a continued fixed gaze to confuse the vision, and of a fixed idea and expectation to confuse and bewilder the mind.

It is well known that the undue excitement of an organ disturbs the normal functions of such organ; and that in a state of fever, delirium tremens, and various morbid states of the nervous system, and even in the healthy state during dreaming, the patient imagines that he feels and sees, or hears all sorts of forms, colours, sounds, etc. We do not, on that account, subscribe our belief in the reality of the objects, or peculiar attributes he has seen, heard, or felt, or the imaginary feats he has accomplished. In this case we estimate the phenomena as mental and morbid delusions; and such I apprehend ought to be our conclusion in reference to these extraordinary and startling allegations.

Inasmuch as patients can throw themselves into the nervous sleep, and manifest all the usual phenomena of mesmerism, through their own unaided efforts, as I have so repeatedly proved by causing them to maintain a steady fixed gaze at any point, concentrating their whole mental energies on the idea of the object looked at; or that the same may arise by the patient looking at the point of his own finger, or as the Magi of Persia and Jogi of India have practised for the last 2,400 years, for religious purposes, throwing themselves into their ecstatic trances by each maintaining a steady fixed gaze at the tip of his own nose; it is obvious that there is no need for an exoteric influence to produce the phenomena of mesmerism. The agency may be entirely personal or subjective, and in such cases as I have illustrated by extracts from Ward's History of the Hindoos and the Dabistan, through certain associations of ideas, such self-mesmerized patients can see and imagine as great, or indeed far greater wonders than are recounted by our most successful mesmerists of modern times, with the additional aid of their alleged mesmeric fluid. In proof of this I beg to refer to my paper in the Medical Times, page 272, vol. XI. The great object in all these processes, is to induce a habit of abstraction or concentration of attention, in which the subject is entirely absorbed with one idea, or train of ideas, whilst he is unconscious of, or indifferently conscious to, every other object, purpose, action.

I had long been familiar with the fact, that during a certain stage of hypnotism, patients may be made to give various manifestations, or declarations of their feelings and emotions, according to previously existing ideas, or suggestions imparted to them during the sleep; and, moreover, that such associations once formed, were liable to recur ever after, under a similar combination of circumstances. As occurs in ordinary dreaming, they seem generally at once to adopt the idea as a reality, without taking the trouble of reasoning on the subject as to the probability of such ideas being only imaginary; and their extreme mobility in the hypnotic state at a certain stage renders them prompt with their corresponding physical response. In proof of this, and how readily those inattentive to these facts may misapprehend what they see realized in such cases, I beg to submit the following interesting illustration. When in London lately, I had the pleasure of calling upon an eminent and excellent physician, who is in the habit of using mesmerism in his practice, in suitable cases, just as he uses any other remedy. He spoke of the extraordinary effects which he had experienced from the use of magnets applied *during the mesmeric state,* and kindly offered to illustrate the fact on a patient who had been asleep all the time I was in the room, and in that stage, during which I felt assured she could overhear every word of our conversation. He told me, that when he put the magnet into her hands, it would produce catalepsy of the hands and arms, and such was the result. He wafted the hands and the catalepsy ceased. He said that a mere touch of the magnet on a limb, would stiffen it, and such he proved to be the fact.

I now told him that I had got a little instrument in my pocket, which although far less than his, I felt assured would prove quite as powerful, and I offered to prove this by operating on the same patient, whom I had never seen before, and who was in the mesmeric state when I entered the room. My instrument was about three inches long, the thickness of a quill, with a ring attached to the end of it. I told him that when put into her hands, he would find it catalepsized both hands and arms as his had done, and such was the result. Having reduced this by wafting, I took my instrument from her, and again returned it, in *another position*, and told him it would now have the very reverse effect —that she would not be able to hold it, and that although I closed her hands on it, they would open, and that it would drop out of them, and such was the case,—to the great surprise of my worthy friend, who now desired to be informed *what I had done to the instrument to invest it with this new and opposite power.* This I declined doing for the present; but I promised to do so, when he had seen some further proofs of its remarkable powers. I now told him that a touch with it, on either extremity would cause the extremity to rise and become cataleptic, and such was the result; that a second touch on the same point would reduce the rigidity, and cause it to fall, and such again was proved to be the fact. After a variety of other experiments, every one of which proved precisely as I had predicted, she was aroused. I now applied the ring of my instrument on the third finger of the right hand, from which it was suspended, and told the doctor, that when it was so suspended, it would send her to sleep. To this he replied "It never will," but I again told him that I felt confident that it would send her to sleep. We then were silent, and very speedily she was once more asleep. Having aroused her, I put the instrument on the second finger of her left hand, and told the doctor that it would be found she could not go to sleep, when it was placed there. He said he thought she would, and he sat steadily gazing at her, but I said firmly and confidently that she would not. After a considerable time the doctor asked her if she did not feel sleepy, to which she replied, "Not at all." "Could you rise and walk?" When she told him she could, I then requested her to look at the point of the forefinger of her right hand, which I told the doctor would send her to sleep, and such was the result; and, after being aroused, I desired her to keep a steady gaze at the nail of the thumb of the left hand which would send her to sleep in like manner, and such proved to be the fact.

Having repaired to another room, I explained to the doctor the real nature and powers of my little and apparently magical instrument,—that it was nothing more than my *portmanteau key and ring*, and that what had imparted to it such apparently varied powers was merely the predictions which the patient had overheard me make to him, acting upon her in the peculiar state of the nervous sleep, as irresistible impulses to be affected, according to the results she had heard me predict. Had I predicted that she would see any flame, or colour, or form, or substance, animate or inanimate, I know from experience that such would have been realized, and responded to by her; and that, not from any desire on her part to impose upon others, but because she was self-deceived, the vividness of her imagination in that state, inducing her to believe as real, what were only the figments of fancy, suggested to her mind by the remarks of others. The power of suggestions of this sort also, in paralyzing or energizing muscular power is truly astounding; and may all arise in perfect good faith with almost all patients who have passed into the second conscious state, and with some, during the first conscious stage; and with some weak-minded, or highly imaginative or credulous and con-

centrative people, *even in the waking condition.* The latter constitutes that class of subjects who manifest what are called the "vigilant phenomena." The true cause of these "vigilant phenomena"
is not a physical influence from without, but a mental delusion
from within, which paralyzes their reason, and independent
volition, so that for the time being they are mere puppets in the
hands of another person by whom they are irresistibly controlled, so
that they can only see, or hear, or taste, or feel, or act, in accordance with his will and direction. They have their whole attention fixed on what may be said or signified by this alleged superior power, and consequently perceive impressions through the
excited state of the organs of sense, called into operation, which
they could not perceive in their ordinary condition; and this
sort of clairvoyance or thought-reading, the mesmerists attribute
to some special influence, such as the new inponderable of Reichenbach. So soon as patients can be made to believe that in the
waking state, the evidence of their senses is more trust-worthy
than mere ideal or suggested impressions; and that they can really
exercise their own independent powers in opposition to the alleged power of the will of another, through auricular suggestions
or passes, and other manoeuvres, it will instantly be found that
the spell is broken, and that rational beings can no longer be
magnetically tied together, or to chairs, or tables, or the floor;
or made to see an object of every colour and hue, or meta-
morphosed into every nature, form, or creature, the operator
may incline and indite. It may have been interesting enough to have
demonstrated that the human mind could be so subjugated and
controlled; but, as I have formerly said, and now repeat, I do not
consider the *continual repetition* of such experiments in the waking state, as at all proper, or free from the danger of throwing
the faculties of the mind of such subjects into a permanently
morbid condition.

It would be inconsistent with the scope of this paper to enter
into an elaborate detail of my views as to the philosophical explanation of the modes of exciting and varying certain trains of
ideas, and their consequent manifestations during the nervous
sleep. The inquiry is not only curious, but also one of great inter-

est, in respect to the power of the mind in controlling physical action, and of physical impressions in re-acting on the mind. I have given a pretty ample discussion on these topics in a second edition of my little work on hypnotism, now preparing for the press, to which I beg leave to refer those who feel desirous of prosecuting the inquiry, and particularly those who desire to do so for curative purposes.

In conclusion, I beg particularly to remark, that, whilst my experiments and observations are opposed to the *theoretical* notions of Baron Reichenbach and the mesmerists, in all the more important points, they directly confirm the reality of the facts, as to the power which we possess of artificially producing certain phenomena by certain processes; as also of intensifying effects which arise in a minor degree, spontaneously, or by the patient's own unaided efforts. They allege that the exciting cause is the impulsion into the body of the patient from without of a portion of this new force; whilst I attribute it to a subjective or personal influence, namely, that of the mind and body of the patient acting and reacting on each other in a particular manner, from an intense concentration of inward consciousness on one idea, or train of ideas, which may, to a certain extent, be controlled and directed by others. The latter power, however, merely arises from the mental and physical impressions producing still greater concentration of the patient's attention in a particular direction; that is to say, by concentrating their attention to the point over which they see anything drawn, or upon which a mechanical, calorific, frigorific, or electric impression is made, whereby a greater supply of nervous influence, blood, and vital action, is drawn to the part *from the physical and mental resources of the patient himself,* and *not* from the person or substance exciting those physical impressions. They enable the patient more effectually to concentrate his own vital powers, and thus to energize function; on the same principle as a patient afflicted with anaesthesia, or loss of feeling, is able to hold an object in his hand whilst he looks at it, but will allow it to drop when his eyes are averted.

It is worthy of particular remark, that my researches prove the power of concentration of attention, as not only capable of changing physical action, so as to make some patients, in the wide waking state, imagine that they see and feel from an *external* influence what is due entirely to an *internal* or *mental* cause; but I have extended the researches, so as to prove, that the same law obtains in respect to all the other organs of special sense, and different functions of the body. My theoretical views, therefore, instead of diminishing, rather enhance the value of this power as a means of cure. They strikingly prove how much may be achieved by proper attention to, and direction of, this power of the human mind over the physical frame, and vice versa, in ameliorating the ills which flesh is heir to. I beg further to remark, in support of my views, that in the experiments of Baron Reichenbach, and the mesmerists generally, all which I have endeavoured to prove as requisite for the production of the phenomena referred to, is necessarily brought into play during their processes, *in super-addition to their alleged mesmeric fluid, or new force;* of the latter, therefore, under such circumstances, I maintain that we have, as yet had no direct and satisfactory proof; and it is unphilosophical to attribute to a new and extraneous force what can be readily accounted for from the independent physical and psychical powers of the patient, which must necessarily be in active operation, along with their processes, and alleged new imponderable.

The results of my experiments moreover satisfactorily prove the *unity* of the *mind;* and the remarkable power of the soul over the body.

3, St. Peters Square Manchester, July, 1846

James Braid

In "The Physiology of Fascination", James Braid indicates that he had a perfectly clear concept of the suggestion technique, the credit for the discovery of which is usually given to Bernheim. Further in this work, Braid introduces the term *monoideism* to describe the condition in which the mind is possessed by a dominant idea. One canot fail to note the relationship between this concept and the "idee fixes" propounded by Janet some years later.

Braid also introduced the term *psychophysiology* to cover all those phenomena which result from the interaction of mind and body, and indeed his many references to the interaction of mind and matter will earn him the title of the first research worker in the field of psychosomatic medicine.

In "The Critics Criticised," Braid describes cases of self-hypnotism or instances of individuals entering a hypnotic state without being influenced by any other person. If one takes this in conjunction with the view which he expresses in "The Physiology of Fasination"—that man, like other animals, is influenced by irrational impulses based on fascination—we realize that Braid recognized how the mind of man is at times, as it were, unconsciously infected with noxious ideas. He describes in some detail examples of conflict between the will or reasoning power and the unreasoned and often destructive impulses arising out of the emotion of fear.

THE PHYSIOLOGY OF FASCINATION*

The power possessed by serpents to fascinate birds has always been a source of interest and admiration to the curious. That a crawling reptile, such as a serpent, doomed to move pronely on the earth, should possess the craft and power, by the mere fixed gaze of its glaring eyes, irresistibly to draw down from their proud aerial perch the very fowls of heaven, which cleave the air with rapid wing far beyond the reach of the sportsman's tube, seems to proclaim this as one of the most remarkable of nature's

---

*Braid, James: *The Physiology of Fascination and the Critics Criticised.* Manchester, Grant & Co., 1855.

laws, which has ordained that extremes should meet. The question therefore arises, by what means is this remarkable result effected? Is there any magnetic attraction in the eye of the serpent by which the bird is drawn? Or is it the result of any poisonous emanation projected by the serpent? Is it a voluntary, or an involuntary process by which the creature approaches and falls an easy prey to its fell destroyer?

Without occupying your time by entering into any elaborate history of the various speculations which have been advanced on this subject by different authors, I shall at once proceed to state what appears to me to be the true explanation of the phenomenon—one which is quite in accordance with nature's laws, and which, moreover, explains, on scientific principles, some remarkable phenomena observed even in man.

From various observations which I have read and heard on the subject, I feel satisfied that the creatures fascinated do not *voluntarily* surrender themselves to their fate; and this, I consider, is proved by the agitation and alarm which many of them display when advancing to meet their fate; viz., their plaintive cries, and the agitation of their bodies, and the instant escape which they make when any circumstance has occurred to avert from their sight the glaring eyes of the serpent. Their ability to escape so speedily, moreover, under such circumstances, proves that the charm had not been the result of any poisonous emanation proceeding from, or projected by, the serpent. After due consideration, I feel satisfied that the approach and surrender of itself by the bird, or other animal, is just another example of the *monoideodynamic,* or unconscious muscular action from a dominant idea possessing the mind, which I was the first to publish as the true cause of "table-turning," and which has since been confirmed by others, and most satisfactorily so by the report of the medical committee published in the *Medical Times and Gazette,* and by Professor Faraday, in the London *Times* newspaper, and in the *Athenoaum,* which contained reports of this acute and profound philosopher's ingenious experiments, and unexceptionable physical tests, for determining the question according to this view.

The law upon which these phenomena are to be explained has long been familiar to me, from observations made during my investigation of hypnotic and mesmeric phenomena, and it is simply this—that when the attention of man or animal is deeply engrossed or absorbed by a given idea, associated with movement, a current of nervous force is sent into the muscles which produce a corresponding motion, not only *without* any conscious effort of volition, but even in opposition to volition, in many instances; and hence they seem to be irresistibly drawn, or spell-bound, according to the purport of the dominant idea or impression in the mind of each at the time. The volition is prostrate; the individual is so completely *monodeised,* or under the influence of the dominant idea, as to be incapable of exerting an efficient restraining or opposing power to the dominant idea; and, in the case of the bird and serpent, it is first wonder which arrests the creature's attention, and then fear causes that *monoideo-dynamic* action of the muscles which involuntarily issue in the advance and capture of the unhappy bird. This is the principle, moreover, which accounts for such accidents as are frequently witnessed in the streets of every crowded thoroughfare, where some persons, when crossing the streets amidst a crowd of carriages, not only become spell-bound by a sense of their danger, so that they cannot move from the point of danger, but it even sometimes happens that they seem impelled to advance forward into the greater danger from which they are anxious to escape, and from which a person with more self-possession or presence of mind may be fired, by the very sense of his danger, to escape, by making an incredible bound— his natural powers having become stimulated to unwonted energy, by a lively faith having taken possession of his mind as to his capability to accomplish such a feat. It is this very principle of involuntary musclar action from a dominant idea which has got possession of the mind, and the suggestions conveyed to the mind by the muscular action which flows from it, which led so many to be deceived during their experiments in "table-turning," and induced them to believe that the table was drawing them, whilst all the while they were unconsciously drawing or pushing it, by their own muscular force. As already remarked, it is upon this principle that the bird is drawn to its fell destroyer, and that human beings may appear deliberately and intentionally to leap over precipices, and cast themselves from towers, and other situations, not only of danger, but of certain destruction. It is also upon the same principle that some individuals may be brought so much under the control of others, through certain audible, and visible, and tangible suggestions by another individual, as is seen in the phenomena exhibited in the waking condition, in what has been so absurdly called "electro-biology." The whole of these phenomena of "electro-biology," of "table-turning," the gyrations of the odometer of Dr. Mayo, of the magnetometer of Mr. Rutter, the movements of the divining-rod, and the supposed levity of the human body lifted on the tips of the fingers of four individuals, as described by Sir David Brewster, the fascination of serpents, the evil eye and witchcraft, and the charm by which a fowl may be fixed and spell-bound by causing it to gaze at a chalk line, or strip of coloured paper, or of white paper on a dark ground—all come under the same category, namely, the influence of a dominant idea, or fixed action of attention, absorbing, or putting in abeyance for the nonce, the other and great controlling power of the mind— the *will*.

The following is an interesting example of a person becoming spell-bound through a dominant idea excited through the suggestion of a second party. The anecdote was communicated to me by a highly scientific friend, as an event which occurred in his own family circle. His grandfather resided in the country, and on going into his orchard one Sunday morning, he described a boy who had climbed up into one of his apple trees, and was then in the attitude of laying hold of an apple. At this moment the gentleman addressed the boy in a *stern* manner, declaring that he would *fix him there* in the position he was then in. Having said so, the gentleman left the orchard and went off to church, not doubting that the boy would soon come down and effect his escape when he knew the master of the orchard was gone. However, it turned out otherwise; for, on going into the orchard on his return from church, he was not a little surprised to find that the boy had been spell-bound by his declaration to that effect—for there he still remained, *in the exact attitude in which he left him, with his arm outstretched, and his hand ready to lay hold of the apple.* By some farther remarks from this gentleman the spell was broken, and the boy allowed to escape without further punishment.

My investigations have proved, beyond all controversy, that by these means the ordinary mental and physical functions may be changed, so that the subject shall lose his freedom of action, and that *all* the natural functions may be either excited or depressed with great uniformity, even in the waking condition, according to the dominant idea existing in the mind of man or animal at the time, whether that has arisen spontaneously, had been the result of previous associations, or of the suggestions of others. The whole of the subsequent abnormal phenomena are due entirely to this influence of dominant ideas over physical action, and point to the importance of combining the study of psychology with that of physiology, and *vice versa.* I believe the attempt made to study these two brances of science so much apart from each other, has been a great hindrance to the successful study of either.

With the view of simplifying the study of the reciprocal actions and re-actions of mind and matter upon each other, which have hitherto been comprised under the vague terms, reverie, animal magnetism, mesmerism, hypnotism, electrobiology, etc., I beg leave to suggest the adoption of the following terms. After having convinced myself, by numerous experiments and careful observation and reflection, that the phenomena of the so-called animal magnetism, or mesmerism, did not result from any influence, *ab extra*, of a magnetic fluid or force, projected from the body of the mesmerizer, and passing into and charging the body of the subject with its peculiar properties and powers, but, on the contrary, that the condition arose from influences existing within the patient's own body, viz., the influence of concentrated attention, or dominant ideas, in modifying physical action, and these dynamic changes re-acting on the mind of the subject, I adopted the term *hypnotism,* or nervous sleep, in preference to mesmerism, or animal magnetism. This term has met with most favourable consideration from many able writers on the subject; still it is liable to this grave objection—that it has been used to comprise not a *single* state, but rather a series of stages or conditions, varying in every conceivable degree, from the slightest reverie, with high exaltation of the functions called into action, on the one hand, to intense nervous coma, with entire abolition of consciousness and voluntary power, on the other; whilst, from the latter condition, by very simple, but appropriate means, the subject is capable of being partially restored, or entirely roused, to the waking condition. By this means, I maintain that the operator does not communicate any surcharge of a magnetic, odylic, electric, or vital fluid or force from his own body to that of the subject, as the real and efficient cause of the phenomena which follow in altering or modifying physical action and curing disease; but I hold that he acts merely as the engineer, by various modes exciting, controlling, and directing *the vital forces* within *the patient's own body,* according to the laws which regulate the reciprocal action of mind and matter upon each other, in organized and living beings, in the present state of our existence.

I am well aware that, in correct phraseology, the term *hypnotism* ought to be restricted to the phenomena manifested in patients who actually pass into a state of sleep, and who remember nothing on awaking of what transpired during their sleep. All short of this is mere reverie, or dreaming, however provoked; and it, therefore, seems highly desirable to fix upon a terminology capable of accurately characterizing these latter modifications which result from hypnotic processes. This is the more requisite from the fact that, of those who may be relieved and cured by hypnotic processes of diseases which obstinately resist ordinary medical treatment, perhaps not more than one in ten ever passes into the state of oblivious sleep, during the processes which they are subjected to. The term *hypnotism,* therefore, is apt to confuse them, and lead them to suspect that, at all events, *they* cannot be benefited by processes which fail to produce the most obvious indication which the name imports. After much reflection on the subject, it has occurred to me that the object in view might be attained very satisfactorily as follows:—Let the term *hypnotism* be

restricted to those cases alone in which, by certain artificial processes, oblivious sleep takes place, in which the subject has no
remembrance on awaking of what occurred during his sleep, but
of which he shall have the most perfect recollection on passing into
a similar stage of hypnotism thereafter. In this mode, *hypnotism*
will comprise those cases only in which what has hitherto been
called the double-conscious state occurs; and let the term *hypnotic
coma* denote that still *deeper* stage of the sleep in which the patient
seems to be quite unconscious at the time of all external impressions, and devoid of voluntary power, and in whom no idea of
what had been said or done by others during the said state of
hypnotic coma can be remembered by the patient on awaking,
or at *any* stage of *subsequent* hypnotic operations. Then, inasmuch
as I feel satisfied that the mental and physical phenomena
which flow from said processes result entirely from the mental
impressions, of dominant ideas, excited thereby in the minds of
the subjects, changing or modifying the previously existing physical
action, and the peculiar physical action thus superinduced re-
acting on their minds—and that, whether these dominant, expectant ideas existed in the minds of the subjects previously, or were
suggested to them after passing into the impressible condition, by
audible suggestions or sensible impressions excited by manipulations of a second party—under these circumstances, I consider
the following terms calculated to realize all the precision which
we need desire on this point:

Let *monoideology* indicate the doctrine of the influence of
dominant ideas in controlling mental and physical action.

Then *monoideism* will indicate the condition resulting from the
mind being possessed by a dominant idea.

To *monoideise* will indicate the act of performing processes for
inducing the state of *monoideism*.

Monoideiser will indicate the person who *monoideises*.

Monoideised will indicate the condition of the person who is in
the state of *monoideism*.

And *monoideo-dynamics* will indicate the mental and physical changes, whether of excitement or depression, which result from the influence of *monoideism.**

And, finally, as a generic term, comprising the *whole* of these phenomena which result from the reciprocal actions of mind and matter upon each other, I think no term could be more appropriate than *psychophysiology.*

It must be obvious that these terms would comprehend every conceivable variety of phenomenon, according to the function of the part on which the dominant idea of the subject might be concentrated, and the liveliness of his faith. Thus, let the mind of the subject be engrossed with the notion that he is to be irresistibly drawn, repelled, paralyzed, or catalepsed, and the monoideo-dynamic or ideational condition of the muscles corresponding with this idea will take place, without any conscious effort of volition of the subject to that effect. It was, moreover, this very ideational or unconscious muscular action, which was the cause of "table-turning," which so much excited the public mind two years ago. The experimenters perceived the fact that the table moved, but, not being conscious of putting out any voluntary effort, they imagined that the table was drawing them, whilst all the while their own muscles were imparting the requisite impulse to the table, although they were unconscious that they were doing so.

It was in 1841 that I first undertook an experimental investigation for the purpose of determining the nature and cause of mesmeric phenomena. Hitherto it had been alleged that the mesmeric condition arose from the transmission of some magnetic

---

*In order that I may do full justice to two esteemed friends, I beg to state, in connection with this term *monoideo-dynamics,* that, several years ago, Dr. W.B. Carpenter introduced the term *Ideo-motor* to characterize the reflex or automatic muscular motions which arise merely from ideas of volition. In 1853, in referring to this term, Dr. Noble said, "*Ideo-dynamic* would probably constitute a phraseology more appropriate, as applicable to a wider range of phenomena." In this opinion I quite concurred, because I was well aware that an idea could *arrest* as well as *excite* motion automatically, not only in the muscles of voluntary motion, but also as regards the condition of *every other function of the body.* I have, therefore, adopted the term *monoideo-dynamics,* as still more comprehensive and characteristic as regards the true mental relations which subsist during all dynamic changes which take place, in every other function of the body, as well as in the muscles of voluntary motion.

fluid, or occult influence, fluid, or force, projected from the body of the operator, impinging upon, and charging the body of the patient. However, I was very soon able to demonstrate the fallacy of this *objective influence* theory, by producing analogous phenomena simply by causing subjects to gaze with fixed attention for a few minutes at inanimate objects. It was thus clearly proved that it was a subjective influence, resulting from some peculiar change which the mind could produce upon the mental and physical functions, when constrained to exercise a prolonged act of fixed attention. I therefore adopted the term hypnotism, or nervous sleep, to characterize the phenomena producible by my processes. I became satisfied that the hypnotic state was essentially a state of mental concentration, during which the faculties of the *mind* of the *patient* were so engrossed with a single idea or train of thought as, for the nonce, to render it dead or indifferent to all other considerations and influences. The consequence of this concentrated attention, again, to the subject in hand, intensified, in a correspondingly greater degree, whatever influence the mind of the individual could produce upon his physical functions during the waking condition, when his attention was so much more diffused and distracted by other impressions. Moreover, inasmuch as words spoken, or various sensible impressions made on the body of an indivdual by a second party, act as suggestions of thought and action to the person impressed, so as to draw and fix his attention to one part or function of his body, and withdraw it from others, whatever influence such suggestions and impressions are capable of producing during the ordinary waking condition, should naturally be expected to act with correspondingly greater effect during the *nervous sleep,* when the attention is so much more concentrated, and the imagination, and faith, and expectant ideas in the mind of the patient are so much more intense than in the ordinary waking condition. Now, this is precisely what happens; and I am persuaded that this is the most philosophical mode of viewing this subject; and it renders the whole clear, simple, and intelligible to the apprehension of any unprejudiced person, who may at once perceive that the real object and tendency of the various processes for inducing the state of *hypnotism* or *mesmerism* is obviously to induce a state of abstraction or concentration of attention—that is, a state of monoideism—whether that may be by requesting the subject to look steadfastly at some unexciting, and empty inanimate thing, or ideal object, or inducing him to watch the fixed gaze of the operator's eyes, his pointed fingers, or the passes or other manoeuvres of the mesmerizer.

In passing into sleep, moreover, reason and will, the *highest* powers of mind, are the *first to wane*—as is beautifully illustrated in the writings of Dr. W.B. Carpenter, well-known as one of our ablest writers on physiology—and thus the imagination gains the ascendancy, and careens in unbridled liberty; and, as the cerebro-spinal functions or reflex actions become more excitable at a certain stage of the sleep, just when the controlling power of the will, which is a cerebral function, is withdrawn, a very interesting series of phenomena may be elicited in the functions of the patient by those who thoroughly understand the subject, and how to regulate and control them; and thus various diseases may be speedily and safely relieved and cured by judicious and suitable manipulations and suggestions, which are not at all amenable to ordinary medical treatment. In this manner cases may be cured in a few minutes, or in a few days, which, by ordinary treatment, by the administration of drugs, prescribed by the ablest members of the profession, or when left to nature, may require not only weeks or months, but years to effect a recovery. It was to such cases as these that I referred in my article on "Hypnotic Therapeutics," which was published in the *Monthly Journal of Medical Science,* for July, 1853, where I said, "The most striking cases of all, however, for illustrating the value of the hypnotic mode of treatment, are cases of hysteric paralysis, in which, without organic lesion, the patient may have remained for a considerable length of time perfectly powerless of a part, or of the whole body from a dominant idea which has paralyzed or misdirected his volition. In such cases, by altering the state of the circulation, and breaking down the previous idea, and substituting a salutary idea of vigour and self-confidence in their place (which can be done by audible suggestions addressed to the patient, in a confident tone of voice, as to what *must and shall be realized by the processes he has been subjected to,* on being aroused in a few minutes thereafter, with such dominant idea in their minds, to the astonishment of themselves, as well as of others, the patients are found to have acquired vigour and voluntary power over their hitherto paralyzed limbs, as by a magical spell or witchcraft. Assuredly such cures are as important as they are interesting and surprising, because such cases may resist ordinary modes of treatment for paralysis for an indefinite length of time; but still the rationale is simple enough when viewed according to the principles which I have already explained, of the influence of an expectant, dominant idea, *either exciting or depressing natural function, according to the faith and confidence of the patient."*

Cases of this sort are by no means rare, and are obviously closely allied to fascination. Is it not an important boon, therefore, which science has achieved in discovering such a simple, safe, speedy, and certain mode of curing such affections; and that the same principle of a strongly excited dominant idea, which is so fatal to the unhappy fascinated bird, can, by judicious management, be turned to such salutary purposes for the relief and cure of suffering humanity?

PREFACE TO THE CRITICS CRITICISED*

The following remarks were sent for publication in the *Association Medical Journal,* as that appeared to me to be the most natural medium for a member of the Provincial Association to publish his defence against wrongs inflicted upon him in the pages of such a journal as the *Zoist,* which habitually refuses to publish replies to attacks upon others which have appeared in that journal. The Editor of the *Association Journal,* however, declined to publish my communication, from his unwillingness to have any controversy on the subject in question in the *Journal,* at a time when he thought it contained more controversy than was desirable on Association Policy. Under the circumstances stated, that the Editor of the *Zoist* excluded all rejoinders from

---

*Braid, James: *The Physiology of Fascination and the Critics Criticised.* Manchester, Grant & Co., 1855.

me to former attacks in his journal, the publication of my remarks in the *Association Journal* would not necessarily have imposed on the Editor any obligation to publish a reply in the
*Association Journal*s and, moreover, independently of the controversial style of my communication, I considered that the observations embraced illustrations of a psycho-physiological character
which would have proved a useful postscript to may late publication in the *Journal,* "On the Nature and Treatment of Certain
Forms of Paralysis," and with that view they are now published in
this separate form, for distribution amongst my professional and
other friends who take an interst in the inquiry. Moreover, in
order that I may accommodate my fellow associates, with whom I
am not personally acquainted, to the utmost in my power, I have
caused a few extra hundred copies to be thrown off, and given
instructions to the printer to send copies by post, at cost price,
to any member of the Association who may enclose his address,
with three postage stamps, to Grant and Co., Printers, Corporation
Street, Manchester.

THE CRITICS CRITICISED

In the *Quarterly Review* for September, 1853, an article appeared on Electro-Biology and Mesmerism. In general estimation
the said article was regarded as one of the most able and lucid
expositions which had ever been published on this interesting and
recondite inquiry.

The *Zoist* for 1854 contained some furious articles as criticisms
on the above article in the *Quarterly*. The work referred to being
very little known or read, it may be as well for me here to explain
that the *Zoist* is a small quarterly journal, devoted chiefly to the
enthusiastic advocacy of mesmeric doctrines and practices, and the
laudation of mesmerists, and to the persecution, misrepresentation and abuse, of all who dare to differ from their dogmas.
Whilst theoretically differing from the mesmerists as to the
mode of explaining the curative results which flow from certain
processes, and from the general policy of their proceedings, I have
great pleasure in thus publicly stating that the *Zoist* has been the

medium of recording many splendid cures effected by the *so-called* Mesmeric treatment.

In these articles in the *Zoist* Dr. Carpenter and myself were assailed, in the coarsest terms, as conjoint authors of the said review, in which they represented me, in addition to other charges, as blowing my own trumpet, anonymously, "as a quack advertisement, with a purpose, and with the hope of turning *something* into profit." Now, inasmuch as I never wrote a single line of the said article, nor ever saw a single line of it in manuscript or in proof, I wrote a short notice of this fact, intended for publication, as I was unwilling to appropriate to myself any share of the credit due entirely to Dr. Carpenter, he having been the *sole* author of that very lucid exposition of the subject.

Unwittingly, however, these *Zoisters* have paid me a very high compliment by the said attack, for I cannot feel it otherwise than a great compliment to find that a gentleman of Dr. Carpenter's mark, who had enjoyed many opportunities of investigating along with me my various opinions, and the practical illustrations as the reasons thereof, had so thoroughly set forth my views in the said article as to have led even the clairvoyant carping critics in the *Zoist* to suppose that certain portions of it must have been written by myself, "with a purpose, and with the hope of turning *something* into profit;" for it is obvious that Dr. Carpenter must have had too much respect for his own reputation to have published anything merely to serve me, or any one else, which he believed to be erroneous.

Having read to a mutual friend what I had written for publication as an act of justice to Dr. Carpenter, so that I might not appropriate to myself, through silence, any share of what was his especial property, that friend dissuaded me from publishing it, by assuring me that he *knew* Dr. Carpenter felt quite indifferent regarding any misrepresentation or scurrility which might be published against him in *such* a work as the *Zoist*. That being the case I withheld it, as I had myself so long been accustomed to misrepresentation and abuse in that print; for, with one or two exceptions, my name has never been introduced into the *Zoist* but with the view of misrepresentation and the grossest abuse, whilst they refused to publish a single line from me to correct their misrepresentations—that, personally, I felt quite regardless of their unwarrantable assaults on myself in that instance.* Now however, that the Rev. G. Sandby, vicar of Flixton, Suffolk, a gentleman who had formerly referred to my labours in a kind and liberal spirit, has once more renewed the charge of my being one of the writers of said article—for he writes in the *plural*—and has resorted to very unfair means in order to misrepresent me and my views, I deem it my duty at once distinctly to avow, through the press, that *I* had *no share whatever in the authorship of the said article* in the *Quarterly Review.*

Having recorded the above declaration, I now beg leave to add a few remarks on the Rev. Mr. Sandby's strictures. Seizing the occasion of a blind woman having been relieved of severe pain in the breast from a bruise, by passes made over the seat of the pain without contact, and of her having been relieved, on another occasion, of rheumatism of the knees, and an unpleasant heat in the head,

---

*The following are a few additional illustrations of the dignity of diction, meekness, modesty, and love of truth, displayed by these *Zoist* reviewers.

"The author, or rather authors, stand forth confessed by their very mannerisms. The materials tell us by their quality what handicraftsmen have been employed. A fancy carpenter, who well understands the knack of dovetailing his own semi-scientific views into the discoveries of others, and of then overlaying them with a smooth veneer, and a practical embroiderer, who contrives on every occasion to Braid and twist his one-sided facts into consequences, *which he knows are not true,* would seem to have been at work upon the fabric."

This base imputation upon my veracity I repel as the mere invention of this unscrupulous and malicious anonymous slanderer, and I can confidently appeal to all who know me that I am ever most scrupulous in adhering to what I *believe* to be true. — J.B. "Again, these humble — most humble, highly informed — very highly informed, far sighted — very far sighted, modest — very modest writers — *par nobile* — each *alter idem,* two writers in one, of the article in the *Quarterly Review.*"

Again, "Mr. T. castigates and ridicules (the *Quarterly* reviewer) charmingly — though, perhaps, the sin is not ignorance, but wilful and most unprincipled ignoring, which arises from the lowest and worst of feelings."

And again, "Mr. T. has no mercy upon the conceit of the superficial, flimsy reviewer, for his refusal to be taught by those who are only qualified to teach him, and ridicules him in a way calculated to make him feel, did not his conceit—his enormous development of self estem—render him as insensible to the exquisite ridicule as the thickness of the skin of the sagacious, rhinoceros to a bullet from a Minie rifle."—Page 19.

Nothing could be more unwarrantable than the editor of the *Zoist* to assume that I was one of the writers of the article in the *Quarterly Review,* and charge me with wilfully withholding all allusion to communications published in the *Zoist,* for he well knew that, four or five months previously, to wit in 1853, I sent him a copy of my "Hypnotic Therapeutics," in the appendix to which I criticised and controverted opinions of its leading contributors on "table-turning," and the Od force, vix., the Rev. Mr. Sandby, the Rev. Mr. Townshend, Dr. Elliotson, and Dr. Ashburner, but neither the editor nor any of these gentlemen have yet attempted to refute my arguments in opposition to their dogmas. I was the first to publish the unconscious muscular action theory of *table-turning,* and I still maintain that *that* is the true explanation of the phenomenon; and I moreover contend that nothing short of my opponents performing successfully the crucial experiments which I proposed—viz., lifting a small weight, such as an ounce of lead, copper, wood, or marble, from the centre of a table, and holding it suspended in the air, say twelve inches above the table, by the force of the will alone of ten or twenty efficient table-turners, when no human hand is near it, nor any mechanical contrivance has been had recourse to for lifting it—can reasonably satisfy any candid inquirer after truth. Nothing but the *non-contact* plan can, with certainty, guard against the fallacy of unconscious muscular action.

Some misrepresentations as to the results of my processes in the hands of mesmerists are mere repetitions of charges, all which I long ago proved to be caused by their *mismanagement of my processes,* and then blaming hypnotism for the results of their own blunders, or *intended misdirections.*—J. Baird.

The following extracts are avowedly from the pen of Dr. Elliotson contrasting himself with Sir James Clark, Bart., and they occur in the very next article to that in which the attack was made upon Dr. Carpenter and myself. Dr. Elliotson says—for his name is appended to the article—"me, who stand quite as high, I trust, as a physician as himself, through neither a baronet nor a royal physician. *** I have examined hundreds of abdominal enlargements, and never once made a mistake; and could not, I think, by any possibility make a mistake, when the size was not trifling."

"Let Sir James Clark remember that he is only a lucky man. His rise and progress have not been from hard work in hospitals, for he has never, like me, been physician to any hospital, nor from teaching successfully, for he was never, like me, been a lecturer in a large medical school, or a lecturer at all; whereas, I raised the Medical-School of St. Thomas's from nothing to a high condition, and that of University College from a fallen state to a very high condition, from which each fell as soon as I left it. Nor has he risen from writing anything worth reading. *** He has only been a lucky man."

"I never considered it an honour to meet Sir James Clark. I never gained an idea, or heard a sagacious remark from him. *** When a young man, he went out a very awkward Scotch body to take care of the son of a gentleman of rank and furtune."

When such is the style and manner of attacking a man like Sir James Clark adopted by Dr. Elliotson, the *Magnus Apollo* of the *Zoist,* what is to be expected from his associates and devotees, who attack others and fight mesmeric battles under the leadership of such a commander-in-chief?

by "rapid tractive passes over the feet," and "common down passes, at the distance of three feet, for ten minutes," when, of her own accord, she said, " ' I feel a fine glow all over me, especially in the knees—most in this one,' pointing to the chief offender." Having still further stated that the patient was *blind;* that the pain left her at the time the passes were being made by Mr. Plowman, without her knowledge, or one word having been said to her on the subject; and that a Mr. Neilson produced an impression on the same *blind* woman, on a subsequent occasion, without informing her of his intention, simply "by mesmerizing the *feet,* at the distance of three feet, when he caused a sensation of coldness in the *head;*"—having made these statements, the Rev. Mr. Sandby then triumphantly asks—"Now, in what manner will our opponents explain away the above facts? What is their *rationale?* How does their hypothesis apply? What is the grand physiological principle which is to solve and settle this case?"

Now, in my opinion these are all fair and legitimate queries; and, far from acting according to Mr. Sandby's expectation and prediction, that these gentlemen "will simply say, 'We are mistaken in our facts,'" and so on, as represented in page 289, I readily admit that I have no doubt whatever that the *facts,* are stated in this case, are *quite true in every particular as there set forth;* and I have great pleasure, moreover, in giving *my rationale,* and pointing out what appears to *me* "the grand physiological principle which is to solve and settle this case;" and that this can be done too independently of "Mr. Braid's *starting process,* expectant attention, or dominant ideas," or a mesmeric fluid or force. Had expenctant attention or dominant ideas been excited in the mind of the patient, however, by audible suggestions, I doubt not the satisfactory results would have been still *more speedily* realized.

At page 288 the Rev. Mr. Sandby says: "For instance, will Mr. Braid, who contends that the so-called mesmeric effects are produced by the patient being made to concentrate his vision on some object for a certain time, assert that the *staring process* was the secret of Mr. Plowman's success? Did the gaze of the *blind*

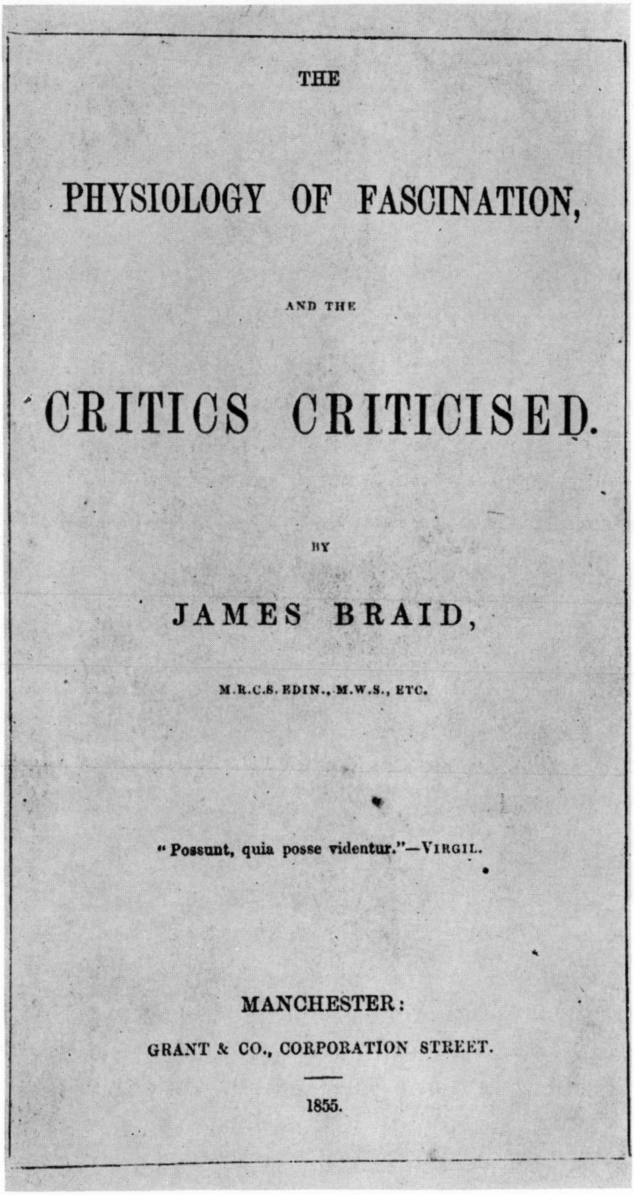

THE

PHYSIOLOGY OF FASCINATION,

AND THE

CRITICS CRITICISED.

BY

JAMES BRAID,

M.R.C.S. EDIN., M.W.S., ETC.

"Possunt, quia posse videntur."—VIRGIL.

MANCHESTER:

GRANT & CO., CORPORATION STREET.

1855.

FIGURE 13. Title page from James Braid's *The Physiology of Fascination and the Critics Criticised,* published in 1855.

woman excite her nervous temperament, and influence her system
so potentially?"

Now, I felt extremely sorry—chiefly on his *own* account—to
find that the Rev. G. Sandby had made such an attack upon me,
as that contained in the above paragraph; because it was quite
unworthy of a gentleman of his sacred office, and of his high
talents and attainments; indeed it was unworthy of *any* man who
wished to act the part of an honourable and fair controversialist,
as I shall now proceed to prove; for here, be it observed, the Rev.
gentleman wishes to represent me as contending that fixation of
the *visual organ,* or the "staring process" is the *sole* cause of the
phenomena, which result during hypnotic and mesmeric processes.
Now, with what propriety could he do this when he knew that, at
age 31 of my work on hypnotism, which was published *twelve
years ago,* I said "As the experiment succeeds with the *blind,* I
consider it not so much the optic, as the sentient, motor, and
sympathetic nerves, and the *mind* through which the impression
is made"? Such were my recorded sentiments and experience
twelve years ago; and I have published various remarks since tending to confirm them; and proving, moreover, that whatever produces a *new* impression, will modify or change *existing function,*
whether that new impression may be of a mental or physical
nature, and whether it may have arisen from a sensible impression
by fanning or breathing on, or wafting with the natural hand, with
some artificial contrivance, or the gentle blast from a pair of
bellows, or from audible suggestions or sensible impressions directing the circulation to certain parts, and withdrawing it *from*
others—thus stimulating or depressing function—these natural results, however, being greatly influenced by dominant ideas or expectant attention, either originating from audible suggestions of
another person present, or from previous convictions and belief
on this point in the patient's own mind. Moreover, whatever
changes sensation changes also the circulation, secretion, and the
capillary circulation and general function of the part so impressed,
and, concurrently, the whole of the other functions of the body
become modified in a greater or lesser degree, and that whether
the primary impression resulted from a mental or from a physical

influence. The brain, moreover, receives many impressions which subsequently influence the mind as conscious impressions, although they were not perceived at the moment when they were conveyed to the brain through the organs of sense; and impressions too slight to be conveyed to the brain at all, so as ever to become the objects of consciousness, may nevertheless be adequate to produce a *local* influence on the organic nerves and capillaries, and thus alter existing normal or morbid function.

As regards the influence of passes, again, I have fully admitted that, independently of the mechanical influence produced thereby, by the agitation of the air or by touch, they may also produce impressions in some cases through the influence of temperature or electric agency, as it is an undoubted fact that a change in the electrical polarity takes place from the mere proximity or contact of every substance in nature, animate or inanimate, independently of any occult, magnetic, or odylic force, such as the mesmerists contend for. That electricity, however, was not the chief or important agency was obvious, I remarked, from this fact, that I have found similar results to arise from touching a patient with a glass rod, 3½ ft. long, or from making passes with an artificial hand attached to the end of the said glass rod, as when doing so with my own hand or any other conductor of electricity.

Now, bearing these facts in mind, will the Rev. G. Sandby presume to say that because the poor woman, Ann Donaldson, was *blind,* and was not expecting any mesmerizing process to take place, that *therefore* she *could* not be influenced in her organic functions and sensations by the agitation of the air by the passes made over the painful part, or over the feet, so as to draw the circulation to the feet, and thus relieve the oppressed brain, unless there was some *occult agency at work,* such as a mesmeric fluid or force projected from the body of the operator and charging the body of the blind woman? Is Mr. Sandby not aware, moreover, that feeling, hearing, and smell are generally prodigiously exalted in blind people, to compensate for their loss of sight: and that from *this* cause his notable example, Ann Donaldson, was the more likely to be easily affected by the passes, irrespectively of the transference to her body of any magnetic fluid or force from the body of the operator?

Again, is Mr. Sandby not aware that very slight impressions may be sufficient to change existing physical action, through their influence on the organic nerves, which preside over nutrition and special function, so slight as not even to excite consciousness? And is he not aware that organic changes may be effected through mental or physical impressions so slight that although sufficiently intense to excite consciousness slightly at the time, nevertheless are too faint to make a lasting impression on the memory? Is the Rev. Mr. Sandby not aware that he may be seated at an open window, and so engaged in reading or study, or in conversation, as not to perceive that such effect is being produced upon his frame by the cold draught of air to which he is exposed, as may issue in rheumatism, inflammation of his eyes, or ears, or nose, or glands, or throat, or lungs, or any other organ of his body most predisposed to take on morbid action? Is he not aware that kindness and earnestness in his manner of addressing a suffering fellow-mortal, enforced by the *gentle movement* of his hand *the more completely to arrest the patient's attention,* may so withdraw it from his past and present sufferings as to give a turn to *existing* morbid function, and thus effect a crisis, without any magnetic, odylic, or nervous, or vital force, extruded from the body of the operator, and entering into and charging the body of the patient with its peculiar properties and powers?

And again, is the Rev. Mr. Sandby not aware that patients may be affected, even during sleep, from infancy to old age, by passes, or by the mere breath of heaven—as by the gentle zephyr fanning their frames—so as to excite various effects, visible or invisible, which may not be remembered by the sleepers on awaking? And is he not aware, moreover, that a patient may fall asleep with one side of his face exposed to a draught of cold air, and although unconscious of its influence at the time, and during his sleep, have, on awakening, most convincing physical proof of its influence, from his face being drawn to the *opposite* side, through paralysis of the portio dura, caused by the continued stream of cold air impinging agains the trunk and ramifications of that nerve?

Now, it is just because a *blind* patient is *"not* like a piece of sulphate of iron, which we can find at any moment in our laboratory, and heat up in the retort at will, and because it is a material of a far more delicate and sensitive nature," that the passes of Mr. Plowman and Mr. Neilson were so effective in changing the organic functions in the frame of Ann Donaldson—and that even independently of any occult agent of the nature alleged by the Rev. Mr. Sandby and other mesmerists. Such is *my* "verdict, and the reasons thereof."

As to Dr. Esdaile's case with the blind man, I shall leave it in the safe keeping of Dr. E. and the Rev. Mr. Sandby; but as to Dr. Gregory's case it proves *too much* for Mr. Sandby's purpose; for, as *this* blind man went to sleep when another gentleman was trying, *at some distance, unknown to this blind man,* to put *another* person to sleep, this fact furnishes strong proof that this blind man was one of those subjects who are liable to be affected entirely through the imagination, expectant attention, or a dominant idea and habit; and he might just as likely have been affected in this way when Dr. Gregory fixed his silent gaze upon him as in the instance referred to with the other gentleman. Moreover, the other case referred to by Mr. Sandby very probably was a person of the like susceptibility.

I think, by the foregoing remarks, I have fully satisfied the requirements of the Rev. G. Sandby where he says—"We call upon the adherents of the suggestive theory, first to examine our evidence respecting the facts as rigidly as they wish, and then give in their verdict, and their reasons thereof;" and I maintain that the case of "Ann Donaldson, the poor blind Scotch woman of Greenside" has *not* overthrown *my* theory, nor has it established the *mesmeric* theory; and I further maintain, that it is to the dogmatic mesmerists and lovers of the marvellous, and not to me and others who have espoused my views, that the Rev. gentleman's strictures in his concluding paragraph properly apply, as aiming at "laying down positive laws for universal application, and yet omit in their calculations an essential part of the argument, and all the most important facts which militate against their conclusions."

I quite concur in the Rev. Mr. Sandby's observations when he says, "Different minds are of course differently constituted, and observe the same facts after a different fashion. What looks feasible to one man looks preposterous to another." I have never, however, said that the *whole* results are the products of the imagination, nothing but the fancy of the brain, the staring process, fixed gaze, or dominant ideas; but I have attempted to demonstrate how far these and other influences co-operate toward explaining various phenomena attributed by the mesmerists to some more mysterious power; and I do maintain that, so far as I have *seen* and believe, the whole results can be accounted for upon the principles of the reciprocal action of mind and matter, of the patient's own body, upon each other, modified and directed by external circumstances, sensible impressions, audible suggestions, and dominant ideas, irrespective of any magnetic, odylic, nervous, vital, or occult force passing from the operator to the patient, as the all-efficient cause, as has been contended for by the mesmerists.

Having thus disposed of the Rev. Mr. Sandby, I beg leave now to address a few words to another champion of occult mesmerism. The Mr. T. referred to in the note, *ante,* is the Rev. C.H. Townshend, who was so moved by the "heavy blow and great discouragement" inflicted on mesmerism by the article in the *Quarterly Review,* as induced him forthwith to come to the rescue, by perpetrating a five shilling volume to stem the torrent set in against his mesmeric notions. Mr Townshend's main argument was based upon what he deemed an impregnable dogma about the influence of the *personal presence of the operator,* or, as he styles it, of "the man in the room." As it appears to me that a few simple and obvious examples may be adduced, capable of demolishing this all-powerful argument of "the man in the room"—either as operator or sceptic—I shall venture to enter the lists even with this great champion for occult mesmerism.

Mr. Townshend says—"I cannot see how phenomena that are induced by *any* methods of which a human being is the employer can apply to the present question. Whatever may be their quality they have been originated, and are wielded, by the presence, the commands, the prescriptions of a human being. *There is the man in the room.* You cannot get rid of him. * * * Without the hypnotist or biologist the phenomena do *not* occur. Thus have we seen that the reviewer's handle to his theory does not truly fit the occasion, just because of *the man in the room."*

Now, in refutation of these dogmas, I beg leave to state that, at the very first public lecture delivered by me in 1841, in order to prove the *fallacy of such a fancy,* three of my patients put themselves into the hypnotic state in succession, when I was not only not in the *room,* but when I was actually in *another* room at a considerable distance from that in which they were, and I only came in after it was announced to me that they had gone to sleep by *their own unaided efforts,* as can be testified by at least six hundred witnesses. My proof, however, does not rest upon these cases only, for I have since had innumerable examples of equally successful results with many other subjects; and I can, moreover, readily adduce other cases of the sort *any* day. Will the *Zoist* presume to say that in any of these cases Mr. Braid was "making mesmeric passes (I made no passes at all) and *looking hard at his patients as he always has done,* while *making them stare?"* I am, therefore, warranted in retorting on the Rev. Mr. Townshend that in these instances we *had* got rid of *"the man in the room,"* and that *without* the hypnotist the phenomena *did occur;* and consequently that *Mr. Townshend's* "handle to his theory does not truly fit the occasion, just because *the man was"* NOT *"in the room."*

The self-induced trance of the Fakirs in India, in like manner, furnishes ample proof in point.

Nor was it the influence of my *will;* for I purposely directed my attention to *other* matters, the more satisfactorily to prove that the influence was entirely subjective.

But perhaps Mr. T. will wish to argue, that although the patients were not influenced by my *presence in the room, my commands and prescriptions,* before leaving the room, had produced the results. However, I am prepared to rebut that argument also, by other examples. Thus, a patient whom I had previously cured, by hypnotism, of rheumatism and opacity of the cornea, when at a distance of five and one-forth miles from me, put herself into the state, *unknown to me,* to convince someone that the effect could be produced by her own efforts, without my knowledge or any special influence communicated by me to the patient. The following is another example in point. A lady whom I had hypnotized, with great relief to her sufferings, after the failure of some noted mesmerists by their "old established modes of mesmerizing," became curious to know whether the results might not after all arise from some *occult* influence projected from my body during my personal attendance; and, in order to satisfy her mind upon this point, she one day repaired to her room alone, and sat down and fixed her attention in all respects as when I used to be present; the result of which was that she fell asleep in her chair, where she was found fast asleep an hour or two afterwards by her friends, who went in search of her, and could not comprehend the cause of her long absence.

I shall only give one more example, embracing the waking phenomena. In October, 1856, I exhibited the power of suggestion and dominant ideas over certain subjects in the waking state, by requesting a gentleman of high intelligence to lay his hand on the table, when, through my audible suggestion, his hand was instantly so firmly fixed to the table that neither his own volition nor the physical efforts of others could separate them. By blowing on the hand it was instantly set free; and on being now requested to extend his arm above the table, I then told him to put it down if he could—so emphasized as to suggest the idea that he could *not.* He now put forth a strong effort to put his arm down, when the arm became rigidly cataleptic in its extended position, and his other extremities became quite rigid also, notwithstanding he was wide awake, and had undergone no process whatever that day. The Earl of Carlisle was present, and tested him, as well as Professor Gregory, and others. These experiments in the waking state very much astonished most of those present; and Professor Gregory immediately jumped to the conclusion that it resulted from the influence of my extraordinary magnetic force over the said gentleman when I was near to him, or—in Mr. Townshend's phraseology—that it was the all-controlling influence of *"the man in the room."* I repudiated the notion of it having resulted from any such occult agency; but Dr. Gregory insisted so much in favour of the occult theory that, some days thereafter, when this gentleman was at his own home, which is thirteen miles from Manchester, he resolved to put the matter to the proof by experimenting upon himself when no one else was in the room with him, and when I could know nothing of his intentions—for he had been led by Dr. Gregory's remarks to suppose that it was just *possible,* after all, that, when present, I *might* have some occult power over him. Well, in his solitary apartment this gentleman laid his hand on the table, as in the former instance, and instantly his arm became firmly and involuntarily fixed in that position. However, his other hand and arm being free, he applied the other hand to rub the cataleptic arm, and thus set himself at liberty; and then he felt satisfied that my explanation was correct, that it was merely the result of a dominant idea and habit, and that Professor Gregory's opinion was erroneous in alleging that, on the former occasion he had been affected through some *occult* agency emanating from me as *"the man in the room."*

I have long felt convinced that the *odium mesmericum* was as inveterate as the *odium theologicum;* what then must be my perilous position, when so hardly and inveterately assailed by the *odium mesmericum* and *theologicum* combined? Still, however, I entertain a confident hope that time, which is the great reformer, will ultimately give in her verdict in favour of my psychophysiological theory.

JAMES BRAID

Rylaw House, Manchester,
23rd October, 1855

J. P. Philips

Hypnotism, as Braid has well defined it, consists in the action produced on the subject by the steadiness of his gaze maintained by attention. This action may be obtained through whatever object the eyes are to be persistently fixed upon. In 1860, Dr. Philips, taking up Braid's theory, known as *braidism,* and willingly discarding mesmerism, presented it as capable of producing fascination—a fact which he practically demonstrated.

In the remotest antiquity, this was practiced by the Joquis of India, who kept pertinaciously looking at the tips of their noses or at some imaginary point in space, until a kind of trance was produced, during which they pretended having become united to Divinity.

The monks of Mount Athos procured hypnotism by staring at their umbilici. Among the Arabs, the "inspired" Aissaouias had recourse to other means. Braid used a cork, and Dr. Philips first made use of a silver coin but later adopted the hypnotic disc. The disc is made of metal; ordinarily of zinc, and is the size of a quarter or a small florin. It is convex on both sides, and traversed in the center by a piece of copper wire, three or four lines in diameter. This red point on a gray field catches the eye, which is the part of the head aimed at. Anything producing a like result may serve as a substitute.

After causing the subject to be seated, the disc is placed in his hand, which rests flat on his knees, and he is told to keep his eyes constantly fixed on it. This constitutes the whole process.

Dr. Philips theorized that a great number of persons he treated by means of the disc feel a peculiar sensation. This sensation consists of a kind of tingling in the palm of the hand, at the part covered by the disc, which feeling follows the direction of the principal nerves of the arm until it comes to the head, where the subject experiences a strange feeling, as though a great tranquility had overcome him. Dr. Philips estimates that one in fifteen can experience the effects of this method.

After receiving further development and being practiced for

several years, especially in America, braidism was given up, when, in 1859, Velpean brought the question before the Academie de Medecine, by presenting hypnotism as a kind of anesthetic capable of being substituted for ether or chloroform, a use to which magnetism had already been put.

A COURSE IN THE THEORY AND PRACTICE OF BRAIDISM OR NEUROHYPNOTISM*

First Conference

Ladies and Gentlemen,

I have to tell you about facts singularly remarkable. Yesterday still, serious men were only talking of it with scorn or very softly; today, by a sudden comeback of fortune, these facts have the privilege of exciting to the highest degree the interest of the scholarly world and of provoking it to active research. Thanks to the bold initiative of a few young members of the medical education, they are finally entering into official science, on which doors they knocked in vain for fifty years. Honour then to those intelligent professors! Through them medicine has just annexed to her "domaine" a whole new region destined perhaps to become her most beautiful and her richest possession. But at the same time, glory to the lost children of progress! More devoted than prudent, the latter have not waited to enter the tilt, for the chances of combat to be announced, and jealous of bequeathing to humanity a salutary truth, they have undergone some long tests without giving way.

All sciences really worthy of the name, that is to say which present us with some systematic groups of truths rigorously established by experience and reason, susceptible to useful application, had in the beginning the shadow sanctuary of superstition; all, at their origin, were "occult sciences". The philosophical mind put centuries of effort in delivering them from the hindrance

---

*Philips, J.P.: *Cours Theorique et Pratique ou Hypnotisme Nerveux*. Considere dans ses Rapports avec la Physiologie, la Psychologie, et la Pathologie, et dans ses applications a la Medecine, a la Chirurgie, a la Physiologie Experimentale a la Medecine Legale et a l'Education par Le Docteur J.P. Philips. Paris, J.B. Baillere et Fils, 1860, pp. 1-23.

of the mystical hypothesis, which from all phenomena make a prodigy and in any effect wants to see no other cause than the immediate action of an arbitrary will of a supernatural and unfathomable will, true "deus ex machina" whose sovereign fantasies would be the whole code of nature. Several of them have stripped away their swaddling clothes hardly more than 200 years ago, and there is one which still hasn't been able to succeed in getting free of them. The facts that this occult science of our time confirms, and the methods that it uses, have been observed or put to use in the most distant lands and among all people. They were studied by the greatest thinkers of antiquity, and they have preoccupied very much the first founders of modern science, not excepting Bacon, the illustrious father of experimental critics. In the eighteenth century philosophy brings its immortal revendication in favor of the imprescriptible and unlimited rights of human reason. But the excess of its zeal carries it beyond the goal; meeting those facts of an order entirely different, facts entirely unexplained and generally reputed to be unexplainable, it sees in them a denial of its proposition; before the moral impossibility of refuting the latter, it rejects the former. It had not understood that a problem however inaccessible to the intelligence that it seems to be at first, does not suppose a native infirmity of the reason, but simply our ignorance or the imperfection of our means of analysis.

Anyway, facts are facts, all the same, and we could not imagine a pretension more ridiculous than demanding that they change or disappear to make room for the capricious creations of our preconceived theories. The sentence of the eighteenth century must therefore be brought back: it is time that the positive science opens for the exploration of her trained searchers this land of the marvelous whose richness was uselessly signalled to it by many enlighteners, but in which it refused to see anything other than the fabulous country of chimera. May the experimental and rational method carry then boldly its torch in the shadows of the marvelous: this night, dear and propitious to the owls of the intelligence, but full of dispair for philosophy, will dissipate; in place of its faded phantoms we will see appear a whole new order of biological phenomena, and perhaps the mystery of life will find itself enlightened as far as those depths so dark where all the sources of truth are going to be lost. A trouble of the innervation being able to spread itself from the apparent suppression of all nervous activity to an excessive exaltation and to surprising modifications that are enigmatical on the sensibility of the thought and of motivity, such is the general character of the phenomenon that we will have to consider in its physiological essence, and in the artificial means with the help of which we succeed in provoking it. This striking manifestation of the hidden virtualities of human nature was the basis of the cult in antiquity.

It surrounded with its prestige the sacerdotal authority and it was the voice of the oracles. It constituted the deepness of the secret medicine of the Brahmans, of the therapeutics of the Asclepiades, of the mystical doctors of the School of Alexandre. By it are explained most of the prodigies attributed to the ancient and modern thaumaturgists, and profane, and sacred, it furnished an experimental confirmation of the accounts which occupy a place so considerable in the annals of the Middle Ages concerning the works of the enchanters, of the magicians and of the sorcerers; it is the justification of mesmerism and the condemnation of its blind or clairvoyant detractors.

In the sixteenth century, the critical mind undertook the examination of this mysterious phenomenon; Cardan, Maxwell, Wirdig, Paracelcus, Van Helmont, tried to make this phenomenon enter into the framework of general physics. Later, the investigations of those men of genius are again attempted by Mesmer, who must then share with them the merit of having exposed to the light of day of scientific discussion, a whole order of natural facts obscured until then, and struck with sterility by mysticism.

This study has been pursued since then without interruption, and for a certain number of years it excites the multitude; but the scholars turned away with scorn and as if they were afraid of soiling themselves; to them then goes all the blame for some of the serious and high level research which they completed in its entirety; those scholars have often been compromised by the zeal of ignorance or by some unworthy speculations; if they have dragged themselves through the maze of empiricism they have gone astray in the aberrations of fantasy.

We must ascertain however that a few notables, in medicine and in the natural sciences, have dared to brave the forbidden, or what was forbidden on this field of exploration by scientific routine.

Those honorable dissidents have been seen in the chairs of the Faculty, at the Academy of Medicine, and even in the Chair of its President. The honored names of Mr. Jules Cloquet, Rostan, Husson, Lordat, are presenting themselves naturally to your minds. Among the foreigners, we would not lack any illustrations to quote you. They would be, for the country of Germany, a distinguished chemist, M. de Reichenbach; an eminent doctor, M. le Doctor Frank, and many renowned Doctors of the Academy of Berlin. Belgium would name us M. Jobard who is, in spite of very much wit, a consummate scholar. On the other side of the Channel, we would mention Doctor Gregory, pupil of Liebig and a very esteemed professor from the University of Edinburg; Doctor Elliotson, one of the most considered practitioners of London, who sacrificed voluntarily to his new medical convictions, one of the richest clientelles of this metropolis; Doctor Esdaile, who was for a long time, and until his death, at the head of the Principal Hospitals of Calcutta. Italy would present us several of its able physiologists; United States would offer us its great chemist, the venerable Doctor Hare, whose numerous discoveries have considerably contributed to the progress of chemistry and physics.

But the proscribed faith did not have only a few rare admitted followers in official science, it included above all Nicodemes in great number. If my information is exact, half of the members of the Academy of Medicine belonged to this last category, reciprocally unbeknownst and among them were two of the professors the most renowned of the School of Paris. Finally an unexpected crisis came to change suddenly the face of things: Mm. Azam and Broca, professors and surgeons of the hospitals, announced to the Academy of Medicine the anesthetic properties of hypnotism: the Academy, whose innocence suspected no fraud, welcomed favorably this "astonishing discovery"! But the newcomer was nothing else however than an intrusion of old knowledge which had not been recognized under its perfidious disguise, and which M. Velpeau himself, deceived like all the others, had hastened to cover with his reassuring patronage. The prohibited merchandise comes then into franchise in a new pavillion, and under the pretext of hypnotism the official scholars are able now, without risking their position or their consideration, to give themselves openly to the study of the wonderful; they can, without temerity and without heroism, publish as the results of their personal observations, a multitude of facts which, "from the science", were only absurd fables six months ago. Already the most accredited medical journals and medical publications are giving the honor of their first page to many communications about which, at another time, they would have willingly sent the authors to the "petites maisons". A revolution in our scientific regime has thus been accomplished; let us be happy about it, Gentlemen, with all the true friends of light and humanity: the genius of the discoveries, so active in our time, was beginning to find too narrow for its wings that cross ceaselessly, the circle where he was enclosed; they have just opened to him a sphere much larger in which he will be able to take his full flight.

It is true that, by an action of unknown essence, but emanating fully from human vitality, man can affect his own organization or the one of his fellow man in a way so as to alter the regular mode of his diverse functions and modify their activity to every possible degree. At all times facts have been reported that answer this question in the affirmative. However the singular nature of those facts, their rarity, which made their recognition difficult, and, on the other hand, the intimate rapport which attaches them to mysticism, had furnished the scholars a pretext to reject them as popular errors undertaken by the fraud of charlatanism or by superstition. But today numberless experiments repeated on every side, and attested to by the most honorable and the most competent men, establish the reality of those things by such a deluge of proofs, that it becomes futile and ridiculous to put them to doubt.

By the revelation that they are bringing us a whole transcendent order of vital properties still ignored in science, by the useful application to which those properties show themselves susceptible, those facts have an importance without equal for anthropology in general, and especially for physiology and medicine. They deserve then, in the highest degree, to be studied by the rigorous processes of scientific analysis. We have made this study, and we come to show to you the results of it.

The object with which we have to occupy ourselves represents a numerous series of phenomena; but they all have, like we have already noted, the same fundamental character, a particular psychosis, and their variety corresponds to the variety of nervous functions. Now the study of those effects is inseparable from that of the artificial processes by means of which one obtains them, and these procedures are diverse. They are divided into two great collateral methods that the public has tried to distinguish by the denominations of "animal magnetism and of hypnotism." But those designations are inexact: the first, because it implies a disputable theory; the second, because it gives falsely to understand that the essential and constant character of the phenomena that it represents is the sleep. To avoid the inconvenience of similar denominations, we think we must substitute respectively those of "Mesmerism" and of "Braidism", following in this a role already consecrated in the classic words of "Galvanism, Voltairism, Faradism" etc.

Mesmerization rests upon a hypothesis which attributes to the will the power to hunt beyond the periphery of the body the nervous influx that it stimulates in the nerves of movement, and to direct this force through space on the living beings that it proposes to affect. A few of the mesmeric effects seem to us to justify this supposition in an absolute manner; there are some others which can find their explanation outside of it. Moreover, it is a subject that we do not have to debate here. We pass then to the examination of the Braidic method, to which those lectures are exclusively given.

In the year of 1841, M. Braid, a Scottish surgeon established in Manchester, having been witness of mesmeric experiences, made in that town by M. Lafontaine, presumed that the results obtained could have for a true and unique cause, not the "animal magnetic fluid", but the "fixation of look and of attention" provoked quite naturally in the subjects by the long series of uniform movements that the hand of the operator executed in passing and re-passing continually in front of their eyes, and which constituted what we designate as "magnetic passes". But let's permit M. Braid himself to expose to us his discovery. I translate.

"My first experiments were conceived in view of proving the falseness of the magnetic theory which states that the provoked phenomena of sleep is the effect of the transmission of the operator on the subject, of some special influence emanating from the first while he makes some touches on the second with the thumb. He looks at him with a fixed stare, while he directs the points of the fingers toward his eyes, and executes some passes in front of him.

"It seemed to me that I had clearly established this point, after having taught the subjects to make themselves fall asleep just by fixing an attentive and sustained look on any inanimate object.

"It was not only a few rare individuals who thus fell asleep upon the first attempt; on one occasion, in the presence of 800 spectators, ten adult males out of fourteen were affected in the same way. All of them had started the experiment at the same time; some of them by turning their eyes on a cork fastened on their foreheads, and making a projection forward, the others by looking at fixed points chosen in the room. At the end of ten minutes the eyelids of ten of these subjects were found to be involuntarily closed. Some of them had retained their consciousness, some others had fallen into a state of catalepsy. Certain were insensible to pinpricks, and several had forgotten upon awaking everything that had happened to them during their sleep. Moreover, three persons in the audience fell asleep without my knowing it, by following the same process, which consisted of keeping their glances fixed upon a point in the room." ("Magic, Witchcraft, Animal Magnetism, Hypnotism, and Electrobiology" by James Braid, M.R.C.S. Edin. C.M.W.S., etc. Third Edition, P. 57 in London, at John Churchill; and in Paris, at Fowler, Palais Royal.)

The indirect part taken by M. Lafontaine in the beginning of hypnotism, of which he has been, I suppose, the first historian, gives him the right to be heard in his turn. Here is what we read in "The Art of Magnetizing", (by Charles Lafontaine, at Germer Bailliere, P. 262):

"Doctor Braid, after having attended my meetings and seeing the effects that I was producing, wanted also to make a name for himself, and to become the creator of a new system, of a new discovery. Soon he began to positively magnetize himself, while still denying magnetism and attributing always to different causes the effects that he was producing with the help of magnetism itself.

"Doctor Braid put a cork on his forehead, which he maintains with a rubber band around his head; he has the subject look at the cork, the subject is thus forced to have his eyes turned upward; all his nerves and all his muscles begin to be tired, the sight grows less clear, eyelids fall, and for an instant cannot be raised. M. Braid then tries to prove by experiences that the subjects are in a state similar to the magnetic state."

Here is the recital of a series of experiments that M. Lafontaine instituted in his turn, to demonstrate the inanity of those of his adversary.

M. Lafontaine having followed the procedures recommended by the latter, (M. Braid) would have obtained only insignificant effects. For he who has realized the means of action of Braidism, this negative result is not surprising coming from an experimenter so badly disposed toward his instrument. M. Lafontaine adds: "However, M. Braid continued his experiments; but to have some positive results, he magnetized with the help of a glass tube, although appearing not to use it, and while attributing the effects he was producing to a cause which did not have anything to do with magnetism. In spite of that, his system fell and did not rise any more."

M. Lafontaine, in this circumstance, has not made any proof of the gift of prophecy; he will rejoice himself about this, we do not doubt. The observations to which he has been able to give himself since he wrote those lines, cannot fail to have modified his judgment. Instead of denying the discovery of his loyal antagonist from Manchester, he should congratulate himself for having furnished the occasion for such a happy discovery of which the mesmerists, and he is without a doubt one of the most skillful of them, are in a better position than anybody else for appreciating and using the advantages of it.

On the other hand, it is less certain for us to say that M. Braid is wrong to contest the reality of all the effects attributed to mesmerism, which he is powerless himself to reproduce, by the use of his own procedures, or to explain with his hypotheses! We are even astonished that so good a mind has persisted so long in what appears to us like a big error.

An inhabitant of New England, M. Grimes, was led in the year 1848, we do not know by exactly what empirical or theoretical means, to some results analogous to the discovery of M. Braid, before having had, so it seems, knowledge of the latter (M. Braid).

I did not know, myself, until those last months, the works of the ingenious Scottish surgeon. I have very much regretted since, the gap that this ignorance left in my book, "Electro-dynamism Vital", where it would have been a pleasure for me, as well as a duty to consider the rights of the inventor, at the same time using his work to the profit of mine.

I certainly had, about twelve years ago, looked over the work of M. Lafontaine, and noticed the passage which I have just read to you; but the way in which the facts are presented had prevented me from giving them the attention that they deserve, and I had completely lost sight of them.

The Electro-Biology, (such is the very ill-chosen name that M. Grimes has given to his method) is in reality only a development of hypnotism. It presents along with it, this remarkable difference, and at the same time has over it this advantage, that it discovers in most of the subjects an appearance refractory to the action of the proceeding of M. Braid, a latent modification developed through them by this application. This modification permits the determination on awakened people the whole series of nervous effects that the hypnotists seek only in the individuals plunged beforehand in a more or less deep sleep. What still characterizes electro-biology, is that while M. Braid, or rather his new French disciples, are asking the effect desired of the spontaneity of the hypnotic state, M. Grimes and his imitators know how to provoke it, at will, by putting into play the influence of vocal suggestion. This wonderful property of the organization, which permits an outside will to direct our ideas, and, by its suggested ideas, to modify our passions, our sensations, our motoricity, and even the exercising of our organic functions, had not been without studied doubters, in a deep manner and fully utilized before the electro-biologists; however the wise inventor of hypnotism had foreseen in this very curious observation that the attitudes imprinted by him on the bodies of his subjects, caused in them to appear the states of the soul of which those attitudes are the natural expression. So, making his subjects to take the attitude of prayer, he was exciting in them a religious feeling, if he extended their arms horizontally, facing downward with fists closed, slightly inclining the head forward, he could see their faces take on a menacing expression, and soon after they were throwing themselves with furor on some imaginary antagonists.

I have not been able to discover the original writings where M. Grimes has discussed his doctrine; I know it only by a very succinct resume, which has been given by a certain M. Stone, from Boston, at the first of a work on Electro-Biology that he had published in London in 1852, and which is a short version of the book published on this subject by another American, M.J.B. Dods. This last book, in spite of its faults, merits being consulted; it has for a title: "The Philosophy of Electrical Psychology", etc., it was edited by Fowler and Wells, in New York. It is composed of twelve "lectures" given by the author before the Congress of the United States, at a semi-official invitation signed by seven members of the Senate. Here is the translation of this invitation; it constitutes a rather curious document for the history of this new branch of science which occupies us here; it offers at the same time an interesting and very characteristic trait of American manners:

"Washington, 12 February, 1850

To Doctor Dods:
Dear Sir,
    Having heard spoken in the most advantageous way of the ex-

positions made by you, in different parts of the Union, on "Electric Psychology", a branch of science which treats, they say, the theory of illness and the reciprocal action of "the mind" and of "matter," we would be most happy if you would give one of your readings on this subject in this city, as soon as it would be possible.

The House of the Representatives, if we can procure it, would be for the accommodation of the members of the Congress and for the public in general, a suitable place for your talk.

> Very sincerely yours,
> George W. Jones, Thomas J. Rusk,
> John P. Hale, Sam Houston,
> H. Clay, H. S. Foote,
> Daniel Webster

Electro-Biology was propagated in the United States by a multitude of professors of whom the majority of them were unfortunately not on a level of a scientific mission. There were to be found among them doctors and ecclesiasticals. If we must believe the reports which without doubt are often very difficult to verify in their authenticity, but which nevertheless rest upon the attestations that do not seem possible to challenge, electro-biology has been applied with the most surprising success to produce unconsciousness in surgical operations, thus in the treatment of illness. We have been seeing for several years, in American newspapers, the advertisements of a dentist from Boston, announcing that in his practice, this less dangerous anesthetic is substituted for chloroform.

Electro-Biology got to England around 1850. Doctor Darling was one of its first proponents. The "éclat" that it produced there covered for awhile the less resounding fame of M. Braid. Nevertheless, those who knew of the results obtained for nearly ten years by the latter (M. Braid), could not keep from recognizing that this American product of recent creation did not essentially differ in any thing despite its superiority in certain ways, the work already ancient issuing from British genius. From there on, without contesting the originality of the discovery of "Electro-biology", but because this discovery was behind by several years to that of "hypnotism", it seemed reasonable to envisage the two proceedings as two progressive states of one and the same art, whose paternity would be devolved from M. Braid. Such was the judgment of the medical scholars of the three realms. The most distinguished scholars of England have studied with care the experiments of M. Braid and of the electro-biologists; they have established the reality of the phenomena that those experiments bring out, and they have proclaimed highly and conscientiously their importance as fearless and reproachless men, like scholars morally worthy of this name. We will cite among them the professors of medicine; J. H. Bennet, Simpson, Carpenter, Alison, Gregory, etc., the Doctor Holland, doctor of the queen, and eminent physician Sir David Brewster, the psychologist Dugald Stewart, etc., etc.

The observations of those gentlemen have been published in special writings or in periodical collections, such as the "Medical Times, the British and Foreign Medico-chirurgical Review (October 1851), the Edinburg Medical and Surgical Journal (1850), the Psychological Journal, Todd's Cyclopaedia of Anatomy and Physiology, Prof. John Hughes Bennet's Lectures, Letters to a Candid Inquirer, by Prof. Gregory, Elements of the Philosophy of the Human Mind," etc.

The special publications of M. Braid are rather numerous, but less extensive; they have the stamp of a positive mind, of a solid knowledge and of the genius of observation; his principal writings have for title: Neurypnology (1843), Observations on Trance, (1845), Witchcraft, Hypnotism, Electro-Biology, (1852).

He, who has the honor to talk at this moment before you, has called the attention of the doctors and of the scholars to the effects of electro-biology by oral and experimental expositions made in Belgium, in Switzerland, in Algeria and in Marseille, throughout 1853. At the request of the many pupils whom I have the honor of having taught, among whom are many distinguished doctors, the subject sketched in those lessons was developed into a lengthy treatise which was presented in Paris in 1855.

Doctor Charpignon, Doctor of the Prisons of Orleans, had written several years before, in the "Journal of the Magnetism", a series of articles on the "Medicine of Imagination." Those studies belong to the history of Braidism in France. On the other hand, M. Littre had given, in his edition of the Dictionary of Nysten, the extract of a long analysis of the proceedings, of the experiments and of the doctrines of M. Braid, contained in the English Encyclopaedia of Todd. The curious revelations of this work, owing to the pen of Doctor Carpenter, had already been reviewed in 1852, in the newspaper "La Presse", by M. V. Meunier, the able and courageous man who rendered them into the language of the layman. Finally a few reviews of my book had appeared in the newspapers of 1856. There, the contingent furnished by the scientific French press was limited to a discussion which, on the other side of the channel, had excited all the medical world.

Thanks to the lassitude of his rare apostles, thanks to the lukewarm attitude of the proselytes too much preoccupied to escape to the glory of martyrdom, thanks to the conservatism of the people whom "the chair has made", thanks to the rarity of moral courage even among the doctors, thanks finally to that truth which is not new and scarcely consoling, that the love of having wins over the love of knowing, the new science rested in its cradle under the thick veils of forgetfulness. When Mm. Azam and Broca came suddenly to put it in the place of honor and fill the world with its name, those gentlemen having tried to reproduce the experiences of hypnotism of which they had read the description in Todd, found themselves suddenly as much sorcerers as M. Braid himself. Led immediately, by a logic of practicians, by experiments of pure research for useful applications, they soon had the satisfaction of announcing to the Academy of Medicine that they had just executed a surgical operation, particularly painful in its nature, in a complete state of insensibility obtained by the processes of Braidism.

One more trait on this historical sketch, and we will be finished.

The history of peoples and of their customs tells us of certain bizarre practices in which until now only indecipherable enigmas have been seen, and which now appear to us as the scattered debris of an antique art which M. Braid would be really only the restorer among us. But let this be said in passing, the adversaries discomfitted of hypnotism seem to have bad grace in bringing to us those belated revelations the goal of which is not to instruct us, but to lower the merit of the intrepid suckers who had known to find again in their genius a treasure that science had lost.

The contemplative asceticism seems to have sought in the long fixity of the sight, the voluptuousness of ecstasy which like others have asked for drunkenness analogous to opium and to hashish.

According to Bernier, of Anquetil Duperron, and of various authors who have described to us the manners of India, the principal devotion of the "Joquis" consist in an operation where it is impossible for us not to recognize the fundamental fact of Braidism; this is a hypnotization by which those mysticals are looking for a way to unify themselves with God, and they effect this by holding still for hours, looking at the end of their nose or at an imaginary point in space. The Christian monks of Mount Athos observed the same practice, with the single difference that they had adopted their navel for the point to regard fixedly, acquiring their name of "Omphalo-Psychiens". The Arabs of the sect of Aissa practice rites of a more violent character, but the efficacy has no other principle, other than the effects which are delirium and an anesthesia either superficial or deep, as I have been able to verify myself.

We meet in Egypt magicians who practice divination by the best characterized Braidism: they pour a few drops of a thick ink into the palm of the hand of the one who consults them, ordering him to plunge his sight into this magic mirror. Visions follow after a more or less long wait. Faith, this "physiological virtue", this mental power which, as I will have to explain to you soon, is one of the two great levers of the action Braidic, plays also the important part, as everybody knows, in the religious thaumaturgy. It has received because of this the title of "Vertu theologale", which translated in the most precise language of science means as a "constitutive force" of our being, whose excitement can exalt all our faculties to an unknown degree, and provoke the most strange effects of anesthesia and hyperaesthesia, and among others, ecstasy, which, following the doctrines of the Brahmans and the ones of Sainte Therese, lifts the soul up to God, and according to Buddhism, can make us taste after this world the supreme beatitude of Nirvana.

We have pointed out certain common practices which are still in the domain of Braidism. It is said that the women of Brittany know how to put their nursing children to sleep by waving before their eyes a little ball of glass suspended by a string above the cradle. A cafe in Besancon possesses on the wall of one of its rooms a miraculous nail which has, they say, the virtue of stopping the hiccoughs, provided that one fixes his eyes on its shining head a few seconds.

The engineer Latil, director of the Forges of Labsann, has told us himself, that he had gotten rid of a stubborn case of hiccoughs, which obsessed him for more than twenty-four hours, at the end of ten minutes by remaining still and contemplative before this precious amulet. Anyway, it seems that this nail is not the only one of its kind; I have, from Doctor Wright, professor of zoology at the University of Dublin, that the recipe of the byzantine cafe-keeper has been in use since time immemorial in the hospitals of Ireland, not precisely to stop the spasms of the diaphragm, but as a general substitute for the somniferic and sedative action of opium.

The experiments of hypnotization on chickens, of which the description has been found in a work, by Pere Kircher, has been reedited enough times by the newspapers lately, so that I will not mention it.

Braidism has the fatal power of any great innovation which, after having put its enemies off the track, manages to humiliate them by pushing them, I do not know by what mysterious goad, to plunge themselves into the powder of the libraries to exhume with a feverish zeal, its titles of nobleness, and to demonstrate by all kinds of means, that what they were still denying yesterday as impossible and absurd, had existed all the time. Such is the case to repeat to M. Braid this consoling reflection of a judicious author: "in the progress of improvements, it is always a good sign of their appreciation when attempts are made to rob the authors of the merit due to them."

SECTION FOUR

Hypnotism in the Late Nineteenth Century

Fredrick Bjornstrom, M.D.
(1833-1889)

A Swedish physician, who in 1887 became interested in hypnosis, was Fredrik Bjornstrom. He was Professor of Psychiatry at the Stockholm Hospital and published his book on hypnotism so that his colleagues as well as the general public might not remain ignorant or prejudiced on the subject.

In his Preface to *Hypnotism, Its History and Present Development,* Dr. Bjornstrom states, "I have decided to try and give an easily comprehensible account of the development and present status of hypnotism, for the benefit of physicians as well as of lawyers and of the interested public; and as my personal experience in the matter is yet too small, I have collected from the best and latest authorities such facts as to me seemed surest, most reliable and most instructive. I have especially illustrated the dark sides of hypnotism, and the many injurious effects upon the physical and psychic life of man, which may result from the abuse of it; and I would strongly advise those who have not had a medical education not to meddle with this agent so dangerous and so difficult to control."

Dr. Bjornstrom was one of the first physicians to warn against the dangers of hypnosis, which can even be utilized today, when so many lay people try to use hypnosis as a therapeutic agent. He adds, "If this treatise shall be the means of inducing more specialists seriously to investigate this subject, and to use their knowledge as an aid in therapeutics; and if by it the public shall be prevented from playing with fire by which oneself or others may be burnt, the object of my unpretentious work will be gained."

The chapter which is representative of his work deals with hypnotism and the law, and raises legal and moral questions which we still are asked by the questioning public today.

HYPNOTISM AND THE LAW*

HYPNOTISM comes in contact with the law at more than one point, and many and intricate are the medico-legal questions which it has already raised. The most important of these questions are:

1. Can the hypnotized be physically or mentally injured by hypnotism?

2. Can the hypnotized fall victim to crime?

3. Can the hypnotized be used in the service of crime as a ready tool without a will?

4. Are the hypnotized responsible?

5. Should hypnotism be prohibited?

To these main questions we will try to give answers, and at the same time will cite explanatory examples.

1. *Can one hypnotized be physically or mentally injured by hypnotism?*

By hypnotism a natural, normal sleep is not produced in a person, but a sleep-like nervous condition, which must be considered rather as a pathological than as a physiological state; rather as a morbid and abnormal than as a healthy and normal condition; in many cases indeed it is more like mental disease than physical health and sound mind. But all morbid, artificially-produced conditions of the nervous system, even if they are soon changed, must cause an over-irritation and weakening of the system, and this in a greater degree the oftener the experiments are repeated. Experience also teaches that nervously weak persons are usually more easily hypnotized, and that the oftener the hypnosis is repeated, the sooner and more easily does it appear in the same individual, because the nervous system grows more sensitive, more irritable and weaker. This weakness may go so far, that hypnosis takes place from the slightest cause, even against one's will, as we have seen in the case of the subject who became cataleptic by merely staring at her reflected image in a mirror. Also an involuntary somnambulistic state can easily arise in one who has often been hypnotized; and of course during that state the subject cannot

---

*From Bjornstrom, Fredrik: *Hypnotism, Its History and Present Development.* Authorized translation from second Swedish edition by Baron Nils Posse. New York, Humboldt Publishing, 1887, pp. 104-115.

freely control his mind or actions. Several cases are on record, where the subjects of professional magnetizers, after only one or two experiments, have become sick and debilitated—and even melancholic and mentally deranged. It is true that hypnotism provides the means by which a cure can often be effected where harm has been done, viz. suggestion; but for all that, prudence insists on a careful handling of a power which can so thoroughly control both the physical and mental life.

We have previously shown how this means can be advantageously used for the improvement of man's character—as a powerful means of moral education. But whether the effect shall be good or bad rests entirely with the operator, and in the hands of an unscrupulous hypnotizer is as likely to be misused as not; for no one is so easily led as a hypnotized subject, and the bad instincts and impulses can be awakened as easily as the noble ones. Bailly's report in 1784 pointed out how easily passions could be awakened by the close contact between the magnetizer and his female subject, especially by the passes then in use and other methods altogether too familiar. Hence it is of the greatest importance that hypnotism be practiced only by honorable, conscientious and pure-minded physicians, who do not misuse the great influence and sympathy which they gain over their patients by this means.

But the hypnotized can be injured not only by the weakening effect of the hypnosis on the nervous system, but also by suggestions of such a kind that with or without the operator's intention they cause injurious and even fatal effects. Even in those not hypnotized imagination can be so strong that they may be frightened to disease or death. The story is told of a young girl, sixteen years of age, who was nearly frightened to death by the joke of a kinsman, merely by his making her believe that she had taken a strong poison instead of a harmless drug. All the symptoms of poisoning were fully developed, when at the last minute she was informed of the joke and was saved.

Quite recently a medico-legal examination was made of a woman who was supposed to have shortened her life by poison. The investigation brought to light the fact that she had taken perfectly harmless insect-powder, in the belief that it was a deadly poison, and as no other cause of death was found, it must be supposed that her imagination as to the efficiency of the powder had caused her death.

With the consent of Napoleon III, a scientist had a criminal tied to a table, with his eyes blindfolded, under the pretext that he was going to open the man's carotid artery and let him bleed to death. With a needle he made a slight scratch on the criminal's neck and had water dropping into a vessel that stood underneath, while all around an awful silence prevailed. The victim, believing that he heard his lifeblood flowing away, really died after six minutes.

A horrible joke by some Scotch students produced the same result.

A disagreeable janitor was one night lured into a room, where he was solemnly tried and sentenced to death by decapitation. The terrified man was led into a corner and placed on a block beside which stood a sharp axe; after his eyes had been blindfolded, he was given a blow on the neck with a wet towel, and when they lifted him up, he was dead.

If such things can take place with waking persons, how much more easily might it not then be done with hypnotized and "suggested" ones.

2. Can the hypnotized fall victims to crime?. .

The unconsciousness and loss of will, which are so easily caused in the hypnotized, can, of course, with the greatest facility be *misused* for immoral and criminal purposes. Rape, murder, robbery, theft, abduction, etc., are then easy to accomplish. In the beginning of this century, the people of India knew that the easiest way to steal children and carry them away was to magnetize them. Such thieves were known in India under the name, *thugs* or *bheels,* and in 1820, a band was discovered whose members, in the course of twenty years, had stolen millions of children. A child recovered at that time was entirely stupid and did not recognize her father until she had been dehypnotized by the ceremonies of the Buddhist priests.

In 1845, a case of this kind was minutely described by Esdaile.

In France some remarkable medico-legal cases have occurred

with reference to crime against morality under hypnosis, one of them combined with abduction; but we do not consider it proper to quote here any details of these horrible and shocking occurrences, which we hope will stand alone in the history of misused hypnotism.

Besides by robbery and theft the hypnotized might easily be deprived of their property in a more delicate manner, so that it would look as if they voluntarily gave it away, if only a powerful suggestion were given in that direction. In this respect Liegeois has made very instructive experiments.

For instance, he said to Miss E., who was very susceptible to suggestions even without being hypnotized and in an apparently normal state: "You know that I have loaned you five hundred francs; you must give me a note for that sum."— "But I do not owe you anything; you have a poor memory, madam; I will remind you of all the circumstances of the loan. Yesterday you asked me for this sum and I gave you a roll of twenty franc pieces. "—Under the influences of his honest expression and decided assertion, she began to hesitate and her thoughts became confused; she searched her memory; finally it obeyed his suggestion and showed her the matter as he had stated it; she acknowledged her debt and wrote a formal note for five hundred francs. As she was of age the note was perfectly valid before the law. Her mother was greatly astonished when she saw the note, and said to her daughter: "You have not told me anything about this loan; where have you spent the money?"—Somewhat embarrassed she looked at Liegeois.— "It is very simple; you have deposited it in the savings-bank."— She acknowledged this as entirely correct.

M. Liegeois, who is Professor of Jurisprudence at Nancy, seems to have a special gift for making women believe that they owe him money, and he does not even need to hypnotize them in order to convince them of it. The following cases were reported in 1884 before *the Academie des Sciences Morales et Politiques.*

"Mrs. O. is a young and very intelligent lady; she has received an excellent education; at first she energetically resisted all suggestion, but gradually yielded. I made her believe that she owed me one thousand francs and asked for her note. She obstinately refused to give it, and declared that she owed me nothing and that she would never acknowledge any debt to me. I insisted. She began to hesitate; she remembered it, acknowledged it before several witnesses, and wrote the note."

On another occasion, when she seemed fully normal, he told the same lady in the presence of her husband and several other witnesses, that she had promised to pay him, on account of her husband's indebtedness to him, one hundred thousand francs. At first she denied that such a thing had ever been mentioned; afterward she searched her memory, finally found that he was right, and wrote a bond for the sum named.

In the same way the hypnotizer can abuse his influence over the sleeper, by compelling him to make out donations or to make his will in the other's favor, and even to take upon himself the worst fictitious crimes.

This is an experiment in that direction by Liegeois.

He made Miss E., who was apparently in a wakeful and normal state, believe that she had killed one of her friends, introduced her to the justice of the peace, who was present, and told her that the questions the latter was going to ask her were entirely serious and that her welfare depended on her answers. "Why have you killed your friend?"—"I was angry with her on account of a dispute." —"With what instrument did you commit the murder?"—"With a knife."—"Where is the body of the victim?"—"At her home." —"You know what penalty befalls you for such a crime?"—"Yes, perfectly; but that makes no difference to me."

There would even be no difficulty in making away with an enemy or objectionable person, in a manner which would not betray the originator of the crime. It is only necessary to hypnotize the victim and to give him the suggestion that he will commit suicide. With the strongest possible love of life he will have great difficulty in resisting such a suggestion.

There is still another way in which the hypnotized can be injured, viz.—by drawing forth under hypnosis confessions and secrets which they would not voluntarily disclose when awake. Of course this may not succeed with all somnambulists, for some are very cautious and reserved and some may even play the hypocrite, and lie and deceive their hypnotizer. But the great majority will prove very frank and outspoken, and during the sleep may much too easily hurt themselves or others by revealing secrets which ought to be kept.

Hence the answer to the second question would be, that the hypnotized may fall hopeless victims to the most criminal and actions of all kinds, not only while they are asleep, but also after they have been awakened, and certain sensitive individuals even without being hypnotized. There lies such an infernal power in the hands of the hypnotizer that every one ought to be strictly forbidden to meddle with hypnotism, except those who assume the responsibilities of a physician and who have the people's welfare and woe in their hands.

3. *Can one hypnotized be used in the service of crime as a ready tool without a will?*

From the cases already mentioned it plainly follows that the hypnotized can by all kinds of suggestions be made not only to harm themselves but also others, and that they may even be irresistibly driven to any crime. It is chiefly in this that the darkest side and the worst dangers of hypnotism are found.

Also of this Liegeois and others have reported some striking experimental proofs. For instance L. made the above-mentioned Miss E. fire a pistol at her own mother, thinking it was loaded.

A young man, twenty-five years old, in whom L. could at pleasure produce catalepsy, anaesthesia, illusions of taste, and positive and negative hallucinations, even without hypnotizing him, was once presented by L. with a white powder, and told that it contained arsenic. "You will immediately go to your aunt's; there you will take a glass of water, pour the arsenic into it, dissolve it well in the water and offer the poisoned drug to your aunt."— "Very well."—In the evening L. was informed that the attempt at poisoning had been punctually performed.

On another occasion, L. chose at random from a party of five or six somnambulists, who met at Liebault's, a Mrs. G., took a revolver and some cartridges, went out into the garden, loaded only one of the chambers, fired it against a piece of pasteboard and returned showing the hole from the bullet. In less than fifteen seconds, he suggested to Mrs. G. to kill with the revolver a Mr. P., an old magistrate, who was present. Without hesitation Mrs. G. fired a shot (from the unloaded pistol, of course) at Mr. P. Immediately questioned by the police inspector, who was in the room, she acknowledged her crime with the utmost indifference. She had killed P. because he did not please her. They might just as well arrest her; she knew very well what punishment she would get; if they took her life, she would go to the other world, like her victim, whom she saw stretched out before her, bathed in his own blood. She was asked if she had not received the idea of murder from Liebault. —No, she had done it from her own impulse; she alone was guilty; she was resigned to her fate; she would submit to the consequences of her crime without complaining.

L. said to Mrs. C.: "There is Mr. D.; he is thirsty; give him this solution which contains arsenic."—She offered him the glass. Quite unexpectedly he asked: "What does this contain?"—She answered frankly: "It is arsenic." (For she was not forbidden to mention this.) New suggestion: "If you are asked, you will answer that it is sugar and water."—At the repeated question she answered: "It is sugar and water." D. emptied the glass.

Finally, we will quote a case which has been reproduced in many French journals, the last time in 1886, in the July number of the then new periodical *Revue Del'Hypnotisme*. The idea of this experiment was borrowed from Jule Clareties' novel, *Jean Mornas*.

Under deep hypnosis the girl X. was ordered to sneak into Mr. F.'s house the next day at a certain hour, and, with precautions not to be discovered, to steal a bracelet, which was lying in a wardrobe at a place minutely described, and to carry it cautiously home to the magnetizer, so that no one would notice that he was in the plot. Under no considerations was she allowed to denounce or betray him. The theft was punctually executed on the following day, with the greatest cunning and caution, and the trinket was delivered. The same evening, the girl was again hypnotized by the Mr. F. who owned the bracelet, who was also a magnetizer and in the conspiracy with the first one; during the hypnosis the following conversation occurred:

"I have been robbed of a bracelet today; you know who the

thief is."—"How can I know that?"—"You cannot be ignorant of it!"—"Why so?"—"Because I am sure you know the thief, tell his name!"—"I cannot."—"But I desire it!"—"And I say that I cannot."—"You know that you have no will here; there is only one—mine; obey!"—(After a silent resistance and evidently with effort) "Well, it is I!"—"That cannot be possible!"—"Yes, it is I!"—"You are not capable of such an action. Then you must have been forced to do it?"—"No!"—"You certainly have not done this of your own accord."—"Yes."—"I do not believe you."—"Well, it was not I."—"Who, then?"—"I will not tell you!"—"But I demand it."—"That makes no difference! I shall sooner yield up my life. I am sorry, for you have always been good to me; but I shall never tell it."

Further attempts to induce her to confess failed through her obstinacy, which however would probably have been broken, if he had persisted long enough. But he proceeded to another experiment during the same hypnosis.

"I seek revenge on somebody; will you help me?"—"Willingly!" —"You know that Mr. Z. " (the first one who magnetized the girl) "is my enemy."—"I should think so!"—"Then you must denounce him. As soon as you have awaked, you will write to the justice of the peace, that you have been accused of stealing a bracelet, but that you are innocent; that Mr. Z is the guilty one, and that you saw him commit the robbery."—"But this is wrong, as it is I who stole the bracelet."—"Never mind; write this."—"Very well! But if it were not true?"—"But it is true; for you are much too honest a girl to have stolen. It is not you! Do you hear? It is not you! I say that it is not you" (with confidence).—"Of course not. It is not I!"—"Mr. Z. is the thief; you have seen him!" (Energetically)—"Yes, I saw him, it is he!"—"You will write to the justice of the peace."—"Yes, immediately; I must denounce him."

Immediately after her awaking, fully convinced of the correctness of the accusation, she wrote and sealed a letter to the justice of the peace put a stamp on it, and was just going to mail it, when she was again hypnotized, in order to prevent this. The letter read as follows:

"To the Justice of the Peace:

"I accomplish a duty. This morning at one o'clock, a bracelet was stolen from Mr. F. For a moment I was accused of it, but unjustly; I swear to it; for I am entirely innocent. The thief—I must mention it, because I saw it all—is Mr. Z. (his full name given). It was done as follows: he sneaked into F.'s parlor at one o'clock; he went through the small entrance on du Four street and he stole one of Mrs. F's bracelets, which was lying in a wardrobe near the window—I saw it. Then he put it into his pocket and went away. I swear that it is as I have stated. He alone is the thief and I am ready to testify to this before the court."

The letter was not dictated, but composed by the girl herself. When she awoke, she had forgotten the whole story; but nothing would have been easier than to order her during her sleep to appear on a certain day and hour—even long afterwards—before a court, and to swear to whatever she had been ordered to testify.

Bottey tells of the following case of suggested theft.

He said to the hypnotized Miss S. R.:—"At about four o'clock today, you will see a gold watch on a table, and you will not be able to resist the temptation of stealing it." At the appointed hour— about seven hours after the hypnosis—B. saw her going to the table, on which he had placed the gold watch. She took it, looked at it, put it back, and repeated these actions several times; finally, after a long internal struggle, she quickly took the watch and put it in her pocket, while she looked around to see if she was detected. Afterwards, when he asked her to return the watch, she showed such mortification on account of her involuntary offence that B. was obliged by suggestion to remove her remembrance of this event.

By suggestion persons can also be made to commit perjury or to bear false witness; and this can be done in various ways; either so that they make an entirely false statement of occurrences which they have really witnessed, or so that they are by retroactive suggestion, so-called, made to believe that they have witnessed occurrences which in reality never took place; or finally, so that they are by suggestive amnesia completely robbed of all memory of what they have experienced.

Thus Bottey, for instance, gave the following suggestive communication to S. during a somnambulistic state: "Three days ago, at 11 P.M., you called on the noted Mr. C. When you arrived at his door, you heard loud quarreling; through the glass door you saw Mr. C. disputing with a lady dressed in furs and wearing a hat with red feathers. You saw C., in a fit of anger, take a dagger out of his pocket and thrust it into the lady's breast. Because you have seen this crime, you must denounce him before the court. When you awake you will remember what I have now told you, and you will make the accusation in writing and ask me to give it to the *procureur*." And that took place: the same day a letter was given to B. for the *procureur,* relating the crime in all its details, the lady's dress not forgotten.

In the same way B. convinced another woman that she had seen a certain gentleman poison an old lady with opium, and when she awoke, she hastened to make the accusation at the proper place. Bottey has also suggested suicide and murder to several. Concerning these he has made the observation that if they were to be performed immediately after awaking they were done more easily and without hesitation. If on the other hand they were not to be performed until several hours or days afterwards, a hard struggle was usually noticed, as also hesitation and resistance against the temptation, to which, however, they almost always finally succumbed.

Once the somnambulist L. was given the order, upon awaking to shoot with a revolver at an imaginary person who would appear before her. The order was punctually executed, and they made a pretence of carrying the corpse out of the room. An hour later Bottey arrived with a friend, who pretended to be a justice of the peace, and who asked why she had killed the innocent person and if possibly B. had not ordered the murder during her sleep. She answered that she was entirely unaware that B. had given her any such order; on the other hand she was convinced that, when she shot at the stranger, she was as if completely mad, and no human power could then have prevented her from committing this crime. But that persons can by positive suggestion be compelled to criminal actions is not all; by negative suggestion they can also be made to neglect their duties and to omit what they ought to do. Thus they can be prevented from writing their name, and even made to forget it, and to forget their duties, etc.; fears have even been expressed, that marriage could in this way be prevented, if, for instance, by suggestion a rival compelled a bride to say nay at the altar.

By the experiments just related and by several similar ones, it has been sufficiently proved that it is possible by hypnotism and suggestion to use others as willing tools for the execution of criminal actions of almost every kind. The danger of this is greatly increased, partly by the fact that the somnambulist, upon awaking, does not remember the contents of the suggestion nor who gave it, while at the same time it is faithfully and irresistibly performed at the appointed hour; partly that there are persons, but fortunately only those who have been hypnotized many times, who, even in an apparently entirely wakeful state are susceptible to hypnotism.

The help a judge could get from the fact that usually the memory of what has happened during one hypnosis reappears during the next, (whereby he would only need to again hypnotize the delinquent in order to draw the truth from him) can, unfortunately be neutralized by the hypnotizer by suggestive amnesia, or an order to forget all that was said during the hypnosis.

To the credit of humanity all these suggested crimes have as yet been confined to the harmless sphere of experimenting, and have hardly appeared in real life. But a judge must nevertheless be on his guard. No one knows what may happen.

4. *Is the one, who acts on account of the suggestion of others, responsible for his actions?*

Those who voluntarily submit to hypnotism are in about the same predicament as those who by alcohol or other narcotic and soporific agents—such as opium, hashish, chloral, chloroform etc.,—voluntarily put themselves into a state of bondage, where they cannot with certainty control their judgment of free will.

Though such a person should be considered as perfectly irresponsible as a natural somnambulist for the actions he executes on account of suggestion, yet if he knew of the danger of which he exposed himself in being hypnotized, and if he submitted to it voluntarily, he has fallen into mental derangement by his own actions, and is then responsible—according to Chapter V. #5 of the Swedish law, which accords impunity only to such a person as *"without any fault of his* has become mentally deranged, so that he does not know what he is doing." But there are also those who can be hypnotized without their knowledge or will, and these must be considered entirely irresponsible. The circumstance before mentioned, that the somnambulists are not so dependent as the cataleptic automatons, but can make resistance, is however so difficult to estimate in each case, that no degree of the somnambulist's responsibility can very well be based on it.

On the other hand it is fully decided that the one most to blame for the suggested crime is the hypnotizer, or the one who has given the suggestion. On him the severest punishment of the law should fall in all its rigor, if he has abused his immense power over his fellow-men.

5. *Should hypnotism be prohibited?*

Before answering this question, we will cast a rapid glance at the present relation of the law to the practice of magnetism or hypnotism in different countries.

We have already seen how Mesmer, although a regular physician, was driven out of Vienna, and with him his new remedy, magnetism. In spite of his connection with Dr. d'Eslon and many other noble patrons, in Paris also he had great difficulty in getting his new method legalized and the official report of the medical faculty, by Bailly, urged its suppression. In 1784 the chief of the Paris police received orders to put a stop to the scandals of the magnetizers. The Revolution swept away the "harmonic" (Magnetic) societies, and not until after the fall of Napoleon did they flourish again; but the public authorities did not care to make regulations for a matter which was declared by all the scientists to lack real solidity. The Paris Academy of Medicine even questioned whether it would be proper for that body to have animal magnetism investigated. However we know from Husson's report that the investigation, which lasted for five years, was both thorough and favorable. But even at that time Husson complained that the physicians had neglected to take this process into their own hands, and that instead, they had allowed impostors and secret societies to work mischief.

On the other hand, the question was treated with less prejudice in the northern countries. Figuier relates that the Emperor Alexander of Russia in 1815 ordered a committee to investigate magnetism. The committee declared magnetism to be a very important agency, but that just on that account it should be practiced only by skillful physicians. And to this end the emperor issued an ukase. In 1817, the king of Denmark signed a resolution of the board of health, which allows magnetism in medical practice, but only on the same conditions as in Russia. In the same year a royal decree was (according to Figuier) published in Sweden, which ordered that these on magnetism would have to be defended for the degree of M.D. (?) We have not as yet found this decree. In the same year (1817), the king of Prussia also signed an order that only licensed physicians would be allowed to practice magnetism, and in the next year the Berlin Academy of Sciences offered a prize of three thousand and three hundred francs for the best treatise on animal magnetism. Although the French government did not take any steps, yet many private scientists came forth to defend magnetism—such as Laplace, Cuvier, Arago, Bertrand, Georget, etc. We have already spoken of Husson's report, which in 1831 was buried in the archives of the Academy of Medicine. A new official report, hostile to Husson and magnetism was sent in 1837 to the Academy by Dubois (of Amiens), and others. The report was received with acclamation by the Academy. Nevertheless Burdin offered a prize of three thousand francs to any one who should prove that he could read without the aid of the eyes or without light. Pigeaire, a veterinary surgeon of Montpellier had a daughter Leonide, who was said to possess this power. He took her to Paris to gain the offered prize. Her seances succeeded admirably before the public, but as, at the final test, the Academy wished to provide the bandage for her eyes, and P. would not allow any other than the one she had used before, the test did not take place; and it was just as well, as Velpeau had shown that he could also read with her bandage. Another aspirant for Burdin's prize, Mlle. Emilie, was found to have copied beforehand the passages in the book which she afterwards read. A third trial, with M. Tests and his somnambulist, failed completely. That after these exhibitions the Academy should have become still more sceptical towards magnetism, is not to be wondered at. On the other hand it was too hasty a decision that the Academy now made, viz.—forever to desist from all meddling with animal magnetism, in the same way as the Academy of Sciences had then refused to have anything further to do with squaring of the circle and perpetual motion.

The negligence of the physicians had for result, that magnetism for several decades fell almost exclusively into the hands of impostors and charlatans, and although, during the last decade, the scientists have at last begun to do their duty in cultivating a field which should become fruitful to science and to the health of man, yet it would hardly be believed how many needs still remain, especially in Paris, where there are said to be about five hundred "Magnetic cabinets," so-called, where the public is cheated in the most shameful manner by professional magnetizers and somnambulists. A description of this swindle would be of great interest but it is not allowed by the limited space of this work. That legislation should seize upon and check such mischief and abuse is self-evident. Some countries have already set a good example and prohibited at least the public exhibitions of professional magnetizers—Italy, Austria and Switzerland, for instance.

It is our opinion that magnetism or hypnotism, the far-reaching effects of which on both the physical and psychical life of the human organism cannot nowadays be denied by any cultivated person, should be dealt with the legislature like deadly poisons. None but licensed physicians should be allowed to practice hypnotism. What would be said if tramps were allowed to travel round and show the power of opium, chloroform, or chloral to put persons to sleep; or the power of strychnia to make one's limbs stiff; or the power of alcohol, belladonna, hashish, etc. to produce strange visions and delirium? We are astonished that hypnotizing in public is not already prohibited in all civilized countries where the question of poisons is regulated by law. On the other hand, hypnotism should be freely allowed in the service of medical science. For its proper practice both the physician's knowledge and the moral responsibility of his position are necessary. In the hand of the physician this two-edged sword can become a great blessing, in that of others an unmitigated evil.

G. Guillain on J. M. Charcot's Life
and Work

This chapter on Charcot's role in the development of the theories of hypnosis is taken from the work of Georges Guillain, M.D., on the life and work of Charcot. We have all read about the schools of Nancy and the school of the Salpetriere and Charcot. The theories of the school of the Salpetriere were discredited by the school of Nancy. During the second International Congress on Experimental Psychology (London, 1892), they had almost ceased to attract attention. Many persons, however, still regard them as affording a satisfactory explanation of hypnotic phenomena.

The following is a summary of these theories: (1) Hypnosis is an artificially induced morbid condition; a neurosis found only in the hysterical. (2) Women are more easily influenced than men; children and old people are insusceptible. (3) Hypnosis can be produced by purely physical means; a person can be hypnotized unknown to himself. (4) Hypnotic phenomena can be induced, transferred or terminated by metals, magnets, and so forth.

Charcot argued that hypnosis and hysteria were identical because during both, the urine is similar. Charcot's subjects were all hysterical, and as the phenomena of waking life are readily induced in hypnosis, Charcot had created a type of hysteria by suggestion. It was stated by the School of Nancy that if the hysterical alone can be hypnotized, we must conclude, from the statistics of suggestibility, that at least 80 per cent of mankind suffer from hysteria.

It was at the Salpetriere school that the idea of classifying the different phases of hypnotic sleep into the lethargic, cataleptic, and somnambulistic stages originated. This classification theory was attacked by the Nancy school which pointed out the insufficiency of its data and cited the confession of one of its supporters that only a dozen cases of hypnosis had occurred in the Salpetriere in ten years (a very large proportion of the experiments had been made on one subject, an inmate of long standing at the hospital).

Charcot did little experimenting himself, and left much of the work to his assistants, failing to check their work before publishing the results. However, because of his high stature and position at that time, he had many followers who would not question his theories or his ability at hypnotizing the patients.

HYPNOTISM*

Although Charcot's work on hysteria and the neuroses had been often unfairly criticized, as I indicated in the preceding chapters, it seems, nevertheless, that his investigations on hypnotism, and metallotherapy, which were published either by him or by his collaborators, are open to justifiable criticism. This part of Charcot's work was, as Professor Pierre Marie called it, "a slight failing." I have endeavored to understand what was behind this "slight failing," a question that I shall dwell on later. Charcot has created a sufficiently imposing scientific monument so that a few imprudences of his later years would not detract in any way from the glory of his edifice. Moreover, as we shall see later, there were some attenuating circumstances that will help us to understand this "slight failing."

It seems that during a certain phase of his life Charot, although he had been the promoter of the clinicoanatomic method and had been very organic in his orientation, nevertheless had been attracted to philosophy and psychology, and to the study of the behavioral correlates of brain function. Therefore he selected, in addition to his medical interns, collaborators who belonged to philosophic disciplines. For example, he wrote: "Until the present, we have been in the habit of treating psychology lightly; it is taught in college, but this is a small superficial kind of psychology which does not serve any useful purpose. Another type of psychology must be created, a kind of psychology which is

*Grateful acknowledgment is expressed to Hoeber Medical Division, Harper & Row, Publishers, for permission to reprint in this book the chapter entitled "Hypnotism," from the publication, *J. M. Charcot, His Life—His Work*, by George Guillain, M.D.

correlated with pathophysiologic studies. We are in the process of building such a psychology with the co-operation of the psychologists, who now wish to expand their activities beyond the so-called introspective methodology of their predecessors. The psychologist of the past locked himself up in his ivory tower, studied himself from within, and made himself the subject of his own investigation. This methodology may have value, but by itself is entirely inadequate. In order to control this type of study of man by himself, we must add a more objective type of study; and in these objective studies, the pathology of the nervous system will play an important role.*"

By this route, Charcot became interested in hypnotism; he was familiar with the previous publications of †Braid (of Manchester) in 1843, Broca (1859), Azam (1860), Mesnet (1860), Lasegue (1865), Bailly (1868), Demarquay and Giraud-Teulon (1868), and Pan de Saint-Martin (1859). At this time the question of hypnotism in general was regarded with suspicion by scientists and exploited by charlatans. Nevertheless, a young physiologist, the future professor Charles Richet, published from 1875 to 1883 in the *Journal de l'Anatomie et de la Physiologie* and in the *Revue Philosophique* of Th. Ribot, a series of studies on hypnotic phenomena, in which he contended that any theory which considers hypnosis only as a prolonged form of chicanery can no longer be sustained.

Charcot* himself explained the purpose of his physiologic and clinical studies in hypnotism. I shall quote from his own text as it was drafted in his "Expose de Titres et Travaux," which was submitted for his candidacy for membership in the Academy of

---

*In 1885, the Society of Physiological Psychology was founded, of which Charcot was President, Paul Janet and Th. Ribot, Vice-Presidents, and Charles Richet, Secretary. This society was made up of physicians, philosophers, writers, and even poets such as Sully Prudhomme. It seemed that the very disciplines which made this group were so dissimilar that the society could not last for long; however, it did organize the first congress of psychology, which was held in Paris in 1889.

†Braid substituted the word "hypnotism" for "Mesmerism" or "animal magnetism," which were previously used.

*Charcot, J.M.: *Expose des Titres Scientifiques.* Paris, 1883, p. 149.

Sciences; in his text Charcot used the third person:

The investigations on hypnotism undertaken at the Salpetriere by Charcot and, under his direction, by several of his pupils, dates from the year 1878. . . . From the very beginning a prudent and conservative orientation was developed and applied to these investigations. This approach was only slightly influenced by the purely arbitrary skepticism practiced by those who, under the pretext of "purely scientific orientation," concealed a prejudice to see nothing and to hear nothing in these matters. At the same time every attempt was made to avoid being attracted by the esoteric or the extraordinary, a peril which in this scientifically unexplored field was encountered, so to speak, at every step of the way. Briefly, the method Charcot adopted for these intense physiologic, and neuropathologic studies can be summarized very simply; instead of allowing himself to be led into a pursuit of the unexpected and the mystic, he decided for the time being to attempt to analyze the meaning of the clinical signs and physiologic characteristics that can be identified among various conditions and phenomena caused by nervous reactions. He further decided to confine himself at first to an examination of the most simple and constant factors, the validity of which was the most easy to demonstrate, and only to investigate later and still with caution the more complex or evasive phenomena; and finally to omit studying systematically, except in a provisional way, those phenomena which are of a much more obscure nature and which for the moment do not appear to correlate with any known physiologic mechanisms. According to Charcot, it is largely because these very simple precautions have often been overlooked that studies of hypnotism as an experimental neurosis, which previously had been almost inaccessible, have not until now borne fruit to the extent anticipated and have not enjoyed everywhere the favorable reception that such studies should merit. Such studies, when properly prosecuted, are certainly destined to bring eventual light to a whole host of questions, not only from a pathologic standpoint but also from the standpoint of physiology and psychology.

The program that Charcot proposed was a very logical one, the methods he designed for the study of hypnotism were quite rational. It seems, however, that neither the program nor the method was ultimately followed.

In the process of hypnotizing patients, Charcot described three chronologic phases: the phase of catalepsy, the phase of lethargy, and the phase of induced somnambulism.

He emphasized the so-called somatic phenomena of the "grand hypnotisme" (deep hypnotic states), particularly the neuromuscular hyperexcitability and cataleptic plasticity. He stated that when a mechanical stimulus was applied to a muscle such as the common superficial flexor of the fingers, this muscle would contract and the fingers would become flexed so that considerable force had to be applied in order to stretch and overcome the power of the muscle contraction. Also, the mechanical excitation of a motor nerve, such as the facial, cubital, or median nerve, would cause a contraction of the muscles innervated by that nerve.

The cataleptic state, on the contrary, was characterized by a plasticity of the muscles. If a violent noise was made in front of a subject in a lethargic state or if an attempt was made suddenly to open his closed eyelids, the subject was able without effort to maintain the most varied types of posture.

Charcot demonstrated that, by giving suggestions to hypnotized subjects, they could be induced to perform posthypnotically more or less reasonable acts. They also could be cured of certain abnormal clinical manifestations.

Charcot also lectured on the influence of magnets and metals on hysteric phenomena; this was called metalloscopy and metallotherapy. For a description of these mechanisms, he relied on investigations pursued by collaborators whose competence in neurology and in psychiatry was open to question.

It is easy to understand why Charcot's lectures on hypnotism enjoyed an undeniable success. First, Charcot was a professor who possessed a unique background; second, he brought to light questions which were of interest not only to physicians but also to philosophers, writers, and to the intellectual public.

Beginning in 1882, all medical journals, philosophic and literary reviews, as well as the daily press carried articles on hypnotism. Special journals were created in France and other countries that were devoted to hypnotism (*Revue de l'Hypnotisme* de *Berrillion Zeitschrift fur Hypnotismus,* etc.).

The studies of Charcot on hypnotism and on its therapeutic effects became the target of serious criticism from the professors of the Faculty of Medicine at Nancy; these scientists placed the notions on hypnotism of the Nancy school in opposition to those of the Salpetriere.

Beginning in 1884, Professor Bernheim (of Nancy) made it known that he had for several years conducted investigations on animal magnetism with a method which he owed to Dr. Liebault (of Nancy). The Nancy approach tended to explain the phenomena of animal magnetism on the basis of psychologic principles with particular reference to the power of ideas. Bernheim said that he understood these phenomena in a way which was quite different from that of the Paris school. The investigations of Professor Bernheim* were continued in the years following with the collaboration of Beaunis, Professor of Physiology at the Faculty of Medicine and of Liegeois, Professor of Law of the Faculty of Law at Nancy. Professor Bernheim attacked the notions of Charcot, denied the existence of Charcot's three phases of hypnotism, and maintained that all these phenomena could be explained as being the results of suggestion. In an article published in 1911 he clearly formulated his ideas as follows:

"The scientists of the Nancy school conclude from their experiments that all the phenomena established at the Salpetriere, the three phases of hypnotism, the neuromuscular hyperexcitability of the lethargic phase, the special muscle spasms induced in the so-called somnambulistic phase, and the transfer of magnetism by metals would not exist if the experiments were conducted under conditions that excluded the use of suggestion. In other words, the subjects did only what they knew they should do, either because they had observed these acts performed by other subjects or because they had heard about them, or in one word because the idea of what should be done had been instilled in their brains by means of suggestion. The hypnotism of the Salpetriere is a cultist type of hypnotism."

Charcot's pupils, Paul Block and Gilles de la Tourette, however,

---

*Bernheim. *De la Suggestion et de Ses applications a la Thérapeutique.* O. Doin, editeur, Paris, 1886.

Bernheim. *Hypnotisme, Suggestion, Psychothérapie.* O. Don, editeur, Paris, 1891.

defended the hypothesis of the school at the Salpetriere. Moreover, at the request of Charcot a conference was held on June 23, 1891, at the Salpetriere under the direction of one of Charcot's most distinguished collaborators, J. Babinski*, who attacked the views of Professor Bernheim.

Professor Pierre Janet† was able to say later: "Charcot's three phases of hypnotism, as Professor Bernheim knew very well ever since 1884 and as he was the first who dared to say, was never anything but a cultists type of hypnotism; it was he (Bernheim) who won the battle."

I believe it would be interesting, both scientifically and psychologically, to cite a few lines written in 1910 by Babinski*, the neurologic scientist, who had proposed a revision of hysteria and who often had attracted attention to the malingering of patients. He wrote: "I practice my profession in good faith. I should like to say the existence of a condition that can be called 'hypnotic sleep' appears quite reasonable to me. It is notably different from all other kinds of sleep, and is susceptible to being easily simulated." With respect to the experiments conducted at the Salpetriere in which Babinski had participated, he added the following words which, since they were written by him, have an importance that cannot be underestimated: "The hypothesis that hypnotism is a vulgar hoax would necessarily mean that there was some sort of conspiracy that would require the connivance of patients who were in daily contact with charlatans. It is difficult to imagine how the secrets of such a mysterious performance could have been guarded for such a long time, without having sprung many leaks . . . Using appropriate methods, I have tried to obtain confessions from old subjects during several different interviews a long time after their discharge from the hospital,

---

*J. Babinski. Hypnotisme et hysterie. Du role de l'hypnotisme en therapeutique. *Gazette Hebdomadaire de Medecine et de Chriurgie*, Juillet 1891.

†Pierre Janet. *Les Medications Psychologiques. Etudes Historiques, Psychologiques et Cliniques sur les Methodes de la Psychotherapie.* Felix Alcan, editeur, Paris, 1919.

*Babinski, J. De l'hypnotisme en therapeutique et en medecine legale. *Semaine Medicale*, 27 Juillet 1910. In J. Babinski. *Oeuvres Scientifiques*, pp. 505-513.

when they would not have any apparent interest in deceiving me, but the results were always negative."

If Charcot's studies on hypnotism are open to criticism on several counts, they were neither useless nor without value; they retain their importance from a viewpoint of therapy and of legal medicine.

Charcot and his collaborators not infrequently used hypnotic suggestions in order to combat certain types of paralyses and other functional disorders; however, Charcot was never unaware of the eventual dangers of this method.

After Charcot's death, Babinski* did not abandon the occasional treatment of hysteric conditions by hypnosis. In 1906, he wrote; "I am of the opinion that the practice of hypnosis can be harmful; it can produce in the mind of a hypnotized subject an idea that he is unbalanced and incapable of resisting the will of another. Therefore, I find it preferable to abstain from its use as a general procedure . . . But when I find myself in the presence of a hysteric syndrome of long duration, which is intractable and has resisted the usual routine methods of treatment (Hydrotherapy, electrotherapy, isolation, etc.), or when a patient after my examination seems skeptical about the usual treatments, I willingly resort to hypnotism, which has given me, as well as many other physicians, remarkable results."

From the medical-legal point of view, Charcot's work on hypnotism has retained its importance. For example, it was common gossip that the hypnotized individual, obedient to the will of the hypnotist, was impelled posthypnotically to follow the commands suggested by the hypnotist, no matter what they were, even though they might be of a criminal nature. The experiments performed at the Salpetriere at the instigation of Charcot showed that the integrity of the psyche of patients in a state of somnambulism is not destroyed and that most patients resist suggestions that offend their consciences. Gilles de la Tourette, Pierre Janet, and Babinski emphasized these factors. Babinski said quite cor-

---

*Babinski, J. Ma conception de l'hysterie et de l'hypnotisme (Pithiatisme). *Conference Faite a la Societe de l'Internat des Hoptiaux de Paris,* seance du 28 Juin 1906. In J. Babinski. *Oeuvres Scientifiques,* pp. 465-485.

rectly that in serious situations hypnotized individuals retain control of their actions to the same degree they possessed in a conscious state. He portrayed this belief, which was the same as Charcot's as follows: "To my knowledge, a woman who would give herself to a man when hypnotized also would do so just as freely when independent of any hypnotic experience; hypnosis does not paralyze the will nor does it bestow on the hypnotizer a power to violate it. The hypnotic trance should not be considered as an excuse for committing rape."

Babinski* in addition paid deep homage to Charcot for his studies on hypnotism:

> About forty years ago, when Charcot engaged in his research, a problem was posed which was called "hypnotism," implying that the use of suggestion conferred a power to the hypnotist over the person hypnotized, a problem that intrigued many intellectuals because of its psychologic ramifications and its social consequences. Many believe that the passivity of the subject, his submission to the will of the one who has "put him to sleep," could extend to the point of forcing the hypnotized person to indulge in a carnal pleasure or even to commit a crime in a compulsive way, without having any sense of guilt, or without being bothered by any sense of responsibility. Charcot, by a series of experiments which were skillfully performed, established in peremptory fashion that the power of suggestion was limited and that even subjects who were most suggestible retained in a hypnotic state a degree of moral sense that was sufficient to resist a suggestion contrary to the moral principles of their waking lives. One need not dwell on the service that he (Charcot) rendered in rectifying an error which, if it had become widespread, could have been exploited to the detriment of society.

Charcot's work in hypnosis had an influence on later studies in psychoanalysis and narcoanalysis. Charcot recognized, in the etiology of neurosis and hysteria, the dynamic role of conscious and unconscious memories (a fire, an attempted rape, a psychic trauma, or a violent emotion). Professor Pierre Janet, who was one of Charcot's collaborators, wrote: "Charcot's lectures on the significance of the recall of traumatic experiences and my own

*Babinski, J. Eloge de J. M. Charcot, pronounce a la Sorbonne le 20 Mai, 1925. In *Revue Neurologique,* Jun 1925, I, No. 6, pp. 746-756.

studies provided the point of departure for a remarkably strong system of knowledge on the interpretation of the dynamics of the neurosis and their treatment. I am referring to the studies of Professor Freud (of Vienna) and of a number of his pupils in psychoanalysis."

Sigmund Freud* himself said that Charcot was the first to furnish a general explanation of hysteric phenomena; he put it this way: "He had the creative idea to reproduce these symptoms in an experimental way among patients by putting them in a hypnotic or a somnambulistic state. He also found that certain paralyses were the result of symbolizations which dominate the mental processes of patients having a special predisposition . . . it was because of Charcot's conceptions that Pierre Janet, Bleuler, and others were able to develop a theory of the neuroses which was acceptable to science."

As a result of the experiments performed at the Salpetriere in hypnotism, certain controversial conclusions were drawn regarding the question of malingering and the influence of suggestions made to the patients,* whether consciously or unconsciously. The Nancy school had every reason to protest as it did. However, I should like to look into the reasons behind what Professor Pierre Marie called "the slight failing" of Charcot. The causes appear to be multiple.

Charcot obviously made a mistake in not checking his experiments. Every morning he made rounds on his hospital service with exemplary regularity and a sense of duty, but, like all physicians of his generation, he did not return to his service in the afternoon. Accordingly his chiefs of clinics, his interns, and other assistants prepared the patients, hypnotized them, and organized the ex-

---

*S. Freud. Charcot. *Wiener Medizinische Wochenschrift,* 1892. Cite par H. Codet et R.

Laforgue. L'Influence de Charcot sur Freud. *Progres Medical,* 30 Mai 1925, pp. 801-802.

*In 1899, about six years after Charcot's death, I saw as a young intern at the Salpetriere the old patients of Charcot who were still hospitalized. Many of the women, who were excellent comedians, when they were offered a slight pecuniary remuneration imitated perfectly the major hysteric crises of former times.

periments. Charcot personally never hypnotized a single patient, never checked the experiments and, as a result, was not aware of their inadequacies or of the reasons of their eventual errors.

Charcot also erred when he opened his clinics on hysteria and on hypnotism not only to physicians but also to a nonmedical public.* The lectures, as I have previously stated, attracted society people, actors, writers, magistrates, and journalists. The presentation of patients in a state of lethargy, catalepsy, somnambulism, as well as patients in the process of having violent seizures, resembled more a theatrical than a scientific performance. Charcot has been justly criticized for these clinics, which were a little too spectacular.

We should take into consideration, however, the attenuating circumstances in this "slight failing" of Charcot.

The pupils and assistants of Charcot also are not free from reproach. Frequently, mingling among Charcot's chiefs of clinic and his interns were students who did not belong officially to his service but who, out of curiosity, attended the afternoon sessions on hypnotism and even suggested that certain experiments be performed. Professor Pierre Janet said that some of these clandestine students took the course in magnetism at the Palais Royal, which were given by the professional and well-known magnetizer, the Marquis de Puyfontaine, who had been introduced

---

*Axel Munthe, an English physician (a naturalized citizen; he was a native of Sweden), who lived several years in Paris, published a book (*The Story of San Michele*. New York, E.P. Dutton & Co., 1930) that enjoyed some literary success and recounts the history of his life. He writes about the Latin Quarter the Salpetriere at the time of Charcot. Chapter 18 of his book (pages 296-313) is devoted to the Salpetriere and Chapter 19 (pages 314-322) to hypnotism. Axel Munthe describes Charcot's amphitheater during his lectures on hypnotism as one filled with physicians, writers, actors, and actresses; he adds that he suspected fraud among the patients. The work of Munthe is, as far as Charcot is concerned, deprecatory. However, it would be wise to question his impartiality. As a matter of fact, as Munthe admits, he brought a hysteric to his own residence in order that he might escape from Charcot's service. Charcot on learning this called for Munthe, threatened him with police action, and had him conducted by one of his chiefs of clinic to the entrance of Salpetriere with the order that in the future he be refused entrance to the hospital. It is quite evident, therefore, that the author of this volume could have borne some resentment toward Charcot.

at the Salpetriere and had communicated with Charcot's collaborators. Many of the hysteric patients offered their services voluntarily for the experiments in order to make themselves more interesting. However, Charcot did not observe the preliminary preparations of the patients and, confident in his staff, accepted the conclusions that he was told had been obtained, even though he had advised that his presentations were taking a bizarre trend.

I cannot ignore, however, a question that has often come to my mind. Charcot had assistants of high scientific caliber, gifted with a penetrating and critical type of mind, who possessed high moral integrity. It seems to me impossible that some of them did not question the unlikelihood of certain contingencies. Why did they not put Charcot on his guard? The only explanation that I can think of, with all the reservation that it carries, is that they did not dare alert Charcot, fearing the violent reactions of the master, who was called the "Caesar" of the Salpetriere.

However, Charcot himself finally understood, even though a little late, that he was being beguiled into an uncertain terrain. Unquestionably in this respect he was influenced by his old chief of clinic and private secretary, Pierre Marie, who always refused to become identified with the experiments on hypnotism*. Charcot developed too his own doubts in the matter; at first they were vague, but later they became better defined. Shortly before his death he decided to revise his entire work on hysteria and hypnotism. But by this time he had frequent attacks of angina pectoris, and he knew that he was very ill.

Georges Guinon, †Charcot's last private secretary, wrote suggestively on this subject:

> I have some very vivid recollections of a conversation that I had with Charcot a short time before his death, a few days before his departure on that fatal journey from which he was never to return. In his office and in his house at Neuilly where he was on vacation at the moment, he spoke to me about the work planned for himself after his return. He told me that his concept of hysteria had become

---

*Oral communication made to me in 1901.
†Guinon, Georges. Charcot intime. *Paris Medical,* 23 Mai 1925, pp. 511-526.

decadent and his entire chapter on the pathology of the nervous system must be revised. Showing me a sheaf of papers on the corner of the table, he added that he had already begun to collect the essential elements for the accomplishment of this task. Consequently, several years before his pupil, Babinski, majestically took it upon himself, Charcot had foreseen the need of dismembering his theory on hysteria and was preparing himself to dynamite the edifice to which he had personally contributed so much in building. Is it not interesting that perhaps I am the only one today to be aware of this fact, which illustrates so vividly the critical turn of mind that was so characteristic of Charcot?

Hippolyte Bernheim
(1837-1919)

In France, .M. Charcot began his public classes at the School of the Salpetriere, in which he directed attention to the physical states of hystero-epileptics during hypnosis. In contrast to Charcot, Liebault (1823-1904) founded the School of Nancy and developed a psychological approach to the theory of hypnosis based on the influence of suggestion.

Dr. Bernheim, a professor at the School of Nancy, approached the subject and studied it with Liebault. He accepted Professor Liebault's views and published a book, *De La Suggestion,* in 1884. He considered that the physical phenomena produced at the Salpetriere are merely the result of suggestion. Bernheim felt that suggestion was the sole agent and then followed the contest between the Schools of Charcot and of Nancy, which is still unsettled as to the correct interpretation of the problem.

SUGGESTIVE THERAPEUTICS*

Manner of hypnotizing. — Sleep and hypnotic influence. — Variable sensitiveness of subjects. — Classification of the various degrees of sleep according to M. Liebault: — 1st. Drowsiness; — 2d. Suggestive catalepsy; — 3d. Rotatory automatism — 4th. Auditory relation of subject with the operator only; — 5th. Light somnambulism; — 6th. Deep somnambulism. Author's classification: A. — Memory preserved on waking: 1st. Suggestibility to certain acts only. 2d. Inability to open eyes. 3d. Suggestive catalepsy liable to be broken. 4th. Irresistible catalepsy. 5th. Suggestive contraction. 6th. Automatic obedience. B. — Memory lost on waking, or Somnambulism. 7th. Without susceptibility to hallucinations. 8th. Susceptibility to hallucinations during sleep. 9th. Susceptibility to hypnotic and post-hypnotic hallucinations. Varieties: — Suggestion without sleep. Definition of hypnotism — Of fascination: — Of waking — Proportion of subjects susceptible to hypnotism.

I proceed to hypnotize in the following manner.

I begin by saying to the patient that I believe benefit is to be

---

*From Bernheim, H.M.: *De la Suggestion et de Ses Applications a La Thérapeutique.* Second edition revised and augmented (Octave Doin, Ed.). Paris, 1888, Vol. 1, pp. 1-29.

derived from the use of suggestive therapeutics, that it is possible to cure or to relieve him by hypnotism; that there is nothing either hurtful or strange about it; that it is an ordinary sleep or torpor which can be induced in everyone, and that this quiet, beneficial condition restores the equilibrium of the nervous system, etc. If necessary, I hypnotize one or two subjects in his presence, in order to show him that there is nothing painful in this condition and that it is not accompanied with any unusual sensation. When I have thus banished from his mind the idea of magnetism and the somewhat mysterious fear that attaches to that unknown condition, above all when he has seen patients cured or benefited by the means in question, he is no longer suspicious, but gives himself up, then I say, "Look at me and think of nothing but sleep. Your eyelids begin to feel heavy, your eyes tired. They begin to wink, they are getting moist, you cannot see distinctly. They are closed." Some patients close their eyes and are asleep immediately. With others, I have to repeat, lay more stress on what I say, and even make gestures. It makes little difference what sort of gesture is made. I hold two fingers of my right hand before the patient's eyes and ask him to look at them, or pass both hands several times before his eyes, or persuade him to fix his eyes upon mine, endeavoring, at the same time, to concentrate his attention upon the idea of sleep. I say, "Your lids are closing, you cannot open them again. Your arms feel heavy, so do your legs. You cannot feel anything. Your hands are motionless. You see nothing, you are going to sleep." And I add in a commanding tone, "Sleep." This word often turns the balance. The eyes close and the patient sleeps or is at least influenced.

I use the word sleep, in order to obtain as far as possible over the patients, a suggestive influence which shall bring about sleep or a state closely approaching it; for sleep properly so called, does not always occur. If the patients have no inclination to sleep and show no drowsiness, I take care to say that sleep is not essential; that the hypnotic influence, whence comes the benefit, may exist without sleep; that many patients are hypnotized although they do not sleep.

If the patient does not shut his eyes or keep them shut, I do not require them to be fixed on mine, or on my fingers, for any length of time, for it sometimes happens that they remain wide open indefinitely, and instead of the idea of sleep being conceived, only a rigid fixation of the eyes results. In this case, closure of the eyes by the operator succeeds better. After keeping them fixed one or two minutes, I push the eyelids down, or, stretch them slowly over the eyes, gradually closing them more and more and so imitating the process of natural sleep. Finally I keep them closed, repeating the suggestion, "Your lids are stuck together; you cannot open them. The need of sleep becomes greater and greater, you can no longer resist." I lower my voice gradually, repeating the command, "Sleep," and it is very seldom that more than three minutes pass before sleep or some degree of hypnotic influence is obtained. It is sleep by suggestion,—a type of sleep which I insinuate into the brain.

Passes or gazing at the eyes or fingers of the operator, are only useful in concentrating the attention. They are not absolutely essential.

As soon as they are able to pay attention and understand, children are as a rule very quickly and very easily hypnotized. It often suffices to close their eyes, to hold them shut a few moments, to tell them to sleep, and then to state that they are asleep.

Some adults go to sleep just as readily by simple closure of the eyes. I often proceed immediately without making use of passes or fixation, by shutting the eyelids, gently holding them closed, asking the patient to keep them together, and suggesting at the same time, the phenomena of sleep. Some of them fall rapidly into a more or less deep sleep.

Others offer more resistance. I sometimes succeed by keeping the eyes closed for some time, commanding silence and quiet, talking continuously, and repeating the same formulas; "You feel a sort of drowsiness, a torpor; your arms and legs are motionless. Your eyelids are warm. Your nervous system is quiet; you have no will. Your eyes remain closed. Sleep is coming, etc." After keeping up this auditory suggestion for several minutes, I remove my fingers. The eyes remain closed. I raise the patient's arms;

they remain uplifted. We have induced cataleptic sleep.

Others are more rebellious, preoccupied, unable to give themselves up: they analyze their own feelings, are anxious, and say they cannot sleep. I command them to be calm. I speak only of drowsiness, of sleepiness. "That is sufficient," I say, "to gain a result. The suggestion along may be beneficial even without sleep. Keep perfectly quiet and do not worry." When a patient is in this frame of mind, I do not try to get cataleptiform effects, because, being only drowsy yet always awake, always apt to regain full consciousness, he is easily roused out of this state. Sometimes then, satisfied with a doubtful state of somnolence, and without wishing to prove if the patient is really influenced, I leave him to himself, asking him to remain in this condition for some time. Some remain under this influence for a long period without being able to say whether they have done so voluntarily or involuntarily. Generally during the second or third seance I succeed by means of this suggestive education which the patient has had, in inducing a more advanced stage of hypnotic influence which is no longer doubtful but accompanied with suggestive catalepsy or even with somnambulism.

Whilst with some patients success is more readily obtained by acting quietly, with others quiet suggestion has no effect. With these, it is better to be abrupt, to restrain with an authoritative voice the inclination to laugh, or the weak and involuntary resistance which this manoeuvre may provoke.

Many persons, as above stated, are influenced at the very first seance, others not until the second or third. After being hypnotized once or twice, they are speedily influenced. It is often enough to look at such patients, to spread the fingers before the eyes, to say, "Sleep," and in a second or two, sometimes instantly, the eyes close and all the phenomena of sleep are present. It is only after a certain number of seances, generally a small number, that the patients acquire the aptitude for going to sleep quickly.

It occasionally happens that I influence seven or eight persons successively, and almost instantly. Then there are others who are refractory or more difficult to influence. I only try for a few minutes. A second or third seance often brings the hypnosis which is not obtained at first.

Patients in whom hypnotic suggestibility is very well developed, fall asleep, however slight may be the idea of sleep that is given them. They can be hypnotized by correspondence,—for example, by assuring them that as soon as they have read a letter they will fall asleep. They can be hypnotized by means of the telephone, as M. Liegeois has shown. No matter what voice conveys the suggestion it produces its effect.

Some people can be hypnotized with chloroform before they are really under its influence. All surgeons have seen patients go to sleep suddenly without any period of excitement, after a few breaths of the anaesthetic and before it certainly has done its work. I have noticed this fact in some of my own patients whom I have chloroformed in the presence of the dentist in order that a tooth might be extracted. Profiting by this observation, each time I use chloroform I take care to suggest to the patient before he has taken the first inspiration that he will fall asleep quietly and quickly. In some cases the hypnotic sleep thus comes before the anaesthesia. If it is deep enough to cause complete anaesthesia, as I have seen it, the operation can be performed without delay; if not, I keep on giving chloroform until the anaesthesia is complete, which takes place more rapidly, because aided by suggestion. By acting in this manner, I also prevent the period of excitement in these cases.

It is wrong to believe that the subjects influenced are all weak-nerved, weak-brained, hysterical, or women. Most of my observations relate to men, whom I have chosen on purpose to controvert this belief. Without doubt, impressionability varies. Common people, those of gentle disposition, old soldiers, artisans, people accustomed to passive obedience, have seemed to me, as well as to M. Liebault, more ready to receive the suggestion than preoccupied people, and those who often unconsciously oppose a certain mental resistance. Cases of insanity, melancholia, and hypochondria are often difficult or impossible to influence. The idea of being hypnotized must be present; the patient must submit entirely to the hypnotizer, using no cerebral resistance; then, I repeat, experience shows that a very large majority of people are easily influenced.

I have hypnotized very intelligent people belonging to the higher grades of society, who were not in the least nervous, at any rate in the sense in which that word is commonly used. Doubtless, it is often impossible to influence people who make it a point of honor to show that they cannot be hypnotized, that they have minds better balanced than others, and that they are not susceptible to suggestion, because such persons do not know how to put themselves into the psychical state necessary to realize the suggestion. They refuse to accept it, consciously or unconsciously; in fact they oppose a kind of counter-suggestion.

The degree of influence produced varies according to the subject. The following is the classification of the various degrees proposed by M. Liebault.

Some subjects experience only a more or less pronounced dulness, a heaviness in the lids, and sleepiness. This occurs in the smallest number of cases; it is the first degree of M. Liebault. This sleepiness may vanish as soon as the operator's influence is withdrawn. In some cases it lasts for several minutes, in others longer, an hour, for instance. Some subjects remain motionless. Others move a little, and change their position, but still remain sleepy. At the following seances, this condition may pass to a more advanced degree, though often one cannot go beyond that first attained. For example, in the case of a woman, I induced more than a hundred times a sleepiness lasting from half an hour to an hour, but only this somnolence of the first degree.

In some cases, somnolence, properly so-called, cannot be induced, but the eyelids remain closed and the patients cannot open them. They speak, answer questions, and assert that they are not asleep, but I say, "You cannot open your eyes." They make fruitless efforts to do so. The lids are as if cataleptic. It has seemed to me, though I cannot state it as a fact, that this form of hypnotism is more frequent in women than in men. One woman made strange efforts to open her eyelids. She laughed and spoke fluently. I repeated, "Try to open them." She used all her force of will without succeeding, until I brought the charm to an end by saying, "You may open them."

I consider this also a variety of the first degree.

In the second degree, the patients keep their eyes closed. Their limbs are relaxed, they hear everything that is said to them as well as what is said around them, but they remain subject to the inclination to sleep. Their brain is in the condition called by magnetizers, hypotaxic, or charmed.

This degree is characterized by suggestive catalepsy.

By this word the following phenomenon is meant. If, as soon as the patient falls asleep, the limbs being relaxed, I lift his arm, it stays up; if I lift his leg, it remains uplifted. The limbs passively retain the positions in which they are placed. We call this suggestive catalepsy, because it is easy to recognize that it is purely psychical, bound up in the passive condition of the patient, who automatically keeps the attitude given just as he keeps the idea received. In fact, in the same or in different patients, one sees the phenomenon more or less marked according to the depth of the hypnotic influence and the psychical receptivity. At first, this cataleptiform condition is hardly apparent. The lifted limb remains up a few seconds, but falls down afterward with a certain hesitancy; or the fore-arm only remains lifted. If one wishes to lift up the whole arm, it falls down again. The individual fingers do not keep positions into which they are put, but the entire hand and the fore-arm remain fixed.

With some patients, for example, if one arm be quickly raised and let alone, it falls back again, but if it is held up for a few seconds to fix the idea of the attitude in the brain, so the speak, then it remains up.

Finally, with others, catalepsy is only obtained through a formulated verbal suggestion. The person hypnotized has to be told, "Your arms remain up. Your legs are up." Then only do they remain so. Some keep the new position passively, if nothing is said to them, but if they are dared to change it they regain consciousness, so to speak, call upon their dull will power, and drop the limb. Then they often wake up. These cases constitute the intermediate phases between the first and second degrees.

Most cases, on the contrary, in spite of every effort cannot alter the attitude impressed upon them.

The progressive development of suggestibility can thus be traced by the special phase of the cataleptiform condition. In a vast number of cases this condition is very pronounced from the first. After a patient has been hypnotized for the first time, the limbs keep the position imposed without the necessity of formulated suggestion. They remain fixed, sometimes as long as the hypnotic condition lasts, sometimes falling down again slowly, gradually, at the end of a few minutes, a quarter of an hour, half an hour, or a still longer period.

On waking again, some patients who have not gone beyond the second degree, imagine that they have not been asleep because they remember everything they have heard. They believe that they have been influenced from a wish to be obliging, but if the experiment is repeated, suggestive catalepsy again appears. If this is not sleep, it is at least a peculiar psychical condition which diminishes the force of cerebral resistance, and which renders the mind receptive to suggestion.

In the third degree the drowsiness is more pronounced. Tactile sensibility is diminished or destroyed. Aside from suggestive catalepsy, the patient is capable of making automatic movements. I move both arms, one about the other. I say, "You cannot stop." The arms keep up the rotation for a longer or shorter time or indefinitely. The patient hears everything that is said around him.

In some cases this automatic rotation follows the impulse given to the arms. The verbal suggestion is not necessary. In cases of this degree, suggestive contracture can also be brought about.

The fourth degree is characterized, in addition to the preceding phenomena, by the loss of relationship with the outer world. The patients hears what the operator says, but not what the others around him say. His senses are only in communication with the operator. They are, however, susceptible of being put into relationship with any one.

The fifth and sixth degrees—characterized according to M. Liebault, by forgetfulness, upon waking, of all that has happened during sleep—constitute somnambulism. The fifth degree is light somnambulism. The patients still remember in a vague sort of way. They have heard some things confusedly; certain memories awake spontaneously. Destruction of sensibility, suggestive catalepsy, automatic movements, hallucinations caused by suggestion, —all these phenomena of which we shall speak later in greater detail, reach their greatest expression.

In deep somnambulism, or the sixth degree, the remembrance of all that has happened during the sleep is absolutely destroyed and cannot revive spontaneously.

We shall see later that these memories can always be revived artificially.

The patient remains asleep according to the operator's will, becoming a perfect automaton, obedient to all his commands.

This division of hypnotic sleep into several degrees, is purely theoretical. It permits us to classify each patient influenced, without making a long description necessary. There are variations and cases intermediary between the several degrees. All possible transitions may be noticed from simple drowsiness and doubtful sleep to the deepest somnambulism.

I add that docility to suggestion and the ease with which diverse phenomena are provoked, are not always in proportion to the depth of the hypnotic sleep. Certain patients sleep lightly, answer questions, remember everything upon waking. Nevertheless, contracture, insensibility, automatic movements, ordered or communicated, therapeutical suggestions, succeed well with them. This will be easy to understand when I have spoken of suggestion in the waking condition.

Others, on the contrary, fall into a deep, heavy sleep and remember absolutely nothing upon waking. While they are asleep they can be questioned in vain,—tormented with questions, yet they remain inert. Suggestive catalepsy is very difficult to induce in these cases. The arms are held up only for a short time. Suggestions, actions, illusions, hallucinations, commands to be carried out upon waking, are not realized; we might suppose they are not in relation with the operator; however, it is enough to pronounce the word, "awake," for them to wake spontaneously;—an evident proof that this relationship does exist. In several cases where sleep was such as I have just described, I have obtained immediate therapeutic effects through auditory suggestion. Return of sensibility, disappearance of melancholy, increase in muscular strength measured by the dynamometer, prove that in spite of their apparent inertia, they have been in relationship with me during the sleep.

Others, finally, answer all questions, speak fluently, and appear wide awake, except that the eyes are closed. They are not cataleptic or only slightly so. Neither hallucinations nor illusions can be provoked in them, but nevertheless on waking, amnesia is complete.

Each sleeper has, so to speak, his own individuality, his own special personality. I only wish to emphasize that the aptitude for realizing suggestive phenomena is not always proportional to the depth of the sleep.

Such is the classification of the various degrees of induced sleep as pointed out to my be Dr. Liebault and published in the first edition of this book. I have, indeed, been able to confirm the truth of the facts so well observed by my colleague.

I believe, however, that it is interesting to consider these facts from a wider point of view, and to give to the word hypnotism a more extended meaning than that of induced sleep.

The observations I am about to make, far from striking a blow at M. Liebault's idea, really go to confirm it, by showing that suggestion is the key-stone of the arch of all hypnotic manifestations.

In the first place, investigation reveals the following:

Some patients influenced by hypnotism, have no recollection of what has passed as soon as they return to their normal condition. Everything is a dead letter. This is the first category.

Others retain a vague or incomplete memory. Certain facts remain, others are obliterated. Some have heard talking, but do not remember what has been said; or, they have heard the remarks of the operator, but not those of others. This is the second category.

Finally, others remember everything that has occurred. Among these, some are conscious of being stupid, drowsy, or sleepy, and yet they may have heard everything, but were not able to make any movements, and could not throw off their drowsiness. Others have no consciousness of drowsiness. They say that they have been aware of all that was going on, and that their minds are alive to all that has been said and done. They say they have not slept and in fact, the particular condition in which they have been, could not be called sleep; at least, nothing proved that there has been a real sleep. These different conditions constitute the third category.

It is with patients of the first category, with those who have lost all memory, or nearly all, upon waking, that the induced hypnotic phenomena are the most numerous and the most pronounced; that is to say, with these cases suggestibility is most marked. In them catalepsy, automatic movements, analgesia, sensorial illusions, hypnotic hallucinations, and occasionally even post-hypnotic hallucinations can often be determined. Nevertheless, this is not constant.

I have seen patients (I record an example later) sleep quite deeply, or at least be so profoundly influenced as to have all memory destroyed upon waking; nevertheless, neither catalepsy, anaesthesia, nor hallucinations could be induced. Amnesia upon waking was the only symptom which appeared to indicate this sleep, although some of these subjects could speak fluently while in the hypnotic condition.

On the other hand, I have seen patients in whom catalepsy, anaesthesia, and hallucinations could be induced while they (the subjects) were in the hypnotic condition and who, upon returning to their normal state, retained the recollection of everything. But such cases constitute a minority. As a rule, suggestibility is more decided if there is amnesia upon waking.

All patients who are hypnotized do not sleep. In some cases sleep is only partial, or doubtful. I also believe that it is better, in order to get a true conception of the phenomenon, to use the words, hypnotic influence, instead of hypnotic sleep, and to say that this influence manifests itself in different patients by symptoms varying according to the degree and individual way in which they are influenced by suggestion. From this point of view each patient represents a special individuality with regard to suggestion, and the number of divisions or degrees corresponding to the diverse hypnotic influences can be multipled indefinitely.

In order to fix the ideas by a slightly schematic classification but embracing the majority of the facts, I shall adopt the following division of the different degrees of the hypnotic condition.

First Degree.—The patient does not exhibit catalepsy, anaesthesia, hallucinations, nor sleep, properly so-called. He says he has not slept, or that he has been only more or less drowsy. If sleep is suggested to him, he is content to remain with his eyes closed. He must not be dared to open his eyes, however, because then he opens them. The influence obtained may appear as naught or as doubtful, yet it exists; because if neither sleep, catalepsy, nor any other manifestations may be provoked, suggestibility can nevertheless assert itself through other influences. For example, a suggestion of heat on a determined part of the body may be induced, certain pains may be destroyed, and evident therapeautic effects may be obtained.

I have succeeded in some cases, to all appearance refractory, in inducing all the regular manifestations of hypnotism, by suggestion, causing pains of a muscular or inveterate nervous character to disappear,—evident proof that suggestibility exists for certain organic activities.

Second Degree.—The patient has the same appearance as in the preceding degree and present the same negative symptoms. If sleep is suggested, he remains with his eyes closed without really sleeping, or is only drowsy; but he differs from the subjects of the preceding degree in that he cannot open his eyes spontaneously if he is dared to do so. Here the influence is evident.

Third Degree.—The patient is susceptible to suggestive catalepsy whether the eyes are open or shut and whether he is drowsy or wakeful. As we have already stated, this catalepsy varies in intensity. In the degree of which we are speaking, the patient retains the position induced or suggested, unless challenged to alter it. If he is challenged, he regains consciousness, so to speak, and succeeds in changing his position by an effort of the will. To a superficial observer the influence may appear doubtful, but this is no longer the case, if, upon repeating the experiment, it is shown that the patient keeps his passive position from inertia, so long as his dormant will is not roused.

Fourth Degree.—In this degree, the suggestive catalepsy is more pronounced and resists all efforts on the part of the subject to break it. The influence is evident. The subject may be convinced that he is influenced by showing him that he cannot alter the position induced.

Besides this, suggestive catalepsy and automatic rotatory movement in the upper extremities may sometimes be induced, which may continue for a long time. In some cases this motion is obtained by simply communicating the impulse. In others, verbal suggestion is necessary to continue the movement. As in catalepsy, some patients succeed in checking the motion by an effort of the will if they are dared to do so; others do not succeed in spite of all effort.

Fifth Degree.—In addition to the cataleptiform condition, accompanied or unaccompanied by automatic movements, contractures varying in degree may be induced by suggestion. The patient is dared to bend his arm, to open his hand, to open or shut his mouth, and he cannot do it.

Sixth Degree.—The patient exhibits moreover a more or less marked docility, or automatic obedience. Though inert and passive if left to himself, he rises at a suggestion, walks, stands still if ordered, and remains fixed to a spot when told that he cannot advance.

As in the preceding degrees, he is susceptible neither to sensorial illusions nor to hallucinations.

The subjects in these different categories remember everything upon waking. Some, however, are conscious of having slept. They remain inert, passive, without spontaneity and without initiative. This is the case of such a degree, that they cannot be roused from their torpid state until the intellectual initiative regains the upper hand, and they come out of the condition spontaneously. Some do not know whether they have really slept, and others positively state that they have not been asleep. But in cases included under the last three degrees, the patients can be convinced that, if they have not slept, they have been at least influenced.

Between a perfectly conscious condition and deep sleep all transitions exist. It is certain that in many subjects belonging to these different categories, intelligence and sensibility remain active during the hypnosis. Others have only certain symptoms of the sleep: the lack on initiative, inertia, sensation of drowsiness and the closed eyelids, or their minds reacting to the operator whom they answer and obey, seem uninfluenced by other people whom they do not appear to hear, and to whose questions they give no answers.

It is often difficult to penetrate the psychical condition of the subjects hypnotized. Observation requires nicety, and analysis is subtle. Some cases are doubtful, simulation is possible and easy, and it is still easier to believe in simulation where it does not exist. Certain subjects, for example, keep their eyes closed while the operatior is hypnotizing them. When he ceases to look at them, their eyes open, and close quickly when he again fixes his gaze upon them. There is every appearance of deceit. The assistants believe it is a fraud. They pity the operator's naive credulity and think the subject is deceitful, or that he is acting to oblige the operator.

This occurs daily in the presence of my pupils. I show them, however, that the subject is not deceiving me, and that I am not imposed upon, by hypnotizing him again and inducing catalepsy or contracture out of which I challenge him to come, requesting him at the same time, not to think of obliging any-one.

This tendency which certain subjects have to open their eyes again, and come out of their inertia as soon as the operator ceases to influence and watch them, this apparent pretending which is especially frequent in children, exists even in certain somnambulists, and one would swear that deception had been practised in these cases. Nevertheless the subjects remember nothing upon waking.

The majority of patients, however, remain with eyes closed for some time, apparently or actually asleep. They only open their eyes after the influence has worn off or when they are told to awake.

Considering these facts, I cannot repeat too often that the hypnotized subject is not a lifeless corpse or a body in a state of lethargy, for even though he is inert he hears, is conscious, and often shows signs of life. We may see him laugh or try to smother a laugh. He may remark upon his condition. He sometimes pretends that he is cheating or that he is trying to be obliging. Behind the doctor's back he boasts in good faith that he has not slept but has only pretended to sleep. He is not always aware that he is unable to pretend and that his disposition to oblige is forced upon him, and is due to a weakening of will or of his power of resistance. The majority, however, finally become aware of this want of power. They feel that they are influenced. They are conscious of having slept even when memory is preserved upon waking.

In the degrees of which I shall now speak there is no longer any uncertainty as to the hypnotic influence, for there is amnesia upon waking which is sometimes complete, sometimes partial.

The subject remembers imperfectly. He knows that he has heard voices but does not know what has been said. He recalls some things. Other incidents of his hypnotic life are obliterated. These degrees of hypnotism in which memory is destroyed upon waking, we call somnambulism. In certain cases, somnambulism lasts only during particular moments of the hypnosis. Here there is sleep; if by sleep we mean that condition of the mind which leaves behind it forgetfulness of all that has occurred during its existence. It is in this somnambulistic condition that we find subjects susceptible to hallucinations, analgesia, and suggestions of acts. Suggestibility here reaches its highest development. There are many variations however in this condition.

Seventh Degree. —Cases in which there is amnesia upon waking, but in which hallucinations cannot be induced, I consider as belonging to this degree. Almost all somnambulistic subjects in this degree are susceptible to catalepsy, contractions, automatic movements and automatic obedience. One or the other of these phenomena, however, may be wanting. Sometimes all are absent, but this is exceptional, as we have said. Amnesia upon waking is the only symptom characteristic of somnambulism. The eyes may be open or shut in this as in the following condition.

Eighth Degree. —There is amnesia upon waking as well as a great number of the phenomena observed in the preceding degrees. Susceptibility to hallucination during sleep is increased, but post-hypnotic hallucinations cannot be induced.

Ninth Degree. —Amnesia upon waking with the possibility of inducing hypnotic and post-hypnotic hallucinations.

These hallucinations are more or less complete and distinct. They may succeed with certain senses; for example, the olfactory and auditory, but not with others, as the visual. In many cases all the most complex hallucinations are perfectly carried out. Many more phases could be mentioned, according to the power of mental representation, which in each subject calls forth images with greater or less clearness and vividness.

More or less complete suggestive anaesthesia or analgesia may be met with in all degrees of hypnotism. It is generally more frequent and more pronounced in instances of the degrees last mentioned; those in which there is deep somnambulism and where there is great aptitude for hallucinations.

By stating the facts in this way I believe I come nearer the truth. Hypnotism manifests itself in different subjects in different ways. There may be simply drowsiness, or other induced. sensations, as heat, pricking, etc. This is the lightest influence. We have more marked effects when suggestion affects motility; develops the cataleptic condition, the inability to move, contraction and automatic movements. It is still more decided when it affects the will and causes automatic obedience. All these manifestations of motion, will, and even sensibility can be affected by suggestion with or without sleep, and even when it is powerless to induce sleep. In a more intense degree, suggestion produces sleep or an illusion of sleep. The subject convinced that he is sleeping, does not remember anything upon waking. In general, the more advanced degrees of suggestion affect the sensorial and sensory spheres — memory and imagination.

Illusion may be created and destroyed, and the imagination may call forth the most varied memory pictures.

I insist upon the fact that all or some of these suggestions may be realized with or without sleep. Other suggestions may succeed where that of sleep itself remains useless, for the sleep is also nothing but a suggestion. It is not possible in all cases, and it is not necessary in cases of good somnambulism in order to obtain the most diverse phenomena. They can be dissociated, so to speak, from sleep. Catalepsy, paralysis, anaesthesia, and the most complex hallucinations may be realized in many cases without the necessity of preceding these phenomena by sleep. Susceptibility to suggestion occurs in the waking state.

To define hypnotism as induced sleep, is to give a too narrow meaning to the word, —to overlook the many phenomena which suggestion can bring about independently of sleep. I define hypnotism as the induction of a peculiar psychical condition which increases the susceptibility to suggestion. Often, it is true, the sleep that may be induced facilitates suggestion, but it is not the necessary preliminary. It is suggestion that rules hypnotism.

I have tried to show that suggested sleep differs in no respect from natural sleep. The same phenomena of suggestion can be obtained in natural sleep, if one succeeds in putting one's self into relationship with the sleeping person without waking him.

This new idea which I propose concerning the hypnotic influence, this wider definition given to the word hypnotism, permits us to include in the same class of phenomena all the various methods which, acting upon imagination, induce the psychical condition of exalted susceptibility to suggestion with or without sleep.

Such is the case, for example, with fascination induced by a brilliant object, or by the gaze. The latter form of fascination, used for the first time by Donato, has since been described by Bremaud. I have also seen it applied by Hansen. Donato, who operates especially upon young people, proceeds in the following manner. He asks the subject to lay the palms of his hands upon his own, stretched our horizontally, and to press downward with all his might. The subject's whole attention and all his physical force are absorbed in this manoevre. All his innervation, so to speak, is concentrated in this muscular effort, and so the distraction of his thoughts is prevented. "The magnetizer" says Bremaud, according to Donato, "look at him sharply, quickly, and closely, directing him by gesture (and by word, if need be) to look at him as fixedly as he is able. Then the operator recedes or walks around the patient, keeping his eyes fixed upon him and attracting his gaze, while the subject follows him as if fascinated, with his eyes wide open, and unable to take them from the operator's face. If once carried away by the first experiment, the simple fixation of the gaze suffices to make the subject follow. It is no longer necessary to make him first place his hand on the operator's."

Here we have to do with simple suggestion by gesture. When the magnetizer fixes his eyes upon the subject's, the latter understands that he must keep his eyes fixed and must follow the operator everywhere. He believes that he is drawn toward him. It is a suggestive psychical fascination and not physical in the least. I have seen the experiment unsuccessful with the best somnambulists when they did not understand the meaning of the operator's gesture. In such cases, the experiment may be made to succeed by imitation, if the subject has seen it performed successfully in his presence upon someone else. This then is suggestion by imitation.

Among subjects thus fascinated, some submit to the influence without sleep, just as those do who are hypnotized by another method. They are susceptible to suggestions in the waking condition. They remember afterward what they have done; they do not know why they were unable to keep from following and gazing at the operator. Others remember nothing at all after they are waked by blowing upon the eyes or by a simple word. They do not know what has happened, they have been in a somnambulistic condition with their eyes open. In this somnambulistic fascination, catalepsy and hallucinations may be induced. In these same subjects, catalepsy or hallucination may often be induced by a simple word, a gesture, or a position communicated to them without any previous fascination.

Fascination, then, does not exist as a special condition. It is always hypnosis, that is to say, an exalted susceptibility to suggestion induced by an influence exercised over the subject's imagination. Whether this influence reaches the sensorium through eye, speech, or touch, etc., the psychical condition obtained is always the same. It is always a susceptibility to suggestion which varies in degree in different individuals, and this degree depends less upon the method employed than upon the special impressionability of the subject.

The awaking may be spontaneous. Subjects who sleep lightly at the first seance, sometimes have a tendency to awake quickly. It is necessary to hold their eyelids closed, or to say from time to time, "sleep," in order to keep them under the charm. The habit of sleep is very soon acquired by the organism. The subject no longer wakes while the operator remains at his side; he may awake as soon as the operator's influence is withdrawn. The majority of subjects left to themselves sleep on for several minutes, for half an hour, or even for one or more hours. I allowed one of my subjects to sleep fifteen hours, another eighteen.

In order to awake the subject immediately, I use verbal suggestion, in the same manner as when sleep is to be induced. I say "It is over; wake up," and this suffices, even when uttered in a low voice, to awake subjects who have already been hypnotized several times, immediately.

In some cases it is necessary to add, "Your eyes are opening; you are awake." If that is not enough, blowing once or twice on the eyes causes the subject to wake. I have never had to resort to other methods, such as sprinkling cold water on the subjects. The awaking has always been easy.

At times there is nothing so strange as this awaking. The subject is in deep sleep. I question him and he answers. If he is naturally a good talker, he will speak fluently. In the midst of his conversation I suddenly say, "Wake up." He opens his eyes, and has absolutely no rememberance of what has happened. He does not remember having spoken to me, though he was speaking, perhaps, but one tenth of a second, before waking. In order to make the phenomenon more striking, I sometimes wake a patient in the following way. "Count up to ten. When you say ten aloud, you will be awake." The moment he says ten, his eyes open; but he does not remember having counted. Again I say, "You are going to count up to ten. When you get to six you will wake up, but you will keep on counting aloud up to ten. When he utters the word six, he opens his eyes but keeps on counting. When he has finished I say, "Why are you counting?" He no longer remembers that he has been counting. I have repeated this experiment many times with very intelligent people.

It is necessary to proceed cautiously with certain hysterical subjects, avoiding touching painful points, and exciting the hysterogenic zones, lest an hysterical crisis be produced. The hypnotic sleep may in this way give place to hysterical sleep, and the operator is then no longer in relationship with the subject. Suggestion has then no effect.

Some subjects remain sleepy when they wake up. If the operator waves his hand once or twice before the eyes, he may dispel this drowsiness. Others complain of heaviness in the head, and of a dull headache or of dizziness. In order to prevent these various sensations say to the subject before waking him, "You are going to wake up, and you will be perfectly comfortable; your head is not heavy, you feel perfectly well," and he awakes without any disagreeable sensation.

Some subjects can be awakened by suggestion after a specified time. It is enough to say, "You will awake in five minutes." They wake precisely at the moment suggested. They have a correct idea of time. Some subjects have no accurate idea of time and awake before the moment suggested. Some too, forget to awake. They remain in the passive condition and appear unable to come out of it spontaneously. It is necessary to say, "Wake up" in order to have them do so.

Many subjects upon waking rub their eyes, look wildly about, and are conscious of having slept deeply. Others open their eyes suddenly, not remembering what has passed, and do not know that they have been asleep. They are like epileptic patients who have been unconscious and ignore the void which has come into their state of normal consciousness. "Have you slept?"—"I do not know, I ought to believe it if you say so." Or, they are convinced that nothing abnormal has happened to them, and deny that they have been influenced.

The following table, made from a considerable number of cases and presented to M. Dumont by M. Liebault, gives an idea of the proportion of patients of all ages, of both sexes, and of all temperaments subdivided into the different categories of sleep.

YEAR 1880 1012 PERSONS HYPNOTIZED.

Refractory	27	Very deep sleep	230
Somnolence, heaviness	33	Light somnambulism	31
Light sleep	100	Deep somnambulism	131
Deep sleep	460		

It is doubtless necessary to take account of the fact that M. Liebault operates chiefly upon the common people who come to him to be hypnotized and who, convinced of his magnetic power show greater cerebral docility than more intelligent people. Perhaps the number of cases influenced would be less without these favorable and predisposing conditions. I have been able to prove, however, that refractory subjects constitute a small minority, and I succeed in hypnotizing subjects at the first seance daily who come to my office with no idea what the hypnotic sleep is.

According to this statistical table and another, also covering a year's time, prepared by M. Liebault and mentioned by M. Beaunis, the number of somnambulists in one hundred subjects chosen at random may be considered as from fifteen to eighteen.

Persons who can be hypnotized, and who, when they wake, have no recollection of what has happened during their sleep, we call somnambulists. It seems to me that this proportion may be considerably increased if the sleeping subject is told, "When you wake, you will remember nothing." In a certain number of cases, amnesia is thus produced by suggestion.

From this same table of M. Beaunis, it appears that the proportions of subjects that can be hypnotized are about the same in men as in women, and particularly that the proportion is nearly the same as regards somnambulism, contrary to current opinion.

18, 8 per cent. in men; 19, 4 per cent. in women.

The following table, prepared by M. Beaunis from the above mentioned statistics, shows the percentage of subjects exhibiting the different degrees of sleep at different periods of life.

AGE	Somnam-bulism	Very Deep Sleep	Deep Sleep	Light Sleep	Sommo-lence	No Influ-ence
Up to 7 years	26,5	4,3	13	52,1	4,3	
From 7 to 14 years	55,3	7,6	23	13,8		
From 14 to 21 years	25,2	5,7	44,8	5,7	8	10,3
From 21 to 28 years	13,2	5,1	36,7	18,3	17,3	9,1
From 28 to 35 years	22,6	5,9	34,5	22,6	13	5,9
From 35 to 42 years	10,5	11,7	35,2	17,8	5,8	8,2
From 42 to 49 years	21,6	4,7	29,2	28,2	9,4	12,2
From 49 to 56 years	7,3	14,7	35,2	27,9	10,2	4,4
From 56 to 63 years	7,3	8,6	37,6	18,8	13	14,4
From 63 and onward	11,8	8,4	38,9	20,3	6,7	13,5

M. Beaunis shows that the striking point in this table is, the great proportion of somnambulists in childhood and youth. (26, 5 per cent., from 1 to 7 years, and 55, 3 per cent., from 8 to 14 years.)

It is noticeable also that during these two periods of life, all the subjects, without exception, have been more or less influenced. In old age, on the contrary, the number of somnambulists is observed to decrease, but always remains at a relatively high figure (7 to 11 per cent.).

Sigmund Freud

HYPNOSE (1891)

(A) German Editions:
1891 In Anton Bum's 1891) *Therapeutisches Lexikon*, 724-732.
1900, 3rd Ed., 1, 1110-19.)

The second and third editions are unaltered, except for a very few extremely small corrections, mainly typographical. The present translation, by James Strachery, is the first into English.

The following article was a signed contribution to a medical dictionary and had been entirely overlooked till it was discovered in 1963 by Dr. Paul F. Cranefield, Ph.D., the Editor of the *Bulletin of the New York Academy of Medicine*. Our thanks are due to him for drawing our attention to it and supplying us with photostats. Nothing seems to be known of the circumstances of its composition.

HYPNOSIS*

It would be a mistake to think that it is very easy to practise hypnosis for therapeutic purposes. On the contrary, the *technique* of hypnotizing should have learnt it from a master of the art and even then will require much practice of his own in order to achieve successes in more than a few isolated cases. Afterwards, as an experienced hypnotist, he will approach the matter with all the seriousness and decisiveness which spring from a consciousness of undertaking something useful and, indeed, in some circumstances necessary. The recollection of so many cures brought about by hypnosis will lend his behaviour towards his patients a certainty which will not evoke in them too an expectation of yet another therapeutic success. Anyone who sets about hypnotizing half sceptically, who may perhaps seem comical to himself in this situation, and who reveals by his expression, his voice and his bearing that he expects nothing from the experiment,

*Grateful acknowledgement is expressed to Sigmund Freud Copyrights Ltd., The Institute of Psycho-Analysis and the Hogarth Press Ltd., for permission to reprint "Hypnosis," from Volume I of the *Standard Edition of the Complete Psychological Works of Sigmund Freud*.

will have no reason to be surprised at his failures, and should rather leave this method of treatment to other physicians who are able to practise it without feeling damaged in their medical dignity, since they have convinced themselves, by experience and reading, of the reality and importance of hypnotic influence.

We should make it a rule not to seek to impose hypnotic treatment on any patient. A prejudice is widespread among the public (actually supported by some eminent, but in this matter inexperienced, physician*) that hypnosis is a dangerous operation. If we sought to impose hypnosis on someone who believed this assertion, we should probably be interrupted, after no more than a few minutes, by disagreeable occurrences, which would arise from the patient's anxiety and his distressing feeling of being over-powered, but which would quite certainly be regarded as results of hypnosis. Whenever, therefore, a violent resistance arises against the use of hypnosis, we should renounce the method and wait till the patient, under the influence of other information, becomes reconciled to the idea of being hypnotized. On the other hand, it is not at all unfavourable if a patient declares that he is not afraid of hypnosis, but that he does not believe in it or does not believe that it can be of use to him. In such a case we say to him: "I do not require your credence, but only your attention and some compliance at the start." And as a rule we find excellent support in this indiffernt mood of the patient. On the other hand, it must be said that there are people who are hindered from falling into hypnosis precisely by their willingness and their insistence upon being hypnotized. This is completely out of harmony with the popular view that "faith" is a factor in hypnosis, but such are the facts. We may in general start from the assumption that everyone is hypnotizable; but every individual physician will be unable to hypnotize a certain number of people under the conditions of his experiments, and will often be unable to say where his failure lay. Occasionally one procedure is successful in achieving something which seemed to be impossible with another one, and the same is true of different physicians. We can never tell in advance

---

*(Cf. Freud's criticism of Meynert in his review of Forel, p. 92 ff. above.)

whether it will be possible to hypnotize a patient or not, and the only way we have of discovering is by the attempt itself. There has been no success hitherto in bringing accessibility to hypnosis into relation with any other of an individual's attributes. All that is true is that sufferers from mental disease and degenerates are for the most part not hypnotizable, and neurasthenics only with great difficulty; it is untrue that hysterical patients are unadapted for hypnosis. On the contrary, it is precisely the latter in whom hypnosis comes about in response to purely physiological measures and with all the appearance of a special physical condition. It is important to form a provisional judgement of the psychical individuality of a patient whom we wish to hypnotize; but general rules on this particular point cannot be laid down. It will be clear, however, that there is no advantage in beginning a medical treatment with hypnosis, and that it is better first of all to gain the patient's confidence and to allow his distrust and critical sense to blunt themselves. Anyone who enjoys a great reputation as a physician or as a hypnotist can, however, do without this preparation.

Against what illnesses are we to make use of hypnosis? Indications on this are more difficult than in the case of other methods of treatment, since individual reaction to hypnotic therapy plays almost as great a part as the nature of the illness that is to be combated. In general, we shall avoid applying hypnotic treatment to symptoms which have an organic basis and shall employ this method only for purely functional, nervous disorders, for ailments of psychical origin and for toxic as well as other addictions. We shall, however, become convinced that quite a number of symptoms of organic diseases are accessible to hypnosis and that organic change can exist without the functional disturbance which proceeds from it. In view of the dislike of hypnotic treatment prevailing at present, it seldom comes about that we can employ hypnosis except after all other kinds of treatment have been tried without success. This has its advantage, since we come to know in this way the true sphere of action of hypnosis. We can of course also hypnotize for purposes of differential diagnosis: for instance, when we are in doubt as to whether certain symptoms relate to hysteria or to an organic nervous illness. This test, however, is of some value only in cases where the outcome is favourable.

When we have made our patient's acquaintance and established the diagnosis, the question arises of whether we are to undertake the hypnosis in a *tete-a-tete* or to introduce a trustworthy third person. This measure would be desirable to protect the patient from an abuse of hypnosis as well as to protect the physician from being accused of it. And both of these things are on record. But it cannot be applied universally. The presence of a woman friend, of the patient's husband, and so on, often disturbs the patient very considerably and decidedly diminishes the physician's influence. Moreover the subject-matter of the suggestions which are to be imparted in the hypnosis is not always suitable for conveyance to other people closely connected with the patient. The introduction of a second physician would not have this disadvantage, but it increases the difficulty of carrying out the treatment so much that it becomes impossible in the majority of cases. Since it is the physician's foremost duty to be of assistance by means of hypnosis, he will in most cases renounce the introduction of a third person and will lump in the danger that has been mentioned with the others that are inherent in the practice of the medical profession. The patient, however, will guard herself by not allowing herself to be hypnotized by any physician who does not seem to deserve the fullest confidence.

On the other hand, it is of the greatest value for the patient who is to be hypnotized to see other people under hypnosis, to learn by imitation how she is to behave and to learn from others the nature of the sensations during the hypnotic state. In Bernheim's clinic and in Liebeaul's out-patient clinic at Nancy, where every physician can obtain enlightenment concerning the results of which hypnotic influence is capable, hypnosis is never conducted in a tete-a-tete. Every patient who is making his first acquaintance with hypnosis watches for a while how older patients fall asleep, how they are obedient during hypnosis and how, after waking up, they admit that their symptoms have disappeared. This brings him into a condition of psychical preparedness, which causes him, for his part, to fall into deep hypnosis as soon as his turn comes. The objection to this procedure lies in the fact that the ailments of each individual are discussed before a large crowd, which would not be suitable with patients of a higher social class. Nevertheless, a physician who wishes to treat by hypnosis should not renounce this powerful assisting factor, and should, so far as this is possible, arrange for the person who is to be hypnotized to be present first at one or more successful hypnotic experiments. If we cannot count on the patient hypnotizing himself by imitation as soon as we give him the signal, we have a choice between various *procedures* for bringing him under hypnosis, all of which have in common the fact that they recall falling asleep through certain physical sensations. The best manner of proceeding is as follows. We place the patient in a comfortable chair, ask him to attend carefully and not to speak any more, since talking would prevent his falling asleep. Any tight clothing is taken off and any other people present are placed in a part of the room where they cannot be seen by the patient. The room is darkened, silence is preserved. After these preparations, we sit down opposite the patient and request him to fixate two fingers on the physician's right hand and at the same time to observe closely the sensations which develop. After quite a short time, a minute, perhaps, we begin to talk the patient into feeling the sensations of falling asleep. For instance: "I see that things are going quickly in your case: your face has taken on a rigid look, your breathing has become deeper, you have grown quite peaceful, your eyelids are heavy, your eyes are blinking, you can no longer see clearly, you will have to swallow soon, then you will close your eyes—and you are asleep." With these and similar words we are already well into the process of "suggesting", as we call such persuasive remarks during hypnosis.* But we are only suggesting sensations and motor processes such as occur spontaneously at the onset of

---

*Unlike French and English (in which the technical use of the term "suggestion" was derived from its everyday use) German adopted the word first in its technical sense and only subsequently and rarely introduced it into ordinary language.

hypnotic sleep. We can convince ourselves of this if we have someone before us who can be put under hypnosis by fixating alone (the method of Braid), in whom, accordingly, the fatigue of the eyes, owing to the straining of attention and its diversion from other impressions, brings on the sleep-like state. First the patient's face assumes a rigid look, his breathing deepens, his eyes grow moist and blink frequently, one or more swallowing movements occur, and finally the eyeballs turn inwards and upwards, the eyelids fall, and hypnosis is there. The number of such people is very considerable; if we observe that we have someone of this kind before us, we shall be well-advised to keep silent or only to give occasional help with a suggestion. Otherwise we should merely be disturbing the patient who is hypnotizing himself, and, if the succession of suggestions does not correspond to the actual course of his sensations, we should be provoking contradiction. In general, however, it is advisable not to wait for a spontaneous development of hypnosis but to encourage it by suggestions. These must, however, be given energetically and in rapid succession. The patient should not, as it were, come to his senses: he should not have time to test whether what is said to him is correct. We do not need more than from two to four minutes for his eyes to close; if they have not closed spontaneously, we close them by pressure on them, without showing surprise or annoyance at their spontaneous closure not having come about. If the eyes then remain closed, we have as a rule achieved a certain degree of hypnotic influence. This is the decisive moment of all that is to follow.

For one of two possibilities has come about. The first alternative is that the patient, by fixating and listening to the suggestions, has really been brought under hypnosis, in which case he remains quiet after the closure of his eyes. We may then test him for catalepsy, give him the suggestions called for by his ailment, and thereupon awaken him. After waking up he will either be anamnestic (that is to say, he has been "somnambulistic" during the hypnosis), or he will retain his memory completely and report on his sensations during the hypnosis. Not infrequently a smile appears on his features after we have closed his eyes. The physician should not be put out by this; as a rule it only means that the person under hypnosis is still able to form a judgement on his own state and finds it queer or comical. The second alternative, however, is that no influence, or only a slight degree of it, has been established, while the physician has behaved as though he had a successful hypnosis before him. Let us picture the patient's mental state at this point. He has promised at the start of the preparations to stay quiet, not to speak any more and to give no indication of confirmation or denial; he now notices that, on the basis of his consent to this, he is being told that he is hypnotized; he is irritated at this, feels uncomfortable at not being allowed to express his irritation; no doubt, too, he is afraid that the physician will begin suggesting to him too soon, in the belief that he is hypnotized before he is. And now experience shows that, if he is not really hypnotized, he does not keep to the compact we have made with him.* He opens his eyes and says (resentfully, as a rule): "I am not in the least asleep!" A beginner would now regard the hypnosis as a failure, but someone with experience will not lose his composure. He will reply, not in the least angrily, as he once more closes the patient's eyes: "Keep still. You have promised not to talk. Of course I know that you are not 'asleep' nor is that in the least necessary. What would have been the sense of my simply making you fall asleep? You would not understand when I speak to you. You are not asleep, but you are hypnotized, you are under my influence; what I say to you now will make a special impression on you and will be of use to you." After this explanation, the patient usually becomes quiet and we make the suggestions to him; for the moment we abstain from looking for physical signs of hypnosis, but, after this so-called hypnosis has been repeated a number of times, we shall find that some of the somatic phenomena which characterize hypnosis will emerge.

In many cases of this kind it remains to the end doubtful

---

*Cf. a phrase in one of the very last of Freud's papers, "Analysis terminable and interminable" (1937C (Standard Ed. 23, 239: "During the work on the resistances the ego withdraws . . . From the agreement on which the analytic situation is founded."

whether the state we have provoked deserves the name of "hypnosis". We should be wrong, however, if we sought to restrict the making of suggestions to those other cases in which the patient becomes somnambulistic or falls into a deep degree of hypnosis. In cases like these, which in fact only have the *appearance* of hypnosis, we can achieve the most astonishing therapeutic results which, on the other hand, are not to be obtained by "waking suggestion". Here too, therefore, it must nevertheless be a question of hypnosis—whose only purpose, after all is the effect which is brought about in it by suggestion. If however, after repeated attempts (from three to six) there is neither a hint of success nor any of the somatic signs of hypnosis, we shall give up the experiment.

Bernheim and others have distinguished several degrees of hypnosis, whose enumeration is of little value in practice. What is of decisive importance is only whether the patient has become somnambulistic or not—that is, whether the state of consciousness brought about in the hypnosis is cut off from the ordinary one sufficiently sharply for the memory of what occurred during hypnosis to be absent after waking. In these cases the physician can deny the reality of the pains that are present, or of any other symptoms, with the greatest decision—which he is as a rule unable to do if he knows that a few minutes later the patient will say to him: "When you said I no longer had any pains, I did have them all the same and I still have them now." The hypnotist's efforts are directed to sparing himself contradictions of this sort which are bound to shake his authority. It would therefore be of the greatest importance for treatment if we possessed a procedure which made it possible to put *anyone* into a state of somnambulism. Unluckily there is no such procedure. The chief deficiency of hypnotic therapy is that it cannot be dosed. The degree of hypnosis attainable does not depend on the physician's procedure but on the chance reaction of the patient. It is very difficult, too, to deepen the hypnosis into which a patient falls, though this usually happens when there are frequently repeated sessions.

If we are not satisfied with the hypnosis attained, we shall look for other procedures when the treatment is repeated. These often work more strongly or continue to work after the influence of the procedure first adopted has grown weaker. Here are some such procedures: stroking the patient's face and body with both hands continuously for from five to ten minutes (this has a strikingly soothing and lulling effect); suggestion accompanied by the passage of a weak galvanic current, which produces a perceptible sensation of taste (the anode in a broad band on the forehead and the cathode in a band round the wrist)—here the impression of being tied up and the galvanic sensation contribute greatly towards hypnosis. We can invent similar procedures at our choice if we only keep the aim before us of arousing, by an association of thought, the picture of falling asleep and of fixating attention by means of a persistent sensation.

The true therapeutic value of hypnosis lies in the *suggestions* made during it. These suggestions consist in an energetic denial of the ailments of which the patient has complained, or in an assurance that he can do something, or in a command to perform it. A far more powerful result than that produced by a simple assurance or denial is achieved if we link the expected cure to an action or intervention (of our own) during hypnosis. For instance: "You no longer have any pains at this place; I press on it and the pain has gone." Stroking and pressing on the ailing part of the body during hypnosis gives excellent support in general to the spoken suggestion. Nor should we neglect to enlighten the patient under hypnosis on the nature of his ailment, to give him reason for the cessation of his trouble, and so on; for what we have before us is not, as a rule, a physical automation, but a being endowed with the power of criticism and capacity for judgement, on whom we are simply in a position to make more impression now than when he is in a waking state. Where hypnosis is incomplete, we should avoid allowing the patient to speak. Motor utterance of this sort dissipates the numbed feeling which vouches for his hypnosis and wakes him up. Somnambulistic subjects may without fear be allowed to speak, walk about and work, and we obtain the most far-reaching psychical influence over them by questioning them under hypnosis about their symptoms and the origin of these.*

Through suggestion we call for either an immediate effect—particularly in treating paralyses, contractures, and so on—or a post-hypnotic effect—that is, one which we stipulate for a particular time after awakening. In the case of all obstinate ailments it is a great advantage to interpolate a waiting period like this (even a whole night) between the suggestion and its execution. Observation of patients shows that psychical impressions as a rule need a certain time, an incubation period, in order to bring about a physical change. (Cf. "Neurosis, traumatic"†. Each separate suggestion must be made with the greatest decisiveness, for any hint of a doubt is noticed by the patient and unfavourably exploited; no contradiction whatever must be permitted and, if we are able, we should insist upon our power to produce catalepsy, contractures, anaesthesia, and so on.

The *duration* of a hypnosis is to be arranged according to practical requirement; a comparatively long continuance under hypnosis—up to several hours—is certainly not unfavourable to success. "That is enough for the present!" We should not fail to give an assurance at the first hypnosis that the patient will wake up without a headache, cheerful and well. In spite of this, it can be observed that, after a light hypnosis, many people wake up with pressure in the head and fatigue, if the duration of the hypnosis had been too short. They have not, as it were, had their sleep out.

The *depth* of a hypnosis is not invariably in direct proportion to its success. We may produce the greatest changes in the lightest hypnosis and, on the contrary, we may have a failure under somnambulism. If the desired success is not achieved after a few hypnoses, a further difficulty is revealed which attaches to this method of treatment. Whereas no patient ventures to be impatient if he has still not been cured after the twentieth electrical session or an equal number of bottles of mineral water, with hypnotic treatment both physician and patient grow tired far sooner, as result of the contrast between the deliberately rosy colouring of the sug-

---

*This is again an allusion to Breuer's method which Freud was already using at the time he wrote this article.

†The reference is to another article in Bum's *Lexikon*.

gestions and the cheerless truth. Here too, intelligent patients can make it easier for the physician as soon as they have understood that in making suggestions he is, as it were, playing a part and that the more energetically he disputes their ailment the more advantage is to be expected for them. In every prolonged hypnotic treatment a monotonous procedure is carefully to be avoided. The physician must constantly be on the look-out for a new starting-point for his suggestions, a new proof of his power, a new change in his hypnotizing procedure. For him too, who has, perhaps, internal doubts about success, this presents a great and in the end exhausting strain.

There is no doubt that the field of hypnotic treatment is far more extensive than that of other methods of treating nervous illnesses. Nor is there any justification for the reproach which asserts that hypnosis is only able to influence symptoms and then only for a short time. If hypnotic treatment is directed only against symptoms and not against pathological processes, it is following precisely the same path which all other therapeutic methods are obliged to take.

If hypnosis has had success, the stability of the cure depends on the same factors as the stability of every cure achieved in another way. If what it was dealing with were residue phenomena of a process that was concluded, the cure will be a permanent one; if the causes which produced the symptoms are still at work with undiminished strength, then a relapse is probable. The employment of hypnosis never exclude that of any other treatment, dietetic, mechanical, or of some other sort. In a number of cases—namely where the symptoms are of purely psychical origin—hypnosis fulfills all the demands that can be made of a causal treatment, and in that case questioning and calming the patient in deep hypnosis is as a rule accompanied by the most brilliant success.

Everything that has been said and written about the great *dangers* of hypnosis belongs to the realm of fable*. If we leave on one side the misuse of hypnosis for illegitimate purposes— a possibility that exists for every other effective therapeutic method

---

*These are discussed at length in the first part of the Forel review (p. 92 ff. above).

—the most we have to consider is the tendency of severely neurotic people, after repeated hypnosis, to fall into hypnosis spontaneously. It is in the physician's power to forbid this spontaneous hypnosis, which would seem to come about only in very susceptible individuals People whose susceptibility goes so far that they can be hypnotized against their will, can also be protected fairly completely by a suggestion that only their physician will be able to hypnotize them.

Sigmund Freud

EIN FALL VON HYPNOTISCHER HEILUNG NEBST BEMERKUNGEN UBER DIE ENTSTEHUNG HYSTERISCHER SYMPTOME DURCH DEN "GEGENWILLEN" (1892)

(A) German Editions:

1892-93 Zeitschr. Hypnot., 1 (3), 102-7, (4), 123-9. (December, 1892 and January, 1893)

1925   G. S., 1, 258-272.

1951   G. W., 1, 3-17.

(B) English Translation:

1950   "A Case of Successful Treatment by Hypnotism" C. P., 5, 33-46. (Tr. James Strachey.)

The present translation is a slightly corrected version of the one published in 1950.

This paper was almost exactly contemporaneous with the Breuer and Freud "Preliminary Communication" (1893A). Some of the ideas in it (e.g., the "counter-will") have a place in Freud's later work, and it forms something of a link between his writings on hypnotism and those on hysteria upon which he was embarking. The view that "a moment if disposition to hysteria" —in this instance, physical fatigue — provides the opportunity for the counter-will to assert itself suggests the influence of Breuer and the "hypnoid state."

A CASE OF SUCCESSFUL TREATMENT BY HYPNOTISM

With Some Remarks on the Origin of Hysterical Symptoms Through "Counter-will"*

I propose in the following pages to publish an isolated case of a successful treatment by hypnotic suggestion because, owing to a number of attendant circumstances, it was more convincing and more lucid than the majority of our successful treatments.

I have been acquainted for many years with the woman whom I was thus able to assist at an important moment of her existence,

---

*Grateful acknowledgment is expressed to Basic Books, Inc. for permission to reprint Chapter III, Volume 5 of *The Collected Papers of Sigmund Freud,* edited by Ernest Jones, M.D., Basic Books, Inc., Publishers, New York, 1959.

and she remained under my observation for several years afterwards. The disorder from which she was relieved by hypnotic
suggestion had made its first appearance some time earlier. She
had struggled against it in vain and been driven by it to a renuncia-
tion which, with my help, she was spared on a second occasion.
A year later the same disorder appeared yet again, and was once
more overcome in the same manner. The therapeutic success was
of value to the patient and persisted as long as she desired to carry
out the function affected by the disorder. Finally, it was possible
in this case to trace the simple psychical mechanism of the disorder and to bring it into relation with similar happenings in the
field of neuropathology.

It was a case, if I may now cease talking in riddles, of a mother
who was unable to feed her new-born baby till hypnotic suggestion
intervened, and whose experiences with an earlier and a later child
provided controls of the therapeutic success such as are seldom obtainable.

The subject of the following case history is a young woman
between twenty and thirty years of age with whom I happen to
have been acquainted from her childhood. Her capability, her
quiet common sense and her naturalness made it impossible for
anyone, including her family doctor, to regard her as a neurotic.
Taking the circumstances that I am about to narrate into account,
I must describe her, in Charcot's happy phrase, as an *hysterique
d'occasion*. This category, as we know, does not exclude the most
admirable combination of qualities and otherwise uninterrupted
nervous health. As regards her family, I am acquainted with her
mother, who is not in any way neurotic, and a younger sister who
is similarly healthy. A brother suffered from a typical neurasthenis
of early manhood, and this ruined his career. I am familiar with
the aetiology and course of this form of illness, which I come
across repeatedly every year in my medical practice. Starting originally with a good constitution, the patient is haunted by the
usual sexual difficulties at puberty; there follow years of overwork
as a student, preparation for examinations, and an attack of gon-
orrhoea, followed by a sudden onset of dyspepsia accompanied by
obstinate and inexplicable constipation. After some months the

constipation is replaced by intracranial pressure, depression and incapacity for work*. Thenceforward the patient grows increasingly self-centered and his character more and more restricted, till he becomes a torment to his family. I am not certain whether it it is not possible to *acquire* this form of neurasthenia with all its elements and therefore, especially as I am not acquainted with my patient's other relatives, I leave it an open question whether we are to assume the presence in her family of a hereditary disposition to neurosis.

When the time approached for the birth of the first child of her marriage (which was a happy one) the patient intended to feed the infant herself. The delivery was not more difficult than is usual with a primiparous mother who is no longer very youthful; it was terminated with forceps. Nevertheless, though her bodily build seemed favourable, she did not succeed in feeding the infant satisfactorily. There was a poor flow of milk, pains were brought on when the baby was put to the breast, the mother lost appetite and showed an alarming unwillingness to take nourishment, her nights were agitated and sleepless. At last, after a fortnight, in order to avoid any further risk to the mother and infant, the attempt was abandoned as a failure and the child was transferred to a wet-nurse. Thereupon all the mother's troubles immediately cleared up. I must add that I am not able to give a medical or eye-witness account of this first attempt at lactation.

Three years later a second baby was born; and on this occasion external circumstances added to the desirability of avoiding a wet-nurse. But the mother's attempts at feeding the child herself seemed even less successful and to provoke even more distressing symptoms than the first time. She vomited all her food, became agitated when it was brought to her bedside and was completely unable to sleep. She became so much depressed at her incapacity that her two family doctors — physicians of such wide repute in Vienna as Dr. Breuer and Dr. Lott — would not hear of any prolonged attempt being made on this occasion. They recommended that

---

*These include symptoms by which Freud was later to distinguish neurasthenia proper from anxiety neurosis. Cf. his first paper on anxiety neurosis (1895B), *Standard Ed.*, 3, 90.

just one more effort should be made — with the help of hypnotic suggestion; and, on the evening of the fourth day, they saw to it that I was brought in professionally, since I was already acquainted with the patient.

I found her lying in bed with flushed cheeks and furious at her inability to feed the baby—an inability which increased at every attempt but against which she struggled with all her strength. In order to avoid the vomiting, she had taken no nourishment the whole day. Her epigastrium was distended and was sensitive to pressure; palpation revealed abnormal motility of the stomach; there was odourless eructation from time to time and the patient complained of having a constant bad taste in her mouth. The area of gastric resonance was considerably increased. Far from being welcomed as a saviour in the hour of need, I was obviously being received with a bad grace and I could not count on the patient's having much confidence in me.

I at once attempted to induce hypnosis by ocular fixation, at the same time making constant suggestions of the symptoms of sleep. After three minutes the patient was lying back with the peaceful expression of someone in profound sleep. I cannot recollect whether I made any tests for catalepsy and other symptoms of pliancy. I made use of suggestion to contradict all her fears and the feelings on which those fears were based: "Have no fear! You will make an excellent nurse and the baby will thrive. Your stomach is perfectly quiet, your appetite is excellent, you are looking forward to your next meal," etc. The patient went on sleeping while I left her for a few minutes, and when I had woken her up showed amnesia for what had occurred. Before I left the house I was also under the necessity of contradicting a worried remark by the patient's husband to the effect that a woman's nerves might be totally ruined by hypnosis.

Next evening I was told something which seemed to me a guarantee of success but which, oddly enough, had made no impression on the patient or her relations. She had had a meal the evening before without any ill effects, had slept peacefully and in the morning had taken nourishment herself and fed the baby irreproachably. The rather abundant midday meal, however, had been too much for her. No sooner had it been brought in than her former disinclination returned; vomiting began even before she had touched it. It was impossible to put the child to her breast and all the objective signs were the same as they had been when I had arrived the evening before. I produced no effect by my argument that, since she was now convinced that her disorder *could* disappear and in fact *had* disappeared for half a day, the battle was already won. I now brought on the second hypnosis, which led to a state of somnambulism as quickly as the first, and I acted with greater energy and confidence. I told the patient that five minutes after my departure she would break out against her family with some acrimony: what had happened to her dinner? Did they mean to let her starve? How could she feed the baby if she had nothing to eat herself? And so on.

When I returned on the third evening the patient refused to have further treatment. There was nothing more wrong with her, she said: she had an excellent appetite and plenty of milk for the baby, there was not the slightest difficulty when it was put to her breast, and so on. Her husband thought it rather queer that after my departure the evening before she had clamoured violently for food and had remonstrated with her mother in a way quite unlike herself. But since then, he added, everything had gone all right.

There was nothing more for me to do. The mother fed her child for eight months; and I had many opportunities of satisfying myself in a friendly way that they were both doing well. I found it hard to understand, however, as well as annoying, that no reference was ever made to my remarkable achievement.

But my time came a year later, when a third child made the same demands on the mother and she was as unable to meet them as on the previous occasions. I found the patient in the same condition as the year before and positively exasperated with herself because her will could do nothing against her disinclination for food and her others symptoms; and the first evening's hypnosis only had the result of making her feel more hopeless. Once again after the second hypnosis the symptoms were so completely cut short that a third was not required. This child too, which is now eighteen months old, was fed without any trouble and the mother has enjoyed uninterrupted good health.

In face of this renewed success the patient and her husband unbent and admitted the motive that had governed their behaviour towards me. "I felt ashamed," the woman said to me, "that a thing like hypnosis should be successful where I myself, with all my will-power, was helpless." Nevertheless, I do not think either she or her husband have overcome their dislike of hypnosis.

I shall now pass on to consider what may have been the psychical mechanism of this disorder of my patient's which was thus removed by suggestion. I have not, as in certain other cases which I shall discuss elsewhere,* direct information on the subject; and I am thrown back upon the alternative of deducing it.

There are certain ideas which have an effect of expectancy attached to them. They are of two kinds: ideas of my doing this or that—what we call *intentions*—and ideas of this or that happening to me — *expectations* properly speaking. The effect attached to them is dependent on two factors, first on the degree of importance which the outcome has for me, and secondly on the degree of uncertainty inherent in the expectation of that outcome. The subjective uncertainty, the counter-expectation, is itself represented by a collection of ideas to which I shall give the name of "distressing antithetic ideas". In the case of an intention, these antithetic ideas will run: "I shall not succeed in carrying out my intention because this or that is too difficult for me and I am unfit to do it; I know, too, that certain other people have also failed in a similar situation." The other case, that of an expectation, needs no comment: the counter-expectation consists in enumerating all the things that could possibly happen to me other than the one I desire. Further along this line we should reach the *phobias,* which play so great a part in the symptomatology of the neuroses. But let us return to the first category, the intentions. How does a person with a healthy ideational life deal with antithetic ideas against an intention? With the powerful self-confidence of health, he suppresses and inhibits them so far as possible, and excludes them from his associations.

---

*A reference to the Breuer and Freud "Preliminary Communication" (1893A) which was on the point of appearing.

This often succeeds to such an extent that the existence of an antithetic idea against an intention is as a rule not manifest, but is only made probable when we come to consider the neuroses. On the other hand, where a neurosis is present—and I am explicitly referring not to hysteria alone but to the *status nervosus* in general—we have to assume the *primary presence* of a tendency to depression and to a lowering of self-confidence, such as we find very highly developed and in isolation in melancholia. In neuroses, then, great attention is paid (by the patient) to antithetic ideas against intentions, perhaps because the subject-matter of such ideas fits in with the mood of the neurosis, or perhaps because antithetic ideas, which would otherwise have been absent, flourish in the soil of a neurosis.

When this intensification of antithetic ideas relates to *expectations,* if the case is one of a simple *status nervosus,* the effect is shown in a generally pessimistic frame of mind; if the case is one of neurasthenia, associations with the most accidental sensations occasion the numerous phobias of neurasthenics. When the intensification attaches to *intentions,* it gives rise to the disturbances which are summed up under the description of *folie du doute,* and which have as their subject-matter distrust of the subject's own capacity. Precisely at this point the two major neuroses, neurasthenia and hysteria, each behave in a different manner characteristic of each. In neurasthenia the pathologically intensified antithetic idea is combined with the volitional idea into a *single* act of consciousness; it substracts from the volitional idea and brings about the weakness of will which is so striking in neurasthenics and of which they themselves are aware. The process in hysteria differs from this in two respects, or possibly only in one. (Firstly,) in accordance with the tendency to a *dissociation of consciousness* in hysteria, the distressing antithetic idea, which seems to be inhibited, is removed from association with the intention and continues to exist as a disconnected idea, often unconsciously to the patient himself. (Secondly,) it is supremely characteristic of hysteria that, when it comes to the carrying out of the intention, the inhibited antithetic idea can put itself into effect* by innervation of the body just as easily as does a volitional idea in normal circumstances. The antithetic idea established itself, so to speak, as a *"counter-will"*, while the patient is aware with astonishment of having a will which is resolute but powerless. Perhaps, as I have said, these two factors are at bottom one and the same: it may be that the antithetic idea is only able to put itself into effect because it is not inhibited by being combined with the intention in the way in which the intention is inhibited by it.†

If in our present case the mother who was prevented by neurotic difficulties from feeding her child had been a neurasthenic, her behaviour would have been different. She would have felt conscious dread of the task before her, she would have been greatly concerned with the various possible accidents and dangers and, after much temporizing with anxieties and doubts, would after all have carried out the feeding without any difficulty; or, if the antithetic idea had gained the upper hand, she would have abandoned the task because she felt afraid of it. But the hysteric behaves quite otherwise. She may perhaps not be conscious of her fear, she is quite determined to carry her intention through and sets about it without hesitating. Then, however, she behaves as though it was her will not to feed the child on any account. Moreover, this will evokes in her all the subjective symptoms which a malingerer would put forward as an excuse for not feeding her child: loss of appetite, aversion to food, pains when the child is put to her breast. And, since the counter-will exercises greater control over the body than does conscious stimulation, it also produces a number of objective signs in the digestive tract which malingering would be unable to bring about. Here, in contrast to the *weakness* of will shown in neurasthenia, we have a *perversion* of will; and, in contrast to the resigned irresoluteness shown in the former case,

---

*"Sick objektiviert". Literally, "makes itself objective". In his own abstract of this paper (Freud, 1897B), Freud uses the word "Realisierung", "Making real." (*Standard Ed.* 3, 243.)

†In the interval between writing this and correcting the proofs, I have come across a work by H. Kaan (1893) containing similar arguments.

here we have astonishment and exasperation at a disunity which is incomprehensible to the patient.

I therefore consider that I am justified in describing my patient as an *hysterique d' occasion* since she was able, as a result of a fortuitous cause, to produce a complex of symptoms with a mechanism so supremely characteristic of hysteria. It may be assumed that in this instance the fortuitous cause was the patient's excited state before the first confinement or her exhaustion after it. A first confinement is, after all, the greatest shock to which the female organism is subject, and as a result of it a woman will as a rule produce any neurotic symptoms that may be latent to her disposition.

It seems probable that the case of this patient is a typical one and throws light upon a large number of other cases in which breast-feeding or some similar function is prevented by neurotic influences. Since, however, in the case I have reported I have only arrived at the psychical mechanism by inference, I hasten to add an assurance that I have frequently been able to establish the operation of a similar psychical mechanism in hysterical symptoms *directly,* by investigating the patient under hypnosis.*

Here I will mention only one of the most striking instances. †Some years ago I treated a hysterical lady who showed great strength of will in those of her dealings which were unaffected by her illness; but in those which *were* so affected she showed no less clearly the weight of the burden imposed on her by her numerous and oppressive hysterical impediments and incapacities. One of her striking characteristics was a peculiar noise which intruded, like a *tic,* into her conversation. I can best describe it as a singular clacking of the tongue with a sudden interruption of the convulsive closure of her lips. After observing it for some weeks, I

---

*See the preliminary communication by J. Breuer and S. Freud (1893A) on "The Psychical Mechanism of Hysterical Phenomena", which is appearing at the same time as the present paper.

†This patient, Frau Emmy von N., was subsequently made the subject of the second case history in Breuer and Freud's *Studies on Hysteria* (1895D). See especially *Standard Ed.,* 2, 49, 54, 57-8 and 91-2. Her case is also referred to briefly in the "Preliminary Communication", ibid., 2, 5. The accounts differ in their details.

once asked her when and how it had first originated. "I don't know when it was," she replied, "Oh! A long time ago." This led me to regard it as a genuine *tic,* till it occurred to me one day to ask the patient the same question under deep hypnosis. This patient had access under hypnosis (without there being any necessity to suggest the idea to her) to the whole store of her memories—or, as I should prefer to put it, to the whole extent of her consciousness, which was restricted in her waking life. She promptly answered: "It was when my younger girl was so ill and had been having convulsions all day but had fallen asleep at last in the evening. I was sitting beside her bed and thought to myself: "Now you must be absolutely quiet, so as not to wake her." It was then that the clacking came on for the first time. Afterwards it passed off. But once, some years later, when we were driving through the forest near . . . , a violent thunderstorm came on and a tree-trunk beside the road just in front of us was struck by lightning, so that the coachman had to rein in the horses suddenly, and I thought to myself: "Now, whatever you do, you mustn't scream, or the horses will bolt." And at that moment it came on again, and has persisted ever since." I was able to convince myself that the noise she made was not a genuine *tic,* since, from the moment it was in this way traced back to its origin, it disappeared and never returned during all the years I remained in contact with the patient. This, however, was the first occasion on which I was able to observe the origin of hysterical symptoms through the putting into effect of a distressing antithetic idea — that is, through counter-will. The mother, worn out by anxieties and her duties as a nurse, made a decision not to let a sound pass her lips for fear of disturbing her child's sleep, which had been so long in coming. But in her exhausted state the attendant antithetic idea that she nevertheless *would* do it proved to be the stronger; it made its way to the innervation of the tongue, which her decision to remain silent may perhaps have forgotten to inhibit, broke through the closure of her lips and produced a noise which thenceforward remained fixated* for many years, especially after the same course of events had been repeated.

There is one objection that must be met before we can fully understand this process. It may be asked how it comes about that it is the *antithetic* idea that gains the upper hand as a result of general exhaustion (which is what constitutes the disposition for the process.) I should reply by putting forward the theory that the exhaustion is in fact only a *partial* one. What are exhausted are those elements of the nervous system which form the material foundation of the ideas associated with the primary consciousness; the ideas that are excluded from that chair of associations — that is, from the chain of associations of the normal ego — the inhibited

---

*"Fixiert." Is this word used in its everyday sense of "fixed"? Or is it used in the more technical sense of "fixated"? The question is a constant plague to the translator at this period. Freud uses the word in a variety of ways. We have already come across "Fixierung" in quite another sense, as used by hypnotists, to mean "a concentrated stare". (See the Preface to the Bernheim translation (1888-9), p. 80 above, the review of Forel (1889A), p. 96 above, and the encyclopaedia article on "Hypnosis" (1891D), p. 108 above.) Leaving this special sense on one side, we come to a number of cases, such as the present one, in which the word is used in something that approaches the ordinary sense of "permanently set" or "established". See for instance, the early lecture on the "Preliminary Communication" (1893H), *Standard Ed.*, 3, 32, where, as here, a symptom becomes "fixated"; or the French paper on motor paralyses (1893C), p. 172 below, where an idea is "fixated" to a memory; or, another instance of a symptom being "fixated", the second paper on the neuropsychoses of defence (1896B), *Standard Ed.*, 3, 174. A more doubtful case will be seen in Draft L of the Fliess papers, dating from 1897 (p. 249 below); but an instance in the "Dora" case history (1905E 1901) ibid., 7, 56 and several in the *Three Essays* (1905D)—especially ibid., 7, 235—show that the final psychoanalytic sense of a developmental stoppage has been reached. It should be noted that in this psycho-analytic sense the word still has two uses—fixation of an instinct to an object and fixation of an instinct at some particular point in its development. These two uses correspond to the two kinds of temporal regression which are described below in Appendix A to the *Project* (p. 345). Indeed, as is shown (with references) in the same passage, there is the closest clinical connection between fixation and regression in these senses. Finally, mention must be made of the very exceptional occurrence of the word "Fixierung" in the sense of "record" or "recording". It appears thus in Chapter VII (B) of *The Interpretation of Dreams* (1900A), *Standard Ed.*, 5, 539 but thereafter not, it seems, till *Moses and Monotheism* (1939A), *idbid.*, 23, 62 and *An Outline of Psycho-Analysis* (1940) 1938), ibid., 23, 160. In all these last passages we have translated the word "record". (Cf. also Letter 52 to Fliess, p. 234, N. 3 below).

and suppressed ideas, are not exhausted, and they consequently predominate at the moment of disposition to hysteria.

Anyone who is well acquainted with hysteria will observe that the psychical mechanism which I have been describing offers an explanation not merely of isolated hysterical occurrences but of major portions of the symptomatology of hysteria as well as of one of its most striking characteristics. If we keep firmly in mind the fact that it is the distressing antithetic ideas (inhibited and rejected by normal consciousness) which press forward at the moment of disposition to hysteria and find their way to the somatic innervation, we shall then hold the key to an understanding of the peculiarity of the deliria of hysterical attacks as well. It is owing to no chance coincidence that the hysterical deliria of nuns during the epidemics of the Middle Ages took the form of violent blasphemies and unbridled erotic language or that (as Charcot remarked in the first volume of his *Lecons du Mardi*) it is precisely well-brought-up and well-behaved boys who suffer from hysterical attacks in which they give free play to every kind of rowdiness, every kind of wild escapade and bad conduct*. It is the suppressed—the laboriously suppressed—groups of ideas that are brought into action in these cases, by the operation of a sort of counter-will, when the subject has fallen a victim to hysterical exhaustion. Perhaps, indeed, the connection may be a more intimate one, for the hysterical condition may perhaps be *produced* by the laborious suppression; but in the present paper I have not been considering the psychological features of that condition. Here I am merely concerned with explaining why—assuming that there is a state of disposition to hysteria—the symptoms take the particular form in which we in fact observe them.

The emergence of a counter-will is chiefly responsible for the daemonic characteristic which hysteria so often exhibits—the characteristic, that is, of the patients' not being able to do something precisely when and where they want to most passionately, of

---

*The nuns and well-behaved boys appear several times at this period: e.g., in the "Preliminary Communication" (1893A), *Standard Ed.*, 2, 11, in Freud's technical section of *Studies on Hysteria*, ibid., 249, in his early lecture on hysteria (1893H), ibid., 3, 38, as well as in one of his footnotes to his translation of Charcot's *Lecons du Mardi* (1892-4), p. 138 below, and again on p. 153.

doing the exact opposite of what they have been asked to do, and of being obliged to cover everything they most value with abuse and suspicion. The perversity of character shown by hysterical patients, their itch to do the wrong thing, to appear to be ill just when they most want to be well—compulsions such as these (as anyone will know who has had to do with these patients) may often affect the most irreproachable characters when for a time they become the helpless victims of their antithetic ideas.

The question of what becomes of inhibited intentions seems to be meaningless in regard to normal ideational life. We might be tempted to reply that they simply do not occur. The study of hysteria shows that nevertheless they *do* occur, that is to say that the physical alteration corresponding to them is retained, and that they are stored up and enjoy an unsuspected existence in a sort of shadow kingdom, till they emerge like bad spirits and take control of the body, which is as a rule under the orders of the predominant ego-consciousness.

I have already said that this mechanism is supremely characteristic of hysteria; but I must add that it does not occur only in hysteria. It is present in striking fashion in *tic convulsif,* a neurosis which has so much symptomatic similarity with hysteria that its whole picture may occur as hysteria that its whole picture may occur as a part-manifestation of hysteria. So it is that Charcot, if I have not completely misunderstood his teachings on the subject, after keeping the two separate for some time, could only find one distinguishing mark between them—that hysterical *tic* disappears sooner or later, while genuine *tic* persists. The picture of a severe *tic convulsif* is, as we know, made up of involuntary movements frequently (according to Charcot and Guinon, always) in the nature of grimaces or of performances which have at one time had a meaning—of coprolalia, of echolalia and of obsessive ideas belonging to the range covered by *folie du doute.* It is, however, surprising to learn that Guinon, who had no notion whatever of entering into the psychical mechanism of these symptoms, tells us that some of his patients arrived at their spasms and grimaces because an antithetic idea had put itself into effect. These patients reported that on some particular occasion they had seen a similar *tic* or a comedian intentionally making a similar grimace, and felt afraid that they might be obliged to imitate the ugly movements. Thenceforward they had actually begun imitating them. No doubt only a small proportion of the involuntary movements occurring in *tics* originate in this way. On the other hand, it would be tempting to attribute to this mechanism the origin of coprolalia, a term used to describe the involuntary, or rather, the unwilling ejaculation of the foulest words, which occurs in *tics*. If so, the root of coprolalia would be the patient's perception that he cannot prevent himself from producing some particular sound, usually a "h'm h'm". He would then become afraid of losing control over other sounds as well, especially over words such as any well-brought-up man avoids using, and this fear would lead to what his feared coming true. No anamnesis confirming this suspicion is quoted by Guinon, and I myself have never had occasion to question a patient suffering from coprolalia. On the other hand, I have found in the same writer's work a report upon another case of *tic* in which the word that was involuntarily spoken did not, exceptionally enough, belong to the coprolalic vocabulary. This was the case of an adult man who was afflicted with necessity of calling out "Maria!" When he was a schoolboy he had had a sentimental attachment to a girl of that name; he had been completely absorbed in her, and this, it may be supposed, predisposed him to a neurosis. He began at that time to call out his idol's name in the middle of his school classes, and the name persisted with him as a *tic* half a lifetime after he had got over his love-affair. I think the explanation must be that his most determined endeavour to keep the name secret was reversed, at a moment of special excitement, into the counter-will and that thereafter the *tic* persisted as it did in the case of my second patient. If my explanation of this instance is correct, it would be tempting to derive coprolalic *tic* proper from the same mechanism, since obscene words are secrets that we all know and the knowledge of which we always try to conceal from one another.*

---

*I will merely add a suggestion that it would be repaying to study elsewhere than in hysteria and *tic* the way in which the counter-will puts itslef into effect—an event which very frequently occurs within the limits of the normal. This is an anticipation of *The Psychopathology of Everyday Life* (1901B), where, almost ten years later than this paper, the "counter-will" reappears (*Standard Ed.*, 6, 154 and 275). It occurs once more, also in connection with parapraxes, in Lecture IV of the *Introductory Lectures* (1916-17), *Standard Ed.*, 15, 71, ff.

Ralph Harry Vincent

Many theories were proposed by the practitioners of hypnosis at the turn of the century. Animal magnetism was still being expounded by members of the Royal Society of Medicine as being the work of charlatans and magicians. So that hypnosis could be better understood, practitioners like Vincent tried to explain it through physiology and physiological processes.

The following article is one of the chapters of his popular treatise on the *Elements of Hypnotism,* and is in itself a good review of the physiology of the nervous system.

THE PHYSIOLOGY OF HYPNOSIS*

Nature of nervous action—the nervous mechanism—Anatomical differentiation—Functional differentiation—Structure of cerebrum—The white and grey matter—The combination of neurons—Structure of a neuron—The spinal cord—Course of a motor impulse—The ganglionic system—The nervous mechanism of the various organs—The heart—Stimulation of the vagus—Division of the cervical sympathetic—The submandibular gland—The relations between the psychical and physical—Various kinds of nervous action—Inaptic, aptic, conscious—"Reflex" action—Experimental differentiation of actions—Interpretative and non-interpretative—"Automatic" actions—Unconscious psychical action—The basis of classification—Hypnosis in relation to psychology—Modification attending the induction of hypnosis—The mental function—The neuronic group—Inhibition—Suggestion in the normal state and in hypnosis—The course of the stimulus; its terminal dissipation—Hallucination—Memory—The place of hypnotism in scientific knowledge.

In order to obtain an accurate view of technical relations of the hypnotic to the normal condition, it is necessary to have a clear conception of the nature of nervous action, of the structure of and function of the nervous system, of the interdependence which exists between the various organs of the body and the central nervous mechanism, and of the character of this interdependence. Many writers have given clear accounts of the nervous mechanism of the

---

*From Vincent, Ralph Harry: *The Elements of Hypnotism.* The Induction, the Phenomena, and the Physiology of Hypnosis, 2nd ed. London, Paul Kegan, Trench, Trubner and Co., 1897, pp. 155-199.

body; the distribution of the nerves has been described with an accuracy and detail, leaving nothing to be desired; but while one has concerned himself with the structure and another with the function, the meeting-place of the two seems to have been in some respects singularly neglected. The general conception of the nature and extent of nervous action is thus faltering and inadequate; our terms are vague, mean too little or too much, and are too often used with but a faint glimpse of their meaning. A general consideration of nervous anatomy would here be impossible and in tracing the outlines of the distribution of the system in man, we shall do no more than is absolutely necessary for the purpose of the argument we wish to establish and for an indication of the paths by which a psychical stimulus becomes translated into a physical fact.

The human nervous system has a wide extension throughout the body, its ramifications blending with almost every structure; from anatomical and physiological points of view it is divided into distinct parts. The brain, including the cerebrum, cerebellum, pons Varolii, and medulla oblongata; the spinal cord with the peripheral nerves, and the ganglionic or sympathetic visceral chain. To the cerebrum belongs the functions of intellect, will, emotion, and in fact, all of the great physical processes; possessing these functions it necessarily has the control of the voluntary movements of the body, and coming to it, for its information, from the whole of the periphery are the varied stimuli derived from the outside world by the special senses of sight, hearing, touch, smell, and taste. Thus we have at once a marked differentiation of the functions of the brain into two sorts—(1) the psychical, and (2) that connected with the issuing and receiving of impulses, and accordingly we find corresponding anatomical distinction. If we take a section through a hemisphere of the cerebrum, we find the central portion hard, comparatively resistant to the knife, dense in texture, and of a whitish appearance; external to this is a convoluted margin, composed of a darker substance, soft to the touch, more easily pliable than the white matter, and dipping with some irregularity into the white layer beneath it. The central white matter consists of the nerve fibres coming from and going to the grey matter, and the difference of texture in this substance is due to the sheaths (the medullary sheath) in which the fibres are enclosed; the darker substance (the grey matter) is chiefly characterized by the presence of large numbers of nervous cells, together with a certain proportion of medullated and non-medullated nerve fibres.

The fundamental component of the cerebrum is the combination of a multitude of neurons, the total number of which has been estimated at about two thousand million. Each neuron is composed of a cell body, protoplasmic processes (dendrons), and the "axis-cylinder" process. The protoplasm of each neuron is distinct from that of every other, the only connection obtainable being by virtue of the proximity or contact of the dendrons. It is by means of these protoplasmic dendrons, which are a constituent of the neuron itself, that the impulses are finally conducted to the the neuron, whilst the efferent impulses leave the neuron by the axis-cylinder process.

This process leaving the neuron gives off at intervals collateral branches which run at right angles to the process. The collaterals split up into the finest fibres which, with the dendrons of another neuron, form arborization. The neurons and the dendrons constitute, as has been said, the grey matter of the brain, whilst the axis-cylinder processes are chiefly found in the white matter. The nerves must pass through various structures before reaching their termination; the impulses to the periphery pass downwards through the medulla oblongata to the spinal cord. And here there is a change in the relations of the grey to the white matter. Taking a cross-section of the spinal cord, which, however, varies somewhat according to the level at which the section is taken, we find the grey internal to the white matter; the white consisting as before of nerve-fibres, and the grey of neurons intermingled with nerve-fibres, about to form arborescence around other neurons. Taking one-half of the section, we find the grey matter forms an anterior prominence, very definitely marked and termed the anterior cornu, whilst the posterior portion, more tapering and somewhat less definite in character, is termed the posterior cornu. The afferent nerve-fibres (the nerves going to the central nervous system from the periphery) enter the posterior cornu, and leaving the anterior cornu are the fibres conveying motor impulses to the periphery. These nerves leaving or entering the cord form two separate bundles known as the anterior and posterior nerve-roots, the posterior root bearing on it a ganglionic enlargement; the two roots then become united into one large nerve trunk, containing both afferent and efferent fibres. The nerve-fibres enter or leave the grey matter, and thus there is outside the grey matter of the cord the white matter consisting of medullated nerve-fibres.

We may now be able to trace the course of a motor impulse starting from the cerebral cortex. Starting from a neuron, it passes down the axis-cylinder process; this process now crosses to the opposite side of the cord, and at a certain level passes into the grey matter, where it breaks up into an arborescence round the dendrons of a neuron: from this neuron an axis-cylinder is produced, which passes down a nerve-truck, and finally breaks up in the muscle which it supplies. It is thus easy to perceive the elaboration of the mechanism involved in a single movement. As we have seen, the distal axis-cylinder gives out collateral branches which arboresce with other neurons, whilst the termination of the first axis-cylinder is surrounded with arborescing fibres; and from this neuron the second axis-cylinder proceeds, giving out before leaving the cord other collateral branches. We are able, therefore, to see that for the simplest movement the combination of many neurons is necessary, and a specific movement is brought about by the specific combination of these neurons, the activity of which is requisite for the performance of the movement.

The course and distribution of the sensory nerves need not here be described, since, though differing in detail, the principles underlying their structure and course are essentially the same. For the same reason we have not discussed the course of the cranial nerves; there is, however, one special branch of the nervous system which plays so important a part in the adjustment of the organs to the immediate requirements of the organism that a short description may be useful. The "sympathetic" or "ganglionic" part of the nervous system consists of (1) a series of ganglia connected together by intervening cords, extending from the base of the skull to the coccyx, one on each side of the middle line of the body, partly in front and partly on each side of the vertebral column; (2) of three great gangliated plexuses or aggregations of nerves and ganglia, situated in front of the spine in the thoracic, abdominal viscera; and (3) of numerous nerve-fibres. These latter are of two kinds— communicating, by which the ganglia communicate with each other and with the cerebro-spinal nerves; and distributory, supplying, in general, all the internal viscera and the coats of the blood-vessels. By means of this distribution every organ and gland in the body is governed and regulated. The distribution and course of the ganglionic system is elaborate and complex, and for an adequate description of the anatomy of the nervous system the reader is referred to the anatomical works (Quain, Gray, etc.). On anatomical grounds, therefore, we have every reason to assign to the nervous system functions much higher than those involving the mere conduction and dissemination of impulses; from the specific combinations of neurons already referred to, from the presence of multitudinous ganglia, and from the elaboration of the system, we have evidence of a mechanism which is selective, purposive, and adaptive in its functions. We may now consider the method of action as regards the organic functions, since, without a knowledge of the nature of these processes, we shall not be able to realize the nature of the changes induced as a result of hypnotic suggestion.

To consider the nervous mechanism of each organ in detail would be an unnecessary labour, and we, therefore, may select a few examples, from which a clear idea may be gained of the general characters of the methods by which each part of the body is regulated to meet the demands made on it. Selecting, then, the heart as the most important organ, we may briefly discuss the paths of innervation and control as demonstrated by experiment on various animals. The heart is constantly regulated to the organic needs mainly through two channels; the sympathetic system conveying to it the accelerating or augmenting impulses, whilst the inhibition of the heart is maintained by the nervous impulses passing down the vagus nerve. At first sight such a double mechanism as this might appear unnecessary; it would seem simpler for the heart to have been provided with merely an augmenting mechanism, which should serve for the occasion when undue exertion on the part of the heart was called for; but it is, in fact, the inhibitory apparatus which plays the more important part, and which, throughout the body, has the most powerful and striking influence. Thus, under normal circumstances, the heart is working at only a comparatively small percentage of its real power, being restrained by the constant inhibitory impulses reaching it through the vagus, so that on some further effort of the heart being required, this is not provided for so much by an exhausting series of augmenting stimuli, which would correspond in some degree to the flogging of a wearying horse, but by the adjustable withdrawal of inhibitory influences; thus permitting the heart to respond to the calls made upon it without undue strain. We shall find that this action of inhibition has a profound influence on all the functions, from the most physical to the most psychical; and as the etiology of hypnosis largely depends on the alteration in the nervous balance of inhibitory impulses, we must refer to certain experiments in this direction.

If the vagus nerve in a frog be stimulated by means of an interrupted current, the normal beating of the heart will be interrupted, the heart ceases to contract, and the heart-muscle is completely relaxed; on the withdrawal of the stimulus the heart begins to contract, at first feebly, but in a short period with greater strength than before the stimulation; and this experiment may be repeated many times with precisely the same result. We here have a clear demonstration of the nature of impulses passing down the vagus to the heart: they are not impulses of a motor or innervating character, but perform the function of a regulatory inhibition.

Two experiments may be quoted as indicative of the nervous control of the whole of the vasomotor system, and of the process of secretion. The regulation of the blood supply to a part, and consequent, to a great extent, of the activity of that part is maintained by a compensatory mechanism similar to that of the heart. If, in a rabbit, the cervical sympathetic be divided, the vessels on that side of the head dilate, the whole of the region affected becomes engorged with blood, and the temperature is raised. On stimulation of the central end of the divided nerve, the dilated vessels contract, the engorgement disappears, and the temperature returns to normal; the sympathetic system is thus seen to exert a constrictive action on the blood-vessels, thus maintaining a tonus and, consequently, an adequate blood-pressure. The most convincing experiments have, however, been performed upon the submandibular gland of the dog. . . . The nervous supply of this gland is derived from two channels—the chorda tympani and the sympathetic. If the chorda tympani be divided, on stimulation of the peripheral end, a copious secretion from the gland ensues. The copius secretion thus obtained from the duct is clear and liquid. Simultaneously with the increased secretion the gland itself becomes hyperaemic, the blood-vessels dilate, and the blood-flow is more rapid; thus the chorda tympani contains fibres from a vaso-dilatator neuronic group, and other fibres from a secreto-motor group. On the other hand, when the cervical sympathetic is stimulated the arteries are constricted, the escape of blood from the veins is small, whilst the secretion of a gland is scantier and altered in character, being much more viscid and more albuminous. The sympathetic thus contains fibres from a vaso-constrictor group, and other fibres from a secreto-motor group. If the chorda tympani and the sympathetic be stimulated together, then the alteration and the secretion partake of both characters, the secretion being fairly copious in amount and viscid in character. With the above as a rapid survey of the nature of the proximal mechanism, we may now proceed to a discussion of the higher mechanism involved in the origination or interpretation of stimuli—of the relations between the psychical and the physical.

Let us at once explain that by the term "psychical" we do not desire to endorse any of the various ideas connected with the word "soul"; we use the word simply to represent the non-physical aspects of nervous action. The various ideas connected with the "mind" and the "soul" are very confusing; but even as an hypothesis the doctrine of the soul would lend us no assistance, but would only needlessly involve an already complex question. We shall then regard the mind as one of the functions of a certain part of the nervous system, and, indeed, it will become evident in the course of discussion how impossible it must be to essentially separate the psychical processes from the physical. Yet in endeavouring to place before the reader a systematic view of the relations of the various forms of nervous activity, we shall have reason to differ from the teaching of the accepted schools of physiological psychology, and it is only just to the reader to say that though the theories here advanced have not been put forward without consideration, they fail to harmonize with the conclusions of many of the leading authorities in material respects.

The various kinds of nervous action may all be classed under three leads:

1. Acts, constant, unmodified by reason of special adaptation to alter environment. Inaptic.
2. Acts, accompanied by adaption to altered environment; purposive; unassociated with a conscious process. Aptic.
3. Acts, associated with a conscious process.

The student of physiological psychology regarding this classification from the accepted standpoint will at once notice that the differential elements vary from those usually put forward as the criteria of classification, and moreover, he will hardly be prepared to sanction the disappearance of the one term more relied upon than any other, viz., the term "reflex." Our reasons for this alteration will appear in the course of the argument.

The first class of nervous actions may be represented by the action which follows irritation of the cornea; the eyelid immediately closes; the action is altogether independent of consciousness; volition has no power to prevent it; it is a definite muscular response to a definite stimulus; so long as the nervous mechanism is intact it will occur, entirely independent of and beyond the control of the individual.

The second class includes actions which are more complicated and are adaptive. Moreover, an essential feature in this class is the presence of more or less elemental psychical action. Inasmuch, however, as the possibility of psychical action without consciousness is energetically denied by many authorities, we shall reserve the description and discussion of this special elimination till later.

The third class comprises all those actions of which a conscious process is an essential feature. We have avoided the term "reflex" action; not indeed, that we are unwilling to use it when properly applied, but for the reason that reflex actions do not belong exclusively to the class of inaptic actions, but to all three classes, and to none more so than the class comprising the acts of consciousness. The most important point of our discussion will necessarily turn upon the fundamental distinction existing, in the writer's opinion, between the inaptic and aptic classes of action, and inasmuch as this distinction is not generally admitted, we must refer to experiments illustrating this differentiation. If we destroy the brain of a frog as far down as the medulla oblongata, leaving the animal otherwise intact, we shall have an animal in whom all the nervous reaction to be obtained by experiment must necessarily take place in that portion of the nervous system not destroyed, i.e., the spinal cord and the peripheral nervous system in connection with it. With the animal in this condition we can readily obtain the class of action called "reflex." If the tip of any toe of the right foot be pinched, the right leg is immediately drawn up; if a toe of the opposite foot be pinched, then the opposite leg is drawn up. Now this is a constant simple reaction to stimulus; it is a physical property of the nervous mechanism existent in the spinal cord; the nervous system takes no cognizance of its adaptation to the circumstances; so long as the same stimulus be applied, so long will this act take place, "constant and unmodified by altered environment." It is a type, therefore, of the inaptic class. On elaborating the experiment, we notice the same constant reaction to stimulus as before, but we find that the conditions of the animal to its environment will effect the response of the brainless frog. A small piece of paper is moistened with glacial acetic acid and is applied to the skin of the inner side of the thigh; the leg on this side is at once violently drawn up, and the foot of the leg is swept over the spot where the irritation is so as to remove the paper. Now place the paper, moistened as before, on the side of the frog and hold the leg on the same side; at first, the frog will attempt to free this leg in order to remove the irritant; then, realizing this is impossible, he struggles to remove it by means of the other leg, and after possible several futile attempts, succeeds. Are these last two actions merely complications of the one first quoted; are they essentially the same, or can we name any fundamental distinction existing between them? The answer to this is highly controversial and varies according to the position taken up by the various writers. Ziehen, to whose work the reader is referred for a very able and lucid exposition of the opposing argument, takes up a position which, in the writer's opinion, is altogether fallacious from his persistence in refusing to any nervous process the name or function of "psychical" unless it be accompanied with consciousness, a position which, however widely it may be held, appears to us to be founded on an altogether gratuitous and confusing assumption. In the case of the brainless frog, there can be no consciousness; there can "therefore" be no "psychical" processes taking place, consequently all the phenomena are physical in nature; that part of the nervous system still intact can have no perception of altered conditions, it does alter its reactions. We are told that the actions are due simply to a complication of reflex processes. This "complication," however, begs the question, for what we have to decide is the reason for these complications. No one will deny that the movements in the last experiment are more complicated than those in the first.

We must then discuss the reason for this complication, and in doing so, we must necessarily examine the position of the opposite school. To the question whether there can be any intermediate stage between the physical and the conscious states of the nervous system, Ziehen gives a decided answer. "All and only the phenomena which are imparted to our consciousness are psychical. . . . The sensation of sight itself is psychical in so far as it affects our consciousness"; and again: " 'Psychical' and 'conscious' are for us, at least, at the beginning of our investigations, identical." Now, all this depends on the meaning that we attach to the word "psychical", and let us say at once that, whilst all the higher psychical processes are necessarily part of a conscious process, yet the essential qualities of a psychical process do not, in our opinion, require the co-existence of consciousness. Any function which has to do with interpretation of impulses cannot be classed in the same category with a reaction of a merely physical nature, even though, as we are willing to admit, the interpretative function is equally a reaction to a stimulus; indeed, consciousness itself is such a reaction; but whilst in the case of the physical reaction we have nothing more than the simple unmodified reaction, in the case of the interpretative reaction we have a new element present, depending on the interposition of an agency quite foreign to the physical reaction. So obvious is this that Stirling, who describes the various experiments with the pithed frog, puts them under two headings. The simple withdrawal of the leg on pinching the toe he includes in the heading "Reflex Action"; whilst the removal of the irritant is placed under the significant heading "Chemical Stimulations—Purposive Characters of Reflex." In a work dealing with the purely practical and experimental side of physiology this is somewhat curious, and the reference to the "purposive characters" would appear to indicate that in a greater or less degree the writer draws some distinction between the two classes of actions.

It might appear at first sight wiser to introduce an intermediate term and thus avoid the confusion caused by using the word "psychical" in a manner different from that of other writers. And since there is a real distinction existing between a conscious and an unconscious act, we have referred the unconscious psychical process to the aptic class. But in this class the psychical feature is always present in a more or less elemental form, and consequently the term is common to the aptic and the conscious actions.

The actions comprised in the aptic class are so various that in the present state of our knowledge it is almost impossible to give an accurate definition which shall neither exclude too much nor include too little; yet in the case of a typical inaptic action of the first class and a typical aptic action there can be little difficulty in arriving at their classification. If we find an action which must have required for its performance a perception of the present environment, an estimation, more or less complete, of the circumstances under which the action is to be performed, and a modification of the action to meet the existing conditions, then, since we cannot conceive the qualities of perception, estimation, and deduction as physical qualities whilst on the other hand they definitely correspond with our conception of the immaterial nervous phenomena, we consequently can only classify them as psychical.

So prominent is the differentiation of these processes that the writers seeking refuge in "reflex action" have found it necessary to provide some way out. Ziehen quotes two experiments performed by Goltze, which well illustrate the difficulties under which the advocates of "reflex action" labour. "If after having removed the cerebrum of a frog we touch the cornea of the brainless animal with a coughing-needle, the first reflex motion is the closing of its eyelid. If we repeat or intensify the stimulation the animal will strike the needle aside with the corresponding front foot. A still further increase causes the head and trunk to be turned away from the irritant. Finally upon constantly increasing both the frequency and the intensity of the irritation, the animal will retire to some other place." Now if similar responses had taken place, say, in a healthy boy with an intact nervous system, could we class these as physical reactions? Yet in the case of the frog, because the cerebrum has been removed, we are to argue that there can be no consciousness; without consciousness there can be no psychical actions, and consequently the whole process is one corresponding with the simple physical reaction to a simple stimulus—the whole argument depending upon the fallacious identification of consciousness with psychical activity. Still even the erroneous limitation of "psychical" has to give way, and Ziehen in describing the next experiment takes refuge in the descriptive but question-begging term, "automatic acts or reactions." A frog is taken and its cerebrum destroyed, leaving the optic thalamus intact. A prick on its foot easily causes it to leap off. "If we place an obstacle in the path of its retreat it avoids the obstruction, or, in rare cases, clears it with a well measured bound." Whatever name we care to give to these processes they are essentially adaptive; they connote the elements of preception and deduction. As examples of psychical action without consciousness we can quote almost innumerable examples in ourselves. For instance, we may take the common instance of absent-mindedness, where the consciousness is fully occupied with an idea and cannot, in consequence, respond for some little time to another stimulus. Whilst in this absent-minded condition the person is addressed by a friend; at the time he gives no sign of having heard the remark; after an appreciable interval his consciousness is affected, and he replies.

Between the line of the remark and the time of the reply, what has taken place? The stimuli afforded by the spoken words have been transmitted to the proper group; the exact nature of the stimuli has been appreciated; the memory has identified the words and supplied this meaning; all this must have happened at the moment, for the auditory stimulus could not well gain a reaction when the stimulus had ceased to exist; thus without any conscious process the stimulus has been received and appreciated; after a period of shorter or longer duration comes the action due to the conscious process, without which the reply could not be formulated. To quote other examples would be to fill our pages with unnecessary material, since phenomena of a similar nature will readily occur to the reader—e.g., the playing of an instrument, the consciousness being engaged in some other direction; the performance of elaborate movements without any distinct consciousness of their performance, yet all of them dependent on some of the most psychical of combinations as the combination of perception, memory, and the like.

The view here put forward with regard to the nature of nervous action thus differs, in material particulars, from any of the current theories. Now we may briefly summarize the distinctions. The views depending upon the assumption of an "entity" inhabiting the body, and commonly called the "soul," must be at once dismissed, since, in their origin and advocacy, they do not depend on scientific investigation; the argument as to the necessity of a "soul" for the production of thought is equally applicable as an argument for the existence of a "soul" controlling and supervising the processes of gastric digestion; moreover, it is only as we have been able to rid ourselves of this and similar superstitions that any progress has been made in the study of the mental processes.

The only method by which we can arrive at a sure knowledge of the etiology and physiology of nervous action is by a study of the organ to which this function belongs. We thus rely entirely on the psychology which is physiological in its arguments and methods; when, however, we come to examine the details of the processes in this manner we are bound to differ from many of the writers on physiological psychology in matters of moment, though, at the same time, we would acknowledge the great and lasting value of their work. And the first point on which we join issue is in their method of regarding and treating what they term "Reflex action." The use of the term is to express the constant reaction to a constant stimulus, the simple actions, such as the one above referred to, are classed as "reflex." But such a limitation is altogether artificial and confusing; so far from such a reaction being limited to the simple movements, the law of a constant reaction to a constant stimulus applies with equal force to the highest cerebral functions. When we see a friend—can we help seeing him? Why, because the response to the stimulus is in a conscious process, should we exclude it from the class of reflex actions? The stimulus is present, the reaction to the stimulus is present, and the relation is constant. When we hear a piano-organ, we recognize the sounds and their origin, though we do not see the instrument or the player, and we cannot help recognizing them; we find it impossible to avoid the effects they produce on us. The higher cerebral processes, it is true, are much more complicated; each state of consciousness is modified by stimuli belonging to the present environment, which can probably never be repeated in their exact order, number, and rotation; but each separate stimulus produces its separate response, and for every one that we can isolate we can obtain the same evidence of a constant response to a constant stimulus. Therefore, not some, not many, but all nervous actions are "reflex" actions. If, however, we thus include all the nervous processes within this term, it must lose all its value as a classified category term for certain of the elementary functions, and this is the reason for its avoidance in our suggested classification. Thus with regard to the etiology of the phenomena, our position is simple; whether or not the action corresponds to any one of Ziehen's three classes—"(1) Motions constant and generally following; results from one or more external stimuli—no psychical correlative. (2) Motion modified by one or more intercurrent stimuli; generally following—no psychical correlative (3) Motion results directly or indirectly from one or more external stimuli; modified by the association of intercurrent sensations and ideas; generally following—with psychical correlative." They all obey the same law of constancy; the precise response depending on the part stimulated, the paths through which the stimulus passes, and the point at which it terminates.

In the preceding, therefore, we have sought to classify the actions, not according to their ultimate etiology, which is essentially the same in all, but according to the nature of the processes involved in the response made to the stimulus.

If the response by one which is "physical," i.e., giving no evidence of modification due to the external environment, we include it in the elementary class of nervous action—the inaptic. If the response be of such a nature as to show that there has been a modification due to the environment of the moment, but without consciousness, then we have an easily appreciable distinction as our basis for a second classification—the aptic. Finally, if the response be associated with a conscious process, we again have a real and definite distinction upon which to rely for the third and last class.

But the student will readily perceive that our distinction between the first and second classes, whilst definite enough in many marked cases, is certainly vague in others. Indeed, we admit at once that taking all the actions belonging to cases 1 and 2 together, it would be very difficult, if not impossible, to definitely relegate some actions to either class; there would remain a certain percentage of indeterminate phenomena. Admitting this, we cannot pretend that the classification is a perfect one. Still further, when we consider the terms "unmodified by reason of adaptation to altered environment" we may meet with the criticism that in the simplest cases cannot materially alter the environment so as to affect the response, without at the same time altering the stimulus. Again, perhaps we should regard the simple "reflexes" as adaptive; unquestionably they are of service to the organism; the loss of the "corneal reflex" may and often does result in serious injury to the eye; the withdrawal of the frog's foot on pinching it may also be considered as adaptive; but all this is probably developmental in its origin and can be so explained; then there are many "reflexes" of no use to the organism, though equally of developmental origin, as for example, the gluteal, cremasteric, abdominal, epigastric and scapular "reflexes." So far, therefore, as this class of actions is

adaptive or "fitting," they are so from developmental consideration, and not from any spontaneous recognition of and adaptation
to the present environment; whereas a typical aptic action is
characterized by the recognition of circumstances which require
to be taken into account. For our purpose it matters little as to
the exact point at which we may deny or admit the interposition
of an unconscious intelligence, so long as we recognize that amongst
the functions of the nervous system one of the most important parts
is played by this unconscious intelligence. So much in observation
and experiment is conclusive in this direction that we make little
apology for the intrusion of the term—unconscious psychical actions.

So far, we have relied mainly on experiments conducted on
animals; but if we are to pursue our studies in direct application to
human psychology it is above all things necessary that we should
experiment on the human subject. And in this direction the most
promising field is in the study of the hypnotic state; for here we
have a condition which is a remarkable deviation from the normal
condition, yet in which every action performed in normal life can
equally be performed. Psychologists have profited but little from
the opportunities open to them for various reasons; the experimental use of hypnotism requires a good deal of practical experience
and a precise knowledge of the condition; physiologists being, as a
boy, devoid of this practical experience, have put forward theories
which are evidently the results of casual and inexact observation, and not infrequently appear to be founded on their knowledge of the normal nervous processes rather than on any actual
knowledge of the hypnotic state. Having dealt in as brief a manner as possible with the structure and function of the nervous system, regarded as a whole, we shall now turn our attention to the
modifications effected by the induction of hypnosis, with especial
reference to the physiology of the modifications thus induced. The
phenomena of hypnosis we discuss separately, and we shall only
refer to this instance to such of the phenomena as may be necessary
to the course of the argument.

The attention of physicians and physiologists has been directed
towards what is termed the influence of the "Mind" upon the
"Body," and in numerous works we find references to the ef-

fects of "suggestion" in the waking state; still further, we recognize the effects of emotions on the normal process, the effect, for instance, of fear in preventing the flow of saliva; the effect of nervous emotion on the gastro-intestinal tract, and many others. In a vague and unsatisfactory way these are classed as examples of a condition in the body sympathetic with that in the mind. These theories involve a misconception of which it is difficult to get rid. In our description of the anatomy and distribution of the nervous system no reference was made to any distribution of neurons or fibres whose function, pure and simple, was mental. So far as our anatomical and histological knowledge of the nervous system goes, we can point to no group which does not either receive sensory impulses or from which motor impulses do not emanate Indeed, if from anatomical considerations we were to attempt a localization of the mind, we should rather place it in the arborescing dendrons than in any other situation. But so far from seeking to attempt any such localization of the mental functions it will be seen that we have every reason to believe that there is no such separation physiologically considered. Thus the neuron which receives the sensory stimulus, the neuron which discharges the motor impulse, and the arborescence connecting the two, are also psychical in function, either separately or as a group. This conclusion is not derived from that fruitful source of error, introspection, but partly from a consideration of the structure of the nervous system, partly from a consideration of the normal nervous phenomena, but chiefly from the writer's study and observation of the hypnotic phenomena. If there be any reason for the opinion above expressed, the importance of a knowledge of nervous-anatomy will be easily realized, and it will be essential to bear in mind the anatomical and physiological details referred to in the earlier parts of this chapter.

The group of neurons must then be regarded as an organic unit capable of sensation, ideation, emotion, volition, and motion, in other words, capable of psychical and physical activity. With this group some others are in arborescent connection. We have at once on this conception a clearer view of the phenomena of the nervous system; emotion betrays itself in muscular movement, as movement betrays itself in emotion; the psychical actions of the organism correspond with the physical, and the physical actions with the psychical actions of the organism, not because the one acts on the other, not, therefore, because of the influence of the "Mind" on the "Body," but because the processes are the results of the neuronic groups in action.

Here, however, we must indicate the limitations which govern the action of the group, for, though well acquainted with the muscular element of consciousness, we are equally familiar with the idea, the reflection or thought which causes no appreciable physical reaction, and with the movement which is unassociated with a conscious process; for the laws of inhibition apply with equal force to the nervous system itself, and the following examples illustrate this. In the case of a severe fright the stimuli are so strong, and produce such a violent reaction, that the ordinary inhibitory forces are not strong enough to meet the case; the inhibitory power is withdrawn from the general system and centralized upon the higher cerebral groups; concomitantly with this withdrawal of inhibition, the heart, no longer restrained by the retarding inhibitory influences passing down the vagus, beats more rapidly and more strongly, and we have the "thumping" heart as a consequence of this withdrawal. Again, in the case of diseases causing an atrophy of the nervous tracts leading from the brain, and consequently causing a shutting-off of the inhibition, the "reflex" actions are increased, and others are developed, which in the normal subject are not present.

In the case of the neuronic group we have a twofold phase of inhibition: the physical and the unconscious psychical are restrained within their paths, so that with normal stimuli their reactions will correspond completely to the stimulus; the energy represented by the stimulus will have entirely disappeared in the unconscious sphere, and there will be in consequence no disturbance of the conscious elements of the group. Should, however, the stimulus be too strong to be dissipated in this manner, then the consciousness will be affected according to the degree of excess in the stimulus; in the manner we may have, (1), A stimulus causing action belonging to either the first or the second class of nervous actions. (2), A stimulus, which, being in excess, is dissipated in an affection of the consciousness. (3), A violent stimulus, the excess of which is so great as to affect the consciousness violently. (4), A stimulus which tends to affect the consciousness first, and does not directly cause physical or unconscious psychical reaction, unless in excess (e.g. special sensation). In this manner we might easily multiply the possible varieties, thus two stimuli may be combined, as for instance, (1) and (4), and the consciousness is affected by the sensation of touch, whilst the other actions are accompanied by no conscious process.

We have, therefore, a very delicate mechanism kept in adjustment by inhibition; in the normal state, subject to withdrawal and increase of the inhibitory impulses, and with momentary variations in the balance between the processes attended and those unattended with consciousness. In the nervously irritable we have a condition of weak inhibitory power, with the result that normal stimuli produce abnormal reactions; the balance may be altered by means of drugs, such as alcohol, cannabis indica, and in various conditions such as sleep, coma, etc., so that we are well acquainted with conditions in which the normal balance is more or less interfered with. The interference may be quite within physiological bounds, or in its nature and degree, may become a pathological condition. From a consideration of the phenomena we shall be easily able to deduce the purely physiological nature of the modifications induced in normal hypnosis.

In the account of the phenomena of hypnosis in an earlier chapter, stress was laid on the change which occurs in the hypnotized subject apart from the effects of suggestion. The changes in the pulse and respiration are comparatively trivial, since they may occur in many normal conditions, but the altered condition of the consciousness is exceedingly important. The disappearance of normal irritability, the acute passivity, and the lack of attention to the external on the part of the subject, are all evidences of a profound change in the nervous system. This alteration is spontaneous; it has not been caused by the action of drugs or by increasing or decreasing the metabolism of any particular portion of the nervous system, but has resulted from a cerebral change produced as a result of the various stimuli brought into action in inducing hypnosis.

All this has been brought about as a consequence of the abnormal form of inhibition induced, which tends to limit the action of the higher psychical functions to the least degree possible, and this is still true, even in the case of hallucinations and the effects of other suggestions which might appear to be due to an increased ideation.

Most of the theories propounded in explanation of the phenomena of hypnosis have been put forward by physiologists who, however eminent in the branch of science which they have studied, have apparently not had opportunity of systematically observing the hypnotic phenomena. The commonest and most improbable is the theory which assumes a psychical exaggeration; the subject is "preoccupied" with the idea given to him by the suggestion; so increased are his powers of ideation that the developments of the idea are manifested in every direction; he is told he sees till he believes he really does, and so forth. This theory, put forward in many ways and with various modifications, is, in the writer's opinion, untenable. Whatever may be the cause of the hypnotic phenomena, we are assured that any explanation proceeding on these lines is wide of the mark. The symptoms in hypnosis when accurately studied point in quite the opposite direction. If we say to a person in the normal condition, "Your left arm is stiff; you cannot bend or move it," we may cause amusement or surprise in the individual, but the arm is as capable of movement as before, and remains in every way normal. If, on the contrary, we make such a suggestion to a person in a moderately deep hypnosis, the effect is markedly different; there is no evidence of surprise or any other emotion on the part of the subject; he does not reply, and from the appearance of his features he does not appear to have heard the remark; as far as his general appearance gives us any information, his consciousness has not been affected by the words spoken; but, on the other hand, the arm is affected; it is quite stiff, immovable by any muscular contractions of the subject's muscles, and only with great difficulty to be moved by another person.

So far, then, as the higher cerebral functions are concerned, the excess is all in the normal person; it is the physical reaction which is here distinctive of hypnosis.

Having previously demonstrated the play of inhibition in the psychical as well as in the physical functions of the brain, we are now in a position to represent physiologically the differences in the course of the suggestions in the two cases. Taking the case of the suggestion of stiffness of the arm made to the normal person, . . . the stimulus is dissipated in the formation of ideas connected with the suggestion, and it is, therefore, the conscious function of the neuronic group which acts in response to the stimulus. In the case of the suggestion made to the hypnotized subject, there is no ideation; the subject does not consider the possible truth or untruth of the suggestion; its reasonableness, or the reverse; for those functions are inhibited. Those paths being thus shut off, the stimulus must be dissipated in the other functions of the neuronic group, and these are the physical.

Yet the inhibition of the conscious process is not complete; for obviously before the motor effect can be produced the meaning of the suggestion must be appreciated; but this is an attendant process, unassociated with the development of ideation. In the same way the inhibition, in the normal state, of the motor functions is not complete; for associated with the consciousness and ideation caused by the suggestion, is the motor part of the emotion of surprise; etc., with which the suggestion was received.

The principles here enunciated enable us to gain a more thorough appreciation of the processes employed in the execution of suggestions which are psychical in their nature. It may appear difficult to apply our theory to these conditions, which are especially characterized by the action of the higher groups, such as those employed in hallucinations, illusions, etc.; especially may this appear to be the case when we have to do with increased sensory powers. But when we realize the limitations which surround the exhibition of these phenomena, we shall find that they present no difficulty, and that in many points they lend a striking confirmation to the views here expressed.

One of the most noteworthy features in a posthypnotic hallucination is the completeness with which it possesses the individual. If we take an ordinary uneducated boy, and suggest to him that when he wakes up he will find himself a certain eminent actor, we notice that he takes to the part with a readiness which appears astonishing. Not that his powers of elocution or acting are, in themselves, increased; but all the influences which would restrain him were he "acting" are absent. There is no self-consciousness; nor consideration as to whether he is interesting his audience; all his ideas are turned in the direction of the idea which has been suggested to him. Moreover, it is not concerned with any volitional energy on his part; he would be amazed at the person who told him he was not the actor in question. He would be in the same frame of mind as we should be were we told that we were not ourselves. The reason of his condition is as follows. We have already explained that in the appreciation of the suggestion the consciousness of the hypnotic subject is not interfered with, so that we have a full and free play of the subject's ideation and emotion with reference to the suggestion which is their stimulus; but there is still, not only in theory, but, as we have seen, in fact, a marked limitation to the action of his consciousness with reference to the suggestion in directions other than that indicated by the suggestion. Coincident with the inhibition of one set of functions, there is an increased capability of action in the others; the result we may represent almost mathematically. The stimulus, instead of being dissipated amongst an indefinite number of neuronic groups, or parts of groups, is confined to those whose function is the pure appreciation of the stimulus; the other groups whose function is the consideration of the reasonableness of the suggestion and the development of the stimulus in other conscious directions are inhibited. Let us represent the stimulus by 5; in the hypnotic state, the 5 is confined to, and therefore being dissipated in, one department of conscious activity. In the normal state the 5 is dissipated in various directions, and assuming that there are at least twice as many neuronic groups in conscious action as there are in hypnosis, we may safely divide the 5 by 2 to represent the share of any one function; but, further, the other 2½ would be dissipated not in assisting the execution of the suggestion, but in its consideration, and, consequently, in the retardation and prevention of any execution. Hence, taking this as an example, in hypnosis we have a force represented by 5 acting unrestrained; in normal conditions, with the same stimulus, there is a force of 2½ opposed by a force of 2½.

Many problems of great interest are suggested by the careful examination of the phenomena of hallucinations and illusions belonging to the deeper states; moreover, the probability that the function of memory essentially belongs to the neuronic group connected with the action, and the reasons for this unity of function are clearly brought out in many experiments; but we do not propose to deal at length with the phenomena of hallucination, for while their etiology differs in no wise from the other premises of hypnosis, many other considerations would have to be brought forward which would involve us in a psychological discussion impossible to keep within our limits. But some of the questions may be briefly illustrated. In the experiments where an educated subject was led to spell incorrectly, there was distinct evidence of a conflct between the suggested ignorance of the subject and his actual knowledge. The action of the neuronic group under these suggestions presents some curious problems. Did the subject, for instance, think at the time that "hundrud" was wrong? It was noticeable that before omitting the letter "e" or commiting an error of spelling, there was a momentary but distinct hesitation. The spelling in the specimen reproduced is nearly, though not quite, phonetic, and it is difficult to say whether the suggestion simply had the effect of causing the subject to spell phonetically or whether a more elaborate process was induced. The latter hypothesis appears to be the more probable, and in all cases it would seem that there is a distinct knowledge in the subject's mind of the right form, which, however, is so suddenly and automatically modified, by the action of the suggestion, that he is never conscious of the modification. This kind of ignorance is present to some extent in the normal state; we are not actively conscious of the separate effects produced by the rays from an object striking the eye; we are only aware of the final result, i.e., we see the object.

There is a moment in all hypnotic illusions when, though the subject knows it not, the brain recognizes the truth. If we suggest to a subject that when he sees the letter "a" he shall think it is "b", it is obvious that he must perceive and recognize "a" before he can confuse it with "b". The complexity of the process instituted by any suggestion of this kind is evident when we consider that not only does the apparatus of vision act in the normal manner, but the perception must first act normally before the suggestion can take effect, and when the suggestion has taken effect, the impression remains a psychical one and does not affect the retina of the optic nerve.

It is clear, from the final result of the suggestion, that the psychical impression at once interprets the stimulus of objective reality, according to the original cerebral stimulus supplied by the suggestion. There is present, that is to say, as a result, a condition of the cerebral cells which will accurately adapt the action to the combined effect of the suggestion and the objective stimulus. This was well illustrated in the following experiment:—It was suggested to a subject in hypnosis that at a certain time (about a week later) and at a certain place, he should find that T—was V—and that V— was T—. During the interval there was no confusion in his mind as to their respective personalities; but, at the time and place suggested, coming up to V—, he asked him if he knew where V— was, and, on seeing—just entering the hall, went towards him saying, "Ah, there he is." For the next hour, which was the limit given in the suggestion, it was impossible to disabuse him of the idea; at the expiration of the hour he looked somewhat absorbed in himself and puzzled for a few moments, and then continued his conversation; only, he no longer confused the two persons, and, when challenged with what he had previously been doing, he stoutly denied that he had done anything of the kind. Another experiment of a similar nature may be mentioned. L— and M— are intimate friends. It was suggested, in hypnosis, to L— that M— was V— and that V— was M—. This suggestion was made at 11:30 a.m. and continued entirely effective until 2:30 p.m. when L— was hypnotized again and the impression was removed. The three went for a walk, lunched together, played billiards, etc., L— confusing M— and V— the whole time. In this case L— remembered afterwards all that had occurred, but still retained the impression that what M— had done was V—'s doing, and vice versa. Thus, V— played billiards with him whilst M— marked; but he said (after the removal of the suggestion) that it was M— who played with him and that it was V— who marked, and so forth. These two cases are examples of two distinct post-hypnotic states; in neither case was the subject open to further suggestion. The action of the memoric faculty, in its twofold aspect of the preservation and the reproduction of ideas, is vividly illustrated by some of the phenomena of hypnosis. The observed facts seem to support the view that no impression is ever absolutely effaced from the brain; the faculty of recalling an idea (recollection) may be absent, but the cerebral record is permanent. The two cases quoted previously seem to be hardly capable of explanation of any other hypothesis. The phenomena of memory as seen in the dreaming, sleep-walking, and hypnotic states all point to this conclusion. The faculty of recalling these impressions is, however, generally non-existent when the brain is in a different condition from that in which the impression was made. The recollection of an idea depends upon the ability of the brain to link together its various impressions until it gains a connected whole, of which the part recollected is an essential feature. If, then, by some cerebral modification there be a distinct break in the chain no recollection will be possible. Accordingly there must be some connection between that recollected and the moment of recollection; the link may be supplied in many ways, but if the physiological modification be great so will the difficulty of recollection be correspondingly great. If, therefore, there be a profound physiological change, such as occurs in hypnosis, the probability is that recollection will not be present until that physiological condition is reproduced. This law is adequately illustrated by the phenomena of hypnosis, to which we have referred in the previous chapter.

Moreover, our general knowledge of the memory is brought to a more definite state by considerations resulting from our knowledge of the condition underlying the relations between the physical and psychical action of the nervous system; we may assume that each neuronic group possesses the memory of the stimuli which it has received, and that there is a necessary sensation-memory and motor-memory intimately associated with the recognition of stimuli and with the discharge of the proper motor impulses.

We have attempted in this rapid introduction to the subject of the physiology of hypnosis to place before the student an argument as to its etiology and its relationships with the normal conditions derived almost entirely from observation and experiment. That in so complex a subject we should have adequately considered each phenomenon of importance is not possible, but we have endeavoured to select various examples typical of their kinds and thus illustrated the general principles underlying the nervous adaptation in hypnosis. No doubt we may still be told that the mental processes, and especially those occurring in hypnosis, are so many puzzles interesting though never soluble; but to the student properly acquainted with his subject there is no mystery in hypnosis. Our knowledge is far from complete, but it is only when there is a great deal known about a subject that the incompleteness of our knowledge becomes evident. In hypnosis itself there is nothing mysterious or insoluble; the uncertain elements in it belong to it in common with all those processes connected with the immaterial and imponderable reaction to stimuli. At least we may comprehend the fact that thought is ultimately as much a physical fact as the process of secretion in a gland or the beating of the heart, and that these functions are necessarily associated with one another, not by reason of any impression from the "Mind," but in an exact quantitative relationship. Given the definite stimulus, it may result in high psychical activities and give rise to a thought; with the conscious function debarred from action the stimulus is expressed in other than conscious terms; it is in hypnosis that we can regulate the course of the stimulus and determine its reaction.

Otto Georg Wetterstrand, M.D.

Dr. Wetterstrand's work has appeared in both Swedish and German, and a Russian translation, by Dr. N. Dal, was published in Moscow in 1893. The English-speaking medical profession recognized the value of Dr. Wetterstrand's work as fully as the Europeans did. More practical than theoretical, it offers the results of conscientious and able observation in what is today an important branch of medical science.

The following article appeared in the Swedish language in *Hygiene,* a periodical of the Swedish Medical Society. It created a method of treatment which follows the other processes of healing in practical medicine. This method followed the investigations of Liebault, Bernheim and Forel, and others.

Wetterstrand wrote in his Preface: "It has not been my intention to write a manual or a textbook, but simply to allude to the value of a therapeutic method which so strikingly illustrates the truth of the words: l'esprit gouverne, le corps obeit."

PRACTICAL TEACHINGS OF THE USE OF PSYCHOLOGY IN MEDICINE*
Notes from Clinical Studies with Bernheim, Forel, von Kraft Ebing, Etc.

I

An early train in July 1891, brought me from Strasburg to Nancy. There was a strange comfort in leaving, as an indescribable feeling of uneasiness had grown stronger during my short stay. Impartial in my views, and a perfect stranger, nothing but politeness and kindness had been extended to me. The new Strasburg had elicited my admiration, with its fine private and public buildings—a magnificent university, for instance, an eloquent interpretation of the German love and respect for scientific pursuits. The pride manifested in showing me all this was legitimate, and no exultation struck a discordant note.

---

*From Wetterstrand, O.G.: *Hypnotism and Its Application to Practical Medicine.* Authorized translation by H.G. Petersen, M.D. New York, Putnam; London, Knickerbocker, 1902, pp. 125-152.

Still, one labored under the irrepressible feeling that to bridle utterance, whether of criticism or of praise, would be just as much an act of kindness as of prudence. It was intolerable. A silence of unspoken thoughts made the city mournful and chilly. To watch the characteristic, ill-concealed language of those faces, eyes, gait, and then to think of the terrible effect when the spell eventually breaks! This prison air unnerved me. Just as silent and masked lies the steel girdle around. The rippling surface of the surrounding land looks like a half-forgotten burial-ground, but its undulating lines are the war-god's hieroglyphics. There, in these hidden casemates, are buried at present the weighty arguments of—a future day. And over it all, green waving grass, birds and a fleecy sky.

Speeding on, there were banners and music from the frontier of Nancy. What a contrast between the 14th of July here and there! On several occasions I had partaken of French enthusiasm on that day, but had never before been equally touched by its pathos and meaning. The gay coloring of the crowd thronging the streets on the passing of the troops, and filling the great square to witness their review, was a pleasant welcome to the city which for so many years I had longed to visit. Stanislas Place, surrounded with its magnificently wrought iron gates, opened into the Pepiniere, a park of great rural beauty and rich in shade trees and tastefully arranged flower-beds. Thousands filled it. The military band played, and later in the evening, when numberless lanterns splashed streaks of color upon the animated promenaders, it made one think of the preparation for a carnival.

The next day had sobered this exuberance, and Nancy was again the quiet, easy-going provincial town, claiming no ambitious position otherwise than that accruing from peaceful thrift among its citizens. This was not, however, what attracted me to the place. Nancy had attracted the physician, not the sightseer or inquirer into its patriotic or its industrial status. It reckoned among its citizens men of keen observation, men whose fearless and successful researches had given their names to the scientific world by proclaiming a new departure, apparently in direct opposition to former theories and experience. Liebeault and Bernheim are known to the medical world as advocates of psychological therapeutics based upon rational and honest investigation of psychic possibilities. The result of their experiments is known as "hypno-suggestion." They have gathered around them those who have been willing to try the new, not in contempt of the old, but incited by a spirit of progress that believes in evolutionary phases of existing things. Accordingly there is a constant intellectual growth which necessarily must supersede the old. Therefore the modern world differs in this from generations of the past, (in) that it nurses fewer theories at the expense and refutation of facts. In making Nancy a medical Mecca, the modern physician comes there, not to sit at the feet of any exponent of abstract philosophy, but to observe readily demonstrable facts, to test them, and then discuss the theory which endeavors to furnish an explanation. This purpose animated me when I called upon Professor Bernheim that day.

Rather below middle size and slightly bent at the shoulders, he carries a well-formed head of especially fine frontal development, closely cut hair more gray than white, a moustache and goatee. His eyes have a friendly smile which encourages, and makes a well-modulated voice more sympathetic. He has few, almost no gestures, and the whole impression is one of quiet and modest assurance. He is enthusiastic, but a good listener. Accustomed to contradiction, his discussion is never tainted with bitterness or with obstinacy. He manifests more than polite interest in your views; but, without appearing over-anxious to change them if opposed to his own, he does not tire of justifying the position he has taken.

With these impressions I left his cozy office in Carriere Place, and the congenial professor's *"a demain, Docteur, nous verrons bien des choses!"* opened to me for a long time *l'hopital civil,* whose clinical chief he is, for the nervous section, and where his remarkable experimental studies of hypnotic conditions have advanced practical medicine, not at the expense of innocent lives scientifically tortured, but by judiciously utilizing that subtle power inherent in every human being, which eludes the scalpel, the microscope and all direct material research.

About a hundred patients, male and female, received Professor Bernheim's morning visit in airy wards with large windows where the monotony of white was broken by restful green plants and the patients' pet flowers, many in bloom. From bed to bed we went, and after the individual case was examined, Bernheim would address the sufferer in a gentle, firm voice in no way different from his ordinary conversational rhythm. He told them to sleep either at once or before he left the ward, suggested the alleviation or the disappearance of their pains, made them take imaginary tonics, at times touched the seat of pain, and assured them that when their slumber had ceased—he fixing its duration as well as the right time for it—they then would feel comfortable and in a happier mood.

The ease, one could say elegance, with which the hypnosis was induced, formed a striking feature in itself and differed essentially from what I had previously observed in the clinics in Berlin and Vienna. Professor von Krafft-Ebing, for instance, would look steadily at the patient, even hold his hands or make movements like passes from the vertex down over the eyes, while he verbally and in a rather monotonous but pleasant voice impressed him with what he expected to be the result in regard to either physical or mental sensations. At Nancy the whole change occurred with astonishing rapidity, and often so suddenly that the intervening degrees would escape the observer.

For instance, a patient listens to the record of the last twenty-four hours of his case, and to the Professor's remarks; he is then told that certain painful conditions are going to change during the sleep he now enters upon. He seems perfectly conscious, and you would consider his marked attention to what is told him very natural, and if you ventured to address him think little of his not heeding you. His real condition, if you are aware of it, offers now, however, the opportunity for studying the curious phenomenon of a gradual fading away of his individual self, the primary *ego,* with increasing absorption of its substitute, the *alter ego.* He may one minute hear, but not see or feel, and the next again be completely oblivious to any other extraneous influence except the one upon which his intellectual faculties are riveted, while the sensory impressions are being annihilated. In the time the physical surroundings are undergoing these changes, his intellectual forces being concentrated, and their energy directed toward the result to be obtained, the subject is really brought to utilize his own powers by obeying the will which dictates. It is suggestion in the waking state, dispensing with hypnotic sleep. You can test the actuality of the suggested impressions and, if possible, compare them with the previous ones. The arm which a moment before was paretic, and the force of which the dynamometer registered but a feeble pressure, has received increased strength. At will, you make the various parts of his body anaesthetic or hyperaesthetic.

One case, that of ulcer of the stomach, which I had the advantage of observing for a week, was finally discharged cured from the hospital, and that after many efforts had proved failures in other places. Excruciating internal pains are assuaged by an imaginary lotion, by the direct command not to suffer, and the despondent mood is made calm and hopeful. Both the mental and physical effects thus obtained are the result of the physician's suggestion, and while he uses the hypnotic condition in many cases for the sake of creating a passive state, and thus increasing the subject's suggestibility, it can be dispensed with. The idea, therefore, that to receive a suggestion, which is to be carried out even to an act, necessitates a previous deep unconsciousness, is erroneous in many respects. The patient has entered into the receptive state by what is explained as inhibition of the cerebral cortex, and a potent psychical influence has taken possession of him by directing both the mental and the physical functions.

Professor Bernheim does not reject the idea of thought-transference, but says that with him the experiment has never succeeded. Some of his French colleagues and others, however, have proved this possibility, but its apparently exceptional occurrence had deprived it at present, perhaps, of practical usefulness for therapeutical purposes.

It would be beyond the present intention to enter upon a speculative discussion of the question, almost offensively delicate, as to whether we possess an independent will or not. Much evidence corroborates to strengthen a negative view, because in every case where the individual will finds expression we are more or less ignorant of the causes which have made us act. To sustain the contrary would be more flattering than substantial, and although we may delight in ascertaining that the waves of molecular vibration in our brain produce consciousness, we are still forced to acknowledge our unconsciousness as to the vibratory cause itself. Any controversy in regard to this and also to telepathic possibilities is therefore of no mean interest and may ere long by continued earnest investigation approach a solution. For that purpose we need first of all to divest the subject of its apparent mystery. W. Crookes thinks that we have happily outgrown the preposterous notion that research in any department of science is a mere waste of time. This may be true, but many ideas strange to our own perceptions are continually dwarfed by an opposition which often has no better argument than a leer or affected superiority.

Of late we are informed that Professor Nicolas Tesla has been able to illuminate a room without connecting his lamp with the light source in any ordinary way. The experiment recalls a demonstration, several years ago, by Professor A.E. Dolbear, at the Massachusetts Institute of Technology, in explanation of his telephone. Here conversation was carried on at both ends, although the conducting elements to all appearances were interrupted. Something similar has been observed quite lately between two telephone stations in California. The mystery of all this may find its natural and logical explanation in the fortunate fact of the right conditions being established for ethereal vibration. Have we a more plausible reason in presuming cerebral vibration to be any greater mystery? To us there seems to be a logical sequence and similarity between wireless electric light and speech and wordless suggestion. We necessarily reason from transient effects in trying to seize permanent causes, and even if these effects should present apparent mysteries, to conclude that the whole is an absurdity, would not be justifiable. It may, as Herbert Spencer says, be truth perpetually that accumulated facts lying in disorder begin to assume some shape if an hypothesis is thrown among them, but how often does it not act as an extinguisher instead of as a spark?

The following experience can be vouched for: The day trains between Boston and New York are at certains points of the route less crowded. Such trains offer good opportunities for telepathic experiments. The proper selection of subjects will in many instances be the outcome of failures and successful reflection upon their possible causes. Let us suppose, for instance, a person is sitting several seats in front of you, on your side of the car, near the window, and with his back turned. He reads the paper after having settled comfortably down in his seat. There are fair chances for successful experimenting with anyone thus engaged. The man does not seem to be absorbed exactly, but he reads on doggedly. It is now your turn to substitute some other subject for the prosy article, without necessarily attempting to create poetical visions. Doing so, you will notice that the man becomes fidgety, moves in his seat, drops his paper, turns several times uneasily, and finally, as with fixed purpose, wheels right around and gazes at you in a far from accidental manner. He who has ever seen a hypnotized person when awakening, or when in the post-hypnotic state, will find in this individual's facial expression the same blank, puzzled look of astonishment as if he were unsuccessfully wrestling with an explanation that eluded his mental grasp. You could have told him that it was your work, and that through your will, more powerful at the moment than his self-chosen entertainment, a molecular action had been started in his brain, its vibrations responding to those from your own. Once this pendulum-saving between yourself and your subject, conditions permitting, you may carry the experiment farther. Your mutual positions in the car were guarded here against self-deception as they involved the greatest physical inconvenience possible to him in his change of position at the moment he obeyed the given impulse.

This example leads us to the conclusion that our intellectual faculties can be most easily controlled when the mind is passive, or, as the saying goes, thinking of "nothing." This may happen suddenly as if stormed and captured, or again, by slow degrees as if by a regular siege. The busy mind, on the other hand, resists your thought just as it would your speech. It is a question whether a mind seriously occupied with a potent idea is more or less proof against foreign thought-influence than one revolving kaleidoscopic images of stocks and bonds, fairs, Paderewski, bargain sales, etc. In this last condition a person is a hard subject.

Such apparent immunity from mental access would almost recommend a state popularly known as "giddiness," presuming individual possession without well-defined ideation. It must, however,
be conceded that this places him in line with certain alienated
individuals upon whom suggestive experiments succeed only after
the sacrifice of much time and patience. A person of good com-
mon-sense and not imaginative, but concentrated and accustomed
to discipline, proves an excellent and surprisingly easy subject.

Statistics show men to be about one per cent less susceptible
than women, and this not, as Charcot asserts, among neurotic and
hysterical patients alone. This the Nancy clinic demonstrates daily.
As a physiological fact, the importance of which is evident, we
notice a more marked susceptibility in childhood and youth and
a diminution thereof in advanced age. Suggestion as projected
will is powerful enough to break down intervening obstacles
whenever encountered, but it is no magic *sesame* and manifests
its power only when judiciously and patiently directed. Unconscious mental suggestion and sensitiveness to its promptings have
been well demonstrated in the case of a Bishop or a Cumberland.
While an absolute follower of the Salpetriere school would on
Charcot's authority refer it to fibrillary contractions and vascular
modifications caused by emotional impulse, the Nancy school goes
s step farther, and while agreeing to a physical condition from
psychic causes, it unites this psychic cause with psychic effect, the
third link in the chair of sequences.

In passing through the wards of the Nancy Hospital we naturally perceive that the atmosphere of expectancy greatly aids in
producing the impressions suggested. This Bernheim of course
admits and rejoices in the fact. The therapeutic results lose no
value thereby either as a scientific demonstration or as a blessing
to the inmates. One might just as well say that a patient recovering
rapidly under the treatment of a physician in whom he places
implicit confidence, ought to have submitted his case to some
other of his colleagues toward whom he feels utterly indifferent,
although he recognizes his skill. In fact, the first step toward
hypnosis is thus begun, and the subsequent increase of suggestibility introduced. The patient himself aids by autosuggestion.

From a medical point of view, the novel and curious sight of a whole ward falling asleep according to order was less striking than the awaking, and the conviction through tangible proofs of both physical and mental improvement in most cases.

It must be remembered that these are patients in the City Hospital, and subject to the ordinary regulated routine of every clinic, with every opportunity to follow up their conditions hourly and daily. Consequently here were to be seen both recent and old cases, and the development of the symptoms could not be said to be the effect of imaginary mirage or complacent belief. After one such experience no one will make a boast of his dulness or his prejudice. If an inflammation can be produced by suggestion, is it not just as natural that it could be reduced by the same means? If a person can be talked into the belief that he looks badly and feels poorly, you can also talk him out of it. The mental medicine, its existence and its effects, grief or joy, can be demonstrated by the pathological changes it produces when the patient's assertion leaves you sceptical.

What the American public knows as mind cure and "mental science", every honest and observing physician acknowledges to be fundamentally true, though he strongly opposes their fallacies; this, for instance, that diseases are but products of thought. Adults may be hypochondriacal regarding their bodily status, and physicians often have to dispel diseases resting upon morbid notions, but children cannot therefore with any shadow of logic be said to have thought themselves into a diseased condition. If treated as a question of heredity, however, the subject may find defenders. The modern physician finds it worth his while to give these ideas a thoughtful consideration and does not reckon it a sacrilege to infuse an orthodox mummy with heterodox life. He admits even a layman's ability to produce similar results, but he does not admit his promiscuous endeavors, although he be, as in some instances, a well-trained philosophical mind inspired with noble intentions. There must be as thorough a comprehension as possible of bodily as well as mental functions, normal as well as abnormal; no fanatical enthusiasm and exclusiveness blinding the senses to differentiating shades and the aid most needed. Thus we will not be called upon to witness the appalling tragedy of thought-battles and prayer-conclaves to assuage and save both children and adults under extreme conditions dependent upon medical or surgical skill alone.

In these sentences is therefore also expressed our belief that mind-power and hypno-suggestion are not the all-replacing therapeutical agents, but take their places as powerful adjuvants which enlarge our field of usefulness, and, although at the present time hardly more than empirical, they have already adjusted many of the grosser medical errors to a finer and more scientific standard. Their presence, their action, and their results remind the world of thought of the too often forgotten fact that the human body is not the essential man, and that if considered as an unknown quantity, all hypothetical deductions of a purely material science will be misleading.

II

The great argument to stay both study and practice of hypnotism is the confused idea of its danger. The idea is confused because even at this moment the majority of the medical profession are ignorant of its principles. In the days of Mesmer, etc., the then demonstrated phenomena were most learnedly dubbed fraud, and it remains a curiosity of science that Benjamin Franklin, who had himself experienced the ridicule of his countrymen and the English Academy for his attempts to identify lightning and electricity, should have been one of the committee of savants who, in 1784, in Paris, examined the claims of Mesmerism and condemned it as absolute quackery. The various phases of its development down to the present give evidence of the fact that while serenely ignoring and condemning even tangible proofs, these investigators, blinded by their materialistic zeal, overlooked entirely the presence and importance of that greatest of all magnets—the human will. So, also, when the famous Perkins' metallic tractors were found to be equal to wooden ones, the effect of the former ones was not reduced to an *absurdum*, nor was any benefit derived from the so-called exposure. Its permanent cause, suggestion or auto-suggestion, found no intelligent advocate, and the opportunity was lost in a mass of triumphant self-conceit.

Under such circumstances the lack of information and practical study on the part of physicians incapacitates them for judging of its danger or usefulness. Professor Bernheim and also Professor Forel go even so far as to refuse anyone the right to judge of hypnotism who has not succeeded with at least eighty per cent of those experimented upon. There must first be personal observation and then personal experience. Summing up the result, we would frankly admit the presence of a danger, but such a one as is always co-existent with imperfect knowledge. A surgical instrument is a terrible weapon in a child's hand, and poisonous drugs are usually so when administered by an ignorant or careless person. Abuse does not abolish use. This exaggerated idea of hypnotic danger has been the cause of a convenient laziness on the part of the medical profession at large, and has delayed its intelligent comprehension by the public. It is not enough to criticize and condemn public demonstrations by those whose education would not warrant a lucid explanation. Such criticism reverts, however, when the dignity aroused remains crystallized, and we permit ourselves to be guided by a *priori* conclusions. It must be confessed that just this position has retarded our insight into hypno-suggestive causes and effects, and given valuable material into hands from which only our own progressive ability and the public's appreciation may finally wrest it.

Schiller has given us the yet recognizable features of the student who works only with a need to making his bread, as follows: "Every extension of his bread-science makes him uneasy, because it gives him fresh work or makes what he has learned useless; every important innovation frightens him because it shatters the old-school form, which he took such pains to master, and he is in danger of losing a whole life's work. Who have written more about reformers than the mass of these bread-students? Who impede the progress of useful revolution in the domain of knowledge more than these? Every light that genius kindles, it does not matter in what branch of science, makes their poverty visible. They fight with bitterness, malice and despair, because they fight for their own existence while defending the school system. Therefore, no enemy is more implacable, no colleague more jealous, no calumniator more willing, than the bread-student. Every new discovery within his world of activity, is a loss to him, but a delight and a gain to the philosophic mind. It filled, perhaps, a gap which had deformed the perfection of his thoughts as it placed the last stone wanting in his ideal structure, which it completed. But even should it all go to pieces, and a new line of thought, a new phenomenon, a new undiscovered law of nature destroy his whole scientific edifice, he would, nevertheless, love truth better than his system, and he feels happy to change the old and imperfect form for one new and beautiful."

The species thus described by the German poet is not extinct. For the sake of parallelism, this instance is given: When James Esdaile, a prominent surgeon in H.B.M. Indian Service, registered painless operations under what then, in 1840, was called mesmeric influence, the Royal Medical and Chirurgical Society of London retorted by this classical utterance: "Pain is a wise provision of nature, and patients ought to suffer pain while the surgeon is operating; they are all the better for it, and recover better." The *ergo* was, of course, an absolute condemnation of Dr. Esdaile's methods.

An echo of this was heard in 1890, at the meeting of the British Medical Association, discussing hypnotism in therapeutics. Dr. Norman Kerr, although acknowledging the hypnotic phenomena as facts, called it "false therapeutics" to annul pain by hypnotism, because pain is a message from a diseased part. We need not dwell upon the absurdity and narrowness of the utterance. Even if true that hypnotism exchanges one morbid condition for another, would it not be desirable to welcome the one that gives the least pain? The more the idea of hypnotism is freed from coarse errors, the sooner will it become a real benefit. Unscientific precursors have induced the error of presuming a mental weakness or faulty equilibrium of nervous force in hypnotic subjects. This is contradicted by facts. Some again say that hypnosis can be produced by any means causing fatigue of the senses, just as certain phenomena in the hypnotic state can be made apparent by mechanical irritation. This also is incorrect as a parallel. Hypnosis never occurs without suggestion or auto-suggestion; it is not pathological, but physiological, not in its origin somatic, but psychic. Neurotrophic changes might then also be said to result from the application of a postage-stamp to a person's back, while its vesicatory effect is due to the will-control of motor and sensory centers Fatigue is a factor, not the entity.

When sleep occurs, then first commences the active influence. Suggestion not only prepares but dominates after hypnosis had produced passiveness and receptiveness. Seeing as we do no marked difference between this state and ordinary sleep, we cannot admit that a nervous debilitated condition is caused, resulting in a dynamic modification of the brain. The sleep induced is not abnormal, as it does not create new functions, and the phenomena observed we obtain during both states. There is concentration in both these cases, and the activity of our intellectual faculties is evident either as a dream or as a direct suggestion. It is this cerebral activity during repose that is utilized, and if for the best purpose, one is hardly justified in saying that contact with an organ continually vibrating under external impressions is at any time hurtful as a strain upon conscious cerebration. Such contact may and does prove corrective and strengthening. Forel claims that a sound brain is undersuch circumstances giving the most satisfactory results, as capable of a more clearly defined state of expectancy. A subject awake is able to correct and also to repel an impression or suggestion, while his passive observation in hypnosis seizes upon the projected thought to the obliteration of all others.

The insane as well as the inebriate are difficult subjects for hypnotism or suggestion, chiefly on account of their erratic thoughts, as already alluded to. Nevertheless, here also has suggestion proved successful. Of course, if their brain substance has degenerated, no power on earth can replace anatomically destroyed parts, but the morbid development may be impeded by limitation of the area involved. Certain physiological facts must guide our efforts. So we know that nervous exhaustion, mere physical fatigue alone, does not produce either sleep or hypnosis. Great mental excitement can counteract sleep, although extreme bodily weakness exists; but, at the same time, increased physical weariness can also completely conquer psychic effects. Consent and cooperation are required to hypnotize a person, but for suggestion a peculiar susceptibility is needed.

As the hypnotic state prepares for that of suggestibility, the involuntary subjection of individual thought becomes difficult in the waking state, and more particularly so when the subject is not aware of any such purpose. Time and patience are indispensable, and timid people may rest assured that, only in exceptional cases, a sudden snapping of fingers and an imperative command to sleep, or the insidious infiltration of a stranger's thoughts and will, can have immediate effect. It depends just as much upon the subject as upon the experimenter, and the wonderman, the platform hypnotizer, has gone. Therefore it is mostly after repeated suggestions that the hypnotic and suggestive state can be reached. This fact was clearly demonstrated when new patients arrived, and many of these did not yield quickly to our efforts. Professor Bernheim failed as well as his assistants, and he acknowledges that this is a daily occurrence in his private practice. There is, of course, a way of doing which only repeated experimenting can teach, but all means finally produce the same result. The individuality exercise its influence, whether the more potent concentration or its very quality, most likely both, and this gives, in many instances, the explanation why our patients reap greater and quicker benefit from one physician than from another. In fact it is not the phenomenon of daily life with the examples it offers through the senses. What are emotions but suggestions entering the brain to produce results on our physical or mental conditions? We may therefore see that is is not a necessity, *sine qua non,* to produce a profound sleep as the initiatory step to suggestive therapeutics.

The antidote for a too easy suggestibility is suggestion itself. Bernheim and colleagues using the hypnotic state therapeutically, would invariably suggest before waking the subject that no one should be able to hypnotize him or her except the physician whom they voluntarily wished should relieve their sufferings. Thus the impressibility of a natural disposition, or that provoked by repeated hypnosis, may be limited to its proper sphere of usefulness. Considering the agent as therapeutical and not as a novel mode of entertainment for drawing-room or platform, the danger is lessened.

A safeguard to both physician and patient, moreover, is the presence of a third person, without which no such treatment should be entered upon. Clinical experience has not yet proved any disastrous after-effect as the unavoidable result of hypnosis, and a patient's mental independence has no more been transformed into stupefied docility than it would be as the result of any other anaesthetic, provided no post-hypnotic condition remained to fetter his will. It is, then a physician's duty to superintend this. A gradual waking after having suggested that it should be a pleasant one restores completely a self-conscious equilibrium, and leaves but in few cases a confused sensation, more or less transient, according to individual constitution.

Some investigators have thought to correct or rather to promote hypnosis by the administration of narcotics from the very fact that this condition is often obtained with great loss of time when the method of suggestion alone is employed. We think this gives rise to many physiological obstacles, and an increase of experimenting fraught with real danger. The safe proportion of the animal and the psychic life, their mutual limitations and capacity for independent control, are not at present cognizant to scientific knowledge, and would be apt to pass beyond the aim we desire to reach. If, nevertheless, narcotics have been advocated and even successfully employed where hypnosis otherwise could not be obtained, we must recall that there are numerous cases where, in such dilemma, the mere preparations to anaesthetize have produced its somnolent effect under well-directed suggestion and consequent auto-suggestion. Moreover, aside from its doubtful advisability, we must not forget the subject's own individual predisposition, which it is decidely erroneous to confound with the degree of hypnosis.

Suggestibility is one thing and hypnotic susceptibility is another, and they are not dependent upon each other although they correspond. We have observed persons easily hypnotized, but at the same time manifesting difficulty either in seizing the idea suggested or in acting upon it, from a marked check of the motor or sensory sphere. It is, further, not verified by increasing clinical observations that hysterical subjects are particularly good hypnotic subjects. Nervous affections are predisposing causes, no doubt, but the great number of, in every respect, healthy persons, born of healthy parents, in whom all the hypnotic degrees can be provoked, contradicts the views of Charcot, while strengthening those of Bernheim. On various occasions we have witnessed even a singular resistance on the part of hysterical and neurotic individuals claimed to be such very easy subjects. Of no little importance is it in this connection to know that hypnotism does not create hysterical after-conditions in otherwise healthy people. The attempts which occasionally have been made to emphasize such a possibility are at best based upon a confused definition of hysteria.

The employment of hypno-suggestion has at this moment entered private as well as official practice, and its beneficial results have established the conviction that medical science, with the adjuvants it now possesses, cannot afford to discard its services. No European clinic of any importance is bare of illustrations to prove its right to therapeutical consideration, and lingering prejudice is but an asthmatic argument in the race of weighty facts. It is through such channels and in the hands of the Old World's most eminent teachers that ample time and opportunity to investigate will do more than discussion *ex cathedra* and the monopoly of knowledge. We have spoken of its dangers and we know that legislaturers endeavor to limit them by definite laws. But its use for the social good is also agitated today, and at a recent debate in the Austrian Reichsrath, a member reproached the Minister of Education for the university's lukewarm interest in the question, designating such indifference as a "crime," whereby suffering humanity is deprived of valuable aid. This accusation is made publicly in a country where it is already taught and practised by the most eminent chairs.

Several hundred cases observed during a period of two years give me as a physician a similar right to employ this remedy. Diseases within and outside of hospitals have been relieved and cured by hypno-suggestive therapeutics. They have not been limited to neurotic persons and light cases, but on the contrary in very many instances have been applied to those considered hopeless. Neither would it be right to say that cases benefited through this agent suffer relapses and therefore gain but a temporary good. We have observed the bane of bad habits eradicated by it, leaving an invincible disgust for falsehood, tobacco, alcohol, opium, morphia, etc. Its application may, however, like all other remedial agents, come too late and be merely able to sustain a sinking system. Where nature's resources are not yet all exhausted, and where manhood lingers, its use is certainly not in vain. Such observations are at the disposal of any sceptical but intelligent mind, if facts are required in place of theory.

The medical profession in America has retarded its advance in this direction. Its interest, indeed, ought not to remain limited to club talk or discussion in iron-hooped societies with exclusive studies and purposes. As a liberal science its researches ought to be independent of any watchword placing it in subservience as tyrannical as French fashions and English fads. For those who are timid, there is at the present time sufficient authority to shield any attempt to carry hypno-suggestive therapeutics into legitimate private practice, and our clinics and hospitals should be called upon to instruct in a branch of the healing are—certainly not any more empirical than other honorable and plausible efforts to widen its field.

American contribution to this science has hitherto come almost exclusively from non-medical circles, the papers being often well written and clearly defined, and on many occasions the writer has been singularly impressed by noticing that the Old World's scientists adopt and adapt transatlantic notions in this direction, although not sanctioning them in the original form or acknowledging their primary authority. American medical literature relating to the subject is scarce, and is not quoted abroad as weighty enough to enrich European experience. Still, the American mind is creative, although its blunt crudeness may lack speculative polish; it is observant, and astonishingly intuitive so that often its right choice resembles the result of tact and study. Its obstacle to independent thinking, and that in spite of a "go-as-you-like" principle, is, nevertheless, its timid reliance upon foreign criticism in matters where it is taught yet that it is inferior, which certainly is true, and mainly on account of this acceptance of a subordinate position.

When this idea of deference ceases to impede our progress we may hope to gain respect for our own observations, deductions and conclusions, and not be obliged to sanction them as imported second-hand articles.

III.

At the Second International Congress of experimental psychology held in London in 1892 from the first to the fourth of August, the tendency of its communications and discussions was to decrease the number of theories extant and to throw light on accumulated matter by additional facts and more concise terms. In Europe, where, so far, the clinical study of psychological action has broken through the hiterto wellnigh unassailable stronghold of medical conservatism, the subject claims today not only better qualified advocates within the profession proper, but also a more rational and less prejudiced insight among the intellectual class. This fortunate position is largely due to the absence of any ponderous playing at secrecy and oracular misgivings whenever the problem refuses to fit any scientific strait-jacket. Besides, although there are leaders, there are also independent co-workers suffering on the whole but little from the general apathy and conservative spirit.

Among the communications which attracted most attention at the congress was one by Dr. F. van Eeden of Amsterdam, Holland, who, with his colleague, Dr. van Renterghem of the same city, has made extensive studies at his private clinic. The lessons taught by these experiences he presented in a paper on *The Principles of Psycho-Therapeutics,* and even a fragmentary acquaintance with his remarks will presumably prove useful and interesting reading both to physicians and laymen.

He regrets first that the words hypnotism and hypnosis were ever made use of in connection with suggestive therapeutics, as they have given rise to prejudice, confusion and misunderstanding on the part of those who might have been benefited themselves through benefiting others. The hypnotism of today, or rather that which was brought into existence by the name and authority of so eminent a man as Charcot and then caricatured by stage exhibitions, had as its natural sequence strong opposition and the birth of a more refined and truer view—suggestive or psycho-therapeutics. The fact, however, that it followed in the wake of the Salpetriere hypnotism, has been detrimental to its ready and rational acceptance, and the show-business, according to Dr. van Eeden, had injured it still more even in the eyes of physicians. Concurring as we do in this view, we can but gratefully remember that indifference was thereby stimulated into activity, and that Charcot's demonstrations and hypotheses, though a searching opposition, showed themselves to rest upon too material a basis, and by their abnormal character to divert the observer from any deeper cognizance of the underlying psychic possibilities in man.

While, therefore, at first, physicians, on being taught that this was going to serve as a therapeutic agent, could see but an odd novelty fit for the working of charlatans, it has helped finally to attract, both directly and indirectly, a number of serious investigators. If the profession had given heed to the patient work of Liebeault's modest clinic at Nancy at least ten years earlier than the hypnotic movement at Salpetriere, suggestive therapeutics would have found their way unobstructed by prejudice just as massage, hydro-therapeutics, and electro-therapeutics have done. Today, the mere idea of patients at Liebeault's and Bernheim's clinics having run the risk of danger is more ridiculous than ever, as no unbiased student and practitioner of psycho-therapeutics doubts that the sick can be cured—we say not indiscriminately —by their inherent *vis medicatrix,* guided by proper suggestion and favored at times by an induced somnolent state. This is the reason why the practitioner from the very beginning must keep apart the two notions—hypnotism and psycho-therapeutics.

The question as to whether hypnosis may be considered a normal or abnormal sleep is still an open forum, as we, today, are not even able to define its ordinary aspects. Still we may, without risking our position, admit the hypnosis to be a possibly abnormal state by its anaesthesia and obedience to external impressions without waking. We may require both conditons, as when we wish to perform a surgical or dental operation, to correct stammering speech, subdue writer's cramp, or give movement to paretic or paralytic limbs, etc. Nevetheless, the obedience to external promptings does not make sleep abnormal any more than the act of a sleeping *concierge* who opens the door when the bell rings, the automatic march of a soldier in the field, and the mother attending to the comforts of the child at her side.

From a therapeutic point of view, it would be out of the question, and even freighted with danger, to make our patients, when asleep, needlessly speak, write, walk, or open their eyes. Then we would produce a pathological condition creating nocturnal somnambulism, for instance. Public exhibitions having phenomena only as their aim, have nothing in common with the purpose of the physician to relieve and cure instead of to astonish and gain the applause of a crowd at the expense of persons who more willingly than wisely submit to such experiments. For therapeutic purposes we do not need this abnormal condition wherein a person presents another self impelled by foreign will. Medical suggestive effort can but gain by this very independence of all fictitious existence and rise to a position of unsuspected utility.

The hypnotism of Salpetriere has been the greatest enemy of psycho-therapeutics by frightening both sick and well, and in this fact is to be found the only valid excuse for doctors making such remarks to patients as follows: "Do as you like, but never allow anyone to hypnotize you!" Or, whenever a patient has been successfully treated by psycho-therapeutics: "Well, well, the cure, as you call it, is only apparent, as you will find out at your cost later!" Or this: "Be careful, it is not so innocent a thing as it looks!" A patient retorted: "You do not believe, however, that it would kill me?" "No," answered the physician, "you may not fear that exactly, but what is far worse will happen to you!" Others inform their patients that they would have been cured anyhow, and that this particular treatment had nothing to do with the result. Now, if these remarks were made in the course of general practice, surgical or gynaecological, they would have been put down as disloyal to the profession, and, perhaps, not deemed worthy of any reply. But whether due to ignorance or malignity, such remarks are of far more significance to the practice of psycho-therapeutics. The danger would be similar to that of using a surgeon's instruments, without his knowledge, in performing an autopsy or any operation on a dead body, because speaking thus, with the authority of a physician, his words are suggestions which may profoundly and forever injure a nervous or impressionable person, and distrust once created, all suggestive treatment may afterward prove a failure.

Forel has said that the hypnotic sleep stimulates the suggestibility, because it produces irregular mental action (ataxy of the mind), and that this ataxy, when suggestions are often repeated, may present itself also during the waking state. Nobody would deny this, and we are consequently facing abnormal conditions under which our curative efforts would suffer needlessly. It must be remembered that although such results may be checked by energetic contra-suggestions, it is, nevertheless, true that psychic ataxy is one of the principal symptoms of hysteria. Strictly speaking, therapeutic suggestions would make no person hysterical, but it does not thereby follow that by repeating too often merely experimental suggestions one might now awaken latent hysteria. The physician's insight and the necessity of the case would consequently only suggest what was in harmony with the normal functions of the organism. Therefore it is a fundamental principle to stimulate as little as possible.

Personal experience teaches us the radical difference which exists between treating the ordinary class of patients in dispensaries and hospitals, and treating those of superior intellect in private practice. Whoever has studied suggestive therapeutics at the Nancy Hospital is struck by the facility with which the inmates obey the various suggestions and often repay those efforts with prompt curative results. Under such circumstances, the authority displayed and believed in does away with many words and explanations. The more decided the tone, the more brilliant the effect. If an energetic suggestion fails, then the aim fails also. Otherwise the failure is when the patients are independent, educated, and sceptical; the authoritative tone irritates them and may even appear ridiculous. They will not be subject to any command, and, above all, they will not accept without understanding. An impression is rarely made before the operator has succeeded in giving them a somewhat clear idea of the whole thing.

The future of psycho-therapeutics is threatened by these obstacles, and by the apparently illogical fact that a therapeutic method has been elected which is suitable for one class only and not for all alike. If it were to remain so, the very class among which the greatest number of psychic and nervous diseases prevail the most would reap no benefit. Fortunately we are not limited to one method, that of absolute authority on the part of the physician and blind obedience on the part of the patient. Whenever we meet with obstinate opposition from a well-educated and well-balanced individual, it is neither because of his being afraid nor because he reflects another's contrary opinion; but simply because he does not comprehend the thing in itself, and therefore lacks confidence in what seems to him arbitrary and enforced. We sympathize with such a state of mind; at the same time it becomes our duty to dispel it by generalizing the principles which guide our theories of therapeutic suggestions. Then we will find no difficulty in applying them with as much beneficial result here as in the case of children and persons who are less positive and less educated. Theoretically considered we must to a certain extent abandon the authority system and preserve the independence of the individual instead of being instrumental in its enfeeblement.

Clinical facts speak in favor of such a proceeding inasmuch as the most satisfactory results have been obtained where the patient either knew nothing, or all that at present can be known upon the subject. It ought not to be difficult in either case to gain the patient's ear and interest, especially as the aim in both instances is above any endeavor to control and is decidely in the direction of benefit and aid. While with one class it is simply affirmed that everything will happen as suggested, and that by following instructions all morbid symptoms will disappear, the intelligent and educated patients must be spoken to as the operator would himself wish to be addressed. The ideo-plastic idea, the suggestive theory, must be explained and how it is possible to dominate and cure pathological conditions by ideas and volition. They must be told that no restraint is put upon them, that they are merely shown the way and that their present conditions will change, not by any preponderance of another's will, but as the result of a proper effort to aid by using their own will. They are helped to develop the ideo-plastic faculty, whereby is meant the power that ideas possess to influence physical conditions, as, for instance, the production of cholera symptoms by fright, or that of bleeding marks on hands and feet from profound and continued contemplation of or meditation upon the crucified Saviour's wounds. They are guided by word and thought without restraint, authority, and command.

This seems easy and yet we find just here no slight obstacle. Truly intelligent patients are rare, and the majority possess but half-culture. What is lacking in intelligence and culture is made up in pretension, and unable to understand they are at the same time unwilling to submit to the knowledge of the physician. His task is doubled by being obliged to instruct as well as cure; his tact is required in managing their susceptibilities and ideas of mental independence while exercising his intellectual experience in their behalf. With a good and firm will to surmount these obstacles, much can be achieved, but the assistance of proper direction, exercise, and time is also needed.

IV

The centralization of psychic functions is another principle, the tendency of which must be evident, at least to every psychologist. The equilibrium and order of all collaborating forces are indispensable to maintain the energy and resisting force of the entire organism. The conscious will of the patient must be appealed to. We are justified in saying that whenever a chronic disease is cured under such circumstances it offers the least chances of relapse. It can even be presented as a principle that, in every disease, we have to reckon with this psychic factor just as much as with nourishing diet, cleanliness, and pure air. If such an idea of psychic centralization should be opposed merely on the ground of a belief that only a few cases yield to its influence, the suggestive theory of Bernheim gives both a denial and an explanation.

Suggestion, or rather suggestibility, is composed of two elements: ability to receive an impulse from without, and the ideo-plastic faculty. As these are absolutely independent of each other, we must distinguish between them. There are patients who are very impressionable, and who accept a suggested idea with absolute confidence; the influence, however, of the idea upon their physiological functions is feeble. They do not realize the suggestions, and their morbid symptoms yield with great difficulty, as their ideo-plastic conception is small. Others, on the contrary, accept suggestions slowly, are incredulous and even resist them. Nevertheless, we find that the physiological and pathological processes are easily modified by the psychic influence, sometimes by auto-suggestions. Here, then, the suggestibility in undeveloped and small, being surpassed by the ideo-plastic faculty. Forming, as it does, the very basis of psycho-therapeutics, we have no doubt as to its future, believing that the limits for its action will rapidly reach beyond the present ones, although even these furnish us with illustrations of severe organic diseases yielding to the beneficial influence.

The observations of Liebeault, Bernheim, Berillon, Lloyd-Tuckey, Kongolensy, Wetterstrand, etc., as well as our own experience, have offered numerous proofs. Take, for instance, the improvement of the general bodily functions in pulmonary phthisis as an illustration. The exaggerations which so much marred Professor Koch's first experiments were due to ignorance of the power of suggestion on the part of the great bacteriologist. If he had understood how to separate the suggestive element as an active co-operating factor in his injections, the benefit effected in the beginning would not have been attributed to the lymph, and the final failure would not have been so discouraging. However, although recognizing the existence and power of the ideo-plastic faculty, it is rational to submit it to a conscious volition whenever it can be done in accordance with the physician's discrimination. Above all, the methods in each particular case should be varied with proper guidance and moderation, not because the suggestibility is thereby increased, but because the ideo-plastic faculty is thus developed and placed under the influence of a will that knows and directs its tendencies. What we look for is, therefore, a slight receptivity for outside impulses and as great a centralization of psychic functions and the ideo-plastic capacity as posible. It is rare to find this combination, but it can be attained by training and education.

Experience has taught many, myself included, that the psychic effect for curative purposes was stronger where patients either did not sleep at all or merely submitted to a somnolent sensation that left the senses conscious of what took place and also a clear recollection afterward. So in most cases, a somnolent state, or merely a passive condition, enhances the energy of the psychic force. The attempt may be made to produce a profound sleep in cases of melancholy, anguish, and restlessness and insomnia, but even in such cases the effort is to develop the inherent faculty, commanding sleep whenever the patient desires to rest. It is an important point in the treatment of all neuroses and psycho-neuroses to regulate rest, and it is equally surprising to observe the remarkable results of a persistent and patient impulse. An intelligent patient is finally persuaded to suggest to himself before going to sleep that the effort of his conscious will shall act during the period of repose. Many of us have experienced how easily and correctly we wake up at a time which necessity has suggested to us before retiring. Of course the efficacy of this power may be lost when the patient is left to his own resources for too long a time. The process is so subtle and complicated that numerous causes are apt to interfere with it, such as a mistaken notion, mental depression, defiance, or a foreign influence. The physician's suggestion is then needed in order to avoid a complete relapse. Would anyone raise an objection to this? Are they not patients and he the physician? Or is any therapeutical method known, the results of which exclude all possibility of a relapse?

There is no objection so weak and void of sense as that which accuses psycho-therapeutics of not making absolute and durable cures. Medical practice in general proves our position because no pretended cure of chronic disease by chemical agents is an absolute cure—and for this reason, that nothing gives the assurance of the patient's power of resistance having been increased. On the contrary, it has rather been enfeebled and spoiled by the use of drugs. Some object that all this is nothing particularly new, and that psychic agents have never been discredited. No! the idea itself is not new, and was honored fifty years ago more than of late, as is evident for the works of Ruseland, Johannis Muller, and von Feuchtersleben. What today is new, however, is the method and the firm conviction. Thus, both in the way of science and of application, the idea is new. It has become scientific in its method, which, applied, resulted in a conviction based upon results. Most physicians probably applaud the idea as a beautiful one, but entertain little faith in its practical value. Why? Simply because they ignore recent psychological research and its discoveries, and the more that they are not, as a rule, prepared for it by previous training. Now this imperfect insight into the domain of psychology, side by side with their greater familiarity with physiology and chemistry, has resulted in the fact that the medical practice of today relies principally on mechanical, chemical, and electrical agents, and dares not confide in the power of psychic functions.

As these functions, nevertheless, play a great role in the human organism, medicine as a science alien to this knowledge will never know human nature thoroughly and never be able to give genuine relief and comfort to its ills, but will remain, as at present, incomplete, provisory, and inexact. From this it does not follow that medicine is too materialistic. The natural sciences must necessarily be materialistic, as they embody the knowledge of external phenomena as matter or force, and are observed through the senses. Only that materialism which exaggerates the superiority of these sciences can be said to be the negation of thought itself, much as if we would pretend that paper and ink were of greater importance than the ideas they serve to convey. When Virchow discovered that the body is a combination of infinite collaborating cells, he called our attention to an effect, but their inherent vitality, being confounded with chemical and physical qualities, escaped recognition just as it did the scalpel. The psychic functions, the vibrating vital cause, remained hidden as before. To bring these functions to light, to establish their presence and their action in every individual life, is the mission of the psychology today. The work is in a fair way of advance upon an enlarging basis of solid, scientific facts.

It is characteristic, to say the least, that Dr. van Eeden can in this way voice the sentiments and the experience of a large number of physicians all the world over to whom psychology means more than a curious plaything. We perceive that every day brings us farther from a conservatism that either had no method at all, or, when one was offered, made a wry face and indulged in what was then considered a superior kind of sneer. The subject finds an eager ear now among competent thinkers and practitioners, and has passed beyond the discussion as to whether such facts are reliable. We know they are, and also that they are within the reach of anyone who brings intelligent and patient inquiry to bear upon psychic life. The material is as abundant as the field is extensive. Research of this kind demands many workers and necessarily creates many branches. Our own part, as physicians, is not to engage in speculative philosophy only, but to apply within practical limits whatever our experience has added to the means of combating disease.

Were we only to accumulate facts and come to a standstill before puzzling theories, we would be no better than the miser hoarding riches useless to himself and others. Once sure of possessing reliable and undeniable facts, theories must take care of themselves and will in due time naturally evolve sound teachings. We have, in the meantime, no right to closet ourselves with our experience, simply because we have not succeeded in elaborating the subtle laws which govern them. The mystery may never be unravelled, and may remain as problematical as the source of life itself. Human existence is too short to permit us to lose any opportunity to better the work we are engaged in. We naturally seek the cause of every effect, and it is plausible that we should endeavor to discover it, but no one will gainsay that we may all the same turn effects to practical account before we fully master the theories of them. That is just the position of suggestive therapeutics today, not yet an exact science, but decidedly scientific in its methods and success. Just as little as we who practise this branch of modern medicine do so to the exclusion of the ordinary methods, just as little do we refute the utility of drugs. We use them because we are convinced by experience of their value, but we are often forced to recognize their failure and are anxious to find a better substitute for them. We are equally convinced that the psychic agent removes physical as well as mental obstacles in many instances where the medicines which we relied on were disappointing.

There is particular interest in the emphasis with regard to strengthening the patient's conscious will instead of constantly substituting for it a foreign one. This has ordinarily been a point of crude misunderstanding with many. Psychic no more than general therapeutics need go to the necessity of forced feeding. An exhausted system is taught to take its nourishment, whether mental or physical, by what might be called infused volition which permits his own to play both a receptive and an elective part in the process. There may be many reasons why the individual fails to assimilate at once, but the resistance is rarely of long duration.

The fact also that unconscious sleep is unnecessary in the majority of cases may surprise those whose ideas of suggestive therapeutics are based upon public exhibitions of hypnotic phenomena. Just as in ordinary practice patients are only occasionally submitted to the influence of ether, so also here we may dispense with making the body and the will negative to the extent of unconsciousness. The logic and simplicity of these proceedings ought to commend themselves instead of repelling sympathy. The instinctive impulse which causes desire we will find more potent than the will. A patient's desire to get well has reached the stage of practical incentive when it induces him to confide in a physician, but although his desire has been embodied in a strong motive, his active self-consciousness stops there, and the volitional process lacks firmness as well as ability to become active at the proper moment. Therefore his will may remain feeble at the same time that is desire is strong. Under such circumstances he brings to his physician the very elements which, if intelligently understood and applied, cause an equalization of the psychic functions, thereby establishing the equilibrium of nervous force.

If, on the contrary, a comprehension of what is meant by psychotherapeutics is one-sided and superficial, and one should indiscriminately attempt to produce the unconscious condition, in most instances the result would be that one would be found battling against a weakened desire and an obstinate, even hostile, will. It would, then, surely be fair to surmise that the non-success was due more to our limited resources than to any original difficulty. Such cases are somewhat frequent, and we suspect that the method has done much to render both the physician and his patient weary and discouraged at the same time, as it may have brought the efficacy of the curative agent itself into temporary discredit. Most morbid mental and physical conditions may serve as examples, but among what is termed bad habits, that of morphinism forms a singular exception. Excluding advanced cases, we refer to those who stealthily indulge and furnish themselves plenty of good arguments for so doing. Here the desire as well as the will to stop the practice is blunted. Such a man is irresolute because he knows that the poison is a necessary stimulant. As a rule, he is of a high-strung nature, with aspirations which are continually in conflict with commonplace surroundings. Of good social position, his intellectual work is often of a high order, and must be attended to even when the organism cries for rest. The difficulty consists in awaking the unfortunate's desire, and then his will, to get rid of the habit. How soon a suggestive treatment will be able to remove these obstacles depends upon circumstances; but it does not become necessary to isolate the patients to ordinary cases.

There is one point toward which observers have not always sufficiently directed their attention although it is closely connected with psychic functions and, undoubtedly, has often enough presented itself to most investigators to elicit its recognition. We refer to thought-conveyance as a force in suggestive therapeutics. The audible word is used, and must as a rule serve in all cases in the beginning, but even that, as we know, is inefficacious until a receptive although perfectly conscious condition is established. The impressive state thus created will then admit of seizing the unspoken suggestion, which naturally imprints itself so much more strongly if it is in harmony with the ideas desired to be conveyed to a patient. Of course, this depends upon the individual's degree of suggestibility and the physician's aptitude for mental centralization. But this fact seems to have been generally overlooked or, at least, its practical value has hitherto been somewhat underated. An illustration of this may be taken for my last day at Nancy Hospital, about five years ago.

Following Professor Bernheim on his morning visit through the wards, we were as usual spending some time experimenting upon his great subject, Henriette, so well known to visiting physicians. Leaving her at the first bed in the hypnotic state, we proceeded toward the other end of the ward. During all this time the woman would continuously answer the professor's questions to the other inmates. The logical connection between question and reply was not once interrupted. As the distance became greater, and her words consequently became confused, I felt anxious to ascertain whether the correctness still existed. Placing myself as far from Bernheim as possible without losing the sense of his words, I became convinced that she was able to understand him although the distance was almost double. When near her I was able to hear his voice, which was low, but not to distinguish a single word. Calling the attention of a visiting Russian colleague to this circumstance, I asked him to stand midway between us and to repeat the professor's questions to me in German. The result proved beyond a doubt that she caught easily and clearly the sense of his words. Walking home with Bernheim, I mentioned my experiment to him, and in giving my opinion of the phenomenon, I think I called it telepathy. Strangely enough, he would not accept this and assured me that he had never succeeded in obtaining the desired effect by thought-suggestion alone. Nevertheless, he recognized the fact as related and explained it as due to induced hypersensitive audition, indisputably present in this woman's case, but the question which I then tried to settle was whether the phenomenon did not depend more upon the coming into play of a psychic function than upon an extraordinarily acute sense of hearing.

Having repeated this experience in daily practice, my esteemed teacher's explanation has proved itself only half the truth, because thoughts have actually been answered. Either a patient when in a somnolent state would suddenly ask, "What did you say, doctor?" or, where the comprehension was more distinct, "Yes, I will try," etc. How concentrated the mind would be upon the suggested ideas may be inferred from the fact that external noises, such as passing cars, the ringing of the doorbell, or knocks at the office door, often for long intervals were not perceived by the patients. Thought seems therefore to be no less potent factor because speech does not convey it, if the ability of projecting and receiving it exists.

It can be but a question of time when in this country also, universities, hospitals, clinics, and extended private practice shall give physicians and the public the same facilities and benefits as older seats of learning now do in Europe in regard to suggestive therapeutics. In the first place, tolerance as to ideas is the only way to reach a correct and fruitful understanding of the principles underlying psychic life and functions. Next, psychology cannot be classed among positive sciences, and efforts to do this have retarded results if not obscured the way of them. For the easy-going majority, that waits until pushed forward and has to be assured that such studies are perfectly "respectable," and need neither to be abhorred completely nor approached after the fashion of Nicodemus, no further excuse exists for retaining its present ridiculous attitude, and those who have already been benefited may yet find moral courage to bear testimony to their profitable heresy. The first step to inaugurate this mental progress should belong to the medical profession, which no doubt, procrastinates only to instruct the better.

August Forel, M.D.

The following article, together with others dealing with the psychological, psychophysiological, and therapeutic aspects of hypnotism appeared in the *Zeitschrift fur die Gesamute strafrechtswissenschaft,* under the title of "Der Hypnotismus und Seine strafrechtliche Bedeutung" (Hypnotism and its Forensic Aspects).

Dr. Forel was Professor of Psychiatry and Director of the Provincial Lunatic Asylum in Zurich, Switzerland. He was influenced by the work of Charcot, Liebault, and Bernheim. Forel had great respect for the work of Bernheim, and he referred to Bernheim's classical work, *De la Suggestion et de Ses Applications et la Therapeutique,* as a must for those interested in practicing hypnosis.

In the Preface, Forel stated, "Some regard hypnotism as humhug, and call all hypnotized persons malingerers. This view, I may explain in passing, has been refuted as absurd to the mind of every unbiassed person by the very number of the so-called malingerers. Some believe that the world is being turned upside down and the law endangered, and they wish the police to interfere, to drive away hypnotism like the plague. To the scoffers and the sceptics, I would say, 'test before you judge.' One can only judge hypnotism if one has practised hypnotizing for a considerable time."

Professor Forel hypnotized nearly all his asylum warders; he selected these himself and did not choose them from the ranks of the hysterical. He asserted that every mentally healthy man—and there are more of these than can be counted—is naturally hypnotizable; the most difficult to influence are the insane. Forel also concluded that the mentally unsound, the idiots, are much more difficult to hypnotize than the healthy. Intelligent people with strong wills, so he said, are more susceptible than the dull, the stupid, or the weak-willed.

HINTS TO THE PRACTITIONER ON SUGGESTIVE
TREATMENT AND PSYCHOTHERAPEUTICS*

If one wishes to hypnotize, and especially to obtain therapeutic results by this means, one must first arm one's self with great patience, with enthusiasm, with consistency, with an unhesitating manner, and with the capability of inventing tricks and of originating ideas. Next, one must learn to observe psychologically correctly, and to individualize. Lastly, the determination of the actual diagnosis is necessary, as it is in every other form of treatment. But suggestion itself often offers such an excellent diagnostic means that one is thoroughly justified in applying it for this purpose frequently. The diagnosis of a doubtful case can ofttimes be made from the success or failure of the hypnotic suggestion.

As the foregoing implies, not every medical practitioner is suitable to become a hypnotist. It is true that the personal magnetic fluid, which used to be considered necessary, is a superfluous myth, but everyone does not possess the characteristics and capabilities mentioned above. By far the most potent factor which stands in the way of success is the want of interest and of personal initiative. In this way, if it is not constantly being spurred again into life, one's own mental activity slowly becomes dormant as a result of the unavoidable frictions of everyday life. In this the *vis-inertia,* which adheres so tenaciously to the larger portion of the populace, plays a determining role. The man who attempts to hypnotize in an automatic sort of way, following out a preconceived scheme, will rapidly fail to have results to record as soon as the fascination of the novelty of the thing has passed off, especially if he does not take an intelligent trouble over it. He will go to sleep himself more and more, and his patients will be influenced less and less.

A second factor which prevents success is mistrust, nervousness, fear that others will laugh at him, fear that the hypnotized person will simulate, and misgivings and doubts of all kinds. This second factor, which at first is the most formidable, disappears as soon

---

*From Forel, August, Dr. (Med.): *Hypnotism or Suggestion and Psychotherapy,* translated from the German edition by H.W. Armet. New York, Rebman, 1906, pp. 206-233.

as one gains experience, and then the first factor makes itself felt to the full extent, and must continuously be combated. One can frequently notice, when one is depressed or tired, that one achieves fewer results, for this weakness of the hypnotist is unconsciously recognized by the brain dynamisms of the hypnotized.

One should approach the person to be hypnotized, as Bernheim advises, quite naturally and intent on one's purpose; one explains to him that there is nothing unnatural or uncanny about the procedure, but that it is a characteristic of the nervous system which applies to everybody; one says that he will readily be influenced or fall to sleep. One should avoid long speeches and explanations, and the patient or subject is placed in a comfortable easy-chair. It is best if the chair has no arms, or, failing this, if the arms are well upholstered. The chair is so placed that one side is touching a perpendicular wall, so that one can assist a suggestive catalepsy of the arm, of which one is not quite certain, by leaning the arm against the wall.

One should enjoy the trust and inclination of the person to be hypnotized as far as is possible, or attempt to gain these.

O. Vogt states that he accustoms his patients to the 'rapport' consistently by very brief repeated hypnoses, after which he makes them relate their sensations exactly. In this way he strangles unpleasant autosuggestions in the bud, and at the same time joins his following suggestions to the innocent suggestive results. He avoids, above all things, giving suggestions in such a way that the patient does not realize them at once, or, at all events, soon, and thus prevents, as I do also, awakening or strengthening the idea 'that it does not succeed with him.' At first he only hints at the occurrence of some phenomenon or other, and only suggests this more forcibly after he has noticed the beginnings of the occurrence himself, or learns of it by the statements of the patient. He avoids a commanding tone of voice, so that those who do not want to lose the 'freedom of will' shall not be disturbed. The phenomena of suggestion should be represented, especially to educated persons, as arising quite naturally out of themselves. I entirely approve of this method, and had already employed it, although not quite so consistently.

One should further avoid that the person to be hypnotized is mentally stimulated or excited, or that he is anxious or in a condition of expectant tension. The last named spoils the first hypnosis in a large number of people, and especially in the educated, who imagine all sorts of wonderful things, and expect them to take place. Some persons are afraid that they cannot be hypnotized, and, in consequence, give themselves this autosuggestion, which is frequently extremely difficult to overcome. In this case patience and various tricks must be employed. The first attempt under these conditions frequently fails. One then explains to the person that he was too excited for the moment, that he was taking too keen an interest in the procedure, but that he was already influenced. Sleep was by no means necessary for the action to be attained, and it would come later of its own account. One then speaks only of light dozing, etc. Once, after I had exhausted all my tricks in this way without result with a lady, I appointed another time for her to come to see me, allowed her to get up, and put on her hat, coat, and gloves, and then I got up too, and said to her, apparently without any ulterior motive, 'Sit down again for a moment'; and, with a few rapid and definite suggestions she was hypnotized in a few seconds.

In many cases of this kind the hypnotizing of another person in the presence of the person to be hypnotized acts advantageously. The intention of this, however, must not be noticed, or else the action will be lost.

I wish, on the whole, to recommend the method according to Liebeault-Wetterstrand, which I shall describe presently—the collective hypnotizing.

According to Bernheim's procedure, one requests the patient to sit in the armchair, tells him to look straight into one's eyes for a few seconds, but no longer than one minute, and declares to him loudly and firmly, but in a monotonous tone of voice, that he is going on famously, that his eyes are already moist, his eyelids are heavy, and that he feels a pleasant sensation of warmth in his legs and arms. Then one tells him to look at the thumb and index finger of the hypnotist's left hand, which one depresses unnoticeably, so that the lids follow. If the eyelids fall to of their own account soon, one

has gained one's end. If not, one says, 'close your eyes.' Some practitioners let the patient look at them for a longer time.

One can then continue by following Vogt's procedure, or one can
also lift up an arm, and lean it against the wall or against the patient's head, declaring that it is rigid. It is best to state at once that
the hand of the raised arm will be absolutely irresistibly drawn
against the head, as if the latter was a magnet. Should this not
succeed, one must help a little; one becomes very definite and intent in suggesting; one suggests at the same time disappearance of
thought, obedience of the nerves, feeling well, rest, and slumber. As
soon as one notices that one or other of these suggestions is beginning to work, one must use it and lay emphasis on it, and at times
it will be well to require the patient to indicate his own experience
by movements of the head. Every suggestion which elicits the reply
'Yes' in the early stages is an important achievement, and one
must use it for all the following suggestions: 'You see, it is working
very well. Your slumber is getting sounder. Your arms gets more
and more rigid. You cannot depress it now.' The patient tries to
do so, with some results; one then quickly prevents him from doing
this, and states: 'On the contrary, if you try to bring it down it
only moves towards your head. Look here, I attract it towards your
head,' etc. It is wise to avoid the suggestion of catalepsy of the arm
at first in very critical and refractory people. After some practice,
one soon can recognize when it is safe to risk this.

I regard it as a mistake to make the patient fix his eyes on an
object for long, as a rule. I rarely do this for more than one minute,
and then only at the beginning of the first sitting. Later on, it suffices always to look at the person to be hypnotized for one or two
seconds at the most, and to give the suggestion of sleep at the same
time. As a rule, I simply declare, 'You are asleep,' making a movement of my hand in front of the patient's eyes, and the subject is
immediately hypnotized.

Grossmann * details his method of hypnotizing as follows:

'First of all, I suggest suggestibility to every patient. I find it best
to deal with the sceptic with the following little experiment: I say
to him that I am going to press on his conjunctiva with my finger,

---

*Grossman, *Zeitschrift fur Hypnotismus,* Vol. I, 1892-1893, p. 410.

although he will scarcely believe it, without producing any reflex closure of the lids—that is, without his blinking. The experiment nearly always succeeds, for, as I have pointed out in a previous work,† the conjunctiva of almost every person becomes anaesthetic by fixing at the same time the attention on this sort of suggestion. The fact that the suggestion has succeeded frequently increases the suggestibility to such an extent that the command to sleep, simply following at once on this, suffices to cause hypnosis to appear forthwith. In other cases I get the patient to sit on a chair, without leaning back, or, still better, to rest on a sofa in a half-sitting, half-lying position, and to fix me intently with his eyes for a few seconds. I then suggest to him that feels a sensation of warmth traversing his limbs, and especially that his arms, which are resting on his knees, are becoming as heavy as lead. Having said this, I raise them a little, catching hold of them by the wrists, and cause them to fall suddenly by a slight push of my hands. They fall back on the knees apparently as heavy as lead, and the patient actually feels a marked tiredness in his arms; this I have had confirmed by nearly everyone. If I do not observe the somewhat dazed expression, or trances of it, which may only last for a few seconds, I then employ the principal trick. I ask the patient to close his eyes, or I close them myself quickly; then I seize his wrists, the forearms being flexed upwards, and suggest that he is becoming so tired that he can no longer keep up, but must sink back. I gradually press him backwards myself by imperceptible pushes, until his head is resting on the back of the chair, and, provided that it is still necessary, give the command to sleep.'

It is best to touch the painful part (head, abdomen, etc.) with the right hand, and to declare at the same time that the pains are disappearing; one then asks the patient during the hypnosis about the result, and, if possible, one does not leave off until this is complete—at all events, for the moment. One often has to use several different suggestions, and should possess talent for invention. Everything succeeds at once with persons who are very suggestible, while one has much difficulty with others.

---

†Ibid., 'The Results of the Suggestion Treatment in Influenza,' (Berlin: H. Brieger, 1892).

One must first see that one induces anaesthesia and amnesia after awakening as rapidly as possible. It is true that many cure suggestions succeed without these two results. But one can attain one's aim more rapidly and better, on the average, with them. One usually prevents the patient from carrying over the thread of his conscious logic from the hypnosis to the waking condition, and the reverse, by means of amnesia.

An important duty of the hypnotist is, further, to prevent the harmful results of autosuggestions. Persons who are anxious and nervous, and more especially hysterical persons, are apt to imagine autosuggestions of harmful actions as a result of the first hypnosis. This is particularly likely if they have learned a lot of this kind of thing from newspapers or from other people. They become giddy after the hypnosis, or they feel themselves dazed, or they have a feeling of fear, or headache, trembling, or twitchings appear, which may even increase into convulsions. One must take great care to avoid showing anxiety or concern should such a condition appear, lest one increases and cultivates the autosuggestion thereby. On the other hand, one must state with the utmost firmness and confidence that these things are only stupid little events, which occasionally turn up during the first hypnosis, but which can be removed at once, and which will never again recur. And while one is saying this, one suggests away these phenomena, down to the smallest detail, by means of an immediate renewal of the hypnosis. One must not allow any part of it to remain, and should always remember that everything which is produced by suggestion can also be removed by suggestion, if this is done in time, and if it is not allowed to be retained by autosuggestion or habit. Hypnosis should only be employed for short periods and not frequently for such persons, or for hysterical individuals generally, and only therapeutic suggestions should then be given.

I lay great stress on this procedure. I am absolutely convinced that want of knowledge of this or ignoring it is responsible for the unintentional damages ascribed by hypnosis of which we read in the literature on the subject. I have personally seen a case of trembling and pain in an arm which was produced by this sort of unskilful hypnotizing on the part of an inexperienced young man; it lasted for a few months, but was then completely removed again by suggestion.

In my experience, one achieves more, as a rule, with hysterics by skilfully-applied suggestions during waking than one does by means of formal (announced) hypnosis. The old rule remains the same: kind, consistent, and firm. One must gain the sympathy of the hysterical person, and at the same time require respect from him. One must never scoff at him, or show him any mistrust, repulsion, or contempt, or else one will damage him considerably. But one must be just as careful not to spoil him, and not to attach much importance to his attacks, pains, etc. One speaks confidently of cure, insists that he will obey implicitly, and then one guides him imperceptibly, by tickling his ambition, etc., into an occupied mode of living, and into healthy hygienic habits by giving him therapeutic hygienic suggestions whenever one comes into contact with him. One should employ medicaments as seldom as possible, and never have recourse to narcotics. I wish to deduce the maxim from all these facts that medical practitioners who are still inexperienced in dealing with suggestion, and especially young practitioners who so far have had but little general experience, should avoid attempting their first hypnotic experiments on hysterical persons.

That one can do harm by suggestion, if one wishes to, is obvious, and is only the reverse of the curative action of suggestion. One can suggest headache, disturbances of menstruation, etc., just as well as one can suggest them away. But if one wishes only to do good, one must never speak to a hypnotized person of the possibility of doing harm, and, on the contrary, always state firmly and unconditionally that suggestion can only act for good. In this way one removes the harmful autosuggestions in the best manner, and preserves a healthy suggestive atmosphere around the patient.

One must avoid the 'occurrence of self-hypnosis,' the supposed 'weakening of the will-power,' and other things of this kind, by the same means of counter-suggestion. The dangers of these things are always being held up as arguments against therapeutic hypnotism. Only on one occasion, while I was still a beginner, did a person whom I had hypnotized fall into a hypnotic sleep of his own account. He received such an energetic suggestive lecture from me in return that the affair was not repeated. If one admits the right of existence of such phenomena in one's environments, they will soon be repeated, not only in the same patient (as, for example, in the hypnotized hysterical girl of von Krafft-Ebing), but also in others. This can be seen in Dr. Friedrich's results,* who hypnotizes by false methods and with preconceived notions. But, on the other hand, a self-hypnosis suggested by means of an amulet is not dangerous. However, one must limit the duration of this to a few minutes by means of suggestion, and only allow it to take place through the intermediation of the amulet and for definite treatment purposes, with the permission of the doctor.

One must always suggest perfect health, cheerful mood, good sleep, good appetite, and strengthening of the will. Besides this, one should always bear in mind Bernheim's and Liebeault's rules:

1. To insist on having at least one suitable witness for every hypnotizing, as a protection for the hypnotist as well as for the person hypnotized.†

2. To give the suggestion to all very suggestible persons (somnambulists) that no one else can hypnotize them.

3. Not to hypnotize anyone without first obtaining his spoken permission.

4. Only to give suggestions for therapeutic purposes, as long as legal, scientific, or didactic purposes do not enter into the question.

I have called attention to many baneful suggestions which are exercised unconsciously by medical practitioners by their expressions of face, by their examinations and prognoses.* Bernheim has also done the same. I am fully aware that I once suggested a gastric ulcer to a patient in whom I suspected this condition by having a

---

*Dr. Friedrich, 'Annals of the General Hospital in the Town of Munchen,' 1894. The article of Dr. Friedrich, which is directed against the therapeutic application of hypnotism, proves conclusively that the author has fallen into all the errors which one should avoid, and that he has completely misunderstood the whole question.

†Special exceptions in which absolute mutual trust can be relied on may take place under especial conditions.

*Forel, 'Unconscious Suggestion' (*American Journal of Psychology*, Vol. IV, No. 4, 1893).

serious countenance, and by carefully palpating the region of the stomach, and ordering rest in bed and milk diet. I suggested the site of the pain by means of a pointed question, and the result of my want of knowledge of suggestion at the time was that the patient was confined to her bed for many months of a suggested illness which was not really present. The patient proved herself later on to be an excellent somnambulist. Hysterical cough, hysterical attacks, diseases of the stomach, uterine disturbances, constipation, and nervous disorders of all kinds are frequently suggested in this manner by anxious practitioners, who are apt to take serious views of cases, or are autosuggested by the patients themselves. There is no doubt as to the truth of this.

That one can suggest hysterical attacks, for example, even without using words, by means of unskilful manipulations has long been recognized. We have all reported this, and it has been confirmed by Dr. Friedrich in a striking manner. But when one understands suggestion, one gets accustomed, not to produce it, but to remove it.

On one occasion a hystero-epileptic woman was brought to me with the history of several severe attacks daily during the past seven years, and of total incapability for work. I was called to her during the first attack in the asylum, hypnotized the patient during the attack, and declared that the attacks had definitely ceased from that time, and that the disease was cured. No further attack took place, and after a few weeks the patient left the asylum. For two and a half years she remained perfectly well. She then again complained of some hysterical symptoms, and consulted a doctor. The latter told her during the treatment that the attacks would certainly recur, and the attacks did recur. She then begged to be admitted into the asylum again, and arrived in 1894. I again removed the attacks at once by means of a few hypnoses; she was discharged cured, and has remained well since. Comments on this case are superfluous.

Dr. Weil, of Berlin,* has written an excellent little article on the suggestive action of 'prognosis.' Of course, a bad prognosis, which some practitioners give to the poor patients without consideration, is frequently tantamount to producing a further illness; not in-

---

*Weil, *Zeitschrift fur Hypnotismus*, Vol. I, 1892-1893, p. 395.

frequently it hastens the death of the patient.

Weil reminds us with perfect justification that the patient who says to his medical attendant, 'Doctor, I want to know the whole truth; I am prepared for anything; tell me what I have to expect,' etc., really deceives himself, and, at all events, usually only wishes to hear a comforting lie from the doctor. The medical practitioner must be a psychologist in this case, and his duty, as a rule, is to conceal his conviction, and even to lie at times.* But, besides, every practitioner should realize how far he is from being infallible, and this should help him to allow the patient to retain hope without lying. There exist certain exceptions under definite circumstances, and with very strong-minded characters, which it is the duty of the psychologist to find out.

One must always study the individual suggestibility on one's hypnotized persons closely, adapt one's self to this, and not proceed in accordance with fixed rules.

If one wishes to employ suggestive anaesthesia for surgical purposes, one must first prepare the patient for a few hypnotizings. When he does not feel pricks of the needle in the palm of the hand, or even touching of the cornea, he is ready for the operation; but one must avoid exciting him by extensive preparations for the operation, for one will thus risk completely desuggesting him. I have often seen this. One should hypnotize him beforehand, and represent the operation as a mere nothing or as a joke, and then one should allow it to take him by surprise as far as is possible. During the operation one must continuously go on suggesting anaesthesia and deadness of the affected part.

If the suggestion fails in a person, one should desist after four or five sittings. It sometimes succeeds later, or if another hypnotist tries.

One must not continue to hypnotize a person *ad infinitum* mechanically; one only loses and does not gain anything. One should attempt to attain the maximum effect rapidly in a few sittings. One must then reduce the number of hypnotizings gradual-

---

*Compare Mark Twain "On the Decay in the Art of Lying. Selected Sketches": 'The liar who is most to be pitied is the one who persuades himself that he always speaks the truth, for he lies to himself as well as to others.'

ly, which at first were carried out every day, and then leave off, having represented the result which one has gained as definite and lasting. There are, however, some obstinate cases, accompanied by a small degree of suggestibility, in which one succeeds after a long time, if one perseveres. Still, everything has its limits. If the patient fails to see any further result, he will often become desuggested, and one loses one's influence instead of increasing it. The hypnotist and the hypnotized become tired out. One must always try to find something new, and to bring this to pass until one has achieved one's aim, and then gradually to break off.

The hypnotized often become desuggestionized by autosuggestions, as well as by insinuation of other people or writings which find fault with hypnotism. They frequently become so because the hypnotist himself loses courage and ardour. However, one can usually regain what one has lost by means of a little energy and trouble. It will be found out infrequently that the results are better if one interrupts the sittings for a good long time.

Hypnotism may be applied therapeutically, as Bernheim has rightly pointed out, not only by itself, but also in conjunction with other remedies. Many of these latter can be employed as auxiliary means to suggestion, or directly as the suggestion itself. It is certain that a large number of medicaments from time immemorial have acted solely and only by suggestion. Homeopathy is a speaking instance of this, and electrotherapy is almost as striking an example.

Many a pain which will not budge in response to simple suggestion can be removed by *aqua clorata* or *mica panis*. Bernheim, Moebius, and Wetterstrand have proved most brilliantly that the so-called metallo-therapeutics and a large proportion of electricity only act by suggestion.

I have repeatedly emphasized, and Bernheim has done the same, that suggestion is not a panacea which cures all ills. If one expects everything of it, one will be disappointed. It is of paramount importance for every hypnotizing practitioner never to forget that the first duty which has been imposed on him by his academic studies and by his diploma is the duty of scientific thoroughness, and also of careful examination and making of the diagnosis; but he must remember that neither of these consists in mere scientific terms and belief in authorities. One can attain much by suggestion, especially if one uses it with perseverance, intelligence, and medical knowledge, and if one understands how to combine suggestion with other means. For example, if one does not succeed in curing stammering completely by suggestion alone, one should combine it with a systematic course of exercises (breathing, vowel, and consonant exercises). If one does not succeed in curing a lady of sea-sickness by verbal suggestion alone, one should rock her during the hypnosis thoroughly, and at the same time give her the suggestion of enjoying it. One will then probably succeed. The electric current is an exellent means of applying suggestion, but the holy water of Lourdes, the 'prayer' treatment, Father Kneipp's method, and homeopathy, are not less good. I propose giving a list of those morbid conditions here which seem to me to respond best to suggestion, although the indications have by no means been sufficiently tested, and much will certainly have to be added to it:

Spontaneous somnambulism.

Pains of all descriptions, especially headache, neuralgia, sciatica, toothache which does not depend on an abscess, etc.

Sleeplessness.

Functional paralyses and contractures.

Organic paralyses and contractures (as palliative means).

Chlorosis (extremely favourable).

Disturbances of menstruation (metrorrhagia and amenorrhoea).

Loss of appetite, and all nervous digestive disturbances.

Constipation and diarrhoea (provided that the latter does not depend on catarrh or fermentation).

Gastric and intestinal dyspepsia (including pseudo-dilatation).

Physical impotence, pollutions, onanism, perverted sexual appetite, and the like.

Alcoholism and morphinism (only by the suggestion of total abstinence).

Chronic muscular and arthritic rheumatism, lumbago.

The so-called neurasthenic disturbances.

Stammering, nervous disturbances of the vision, blepharospasm.

Pavor nocturnus of children.

Sickness and sea-sickness, the vomiting of pregnancy.

Enuresis nocturna (often very difficult, on account of the depth of the normal sleep).

Chorea.

Nervous attacks of coughing (also in emphysema).

Hysterical disturbances of all kinds, including hystero-epileptic attacks, anaesthesia, 'phobias," and the like.

Bad habits of all kinds.

All hypochondriacal paraesthesiae, irritable weaknesses, conceptions of impulse, and the like, are more difficult to cure.

According to Wetterstrand, epilepsy, haemorrhages, etc., can also be influenced.

Suggestion may be tried in all pure functional nervous disturbances.

Many other illnesses have been enumerated in the literature of the subject. The reader can read these for himself in the articles by Liebeault, Bernheim, Wetterstrand, Ringier, and others, in the various yearly volumes of the *Zeitschrift fur Hypnotismus* (Leipzig: Ambrosius Barth). The list given above will suffice for everyone to begin with, and later one forms one's own indications. One should, however, also mention the production of anaesthesia for small surgical operations, especially on the fauces and oral cavity, and also for labour.

I was enabled to visit my colleague, Dr. Wetterstrand, in Stockholm in the autumn of 1890; what I saw of his work was so highly interesting and instructive that I trust he will forgive me if I give some details of it here. He has considerably improved Liebeault's method, not only by means of going deeply scientifically into the cases, and by thoroughness and sharper criticism, but also in erecting practical appliances. He has two large rooms, which communicate with one another by means of a door, and in which all conduction of sound is enormously subdued by thick carpets, etc. They contain numerous sofas, armchairs, and couches. From nine to one daily the patients come in streams to Dr. Wetterstrand; they are first carefully examined, and if they are found to be suitable cases, conducted into the two rooms. First, those patients who have previously been hypnotized are again treated. The suggestions are whispered into their ears by Wetterstrand so softly that only the person for whom they are intended can hear them. In this way Wetterstrand achieves the powerful suggestion action of the sight of the number of people being so rapidly put to sleep, and avoids the disturbance of the mass action of the suggestions—*i.e.,* of each suggestion, which is only suitable for one patient, but which is heard by the others, as in Nancy. If Wetterstrand wishes to give one suggestion to two or more patients, he raises his voice correspondingly. The newly-arrived patients look about them with astonishment, and see how all the others go to sleep in response to the slightest sign or awaken again, and observe the beneficial results. When Dr. Wetterstrand comes to them after a considerable time, they are already so far suggested that the hypnosis practically never fails. He owes his excellent results to his method (97 per cent of all the patients, numbering some 3,148, were hypnotically influenced, against only 3 per cent who remained uninfluenced). Wetterstrand prefers to allow his patient to sleep for a long time, and believes that it is more advantageous to produce as deep a hypnosis as possible, with amnesia. I agree with him. I have witnessed some astonishing cures in his practice, and am convinced that they are due, not only to his striking personality, his consistency, and his patience, but also to a great extent to his excellent method. I had recognized long before that I lost a considerable portion of the advantages of the suggestion in the way in which I used to hypnotize some patient or other, accidentally, as it were, in the interval between various other work. It was impossible for me to have managed it otherwise. But I had never realized how the majority of failures could be avoided by his method so clearly until I visited Wetterstrand. One ought to devote one's self entirely for hours to the matter; one should allow each patient to influence the other, and, at the same time, one should observe and take notes on everything without missing a single advantage or hint which would lead to a deeper action in each patient. In this way one will achieve the maximum action for every patient. While I was with Wetterstrand I saw a hypochondriacal melancholic influenced within a short time by his perseverance and by the surroundings. This is one of the most difficult results to obtain. In reading Wetterstrand's book*—*e.g.*, in the passage where he describes his unique cures of morphinism—some people may become very sceptic. If I had not seen him operate, I should very probably have entertained considerable doubts. But it is only in respect of the epilepsy cases that I still harbour any doubts, and these arise from the question of the diagnosis.

I wish to express considerable reserve with regard to this last-named point. I certainly believe that only certain cases are curable by suggestion. In one case, with a long aura, I have since succeeded in controlling the aura and in curing the epilepsy. Carl Graeter succeeded in recalling the memory of an amnesic period in an extremely instructive case of an epileptic, without the least doubt, by means of hypnosis. But the epilepsy was not cured.

Both Wetterstrand and Bernheim emphasize that one is apt greatly to undervalue the palliative action of suggestion in producing sleep and in quieting pain in severe incurable diseases, such as tuberculosis, cancer, etc. I would wish to add that one underestimates very vastly its enormous value in everyday medicine as an aperient, as a means of procuring appetite and sleep, and as a regulator of digestion, secretion, and menstruation.

It is invaluable in these conditions, and is quite harmless, in contradistinction to the scandalous abuse which so many practitioners make of narcotics and alcohol. One can produce sleep even in high fever by suggestion.

Ringier* has divided the 210 cases which he has treated into the following groups:

1. Dynamic neuroses, of a motor, vasomotor, and secretory nature.
2. Dynamic sensory neuroses, neuralgias.
3. Sleeplessness.
4. General cerebral neuroses (or mild psychoses).
5. Rheumatic affections.

---

*Wetterstrand, "Hypnotism and its Application in Practical Medicine" (Vienna: Urban and Schwarzenberg, 1891).

"Graeter, "A Case of Epileptic Amnesia removed by Hypnotic Hyperamnesia," *Zeitschrift fur Hypnotismus,* Vol. VIII, No. 3, 1897.

*Ringier, "Results of Therapeutic Hypnotism in Country Practice" (Munchen: Lehmann, 1891).

6. Intoxications.

7. Various cases.

Of these:

		Cases.
(1)	Cured, with a report later that the cured had lasted	73
(2)	Cured, without a subsequent report	15
(3)	Considerably improved, with or without subsequent report	64
(4)	Somewhat improved, with or without subsequent report	19
(5)	Failure of the hypnosis, or not improved	25
(6)	Interruption of treatment, mostly early	12
(7)	Hypnosis for surgical cases	2
	Total	210

Ringier complains with justification about the unsatisfactory results of the frequent early interruption of the treatment in country practice. The majority of the improved would have undoubtedly been cured if they had persevered.

Among the number of interesting tables, the following deserve special notice: 27 recurrences among the considerably improved, 9 recurrences among the slightly improved, so that he had 36 recurrences, all of which belong to the patients who were only improved.

Degree	Cure with subsequent report	Cure with -out report	Consider -able im -provement	Slight improve -ment	Failure
	Per cent	Per cent	Per cent	Per cent	Per cent
Somnolence	18.75	—	6.25	6.25	43.75
Hypotaxis	24.45	8.62	31.89	14.21	12.07
Somnambulism and deep sleep	48.05	5.19	33.76	6.49	5.19

Of 209 hypnotized persons (in one case there are no details on these points), 16 fell into the condition of somnolence, 116 fell into the condition of hypotaxis, and 77 fell into the condition of somnambulism or deep sleep.

In addition to this, Ringier met with 12 completely refractory persons out of a total of 221; in these a suggestive treatment could not be undertaken on this account.

The results, expressed in percentages, work out as follows:

Refractory	5.43
Somnolence	7.24
Hypotaxis	52.49
Somnambulism and deep sleep	34.84

The duration of the treatment, expressed in the number of sittings, is given as follows:

In 94 cases only 1 sitting.
In 43 cases only 2 sittings.
In 23 cases only 3 sittings.
In 12 cases only 4 sittings.
In 4 cases onlp 5 sittings.
In 8 cases only 6 sittings.
In 1 case only 7 sittings.
In 4 cases only 8 sittings.
In 21 cases more than 8 sittings.

Of the last-named, one case was treated in thirty-five sittings, one in twenty-one, and one in twenty, while all the rest were treated in less than twenty sittings.

These tables disprove most conclusively the contention of our adversaries who try to compare suggestive therapy with the morphine habit.

The above are only a few summary extracts of some of the many tables which Dr. Ringier has compiled with the utmost statistical exactness from all points of view, and which show the matter in a critical light. His chief aim was to adhere strictly to objective observation, and not to allow his results to appear too favourable. The results confirm those of his predecessors and mine.

I used to teach suggestive therapy in my out-patient class for medical students in Zurich every Saturday from 2:30 to 4. The patients were derived from the town. I first examined them, and then, imitating Wetterstrand's example, made them all sit in armchairs in the presence of the students. I began with those who had already been hypnotized previously, and thus I saved myself from having to prepare the new patients. When the new patients' turns arrived, they were, as a rule, already so much influenced that they fell asleep at once. Like Bernheim, I explained to the apparently refractory patients that they were already influenced, and that sleep was not necessary in their cases. I then employed amulets, pieces of metal and the like at times, together with suggested currents; in this way nearly all of them became hypnotized after one or two sittings (some of them, I must admit, however, only became hypotactic). I have not prepared a statement of the cases and results, on account of want of time, although I obtained very good therapeutic results. I may point out that these results were obtained in this simple way in spite of the disturbing presence of the students (many of the patients were embarrassed by this), in spite of the fact that I only hypnotized once a week (sometimes twice in the most difficult cases), and in spite of the necessity of giving the suggestions aloud for teaching purposes, as well as in spite of the unsuitable quality of the cases.

From the year 1898 to 1905 I have only occasionally treated a few patients in Chigny, in the country, by suggestion according to Wetterstrand's system. In all, the number of patients has reached 236. Of these, only 4 proved themselves to be absolutely refractory (1.7 per cent); 19 (8.0 per cent) because only more or less somnolent; 146 (61.9 per cent) became hypotactic; and 67 (28.4 per cent) became somnambulic. A large number were unsuitable, hopeless cases; others only came once or twice, and then stayed away, so that the statistics of the results and failures do not prove much. The number of somnambulists would have been considerably increased if the material had been better and if they had had more patience.

In summing up the cases, one finds the following (c.-cured, i.-improved, u.-uninfluenced):

1. Actual psychoses, 20 cases, naturally without any visible result. In 2 cases of paranoia, however, the subjective symptoms were materially improved. Both of them employed me to hypnotize them.) One idiot was cured of his migraine. In one case of deeply-rooted periodic melancholia I succeeded in stopping the attacks as they were setting in by suggestion for a time, after the onset of the attacks had first been delayed. After the course of some weeks, however, they again returned. Ringier had succeeded some time ago in curing a mild early case of periodic melancholia, which I myself had diagnosed, by suggestion applied in the intervals.

This does not prove much. But these observations are nevertheless worth recording.

2. Various psychopathies (constitutional). By 'cured' I mean the curing of the pathological symptoms for which I was consulted in these cases. There was 23 cases, of which 1 was refractory and 2 failed to turn up a second time. Of the remaining 20, c.-6, i.-8, and u.-6.

3. Hypochondriasis, 18 cases. One patient disappeared immediately, and of the remainder, c.-4, i.-7, and u.-6.

4. Hysteria, 29 cases. One patient failed to return. Of the remaining 28, c.-15, i.-8, and u.-5.

Two hysterical married people were already improved, but nagged each other with autosuggestions, and, in consequence, went away uncured.

5. Astasia-abasia (a nervous disturbance of standing and walking, mostly due to hysteria), 1 case: improved.

6. Delusions of impulse, 4 cases: c.-1, 1 disappeared, u.-2 (these latter also did not return after a short time).

7. Stammering, 4 cases: i.-3, somewhat improved-1.

8. Blepharospasm, 1 case: improved.

9. Facial nauralgia, 2 cases: c.-1, somewhat improved-1.

10. Epilepsy, 5 cases: uninfluenced.

11. Intercostal neuralgia, 1 case: cured (a female aged seventy-three).

12. Writer's cramp, 2 cases: i- 1, u-1.

13. Cardiac neuroses, 2 cases: cured.

14. Various neuroses, 14 cases: c.-5, i-3, and u.-6.

15. Sleeplessness, 22 cases, of which 1 was refractory and 1 failed to return. Of the remaining 19 cases, c.-14, i-5.

16. Enuresis nocturna, 7 cases: c.-2, i.-4, 1 disappeared.

17. Profuse menstruation of increased frequency, 4 cases: c.-3, and i.1. In one case the menses were definitely regulated for the first of each month, and to last for three days.

18. Obstinate cephalalgias, 2 cases: c.-2. One case was associated with contracted kidney and albuminuria, and, notwithstanding this, was permanently cured. Two further cases were due to overwork at school. One of these was that of a young man who

was suffering so severely that he was nearly compelled to give up his studies. I succeeded in again making him capable of working well after a fortnight, so that he passed his matriculation a few months later, without any return of the headaches.

19. True neurasthenia (according to Beard)—*i.e.*, cerebral exhaustion following overwork—3 cases: c.-2, a little improved-1. The last case was not a pure one; it was complicated with satyriasis and psychopathy. But in its place one could include the two cases tabulated under 18. A psychopathic disposition was discernible in all the cases, although this was not extreme. In three of the four pure cases the cause lay in overwork at school on the classical side, while in one the cause of the exhaustion lay in overwork at school on the modern side; in all four the pupils were preparing for an examination. I suggested to the subjects in all cases to leave off learning things 'off by heart,' and also to follow their school-work as an intellectual game, in which they should take a great interest in their subjects. I further suggested away the examination nervousness, and substituted for this good sleep, good appetite, and coolness, presence of mind, and ease at the examination. This had the desired result, and was both in place and justifiable in connection with the ante-diluvian system of study and examination which is unfortunately still common, and which is especially to be met with in our classical schools (Gymnasien).

20. Impotence, 4 cases: c-3, u.-1. One of the cases occurred in a married man who was formerly continent, but who was psychopathic. During his whole life he had only had pollutions during sleep, but had not experienced orgasm during waking. Thus, he suffered from impotentia coeundi, in spite of libido. I first succeeded in obtaining good erections during hypnosis. Then the complications in the wife were dealt with by operation (hymen and vaginismus). Coitus was not quite successful during the hypnosis, but, as the result of suggestion, was attained after consistent stages in the course of time. Two pregnancies of the wife have assured the result already; the children are healthy.

21. Constipation, 8 cases: c.-4, i.-2, u.-2. (among the last there was one case in which I was only able to produce slight somnolence).

22. Perverse sexual appetite,* I acquired case, with excellent result. Normal libido, with dreams corresponding to this, was obtained. Supposed cases, 7. i.-4, u.-3.

23. Sciatica, 4 cases: c.-1, u.-3. The latter three patients interrupted the treatment after one or two sittings.

24. Digestive disturbances, 5 cases. One case disappeared.

25. Chorea, 2 cases: i.-1, u.-1.

26. Chlorosis, 1 case: cured.

27. Pneumatic pains, 2 cases: cured.

28. Osteo-arthritis, 1 case, which was not cured, as was to be expected. The patient was only hypnotized a few times, in order to satisfy her desire for this.

29. Asthma, attacks of giddiness, "area celsi," with neuropathy, 4 cases, all not cured. One curable case disappeared at once, and one incurable case did likewise. In one case of asthma which had previously been successfully treated by a colleague of mine, disturbing phenomena appeared as the result of the long way the patient had to come, and these led to autosuggestions and failures. The fourth case was that of a severe, almost idiotic psychopathic condition.

30. Phobias, 5 cases: c.-3, and i.-2.

31. Sexual anaesthesia, 2 cases: uninfluenced. In one case, which, however, was not quite complete, a very slight improvement was noticed.

32. Onanism, 6 cases: c.-2, and i.-4.

33. Sexual hyperaesthesia, 2 cases: c.-1, and i.-1.

34. "Exhibitionism," 1 case: improved.

35. "Paederosis" (sexual impulse directed towards children), 1 case: not cured.

36. Nervous diarrhoea, 2 cases, both of which were cured. The one case was complicated by opium-poisoning, due to a prescription error on the part of a practitioner.

37. Lumbago, 1 case: cured.

---

*I only employ suggestion in congenital cases from ethical reasons, to lessen the impulse and to soothe, etc. I regard the attempt to divert impulse toward the opposite sex as inadmissible, and the same applies to marriage (see Forel, "The Sexual Question," E. Rheinhardt, Munchen, 1905.) For this reason, one cannot speak of a cure in these cases.

38. Pathological jealousy, 1 case: cured.

39. Alcoholism, 1 case: improved.

40. Myelitis, 1 case. I attempted to allay the pains, in response to the urgent requests of the patient's family. Occasionally there was a slight symptomatic result, but the case must be tabulated under "not cured." The patient, a female, was fairly suggestible.

41. Paedogogic treatment, 1 case. A ten-year-old schoolboy, who got up to boyish pranks, and was inattentive, as a result partly of the pedantic method of teaching, and partly of the suggestions of other naughty boys. The result was marked.

I refer the reader for further hints on practical suggestive treatment to the *Zeitschrift fur Hypnotismus* (1892 to 1901), edited by Dr. Oscar Vogt. The interesting casuistic and critical articles of Messrs. Brodmann, Bruegelmann, Loewenfeld, Rauschburg, Delius, Tuckey, Bonjour, Ringier, Bramwell, Baur, Graeter, Monier, Inhelder, Hilger, van Straaten, Seif, Cullerre, and others, ought to be mentioned here. I cannot enter into the details of these articles in this place; all of them appear in the journal named above. The *Zeitschrift* has recently been amalgamated with the *Journal fur Psychologie und Neurologie,* under the same editorship.

Alcoholism and Morphinism.—Lloyd Tuckey* and Hirt recommend suggestion in the treatment of alcoholism. I must caution against a crass misunderstanding in this place. It is an absolutely idiotic and harmful undertaking to try to convert a "soaker" into a moderate drinker by means of suggestion, as Hirt advises. One sins against the First Commandment for a lasting result of the suggestion therapy, by allowing the damaging cause of the illness to persist after the result. There are, it is true, no rules without exceptions, and it is possible that in rare cases a not consummate drinker may be rendered moderate in this way, provided that he has been led to abuse alcohol as a result of definite circumstances, and not from hereditary causes nor from psychopathic conditions. But in the large majority of cases one will experience relapses sooner or later, on account of the contrasuggestion induced by the enjoyment of alcohol and by being "sociable." I have observed this

---

*Tuckey, "The Value of Hypnotism in Chronic Alcoholism", (London: Churchill, 1892.)

repeatedly in drunkards, who attempt to begin again to drink moderately. The majority of drunkards are, besides, individually predisposed, and become incapable of resisting alcohol from habit. If suggestion is, therefore, to be of real use in the treatment of alcoholism, one must suggest definite and complete abhorrence of all spirituous liquors, life-long total abstinence from the same, and, if possible, the joining a temperance society. Tuckey agrees with me in this respect; and the secret of the renowned and costly "gold cure" of alcoholics by Keely is undoubtedly to be found in this idea. Keely did not suggest moderation for his patients; he suggested complete abhorrence for all spirituous liquors.

One does the same in the treatment of the morphine habit, except for the belonging to a society. But there is no tempting sociability, no compulsion to drink in company for the morphine takers, as there is for alcoholists. For this reason the suggestive sociability of the temperance society, which is devoid of alcohol, is so important for the latter.

I myself have converted many a drunkard to abstinence by means of suggestion. Still, as Bonne* has justly said, the abstaining medical practitioner suggests infinitely better, since his example and his inward conviction assist the suggestion. I have shown the good results statistically of suggestion in alcoholism as long ago as in 1888.†

---

*Bonne, Wien. Med. Presse, No. 45, 1901.
†Forel, *Munch. Med. Woch.*, No. 26, 1888.

Selected Bibliography

ANONYMOUS: *Lettre de M. A.—A M. B.—Sur le Livre Intitule*: *Recherches & Doutes sur le Magnetisme Animal de M. Thouret.* Ce 22 Aout 1784. Bruxelles, 1784.

Thouret, a member of the Paris medical faculty, in his very learned work had shown that animal magnetism had its predecessors far back in history: against his intention, it was regarded by the mesmerists, therefore, as a confirmation of their theories. The author of the present letter does not agree with this position, however. He regards mesmerism as something entirely new and original.

ANONYMOUS: *Lettre sur la Mort de M. Count de Gebelin.* Paris, 1784.

Count de Gebelin (1728-1784), one of the most learned men of his time, had experienced actual relief in his last illness through a first treatment by Mesmer but soon returned to the latter in a state of shock and died a few days later. An autopsy was performed, an official report of which is here appended. Signed by five physicians, it clearly shows that the patient's condition had been so grave that magentism could not save him, but that it also did not kill him as Mesmer's enemies had been quick to conclude.

ANONYMOUS: *Prophétie Dont l'Accomplissement Paroit Devoir être Assez Prochain.* 1784.

This is a rather spirited and very rare satire. It is predicted that a man will make his appearance who will make it known that old nature watches with still greater care over the preservation of men than the royal medical society, and all physicians and apothecaries will disappear from this earth.

Archiv für den Thierischen Magnetismus. Altenburg, etc., 1817-1821, vols. 1-10.

Great prominence and influence was achieved by the magentic doctrine in Germany during the second, third, and fourth decades of the nineteenth century. The adherents of mesmerism created a literary forum for their views in the *Archiv für den Thierischen Magnetismus,* which appeared from 1817-1824. This journal contained original papers, clinical observations, and reviews.

AZAM, C.M. ETIENNE: Hypnotisme et Double Conscience. Origine de leur étude et divers, travaux sur des sujets analogues. Préface de Paul Beri, Charcot et Ribot. Paris, 1893.

This book contains interresting documents on periodic amnesia.

BARAGNON P. PETRUS: *Étude du magnétisme.* Animal sous le point de vue d'une exacte pratique, suivie d'um mot sur lo rotation des tables. Paris, Toulouse, 1853.

This book contains a chronological history of magnetism.

BARTH, GEORGE: *What Is Mesmerism?* The Question Answered by a Mesmeric Practitioner; or Mesmerism Not Miracle. An attempt to show that mesmeric phenomena and mesmeric cures are not supernatural, to which is appended useful remarks and hints for sufferers who are trying mesmerism for a cure. London, 1853. First edition.

BERGASSE, NICOLAS: *Considerations sur le Magnetisme Animal, ou sur la Théorie du Monde et des étres organises.* D'aprés les principes de M. Mesmer. Avec des pensées sur le mouvement, par M. le Marquis de Chatellux, de l 'Académie Franciose. The Hague, 1784.

Bergasse (1750-1832), a famous French lawyer, edited most of the works which Mesmer published in French. The two men later quarreled, and Bergasse wrote against Mesmer; the above title was one of the reasons for their final separation.

BERILLON, EDGAR: *Hypnotisme Experiméntal La dualite cérébrale et l'indépendance Fonctionelle des Deux Hemispheres Cérébraux.* Paris, 1884.

Berillon writes about experimental hypnosis in relation to anatomy, physiology, embryogeny, cerebral thermometry, mental pathology, psychology. He also discusses the dream, hysteroepilepsy, suggestions, catalepsy, illusions, and hallucinations.

BERNHEIM, HIPPOLYTE MARIE: *De la Suggestion et de Ses Applications a la Thérapeutique.* Paris, 1888. Second edition (revised and augmented).

BERNHEIM, HIPPOLYTE MARIE: *Hypnotisme, Suggestion, Psychothérapie.* Etudes nouvelles. Paris, 1891. First edition.

Like Liebeault, Bernheim (1840-1919) studied the scientific application of hypnotism and substituted verbal for sensory stimuli; he interpreted hypnotism and its consequent phenomena as being the result of suggestion. Freud translated this work into German (1892).

BERSOT, ERNEST: *Mesmer et le Magnétisme Animal.* Paris, 1853.

Bersot presents biographical and historical data of Mesmer and mesmerism up to 1837, followed by a critical presentation of the essence of animal magnetism.

BERTRAND, ALEXANDRE: *Du Magnétisme Animal en France.* Et des judgements du 'en ont porte les sociétés savantes, avec le texte des divers rapports faits en 1784 par les commissaires de l'Academie des Sciences de la Facult'é et de la Société Royale de Médicin et une analyse des dernieres seances de l'Académie Royale de Medécine et du rapport de M. Hussons; suivi de considerations sur l'apparition de l'Extase, dans les traitements magnétiques. Paris, 1826.

This book caused a sensation, on its appearance, for containing views contrary to those which Bertrand (1795-1831), a physician, had previously professed. He maintains in this book that a magnetic fluid does not exist. The book is also valuable because it contains reprints of the famous Academy report on Animal Magnetism which was written by Lavoisier, and of the so-called secret report on the subject which was submitted at the time to the king but published for the first time fifteen years later in 1788.

BERTRAND, ALEXANDRE: *Traite du Somnambulisme* Et des différentes modifications qu'il présénte. Paris, 1823.

This book was the first general treatise on the subject to appear in France. Bertrand (1795-1831), a physician, recognized four different kinds of somnambulism: essential, symptomatic, artificial, and ecstatic, a classification not in use today.

BILLOT, G.P.: Recherches Psychologiques sur la Cause des Phénoménes *Extra-ordinaires Observes chez les Modernes Voyans.* Improprement dits somnambules magnétiques, ou correspondence sur le magnétisme vital, entre un solitarie et M. Deleuze. Paris, 1839.

This curious work was the first to deal with the materialization of objects in connection with somnambulistic experiments (thyme branches, fragments of the bones from martyred people, etc.). Deleuze (1753-1825), who was one of the most prominent adherents of mesmerism in France, expresses his belief in these phenomena.

BINET, ALFRED: *La Psychologie du Raisonnement*. Recherchés experimentales par l'hypnotisme. Paris, 1886. First edition.

Binet (1857-1911), in this work, was still strongly under the influence of sensualism, yet he soon came to the conclusion that there are experiences of consciousness which are not traceable to sensory impressions. Thus, he was led to his famous study of intelligence and on to the Binet scale for measuring intelligence, an achievement that has made his name familiar even to laymen all over the world.

BJORNSTROM, FREDERICK, M.D.: *Hypnotism: Its History and Present Development*. Authorized translation from the second Swedish edition, by Baron Nils Posse. New York, 1899.

This popular exposition of the subject was published before the turn of the century. Bjornstrom was the Professor of Psychiatry at Stockholm.

He included a Selected Bibliography of the major works which were published at that time.

BLANC, HIPPOLYTE: *Le Merveilleux Dans le Janesnisme, le Magnétisme, le Méthodisme et le Baptisme Americain; l'Epidemie de Morzine, le Spiritisme*. Recherchés nouvelles. Paris, 1865. First edition.

Blanc gives an interesting and well-documented survey of the history, the phenomena, and the theory of animal magnetism.

BONNET, GERAUD: *Les Merveilles de l'Hypnotisme*. Considerations, Theoriques et Applications Diverses. Paris, 1901.

Of particular interest are the historical observations—the first chapter dealing with the antiquity of hypnotism, including such figures as Paracelsus, van Helmont, Mesmer, Puysegur, Braid, and Charcot; the second chapter being entirely devoted to the method of Braid; and with further historical and theoretical discussions throughout (Ampere, Liebeault, Loysel, Esdaile, Bernheim, etc.).

BOTTEY, FERNAND: *"Le Magnétisme Animal"*. Etude Critique et Expérimentale sur l'Hypnotisme ou Sommeil Nerveux. Provoque chez les sujets sains, léthargie, catalepsie, somnambulisme, suggestion, etc. Paris, 1884. First edition.

Particularly valuable is the short historical introduction which traces the precursors of mesmerism to antiquity.

BRAID, JAMES: Braid on Hypnotism: *Neurypnology; or the Rationale of Nervous Sleep, Considered in Relation to Animal Magnetism or Mesmerism*. Illustrated by numerous cases of its successful application in the relief and cure of disease. A new edition edited with an introduction biographical and bibliographical embodying the author's later views and further evidence on the subject by Arthur Edward Waite. London, 1899; BRAID JAMES: *Neurypnology; or, the Rationale of Nervous Sleep, Considered in Relation with Animal Magnetism*. Illustrated by numerous cases of its successful application in the relief and cure of disease. London, 1843.

Braid (1795-1860) inaugurated modern *hypnotism*, the word itself being introduced by him. His theories were adopted by Broca, Charcot, Liebault, and Bernheim; thus he founded the French school.

BRAID, JAMES: *The Physiology of Fascination and the Critics Criticised.* Manchester, Grant & Co., 1855.

This booklet consists of the two pamphlets, "The Physiology of Fascination" and "The Critics Criticised", which were published after Braid's work entitled *Neurypnology.* In "The Physiology of Fascination", Braid indicates that he had a perfectly clear concept of the suggestion technique even before Bernheim. He introduced the term *mono-ideism* to describe the condition in which the mind is possessed by a dominant idea.

Baird also introduced the term *psychophysiology* to cover all those phenomena which result from the interaction of mind and body.

BRAID, JAMES: *The Power of the Mind Over the Body.* London, John Churchill, 1846.

James Braid was the first serious critic of the researches of Baron Reichenbach, and he wrote the pamphlet, *The Power of the Mind Over the Body,* to show that his experiments and researches are opposed to the *theoretical* notions of Baron Reichenbach and the mesmerists.

This work is one of the most interesting of Braid's publications, and it contains some of his most sagacious experiments; Braid should be given credit for the formulation of the theories of suggestive therapeutics.

BRAID, JAMES: *Satanic Agency and Mesmerism Reviewed.* In a letter to the Rev. H. Mc. Neile, A.M. of Liverpool, in reply to a sermon preached by him in St. Jude's Church, Liverpool, on Sunday, April 10th, 1842. Manchester, Simms and Dinham, and Galt and Anderson, 1842.

This little booklet covers twelve pages, and in it Braid laid the foundation of *medical hypnotism.* No copy of the book can be traced in the United States or in England. In this book, Braid demonstrated that the various phenomena attributed to animal magnetism could be attained by simple suggestion.

In this, his first work on *mesmerism,* Braid coined the word, "hypnotism," to replace "mesmerism," and his first use of the word occurs in this work, and not, as is generally believed, in his later work, *Neurypnology.*

BRAID, JAMES, AND PREYER, THIERRY WILHELM: *Die Entdeckung des Hypnotismus.* Nebst einer ungedruckten original Abhandlung von Braid in Deutscher Uebersetzung. Berlin, 1881.

Braid (1795-1860) inaugurated modern hypnotism. Preyer (1841-1897) translated the above essay on hypnotism from a manuscript which had been entrusted to him. It was written in the year of Braid's death. The eassay contains additions to Braid's classic *Neurypnology* of 1843, along with many historical references.

BRAMWELL, J. MILNE: *Hypnotism and Treatment by Suggestion.* New York, 1910.

Bramwell practiced hypnotism in England at a time when it was introduced into the practice of medicine by single individuals more or less widely scattered over the Continent and England.

BRAMWELL, J. MILNE: *Hypnotism, its History, Practice and Theory.* London, 1903. First edition.

"Bramwell, the English psychotherapist, expressed the growing recognition of the part of practicing physicians of the number of mental cases that could be handled without recourse to the asylum. 'Until I began hypnotic practise' (circa 1889), he wrote (in the present work), 'I had no conception of the number of people whose lives were made miserable by morbid ideas' (obsessions and phobias). The old question of home versus asylum treatment was being revived; opinion slowly veered away from the accepted conclusion that mental patients should be separated from their families and housed in asylums."—Bromberg.

CAPERN, THOMAS: *The Mighty Curative Powers of Mesmerism.* Proved in Upwards of One Hundred and Fifty Cases of Various Disease. London, 1851. First edition.

The cases range from tic douloureux, paralysis, epilepsy, St. Vitus's dance to emaciation and debility in children. The author calls himself, on the title page, secretary and resident superintendent of the Mesmeric Infirmary.

CAULLET DE VEAUMOREL: *Aphorismes de M. Mesmer.* Dictes a l'assemblée de ses éléves et dans lesquels on trouve ses principles, sa theorie et les moyens de magnétiser: le tout formant un corps de doctrine, développe en trois cents quarante-quartre paragraphes, pour faciliter l'application des commentaires au magnétisme animal. Troisieme edition revue, corrigee et considerablement augmentee. Paris, 1785.

This curious work contains the details of the manner of treatment of various illnesses by animal magnetism. De Veaumorel's work appeared early in the history of animal magnetism and was published after the report of the Commissioners who investigated animal magnetism as practiced by d'Eslon and Mesmer.

CHARPIGNON, JULES: *Physiologie, Medécine et Metaphysique du Magnétisme.* Orleans, 1841.

This book represents an effort to explain the phenomenon of magnetism scientifically.

CHASTENET DE PUYSÉGUR, AND AMAND MARC JACQUES MARQUIS DE: *Details des Cures Operées a Buzancy, Pres Soissons, par le Magnétisme Animal.* Soisson, 1784.

This work contains some sixty-two case reports of cures effected by Puységur in collaboration with his brother Maxime at Soissons. Also included are a testimonial letter of a Soissons salt-tax collector who expresses his convictions as to the beneficial effects of magnetism; a letter from Puysegur to a fellow magnetizer, Nicolas Bergasse, about his operations; the extract of a letter of a Father Gerard; and a report on the cure of a two-year-old child.

Puysegur (1751-1825), a pupil of Mesmer, is remembered as an excellent magnetizer; he discovered magnetic somnambulism.

CHASTENET DE PUYSEGUR, AND AMAND MARC JOSEPH DE MARQUIS: *Du Magnétisme Animal Considéré dans ses Rapports avec Diverses Branches de la Physique Generale.* Paris, 1807.

Comparative studies form the subject of this volume. It also contains some interesting letters from Lavater and others to the author. This work is a good example of a review of the history and the work in detail concerning the main cures performed with the use of animal magnetism.

CHASTENET DE PUYSEGUR, AND AMAND MARC JOSEPH DE MARQUIS: *Recherchés*

Expériences et Observations Physiologiques sur l'Homme dans l'Etat de Somnambulisme Naturel. Et dans le Somnambulisme Provoque par l'cte Magnétique. Paris, 1811.

The Marquis de Puységur (1752-1825), a pupil of mesmer, discovered, or at least elucidated, the phenomenon of magnetic somnambulism.

CHASTENET DE PUYSEGUR, LE COMTE MAXIM DE: *Lettre de M. Le C— de C—a M. le P—E——de S—,* 1784.

This letter is edited by a partisan of Mesmer who signs himself D.M.B. It is supposed to be addressed to the Archbishop of Stasbourgh; it speaks out in favor of animal magnetism and the theory of the magnetic fluid. The editor has added at the end the report of a cure effected by Puysegur, attested by eight Navy physicians at Brest.

CHASTENET DE PUYSEGUR, LE COMTE MAXIME DES: *Rapport des Cures Opérèes a Bayonne par le Magnétisme Animal.* Adresse a M. l'Abbé de Poulouzat, Conseiller-Clerc au Parlement de Bordeaux. Avec des Notes de M. Duval d'Esprèmenil, Corseiller au Parlement de Paris. Bayonne et Paris, 1784.

The author reports how he was induced to magnetize in public, during his regiment's drill sessions, on one of its officers who was attacked by an apopletic stroke and on a small dog wounded by a fall. This shows that magnetization of animals at that time was already established. Puysegur soon had more patients than he could handle. The results of his cures were established in official form before a commission of officers, physicans, and civic officials.

CHEVREUL, EUGENIA: *De la Baguette Divinatoire.* Du pendule dit explorateur et des tables tournantes, au point de vue de l'histoire, de la critique et de la methods experiméntale. Paris, 1854. First edition.

Chevreul (1786-1890), the famous French chemist, has here collected all the bona fide documents and observations relating to transcendental psychology which he considered as exact, but he explained them with psychological causes, a kind of exteriorization of willpower. There are pencil annotations and underscorings throughout.

COLLYER, ROBERT H., MD.: *Psychography, or the Embodiment of Thought;* with an Analysis of Phreno-Magnetism, "neurology," and Mental Hallucination, including Rules to govern and produce the Magnetic State. Philadelphia, New York, Boston, 1843.

According to the title page, the author was a member of the Massachusetts Medical Society and was a former pupil of Dr. John Elliotson.

COLQUHOUN, JOHN CAMPBELL: *Report of the Experiments on Animal Magnetism, Made by a Committee of the Medical Section of the French Royal Academy of Sciences.* Read at the meetings of the 21st and 28th of June, 1831; translated, and for the first time published; with a historical and explanatory introduction and an appendix. Edinburgh, 1833. First edition in English.

Colquhoun (1785-1854), while studying law and philosophy in Germany, had acquired a taste for the investigation of the phenomena of animal magnetism which were just beginning to attract the attention of scientific men. In 1831, a report on the subject was read before the Paris Academie des Sciences, in which it was pronounced worthy of systematic investigation.

This report Colquhoun translated and published with a historical introduction and an appendix of his own research. It became the basis of a work entitled, *Isis Revelata* (Edinburgh, 1836).

COUNTESS C—DE ST. DOMINIQUE: *Animal Magnetism, (Mesmerism) and Artificial Somnambulism*: Being a Complete and Practical Treatise on That Science, and Its Application to Medical Purposes. Followed by Observations on the Affinity Existing between Magnetism and Spiritualism, Ancient and Modern, published for the Authoress, 1874.

The Introduction contains a historical survey of the subject; the last chapter discusses its legal aspects, mentioning in particular insensibility produced by magnetic fascination in criminal assault cases; it is also briefly stated that the phenomenon of insensibility may be availed of in surgical operations.

CSANADY, STEPHAN: *Medicinische Philosophie und Mesmerismus*. Leipzig, 1860. First edition privately published by the author, a "magnetizer."

DALLOZ, A.L.J., L'AINE: *Entretiens sur le Magnètime animal et le Sommeil Magnetique dit Somnambulisme*. Devoilant cette double doctrine, et pouvant servir a en porter un jugement raisonné. Paris, 1823. First edition.

This book contains a number of experiments and some facts about magnetization from the distance.

DELEUZE, J.P.F.: *Defense du Magnétisme Animal Contre les Attaques Dont il est l'Objet Dans le Dictionnaire des Sciences Médicales*. Paris, 1819. First edition.

This publication is a defense of mesmerism. Deleuze, Puysegur's most distinguished pupil, was one of the first to draw attention to the human will in connection with magnetic phenomena. Later, his wide experience with somnambulists led him to the conclusion that the magnetizer's will was the essential factor in any treatment. More than that, he established the early theories about the phenomena we now call posthypnotic suggestion.

DELEUZE, J.P.F.: *Histoire Critique du Magnétisme Animal*. Paris, 1813.

Deleuze (1753-1835) approached the subject entirely scientifically. Librarian to the French Natural History Society, he was a scholar and scientist of considerable repute; this is the best history, even to date, of mesmerism.

DELEUZE, J.P.F.: *Histoire Critique du Magnétisme Animal*. Paris, 1819. Second edition.

This publication is indispensable for a library on the subject, the work was even accepted by the opponents of mesmerism. The first volume deals with the history and practice of magnetism; the second volume contains analyses of, and extracts from, the most important works on magnetism published before 1813 (the date of the first edition of the present title), with a number of valuable notes.

DELEUZE, J.P.F.: *Instruction Pratique sur le Magnétisme Animal;* Suivie d'une letter écrite a l'auteur par un médecin éstranger, Paris, 1825. First edition, very rare.

An important work on the use of mesmerism in medicine with documented accounts of attempted and apparently successful cures, facts which could not be neglected. Deleuze (1753-1835), who was also the author of the best history, ever to date, of mesmerism, approached the subject entirely scientifically. He was librarian to the French Natural History Society, and was a scholar and scientist of considerable repute.

DODS, JOHN BOVEE: *The Philosophy of Electrical Psychology.* In a course of twelve lectures. New York, 1850. Steretype edition.

Dods (1795-1872), an American Universalist minister and amateur physician, was mainly interested in the medical problems connected with mental disorders; he was one of the first to use electricity for therapeutic purposes. He tried to explain psychic phenomena neurologically, emphasizing the "automatic action of the cerebellum" under some sort of electrical influence. He had vague ideas about the role of nerve centers in hypnotism and had several other general theories. The precise mechanism, however, he failed to understand. He finally joined the Spiritualist movement and church.

DODS, JOHN BOVEE: *The Philosophy of Mesmerism and Electrical Psychology.* Comprised in two course of lectures (eighteen in number) complete in one volume. Edited by J. Burns. London, 1876.

DUPOTET DE SENNEVOY, BARON: *Cours de Magnètisme Animal,* Paris, l'Athénée Central, 1834.

DUPOTET DE SENNEVOY, BARON: *Therapeutique Maqnétique, Régles de l'Applecation du Magnétisme Animal a l'Experimentation Pure et au Traitment des Meladies. Spiritulisme son Principe et ses Phénemenes.* Paris, 1863.

This book is one of the best works written on the subject of therapeutic magnetism. It also introduces the phenomenon of mysticism and spiritualism which entered the picture in curative practice as we know it today.

DUVAL D'EPREMESNIL, JAN JACQUES: *Reflexions Preliminaries, a l'Occasion de la Piece Intitulee, les Docteurs Modernes, Jouee sur le Theatre Italien, le Seize Novembre* 1784.

The author of this short note (3 pages) shows his indignation at Mesmer's having been represented on the stage.

ELLIOTSON, JOHN: *Numerous Cases of Surgical Operations Without Pain in the Mesmeric State:* With Remarks upon the Opposition of many Members of the Royal Medical and Chirurgical Society and others to the Reception of the Inestimable Blessings of Mesmerism. London, Cantab., F.R.S., 1843.

This book was written by John Elliotson, an English surgeon, who felt that there was a great deal of merit to the use of animal magnetism for the relief of pain in surgical procedures. He was refused appointments on the staffs of the various hospitals in London and elsewhere, and finally opened his own mesmeric hospital for the continuation of his practice of mesmerism.

He lost his membership in the Royal Medical and Chirurgical Society after he was warned to discontinue the practice. He continued, however, and published *The Zoist* a publication for what was then called "cerebral physiology." The publication also contained the work which was being done at that time in phrenology. The magazine was published for about thirteen years before it was discontinued.

ELLIOTSON, JOHN (Ed.): *The Zoist,* A Journal of Cerebral Physiology and Their Applications to Human Welfare. A series from its commencement in March 1843, to January 1847.

This journal was edited by Dr. Elliotson; it contains numerous articles by him and by other doctors practicing mesmerism, describing cures of insanity with mesmerism and patients in the mesmeric state having surgical operations without pain.

ENNEMOSER, JOSEPH: *Anleitung zur Mesmerischen Praxis*. Stuttgart und Tubingen, 1852. First edition of Ennemoser's famous text.

ENNEMOSER, JOSEPH: *Der Magnetismus in Verhaltnisse zur Natur und Religion*. Stuttgart und Tubingen, 1842. First edition, a historical and critical presentation of animal magnetism, or mesmerism.

Ennemoser (1787-1854), an Austrian physician who practiced as a physician in Munich was one of the most extreme adherents of mesmerism in Germany.

ESDAILE, JAMES: *Mesmerism in India, and its Practical Application in Surgery and Medicine*. London, 1846.

Esdaile (1808-1859) performed a variety of surgical operations on Hindus, upon many of whom he appears to have successfully induced hypnotic anesthesia. However, his similar attempts with Europeans were not successful.

FLINT, HERBERT L.: *Practical Instruction in Hypnotism and Suggestions*. Chicago Flint and Flint, 1903.

The first edition of this publication is an interesting and extremely rare item of hypnosis curiosa. The author, who maintained a "College of Hypnotism" in Cleveland, Ohio, laid in two testimonial broadsides: one is large folio, printed on both sides, containing the testimony of twenty-two of Flint's pupils as to the merits of his course, sixteen of them accompanied by portraits of the persons in question; and the other, printed on one side only, represents the testimony of one Thomas F. Adkin of Rochester, New York, with his portrait.

FLITTNER, CHRISTIAN GOTTFRIED: *De Mesmermi Vestigiis apud Veteres*, Berlin, 1820. First edition, rare.

The author tries to show that mesmerism had its roots in antiquity (India, Egypt, Greece, Rome).

Flittner (1770-1828) was for eight years pharmacist and lecturer on pharmacology at the newly founded veterinary school in Berlin. On his death, he owned three bookshops and a pharmacy. His literary activity also covered a great variety of nonmedical subjects.

FOISSAC, PIERRE: *Rapports et Discussions de l'Académie Royale de Medécine sur le Magnétisme Animal, Receillis par un Sténographe et Publies avec des Notes Explicatives*. Paris, 1833.

This book reports details of the work of the two commissions on animal magnetism of 1826 and 1831. The author has added notes on Mesmer, Deleuze, Puysegur, Bertrand, Virey, Husson, Recamier, as well as on catalepsy, nervous diseases, Gall's opinions on magnetism, Broussais, Frapoart, etc. This historical section is particularly interesting.

FOISSAC, PIERRE: *Second Memoire sur le Magnétisme Animal*. Observations particulieres sur une sonambule présentee a la commission nommee par l'Academie Royale de Medicine pour l'examen du magnetisme animal. Paris, 1826.

Although he does not consider magnetism a universal remedy, the author believes to have cured a number of reputedly incurable conditions by its application.

FOREL, AUGUST, M.D.: *Hypnotism or Suggestion and Psychotherapy*. A Study of the Psychological, Psycho-Physiological and Therapeutic Aspects of Hypnotism. First edition in English translated from the fifth German edition by H. W. Armit. London, New York, 1906. First edition, 1889.

FOVEAU DE COURMELLES, FRANCOIS: L 'hypnotisme. Paris, 1890. First edition.

This gives a very good historical survey of all the scientific methods of magnetism and hypnotism. Special chapters are devoted to the schools of the Salpétriere at Nancy (Liebault) and the Charite of Paris (Charcot), another to the anesthetizing effects of hypnotism.

FRANKLIN, BENJAMIN, et al.: *Rapport des Commissaires,* Chargés par le Roi, de l'Examen du Magnétisme Animal. Imprimé par ordre du Roi. Paris, Imprimerie Royale, 1784. First edition.

This is the orginal appearance, printed at the King's press in the Louvre, of the report which dealt the death blow to mesmerism in Paris. It contains the results of an investigation of the practices of Mesmer, or rather of his disciple, d'Eslon, undertaken by a commission from the Faculte de Medecine and the Academie Royale des Sciences by order of Louis XVI. Franklin was president of this commission, and this report usually goes under his name. It seems to be written in the style of Lavoisier, the great chemist and academician, who was one of the other members of the commission.

After carefully conducted experiments, the commissioners concluded that animal magnetism, as claimed by Mesmer, did not exist, and that its apparent successes were to be explained by suggestion and imagination.

FRANKLIN, BENJAMIN, et al.: *Report of Dr. Benjamin Franklin and the other Commissioners, Charged by the King of France, with the Examination of the Animal Magnetism, as now Practised at Paris.* Translated from the French, with a Historical Introduction by William Godwin. London, 1785. First edition in English published one year after its appearance in Paris. Laehr, Vol. II, p. 862. Ford 361. (Duveen and Klickstein: *A Bibliography of the Works of A.L. Lavoisier,* p. 228.)

By order of Louis XVI, a commission was appointed from the Faculte de Medecine and the Academie Royale des Sciences to investigate the practices of Mesmer, or rather of his disciple d'Eslon. After carefully conducted experiments, the members concluded that animal magnetism, as claimed by Mesmer, did not exist, and that its apparent successes were to be explained by suggestion and imagination. The report of their findings, which dealt the death blow to the movement in Paris, usually goes under Franklin's name. Franklin, at that time at the height of his career as the representative of the United States at the court of Louis XVI, had attained some reputation as an authority on mesmerism. He had known Mesmer some years earlier and was familiar with his practices. Franklin was president of the commission but was ill with the gout in his home at Passy; the other members of the commission actually conducted the necessary experiments. One of the leading commissioners was the great chemist and academician Lavoisier, and the published report seems to be written in his style. In the above translation, this famous report is preceded by the translation of a report of the Societe Royale de Medecine, referring to its own simultaneous investigation of animal magnetism. The Historical Introduction was written by the translator.

FREUD, SIGMUND and BERNHEIM. HIPPOLYTE MARIE: *Die Suggestion und ihre Heilwirking*. Autorisirte deutsche Ausgabe von Sigm. Freud. Zweite, umgearbeitete Auflage besorgt von Max Kahans. Leipzig and Wien, 1896.

This is one of Freud's rare translations from the French.

GALART DE MONTJOYE: *Lettera sul Magnetismo Animale*. Ove si esamina la conformita delle opinioni de'Popoli antichi e moderni, de'Sapienti, e specialmente del Sig. Bailly con quelle del Sig. Mesmer, ed ove si paragonano queste stesse opinioni colla Relazione de' Commissarj incaricati dal Re all'esame del Magnetismo Animale; indirizzata al Sig. Bailly. Cremona, 1785. First edition in Italian. (First French edition, Paris and Philadelphia, 1784.)

This is called an honest defense of animal magnetism against the famous report on mesmerism by members of the French Academy of Sciences and of the Paris medical faculty.

GAUTHIER, AUBIN: *Traité Pratique du Magnétisme et du Sonambulisme*. Paris, 1845.

GAUTHIER, LOUIS PHILIBERT AUGUSTE: *Recheres Historiques sur l'Exercice de la Medecine dans les Temples chez les Peuples de l'Antiquite*. Suivies de considerations sur les rapports qui peuvent exister entre les guerisons qu'on obstenait dans les anciens temples, a l'aide des songes, et le magnétisme animal, et sur l'origine des hopitaux. Paris, 1844.

In several chapters the medical use of dreams in ancient Greece and Rome is discussed, and the view of modern adherents of animal magnetism is refuted to the effect that the priests in the ancient temples practiced magnetism and somnambulism; the author is of the opinion that cures were effected by the influence of the imagination on the nervous system. Gauthier (1792-1850), a Lyons physician, wrote several works on medicohistorical subjects.

GERALD, JULES: *Magnétisme Organique*. Le magnétisme a la recherche d'une position sociale. Sa theoriesa crtiique—sa pratique. Paris, 1866.

Dedicated to the Baron du Potet—an adherent of, and a prolific writer on, animal magnetism—this book contains a defense of attacks made against him. At the same time, it contains a declaration of faith in its tenets, an exposition of theories and practices, together with considerable historical material. The author was a Paris physician.

GERLING, REINH: *Hypnotische Unterrichtsbriefe*. Zur Einfuhrung in die Prixis des Hypnotismus nebst Anleitung zur Abhaltung eines Experimental—Vortrages uber Hypnose and Suggestion. III. Erweiterte Auflage, 13-17. Tausen, Oranienburg—Berlin, n.k. c. 1895.

The author discusses the methods of Bernheim and Liebeault among others.

GESSMANN, G.: *Magnetismus und Hypnotismus*. Eine Darstellung dieses Gebietes mit besonderer Berucksichtigung der Beziehungen zwisch dem mineralischen Magnetismus und dem sogenannten thierischen Magnetismus oder Hypnotismus. Wien. Pest, Leipzig, 1887.

GIRARDIN, S.: *Lettre d'un Anglais a un Francois sur la Découverte du Magnétisme Animal;* et Observations sur Cette Lettre. Paris, Bouillon, 1784.

In this enthusiastic endorsement of Mesmer and his theories—Mesmer is called "the eagle, the king of birds, who will triumph." Girardin was secretary of the Societe de l'Harmonie.

GRIMES, J. STANLEY: *The Mysteries of Human Nature Explained by a New System of Nervous Physiology:* to which is added, A Review of the Errors of Spiritualism, and Instructions for Developing or Resisting the Influence by which Subjects and Mediums are Made. Buffalo, 1857. First edition.

This is a study of occult phenomena, giving special attention to the errors of spiritualism. Grimes (1807-1903), who has been called the "erratic philosopher," and who taught for a period medical jurisprudence in the Castleton Medical College and in Willard Institute, the first woman's college established in the United States, was mainly interested in wide speculative problems of science and pseudoscience. He was one of the first American evolutionists, *one of the first American investigators of mesmerism to reach constructive conclusions,* and a stout opponent of superstition. His attention was early attracted by phrenology. *He showed himself to be in advance of his time by ascribing mesmerism to the power of suggestion,* but he introduced an occult fluid of his own and argued that the seat of consciousness was to be found in the medulla oblongata.

HALLE, JOHANN SAMUEL:*Magie, oder die Zauberkrafte der Natur,* so auf den Nutzen and die Belustigung angewandt werden. Berlin, 1784-1786; HALLE: *Fortgesetzte Magie, oder Zauberkrafte der Natur,* Berlin and Vienna, 1788-1802.

This rare compilative work contains reports on scientific advances of the time in all fields, in popular form, and descriptions of experiments. There are observations on electricity, chemistry, *magnetism,* medicine, mechanics, optics, aeronautics, pyrotechnics, meteorology, etc., in general, and on a medley of such subjects as beer, wine, liquor, amber, bees, blindness, Caliostro, *Franklin,* precious stones, colors, Faust, finger language, ghosts and spirits, glass, inoculation, coffee, potatoes, the piano and the organ, engraving and painting, metals, steel, pomiculture, paper, pearls, chess, apparent death, gun powder, swimming, silk, silhouettes, speaking machines, toothache, and sugar, in particular.

Of special interest are the many *medical references,* the majority of which are *related to mental and nervous diseases and their treatment* (the therapeutic uses of electricity and *magnetism,* opium, sleeping drugs, and remedies against epilepsy, paralysis, apoplexy, physical causes of mental derangement, *animal magnetism,* pyromania, hydrophobia, *somnambulism,* etc.).

KIRCHER, ATHANASIUS, S.J.: *Physiologica Kircheriana Experimentalis, Qua Summa Argumentorum Multitudine et Varietate.* Naturalium rerum scientia per experimenta Physica, Mathematica, Medica, Chymica, Musica, Magnetica, Mechanica comprebatur atque stabilitur. Quam ex vastis operibus. Adm. Revdi. P. Athanasii Kircheri extraxit, et in hunc ordinem per classes redegit Romae, Anno MDCLXXV. Joannes Stephanus Kestlerus Alsata, Authoris discipulus, et in re litteraria assecla, et coadjutor. Amsterdam, 1680.

This first edition of extracts from Kircher's (1602-1680) works includes the first recorded experiment on hypnotism in animals. Kircher was a Jesuit father whose name is linked with that of Fracastoro in the history of contagious diseases. He became the friend of popes and cardinals, and was considered one of the most learned men of his age. His literary activity was enormous, and all his books had a tremendous success.

KLUGE, CARL ALEXANDER FERDINAND: *Versuch einer Darstellun des animalischen Magnetismus als Heilmittel.* Berlin, 1811 (2 parts in 1 vol.). First edition.

This textbook of mesmerism for physicians was written by Kluge (1782-1844) since he found no work extant in the literature of the time appropriate for practical use of this system which, as he says, had been drawn from oblivion by Mesmer, but which was also driven by him and his first followers to charlatanism and had to be freed of much dross. Kluge, at that time professor and head surgeon at the Pepiniere in Berlin (the obstetrical clinic of the Charite), was a pupil of Hufeland, had become interested in animal magnetism as a therapeutic means, knew the contemporary literature on the subject, and had practiced it for some time.

MESMER, FRANZ ANTON AND BERGASSE, NICOLAS: *Considerations sur le Magnétisme Animal, ou sur la Théorie du Monde et des Êtres Organises.* D'apres les principes de M. Mesmer. Avec des pensées sur le mouvement, par M. le Marquis de Chatellux, de l'Académie Francoise. The Hague, 1784. First edition. Bound with: Doutes D'un Provincial. *Proposes a MM. les Medecins-Commissaires, charges par le Roi, de l'examen du Magnétisme Animal.*

I. Bergasse (1750-1832), a famous French lawyer, edited most of the works which Mesmer published in French. The two men later quarreled, and Bergasse wrote against Mesmer; the above title was one of the reasons for their final separation. Although Bergasse defended Mesmer against all the attacks to which the latter was exposed at the time, he discussed in his treatise some of the theories of animal magnetism, and Mesmer resented this revelation of his ideas, which he considered his personal property. The book also contains some valuable information regarding the famous subscription of one hundred Louis d'or arranged by one hundred of Mesmer's followers for the propagation of mesmerism.

II. This work is an anonymous attack on the medical commissioners of animal magnetism, with proposals on how the investigations should actually have been conducted, not on men and women, but on plants, animals, and children.

MESMER, FRANZ ANTON: *Lettres de M. Mesmer, a M. Vicq-d'Azyr, et a Messieurs les Auteurs Du Journal de Paris.* Bruxelles, 1784.

Mesmer had previously published several notes in the *Journal de Paris,* and believed he had to answer an attack on him by Vicq-d'Azyr which has appeared in the same periodical. As the editors of the paper did not want to meet Mesmer's conditions for publication, the latter decided to have the note separately printed preceded by another which had actually appeared in the *Journal de Paris.* Reference seems to be made in these notes to the first commission for the investigation of the magnetic treatments of 1778, which came to nothing.

MESMER, FRANZ ANTON: *Lettre d'Un Medécin de Paris, a Un Medécin de Province.* Paris, 1784.

The letter reports the strange agreements made between Mesmer and his disciple d 'Eslon.

MESMER, FRANZ ANTON: *Mémoire sur la Découverte du Magnétisme Animal.* A Geneve; et se trouve a Paris, 1779. First edition.

This is the basic historic document for the history of mesmerism. It was written by Mesmer (1734-1815) soon after his arrival in Paris, hoping that this memorandum would gain him the interest of the French Academy of Sciences, which it failed to do however.

Mesmer's work served as a basis for the more scientific development of suggestion in treatment, which has been termed after him, *mesmerism*. He did not realize that his clinic in Paris was being used as a meeting place for all sorts of perverts. Following an inquiry instituted by Louis XVI, his career came to an abrupt end.

MESMER, FRANZ ANTON: *Réglemens des Sociétiés de l'Harmonie Universelle.* Adoptés par la Société de l'Harmonie de France, dans l'Assemblée générale tenue à Paris, 13, 12 Mai, 1785. Paris, 1785.

Author's presentation copy to the royal treasurer. It opens with a letter from Mesmer to all the club members and contains in four sections the rules of the society. Nothing could be said or done without Mesmer's approval.

(Mesmerism), *Esquisse de la Nature Humaine expliquee par le Magnétisme Animal;* precedee d'un apercu du systeme general de l'univers, et contenant l'explication du somnambulisme magnetique, et de tous les phenomenes du magnétisme animal. Paris, 1826.

Parts I and II deal with the physical aspects of animal magnetism and of its occurrence in the universe; the third and largest part is devoted to its influence on man and its nature. There are sections on the nervous fluid, on intelligence, sensibility, imagination, sleep, and wakefulness, imbecility, madness etc.

MEYER, JOHANN FRIEDRICH VON: *Hades.* Ein Beytrag zur Theorie der Geisterkunde. Nebst Anhangen: Offentiliche Verhandlungen uber Swedenborg und Stilling, ein Beyspiel des Ahnungsvermogens und einen Brief des jungern Plinius enthaltend. Frankfurt am Mayn, 1810.

MILLER, HUGH CRICHTON, M.D.: *Hypnotism and Disease.* A Plea for Rational Psychotherapy. Boston, The Gordon Press, 1912.

Dr. Miller has made the daring innovation in England of collective hypnotization, which he found distinctly helpful in many cases. Another of his innovations was the systematic employment of bromides and other sedative drugs as an aid to hypnosis and preparation for suggestion, to be used especially in the treatment of alcoholism and drug habits.

MONTEGRE, ANTONINE FRANCOIS JANIN DE: Du Magnétisme Animal et de Ses *Partisans,* ou Recueil de Pieces Importantes sur cet Objet, Precede des Observations, Recemment Publiees. Paris, 1812.

This little-known publication on animal magnetism contains reprints of the famous report on mesmerism by the commissioners from the Paris Academy of Sciences and the medical faculty—Franklin, Lavoisier, *et al.* of 1784— as well as of the "secret report" drawn up by the commissioners for the king's personal use only but published for the first time in 1799 in the first volume of N. Francois de Neufchateau's *Conservateur,* since it was considered unsuitable for general distribution in that it revealed the erotic sexual elements underlying the phenomena observed and discussed.

NEWHAM, WILLIAM: *Human Magnetism;* its Claims to Dispassionate Inquiry. Being an Attempt to Show the Utility of its Application for the Relief of Human Suffering. London, 1845. First edition.

Newham (1790-1865), a physician who had been a favorite pupil of Sir Astley Cooper, was much interested in mental and spiritual phenomena.

NOLLET, JEANE ANTOINE, ABBE: *Essai Sur Electricitédes Corps.* Paris, 1765.

Curative powers attributed to magnetic application of the loadstone are described. Nollet felt that there was more to be investigated but that the understanding of the treatment of the diseases with magnetic electricity was positive in its actions.

PASSAVANT, JOHANN CARL: *Untersuchungen uber den Lebensmagnetismus und das Hellsehen*. Zweite umgearbeitete Auflage. Frankfurt am Main, 1873.

This work is based on lectures which Passavant (1790-1857) held on the subject in Frankfurt during the years 1819 and 1820; he considers its physiological, medical, and psychological aspects.

PETIAU, ABBE: *Autres Reveries sur le Magnétisme Animal;* a un Académicien de Province. Bruxelles, 1784.

Attributed to the Abbe Petiau, this is a critique of the famous academy report, and at the same time a defense of Mesmer against d'Eslon.

PIGEAIRE, J.: *Puissance de Électricite Animale.* Ou du Magnetisme Animal Vital et de Ses Rapports avec la Physique la Physiologie et la Medécine. Paris, 1839.

PODMORE, FRANK: *Mesmerism and Christian Science*. Philadelphia, 1909.

This work is a description of the various phases of mesmerism tracing the successive attempts by those who came after Mesmer and its culmination in the Christian Science movement.

Podmore (1855-1910) was keenly interested in psychical research; he argued for theories of psychological, as opposed to spiritualistic, causality, and for a far-reaching application of the hypothesis of telephathy. He was one of the founders of the Fabian Society.

PREYER, THIERRY WILHELM: Der Hypnotismus. Vorlesungen gehalten an der K. Friedrich-Wilhelms-Universitat zu Berlin. Nebst Ammerkungen und einer nachgelassenen Abhandlung von Braid aus dem Jahre 1845. Wien und Leipzig, 1890. First edition.

Preyer (1841-1897) is best known for his lactic-acid theory of sleep and for his work in child psychology. James Braid (1795-1860) inaugurated modern hypnotism, the word itself being introduced by him (1843); his paper, which is here published posthumously for the first time, in German translation, deals with the differences between nervous sleep (i.e. hypnotism) and natural sleep.

Proceedings of the Society for Psychical Research. Vol. I, 1883 to Vol. L., 1956

QUACKENBOS, J.D.: *Hypnotic Therapeutics in Theory and Practice, with Numerous Illustrations of Treatment by Suggestion*. United States, 1908.

Revue de l'Hypnotisme—Experimental et Therapeutic (Psychologie, Pedagogie, Medécine Legale, Maladies Mentales et Nerveuses). De la 1're annee, 1857-1894; 8 vols. relies et de 1896 a 1914; 18 vols. broches.

Herein is a very interesting review of collaboration of such prominent men as Charcot, Bernheim, Berillon, and Loire.

RICE, NATHAN LEWIS: Phrenology Examined, and shown to be Inconsistent with the Principles of Physiology, Mental and Moral Science, and the Doctrines of Christianity. Also, an *Examination of the Claims of Mesmerism*. New York, 1849. First edition.

Rice (1807-1877), the eminent Presbyterian clergyman, attacks mesmerism as much as he does phrenology.

ROLFI, PIE-MICHEL: *La Magie Moderne on l'Hypnotisme de Nos Jours*. Tradiut de l'Italien par l'Abbe H. Dorangeon. Paris, 1902.

SARRAZIN DE MONTFERRIER, ALEXANDRE ANDRE VICTOR (pseudonym: de Lausanne): *Des Principes et des procedes dus Magnétisme Animal, et de Leurs Rapports avec les Lois de la Physique et de la Physiologie.* Paris, 1819 (2 vols.). First edition.

This is an important work on animal magnetism. The first volume, according to Caillet, has been attributed by Mialle to a Monsieur de Bruno. The author here shows himself in agreement with the doctrine of animal spirits applied to an animalized magnetic fluid.

The second volume deals with the magnetic treatment of diseases and gives a number of cures. Chapter Six represents a brief history of animal magnetism and of Mesmer, including accounts of his discovery, his difficulties in Vienna, his arrival in Paris, his rejection by the Paris faculty, his controversy with his disciple, d'Elson, the report of the royal commissioners, etc. Some parts of this volume had been published previously in the *Annales du Magnétisme.*

Sarrasin (or Sarrazin) de Montferrier (1792-1863)—magnetizer, mathematician, and publicist—is better known among the partisans of magnetism under his pseudonym "de Lausanne." He edited almost single-handedly the first volumes of the *Annales du Magnétisme* (1814) and was one of the founders of the Société Parisienne de Magnétisme. Later he undertook the publication of an *Encyclopédie Mathématique,* of which one volume only ever appeared.

This is a fine copy in contemporary bindings; on title pages and half titles appears the stamp of the Bibliotheque du Chateau de Sercy.

SCHODER, JOHANN AND OROSZ ANTON VON: *Schoderiana oder kurzgefasste Beschreibung von mehr als zwei hundert sehr interessanter and theilweise komplizierter Krankheitsfalle und des durch die Behandlung derselben mittelst des nach der Manier des Herrn Doctor Johann Schoder angewendeten Magnetismus erzielten Resultates.* Aus den arztlichen Vormerkungs-Protokollen des Herrn Doktors mit seiner besonderen Bewilligung zum Besten der leidenden Menschheit gesammelt, als ein nutzliches und trostbringendes Nachschlagebuch fur Franke jeder Gattung zusammengestellt und mit einigen fur den Patienten wissenswerthen Notizen versehen. Wien, 1850.

SCHWARZSCHILD, HEINRICH, M.D.: *Magnetismus, Somnambulismus, Clairvoyance.* First edition. Cassel, 1853.

Volume I contains the history of animal magnetism from Mesmer to Justinus Kerner; Volume II represents and evaluates its manifestations; remarks about the most recent developments, particularly in England (Elliotson) and America (Bushnell, Edmonds, Fowler, Charles Lee, etc.) are appended. The author considers animal magnetism cautiously as a possible therapeutic procedure in certain mental and physical conditions if practiced by qualified physicians, not by charlatans. Schwarzschild (1803-1878) was a physician-poet at Frankfurt-on-the-Main.

SEXTUS, CARL: *Hypnotism, Its Facts, Theories and Related Phenomena,* with Explanatory Anecdotes, Descriptions and Reminiscences. Chicago, 1895. Third revised edition.

Described is a late outgrowth of mesmerism by one of its practicers; it is here called "Puysegurian Somnabulism," after the French Marquis de Puysegur, whom Sextus regarded as the real discoverer of artificial somnambulism. Much attention is paid to the relation of hypnotism to society in its moral and legal aspects.

SINNETT, ALFRED PERCY: *The Rationale of Mesmerism*. Boston, Houghton, 1892.
 Sinnett's presents the first American edition of this interpretation of mesmeric phenomena by a theosophist.

SUNDERLAND, LA ROY: *Pathetism;* with Practical Instructions; Demonstrating the Falsity of the Hitherto Prevalent Assumption in Regard to What Has Been Called "Mesmerism" and "Neurology," and Illustrating those Laws Which Induce Somnambulism, Second Sight, Sleep, Dreaming, Trance, and Clairvoyance, with Numerous Facts Tending to Show the Pathology of Monomania, Insanity, Witchcraft, and Various Other Mental or Nervous Phenomena. New York, 1843. First edition.
 Sunderland (1804-1885) was instrumental in organizing the first anitslavery society in the Methodist Church, from which he withdrew, however, in 1842. Caught up in the restless reformism of the forties, he supported successively mesmerism, Grahamism, and faith-healing, and invented a faith of his own which he called *pathetism*.

SWINDEN, J. H.: *Recueil de Memoire sur l'Analogie de l'Electricité et du Magnétisme*. A la Haye, 1784 (in 3 vols.).
 This is the most complete and valuable contemporary account of current theory and practice in the fields of electricity and magnetism.

TARDY DE MONTRAVEL: *Journal du Traitement Magnétique*. Loudres, 1786.

TESTE, ALPHONE: *Les Confessions d'un Magnétiseur*. Suivies d'une consulation medico-magnetique sur des cheveux de Mme. LaFarge. First edition, 1848.
 These are not memoirs of the author but somnambulistic scenes in the form of short stories or novels.
 Teste, born in 1814 was a French physician, a magnetizer, and homeopath.

THOURET, MICHEL AUGUSTIN: *Récherches et Doutes sur le Magnétisme Animal,* Paris, 1784. First edition.
 This is an important work by a distinquished physician. In the burst of excitement over the supposed remarkable cures of Mesmer, Thouret was the first to attempt to assess the importance of mesmerism and trace its history. The book was read and approved by a council of the Society of Medicine which included Geoffroy, de Fourcroy, and Vicq-d 'Azyr. Their sixteen-page report is included.

TISSART DU ROUVRE, MARQUIS DE: Nouvelles Cures Opèrées par le Magnétisme *Animal*. Paris, 1784.
 An unsigned Preface announces the publication in three parts of a course containing the complete system of mesmerism, without indicating its author. A printed work of this kind is not recorded. The cures which are reported were accomplished at Beaubourg in Brie with the help of a magnetized tree. There is some connected material with, first of all, a report of a Dr. Giraud on the condition of the patients admitted to the free treatments established by him at the Hotel de Coigny—it is addressed to Mesmer.

TOWNSEND, REV. CHAUNCY HARE: *Facts in Mesmerism, or Animal Magnetism.* With Reason for a Dispassionate Inquiry Into It. First American edition, with an Appendix, containing the report of the Boston Committee on Animal Magnetism. Boston, 1841. First American edition.

The work is dedicated to John Elliotson. The author, who was not a medical man, has treated mesmerism as a phenomenon of human nature rather than as a curative means. Townsend (1798-1868), a poet, was a friend of Charles Dickens—whom he made his literary executor—and a collector of precious stones, coins, cameos, pictures, watercolors, and drawings. He published several books on the subject of mesmerism which were valued in their day.

TUKE, DANIEL HACK, *M.D.*: *Sleep-walking and Hypnotism.* London, 1884. First edition.

A psychological study of "artificial somnambulism," a subject in which Tuke's interest had extended over many years, after he had witnessed at the Paris Salpetriere, in 1878, the direct application of "braidism," by Charcot, to patients under his care.

According to Zilboorg, "the history of Tuke's professional life is in more than one respect the history of English-speaking psychiatry . . . He took care to be acquainted with the various trends of his day and studied what he called Braidism, or 'artificial insanity' " (hypnotism).

Author's presentation copy, inscribed by him on title page to "Dr. Barlow." This *may* have been Sir Thomas Barlow (. . . .-1945), known for his description of infantile scurvy (Barlow's disease).

UNDERHILL, SAMUEL, *M.D.*: *Underhill on Mesmerism.* With Criticism on its Opposers and a Review of Humbugs and Humbuggers, with Practical Instructions for Experiments in the Science—Full Directions for Using it as a Remedy in Disease—How to Avoid all Dangers. The Philosophy of Its Curative Powers, How to Develop a Good Clairvoyant. The Philosophy of Seeing Without Eyes. The Proofs of Immortality Derived from the Unfoldings of Mesmerism—Evidence of Mental Communication Without Sight or Sound, Between Bodies Far Apart in the Flesh—Communion of Saints, or with the Departed. (First published in 1868.) Republished, Nevada, Mo., 1902.

This is a rare and curious work on animal magnetism as an exact medical science and including phrenology, neurology, and clairvoyance; the introductory matter contains much about the early history during the time of Mesmer and of later developments in the Nineteenth century.

WETTERSTRAND, OTTO GEORG, *M.D.*: *Hypnotism and Its Application to Practical Medicine.* Authorized translation (from the German edition) by Henrik G. Petersen, M.D., Together with medical letters on hypno-suggestion, etc., by Henrik G. Petersen, M.D. New York, Putnam; London, Knickerbocker, 1902.

Wetterstrand, a Swedish psychotherapist, in expressing the growing conviction that it was very difficult to influence hysterics with suggestive techniques, pointed out in this work that "in one sense" hysterics were helped by a "firmly rooted auto-suggestion."

WOLFART, KARL CHRISTIAN: *Erlauterungen zum Mesmerismus.* Berlin, 1815. First edition (dedicated to Mesmer).

Wolfart (1778-1831) had been sent by the Prussian government to Mesmer in Switzerland as member of a commission, of which Hufeland was the chairman, in order to get instruction in animal magnetism from its orginator. He remained one of its most ardent adherents and promoters throughout his life and published several works on the subject in an attempt to incorporate it scientifically and practically with the whole of medical science. The present volume, the direct result of Wolfart's studies with Mesmer, contains also a short biography on Mesmer.

ZIMMERMANN, W.F.A.: *Magnetismus und Mesmerismus oder Physische und Geistige Krafte der Natur,* Leipzig, 1850. Der mineralische un thierische Magnetismus sowohl in seiner wirklichen Heildraft, als in dem Missbrauch, der von Betrugern und Narren damit getrieben worden, im Zusammenhange mit der Geisterklopferei—der Tischruckerei—dem Spiritualismus dargestellt. This is popular treatise on magnetism, mesmerism, and spiritualism.

Name Index

Abercrombie, 329
Adelon, 161, 199
Aesculapides, 180
Akers, 356
Alcock, A. W., 245
Alexander, E., 230
Alexandre, 393
Alison, W. P., 402
Ampere, M., 245
Anseaume, 97
Arago, M., 422
d'Arcet, 28
  report on animal magnetism, 82-127
Asclepiades, x, 393
Ashburner, J., 379
  introduction to Reichenbach volume, 257-266
Atkinson, E., 247, 314
Azam, C. M. E., 394, 403, 427, 569

Babinski, J., 431, 432, 433, 437
Bacon, F., 392
Baillie, M., 217
Bailly, J. S., 28, 127, 411, 421, 427
  report on animal magnetism, 82-127
Baker, H., 229, 230
Balassa, 154
Barth, A., 48, 557
Barton, J. R., 154
Bauer, cure by Mesmer, 44
Beale, E., 234-237
Beaunis, H.-E., 430, 458, 459
Bennet, J. H., 402
Berard, A., 151
Berillon, E., 536, 570
Bernheim, H. M., 269, 365, 430, 431, 463, 467, 513-517 passim, 520, 523, 526, 528, 531, 535, 536, 542, 544, 546, 547, 552, 555, 557, 559, 561, 570
  description, 515
  suggestive therapeutics, 438-459
Bernier, F., 404
Bertrand, A., 17-18, 273, 274-275, 293, 422, 570

Binet, A., 151, 571
Bjornstrom, F., 409-424, 571
Blake, J. A., 245
Bleuler, E., 434
Block, P., 430-431
Blundell, J., 219
Bonjour, G. H., 566
Bonne, P., 567
Bonvart, M., 93
de Borie, M., report on animal magnetism, 82-127
de Bory, M., 28
Bottey, F., 418-419, 571
de Boulanger, 51
Bourdois, M., 161
Boyle, R., 198
Braid, J., Dr., v, vi, 17, 27, 28, 390, 396-405, 427, 465, 571, 572
  The Critics Criticized, 375-389
  Neurypnology . . . , 269-316
  The Physiology of Fascination, 365-375
  Satanic Agency . . . , 317-330
  writings, 402
Braid, J., Mrs., 281-282
Bramwell, J. M., 566, 572-573
Bremaud, P., 454-455
de Breteuil, 199, 200, 202
Breuer, J., 472, 474
Brewster, D., 368, 402
Broca, P., 269, 394, 403, 427
Broderip, 153
Brodie, B., 245, 314
Brodmann, 566
Brookes, H., 274
Brougham, H., 211
Brown, B., 280
Brown, T., 329
Bruegelmann, P., 566
Buckley, H. T., 262
Burdin, C., 19, 161, 200, 422-423
Burggrav, J. G., xi, xiii
Burrows, G., 245
Buzanci, 134

589

Subject Index

Stare, effect, 390, 396-397
Stars, influence, 31
Statistics, 458, 459, 560-566
Stockholm Hospital, 409
Stockport Chronicle, 286
Suggestion, 438-459, 464-465, 468-469, 503,
   509-510, 524-527 *passim,* 432-536 *passim*
   case described by Freud, 472-486
   criminal influence, 412-420
   dangers, 553
   effect, 430, 434
   hypnotized subjects, 429
   power of, 388
   technique, 365
   therapeutics, 541, 543, 545-567
     Bernheim's views, 438-459
   wordless, 518
   see also Imagination, Mental states, and
     Obedience
Surgery,
   hypnotic procedure, 554
   under hypnotism, 403
   under magnetic sleep, 166-167
   under mesmerism, 21-22, 24-25, 242-249,
     252-253, 524
   see also Curative mesmerism, and Medi-
     cal aspects
Swabia, Mesmer's cures, 45
Sweden, 557
   Bjornstrom, 409-424
   law, 421
   magnetism ruling, 422
   Wetterstrand's writings, 513
Swedish Medical Society, 513
Switzerland, 402, 423, 544, 561
Swooning, 119
Sympathetic system, 490-491, 493

T

Table-turning, 368, 372, 379
Taming wild animals, 155-156
Tests, 423
Theosophical Society of Simla, India, 5
Therapy,
   hypnotism, 472-486, 513-543
     indications for, 462-463
   psychological, 513-543
   suggestion, 438-459, 545-567

Thought, physical results, 535
Thought-transference, 517
Thugs, 412
Tic, 480-481, 484-485
Tic Douloureaux, 313
   cure, 328
Todd's Cyclopaedia of Anatomy . . ., 402
Tooth extraction, under hypnotism, 328
Torrida dipsas, 152
"Traité Pratique du Magnétisme . . .," 20
"Traité Théorique . . . du Magnétisme
   Animal," 12
Trance, 390, 402
   depth for surgery, 254-255
   self induced, 359
Treatment, hypnotism by Freud, 472-486
Trees,
   animal magnetism experiments, 107-108
   mesmerization, 283
   use in cures, 63-64

U

Ulcer, cure by hypnosis, 517
United States, 394, 399, 400-402, 518, 521,
   529
   Harmony Societies, 76
   healing achievements, 25, 26
   mesmerists, 26
Universal fluid theory, xii, 129
University College Hospital, 193, 216, 242,
   243, 246, 379
University of Dublin, 405
University of Edinburgh, 394
University of Paris, 31
University of Vienna, 31

V

Vagus nerve, 492
"Vigilant phenomena," 362
Vision disturbances, 556
Visual acuteness, 336
Volatile salts, discovery, xi

W

Waking patient, 456-457
Water, mesmerization of, 23